11/23

Sourcebook of
Korean Civilization
VOLUME I

SOURCEBOOK OF
KOREAN CIVILIZATION

VOLUME I
FROM EARLY TIMES TO THE SIXTEENTH CENTURY

Edited by Peter H. Lee

WITH

Donald Baker
Yongho Ch'oe
Hugh H. W. Kang
Han-Kyo Kim

Columbia University Press, NEW YORK
UNESCO Publishing, PARIS

UNESCO COLLECTION OF REPRESENTATIVE WORKS
KOREAN SERIES

The publication of this work was assisted by a contribution of the Government of the Republic of Korea under UNESCO's Funds-in-Trust Programme.

Columbia University Press   New York; Chichester, West Sussex
UNESCO Publishing   Paris
Copyright © 1993 Columbia University Press

Grateful acknowledgment is made to the following for permission to reprint previously published material:

Jonathan W. Best, for material from "Tales of Three Paekche Monks Who Traveled Afar in Search of the Law," *Harvard Journal of Asiatic Studies* 51:1 (1991).

Cambridge University Press, for Joseph Needham et al., *The Hall of Heavenly Records: Korean Astronomical Instruments and Clocks, 1380–1780* (1986). © Cambridge University Press 1986.

Columbia University Press, for material from Burton Watson, *Records of the Grand Historian of China* (1961), © 1961 Columbia University Press.

Harvard University Press, for Peter H. Lee, *Lives of Eminent Korean Monks: The Haedong Kosŭng Chŏn.* © 1969 by the Harvard Yenching Institute.

Sungbae Park, for excerpt from "Wŏnhyo's Commentaries on the *Awakening of Faith in Mahāyāna,*" Ph.D. dissertation, University of California, Berkeley, 1979.

Michael C. Rogers, for *"P'yŏnnyon Tongnok:* The Foundation Legend of the Koryŏ State," *Journal of Korean Studies* 4 (1982–1983). © 1983 by the Society for Korean Studies.

Royal Asiatic Society Korea Branch, for Hahm Pyong-choon, *The Korean Political Tradition: Essays in Korean Law and Legal History.* © 1967 by Royal Asiatic Society Korea Branch.

Richard Rutt, for "The Lay of King Tongmyŏng," *Korea Journal* 13:7 (1973).

University of Hawaii Press, for material from Robert E. Buswell, Jr., *The Korean Approach to Zen: The Collected Works of Chinul.* © 1983 University of Hawaii Press.

University of California Press, for two diagrams in Laurel Kendall and Griffin Dix, eds., *Religion and Ritual in Korean Society.* Berkeley: Institute of East Asian Studies (1987). © 1987 by The Regents of the University of California.

Library of Congress Cataloging-in-Publication Data

Sourcebook of Korean civilization: v.1—from early times to the sixteenth century / edited by Peter H. Lee ; with Donald Baker . . . [et al.].
   p.   cm. — (Introduction to Asian civilizations)
   ISBN 0–231–07912–5
   1. Korea—Civilization.   I. Lee, Peter H., 1929–   .   II. Series.
DS904.S68   1993
951.9—dc20

92–28502
CIP

Casebound editions of Columbia University Press books are Smyth-sewn and printed on permanent and durable acid-free paper.

Book design by Jennifer Dossin

PRINTED IN THE UNITED STATES OF AMERICA
c 10 9 8 7 6 5 4 3 2

To our current and future colleagues
in Korean studies

Contents

Preface

This book is a comprehensive English language sourcebook of Korean civilization, encompassing social, intellectual, and religious traditions from early times to 1945. By traditions we mean the past systems of thought, beliefs, rules, and customs that the Korean people considered vital to the maintenance and preservation of their society and culture. Therefore our sources are cultural products of specific historical circumstances, institutional practices, and sociopolitical conditions. They reflect the dynasties and eras they helped to fashion: Three Kingdoms and Unified Silla (57 B.C.–935); Koryŏ (918–1392); Early Chosŏn (1392–c. 1600); Late Chosŏn (c. 1600–c. 1860); and Modern (c. 1860–1945).

We have attempted to maintain a sense of proportion and balance throughout, with minor exceptions. Because the paucity of documents dating from the period of the Three Kingdoms would otherwise make an adequate understanding of its institutional and cultural history difficult, most extant materials relating to that period are included. Also, notwithstanding problems relating to technical vocabulary and doctrinal matters, Silla Buddhism requires a balanced representation of its diverse schools and contributions. Korean Buddhism, the state religion for 865 years (527–1392), made seminal contributions to the development of major Buddhist schools in East Asia. For example, the great scholiasts Wŏnhyo (617–686) and Ŭisang (625–702) influenced Fa-tsang (613–696), the systematizer of the Chinese

Flower Garland school; the commentaries of Wŏnch'ŭk (613–696) on such texts as the *Explanation of Profound Mysteries Scripture* exerted a profound influence on early Tibetan Buddhism; and Musang (680–762), the Silla monk of the Meditation school active in the Szechwan region, was the first Ch'an master known to the Tibetans. Great Master Wŏnhyo, whose goal was to harmonize the doctrinal differences of various schools, may be considered the originator of the ecumenical tradition so characteristic of East Asian Mahāyāna Buddhism.

Something should be said about the lack of discussion of Korea's indigenous folk religion. Like the Japanese Shinto, this is a religion without a written scripture. Through random official and unofficial references, we know that ritual specialists called *mu,* a word usually translated as shamans, existed in the Three Kingdoms period. The rapprochement between shamanism and Buddhism in Silla and Koryŏ illustrates how an official religion attempted to incorporate a folk religion to make itself more appealing to the people. During the Chosŏn dynasty, however, ritual specialists were persecuted and marginalized, and they occupied the lowest stratum of society. Only during the twentieth century have they become a subject of ethnographic study. Their songs, hitherto orally transmitted, reveal a polytheistic pantheon of more than three hundred gods, including some from Buddhism and Taoism. Husbands of ritual specialists became entertainers or singers of tales that later developed into the oral narrative art of *p'ansori.* Like the kabuki actors called *kawaramono* (the Riverbed People), the Korean singers, too, were marginalized. We see here how the power exercised by the dominant literati class of the Chosŏn dynasty had specific aims and objectives. Study of the shamanist songs may help to restore the hitherto suppressed knowledge, belief systems, and worldview of this Korean folk religion.

I want to thank the editors for each period who oversaw the organization and completion of their parts. Hugh Kang for Koryŏ; Yŏngho Ch'oe for Early Chosŏn; Don Baker for Late Chosŏn; and Han-Kyo Kim for Modern. I am grateful too for the generous support of our colleagues for this project, which required a strong sense of collaboration. My special thanks go to my colleagues at UCLA, Robert Buswell and John Duncan, who have been valuable critics throughout by reading parts of the manuscript and discussing various points with me and other period editors. I wish to thank Jennifer Crewe and Anne McCoy of Columbia University Press for their patience and encouragement; my editor Don Yoder for his many valuable suggestions; and my student assistants Jong-Myung Kim and Ann Choi for their diligence.

All those who took part in the project join me in thanking the Korean National Commission for UNESCO and its officers, especially Kim Kyut'aek, Pak Pongsik, Cho Sŏngok, Kim Yŏngsik, Chŏng Hŭich'ae, Paek Sŭnggil, Yi Sŭnghwan, and Hŏ Kwŏn, for their continued encouragement and assistance. Begun in 1978 with the compilation in Korean of source readings, the Korean edition, titled *Korean Civilization Through Historical Sources,* was published in five volumes from 1984 to 1986 and comprises 2,383 printed pages. The book has entered its sixth printing in Korea and is widely used in major universities there. The English version, compiled for both the student and general reader, differs in its emphasis and selection, but as the most comprehensive sourcebook in English on Korean civilization, we hope it will prove to be invaluable for courses in Korean civilization, Korean thought, and Korean religion, as well as in comparative philosophy and religion.

Peter H. Lee

Explanatory Note

The romanization of Korean names follows the McCune-Reischauer system and certain suggestions made in *Korean Studies* 4 (1980):111–125. The apostrophe to mark two separate sounds (e.g., *han'gŭl*) has been omitted throughout. For Chinese, the Wade-Giles system is used; for Japanese, we have used Kenkyusha's *New Japanese-English Dictionary* (Tokyo: Kenkyusha, 1974).

Dates for rulers of China and Korea are reign dates without *r*. They are preceded by birth and death dates if required.

Names of places or suffixes (mountains, river, monastery) are translated whenever possible. We have, however, attempted to avoid such pleonasms as Pulguk-sa Monastery, except for such cases as Mount Muak.

For translation of Buddhist terms we have consulted W. E. Soothill and Lewis Hodous, *A Dictionary of Chinese Buddhist Terms, with Sanskrit and English Equivalents and a Sanskrit-Pali Index* (London: Kegan Paul, 1937), and Mochizuki Shinkō, ed., *Bukkyō daijiten* (Tokyo: Sekai seiten kankō kyōkai, 1960–1963). For Sanskrit terms we have followed Sir Monier Monier-Williams, *A Sanskrit-English Dictionary Etymologically and Philologically Arranged with Special Reference to Cognate Indo-European Languages* (Oxford: Clarendon Press, 1899), and Franklin Edgerton, *Buddhist Hybrid Sanskrit Dictionary* (New Haven: Yale University Press, 1953). For Sanskrit titles of works in the Buddhist canonical collections, we have also consulted Hajime Nakamura,

Indian Buddhism: A Survey with Bibliographical Notes (Delhi: Motilal Banarsidass, 1987).

The translation of Chinese institutional titles generally follows Charles O. Hucker, *A Dictionary of Official Titles in Imperial China* (Stanford: Stanford University Press, 1985). The translation of Korean institutional titles, together with Korean names of distance, area, and linear measure, generally follows Ki-baek Lee, *A New History of Korea,* trans. Edward W. Wagner with Edward J. Schultz (Cambridge: Harvard University Press, 1984).

We have avoided using brackets in the translations for the sake of fluency. Allusions to the Chinese canonical works and histories are worked into the translations whenever possible, and sources are indicated in footnotes. Contentious points are also explained in footnotes; the glossary provides Chinese graphs and other basic information for proper nouns and terms. Brackets are retained for interpolated dates in the translations.

Works frequently cited in the notes have been abbreviated according to the list below:

HKC   *Haedong kosŭng chŏn* (T. 50, no. 2065)
HKSC   *Hsü kao-seng chuan* (T. 50, no. 2060)
HPC   *Hanguk pulgyo chŏnsŏ*
HTC   *Hsü Tsang-ching* (Hong Kong reprint of *Dai-Nihon zoku-zōkyō*)
KRS   *Koryŏ sa* (Yŏnse taehakkyo, Tongbanghak yŏnguso edition)
KSGN   *Kŭmgang smmaegyŏng non* (T. 34, no. 1730)
KT   *Korean Tripiṭaka* (Koryŏ taejanggyŏng)
Legge   James Legge, *The Chinese Classics,* 5 vols.
SGSG   *Samguk sagi* (Yi Pyŏngdo edition)
SGYS   *Samguk yusa* (Ch'oe Namsŏn edition)
SKSC   *Sung kao-seng chuan* (T. 50, no. 2061)
SPPY   *Ssu-pu pei-yao*
SPTK   *Ssu-pu ts'ung-k'an*
T   *Taishō shinshū daizōkyō*
VS   *Vajrasamādhi sūtra* (T. 9, no. 273)

Contributors

The translator's initials follow each translated passage.

BW   Burton Watson, Columbia University
DC   Donald N. Clark, Trinity University
ES   Edward J. Shultz, West Oahu College
HK   Hugh H. W. Kang, University of Hawaii at Manoa
JB   Jonathan W. Best, Wesleyan University
JD   John B. Duncan, University of California, Los Angeles
JJ   John C. Jamieson, University of California, Berkeley
JW   Jinwol Lee, University of Hawaii at Manoa
MD   Martina Deuchler, University of London
MK   Michael Kalton, University of Washington at Tacoma
MR   Michael C. Rogers, University of California, Berkeley
PL   Peter H. Lee, University of California, Los Angeles
RB   Robert E. Buswell, Jr., University of California, Los Angeles
RR   Richard Rutt, Falmouth, Cornwall, England
SP   Sungbae Park, State University of New York, Stony Brook
YC   Yongho Ch'oe, University of Hawaii at Manoa

PART ONE

THREE KINGDOMS AND UNIFIED SILLA

CHAPTER ONE

Origins of Korean Culture

The history of human activity in Korea can be traced far into the ancient past. Some of the earliest archaeological finds include Paleolithic remains at Sŏkchang-ni (South Ch'ungch'ŏng), Kulp'ori (Unggi in North Hamgyŏng), Sangwŏn, Haesang-ni, Tŏkch'ŏn (South P'yŏngan), Chech'ŏn (North Ch'ungch'ŏng), and Chŏngok (Kyŏnggi). These finds include mammal bone fossils, scrapers, choppers, and chopping tools. Radiocarbon dating indicates that habitation began between 40,000 and 30,000 B.C. The oldest Neolithic artifacts are primitive pottery found in the lower layer of Tongsamdong, near Pusan, and Unggi in North Hamgyŏng. The use of comb-pattern pottery emerged around 4,000 B.C. Both the Neolithic primitive pottery and comb-pattern pottery people seem to have been clan peoples engaged in gathering, hunting, and fishing.

They were followed by other clan peoples who farmed, used plain pottery, and lived side by side with fishing people. The influence of the former on the latter can be seen in the remains unearthed in Chit'am-ni, Hwanghae (middle of the comb-pattern pottery period), and Tongsamdong—cultivation and hunting are evidenced by carbonized millet at the first site and by the bones of animals at both sites. Finally, the fishing people seem to have been absorbed by the plain-pottery culture. For example, in Mirim-ri and Ch'ŏngho-ri, northeast of P'yŏngyang on opposite shores of the Taedong River, plain coarse pottery and stone axes and knives were unearthed at the former site and comb-pattern pottery and stone net sinkers at the latter. Judging from the coexistence of the fishing and farming people, there might have been some form of economic exchange. Conflicts arising from the process of exchange and the amalgamation of the clans into tribes called for some form of arbitration. Further change in this early Korean society came with the influx of metal culture from the Scytho-Siberian and the Han Chinese civilizations.

Farming techniques improved in the Bronze Age, and rich remains such as semilunar stone knives, stone hoes, and stone axes with grooves are found on the slopes overlooking fertile valleys and plains. People continued to use stone tools in the Bronze Age, while bronze itself was reserved for weapons, sacrificial vessels, and ornaments. This practice suggests the existence of a dual social structure in which peoples possessing superior bronze weaponry expropriated the agricultural production of Neolithic peoples. To distinguish themselves from their subordinates, the members of a superior tribe would proclaim themselves sons of heaven and build imposing dolmens to display their power. Amid such change in social relationships, some form of political power began to grow in the peninsula.

The Foundation Myth

During the Neolithic period, the Tung-i (Eastern Barbarian) tribes, who lived in an area stretching from the Huai River, Shantung peninsula, and southern Manchuria to the Gulf of Pohai and the Korean peninsula, came under the influence of the Shang and Scytho-Siberian civilizations, the latter coming from Central Asia through northern China. The tribes' close ties with these civilizations helped them develop their own Bronze Age. In addition, those along the Huai and on the Shantung peninsula were in contact with the civilization south of the Yangtze. Included among the Tung-i were the Yemaek and Han tribes that constituted the original nucleus of the Korean people. In their eastward migration, these tribes absorbed or pushed out societies distinguished by their production of comb-pattern pottery and became the core of the patternless-pottery society. Linguistically, they are said to be a branch of the Tungusic tribes and thus belong to the Altaic language family. With agriculture as their economic basis, they absorbed the red-pottery and black-pottery cultures, thus building a broad basis for their own civilization. With the fall of the Shang and the rise of the Chou to the west, tribes migrated from along the Huai River and Shantung peninsula to southern Manchuria and the Korean peninsula. Those who reached the Taedong River basin merged with the inhabitants there and formed Old Chosŏn. The illustrations on the stone slabs in the Wu family shrine in Chia-hsiang hsien in Shantung, built in 147, depict the content of the foundation myth—the Tangun legend—as it is recorded in the *Samguk yusa* (Memorabilia of the Three Kingdoms).

The superior bronze culture tribes of Old Chosŏn ruled over those who were still in the Neolithic stage and tried to assert the authority of their tradition and heritage. The natives' worship of the gods of the wind, rain, and cloud, together with their totemic belief in the bear and the tiger, gave way to the worship of the god of the sun. According to the Korean foundation myth, Hwanung came down to the world of man and married a she-bear who bore Tangun, the first ruler of the age of theocracy. The bear cult, the core of the Tangun legend, descends from the Paleolithic period and is still prevalent among the Ainu and some tribes in Siberia. The stone slabs in the Wu family shrine are proof that the legend was not formed at the time of the Mongol invasion of Korea, as has been suggested by some Japanese scholars. The Wu family may have been part of the tribe belonging to the Korean people or of a tribe close to the Northeast Asian people.

According to the version in the *Chewang ungi* (Rhymed Record of Emperors and Kings) by Yi Sŭnghyu (1224–1300), the great king Hwanung gave medicine to his granddaughter so that she would change into a human. She married a god of the sandalwood tree and bore Tangun, an indication that the Tangun legend originated in the north and was transmitted to the south where it absorbed tree worship.

In Iryŏn's *Memorabilia of the Three Kingdoms,* the account of the legend was based on the *Wei shu* and *Kogi* (Old Record). While such Confucian historians as Kim Pusik (1075–1151) rejected the legend, Great Master Iryŏn's inclusion of it is evidence that Buddhism tried to absorb the autochthonous beliefs during its spread in the peninsula. But even Confucian scholars began to acknowledge the importance of their native tradition, as evinced by Paek Munbo (d. 1374), who pointed out that the year 3600 (1267) in the Tangun calendar marked a year of prosperity.

In addition to the *Memorabilia of the Three Kingdoms,* sources that mention the legend include the *Rhymed Record of Emperors and Kings,*

Ŭngjesi chu (Commentary on Poems Written at Royal Command) by Kwŏn Nam (1416–1465), the monograph on geography in the *Sejong sillok* (Veritable Records of King Sejong), and the *Tongguk yŏji sŭngnam* (Korean Gazetteer). The version in the *Memorabilia of the Three Kingdoms* appears to be closest to the original form of the legend. The *Tangun kogi* (Old Record of Tangun) mentioned in the *Veritable Records of King Sejong* may have been the *Kogi* that Iryŏn used. The *Wei shu*, a text otherwise unknown, is not the work written in 551 by Wei Shou of the Northern Ch'i, as it does not contain the legend.

Tangun
[From *Samguk yusa* 1:33–34]

The *Wei shu* tells us that two thousand years ago, at the time of Emperor Yao, Tangun Wanggŏm chose Asadal as his capital and founded the state of Chosŏn. The *Old Record* notes that in olden times Hwanin's son, Hwanung, wished to descend from heaven and live in the world of human beings. Knowing his son's desire, Hwanin surveyed the three highest mountains and found Mount T'aebaek the most suitable place for his son to settle and help human beings. Therefore he gave Hwanung three heavenly seals and dispatched him to rule over the people. Hwanung descended with three thousand followers to a spot under a tree by the Holy Altar atop Mount T'aebaek, and he called this place the City of God. He was the Heavenly King Hwanung. Leading the Earl of Wind, the Master of Rain, and the Master of Clouds, he took charge of some three hundred and sixty areas of responsibility, including agriculture, allotted lifespans, illness, punishment, and good and evil, and brought culture to his people.

At that time a bear and a tiger living in the same cave prayed to Holy Hwanung to transform them into human beings. The king gave them a bundle of sacred mugworts and twenty cloves of garlic and said, "If you eat these and shun the sunlight for one hundred days, you will assume human form." Both animals ate the spices and avoided the sun. After twenty-one days the bear became a woman, but the tiger, unable to observe the taboo, remained a tiger. Unable to find a husband, the bear-woman prayed under the altar tree for a child. Hwanung metamorphosed himself, lay with her, and begot a son called Tangun Wanggŏm.

In the fiftieth year of the reign of Emperor Yao, Tangun made the walled city of P'yŏngyang the capital and called his country Chosŏn.

He then moved his capital to Asadal on Mount Paegak, also named Mount Kunghol, or Kŭmmidal, whence he ruled for fifteen hundred years. When, in the year *kimyo* [1122 B.C.], King Wu of Chou enfeoffed Chi Tzu (Kija) to Chosŏn, Tangun moved to Changdang-gyŏng, but later he returned and hid in Asadal as a mountain god at the age of one thousand nine hundred and eight. PL

Korea in the Chinese Dynastic Histories

The *Wei lüeh* (A Brief Account of the Wei Dynasty), cited by P'ei Sung-chih (360–439) in the *Wei shu* (chap.30), was compiled by Yü Huan around 280–289. The text itself, which contains information on the relationship between Korea (Old Chosŏn) and northern China before the Han dynasty, was lost and only fragments quoted in other texts remain. The following account of the relationship between ancient Korea and the state of Yen cited by P'ei shows the extent of Old Chosŏn's political influence around the third century B.C.

The *Shih chi* (chap. 115) records the development of Old Chosŏn and its successor state, Wiman Chosŏn, as well as the establishment of the four Chinese commanderies in northern Korea. A similar account is in the *Han shu* (chap. 95). The monograph on geography in the *Han shu* (chap. 28) describes the territory of the Han commanderies and tells how native customs changed under the Han administration. The iron culture introduced by the Han colonies resulted in considerable change in the peninsula. While the ruling class had monopolized bronze vessels in the Bronze Age, the iron culture spread rapidly, bringing about pervasive changes in society. The head of a family became the head of a clan; as the number of clans increased, it became more difficult to form a federation strong enough to oppose the ruling power. Since the policy of Han colonies was to obstruct the growth of a leading power in the peninsula, the state of Chin south of the Han River was dissolved, and even the indigenous society, only indirectly controlled by China through trade, could not grow into an independent force.

Thus the ancient Korean states had two aims: to free themselves from Chinese cultural forces and to remain intact in their struggles against other peoples outside the Great Wall. Internally, they had to build a base for uniting the power of clan chiefs and to find a footing for the establishment of a ruling system. The social conditions during this period of travail are best portrayed in the chapter on the Tung-i in the *Hou Han shu* and *San-kuo chih*. The account in the *San-kuo chih* appeared first as a simple narrative; that in the *Hou Han shu*, while based on the former, was retold in a well-ordered manner. The preface to the account in the *Hou Han shu* summarizes the Chinese view of the Tung-i until the third century A.D. However, the account in the *San-kuo chi* is generally considered to be the best source for ancient Korean history.

Yü Huan: Ancient Korea and Yen
[From *Wei lüeh*, in *San-kuo chih* 30:850]

The marquis of Chosŏn, a descendant of Chi Tzu (Kija) of old, saw that with the decline of Chou the ruler of Yen honored himself with the title of king (*wang*) and was about to make an incursion to the east. The marquis of Chosŏn likewise claimed for himself that title of king and was about to make a counterthrust against Yen to show his veneration for the house of Chou. But his great minister Ye remonstrated against this plan, whereupon the marquis desisted. Instead he sent Ye west to use persuasion with the king of Yen, and indeed the latter desisted and did not attack after all.

Later the sons and grandsons of the marquis of Chosŏn became somewhat arrogant and cruel, so the king of Yen sent his general Ch'in K'ai to attack their western quarter; he took more than two thousand *li* of territory, going as far as Manbŏnhan, which he made the boundary; Chosŏn was thereby weakened.

When the Ch'in had unified the world under its control, the emperor sent Meng T'ien to build the Long Wall, reaching to the east of the Liao. At that time the reigning king of Chosŏn was Pi. Fearing that Ch'in would attack him, Pi went through the motions of vassalage to Ch'in but refused to make the court visit. On Pi's death his son Chun succeeded him. Twenty-odd years later, when Ch'en [Sheng] and Hsiang [Yü] rebelled and the world was in chaos, the people of Yen, Ch'i, and Chao in their misery fled in considerable numbers to Chun, who settled them in his western quarter. With Han's enfeoffment of Lu Wan as king of Yen, Chosŏn and Yen bordered each other at the P'ae River.

When Lu Wan rebelled against Han and defected to the Hsiung-nu, the Yen man Wiman fled for his life and, attired as a *hu* barbarian, crossed the P'ae River eastward and surrendered to Chun. He persuaded Chun to let him settle in the western area, so that he would take in refugees from the Middle Kingdom and serve as a buffer for Chosŏn. Having full confidence in him, Chun favored him with an appointment as erudite, presented him with a scepter, enfeoffed him with a hundred *li* of territory, and had him hold the western frontier. Wiman lured refugee groups and his following became quite numerous. He then deceitfully sent a messenger to inform Chun that troops from Han were advancing against him by ten routes; he sought permission to go and serve as Chun's bodyguard. Wiman then went back and attacked Chun, who fought him but was no match for him. MR

Accounts of Chosŏn★
[From *Shih chi* 115:2985–2990]

Wiman, the king of Chosŏn (Ch'ao-hsien), came originally from the state of Yen. When Yen was at the height of its power, it invaded and conquered the regions of Chen-p'an and Chosŏn, appointing officials to rule the area and setting up fortifications along the frontier. After the Ch'in dynasty destroyed the state of Yen, the area fell under Ch'in control, bordering as it did the province of Liao-tung. When the Han arose, however, it regarded the region as too far away and difficult to guard, and rebuilt the fortifications at the old border of Liao-tung, leaving the area beyond, as far as the P'ae (Yalu) River, to be administered by the king of Yen.

When Lu Wan, the king of Yen, revolted and crossed over into the territory of the Hsiung-nu, Wiman fled into hiding. He gathered together a band of a thousand or more followers and, adopting the mallet-shaped hairdo and dress of the Eastern Barbarians, escaped over the eastern border. After crossing the P'ae River, he settled down in the region formerly administered by the Ch'in, moving back and forth along the old border. Little by little he brought under his control the barbarians and Chinese refugees from Yen and Ch'i who were living in the regions of Chen-p'an and Chosŏn and made himself their king, establishing his capital at Wanggŏm (P'yŏngyang).

During the reign of Emperor Hui and Empress Lü, because peace had only recently been restored to the empire, the governor of Liao-tung province agreed to regard Wiman as a "foreign vassal" of the

★ Reprinted, with Korean names in Korean pronunciation, from Burton Watson, *Records of the Grand Historian of China* 2:258–263.

Han if he would guard the frontier against the barbarians and prevent them from raiding the border. Moreover, if any of the barbarian chieftains wished to enter China and pay their respects to the emperor, Wiman was not to hinder them from making the journey. When word of this agreement was reported to the emperor, he gave his approval. As a result, Wiman was able to acquire considerable wealth and military power with which he attacked and conquered the smaller settlements in the area until all of Chen-p'an and Lin-t'un were under his control. His territory by this time measured several thousand *li* square.

In time the rule passed to Wiman's son and then to his grandson Ugŏ (Yu-ch'ü), who induced an increasing number of Han subjects to flee to his kingdom. Neither he nor his father or grandfather had ever journeyed to the capital to visit the emperor, and when the chiefs of Chen-p'an or any of the other various states in the area sent a letter to the throne requesting an audience with the Son of Heaven, they blocked the way and refused to let them pass.

In the second year of Yüan-feng [109 B.C.] the Han dispatched She Ho to rebuke Ugŏ and warn him to mend his ways, but the latter refused to obey the imperial edict. She Ho left the capital of Chosŏn and began his journey home, but when he reached the border and was about to cross the P'ae River, he stabbed and killed Chang, the assistant king of Chosŏn, who had been sent to escort him out of the kingdom. Then he made a dash across the river and back into Han territory. From there he sent a report to the emperor stating that he had killed a general of Chosŏn. The emperor, pleased by this feat, asked no questions but honored She Ho with the post of chief commandant of the eastern sector of Liao-tung province. The king of Chosŏn, angered at this treachery, called out his troops and attacked and killed She Ho, whereupon the emperor gathered together a force of ex-convicts to make an assault on Chosŏn.

In the autumn Yang P'u, the General of the Towered Ships, embarked from Ch'i and crossed the Gulf of Pohai with a force of five thousand soldiers, while the General of the Left, Hsün Chih marched out of Liao-tung to aid in punishing Ugŏ. Ugŏ called out his troops and blocked the passes.

One of Hsün Chih's battalion commanders named To took it upon himself to lead a large number of the troops of Liao-tung on ahead of the rest, and as a result he suffered a severe defeat. Many of his men were routed and fled back to Liao-tung, and To was tried under military law and executed. As a result Yang P'u and his men from

Ch'i were the first to reach Wanggŏm, the capital of Chosŏn. Ugŏ had withdrawn into the city, but when he observed that Yang P'u's force was very small, he marched out and attacked, defeating and routing Yang P'u's army. Yang P'u, having lost most of his men, was forced to flee to the mountains, where he spent ten days or more rounding up the remnants of his army, until he had gathered together a sizable force again. Hsün Chih in the meantime was attacking the Chosŏn army west of the P'ae River, but was unable to break their line or advance any farther.

The emperor, seeing that neither of his generals was accomplishing much, dispatched Wei Shan to threaten Ugŏ with further military action if he did not submit. When Ugŏ received the Han envoy, he bowed his head and apologized for his actions: "I wanted to surrender, but I was afraid that the two generals would go back on their promises of safety and kill me. Now that I see you bear the seals of a genuine envoy, I beg to surrender." To make amends, he also agreed to send his son, the crown prince, to the capital to wait on the emperor and to present a gift of five thousand horses as well as provisions for the Han armies.

The crown prince set off, accompanied by a force of ten thousand men bearing arms, and they were about to cross the P'ae River, when the Han envoy and Hsün Chih, suspecting his intentions, told the crown prince that since he had already surrendered, he ought to order his men to lay down their arms. The crown prince in turn began to suspect that the envoy and Hsün Chih were plotting to murder him and so he did not cross the river, but instead turned around and went back to Wanggŏm. The Han envoy Wei Shan then returned to Ch'ang-an and reported to the emperor on his mission. The emperor executed him.

Hsün Chih once more attacked the Chosŏn army west of the P'ae River and, defeating it, advanced to Wanggŏm, camping in a semicircle around the northwest corner of the city. Yang P'u arrived at the same time with his forces and took up a position south of the city. Ugŏ, however, guarded his city well, and though several months passed, the Han forces had still not succeeded in taking it.

Hsün Chih had formerly served at court and had enjoyed favor with the emperor. Leading an army made up of men from Yen and Tai, he had plunged forward on a wave of victory and many of his soldiers had grown proud and reckless. Yang P'u, on the other hand, had come by sea with his band from Ch'i and had already suffered a number of times from defeat and desertion. In his earlier encounter with Ugŏ he had been shamefully beaten and had lost so many of his men that his soldiers were all afraid of the enemy and he himself was deeply mortified. Thus, although he was now taking part in the siege against Ugŏ, he did everything he could to bring about a peaceful settlement.

Hsün Chih in the meantime made a sudden attack on the city, whereupon the high minister of Chosŏn sent men in secret to discuss plans for a surrender agreement with Yang P'u. Messengers were sent back and forth several times between the two parties, but no final agreement was reached. Hsün Chih repeatedly set a date with Yang P'u for a joint attack on the city, but Yang P'u, anxious to complete arrangements for the surrender as soon as possible, failed each time to put in an appearance. Hsün Chih then began sending envoys of his own to spread discord among the men of Chosŏn and effect a surrender. The men of Chosŏn, however, refused to listen to his offers and continued to favor negotiating with Yang P'u. As a result, relations between the two generals became strained. Hsün Chih, considering the fact that Yang P'u had earlier committed the military sin of losing his army and observing that he was now secretly on good terms with the men of Chosŏn and was making no effort to capture their city, began to suspect that Yang P'u was planning to revolt, but he did not dare at this point to announce his suspicions publicly.

Meanwhile the emperor declared, "Formerly these two generals were unable to make any progress in their campaign, and so I sent Wei Shan as my envoy to persuade Ugŏ to surrender and send the crown prince of Chosŏn to court. But because Wei Shan was not able to conclude the negotiations on his own, he consulted with Hsün Chih and the two of them acted wrongly and in the end upset the whole agreement. Now Hsün Chih and Yang P'u are besieging the city of Wanggŏm and again there seems to be a clash of opinions. That is the reason the affair has dragged on so long without reaching a settlement!" He then dispatched Kung-sun Sui, the governor of Chi-nan, to go and straighten things out, giving him authority to take what measures might be necessary to clear up the matter.

When Kung-sun Sui arrived on the scene, Hsün Chih said to him, "The men of Chosŏn should have given in a long time ago. There appears to be some reason why they refuse to capitulate." He then told him how Yang P'u had failed to appear at the times agreed upon for an attack and related in detail all the doubts that he harbored concerning Yang P'u. "If some action is not taken at once," he said, "I am afraid a major disaster will result. The emperor will lose not only Yang P'u and his men, but they will take sides with Chosŏn and wipe out my army as well!"

Kung-sun Sui agreed with him and, using the imperial credentials he carried, summoned Yang P'u to come to Hsün Chih's camp to plan the next move. Once there, he ordered Hsün Chih's subordinates to arrest Yang P'u and combine the armies of the two generals. When Kung-sun Sui reported his actions to the emperor, the emperor sent back orders to have Kung-sun Sui executed.

With both armies now under his own command, Hsün Chih began to press his attacks on Chosŏn. At this point the prime ministers of Chosŏn, namely Noin (Lu-jen) and Han Ŭm (Han Yin) along with the prime minister of Igye (Ni-ch'i), namely Ch'am (Ts'an), and a general named Wang Kyŏp (Wang Chia), began to plot together, saying, "Originally we had planned to surrender to Yang P'u, but now he has been arrested, and Hsün Chih, who is in command of both armies, is pressing his attacks with increasing intensity. It is unlikely that we can win out against him, and at the same time the king refuses to surrender!" Han Ŭm, Wang Kyŏp, and Noin then fled from the city; Noin was killed on the way, but the others succeeded in surrendering to the Han forces.

In the summer of the third year of Yüan-feng [108 B.C.] Ch'am, the prime minister of Igye, sent men to assassinate Ugŏ, the king of Chosŏn, and to announce the surrender of the state. The city of Wanggŏm, however, had not yet capitulated, and the former high minister of Ugŏ named Sŏngi (Ch'eng I) declared the country once more in revolt and sent men to attack the Han officers. Hsün Chih then dispatched Changgang (Ch'ang-chiang), the son of Ugŏ, and Ch'oe (Tsui), the son of the prime minister Noin, to persuade the people to submit and to execute Sŏngi. Thus Chosŏn was at last conquered and the territory divided into four commanderies. BW

Accounts of the Eastern Barbarians
[From *San-kuo chih* 30:840–853]

The *Book of Documents* says, "To the east they envelop the sea, to the west they encompass the drifting sands." One can indeed use such words to describe the system of the Nine Zones of Submission. But if one proceeds, relying on multiple translation of tongues beyond the

Desolate Region (the outermost zone), it isn't worth the trouble to mark on maps the places where cart tracks reach, nor is there anyone who knows about the strange forms of national customs to be found there. From the time of Yü down to that of the Chou, we have had submission of white jade from the Western Jung, while the Tung-i have rendered the tribute of Suksin (Su-shen). Both remissions have continued to come in for many generations, even from such vast distances as this.

When it came to pass that the Han sent Chang Ch'ien as envoy to the Western Regions, he plumbed the source of the Yellow River and traveled through one state after another. Han then installed a Metropolitan Warden (*tu-hu*) to keep those states under overall control. Since then the affairs of the Western Regions have been fully preserved, so that our official historiographers can set them down in detail. After the Wei state rose up in North China, not all of the states of the Western Regions were able to make their appearance at court; nevertheless the great states like Kucha (Kuei-tzu), Khotan (Yü-tien), Samarkand (K'ang-chü), Wu-sun, Kashgar (Shu-le), Yüeh-chih, Lou-lan (Shan-shan), and Turfan (Chü-shih) never let a year pass without submitting their tribute at court, in much the same way as they had done under the Han. Then when Kung-sun Yüan succeeded his father and grandfather, making three generations of Kung-sun possession of Liao-tung, the Son of Heaven, considering it to be a "sundered region," vested them with management of affairs beyond the sea; thereupon, cut off by the Tung-i, they were unable to communicate with the Chinese. In the middle of Ching-ch'u [237–239], Emperor Ming greatly mobilized his battalions and executed Kung-sun Yüan; moreover he secretly sent forces across the sea and gathered in the commanders of Lo-lang and Tai-fang. After that the outer reaches of the sea were peaceful, and the Tung-i bent low in submission.

Sometime later, when Koguryŏ became refractory and rebellious, Wei further sent an army detachment to visit chastisement upon them. The army went to the end of the earth in exhaustive pursuit: traversing the lands of the Wu-han and Ku-tu (Hsiung-nu), they passed that of the Okchŏ, and having trampled upon the encampments of the Suksin, they gazed eastwards upon the great sea. As our elders tell it, there were people of strange faces, the product of proximity to the sun. Accordingly they surveyed the several states, noting their norms and customs and distinguishing small from great; each had its own name and could be described in detail. Even though there were the principalities of the I and the Ti, the shapes of ritual vessels were retained among them. It would seem that one can indeed have credence in the saying, "When the Middle Kingdom has lost the rites, seek them among the Four Barbarians." Therefore we have placed their states in appropriate order, and have set forth their similarities and differences, in order to supply what the previous histories have not provided. MR

PUYŎ

Puyŏ (Fu-yü) is north of the Long Wall, a thousand *li* distant from Hsüan-t'u; it is contiguous with Koguryŏ on the south, with the I-lou (Ŭmnu) on the east and the Hsien-pi on the west, while to its north is the Jo (Yak) River. It covers an area some two thousand *li* square, and its households number eight myriads. Its people are sedentary, possessing houses, storehouses, and prisons. With their many tumuli and broad marshes, theirs is the most level and open of the Eastern Barbarian territories. Their land is suitable for cultivation of the five grains; they do not produce the five fruits. Their people are coarsely big; by temperament strong and brave, assiduous and generous, they are not prone to brigandage. Their state is ruled by a king, and they name their officials after the six domestic animals: there is the Horse *ka*, the Ox *ka*, the Pig *ka*, and the Dog *ka*; the *taesa*, the *taesaja*, and the *p'aeja*. In their settlements there are powerful people; called "lowly households" by the *ka*, they can all become slaves. The several *ka* separately rule the roads that extend to the four quarters; those of great domain rule several thousand families, those of small several hundred. In eating and drinking they all use ritual vessels; in their meetings they make ceremonial toasts and wash the goblets; bowing and deferring, they ascend and descend.

They sacrifice to heaven using the correct month of Yin (Shang). When there is a great assembly in the state they eat and drink, dance and sing for days on end. Such occasions are called "welcoming drums" (*yŏnggo*). At this time they decide criminal cases and release prisoners. For their dress within their state they favor white; they have large sleeves, gowns, and trousers, and on their feet they wear leather sandals. When they go out from their state, they favor silken brocades and embroidered fabrics to which the chiefs add the fur of the fox, the badger, the monkey, and the white and black sable, and they decorate their headgear with gold and silver. When their translators transmit the words of a Chinese official, they always squat down and, propped on their hands, speak respectfully. In their use of punishments they are very strict: one who kills another must himself die, and the members of his household are made slaves. Thieves must pay a twelvefold indemnity. When a man and a woman have illicit intercourse or a wife is jealous, all are killed. They especially detest jealousy. Having killed a person guilty of such crimes, they expose her body atop a hill to the south of the community; after it has decomposed and the woman's family wants to retrieve it, they are given it only after having paid for it with cattle and horses. Upon the death of his elder brother, a man takes to wife his former sister-in-law, a custom they share with the Hsiung-nu.

The people of their state are good at raising domestic animals; they also produce famous horses, red jade, sables, and beautiful pearls. The pearls (*chu*) are as large as sour jujubes. For weapons they have bows, arrows, knives, and shields; each household has its own armorer. The elders of the state speak of themselves as alien refugees of long ago. The forts they build are round and have a resemblance to prisons. Old and young, they sing when walking along the road whether it be day or night; all day long the sound of their voices never ceases. In the event of military action they also perform sacrifices to heaven. They kill an ox and observe its hoof to divine good or bad fortune; for the hoof to fall apart is considered to be bad luck, for it to come together is considered to be good. When facing the enemy the several *ka* themselves do battle; the lower households carry provisions for them to eat and drink. Upon their death, in the months of summer they always use ice for preservation. When they kill people, they expose their bodies, sometimes as many as a hundred or more. They bury their dead, with full ceremony, in an outer coffin and no inner one. MR

KOGURYŎ

Koguryŏ lies a thousand *li* to the east of Liao-tung, being contiguous with Chosŏn and Yemaek on the south, with Okchŏ on the east, and with Puyŏ on the north. They make their capital below Hwando. With a territory perhaps two thousand *li* on a side, their households number three myriads. They have many mountains and deep valleys and have no plains or marshes. Accommodating themselves to mountain and valley, the people make do with them for their dwellings and food. With their steep-banked rivers, they lack good fields; and though they plow and till energetically, their efforts are not enough to fill their bellies; their custom is to be sparing of food. They like to build palaces. To the left and right of their dwellings they erect large houses, where they offer sacrifices to ghosts and spirits. They also have rituals for numinous stars and for the spirits of the land and grain. By temperament the people are violent and take delight in brigandage. Their state has a king, and among their officials there are: *sangga, taero, p'aeja, koch'u ka, chubu, ut'aesŭng, saja, choŭi, sŏnin,* each graded and ranked according to hierarchy. As an old saying about the Tung-i would have it, they are a separate branch of the Puyŏ. And indeed there is much about their language and other things that they share with the Puyŏ, but in temperament and clothing there are differences. Originally there were five clans: the Yŏnno, the Chŏllo, the Sunno, the Kwanno, and the Kyeru. Originally the Yŏnno clan exercised the kingship, but it became somewhat wasted and weakened, and now the Kyeru clan has replaced it. During Han times drummers and pipers were bestowed upon them. They ordinarily were under the jurisdiction of Hsüan-t'u Commandery, whence they received court vestments and caps; Koguryŏ was ordered to take charge of registering the recipients. Later they became somewhat overbearing and willful and no longer paid visits to the commandery seat. On their eastern border the commandery administration built a small fort and inside it placed the court vestments and caps; at regular times of the year they came and took them. The barbarians still refer to this fort as "Tse-cap kou-lu"—"kou-lu" being the Koguryŏ term for fort.

As for their placement of officials: when there is a *taero* they do not install a *p'aeja,* and vice versa. In the case of the royal family, their Great *ka* are all called *koch'u ka.* Members of the Yŏnno clan originally were rulers of the state; although they are now no longer kings, their legitimate chieftain can still claim the title *koch'u ka* and can also erect an ancestral temple in which to offer sacrifices to the numinous stars and to the altars of the land and grain. The Chŏllo clan by hereditary custom intermarries with the royal clan and is vested with the title of *koch'u.* The several Great *ka* in like manner install their own *p'aeja* and *choŭi* and *sŏnin*; the latter's names are communicated to the king, like the house vassals of our great ministers. In the sessions of their assemblages, however, they are not permitted to line up on the same level with their counterparts of the royal house. Members of the great houses of their state do not till the fields, and those who thus eat the bread of idleness number more than a myriad. It is the lower households who keep them supplied, bearing rice, grain, fish, and salt from afar.

Their people delight in singing and dancing. In villages throughout the state, men and women gather in groups at nightfall for communal singing and games. They have no great storehouses, each family keeping its own small store, which they call a *pugyŏng*. They rejoice in cleanliness, and they are good at brewing beer. When they kneel to make obeisance, they extend one leg; in this they differ from the Puyŏ. In moving about on foot they all run. In the tenth month they sacrifice to heaven in a great national assembly which they call *tongmaeng*. In their public gatherings they all wear colorfully brocaded clothing and adorn themselves with gold and silver. The Great *ka* and the *chubu* wear *tse* caps on their heads that are similar to ours but have no additional crown. Their Small *ka* wear "wind-breakers" shaped like *pien* caps. To the east of their state there is a large cave called the Tunnel Cave. At the great national festival of the tenth month they welcome the Su spirit at its return to the east of the state and offer sacrifice to it, placing a Su spirit of wood on the spirit seat. They have no prisons; when a crime is committed the several *ka* deliberate together, then kill the guilty one and take his wife and children as slaves.

As for their marriage customs, after the words of the contract have been fixed, the girl's family builds a small house behind the big house, which they call "the son-in-law's house." In the evening the son-in-law comes to the outside of the girl's family gate and, naming himself, bows in obeisance, begging permission to approach the girl's room. After he has done this two or three times, the girl's parents allow him to approach the small house and spend the night there. He stores his money and valuables on one side, and after his offspring have grown up, he takes his wife and returns to his own house. Such is the lewdness of their customs. After a man and a woman have already been married, they then make some clothing for the burial of their parents. They bury their dead with full ceremony; their treasure of gold and silver is consumed in funeral expenses. They pile up stones to make grave mounds and plant pine and oak trees before them in rows. MR

EASTERN OKCHŎ

Eastern Okchŏ is located to the east of the great mountains of Kaema in Koguryŏ; its people make their settlements on the shore of the great sea. In shape their land is narrow in the northeast and long in the southwest, where it is perhaps a thousand *li*. It is contiguous on the north with I-lou and Puyŏ, and on the south with Yemaek. Its households number five thousand. They have no supreme ruler, each village having its own hereditary chief. Their language has broad similarity with that of Koguryŏ, though at times there are small differences. . . . Since the chiefs of the Okchŏ's villages all call themselves the Three Elders, one may conclude that their system is that of the prefectures-and-kingdoms of former times. Their state being small and hemmed in between great states, they attach themselves as vassals to Koguryŏ; the latter in turn appoints the Great Man of their midst as *p'aeja,* commissioning him to serve as prime minister to the ruler. They furthermore charge the Great *ka* with responsibility for collection of their taxes: cloth, fish, salt, and edibles from the sea; they deliver these after bearing them on their backs for a thousand *li*. They also send their beautiful girls to become maidservants; they are treated as slaves.

Their land is fair and fertile, facing the sea with its back to the mountains. It is well suited to cultivation of the five grains, and they are good at tilling and planting. The people are simple and direct, strong and brave. Having few oxen and horses, they are adept at fighting on foot, wielding spears. In their eating and drinking, dwelling places, clothing and ritual, they bear resemblance to the people of Koguryŏ. As for their burial practices: they build a great wooden coffin more than ten *chang* in length; opening it at one end, they make a door and therein temporarily bury the newly deceased. They then make a tracing of the body, and when skin and flesh are gone, they take the bones and place them inside the coffin. A whole family shares a single coffin, the wooden surface of which is carved to resemble the living shapes of the dead, as many as are contained inside. They also have tile vessels that they fill with rice and hang on strands beside the coffin door. MR

YE

The state of Ye is contiguous with Chinhan on the south, and on the north with Koguryŏ and Okchŏ; on the east it ends at the great sea. The whole region east of present Chosŏn is its territory. Its households number two myriads. In the olden days Chi Tzu (Kija) proceeded to Chosŏn and composed his teachings in eight articles to instruct them; as a result, the people did not steal though doors and gates were not closed. More than forty generations later the marquis of Chosŏn (Chun) illegitimately claimed the title of king. When Ch'en Sheng and others rose up and the whole world rebelled against Ch'in, people of Yen, Ch'i, and Chao, several myriads in number, fled to Chosŏn. The Yen man Wiman (Wei Man), with drumstick coiffure and the barbarian attire, then came in turn to rule over them. When Emperor Wu of the Han marched against Chosŏn and wiped it out, he divided its territory into four commanderies. From that time forth, barbarian and Chinese were somewhat distinguished from each other. They have no sovereign chief; from Han times on their officials have included Marquis (*hu*), Township Lord (*ŭpkun*), and Three Elders, which have had general control over the lower households. Their elders have long considered that they are of the same stock as the Koguryŏ. Sincere by nature they keep their desires to a minimum, have a sense of shame, and do not beg for alms. In language, usages, and customs they are in general the same as the Koguryŏ, but in their clothing there are differences. Men and women both wear pleated collars, and the men plait silver flowers several inches wide for adornment. . . .

Their custom is to give great importance to mountains and rivers, each of which has certain parts into which people are not permitted to wade indiscriminately. Members of the same clan do not intermarry. They have many superstitions and taboos: in the event of illness or death, they always abandon their old dwelling, rebuild, and resettle. They have hemp cloth, as well as silkworms and mulberry trees, with which they make silk. At dawn they observe the stars and lunar stations to learn beforehand whether the year's crop will be abundant or short. They do not consider pearls or jade to be precious. They always use the festival of the tenth month to do ritual service to heaven; drinking, singing, and dancing day and night, they call this "dancing to heaven" (*much'ŏn*). They also sacrifice to the tiger as to a divine being. If their villages violently transgress upon each other, they are always penalized by exaction of slaves, oxen, and horses; this they call "exaction for outrage." One who kills another must die in retribution; there is little robbery among them. They make spears three *chang* in length, sometimes carried by three men at once. They are capable foot soldiers; the "sandalwood bow" of Lo-lang comes from their land. Their sea produces striped fish-skin, and their land abounds in the patterned leopard; they also produce "under the fruit" horses;[1] these were presented as tribute in the time of Emperor Huan of Han. MR

THE HAN

Han is south of Tai-fang and on the east and west is bounded by the sea; to the south it is contiguous with the state of Wa (Wae). Its territory is perhaps four thousand *li* square. There are three stocks: the first is called Mahan, the second Chinhan, and the third Pyŏnhan, which is the ancient state of Chin. Mahan is to the west of it. Its people are settled on the land and both sow and plant. They know about silkworms and the mulberry and make silk cloth. Each tribe has its own chief, of whom the great ones call themselves *sinji,* those next in status being called *ŭpch'a.* Scattered between the mountains and the sea, their settlements have no inner or outer walls. . . .

By custom they have few rules and regulations. Their national town has a dominant leader, but the people's settlements are scattered, and they are not readily subject to regulation and control. They do not have the ceremony of kneeling to make obeisance. For their dwellings they make grass-roofed earth-chambers shaped like tumuli; the door is on the top, and a whole family lives together inside, with no distinction as to old or young, male or female. In their burial practice they have an inner coffin but no outer coffin. They do not know about riding oxen and horses, their oxen and horses being used exclusively for accompanying the dead. They consider beads of pearls to have great value, sewing them into their clothing as decoration or hanging them from neck and ears. They do not regard gold, silver, brocades, or silks as precious. They are strong and brave by nature. They wear the "tadpole knot" and leave it bare like a shining fishtail. They wear gowns of rough cloth, and on their feet they wear leather sandals. When there is something to be done within their community up to the point where the authorities have walls built, all the young braves and stalwarts gouge out the skin of their backs to string themselves together with a large rope, or, again, they insert through their shin wooden poles about a *chang* in length. They then chant all day as they work, not because they consider the work painful, but to give themselves encouragement; moreover they consider this to be stalwart behavior.

In the fifth month when the sowing has been finished, they always sacrifice to their ghosts and spirits. Coming together in groups they sing and dance; they drink wine day and night without ceasing. In their dancing, several tens of men get up together and form a line; looking upward and downward as they stomp the ground, they move hands and feet in concert with a rhythm that is similar to our bell-clapper dance. When the farmwork is finished in the tenth month, they do the same sort of thing again. They have faith in ghosts and spirits. In each town one man is appointed master of ceremonies for worship of the spirit of heaven, whom they call Lord of Heaven (*ch'ŏngun*). Moreover each commune has a separate town, which they call *sodo*. Here they set up a great tree, from which they hang bells and drums for serving the ghosts and spirits. All manner of refugees who enter there are exempt from extradition. They have a fondness for brigandage. The significance of their setting up *sodo* is similar to that of our Buddhist shrines, but there are differences in the good and evil that they ascribe to what they do. The people of their northern communes that are close to our commandery have a fragmentary awareness of our rites and customs, but those located further away are just like aggregations of prisoners or slaves. They have no rare treasures that are different from ours, and their flora and fauna are about the same as those of the Middle Kingdom. They produce large chestnuts, as big as peaches. They also produce fine-tailed birds whose trails are more than five feet long. Among their men one occasionally sees one who is tattooed. Moreover on the large islands in the sea west of Mahan there are outlanders, very short and small people whose language is not the same as that of the Han. They all bind their hair like the Hsien-pi, but they make their clothing of leather and like to raise oxen and pigs. Their clothing has an upper part but no lower part, and indeed it is almost as if they were naked. They go back and forth by boat, buying and selling in Han. MR

CHINHAN

Chinhan is east of Mahan. In the stories handed down by their elders they describe themselves as refugees of long ago who, fleeing from the labor levies of Ch'in, came over to the Han state; the Mahan then ceded their eastern area to them. They have walls and palisades. The language they speak is not the same as that of the Mahan. "State" they call "country," "bow" they call "arc," "bandit" they call "brigand," and for "pass the wine" they say "pass the goblet"; and they always call each other "fellow." Thus they bear resemblance to the people of Ch'in: their terminology is not only that of Yen and Ch'i. They refer to the people of Lo-lang as *ajan*; since the people of the eastern quarter refer to themselves as *a*, they imply by their use of *ajan* that the people of Lo-lang were originally "our own remnant" people. Still today there are those who call them Ch'inhan. In the beginning they had six communes, and these have subdivided into twelve. MR

PYŎNHAN

Pyŏnhan too consists of twelve communes, and it further includes a number of small separate towns. Each has its own chief; of these the great ones are called *sinji,* and following them are the *kŏmch'ŭk*; then in order of precedence are the *pŏnye,* the *sarhae,* and the *ŭpch'a.* . . . Pyŏnhan and Chinhan together have twenty-four communes; of these the large ones have four to five thousand families and the small ones six to seven hundred. Altogether there are forty to fifty thousand households. Pyŏnhan's twelve communes are under the jurisdiction of the king of Chin. The king of Chin always employs a man of Mahan to exercise rule, and this position is inherited from generation to generation. The king of Chin is not able to set himself up as king over Pyŏnhan. Their land is fine and fertile, well suited to the planting of the five grains as well as millet. The people are familiar with sericulture, and make double-threaded cloth. They use oxen and horses for riding and traction. In their marriage rites and practices distinctions are made between men and women. They part with their dead using the feathers of large birds; this signifies their desire to have the dead fly aloft. Their state produces iron, which the Han, the Ye, and the Wa all come to get. In all their commercial transactions they use iron, just as we in the Middle Kingdom use copper coins. Moreover, they make payments to the two commanderies with it. By custom they take delight in singing, dancing, and drinking wine. They have a stringed zither (*se*) shaped like our bamboo zither (*chu*); in plucking it they also have tonal modulations. When a boy is born, they press down on his head with a stone, wishing that it be flat. That is why the men of Chinhan are now flat-headed. The men and women, being close to the Wa, also tattoo their bodies. They are agile at fighting on foot, and their weapons are the same as those of the Mahan. By custom, when two men on foot meet, both stop and yield the road. MR

THE PYŎNJIN

The Pyŏnjin live scattered among the Chinhan, and they too have walled towns. In their dress and dwellings they are the same as the Chinhan. Their languages and customs are similar, but there are differences in their cult of ghosts and spirits, in that they all set up their kitchen spirit altar to the west of the door. Their Tongno Commune is contiguous with the territory of the Wa. Their twelve communes also have kings. Their men are of large build. They keep their clothing fresh and clean and wear their hair long. They also make a fine-textured cloth in broad bolts. In their usages and customs they are particularly strict and unbending. MR

Founders of Tribal Federations

Along with the rise of the tribal federations of Old Chosŏn and Wiman Chosŏn in the north, there arose a tribal confederation known as Chin in the south by the fourth century B.C. These early entities gave way to the new confederations of Puyŏ, Koguryŏ, and Ye in the north and the Three Han in the south. In addition to breeding cattle and raising crops, the Puyŏ and Koguryŏ were horseriding people with impressive mobility and combat capability, while the people in the south were sedentary. The migrants from the north at the time of the demise of Old Chosŏn stimulated the indigenous society in the south through dissemination of their iron culture and through the enlargement of the economic base that was made possible by this active trade among tribes and the fusion of their cultures.

The foundation myth of Koguryŏ, as recorded in King Tongmyŏng's story, is not a myth of the creation of the world but one of migration, with vestiges of the tradition transmitted from ancient Korea. That the founders of Paekche were a group of migrants from the Puyŏ family is attested by the letter sent to the Northern Wei by King Kaero; by the name of the state, South Puyŏ, given by King Sŏng after transferring his capital to Sabi; by Puyŏ as the clan name of the Paekche king; and by Chinese accounts starting from the *Wei shu*. The protagonist of the legends, however, varies: he is Onjo and Puryu in the *Samguk sagi* (Historical Record of the Three Kingdoms); Kuta'e in the *Chou shu;* Tomo in *Shoku Nihongi*. Of these, the account in the *Historical Record of the Three Kingdoms* is most detailed. How the migrants bringing with them the iron culture joined with the natives there to build a state is told in the story of Pak Hyŏkkŏse. As told in the final selection, the Sŏk clan arrived next, and the tribal federation comprising Pak, Sŏk, and Kim ensued.

The Lay of King Tongmyŏng
[From *Tongguk Yi sangguk chip* 3:2a–8a]

In the third year of Shen-ch'üeh of Han,[2]
In early summer, when the Great Bear stood in the Snake,
Haemosu came to Korea,
A true Son of Heaven.
He came down through the air
In a five-dragon chariot,
With a retinue of hundreds,
Robes streaming, riding on swans.
The atmosphere echoed with chiming music,
Banners floated on the tinted clouds.
From oldest times men ordained to rule
Have come down from heaven,
But in daylight he came from the heart of the sky—
A thing never before seen.
In the mornings he dwelt among men,
In the evenings he returned to his heavenly palace.
The ancients have told us
That between heaven and earth the distance
Is two hundred thousand million
Eighteen thousand seven hundred and eighty *ri*.
A scaling-ladder could not reach so far,
Flying pinions could not bear the strain,
Yet morning and evening he went and returned at will.
By what power could he do it?
North of the capital was the Green River,
Where the River Earl's three beautiful daughters
Rose from the drake-neck's green waves
To play in the Bear's Heart Pool.
Their jade ornaments tinkled,
Their flowerlike beauty was modest—
They might have been fairies of the Han River banks,
Or goddesses of the Lo River islets.

The king, out hunting, espied them,
Was fascinated and lost his heart,
Not from lust for girls,
But from eager desire for an heir.
The three sisters saw him coming
And plunged into the water to flee,
So the king prepared a palace
To hide in till they came back:
He traced foundations with a riding whip:
A bronze palace suddenly towered,
Silk cushions were spread, bright and elegant,
Golden goblets waited with fragrant wine.
Soon the three maidens came in,
And toasted each other until they were drunk.
Then the king emerged from hiding;
The startled girls ran, tripped, and fell.
The oldest was Willow Flower,
And it was she whom the king caught.
The Earl of the River raged in anger,
And sent a speedy messenger
To demand, "What rogue are you
Who dares behave so presumptuously?"
"Son of the Heavenly Emperor," replied Haemosu,
"I'm asking for your noble daughter's hand."
He beckoned to heaven: the dragon car came down,
And straightaway he drove to the Ocean Palace
Where the River Earl admonished him:
"Marriage is a weighty matter,
Needing go-betweens and gifts.
Why have you done these things?
If you are God's own heir,
Prove your powers of transmogrification!"
Through the rippling, flowing green waters
The River Earl leapt, changed into a carp;
The king turned at once into an otter
That seized the carp before it could move.
The earl then sprouted wings,
Flying upward, transformed into a pheasant;
But the king was a golden eagle
And struck like a great bird of prey;

The earl sped away as a stag,
The king pursued as wolf.
The earl then confessed that the king was divine,
Poured wine, and they drank to the contract.
When the king was drunk, he was put in a leather bag,
Set beside the girl in his chariot,
And set off with her
To rise to heaven together;
But the car had not left the water
Before Haemosu woke from his stupor
And, seizing the girl's golden hairpin,
Pierced the leather and slid out through the hole,
To mount alone beyond the crimson clouds.
All was quiet; he did not return.
The River Earl punished his daughter
By stretching her lips three feet long,
And throwing her into the Ubal stream
With only two maidservants.
A fisherman saw them in the eddies,
Creatures disporting themselves strangely,
And reported the fact to King Kŭmwa.
An iron net was set in the torrent,
And the woman was trapped on a rock,
A monster of fearful appearance,
Whose long lips made her mute.
Three times they were trimmed before she could speak.
King Kŭmwa recognized Haemosu's wife,
And gave her a palace to live in.
The sun shone in her breast and she bore Chumong[3]
In the fourth year of Shen-ch'üeh.[4]
His form was wonderful,
His voice of mighty power.
He was born from a pottle-sized egg
That frightened all who saw it.
The king thought it inauspicious,
Monstrous and inhuman,
And put it into the horse corral,
But the horses took care not to trample it;
It was thrown down steep hills,
But the wild beasts all protected it;

Its mother retrieved it and nurtured it,
Till the boy hatched. His first words were:
"The flies are nibbling my eyes,
I cannot lie and sleep in peace."
His mother made him a bow and arrows,
And he never missed a shot.

Years passed, he grew up,
Getting cleverer every day,
And the crown prince of the Puyŏ[5]
Began to grow jealous,
Saying, "This fellow Chumong
Is a redoubtable warrior.
If we do not act soon,
He will give trouble later."
So the king sent Chumong to tend horses,
To test his intentions.
Chumong meditated, "For heaven's grandson
To be a mere herdsman is unendurable shame."
Searching his heart, he sought the right way:
"I had rather die than live like this.
I would go southward,
Found a nation, build a city—
But for my mother,
Whom it is hard to leave."
His mother heard his words
And wept; but wiped her glistening tears:
"Never mind about me.
Rather I fear for your safety.
A knight setting out on a journey
Needs a trusty stallion."
Together they went to the corral
And thrashed the horses with long whips.
The terrified animals milled about,
But one horse, a beautiful bay,
Leapt over the two-fathom wall,
And proved itself best of the herd.
They fixed a needle in his tongue
That stung him so he could not eat;
In a day or two he wasted away

And looked like a worn-out jade.
When the king came around to inspect,
He gave this horse to Chumong,
Who took it, removed the needle,
And fed the horse well, day and night.
Then he made a compact with three friends,
Friends who were men of wisdom;
They set off south till they reached the Ŏm,
But could find no ferry to cross.
Chumong raised his whip to the sky,
And uttered a long sad plaint:
"Grandson of Heaven, Grandson of the River,
I have come here in flight from danger.
Look on my pitiful orphaned heart:
Heaven and Earth, have you cast me off?"
Gripping his bow, he struck the water:
Fishes and turtles hurried, heads and tails together,
To form a great bridge,
Which the friends at once traversed.
Suddenly, pursuing troops appeared
And mounted the bridge; but it melted away.
A pair of doves brought barley in their bills,
Messengers sent by his mysterious mother.
He chose a site for his capital
Amid mountains and streams and thick-wooded hills.
Seating himself on the royal mat as King Tongmyŏng,[6]
He ordered the ranks of his subjects.
Alas for Songyang, king of Piryu,
Why was he so undiscerning?
Was he a son of the immortal gods,
Who could not recognize a scion of heaven?
He asked Tongmyŏng to be his vassal,
Uttering rash demands,
But could not hit the painted deer's navel,[7]
And was amazed when Tongmyŏng split the jade ring;
He found his drum and bugle changed
And dared not call them his;[8]
He saw Tongmyŏng's ancient pillars,
Then returned home biting his tongue.[9]
So Tongmyŏng went hunting in the west,

Caught a tall snow-white deer,
Strung it up by the hind feet at Haewŏn,
And produced a great malediction:
"Let heaven pour torrents on Piryu,
And wash away his capital.
I will not let you go
Till you help me vent my wrath."
The deer cried with sounds so piteous
They reached the ears of heaven.
A great rain fell for seven days,
Floods came like Huai joined with Ssu;
Songyang was frightened and anxious.
He had thick ropes stretched by the water,
Knights and peasants struggled to clutch them,
Sweating and gaping in fear.
Then Tongmyŏng took his whip
And drew a line at which the waters stopped.
Songyang submitted
And thereafter there was no argument.
A dark cloud covered Falcon Pass,
The crests of the ridges were hidden,
And thousands upon thousands of carpenters
Were heard hammering there.
The king said, "Heaven for me
Is preparing a fortress up yonder."
Suddenly the mist dispersed
And a palace stood out high and splendid,
Where Tongmyŏng ruled for nineteen years,
Till he rose to heaven and forsook his throne.[10] RR

King Onjo of Paekche
[From *Samguk sagi* 23:207–208]

The father of King Onjo, the founder of Paekche, was Ch'umo
or Chumong. He fled from North Puyŏ to escape troubles and went
to Cholbon Puyŏ, whose king had no son but had three daughters.
Knowing that Chumong was extraordinary, the king presented his
second daughter to him in marriage. Shortly thereafter the king died
and was succeeded by Chumong. Chumong had two sons, Piryu and
Onjo.

When Yuri, a son of Chumong, born in North Puyŏ, came to Cholbon Puyŏ and became heir to the throne, Piryu and Onjo were afraid of being rejected by their half brother and traveled south with ten counselors, including Ogan and Maryŏ. Many followed them. Upon reaching Hansan, they climbed Pua Peak (Mount Samgak) to find a place to settle. When Piryu wished to settle by the sea, the counselors advised him: "The land south of the Han borders the Han River to the north, takes to a high mountain to the east, views a fertile marsh to the south, and is separated by a great sea to the west. Its natural fastness is unparalleled, a place fit for your capital." But Piryu did not listen. He divided the people and went to Mich'uhol (Inch'ŏn) to settle. Onjo set up his capital at Hanam Wiryesŏng (Kwangju), made ten counselors his assistants, and named his country Sipche. This was in the third year of Hung-chia of Emperor Ch'eng of the Former Han [18 B.C.].

Because the land of Mich'uhol was wet and its water salty, Piryu could not live in comfort; when he returned and saw Wirye firmly established and its people happy, he died of shame and remorse. His followers pledged allegiance to Wirye and joyfully came to submit, and hence the country was named Paekche. Like Koguryŏ, the ruling family of Paekche stems from Puyŏ, which they adopted as their clan name.

Another account names King Piryu as the founder. His father was Ut'ae, a grandson of Haeburu, king of North Puyŏ, and his mother Sosŏno, the daughter of Yŏnt'abal of Cholbon. By Ut'ae Sosŏno bore two sons, the eldest being Piryu and the second Onjo. When Ut'ae died, Sosŏno remained a widow in Cholbon. Later Chumong, not being accepted by North Puyŏ, moved south to Cholbon in the second month of the second year of Chien-chao of the Former Han [37 B.C.]. He made Cholbon his capital, called his country Koguryŏ, and took Sosŏno as his wife. She helped him found his state and was loved by him; he also treated her two sons as his own.

When Yuryu, Chumong's son from his earlier marriage to Lady Ye, came, he was made heir apparent. Thus he succeeded to the throne. Thereupon Piryu said to Onjo, "When the great king first came here to flee from the adversity in Puyŏ, our mother used up her fortune to help him found his country. She worked hard. Now that the great king is dead, the country is Yuryu's. We cannot stay here, depressed and useless as a wen. It is better to go south with Mother, choose a site, and hold our court there." With Onjo and his followers, he crossed the P'ae (Yesŏng) and Tae (Imjin) Rivers to Mich'uhol (Inch'ŏn), where he lived.

The *Pei shih* and *Sui shu* say that Kut'ae [Koi, 234–286], Tong-myŏng's descendant, was benevolent and faithful to the utmost. He first set up his country in the area of Tai-fang Commandery. The Chinese governor of Liao-tung, Kung-sun Tu [d. 204], presented his daughter to him in marriage. Thus did Paekche become a power among the Eastern Barbarians. PL

Pak Hyŏkkŏse, the Founder of Silla

[From *Samguk yusa* 1:43–45]

In olden times Chinhan had six villages, each belonging to a separate clan whose ancestor was said to have descended from heaven. . . .

On the first day of the third month of the first year, *imja*, of Ti-chieh of the Former Han [69 B.C.], the ancestors of the six villages, together with their children, gathered by the shore of the Al River. They said, "Because we have no ruler above to govern the people, the people are dissolute and do only what they wish. We should seek out a virtuous man to be our king, found a country, and lay out a capital."

When they climbed to a height and looked southward, they saw an eerie lightninglike emanation by the Na Well under Mount Yang, while nearby a white horse kneeled and bowed. When they reached the spot they found a red egg; the horse neighed and flew up to heaven when it saw men approaching. When the people cracked the egg open, they discovered within a beautiful infant boy with a radiant visage. Amazed by their discovery, they bathed the infant in the East Spring, and then he emitted light. Birds and beasts danced for joy, heaven and earth shook, and the sun and the moon became bright. They named the child King Hyŏkkŏse, or Bright, and titled him *kŏsŭrhan,* or king.

The people congratulated one another and said, "Now that the Son of Heaven has come down to be among us, we must seek a virtuous queen to be his mate." That day a hen dragon appeared near the Aryŏng Well in Saryang district and produced from under her left rib an infant girl. Her features were unusually lovely, but her lips were like the beak of a chick. Only when the girl was given a bath in the North River in Wŏlsŏng did the beak fall off. The river was then called Palch'ŏn. The people erected a palace at the western foot of Mount South and reared the two wondrous infants together. Since the boy had been born from an egg in the shape of a gourd, *pak* in Korean, they gave him the surname Pak; the girl was named after the well where she was born.

When the two reached the age of thirteen in the first year, *kapcha*, of Wu-feng [57 B.C.], the boy became king and the girl became queen. They named the country Sŏrabŏl, Sŏbŏl, Sara, or Saro. And because of the circumstances surrounding the queen's birth, the country was also called Kyerim, or Forest of the Cock, to commemorate the appearance of the hen dragon. According to another story, the country was so called because a cock crowed in the woods when Kim Alchi was found during the reign of King T'arhae. Later, Silla became the official name of the country.

After a sixty-one-year reign, Hyŏkkŏse ascended to heaven, and after seven days his remains fell to earth. His queen is said to have followed him. The people wished to bury them in the same tomb, but a large snake appeared and stopped them. So the remains of each were divided into five parts and buried. Called Five Tombs or Snake Tomb, it is the present North Tomb at Tamŏm Monastery. The heir apparent succeeded Hyŏkkŏse as King Namhae. PL

King T'arhae of Silla
[From *Samguk yusa* 1:47–48]

During the reign of King Namhae [4–24], a boat came to anchor off the shores of Karak. King Suro of that country, together with his people, beat drums and shouted to welcome it, but the boat sailed away and reached Ajin Cove in the village of Hasŏji, east of the Forest of the Cock. Just then an old woman appeared on the shore of the inlet. Her name was Ajin Uisŏn, and she was the mother of the fisherman of King Hyŏkkŏse. Espying the boat from afar, she said, "There is no rock in the middle of the sea. Why does a flock of magpies circle there and cry?" She took a skiff and went to investigate. Magpies hovered over the boat, which bore a casket twenty feet long and thirteen feet wide. She pulled the boat and moored it at the foot of a grove of trees. She did not know whether it would be auspicious or not and made a vow to heaven for good luck. Then she opened the casket. She found a handsome boy, seven treasures, and male and female slaves.

After being provided for seven days, the boy said, "I am from the land of Yongsŏng, where there were twenty-eight dragon kings, all born from human wombs. They ascended the throne one after another at the age of five or six, taught the people, and regulated life. We have clans of eight ranks, but all ascended to the throne without elections. My father, King Hamdalp'a, married the daughter of the king of the land of Chŏngnyŏ, but she long remained barren and prayed for a son. After seven years, she gave birth to a huge egg. The great king gathered and consulted his ministers, who said, "We have never heard of a woman giving birth to an egg; surely it is a bad omen." The king had a casket made, put me into it, together with seven treasures and slaves, and loaded it on a boat. He had it launched, and prayed that it would land on a destined place, found a kingdom, and establish a family. A red dragon came to guard the boat until it arrived here."

Then the boy, his staff trailing after him, climbed Mount T'oham with two slaves, built a cairn where he stayed for seven days, and looked around for a suitable place within the city walls to settle. He saw a hill shaped like a three days' crescent moon, an ideal place for a long stay. When he went down and approached the place, it was Lord Ho's residence. The boy devised a ruse: he had whetstone and charcoal buried around the house. The next day, he went to the door and declared that it was the house of his ancestors. Lord Ho denied this, and, after a quarrel without reaching a decision, they brought the case before the authorities. When the officials asked the boy to prove his case, he replied, "We are a family of blacksmiths, but we were away at a nearby village. During our absence some other person occupied our house. I beg you to dig the ground and make a search." They found the whetstone and charcoal, so the house became his. Acknowledging the shrewdness of the boy, King Namhae gave him his eldest daughter in marriage. . . .

Upon the death of King Yuri in the sixth month, *chŏngsa*, of the second year of Chung-yüan of Emperor Kuang-wu [A.D. 57], T'arhae ascended the throne. Because he had taken another's property under the pretext that it was his ancestors', his surname became Sŏk ("old"); or because magpies caused the casket to be opened, the bird radical was dropped from the graph "magpie," leaving the one for Sŏk. His name T'arhae ("remove and undo") alludes to the fact that he came out of an egg from a casket.

After a rule of twenty-three years, he died in the fourth year of Chien-ch'u [A.D. 79], *kimyo,* and was buried on the hill of Soch'ŏn. Later a god said, "Remove my bones." His skeleton was three feet two inches in circumference, his body was nine feet seven inches tall, his teeth were closely set like one tooth, his bones were joined closely —indeed he was a peerless giant. His remains were broken, remade into a statue, and enshrined in the palace. Then a god spoke again, "Bury my bones on Eastern Peak." So he was enshrined there.   PL

CHAPTER TWO

The Rise of the Three Kingdoms

Development of the Three Kingdoms

From the third century, the Three Kingdoms were aware of the existence of the Wei, Shu, and Wu on the mainland. The successive rise and fall of such mainland states and dynasties was strongly felt in the Three Kingdoms since they related to their own fortunes. Koguryŏ, the first to be aware of its place in international politics, was also the first to grow as a state, and it was politically and culturally superior to Paekche and Silla. When the Kung-sun clan encouraged internal dissension in Koguryŏ during the reign of King Sansang, Koguryŏ obstructed the alliance between Liao-tung and Hsüan-t'u. Thus Koguryŏ was able to withstand a Chinese policy aimed at its dissolution. When Silla and T'ang were at odds, the T'ang attempted a similar policy of fostering internal discord in Silla, as attested by diplomatic papers exchanged between the two. Koguryŏ alone was able to see through China's designs and to take advantage of political divisions in the Chinese mainland. The state's negotiations with peoples outside the Wall are another example of Koguryŏ's aggressive diplomacy. Through expansion Koguryŏ extended its sphere of influence to the Moho and Khitan tribes, and the state became the center of Northeast Asia and the leader in the struggle against China. After the fall of the Sui, the founder of the T'ang wondered if Koguryŏ should be treated as a tributary state.[1]

Paekche and Silla, on the other hand, were able to send migrants to Japan to establish political authority there but were unable to subjugate the Japanese. Their foreign policy was aimed at stopping the southward advance of Koguryŏ, and during the struggle among the Three Kingdoms, they turned to the Sui and T'ang for help. The unification of China by the Sui and the rise of the T'u-chüeh Turks prompted Koguryŏ to ally itself with the latter to oppose the former. Then Koguryŏ's ally Paekche established ties with people residing in what later became Japan. The north-south pact among the T'u-chüeh, Koguryŏ, Paekche, and Japan was opposed by the alliance between Silla and the Sui. And as leaders of the two opposing forces, Koguryŏ and Sui came to war in 598 and again in 612–614. At this crucial moment in Koguryŏ's history, its foremost general was Ŭlchi Mundŏk.

The four monuments built when King Chinhŭng of Silla inspected the newly conquered territories in the north, south, and west include those at Ch'angnyŏng (A.D. 561), Mount Pukhan (555), Hwangch'o Pass, and Maun Pass (568). Another monument discovered in 1978, in Chŏksŏng in Tanyang (built about 551), was not built at the time of this inspection but shows how Silla governed that area in the sixth century.

Ŭlchi Mundŏk

[From *Samguk sagi* 44:410–411]

The genealogy of Ŭlchi Mundŏk is uncertain. By nature he was self-possessed, brave, and resourceful. He was also able to write.

During the period of Ta-yeh [605–617], when Emperor Yang of Sui issued an edict declaring war on Koguryŏ, Great General of Left Assisting Guard Yü-wen Shu advanced from the Fu-yü Circuit and Great General of Right Assisting Guard Yü Chung-wen marched from the Lo-lang Circuit and reached the Yalu together with the nine armies. By royal decree Ŭlchi went to the enemy camp, ostensibly to surrender, but in fact seeking to learn the enemy's true strength. Earlier Yü-wen Shu and Yü Chung-wen had received a secret imperial edict ordering them to capture the king of Koguryŏ or General Ŭlchi Mundŏk, if either came. Yü Chung-wen and others intended to detain Ŭlchi, but the Assistant Director of the Right of the Department of State Affairs Liu Shih-lung, as Commissioner of Pacification, vigorously opposed this plan. Thus Ŭlchi was allowed to return home. But the Chinese regretted letting him go and therefore attempted to detain him with a spurious message: "We have something to discuss. Please return."

Ŭlchi did not look back, however, and he finally crossed the Yalu to his home. Both Yü-wen Shu and Yü Chung-wen were very uneasy on account of their failure to detain him. Yü-wen Shu was short of provisions and planned to withdraw. At that time Yü Chung-wen said, "If picked troops are sent to pursue Ŭlchi, we will win fame."

Yü-wen opposed Yü Chung-wen in this, and the latter retorted angrily, "If you, a general with one hundred thousand men at his command, cannot destroy one puny foe, how will you be able to face the emperor?"

Compelled to join forces with Yü Chung-wen, Yü-wen Shu crossed the Yalu in pursuit of Ŭlchi. Noting the famished appearance of the enemy troops, Ŭlchi sought to wear them down by feigning flight at every engagement. Thus the Chinese won seven battles in a day. Trusting to their luck and urged on by their own mutual encouragements, the Chinese finally marched east across the Sal River (Ch'ŏngch'ŏn) and pitched camp on a mountain thirty *ri* from the walled capital of P'yŏngyang. Ŭlchi sent a poem to Yü Chung-wen:

> Your divine plans have plumbed the heavens;
> Your subtle reckoning has spanned the earth.
> You win every battle, your military merit is great.
> Why then not be content and stop the war?[2]

Yü Chung-wen sent Ŭlchi an admonishing reply.

Ŭlchi again sent a message of surrender and told Yü-wen Shu, "If you withdraw, I shall bring our king for an audience with your emperor in his temporary quarters." Because his troops were too tired to fight and because the walls of P'yŏngyang were steep and thick and could not be reduced, Yü-wen Shu decided to raise the siege. The troops withdrew in a square formation.

Ŭlchi sent his troops to attack the enemy on four sides. Now fighting, now marching, when half of the enemy force was at the Sal River crossing, Ŭlchi dealt a severe blow on the rearguard and slew General of the Right Camps Guard Hsin Shih-hsiung. Thereupon the enemy army disintegrated and could not be marshaled again. The soldiers of the nine armies were routed, and they fled four hundred and fifty *ri* to the Yalu in a day and a night. When they crossed the Liao River, the nine armies had numbered three hundred five thousand. Only twenty-seven hundred of these escaped to the walled town of Liao-tung. PL

King Chinhŭng's Monument at Maun Pass
[From *Samguk yusa*, Appendix 14]

If a benevolent wind does not blow, the way of the world perverts truth. And if moral enlightenment is not set forth, evils will vie with one another. Therefore, emperors and kings established their reign titles, cultivated themselves to the utmost, and brought peace to their subjects. I, however, confronting destiny, inherited the foundation of our progenitor and succeeded to the throne. Cautious and circumspect, I was fearful of going against the Way of Heaven. As I basked in heaven's favor, good fortunes were manifested, the spirits of heaven and earth responded, and every enterprise tallied with the norm. Hence, the four quarters entrusted their borders, and we gained extensively in territory and population. Neighboring countries pledged their trust, and envoys of peace were exchanged. The court sympathized with the people and nurtured both old and new subjects. The people now say, "The transforming process of the Way extends outward and its favor pervades everywhere."

Thereupon, in the eighth month, autumn, of this year, *muja* [568], I have inspected the territory under my jurisdiction and inquired into popular feelings. I intend to encourage by rewards the loyal and the trustworthy, the sincere and the talented, those who apprehend danger and those who fight with valor and serve with loyalty. They shall be rewarded with rank and title and honored for their loyal services. PL

Development of Agriculture

The use of cattle and farm tools made of iron greatly increased agricultural production in the Three Kingdoms. Moreover, construction of dams and the establishment of private ownership of land accelerated the growth of landowners among the aristocracy. These landowners increased their holdings by land reclamation or purchase and sale; they built reservoirs and owned the rights to mines. The development of industry and the concentration of the means of production in their hands brought about a major change in society: the division between the aristocracy and the commoners. Thus a rigid class system was born.

The monument erected on the occasion of the completion of a dike in Yŏngch'ŏn sheds light on the living conditions of the villagers, who formed the basic stratum of Silla society, and on the labor mobilization system used by the state. Erected when a reservoir called Luxuriant Dike was built and later repaired, both sides of this monument are inscribed. One side, dated *pyŏngjin*, marks the time of construction, probably 536, the twenty-third year of King Pŏphŭng; the other side, dated Cheng-yüan 14, marks the repair of the reservoir in the fourteenth year of King Wŏnsŏng (798). According to the inscriptions, between the sixth century, when Silla was developing as an ancient state, and the eighth century, when its society began to disintegrate, Silla expended considerable energy implementing irrigation plans. The inscriptions also show the relationship between the central authority and powerful local families, the size of the labor force, and the times of its mobilization. Since the inscription dated 536 is chipped and illegible, the 798 inscription is offered here.

Record of Repair of Luxuriant Dike in Yŏngch'ŏn
[From *Chŭngbo Hanguk kŭmsŏk yumun*, no. 5]

Having repaired Luxuriant Dike, we record it here on the thirteenth day of the fourth month of the fourteenth year of Cheng-yüan, *muin.* Since the bank of the reservoir was damaged, the king dispatched an official with the temporary duty of overseeing the work. The bank's length is thirty-five steps; its height, six steps and three *ch'ŏk;* and its width, twelve steps. The work lasted from the twelfth day of the second month to the thirteenth day of the fourth month, and it was completed during that period. The labor force consisted of 136 axe men and 14,140 soldiers from the Dharma Banner; recruiters from the districts of Chŏrhwa (Yŏngch'ŏn) and Amnyang were—.[3] Overseers were Yŏn, the *sonaesa,* whose local rank was *sanggan* [Rank 6] and court rank was *naemi* [Rank 11]; Sasu, whose court rank was *taesa* [Rank 12]; and Oksun, temporary governor of the district [*kat'aesu*] from Saryang, whose court rank was *naemi.* PL

Political Thought

A major feature of the political life of the Three Kingdoms was the emergence of hereditary lines of kingship as the three entities evolved from loose tribal confederations to centralized monarchies. These royal lines had to achieve for themselves a position superior to the old aristocracy from which they had emerged. This effort was both shaped by and reflected in the political thought of the time, most notably in Confucianism.

In Silla, as shown in the monument at Maun Pass, royal authority was described by means of the kingly way in the *Book of Documents* and Confucian political thought in the *Analects* in order to justify Silla's territorial expansion. In his request to the Sui for military aid, Great Master Wŏngwang also cited the kingly way to justify Silla's position. Moreover, reign titles, such as *kŏnwŏn* (Established Prime) for King Pŏphŭng as well as *kaeguk* (Opened State), *t'aech'ang* (Great Glories), and *hongje* (Vast Relief) for King Chinhŭng, were attempts to rationalize the development of a state by means of Confucian ideology.

Advancement from tribal chief to king required growing power and a broad political base. Ŭl P'aso (d. 203) strove to realize that goal in Koguryŏ. Without being a clan chief, he became state minister under King Kogukch'ŏn (179–196). Ŭl P'aso endeavored to mediate among royal clans and the powerful aristocracy and to establish a fair political base, thereby contributing to the political development of Koguryŏ.

The advocacy of kingly virtue was a means to curb autocratic rule. The fifth, seventh, and fourteenth rulers of Koguryŏ were deposed because of their cruelty. Minister Ch'ang Chori admonished the fourteenth king, Pongsang, for his extravagance and disregard for the welfare of the people. In his admonition, Ch'ang Chori invoked goodness and loyalty to underscore the importance of elements in the Confucian political system that had become popularly accepted. Likewise in Silla, Kim Hujik (fl. 579–631), the erstwhile minister of war, quoted passages from the *Book of Documents* and *The Way and Its Power,* an indication of the influence of Chinese political thought at that time.

Ŭl P'aso

[From *Samguk sagi* 45:419–420]

Ŭl P'aso was a man of Koguryŏ. During the reign of King Kogukch'ŏn [179–196], *p'aeja* Ŏsŭngnyu and *p'yŏngja* Chwagaryŏ, as maternal relations of the ruling house, wielded power and committed misdeeds. The people were outraged. The king was angry and wished to put them to death. Thereupon they rebelled, and the king either banished their followers or had them executed. The king issued a decree: "Recently positions have been awarded through favoritism and promotions granted without regard to the candidate's virtue. This practice has poisoned the people and troubled the royal house. All this is owing to my lack of sagacity. I ask the four enclaves to recommend worthy administrators from their offices."

Thereupon the four districts recommended Allyu of the Eastern Enclave. When the king summoned Allyu to entrust the administration to him, Allyu said, "Your humble subject is simple and stupid and cannot administer state affairs. Ŭl P'aso in Chwamul village in West Yalu Valley is a descendant of Ŭl So, a minister under King Yuri [19 B.C.–A.D. 18]. Though firm of purpose and full of resources, he is unrecognized by the world and works diligently as a farmer to support himself. If Your Majesty wishes to manage state affairs, he is the only man to summon." The king sent for Ŭl P'aso with humble words and extreme courtesy, appointed him as *chungwi taebu,* and added the title of *ut'ae* [Rank 6], saying, "I have inherited the royal work of the former king and occupy a position above the people. But my virtue is small and talent lacking, and I am not governing well. You, sir, have concealed your talents and wisdom and have dwelt long in the country. That you have not shunned me but have come forthwith is not only a joy and a boon to me, but is a blessing to the dynasty and the people. Since I wish to learn from you, devote your mind to the task of teaching me."

Ŭl P'aso intended to offer his life to the country but thought that the title he had been given was not high enough to carry out the work he was to do. To the king he said, "Your subject is a jaded horse. He is unfit for service and cannot receive your commands. I beg Your Majesty to choose a worthy and good person and confer on him a high position so that he might accomplish great things." The king caught the hint and made Ŭl P'aso the state minister in charge of the reins of government.

Under the pretext that the presence of a newcomer had estranged the incumbent ministers, courtiers and members of the royal house hated Ŭl P'aso. The king's message was a stern one: "Anyone, high or low, who disobeys the minister will have his entire clan destroyed." Ŭl P'aso withdrew, saying, "If the times are bad, you live in hiding, and if the times are good, you serve—this is the official's watchword. Now that the king has received me with great kindness, how could I think of returning to my former seclusion?" Ŭl P'aso served the country faithfully. He elucidated official decrees and was circumspect in meting out rewards and punishments. Thus he brought peace to the people and security at home and abroad. The king told Allyu, "Were it not for your advice, I would not have obtained the services of Ŭl P'aso. The current achievements in government stand to your credit." The king appointed Allyu *taesaja*.

In the eighth month, autumn, of the seventh year of King Sansang [203], Ŭl P'aso died. The whole nation mourned his death.   PL

Ch'ang Chori
[From *Samguk sagi* 49:448]

Ch'ang Chori, a man of Koguryŏ, became prime minister under King Pongsang [292–300]. At that time there were frequent border raids by Mu-jung Hui, and the king asked his ministers, "Mu-jung's force is strong and invades our territory. What shall we do?"

Ch'ang replied, "The *taehyŏng* of the Northern Enclave, Konoja, is wise and brave. If you wish to defend the country from foreign invasions and bring peace to the people, Konoja is the only person to employ." When the king made Konoja the governor of Sinsŏng, Mu-jung's forces did not come again.

In the eighth month of the ninth year [300], the king mobilized all adult males above the age of fifteen to repair the palace complex. Suffering from hunger and the fatigue, many began to flee. Ch'ang admonished the king, "Because of repeated national disasters and bad crops, the people have lost their homes. The adult flee to the four directions while the old and the young die in ditches. This is the time to heed heaven, to concern yourself about the people, to be apprehensive and fearful, and to examine yourself with a view to reform. Unmindful of all this, Your Majesty drives the hungry forth and plagues them with public works, contrary to your role as father to the people. Moreover, we have a strong enemy on our border. Should our enemy seize this opportunity to attack, what will become of our dynasty and our people? I beg Your Majesty to consider my words carefully."

The king retorted angrily, "The people must look up to their king. If the palace is not magnificent, we cannot show our majesty. Now you wish to slander me in order to win the praise of the people."

Ch'ang replied, "If the ruler does not relieve the sufferings of the people, he is not good. If a subject does not offer remonstrance, he is not loyal. Having succeeded to the post of prime minister, I cannot help but speak out. How could I have thought of my own reputation?"

Laughing, the king said, "Do you wish to die for the people? I beg you not to mention it again."

Knowing that the king would not mend his ways, Ch'ang withdrew and planned with other ministers to depose him. The king knew that death was inevitable and hanged himself. PL

Kim Hujik's Admonition of King Chinp'yŏng
[From *Samguk sagi* 45:420]

Kim Hujik, the great-grandson of King Chijŭng [500–514], served King Chinp'yŏng [579–632] as *ich'an* and was transferred to the Ministry of Defense. Kim admonished the king, who loved hunting. "The king of olden times," Kim said, "conducted all state affairs, thought deeply about both what lay near at hand and what was distant, accepted the honest admonitions of upright officials, was diligent, and dared not be complacent or thoughtless of his duties. Therefore he was able to achieve the beauty of virtuous government and preserve the country. Now Your Majesty, together with dissolute men and hunters, every day releases hawks and hounds to pursue pheasants and rabbits in the hills and on the plains. The *Lao Tzu* says, 'Riding and hunting/ Makes his mind go wild with excitement.'[4] And the *Book of Documents* says, 'When the palace is a wilderness of lust and the country a wilderness for hunting, . . . the existence of any one of these has ever been the prelude to ruin.'[5] Therefore if your mind is dissolute within, the country will be ruined without. You must reflect on your conduct. I beg Your Majesty to think on this."

The king was recalcitrant. Kim Hujik admonished the king earnestly, but the king would not heed him.

At his deathbed, Kim Hujik told his three sons, "As a subject I have been unable to correct the king's misdeeds. If he does not put an end to his pleasures, he will bring ruin to the nation. This is my great concern. Even though I die, I still wish to awaken him. Bury my bones by the roadside on the king's hunting route." The sons followed their father's wishes.

One day the king was again out hunting. On his way he heard from afar a voice calling, "Please do not go!" Looking back the king asked, "Where does the voice come from?"

The attendant replied, "That is the grave of *ich'an* Kim Hujik," and he reported Kim's last words.

Shedding tears copiously, the king said, "You have not forgotten your loyal admonition even after death. Your love for me is indeed deep. If I do not mend my ways, how shall I see you in the underworld?" Never again did the king go hunting. PL.

Tribal Councils

States were formed through the unification of clan leaders and tribal chiefs, but such a power base also entailed limitations. From their beginnings, each of the Three Kingdoms underwent a similar process, as shown by the five-tribe federation in Koguryŏ and the six-tribe federation in Silla. (There was a five-tribe federation in Puyŏ and a six-tribe federation in Kaya as well, but these were destroyed before they could develop into states.) In Koguryŏ and Silla, the organization of a tribal federation resulted in a ruling power and a hierarchy of official ranks. And the management of a ruling system called for the institution of councils. Silla required unanimous consent for decisions on important matters (*hwabaek,* Council of Nobles), and such deliberations took place at the four sacred places. In addition, there was the South Hall Council where affairs of state were deliberated.

Paekche's *Chŏngsaam* (Administration Rock)—Ch'ŏnjŏng Terrace on Mount Hoap, Puyŏ, South Ch'ungch'ŏng, is the likely site—was the place where important positions were filled and the state minister was elected by vote. In Koguryŏ, the *taedaero* was the chief of the aristocratic council elected for a three-year term (*Hsin T'ang shu* 220:6186); the term for chiefs of offices in Paekche and Koguryŏ was three years as well.

The aristocratic council in Silla was headed by the *sangdaedŭng* established under King Pŏphŭng; as the bureaucratic machinery began to function, however, the *sangdaedŭng*'s role inherited from the chief of the tribal federation weakened. The titles of king in Silla changed from *kŏsŏgan* (the founder), *ch'ach'aung* (the second ruler), *isagŭm* (the third to the eighteenth), and *maripkan* (the nineteenth to the twenty-second), to *wang* (king). The separation of church and state may be seen in such titles as *kŏsŏgan* (chief administrator) and *ch'ach'aung* (chief officiating shaman). *Isagŭm* was used for the chief of the three-clan federation, while *maripkan* (great chief) was reserved for the Kim clan, which monopolized the hereditary right to rule. With the establishment of father-son succession and centralization of power, however, Silla came to use the Chinese title, king. The account in the *Memorabilia of the Three Kingdoms,* which is presented here, best summarizes the development.

Four Sacred Places (Silla)
[From *Samguk yusa* 1:59–60]

Once during the reign of Queen Chindŏk, Lords Alch'ŏn, Imjong, Suljong, Horim, Yŏmjang, and Kim Yusin gathered at Oji Rock on South Mountain to deliberate affairs of state. Thereupon a huge tiger ran out into the meeting place. The lords all rose up in fright, save Lord Alch'ŏn, who laughed and calmly went on with the discussion while seizing the tiger by the tail and dashing it to death. Lord Alch'ŏn sat at the head of the gathering by virtue of his might, but it was the majesty of Lord Kim Yusin that the others most esteemed.

In Silla there were four sacred spots where ministers might gather to discuss important affairs of the state, and any problem of vital importance could be successfully resolved if discussed at one of these. The sacred places were Mount Ch'ŏngsong in the east, Mount Oji in the south, P'ijŏn in the west, and Mount Kŭmgang in the north [Yŏngch'ŏn in North Kyŏngsang]. PL

Administration Rock (Paekche)
[From *Samguk yusa* 2:97–98; 1:59–60]

There was a rock named Administration Rock (also called Ch'ŏnjŏng Terrace) at Hoam Monastery. Before selecting a prime minister, the court would place a sealed envelope containing the names of three or four candidates on this rock and then open it. The candidate whose name was marked with a stamp was chosen as prime minister. Hence the rock was named the Administration Rock. PL

King Namhae

[From *Samguk yusa* 1:45–46]

Namhae *kŏsŏgan* is also called *ch'ach'aung,* "high chief," a title applied only to him. His father was Hyŏkkŏse, and his mother was Lady Aryŏng. His queen was Lady Unje (after Mount Unje, to the west of Yŏngil County, where dwelt the holy mother. She would respond to prayers in times of drought.) King Namhae ascended the throne in the fourth year of Yüan-shih, *kapcha,* of Emperor P'ing of the Former Han [A.D. 4]. After a rule of twenty-one years, he died in the fourth year of Ti-huang, *kapsin* [A.D. 24]. He was the first of Silla's three kings.

The *Historical Record of the Three Kingdoms* says: "In Silla the king was called *kŏsŏgan,* meaning king or a noble person. The king was also called *ch'ach'aung* or *chach'ung.*" Kim Taemun comments: "*Ch'ach'aung* means a shaman in the Silla language. Because a shaman served the spirits and officiated at sacrifices, the people venerated him and called the high chief *ch'ach'aung.* His other title is *isagŭm,* meaning 'king.' "

An old tradition has it that at the death of King Namhae, his son Norye yielded the throne to T'arhae, who then remarked, "I have heard that the holiest and wisest person will have the most teeth," and they bit into a rice cake to see who had the most.

The king was also called *maripkan,* which, according to Kim Taemun, means "seat marker." Posts were set up to indicate the ranks of the king and his subjects.

The criticism section of the *Historical Record of the Three Kingdoms* says: "In Silla one man only was called *kŏsŏgan* or *ch'ach'aung*; those called *isagŭm* numbered sixteen; and those called *maripkan* numbered four."

When, in the last years of Silla, the famous scholar Ch'oe Ch'iwŏn compiled the chronology of emperors and kings, he called the monarchs of Silla "kings" rather than *kŏsŏgan,* a word he probably disdained as vulgar. But in recording the history of Silla it is appropriate to use the native word.   PL

Social Structure

The organization of the ruling structure issuing from the federation of tribal chiefs took the form of the bone rank system.[6] The system had eight classifications:

Holy Bones ⎫ True Bones ⎭	royal clan	Ranks 1–5
six ⎫		Rank 6
five ⎬ aristocracy		Rank 10
four ⎭		Ranks 12–17
three ⎫ two ⎬ commoners one ⎭		no rank

This rigid system of social stratification appears to have taken its final form in the early sixth century, probably as a means of distinguishing the royal line while also protecting the aristocratic status and privileges of the various tribal leaders that were being incorporated into a centralized sociopolitical system. The bone rank system set the top two strata, the Holy Bones and the True Bones, far above the rest of society. Members of the Holy Bone class monopolized the throne until the reign of Queen Chindŏk; those of the True Bone class ruled from kings Muyŏl to Kyŏngsun. Members of both classes could reach the highest rank of *ibŏlch'an,* and only they could occupy the top four ranks. Members of the sixth through fourth head ranks (*tup'um*) could occupy the sixth to the last ranks, each with different privileges and restrictions. A special promotion system allowed them, within limits, to rise faster through the ranks. The bone rank system even dictated what kinds of clothes, carriages, daily utensils, and houses members could have.

As King Hŭngdŏk's edict of 834 shows, the state tried to enforce the system. Sŏl Kyedu, however, a member of the Sŏl clan belonging to the sixth head rank, disliked this rigid class system. In 621, he left Silla for China and took part in a war against Koguryŏ.

King Hŭngdŏk's Edict on Clothing, Carts, and Housing
[From *Samguk sagi* 33:320–326]

There are superior and inferior people, and humble persons, in regard to social status. Names are not alike, for example, and garments too are different. The customs of this society have degenerated day by day owing to the competition among the people for luxuries and alien commodities because they detest local products. Furthermore, rites have now fallen to a critical stage and customs have retrogressed to those of barbarians. The traditional codes will be revived in order to clear the situation, and should anyone breach the law, he will be punished according to tradition. PL

Sŏl Kyedu
[From *Samguk sagi* 47:436]

Sŏl Kyedu was a descendant of a Silla official. Once he went drinking with his four friends, each of whom revealed his wishes. Sŏl said, "In Silla the bone rank is the key to employment. If one is not of the nobility, no matter what his talents, he cannot achieve a high rank. I wish to travel west to China, display rare resources and perform meritorious deeds, and thereby open a path to glory and splendor so that I might wear the robes and sword of an official and serve close to the Son of Heaven."

In the fourth year of Wu-te, *sinsa* [621], Sŏl stealthily boarded an oceangoing ship and went to T'ang China. PL

CHAPTER THREE

Ancient Customs and Religion

I n the societies established by the Three Kingdoms we see a reemergence of the norms of life prevalent in tribal society. Thus Confucian and Buddhist thought began to be understood in the context of tribal rites and customs. In Koguryŏ, for example, upon the death of King Kogukch'ŏn, his youngest brother, Yŏnu, married the widowed queen and became King Sansang. Thereupon, the deceased king's younger brother Palgi rose in revolt on the pretext that his younger brother could not succeed to the throne before him. But Sansang's leviratic marriage to the widowed queen, his sister-in-law, originated from the custom of Puyŏ and could not be censured by Confucian morality.

A major feature of Silla royalty was the tracing of descent through both the paternal and maternal lines. Moreover, endogamy was a common practice among Silla aristocrats. But this Silla custom was likely to invite Chinese censure. Although the mother of King Sosŏng (799–800) was a Kim, her clan name was changed to Sin based on her father's name Kim Sinsul. (The first sin is no. 5712 in Mathews Chinese-English Dictionary; the second sin is Mathews no. 5716.) The clan name of King Aejang's (800–809) mother was reported to be Suk, based on her father's name Kim Sukmyŏng (pronounced Sungmyŏng). The clan name of King Hŭngdŏk's (826–836) wife, the daughter of Kim Ch'unggong, was changed to Pak. Moreover, Silla travelers to T'ang

China used their paternal rather than maternal clan names while in China.

The nature of social order and value systems based on the Silla kinship and marriage system set limits on Silla's understanding of Confucianism. Confucianism was understood not as a social system but as a political ideology that rationalized the ruler's authority. While accepting the Buddhism of the northern dynasties, which conceived of the king as a Buddha, Buddhist institutions neither rejected conquest and territorial expansion nor came into conflict with Confucianism. In the early state, Buddhism helped foster the concept of the state and aided in the understanding of Confucian political thought. This was possible because in the process of translating scriptures into Chinese, a certain amount of Confucianization was inevitable. The introduction of Buddhism meant the importation not only of the religion but also of an advanced Chinese culture because by nature Buddhism was neither closed nor exclusive. The inclusion of monks in the *hwarang* order in Silla indicates that Buddhism provided the social and spiritual basis for Silla to develop as a state.

Ancient Customs

Shamanist beliefs and popular customs in ancient Korea were recorded only after they had lost their functions in upper-class culture. Thus scattered references to the subject not only are fragmentary but have been strongly colored by the Confucian and Buddhist world-views of later times; information preserved in the Korean and Chinese sources (the *Wei chih*) do not antedate the Neolithic Period.

Totemism in the Neolithic period—a belief in the common ancestor of a clan-centered community—may be seen in the worship of the totemic animal: the horse of the Pak clan and the cock of the Kim clan of ancient Silla, for example. Silla's council of nobles (*hwabaek*) and four sacred places, as well as Paekche's council at the Administration Rock (*chŏngsaam*), probably have their origins in ancient clan meetings; Silla's *hwarang* order and Koguryŏ's *kyŏngdang* originate, no doubt, in youth organizations in these states. The harvest thanksgiving festivals in Puyŏ (*yŏnggo*; held in the twelfth month), in Koguryŏ (*tongmaeng*), and in Ye (*much'ŏn*), as well as the Three Han in the tenth month were survivals of the festivals of clan-centered societies. The clan society achieved a degree of economic self-sufficiency, and its religious rites, marriage customs (marriage within a clan was prohibited), and taboos called for minimal legal regulations, such as the eight articles observed in Old Chosŏn of which only three—stipulations against murder, bodily injury, and theft—are known today. Puyŏ's legal provisions dealt with murder, thievery, adultery, and jealousy on the part of a wife. Puyŏ's expansion of protections to include the male head of family may reflect the change from a communal clan to a male-centered family after the introduction of iron. In Koguryŏ, too, a jealous wife was punished with death; for example, Lady Kwanna was placed in a leather sack and thrown into the sea (*SGSG* 17:158–159). The laws of Koguryŏ, Okchŏ, Eastern Ye, and the Three Han may have contained the same provisions, and they were probably observed until the promulgation of the statutes after the Three Kingdoms adopted a Chinese-style administration.

We have noted certain marriage customs and kinship systems that were viewed as incompatible with Confucian morality. One was leviratic marriage (the custom by which the brother or next of kin of a deceased man was bound to marry the widow) as found in Puyŏ and Koguryŏ; another was the offering of one's wife to an esteemed guest (*Han shu* 28A:1657) as practiced in Old Chosŏn and later in Silla until the reign of King Munmu (661–681).

Annual functions originating from prehistoric times were observed in the Three Kingdoms: Koguryŏ's hunting expedition on the third day of the third month, accompanied by the worship of the spirits of great mountains and rivers; Silla's Crow Taboo Day on the fifteenth of the first month, *tano* festival on the fifth of the fifth month, *kawi* on the fifteenth of the eighth month, and thanksgiving festival in the tenth month. Silla's annual rituals originating in agricultural society are still observed today.

Neolithic people believed in animism (shamanism). The most popular among the deified objects of worship were the sun god and the spirits of ancestors. Gods and spirits were either good or evil, the latter bringing misfortune and calamity to human beings. In order to propitiate good ones and exorcise evil ones rituals evolved that included chanting incantations, healing sickness, expelling evil spirits, and praying for a bountiful harvest. Music and dance accompanied these rituals, and sometimes sacrifices were offered, fortunes divined, the clan chief elected, and criminals executed. Religion in the Bronze Age took the form of theocracy. The first ruler in the theocratic society was Tangun of Old Chosŏn. Religious and political leadership separated in the Iron Age, but the use of such titles as *ch'ach'aung* (shaman or chief shaman; later its derivate, *chung,* designated the Buddhist monk) or Buddhist-inspired names for king's titles in Silla reflect the influence of the theocratic rule.

The fusion of Buddhism and native beliefs may be seen in the notion of the "manifestation of the original substance." Gods and spirits of sacred mountains and rivers (in Silla and Paekche and, later, in Koryŏ) were viewed as reincarnations of buddhas and bodhisattvas. Such deities were given Buddhist names in order to naturalize Buddhism; for example, the mother goddess of the earth became the Bodhisattva Sound Observer (Avalokiteśvara). Thus native gods and spirits were regarded as manifestations of the original buddhas and bodhisattvas, and the Bodhisattva Sound Observer was the most popular in the Buddhist pantheon.

King Sansang: The Levirate Custom
[From *Samguk sagi* 16:152–154]

The taboo name of King Sansang [196–227], the younger brother of King Kogukch'ŏn [179–197], was Yŏnu. The *Wei shu* says: "The descendant of Chumong, Wigung, opened his eyes and could see at birth. He was called T'aejo. The present king, his great-grandson, was also able to see at birth. In Koguryŏ similarity is indicated by the word *wi,* hence King Sansang was called Wigung." Because Kogukch'ŏn was heirless, Yŏnu succeeded him.

Upon the death of King Kogukch'ŏn, his queen, formerly named U, kept his death secret and at night went to the house of Palgi, the king's younger brother, and said, "The king has no heir; you should succeed him." Not knowing of the king's death, Palgi said, "Heaven dispenses its favors as it will. Moreover it is indecorous for a lady to travel about at night."

Ashamed, the queen went to Yŏnu, Palgi's younger brother. Yŏnu rose, put on his cap and gown, received the queen at the gate, and gave a banquet in her honor. The queen said, "Now that the king is dead and there is no heir, Palgi should succeed him; but instead he insolently accuses me of treason. That is why I have come."

Thereupon Yŏnu showed more respect and cut his finger while carving the meat. The queen undid her belt and wrapped his injured finger. Before returning to the palace she said, "The night is dark, and

I am fearful. Please take me home." Yŏnu complied. The queen then took Yŏnu's hand and drew him into the palace. The following morning at dawn, the queen lied to the officials and convinced them that the late king had wished Yŏnu to succeed him.

Palgi was furious when he heard the news. He surrounded the palace with soldiers and shouted, "It is proper for a younger brother to succeed an elder brother. You have upset the proper order and usurped the throne. This is a grave crime. Come out at once. If not, your wife and children will be put to death."

Yŏnu closed the palace gate for three days, and none of the people followed Palgi. Anticipating a disaster, Palgi, together with his wife and children, took refuge in Liao-tung and reported to the governor Kung-sun Tu, "I am the brother of Nammu (King Kogukch'ŏn), king of Koguryŏ. Nammu died leaving no heir, but my younger brother Yŏnu has plotted with his sister-in-law and ascended the throne. This is a transgression of the eternal ways of man. In my anger I have come to you. I beg you to give me a troop of thirty thousand to attack and suppress the rebel." Kung-sun Tu complied.

Yŏnu had his younger brother Kyesu lead the defending army, and Kyesu routed the Chinese troops. When Kyesu personally led the van and pursued the fleeing enemy, Palgi asked, "Are you trying to kill your old brother?"

Kyesu was not so heartless as to kill his brother. He said, "It is not just for Yŏnu to have accepted the throne, but are you trying to destroy your own state in a fit of temper? How can you face your own father in the underworld?" Ashamed and remorseful, Palgi fled to Paech'ŏn where he cut his own throat. Kyesu wept bitterly, gave the corpse a hasty burial, and returned.

The king, assailed by mingled feelings of joy and sorrow, received Kyesu in the inner chamber with brotherly rites, saying, "Palgi requested troops from China and invaded our country. His crime was great. You defeated him, but then let him go and spared his life. That was sufficient. But when he committed suicide, you wept bitterly. Are you making of me a ruler without principles?"

Kyesu changed color and holding back his tears replied, "I would like to say a word and beg to be killed."

The king asked, "What is it?"

"Even if the queen made you king with the deceased king's will," Kyesu replied, "you didn't decline it because you lacked a sense of duty to your brothers. In order to display your virtue I buried Palgi. I did not expect that I would incur your anger. If you answer evil with goodness and bury Palgi with brotherly rites, who will call you unjust? Now that I have voiced my true feelings, death will be the same as life. I beg you to put me to death."

Drawing closer to Kyesu with a mild face, the king praised Kyesu's services. "Being unworthy, I harbored a doubt, but your word makes me realize my error. I beg you not to reproach yourself," he said.

When Kyesu rose and bowed, the king too rose and reciprocated. After sharing their mutual delight to the fullest they parted.

In the ninth month the king ordered Palgi's corpse to be received and interred at Pae Pass with royal rites. Because the king obtained the throne with the former queen's help, he did not remarry but made her his queen. PL

Ondal: Hunting Expedition on the Third Day of the Third Month
[From *Samguk sagi* 45:425–427]

Ondal was a man who lived at the time of King P'yŏngwŏn [559–590] of Koguryŏ. He had an absurd countenance but was good-hearted. Being very poor, he would beg food to support his mother and walked through the streets in rags and worn sandals. People called him Foolish Ondal.

At the time the king's young daughter was given to crying, and the king used to joke, "You do nothing but cry and hurt my ears. You can't be a nobleman's wife when you grow up, so I shall marry you off to Foolish Ondal."

When the princess reached the age of sixteen, the king wished to give her in marriage to a man of the noble clan of Ko. "You used to tell me that I am to marry Ondal, but now you won't keep your word," the princess said. "Even a lowly man will keep a promise, so much more should a king. 'The king does not joke,' the saying goes. I cannot obey your misguided command."

The king grew very angry. "If you will not listen to me, you will not be my daughter. Why live with me? Go where you please!" he retorted.

Thereupon the princess tied scores of precious bracelets around her wrist and set forth from the palace. She asked the way to Ondal's house, and upon reaching it she bowed to Ondal's blind old mother and sought to learn where Ondal might be.

"My son is a humble rustic," the mother replied, "you could have no business with him. When I smell you, you are fragrantly scented; when I touch you, your hands are soft as cotton. You must be a noble person. Who has deceived you to come here? My son went to the mountain some time ago to peel elm bark for his food, and he has not yet come back."

The princess went to look for Ondal at the foot of the mountain. There she found him carrying elm bark on his back. She told him why she had come.

He put her off, saying, "This is not what a young girl should do. You can't be human; you must be a fox or a demon. Stay away from me."

He turned his back and walked away. The princess followed him and spent the night by the brushwood door. The following morning she went into the cottage and related her story to Ondal and his mother. Ondal was still suspicious, and his mother broke in, "My son is a rustic, hardly a fitting husband for you, and our humble dwelling is hardly the place for you to make your home."

The princess replied, " 'Even a peck of millet is fit to be pounded, even a foot of cloth is fit to be sewn,' the old saying goes. If we're of one mind, why must we be rich to be married?"

She then sold her bracelets and bought a house and land, slaves, cattle, and utensils, and furnished the house with necessities. When Ondal went to buy a horse, the princess said, "Don't buy the horse in the market. Get one abandoned by the state stable because it is either sick or thin. If you can't find such a horse, buy a good one and later exchange it for a state horse." Ondal did as he was told, and the princess devotedly looked after the animal; it soon grew fat and strong.

It was the custom of Koguryŏ to hold a hunt on the third day of the third month on the hill of Lo-lang and to sacrifice a boar and a deer to heaven and to the deities of the mountains and rivers. That day the king too went hunting, followed by his ministers and soldiers from the five districts. Ondal went along on the horse the princess had reared. He was constantly at the head of the chase and caught the most game. Surprised, the king summoned him, asked his name, and marveled at him.

Shortly thereafter Emperor Wu [560–578] of the Later Chou invaded Liao-tung, and the king met the invaders on the plains of Paesan. Ondal fought courageously in the vanguard and killed scores of the enemy. Seizing an opportune moment, Koguryŏ troops launched a fierce attack on the enemy forces and routed them. When rewards were being distributed, everyone recommended Ondal for the highest honors. The king was greatly pleased and declared, "He is my son-in-law." At last he received Ondal with due ceremony and conferred on him the rank of *taehyŏng* (Rank 5). Thereafter Ondal enjoyed the king's favor, and his fame increased from day to day. PL

The Festival of *Kawi*
[From *Samguk sagi* 1:5]

In the spring of the ninth year [A.D. 32], King Yuri had the names of six districts (*pu*) changed and bestowed surnames upon them. Yangsan district was changed to Yang, with the surname Yi. Koho district became Saryang, with the surname Ch'oe. Taesu district he changed to Chŏmnyang (or Muryang) with the surname Son. Ujin district became Ponp'i, with the surname Chŏng. Kari district was changed to Hanji, with the surname Pae. Myŏnghwal district became Sŭppi, with the surname Sŏl. . . .

The six districts in turn were divided into two groups, and the womenfolk of each group were led by a princess in a game. From the sixteenth day of the seventh month two sides gathered in the village courtyard every day to twist threads from early morning to the second watch. On the fifteenth day of the eighth month, the two teams were rated, and the losing team prepared wine and food to congratulate the winners. Then came songs, dances, and hundreds of games. This was called *kawi*. At that time, a woman from the losing side rose and danced, sighing "*aso, aso*" in a sad but refined tone. Later, the people composed the "Song of Aso" based on her interjection. PL

Crow Taboo Day
[From *Samguk yusa* 1:54–55]

When, in his tenth year, *mujin* [488], the twenty-first King Pich'ŏ (or Soji) traveled to Ch'ŏnch'ŏn Arbor, a crow croaked and a rat squeaked. Then the rat said, "Follow the crow wherever it flies," whereupon the king ordered a horseman to follow the bird. When the horseman had traveled southward to P'ich'on, as far as the eastern foot of Mount South, he stopped to observe a fight between two boars. Thus he lost sight of the crow and began to wander about. Thereupon an old man emerged from a pond and presented the horseman with a letter, on the outside of which was written, "If opened, two people will die; if not, only one man will die."

The horseman took the letter to the king, who said, "If two people are to perish by its being opened, then better not to; let only one die."

Then the astrologer remarked, "The two people are commoners, but the one must be the king." The king harkened to this counsel and opened the letter. It read, "Shoot at the zither case." The king at once returned to the palace and shot an arrow into the case. The box revealed the queen in an illicit affair with a monk whose job was to burn incense and cultivate the faith. Both were put to death.

Thereafter it has been the national custom to be discreet in speech and action and to remain idle on the first boar day, the first rat day, and the first horse day of the first month. On the fifteenth day of the month, called Crow Taboo Day (*taldo*), a day of sorrow and taboo, glutinous rice is even today offered to the bird. The king named the pond Sŏch'ul ("Letter Issuing"). PL

Lord Ch'adŭk: Attendance of a Local Official at Court
[From *Samguk yusa* 2:74–75]

One day King Munmu [661–680] summoned his half brother Lord Ch'adŭk and asked him to act as prime minister to regulate officials and bring peace to the kingdom. The lord replied, "If you wish to appoint me as prime minister, I would first travel in disguise throughout the land to gauge the weight of the corvée and the taxes on the people, and to test the honesty of the officials." The king granted him this.

Wearing a monk's garb and carrying a lute (*pip'a*), the lord left the capital dressed as a householder. He passed through Asŭlla (Myŏngju) and Usu (Ch'unch'ŏn) provinces, Pugwŏn capital (Wŏnju), and reached Mujin province (Haeyang). While the lord was touring the villages, a local official called Angil perceived him to be no ordinary man. Angil invited the lord to his home and entertained him there. At night Angil summoned his two wives and a concubine and said, "If one of you will spend the night with our guest, you and I shall grow old together as man and wife."

Both wives answered, "We would rather part from you than spend the night with a stranger."

The concubine said, "If you will allow me to live with you till the day I die, then I shall do as you ask." Thus she did as the lord wished.

Early the following morning the lord told his host, "I am from the capital, and my home stands between the Hwangnyong and Hwang-sŏng monasteries. My name is Tano. Should you ever visit the capital, be sure to call on me." The lord then returned to the capital to become prime minister.

It was the custom for a local official to be called up for guard duty at various offices in the capital (the *kiin* system of Koryŏ). Soon Angil's turn came, and he proceeded to the capital, but no one there knew the whereabouts of Tano's house. Angil had been standing bemused on the street for a long time when an old man passed by and told him that the house between the monasteries was the palace, and that Tano was none other than the honorable Lord Ch'adŭk. The old man asked whether Angil had made a promise to the lord during his incognito visit to the provinces. Angil told him the truth, whereupon the old man suggested that Angil go to Kwijŏng Gate, west of the palace, and report to a court lady as she was entering or leaving. Angil did this. The lord came forth, took Angil's hand, and led him into the palace. He summoned his wife and had Angil entertained with a feast of more than fifty dishes.

When the story was reported to the king, he decreed that the land below Mount Sŏngbu (or Sŏngsonho) would be used by an official in Mujin province to furnish fuel to the palace, and he prohibited the people from felling trees there. The people therefore dared not intrude and envied Angil's good fortune. The area of the field beneath the mountain was thirty *myo,* enough to plant three bags of seeds. If the harvest of the field was good, then that of Mujin province was also good; and if its crop was poor, Mujin province too suffered a famine. PL

Kim Yusin: Worship of the Three Guardian Spirits
[From *Samguk yusa* 1:60–61]

The eldest son of *Kakkan* Kim Sŏhyŏn, son of *Igan* Horyŏk, was born in the seventeenth year, *ŭlmyo,* of King Chinp'yŏng [595]. His younger brother was Hŭmsun; his sisters were Pohŭi (Ahae) and Munhŭi (Aji). Gifted from birth with the essence of the sun, the moon, and the five stars, he bore on his back the pattern of the seven stars, and miraculous happenings befell him.

At the age of eighteen he mastered the art of swordsmanship and became a *hwarang.* At the time a certain Paeksŏk (White Stone), whose origins were unknown, had belonged to the *hwarang* institution for a number of years. Knowing that Kim Yusin was making plans day and night to attack Koguryŏ and Paekche, Paeksŏk suggested that they both spy out the enemy before making final plans. Kim was pleased and set out with Paeksŏk one night. When the two were resting atop a hill, two girls appeared and followed Kim. When they arrived at Korhwach'ŏn (now Yŏngch'ŏn), a third girl appeared, and Kim spoke happily with the girls together. The girls presented Kim with delicious fruits, and he spoke without reserve. The girls said, "We already know all that you have told us. Please leave Paeksŏk behind and follow us to the forest, where we shall reveal the situation to you in detail." Kim followed the three girls, whereupon they transformed themselves into spirits. "We are the guardian spirits of the three sacred mountains, Naerim, Hyŏllye, and Korhwa. We came to warn you that you are being lured by an enemy spy and to detain you here." With these words they vanished.

Kim prostrated himself in amazement and gratitude before the spirits and returned to his lodging in Korhwa. Kim spoke to Paeksŏk, "I have neglected to bring along an important missive. Let us return and fetch it." Upon arrival in the capital Kim had Paeksŏk arrested, bound, and interrogated.

Paeksŏk confessed, "I am a man of Koguryŏ. Our officials say that Kim Yusin of Silla is a reincarnation of the Koguryŏ diviner Ch'unam. On the frontier between Silla and Koguryŏ is a river that flows backwards. At the king's request, Ch'unam divined, 'The queen acts against the way of the yin and yang, and the river reflects her misdeeds.' The king was baffled and astonished, while the furious queen declared, 'This is a libel by a cunning fox.' She then suggested to the king that they try Ch'unam once more and put him to death if his words should prove false. Thereupon the queen concealed a rat in a box and asked Ch'unam what was inside. 'It contains one rat, or so you think, but in fact there are eight rats in the box.' 'Your answer is wrong, and you shall die,' the queen said. Ch'unam then vowed, 'After I die I shall be reborn as a general who will destroy Koguryŏ.' Ch'unam was beheaded. When the rat's belly was slit open, it was found to contain seven unborn young. Only then did the king and queen realize that Ch'unam had spoken the truth. On the same night the king dreamt that he saw Ch'unam entering the bosom of the wife of Lord Sŏhyŏn (Kim Yusin's mother). When the king recounted this dream to his ministers they said, 'Ch'unam's vow has turned out to be true,' and they dispatched me to lure you to Koguryŏ.''

Kim Yusin beheaded Paeksŏk and offered sacrifices of a hundred delicacies to the three guardian spirits, whereupon they appeared and partook of libations. PL

Peach Blossom Girl, Guardian of the Gate Tower
[From *Samguk yusa* 1:56–57]

The posthumous title of the twenty-fifth king, Saryun, was Chinji, surnamed Kim, whose queen was Lady Chido, the daughter of Lord Kio. Chinji ascended the throne in the eighth year of Ta-chien [576], but after four years of rule he was deposed for misgovernment and lasciviousness.

Before he was deposed, there lived in Saryang district a woman of such beauty that she was called Peach Blossom Girl. The king heard of her, had her brought to the palace, and was about to seduce her. She said, "It is not a woman's way to serve two husbands. To have a husband of my own and to accept yet another, this even a king with all his majesty cannot force upon me."

"What if I were to kill you?" the king asked.

The woman replied, "I would rather be beheaded in the market-place."

The king joked, "If your husband were no more, would it then sit well with you?" "Yes, it would then be possible," the woman replied.

The king then set the woman free, and in the same year he was deposed and died. Three years later, the woman's husband also died.

Ten nights after the husband's death, the king suddenly appeared to the woman and asked her, "You made me a promise long ago. Now that your husband is dead, will you be mine?"

The woman did not consent lightly but consulted her parents, who remarked, "How could you disobey the royal word?" and let her enter the bedchamber. She remained there for seven days, during which time five-colored clouds covered the house and a fine fragrance filled the bedchamber. After the seventh day the king vanished without a trace. The woman became pregnant, and as the time of delivery approached, heaven and earth shook, and a baby boy was born. He was named Pihyŏng. Hearing of the strange incident, King Chinp'yŏng had the baby brought to the palace and reared there. When the boy reached age fifteen, he was given the post of clerk (*chipsa*). When it was learned that the boy was going far afield every night in search of amusement, the king assigned fifty soldiers to keep watch over him. The boy would fly over Wŏlsŏng, go west, and land on a hill above Hwangch'ŏn where he would play with a band of spirits until the ringing of a temple bell at dawn. When he heard this report the king summoned Pihyŏng and asked him, "Is it true that you consort with the spirits?" "Yes," the boy replied. The king continued, "Then have the spirits build a bridge across the stream north of Sinwŏn Monastery." Upon the royal decree Pihyŏng mobilized the spirits, and by morning a stone bridge had been completed. It was called the Bridge of Spirits (Kwigyo).

The king asked the boy again, "Is there any spirit who could return to life and assist me in administration?"

"One named Kiltal is worthy of the task," replied Pihyŏng. The following day the king had Kiltal brought to him and conferred upon him the title of clerk. He proved unequaled in loyalty and honesty.

Kakkan Imjong had no son, and the king had him adopt Kiltal. Imjong had Kiltal build the gate tower south of Hŭngnyun Monastery, and Kiltal slept every night atop the gate. It was then called Kiltal Gate.

One day Kiltal changed into a fox and ran away, and Pihyŏng had the spirits catch and kill him. After this, the spirits feared the name of Pihyŏng and ran away, and the people composed a song: "Here is the house of Pihyŏng,/ The son of the king's spirit./ A gang of flying and galloping spirits,/ Do not stop and linger here." It is a custom to paste the text of the song on the gates to drive away evil spirits. PL

The Introduction of Buddhism

Buddhism was transmitted to each of the Three Kingdoms during their transition from tribal federations to an ancient state: to Koguryŏ in 372, to Paekche in 384, and to Silla in 527. During its dissemination Buddhism absorbed the myths, legends, and shamanist beliefs of the tribes and forged a more systematized religion and philosophy. By offering a way for the people to comprehend the conflicts and contradictions in society, it provided the social and spiritual basis for each of the Three Kingdoms to develop into a state.

From its inception Buddhism was allied with the royal authority.

But this alliance was most conspicuous in Silla, which had the lowest standard of culture and was the last to develop as a state. In Silla, Buddhism became a catalytic force accelerating the growth of the state structure and of royal power. In order to strengthen kingly power, the ruler was viewed as the wheel-turning emperor of the Kṣatriya caste. The twenty-third to twenty-eighth rulers adopted Buddhist names—for example, King Chinp'yŏng adopted the name of Śuddhodana, his queen became Māyā, and Queen Chindŏk became Śrīmālā.

Although Buddhism in Koguryŏ and Paekche also had a nationalist color, these states were more advanced in their cultural standards, familiar with Taoist literature, and distinguished the Buddha Dharma from royal authority. Koguryŏ, which had contacts with the Chinese mainland and Central Asia, adopted the Buddhism that used the method of *ke-yi* (employing Taoist terms to elucidate Buddhist ideas). Likewise, Paekche had contacts with the Han commanderies and the southern dynasties, and the aristocracy was more powerful than the royal house. Thus they were able to uphold the independence of the Buddhist church. Instead of holding Buddhist ceremonies to pray for the protection of the country, monks in Paekche and Koguryŏ specialized in the study of Buddhist doctrines or disciplinary texts (Vinaya) —in Paekche the *Nirvana Scripture* and the *Perfection of Wisdom Scripture* and in Koguryŏ the Three Treatise school. Active Koguryŏ monks include P'ayak, a disciple of Chih-i, who transmitted the T'ien-t'ai school in 596; Sŭngnang, who played a major role in China as a master of the Three Treatise school; and Hyegwan, who founded the same school in Japan.

In Paekche the study of the disciplinary texts flourished; it was founded by Kyŏmik, who had returned from India in 526; three Japanese nuns traveled to Paekche to study it. Studies in the *Nirvana Scripture* continued, judging from the request to the Liang during the reign of King Sŏng (523–554) for commentaries on the text; the Koguryŏ monk Podŏk, who sought refuge in Paekche, further stimulated the study of the same text. Other eminent monks include Hyehyŏn, who did not go to China but whose biography was included in the *Hsü kao-seng chuan* (Further Lives of Eminent Monks); Kwallŭk and Hyech'ong, who went to Japan as experts on the Three Treatise school; and Tojang, who founded the Tattvasiddhi (Jōjitsu) school in Japan.

Early Buddhism in Silla developed under the influence of Koguryŏ. Hyeryang, an exile from Koguryŏ, was made the national overseer of monks (*kukt'ong*), and Chajang, upon returning from the T'ang, succeeded to the position as great national overseer (*taegukt'ong*). Both contributed to the institutional development of the church and the consolidation of Buddhist thought. Chajang also systematized the belief that Silla was the land of the Buddha—that in Silla, a land supposedly chosen and blessed by former buddhas, Buddhism was not a new religion.

Koguryŏ Buddhism

Sŭngnang (end of the fifth to the early sixth centuries), a native of Yodong (Liao-tung) in Koguryŏ, was a master of the Three Treatise (Mādhyamika) school of Nāgārjuna.[1] After its introduction to China by Kumārajīva (344–413) it reached Koguryŏ, and Sŭngnang is said to have studied it and the Flower Garland school. He traveled to Chiang-nan during the period of Chien-wu (494–497) and stayed at Ts'ao-t'ang Monastery on Bell Mountain, north of Nanking, and later at Ch'i-hsia Monastery on Mount She. He expounded the Three Treatises among the teachers of the *Tattvasiddhi* (Treatise on the Completion of Truth), but none could challenge him. Thereupon he propagated the Three Treatises. Subsequently Emperor Wu of the Liang had Sŭngnang teach the Three Treatises to ten students (512). His teaching was continued by his disciple Seng-ch'üan (c. 512) and Seng-ch'üan's disciple Fa-lang (507–581), and Fa-lang's disciple, Chi-tsang (549–623), author of the *San-lun hsüan-i* (Profound Meaning of the Three Treatises; *T.* 45, no. 1852).

The teaching was transmitted by Koguryŏ to Japan—first by Hyeja (Eji; d. 623; in Japan 595–615), Hyegwan (Ekan), and Todŭng (in Japan 629–646). Paekche sent Hyech'ong (Esō) in 595 and Kwallŭk (Kanroku; in Japan 602–624). At Hōkō-ji, Hyeja gave lectures in the presence of Prince Shōtoku. In the same year Hyech'ong arrived and stayed at the same monastery. Kwallŭk stayed at Gangō-ji, where he became *sōjō* (chief executive). Hyegwan, a disciple of Chi-tsang, also stayed at Gangō-ji where he expounded the doctrine of emptiness and was appointed *sōjō*.

Ŭiyŏn's Research into a History of Buddhism
[From *Haedong kosŭng chŏn* 1A:1016b–c]

In 576, Prime Minister Wang Kodŏk of Koguryŏ dispatched the monk Ŭiyŏn to the Northern Ch'i. In Yeh, the capital, Ŭiyŏn met Chief of Clerics Fa-shang and learned from him about the history of Buddhism as well as about the authors and the circumstances surrounding the writing of certain Mahāyāna scriptures. Thus in Koguryŏ more precise knowledge of the origin and nature of Buddhism was deemed important to its study. Devotees' knowledge of the *Daśabhūmika* (Scripture concerning the Ten Stages), *Prajñāpāramitā* (Perfection of Wisdom), *Bodhisattvabhūmi* (Stages of Bodhisattva Practice) and *Diamond Scripture* indicates that these scholars, who earlier had studied the Three Treatise school (Mādhyamika), now desired to learn about the Consciousness-Only school as well. Excerpts from the biography of Ŭiyŏn in the *Lives of Eminent Korean Monks* follow.

The prime minister of Koguryŏ, Wang Kodŏk, had deep faith in the orthodox doctrine and respected Mahāyāna Buddhism. He desired to spread the influence of Buddhism over this corner of the sea. But because he was ignorant of the origin and development of the religion as well as the reign in which it had been introduced from the west, he listed the following questions and sent Ŭiyŏn to Yeh by sea in order to enlighten him. The general contents of the inquiry was as follows: "How many years has it been since Śākyamuni entered nirvana? How many years passed in India before Buddhism was introduced into China? Who was the emperor when it was first introduced? What was his reign title? Also, in your opinion, which state first adopted Buddhism, Ch'i or Ch'en? Please indicate the number of years and emperors since the practice of Buddhism began. Who wrote the treatises on the *Scripture Concerning the Ten Stages,* the *Perfection of Wisdom,* the *Stages of Bodhisattva Practice,* and the *Diamond Scripture?* Is there any biography relating who originated or inspired the composition of these scriptures? I have recorded these questions and await your investigation to cast off my doubts."

Fa-shang answered thus: "The Buddha was born in the twenty-fourth year, *kabin* [1027 B.C.], of King Chao of Chou, whose clan name was Chi. He left home at nineteen and became enlightened at thirty. In the twenty-fourth year, *kyemi* [977 B.C.], of King Mu of Chou, the king heard of one from the west who had been transformed into a human being in order to enlighten living beings, and who had then gone to the west and never returned. Judging from this, Śākyamuni was in this world for forty-nine years. From his nirvana to the present, the seventh year, *pyŏngsin* [576], of Wu-p'ing of Ch'i, fourteen hundred and sixty-five years have elapsed. The scriptures and doctrines of Buddhism were first brought to China during the era Yung-p'ing [58–75] of Emperor Ming of the Later Han and handed down through Wei and Chin. But it was not until the arrival of K'ang Seng-hui at Wu during the era Ch'ih-wu [238–250] of Sun Ch'üan [222–252] of Wu that the teachings of Buddhism were spread and propagated. Bhiksu Asaṅga received a copy of the *Stages of Bodhisattva Practice* from Maitreya, and during the era Lung-an [397–401] of Emperor An [397–418] of Eastern Chin it was translated by T'an-mo-ch'an [Dharmakṣema, 385–433] at Ku-tsang for the king of Ho-hsi, Chü-ch'ü Meng-hsün [401–433]. The *Mo-ho-yen lun* (Great Perfection of Wisdom Treatise) was written by Bodhisattva Nāgārjuna [c. 100–200] and translated, on the order of Yao Hsing [394–416], by Kumā-rajīva [344–413] upon his arrival in Ch'ang-an during the era Lung-an of Chin. The treatises on the *Scripture Concerning the Ten Stages* and the *Diamond Scripture* were compiled by Asaṅga's brother Vasubandhu and first translated by Bodhiruci [c. 508–535] during the reign of Emperor Hsüan-wu [500–515] of the Northern Wei."

In answering these queries, Fa-shang offered evidence and drew references from a wide range of sources. Here I have recorded only the most important points. Ŭiyŏn did not forget the answers for a moment, had superior skill in leading people, and was versed in the mysterious and arcane. His ability in exegesis was inexhaustible, and his reason could master the secret of the joined circles. Once dispelled, former doubts melted away like ice. Now this new, wonderful doctrine shines brilliantly like the dawn, securing the Wisdom Sun in the west and pouring the fountain of dharma into the east. His teaching, like a gold pendant or a string of gems, is imperishable. Was not our master, then, a "ferry on the sea of suffering" and the "middle beam over the dharma gate?" After he returned to his country and promulgated great wisdom, he skillfully persuaded and led the straying masses. His exposition of the doctrine transcends the past and present, and his name has become most famous. Had the master not been endowed with extraordinary talent and blessed with the favors of both the Time and the Way, how could he have achieved such greatness? PL

P'ayak and T'ien-t'ai
[From *Hsü kao-seng chuan* 17:570c–571a]

The Monk P'ayak [562–613] of Mount T'ien-t'ai was a man of Koguryŏ who returned to his country during the time of the Ch'en. He attended lectures on the scriptures in Chin-ling and deeply grasped their essence. When, during the period of K'ai-huang, the Ch'en [557–589] was destroyed, P'ayak toured various places and pursued his studies. At age sixteen he climbed the north face of Mount T'ien-t'ai and sought to receive the meditation dharma from Chih-i [538–597]. Possessed of a keen mind and superior wisdom, P'ayak received a certificate.

"You are qualified to be here," the master said. "Live in a quiet place and cultivate subtle practice. The pinnacle of Mount T'ien-t'ai, sixty or seventy *li* away, is called Hua-ting. That is where I performed my ascetic practices, a place for one who has the root and spiritual capacity for the Great Vehicle. If you go there and learn the Path and make progress in your practice, you are sure to reap great benefits. You must not worry about clothes or food."

Obeying the master's injunction, P'ayak climbed the mountain in the eighteenth year of K'ai-huang [598]. Day and night he practiced the Path, neither sleeping nor reclining. His shadow never emerged once for sixteen years. In the second month of the ninth year of Ta-yeh [613], he suddenly descended from his hermitage, coming first to Fo-lung-shang Monastery. At that time he saw three men following him, clad in white robes and carrying three garments and a begging bowl, but they disappeared in the twinkling of an eye. When he reached Kuo-ch'ing-hsia Monastery, his good friends said to one another, "P'ayak knows that his end is near. His descent is to bid farewell to the masses." In a few days, sitting decorously and self-possessed, he died without illness. He was fifty-two years old.

When P'ayak's bier was carried out through the main gate of the monastery to bid farewell to the assembly, on the way to his burial on the mountain, his eyes opened. They closed again when he reached the mountain. Officials and commoners, those in the household and those gone forth from it, all praised and revered him and desired to achieve enlightenment. When the supernatural auspices portend a being such as this, one can easily guess his miraculous powers on the mountain. Still, because no one witnessed them there, the details are hard to know. PL

Paekche Buddhism

Paekche imported the Buddhism of the southern dynasties of China and focused its study on the Disciplinary (Vinaya) school. The key document shedding light on this aspect is the record of events of Mirŭk Pulgwang Monastery. According to this record, Paekche sent a monk to India to bring back the Sanskrit texts of *Wu-fen lü* and translate and annotate them. This was under King Sŏng (523–554), who adopted the policy of restoration of Paekche power and encouraged overseas trade. The Vinaya texts already translated in China include the *Shih-sung lü* (Vinaya of the Sarvāstivāda school; sixty-one chapters: *T.* 23, no. 1435), *Ssu-fen lü* (Pratimokṣa of the Dharmagupta school; sixty chapters: *T.* 22, no. 1428), *Mahāsāṅghika vinaya* (forty chapters: *T.* 22, no. 1421), and *Wu-fen lü* (Vinaya of the Mahīśāsaka school; thirty chapters: *T.* 22, no. 1421). Only the *Kāśyapīya vinaya* was untranslated. It is uncertain whether the four Vinaya texts were known in Paekche, but Kyŏmik entitled his translation *New Vinaya* (seventy-two rolls) to show that the Koreans had access to the same texts then current in China.

The Disciplinary school in Paekche enjoyed international authority. In 588, three Japanese nuns studied the rules of discipline for three years in Paekche and upon their return became the founders of the Disciplinary school in Japan. Hyech'ong, a Paekche monk, went to Japan in 590 and transmitted the rules to Soga no Umako. Within Paekche itself, a decree was issued in 599 to prohibit the killing of living beings; it was realized by setting free domestic birds and burning the implements used for hunting and fishing.

Kyŏmik and the Disciplinary School
[From *Chosŏn pulgyo t'ongsa* 1:33–34]

In the fourth year, *pyŏngo,* of King Sŏng of Paekche [526], the monk Kyŏmik resolved to seek the rules of discipline and sailed to Central India. He studied Sanskrit for five years at Great Vinaya Monastery in *Saṅghāna and acquired a sound knowledge of the language. He then studied the disciplinary texts thoroughly and solemnly embodied morality (*śīla*) in his heart. He returned together with an Indian monk, Tripiṭaka Master *Vedatta, and brought with him the Sanskrit texts of the *Abhidharma Piṭaka* and five recensions of the Discipline.[2] The king of Paekche welcomed the two at the outskirts of the capital with a plume-canopied carriage and drums and pipes and had them reside at Hŭngnyun Monastery. The king also summoned the country's twenty-eight famous monks and, together with Dharma Master Kyŏmik, had them translate seventy-two rolls of the rules of discipline. Thus Kyŏmik became the founder of the Disciplinary school in Paekche. Thereupon Dharma Masters Tamuk and Hyein wrote commentaries on the rules of discipline in thirty-six rolls and presented them to the king. The king composed a preface to the *Abhidharma* and this *New Vinaya,* treasured them in the T'aeyo Hall, and intended to have them carved on wood blocks for dissemination. The king died, however, before he could implement his plan. PL

Hyŏngwang and the *Lotus Scripture*
[From *Sung kao-seng chuan* 18:820c–821a]

Like Chih-i (538–597), Hyŏngwang (fl. 539–575) was a disciple of Hui-ssu (515–577). Biographies of eminent monks in China call Hyŏngwang a native of Silla, but his life included the period before the demise of Paekche and his activities were centered around Ungju in Paekche. Hence it is proper to consider him a Paekche national. The *Sung kao-seng chuan* (Lives of Eminent Monks Compiled During the Sung) portrays Hyŏngwang as having been praised by Hui-ssu for his grasp of the *Lotus Scripture.* Upon returning home, Hyŏngwang resided on Mount Ong in Ungju, where he practiced the Dharma Blossom *samādhi*[3] and taught the people to believe in the Buddha as a manifestation of the eternal truth and universal salvation. Thus, after Hyŏngwang's return from China, the *Lotus Scripture* was studied and practiced in Paekche during the time of King Mu (600–641). The eminent monk Hyehyŏn made chanting of the *Lotus* a central Buddhist activity.

The monk Hyŏngwang was a native of Ungju in Korea. As a youth—and one of marked intelligence—he abruptly abandoned the secular life and determined to gain access to a religious teacher of high repute. Thereafter he devoted himself to a pure and celibate existence and when fully grown, he resolved to cross the ocean in order to seek training in the meditative methods of China.

Accordingly, he made a journey to the state of Ch'en where, to his good fortune, he visited Mount Heng and met the Reverend Teacher Hui-ssu who opened his understanding to the transience of phenomena and brilliantly elucidated all the matters they discussed. Master Hui-ssu comprehended Hyŏngwang's reasons for having come there and thoroughly instructed him in the "Method of Ease and Bliss" of the *Lotus Scripture*. Hyŏngwang's progress was like that of a supremely sharp awl that meets no impediment and does not deviate from its course; he was as unblemished as a freshly dyed length of cotton cloth. Having requested and received instruction in the method, he was assiduous and meticulous in his practice of it and achieved abrupt entrance into the Lotus Samādhi. When he requested confirmation of this attainment, Hui-ssu verified his accomplishment, saying: "That which you have experienced is genuine and no delusion. Closely guard and sustain it, and your penetration of the dharma will become fuller and more profound. You should now return to your homeland and there establish this efficacious means. It is well 'to dislodge the *ming-ling* caterpillars, so that they may all be transformed into sphex wasps.' "[4] Hyŏngwang, with tears flowing, did reverence to the master.

From that place Hyŏngwang thereafter retraced his steps southward down the Hsi River[5] to the ocean, where he arranged for passage on a large vessel of his native land that soon loaded its stores and set sail. Subsequently, at sea, a multicolored cloud appeared that dazzled the eye, and from this cloud emanated strains of exquisite music that permeated the firmament, while within it could be discerned the scarlet tallies and rainbow-hued insignia of high office. Resounding as it drew near, a voice from deep within the cloud declaimed, "The Emperor of Heaven summons the Korean Dhyāna Master Hyŏngwang!" Hyŏngwang, having clasped his hands together and stepped backwards deferentially, perceived an azure-clad servant who had come forward to escort him. In the space of a short time they entered a mighty palace, and, what is more, the functionaries and guards in attendance there were not human beings! They were none other than finned denizens of the deep and various spirits. One of those present addressed him, saying: "On this day the Emperor of Heaven has descended to the palace of this Dragon King and requests that you, Master, discourse upon the approach to the dharma that you have experienced. We gathered here in this sea palace and would also gratefully receive the master's benefaction." After they proceeded to the sacred hall and Hyŏngwang had mounted the high dais, he lectured as he had been bid. In all he lectured for a span of seven days, but afterwards when the Dragon King did him the honor of personally seeing him on his return way, it was remarkable that his ship had not significantly advanced on its course from the point where he had left it. When Hyŏngwang again climbed onto the vessel, moreover, those on board asserted that since he had been gone no more than half a day had elapsed.

Following his return to Korea, Hyŏngwang settled on Mount Ong in Ungju where initially only a simple hermitage was constructed, but in time this was developed into a full monastery. It is written that "notes of the same key respond to each other,"[6] and so it was that those who wished to attain to the dharma clustered at his gate and opened themselves to his instruction. The carefree and young, those solemnly resolved to adhere to the true Path, even those who still craved for the taste of flesh—they all, like ants in a line, sought him. Among these, there was one who ultimately ascended to a position of eminence and was designated as Hyŏngwang's successor. There was also one who achieved the "Fire Radiance Samādhi," two who achieved the "Water Radiance Samādhi," and even some who became proficient in both of these practices. Those who followed him and distinguished themselves were especially celebrated for their attainments in meditation. In fact, his disciples could be likened to the flocks of birds that haunt Mount Sumeru in that they all were of one color. While Hyŏngwang was yet living, he left Mount Ong and disappeared; where he went is not known.

When the patriarch of Nan-yüeh built an image hall, Hyŏngwang's likeness was one of the portraits of twenty-eight honored masters displayed there. His likeness is also to be seen in the Patriarchs Hall at Kuo-ch'ing Monastery on Mount T'ien-t'ai. JB

Silla Buddhism

Among the versions of the transmission of Buddhism to Silla, an account of Ado, the first missionary, is the most detailed. As Buddhism became the national faith under King Pŏpkong in 527, there arose a belief that Korea was the land of the former Buddha. Ado's mother, for example, remarks to her son, "In the [Silla] capital, there are seven places where the dharma should abide. . . . At these places are ruins of monasteries built during the time of the former Buddha." One such site was found in 534 when the Forest of the Heavenly Mirror was cleared; remains of a stone stupa were excavated elsewhere; and before construction of the national monastery Hwang-nyong, a stone upon which Kāśyapa and Śākyamuni used to sit in meditation was discovered.

Masters Wŏngwang and Chajang devoted their lives to importing an advanced culture from the continent and establishing Buddhism as the state religion. Wŏngwang's close ties to the monarch and the country's expansionist policy may be seen in his simplified form of the bodhisattva ordination consisting of five—rather than ten—commandments he gave to Silla warriors. They contain secular and religious injunctions not to retreat from a battlefield and not to take life indiscriminately. As Great National Overseer, Chajang set up Buddhist discipline and supervised the order. The nine-story stupa at Hwangnyong Monastery, built at his request, was constructed to unify the peninsula and to encourage the surrender of neighboring enemies. The plan was originally suggested by a guardian of the dharma who appeared to Chajang during his study tour in China. As a symbol of national protection (and later as one of the three national treasures), the stupa became the focus of a belief in Silla as the land of the former as well as the present and future Buddha, an impregnable fortress designed to frustrate the territorial designs of enemies.

Ado's Arrival in Silla
[From *Haedong kosŭng chŏn* 1A:1017c–8c]

The monk Ado is said to have been a native of India. Some say he came from Wu, while others hold that he went first to Wei from Koguryŏ and returned to Silla. We do not know which is correct. He was distinguished in manner and appearance, and his miracles were most strange. He held it his duty to travel and convert, and wondrous flowers rained from heaven whenever he preached. At first, during the reign of King Nulchi of Silla, Hŭkhoja arrived in Ilsŏn district from Koguryŏ to enlighten those who had the appropriate karma. Morye, a resident of the district, prepared a secret chamber in his home to receive him. At the time, the Liang [502–557] dispatched an envoy with gifts of garments and incense; but neither the king nor his officials knew the name or use of the incense. The king's messenger, therefore, was sent out with the incense to make inquiries concerning it both inside and outside the country. Once Hŭkhoja saw it, he disclosed its name, saying, "When burnt, it emits a sweet fragrance that will carry one's devotion to the gods and spirits. The title 'sacred' belongs to nothing other than the Three Jewels (*triratna*)—the Buddha, the Dharma, and the Order. If one burns this incense and makes a vow, a response is sure to follow." At that time the illness of the king's daughter took a turn for the worse, and the king ordered Hŭkhoja to burn the incense and make a vow. The princess soon recovered. The king rejoiced and rewarded him amply. Hŭkhoja returned to Morye, and, after giving him all that he had received from the king, said, "I have a place to go; hence I wish to bid you farewell." After that no one knew where he went.

In the time of King Pich'ŏ, Master Ado, together with three attendants, also came to the house of Morye. His appearance was similar to that of Hŭkhoja. After several years, he died a natural death. The three attendants remained reciting scriptures and discipline texts, and occasionally some became converted and practiced the faith.

Yet, according to the old records, on the eleventh day of the third month of the first year of Ta-t'ung of Liang, Ado came to Ilsŏn district, and both heaven and earth trembled. The master, holding a metal staff with gold rings in his left hand and uplifting a jade vessel of supreme response in his right, wearing a colorful cassock, and reciting a revealed truth, came to the believer Morye's house. Morye, surprised and fearful, went out to meet him and said, "Formerly, when the Koguryŏ monk Chŏngbang came to our country, the king and officials regarded his advent as an evil omen and killed him. Another monk, named Myŏlgubi, came after him, and he too was killed. What are you seeking that you should come here? Please come in quickly, lest you be seen by the neighbors." He then took the monk to a secret room and served him with diligence. It happened then that an envoy from the Wu presented five kinds of incense to King Wŏnjong (Pŏphŭng). Ignorant of their use, the king asked the people in the country. When the messenger came to the master, the master told him that they were to be burned to serve the Buddha. Afterward he went to the capital with the messenger, and the king asked him to meet the Wu envoy. The envoy paid him great respect, saying, "Eminent monks are no strangers in this remote country after all." The king, learning through this that the Buddha and his order were to be venerated, issued a decree permitting the propagation of Buddhism.

According to the *Sisa* by Ko Tŭksang, the Liang sent an envoy, Yüan-piao, who presented rosewood incense, scriptures, and images of Buddha. Because no one knew their use, the king made inquiries in all four directions, and Ado took the opportunity to point out the

dharma. Ko Tŭksang comments that Ado twice encountered danger
of death, but that thanks to his supernatural power he did not die but
took refuge in the home of Morye. Thus, whether the envoy came
from Liang or Wu cannot be ascertained. The life of Ado was, moreover, similar to that of Hŭkhoja. But why is this so? A span of some
four hundred and ten years separates the Yung-p'ing period from the
year *chŏngmi* of Ta-t'ung [527]. Buddhism had been in existence in
Koguryŏ for more than one hundred and fifty years, and in Paekche
for more than one hundred and forty.

According to another story, in the *Sui chŏn* (Tales of the Extraordinary) by Pak Illyang [1047–1096], the master's father was a native of
Wei, named Kulma, and his mother a native of Koguryŏ, named Ko
Tonyŏng. During Kulma's stay in Koguryŏ in an official capacity, he
had an affair with Ko Tonyŏng. Later he returned to Wei, leaving her
pregnant. When the master reached the age of five, he had a wondrous
appearance. His mother told him, "You are an unfavored orphan, so
you had better be a monk." The master followed her advice, and on
that very day he had his head shaved. At sixteen, he went to Wei to
visit Kulma and there studied under Master Hsüan-chang. Nineteen
years after ordination, he returned to his mother, who told him: "It is
very difficult to promote the dharma in this country, for conditions
are not yet ripe. Although at this moment there is no oral transmission
of the doctrine in that land of Silla, three thousand months from now
an enlightened king, a protector of dharma, shall hold sway and
greatly advance the Buddha's cause. In the capital, there are seven
places where the dharma shall abide: Ch'ŏngyŏngnim ("Forest of the
Heavenly Mirror"), east of Kŭmgyo (the present Hŭngnyun Monastery); Samch'ŏngi (the present Yŏnghŭng Monastery); south of the
Dragon Palace (the present Hwangnyong Monastery); north of the
Dragon Palace (the present Punhwang Monastery); Sinyu Forest (the
present Ch'ŏnwang Monastery); Sach'ŏnmi (the present Yŏngmyo
Monastery); and the Sŏch'ŏng Field (the present Tamŏm Monastery).
At these places are ruins of monasteries built during the time of the
former Buddha, which escaped earlier destruction. You should go
there, proclaim the mysterious doctrine, and become the founder of
Buddhism. Would that not be wonderful?"

In the second year, *kyemi* [263], of King Mich'u [262–284], the
master, obeying his mother's instructions, went to live in Silla west of
the palace (the present Ŏmjang Monastery). When he asked permission to preach, some thought it strange because this practice was

hitherto unknown, and some even attempted to kill him. He therefore escaped to the village of Sok, the present Sŏnju, and hid in the house of Morok for three years. It happened then that Princess Sŏngguk was ill, and the king sent out messengers everywhere for a healer. The master answered the call, went to the palace, and cured the princess's illness. Overjoyed, the king asked him what he desired. The master replied, "If you will build a monastery in the Forest of the Heavenly Mirror, I shall be well content." The king complied. But the age was crude, the people were stubborn, and it was difficult to make converts. The master at this time used a humble hut as his monastery. Only after seven years were there some who desired to be ordained as monks. Morok's sister, Sasi, became a nun. Therefore, Yŏnghŭng Monastery was erected at Samch'ŏngi where she stayed. After King Mich'u died, his successor did not respect Buddhism and wanted to proscribe it. The master returned to the village of Sok and made a grave for himself. He entered the grave, closed the slab over himself, and died. The sacred religion, therefore, was not practiced in Silla.

Two hundred years later, King Wŏnjong finally propagated Buddhism. This happened just as Tonyŏng had predicted. But from King Mich'u to King Pŏphŭng there were eleven kings. What a discrepancy concerning the dates of Ado's life! Old records must be scrutinized carefully. If Buddhism was practiced under King Mich'u, the master must have been a contemporary of Sundo. In that case, the faith underwent a decline and revived during the Ta-t'ung period of Liang. Hŭkhoja and Yüan-piao, by this reckoning, appeared together, and therefore their careers are described here for the reader's inspection. PL

Pŏpkong Declares Buddhism the National Faith
[From *Haedong kosŭng chŏn* 1A:1018c–1019b]

The monk Pŏpkong was the twenty-third king of Silla, Pŏphŭng [514–540]. His secular name was Wŏnjong; he was the first son of King Chijŭng [500–514] and Lady Yŏnje. He was seven feet tall. Generous, he loved the people, and they in turn regarded him as a saint or a sage. Millions of people, therefore, placed confidence in him. In the third year [516] a dragon appeared in the Willow Well. In the fourth year [517] the Ministry of War was established, and in the seventh year [520] laws and statutes were promulgated together with the official vestments. After his enthronement, whenever the king attempted to spread Buddhism his ministers opposed him with much dispute. He felt frustrated, but, remembering Ado's devout vow, he summoned all his officials and said to them: "Our august ancestor, King Mich'u, together with Ado, propagated Buddhism, but he died before great merits were accumulated. That the knowledge of the wonderful transformation of Śākyamuni should be prevented from spreading makes me very sad. We think we ought to erect monasteries and recast images to continue our ancestor's fervor. What do you think?" Minister Kongal and others remonstrated with the king, saying, "In recent years the crops have been scarce, and the people are restless. Besides, because of frequent border raids from the neighboring state, our soldiers are still engaged in battle. How can we exhort our people to erect a useless building at this time?" The king, depressed at the lack of faith among his subordinates, sighed, saying, "We, lacking moral power, are unworthy of succeeding to the throne. The yin and the yang are disharmonious and the people ill at ease; therefore you opposed my idea and did not want to follow. Who can enlighten the strayed people by the wonderful dharma?" For some time no one answered.

In the fourteenth year [527][7] the Grand Secretary Pak Yŏmch'ok (Ich'adon or Kŏch'adon), then twenty-six years old, was an upright man. With a heart that was sincere and deep, he advanced resolutely for the righteous cause. Out of willingness to help the king fulfill his noble vow, he secretly memorialized the throne: "If Your Majesty desires to establish Buddhism, may I ask Your Majesty to pass a false decree to this officer that the king desires to initiate Buddhist activities? Once the ministers learn of this, they will undoubtedly remonstrate. Your Majesty, declaring that no such decree has been given, will then ask who has forged the royal order. They will ask Your Majesty to punish my crime, and if their request is granted, they will submit to Your Majesty's will."

The king said, "Since they are bigoted and haughty, we fear they will not be satisfied even with your execution." Yŏmch'ok replied, "Even the deities venerate the religion of the Great Sage. If an officer as unworthy as myself is killed for its cause, miracles must happen between heaven and earth. If so, who then will dare to remain bigoted and haughty?" The king answered, "Our basic wish is to further the advantageous and remove the disadvantageous. But now we have to injure a loyal subject. Is this not sorrowful?" Yŏmch'ok replied, "Sacrificing his life in order to accomplish goodness is the great principle of the official. Moreover, if it means the eternal brightness of the Buddha Sun and the perpetual solidarity of the kingdom, the day of my death will be the year of my birth." The king, greatly moved, praised Yŏmch'ok and said, "Though you are a commoner, your mind harbors thoughts worthy of brocaded and embroidered robes." Thereupon the king and Yŏmch'ok vowed to be true to each other.

Afterward a royal decree was issued, ordering the erection of a monastery in the Forest of the Heavenly Mirror, and officials in charge began construction. The court officials, as expected, denounced it and expostulated with the king. The king remarked, "We did not issue such an order." Thereupon Yŏmch'ok spoke out, "Indeed, I did this purposely, for if we practice Buddhism the whole country will become prosperous and peaceful. As long as it is good for the administration of the realm, what wrong can there be in forging a decree?" Thereupon, the king called a meeting and asked the opinion of the officials. All of them remarked, "These days monks bare their heads and wear strange garments. Their discourses are wrong and in violation of the Norm. If we unthinkingly follow their proposals, there may be cause for regret. We dare not obey Your Majesty's order, even if we are threatened with death." Yŏmch'ok spoke with indignation, saying, "All of you are wrong, for there must be an unusual personage before there can be an unusual undertaking. I have heard that the teaching of Buddhism is profound and arcane. We must practice it. How can a sparrow know the great ambition of a swan?" The king said, "The will of the majority is firm and unalterable. You are the only one who takes a different view. I cannot follow two recommendations at the same time." He then ordered the execution of Yŏmch'ok.[8]

Yŏmch'ok then made an oath to heaven: "I am about to die for the sake of the dharma. I pray that righteousness and the benefit of the religion will spread. If the Buddha has a numen, a miracle should occur after my death." When he was decapitated, his head flew to Diamond Mountain, falling on its summit, and white milk gushed forth from the cut, soaring up several hundred feet. The sun darkened, wonderful flowers rained from heaven, and the earth trembled violently. The king, his officials, and the commoners, on the one hand terrified by these strange phenomena and on the other sorrowful for the death of the Grand Secretary who had sacrificed his life for the cause of the dharma, cried aloud and mourned. They buried his body on Diamond Mountain with due ceremony. At the time the king and his officials took an oath: "Hereafter we will worship the Buddha and revere the clergy. If we break this oath, may heaven strike us dead."

In the twenty-first year [534], trees in the Forest of the Heavenly Mirror were felled in order to build a monastery. When the ground was cleared, pillar bases, stone niches, and steps were discovered, proving the site to be that of an old monastery. Materials for beams and pillars came from the forest. The monastery being completed, the king abdicated and became a monk. He changed his name to Pŏp-kong, mindful of the three garments and the begging bowl. He aspired to lofty conduct and had compassion for all. Accordingly, the monastery was named Taewang Hŭngnyun because it was the king's abode. This was the first monastery erected in Silla.

The queen, too, served Buddha by becoming a nun and residing at Yŏnghŭng Monastery. Since the king had patronized a great cause, he was given the posthumous epithet of Pŏphŭng (Promoter of Dharma), which is by no means idle flattery. Thereafter, at every anniversary of Yŏmch'ok's death, an assembly was held at Hŭngnyun Monastery to commemorate his martyrdom. In the reign of King T'aejong Muyŏl [654–661], Prime Minister Kim Yangdo, whose faith was inclined westward, offered his two daughters, Hwabo and Yŏnbo, as maids in the monastery. The relatives of Mo Ch'ŏk, a traitor, were also reduced in rank and made to become servants. Descendants of these two classes of people serve there even today. PL

Wŏngwang Goes to China for Study
[From *Haedong kosŭng chŏn* 1B:1020c–1021b]

The monk Wŏngwang's secular name was Sŏl or Pak.[9] He was a resident of the capital of Silla. At the age of thirteen he had his head shaved and became a monk. His Sacred Vessel was free and magnificent, and his understanding beyond the ordinary. He was versed in the works of the metaphysical school and Confucianism, and he loved literature. Being lofty in thought, he had great disdain for worldly passions and retired at thirty to a cave on Samgi Mountain. His shadow never appeared outside the cave.

One day[10] a mendicant monk came to a place near the cave and there built a hermitage for religious practice. One night,[11] while the master was sitting and reciting scriptures, a spirit called to him: "Excellent! There are many religious people, yet none excels you. Now, that monk is cultivating black art; but because of your pure thought my way is blocked, and I have not been able to approach him. Whenever I pass by him, however, I cannot help thinking badly of him. I beseech you to persuade him to move away. If he does not follow my advice, there will be a disaster."

The following morning the master went to the monk and told him, "You had better move away to avoid disaster. If you stay, it will not be to your advantage."

But the monk replied, "When I undertake to do something opposed by Māra (The Evil One) himself, why should I worry about what a demon has to say?"

The same evening the spirit returned and asked for the monk's answer. The master, fearful of the spirit's anger, said that he had not yet been to the monk but knew the monk would not dare disobey. The spirit, however, remarked, "I have already ascertained the truth. Be quiet and you shall see."

That same night there was a sound as loud as thunder. At dawn the master went out and saw that the hermitage had been crushed under a landslide.

Later the spirit returned and said, "I have lived for several thousand years and possess unequaled power to change things. This is, therefore, nothing to be marveled at." He also advised the master: "Now the master has benefited himself, but he lacks the merit of benefiting others. Why not go to China to obtain the Buddha Dharma, which will be of great benefit to future generations?"

"It has been my cherished desire to learn the Path in China," replied the master, "but owing to obstacles on land and sea I am afraid I cannot get there." Thereupon the spirit told him in detail of matters relating to a journey to the west.

In the third month, spring, of the twelfth year of King Chinp'yŏng [590], the master went to Ch'en.[12] He traveled to various lecture halls, was received, and noted subtle instructions. After mastering the essence of the *Tattvasiddhi* (Treatise on the Completion of Truth), the *Nirvana Scripture,* and several treatises from the *Tripiṭaka,*[13] he went to Hu-ch'iu in Wu, now harboring an ambition that reached to the sky. Upon the request of a believer, the master expounded the *Treatise on the Completion of Truth,* and thenceforth requests from his admirers came one after another like the close ranks of scales on a fish.

At that time Sui soldiers marched into Yang-tu. There the com-

mander of the army saw a tower in flame. But when he went to the
rescue, there was no sign of fire, and he found only the master tied up
in front of the tower. Greatly amazed, the commander set him free.

It was during the period of K'ai-huang [590–600] that the *Mahāyānasaṃgraha* (Compendium of Mahāyāna) was first spread, and the
master cherished its style; he won great acclaim in the Sui capital.[14]

Now that he had further cultivated meritorious works, it was incumbent on him to continue the spread of dharma eastward. Our
country therefore appealed to Sui, and a decree allowed him to return
to his country in the twenty-second year, *kyŏngsin,* of King Chin-
p'yŏng [600] together with the *naema* Chebu and the *taesa* Hoengch'ŏn,
who at that time served as envoys to China. On the sea, a strange
being suddenly appeared out of the water and paid homage to the
master saying: "Would the master please erect a monastery and expound the truth there for my sake, so that your disciples can gain
superior rewards?" The master complied. Because he had returned
after an absence of some years, old and young alike rejoiced, and even
the king declared his pious respect and regarded him as "Mighty in
Kindness."

One day Wŏngwang returned to his old retreat on Samgi Mountain. At midnight the same spirit visited the master and asked him
about his experiences abroad. The master thanked him and said,
"Thanks to your gracious protection, all my wishes have been fulfilled."

"I will not abandon my duty to protect you," the spirit replied.
"You have an agreement with the sea dragon to erect a monastery,
and now the dragon is here with me."

The master then asked where the monastery should be built. The
spirit replied, "North of Unmun, where a flock of magpies are pecking at the ground. This is the place."

The following morning, together with the spirit and the dragon,
the master went to the place and, after the ground was cleared, found
the remains of a stone pagoda. A monastery was erected there, named
Unmun Monastery, and there the master stayed.

The spirit continued to protect the master invisibly until one day he
returned and said, "My end is drawing near, and I want to receive the
bodhisattva ordination so that I might qualify for eternity." The master administered the rites, and they vowed to save each other from
endless transmigration.

Afterward, the master asked if he might see the spirit's manifestation. The latter answered, "You may look to the east at dawn." The master then saw a big arm reach through the clouds to heaven. The spirit spoke, "Now you have seen my arm. Although I possess supernatural power, I still cannot escape mortality. I shall die on such and such a day in such and such a place, and I hope that you will come there to bid me farewell."

The master went to the place as instructed and there saw an old black badger whimper and die. It was the spirit.

A female dragon in the Western Sea used to attend the master's lectures. At the time there was a drought and the master asked her to make rain to alleviate the disaster in the country. The dragon replied, "The supreme deity will not allow it. If I make rain without his permission, I sin against the deity and have no way of escaping punishment."

The master said, "My power can save you from it."

Immediately, the morning clouds appeared on the southern mountain and rain poured down. But thunder from heaven broke out, indicating imminent punishment, and the dragon was afraid. The master hid her under his couch and continued to expound the scriptures.

A heavenly messenger then appeared saying, "I am ordered by the supreme deity. You are the protector of the fugitive. What shall I do if I am unable to carry out my orders?"

The master, pointing to a pear tree in the garden, replied, "She has transformed herself into that tree. You may strike it."

The messenger struck it and then left. The dragon then came out and thanked the master. Grateful to the tree that had suffered punishment for her sake, the dragon touched the trunk with her hand and the tree revived.

In his thirtieth year [608], King Chinp'yŏng, troubled by frequent border raids from Koguryŏ, decided to request help from Sui to retaliate and asked the master to draft the petition for a foreign campaign. The master replied, "To destroy others in order to preserve oneself is not the way of a monk. But since I, a poor monk, live in Your Majesty's territory and waste Your Majesty's clothes and food, I dare not disobey." He then relayed the king's request to Sui.[15]

The master was detached and retiring by nature, but affectionate and loving to all. He always smiled when he spoke and never showed signs of anger. His reports, memorials, memoranda, and correspondence were all composed by himself and were greatly admired throughout the whole country. Power was bestowed on him so that he might govern the provinces, and he used the opportunity to promote Buddhism, setting an example for future generations.

In the thirty-fifth year [613] an Assembly of One Hundred Seats was held in Hwangnyong Monastery to expound the scriptures and harvest the fruits of blessing. The master headed the entire assembly. He used to spend days at Kach'wi Monastery discoursing on the true path.

Kwisan and Ch'uhang from Saryang district came to the master's door and, lifting up their robes, respectfully said, "We are ignorant and without knowledge. Please give us a maxim which will serve to instruct us for the rest of our lives."

The master replied, "There are ten commandments in the bodhisattva ordination. But since you are subjects and sons, I fear you cannot practice all of them. Now, here are five commandments for laymen: serve your sovereign with loyalty; attend your parents with filial piety; treat your friends with sincerity; do not retreat from a battlefield; be discriminating about the taking of life. Exercise care in the performance of them."

Kwisan said, "We accept your wishes with regard to the first four. But what is the meaning of being discriminating about the taking of life?"

The master answered, "Not to kill during the months of spring and summer nor during the six meatless feast days is to choose the time. Not to kill domestic animals such as cows, horses, chickens, dogs, and tiny creatures whose meat is less than a mouthful is to choose the creatures. Though you may have the need, you should not kill often. These are good rules for laymen." Kwisan and his friend adhered to them without ever breaking them.

Later, when the king was ill and no physician could cure him, the master was invited to the palace to expound the dharma and was given separate quarters there. While expounding the texts and lecturing on the truth, he succeeded in gaining the king's faith. At first watch, the king and his courtiers saw that the master's head was as golden as the disk of the sun. The king's illness was cured immediately.

When the master's monastic years were well advanced, he went to the inner court of the palace by carriage. The king personally took care of the master's clothing and medicine, hoping thus to reserve the merits for himself. Except for his monastic robe and begging bowl, the master gave away all the offerings bestowed upon him to the monasteries in order to glorify the true dharma and to lead both the initiated and the uninitiated. When he was near the end, the king tended him in person. The king received his commission to transmit the dharma after the master's death and thus to save the people. Thereupon the master explained the omens to him in detail.

In the fifty-eighth year of Kŏnbok,[16] seven days after the onset of his illness, the master died,[17] sitting upright, in his residence,[18] giving his last commandments in a lucid, compassionate voice. In the sky northeast of Hwangnyong Monastery music filled the air, and an unusual fragrance pervaded the hall. The whole nation experienced grief mingled with joy. The burial materials and attending rites were the same as those for a king. He was ninety-nine years old. PL

Chajang Establishes the Monk's Discipline
[From *Samguk yusa* 4:191–194]

The venerable Chajang [fl. 636–645], surnamed Kim, was the son of Murim, Rank 3 of the True Bone class and a native of Chinhan. His father had served exemplarily in many official positions, but had never had an heir. He then took refuge in the Three Jewels and, in the hopes of begetting a child, supplicated before a thousand-armed and thousand-eyed statue of Avalokiteśvara: "If I beget a son, I will release him from family life so that he may become a ford across the sea of the dharma." Chajang's mother suddenly dreamed that a star had fallen into her bosom, and she conceived. Later, a son was born on the same day as Lord Śākyamuni and he was named Sŏnjongnang. His spirit and ambition were pure and wise. His literary compositions and his ideas developed daily, and he remained unsullied by worldly activities.

Early on, he lost both his parents and came to abhor the dust and clamor of the world. Renouncing wife and children, he donated fields and gardens to be made into Wŏnnyŏng Monastery and dwelled alone amidst the remote escarpments. He did not run from wolves and tigers and cultivated the meditation on dried bones. Becoming somewhat exhausted and vexed, he then built a small hut and covered the walls with thorns and brambles. He sat inside naked and, if he nodded abruptly, he was pricked and pierced. He tied his head to a beam in the roof in order to ward off stupor.

It happened that there was a vacancy at court. Because of his noble birth, he was recommended by public opinion and repeatedly summoned, but he did not proceed. King Chinp'yŏng [579–631] then ordered, "If you do not take office, you will be beheaded." Chajang heard this and replied, "I would prefer to keep the precepts for one day and die rather than to break the precepts for a hundred years and live." This matter was reported to the ruler, who permitted him to leave home to be ordained.

Chajang then retired deep into the cliffs and forests. When his provisions ran out, a strange bird would come to make offerings, carrying fruit in his beak, which he took and ate.

Once in a dream, a heavenly being came and conferred the five precepts on Chajang. He then left the ravines, and the gentlemen and ladies of the villages and towns contended to come and receive the precepts from him.

Chajang lamented to himself that he had been born in a border region and wished to travel to the west to learn the transforming teaching. Therewith, in the third year of Inp'yŏng, pyŏngsin [636], he received royal permission and, together with more than ten of his disciples, such as the monk Sil, traveled west to T'ang, arriving at Ch'ing-liang Mountain.

On the mountain was a clay image of the great saint Mañjuśrī, which, according to the legends of that country, was sculpted by artisans brought by Sakra, the king of the gods. Chajang supplicated before that image and fell into a hypnotic state. In his trance, the image rubbed his head[19] and conferred on him a Sanskrit verse. When he revived, he did not understand what it meant. The next morning, a strange monk came and explained it. He also said, "Even though you study myriads of doctrines, nothing will ever surpass this verse." Then, entrusting him with the Buddha's robe and relics, he vanished. Chajang knew that he had received holy writ. Then, descending to Pei-t'ai and passing T'ai-ho Lake, he entered the capital.

T'ai-tsung [626–649] sent a messenger to cater to his needs and ensconce him in Sheng-kuang Cloister. Though favors and gifts were richly given, Chajang despised this opulence. Upon his request, he went to Yün-chi Monastery on Chungnan Mountain and used an overhanging cliff on its eastern slope for his dwelling. There he lived for three years. Men and spirits received the precepts and miracles took place everyday. To relate all these would make the narrative complicated, and so they are omitted.

Subsequently, he returned to the capital and again received imperial favors. He was granted two hundred rolls of damask to use as capital for the cost of clothing.

During the seventeenth year of Chen-kuan, *kyemyo* [643], Queen Sŏndŏk [632–646] sent a letter to T'ai-tsung requesting Chajang's repatriation. Giving his consent, the emperor invited Chajang to enter the palace and granted him one bolt of damask and five hundred of assorted textiles. The heir apparent also granted him two hundred lengths of textiles and other gifts. As there were still many missing scriptures and images in his native kingdom, Chajang begged to be given a set of the *Tripiṭaka* to take back, as well as all types of banners and streamers and flowered canopies, and anything else that could serve as an object of merit.

Once he arrived in Silla, he received the welcome of the entire country and was ordered to dwell in Punhwang Monastery, where he was provided with generous supplies and protection. One summer he was invited to the palace to discourse on the treatises of the Mahāyāna. Furthermore, at Hwangnyong Monastery, he lectured on the *Text of the Bodhisattva Precepts* for seven days and seven nights.[20] The heaven rained sweet showers, and cloudy mists, murky and nebulous, enveloped the lecture hall. All the fourfold congregation[21] marveled at the wonder.

The court deliberated, "Although the eastern flow of Buddhism has continued for hundreds and thousands of years, there has been a lack of rules and regulations concerning its monastic hierarchy. Without any principles of control, there will be nothing to keep the Saṅgha dignified and pure." By royal order Chajang was appointed to be the Great National Overseer, and it was ordered that all the regulations and plans of the monks and nuns would be the ultimate responsibility of the Saṅgha Overseer.

Chajang used this good opportunity to propagate the religion zeal-ously and encouraged each of the five divisions[22] of the ecclesia to enhance its earlier training through the following measures: recite the precepts each fortnight; hold comprehensive examinations in winter and summer; establish an administrative post to examine whether monks are keeping or transgressing the precepts; furthermore, send investigators out on rounds of the outlying monasteries to admonish the monks on their faults, and ensure that they rigorously and regu-larly maintain the scriptures and images. Thus the protection of the dharma flourished for an entire generation. It was like Confucius, on his return from Wei to Lu, standardizing the music of the odes and hymns so that each was thenceforth perfected. At this time, the Silla people who received the precepts and honored the Buddha were eight or nine households out of ten. The number of those who beseeched to have their hair shaved or requested ordination increased as time passed.

Chajang then founded T'ongdo Monastery and constructed a Precepts Platform with which to ordain those who came from the four directions. He also reconstructed his house in his native village into Wŏnnyŏng Monastery and held a completion ceremony there, where he lectured on the ten thousand verses of the *Flower Garland Scripture*. His lecture inspired fifty-two female seraphim to appear within the audience. Chajang had his disciples plant many trees as testimony to this miracle and, for this reason, called them Trees of Knowledge.

Early on, the Korean style of dress was different from that of China. This matter was brought up for discussion in court and the motion to change to Chinese dress was endorsed. Accordingly, in the third year of Queen Chindŏk, *kiyu* [649], the caps and gowns of the Chinese court were first worn. The following year, *kyŏngsul* [650], the court adopted the Chinese calendar and for the first time used the T'ang reign title of Yung-hui. From that point on, whenever there was an imperial audience, the Silla envoy was placed at the head of the tributary states. All this was due to the achievements of Chajang.

In his twilight years, he left the capital for Kangnŭng prefecture and founded Suda Monastery, where he resided. He dreamed again of a strange monk whose appearance was like that of the monk he had seen at Pei-t'ai. He came and announced, "Tomorrow I will meet you at Great Pine Beach," and he awoke startled. Early in the morning, he went to Pine Beach where, finally, Mañjuśrī appeared. When Chajang asked about the essentials of the dharma, Mañjuśrī replied: "I will meet you again at T'aebaek Mountain at a place that is encoiled with creepers." He then disappeared without a trace.

Chajang went to T'aebaek Mountain in search of him. Seeing a huge python coiled under a tree, he said to his attendant, "This must be Kalbŏnji." He then established Sŏngnam Cloister there and awaited the reappearance of the bodhisattva.

There then appeared an old householder wearing tattered rags and carrying an arrowroot basket containing a dead puppy. He said to the attendant, "I have come to see Chajang."

The disciple said, "In all the time I have served as an attendant, I have never known anyone who called my master by his taboo name. Who are you? Are you insane?"

The householder replied, "Just announce me to your master."

The attendant then went to announce him, but Chajang did not recognize who it was and said, "Perhaps he's insane."

The disciple went out and vituperatively drove the visitor away.

The householder said, "I'm leaving! I'm leaving! How can someone who retains a sense of self possibly see me?" He then turned over his basket and shook it. The puppy was transformed into a jeweled lion-seat. Climbing up and sitting on the seat, the householder departed in a burst of light.

Chajang heard of this and, mustering all his monk's decorum, climbed up South Pass in search of the light. But it was already faint and he could not reach it. Then his body collapsed and he expired. After cremation, his bones were enshrined inside a stone cavern.

During his lifetime, Chajang established monasteries and stupas at ten different sites; and as each one was under construction, some strange and auspicious portent perforce appeared. Because of this, laymen who came to offer their services were as numerous as a crowded marketplace, and they would finish these structures in a matter of days.

Chajang's religious articles, clothes, and leggings, as well as the wooden pillow carved in the shape of a duck which was offered by the dragon of T'ai-ho Lake, and the robes of Lord Śākyamuni are all stored at T'ongdo Monastery. Moreover, in Hŏnyang County there is an Ayu Monastery which is so named because the duck on the pillow had once traveled there and manifested miraculous signs.[23] RB

The Nine-Story Stupa
[From *Samguk yusa* 3:137–139]

When in the tenth year of Chen-kuan, the fifth year of Queen Sŏndŏk [636], Dharma Master Chajang went to study in China and received the teachings of Mañjuśrī, the bodhisattva said, "Your ruler is from India's Kṣatriya caste and has already received the inner and external causes; your people are unlike those of K'ung-kung, but the ruggedness of their mountains and rivers makes them ugly and perverse and prone to espouse perverted views. At times the heavenly god sends down calamities, but the presence of enlightened monks enables your ruler and subjects to be well and the people harmonious." With these words he vanished. Aware that he had beheld the Great Sage in transformation, Chajang wept and withdrew.

While Chajang was passing by the shores of T'ai-ho Lake, a guardian of the dharma emerged from the water and asked him why he had come. Chajang replied that he was in search of enlightenment.

"What difficulties beset your country?" asked the guardian.

"Our country is bordered by Moho to the north and Japan to the south, and Koguryŏ and Paekche often infringe upon our borders. Thus foreign incursions bring hardships to the people," Chajang replied.

"You have as your ruler a woman who has virtue but lacks majesty. Thus do neighboring countries harbor designs upon your own. You must return quickly."

"What can I do to benefit my country?" Chajang asked.

"The dragon, the protector of the dharma at Hwangnyong Monastery, is my eldest son. At the command of the Buddha he is protecting your country. Upon your return, erect a nine-story stupa in the monastery. Then neighboring states will surrender, barbarians will offer tributes, and the royal work will be secured. When the stupa is complete, hold the Assembly of the Eight Prohibitions (*P'algwanhoe*) and grant amnesty to all criminals; then your enemies will be unable to harm your country. For my sake build a monastery to the south of the capital and pray for my happiness; then I too shall repay your kindness."

After presenting Chajang with a piece of jade, the guardian vanished.

On the sixteenth day of the seventeenth year of Chen-kuan, *kyemyo,* [4 September 643], Chajang returned to Silla with such imperial gifts as scriptures, images, cassocks, and silk, and reported to the king about the need to erect a stupa. As the queen deliberated, her ministers advised her to offer precious goods to attract an architect from Paekche. The Paekche architect Abiji arrived and began to work in stone and wood, and the *igan* Yongch'un (Yongsu) supervised the work performed by his two hundred assistants.

But on the day a pillar was erected, Abiji had a dream in which Paekche fell. Perplexed, he stopped working. Then suddenly there was an earthquake and darkness descended, whereupon an old monk and a thug emerged from the gate of the main hall, set the pillar in place, and vanished. With remorse Abiji completed the stupa.

According to the record, the height above the iron plate was forty-two *ch'ŏk* and that below it, one hundred eighty-three *ch'ŏk*. Chajang distributed the hundred relics he had received on Mount Wu-t'ai and enshrined them in the Platform of the Path at T'ongdo Monastery and in the stupa at Taehwa Monastery, thus fulfilling the request of the dragon of T'ai-ho Lake.

With the stupa completed, the kingdom enjoyed peace and the peninsula was unified—such was its efficacy. Later, when the founder of Koryŏ thought to occupy Silla, he remarked that he could not invade that country because of her Three Treasures: the sixteen-foot image of the Buddha, the nine-story stupa at Hwangnyong Monastery, and the jade belt granted by heaven to King Chinp'yŏng. This story recalls yet another concerning the nine cauldrons of the Chou, by which the Ch'u were constrained from attacking to the north.

According to the *Tongdo sŏngnip ki* (Record of the Establishment of the Eastern Capital) by the worthy Anhong, the twenty-seventh ruler of Silla was a queen. She had the Way but lacked majesty, and therefore her neighbors invaded her country. The nine-story stupa was erected at Hwangnyong Monastery south of the palace in order to daunt the enemies of Silla. The first story represents Japan; the second, China; the third, Wu-yüeh; the fourth, T'angna; the fifth, Ŭngyu; the sixth, Moho; the seventh, Tanguk; the eighth, Yŏjŏk; and the ninth, Yemaek. PL

Maitreya and Esoteric Buddhism

The Maitreya cult in Silla was a product of a belief that Silla was the Buddha Land of Maitreya. This version of the Maitreya cult played an important role in Silla Buddhism. Not only was Maitreya ("The Friendly One") the patron saint of the *hwarang*, but members of the *hwarang* class were thought to be reincarnations of Maitreya. Kim Yusin and his group were called "the band of the Dragon Flower tree," a reference to the bodhi tree of Maitreya. By adopting the Buddhist name Pŏbun ("Dharma Cloud"), King Chinhŭng sought to be a wheel-turning king (the ideal Buddhist ruler) in the land of Maitreya. Monk Chinja prayed before an image of Maitreya, asking that the celestial bodhisattva be reborn as a *hwarang* so that he, Chinja, could serve him. Chinja's prayer was answered. The discovery of stone statues of Maitreya at various places and reincarnations of the dead youth in Silla underscore the power of the cult over its devotees. In his poem "Song of Tuṣita Heaven," composed in 760, Master Wŏlmyŏng enjoins flowers to serve Maitreya. Chinp'yo received from Maitreya two special sticks to be used in divination ceremonies. The eighth and ninth sticks, two bones from Maitreya's fingers, represent the two Buddha natures: the innate Buddha nature and that realized through religious practices.

Two types of belief in Maitreya existed in Silla. One was a belief that Maitreya would come down to earth when the wheel-turning king rules, as in the period before the unification. (The *hwarang* Miri was thought to be an incarnation of Maitreya, and Chinja was a member of the clergy who assisted the *hwarang* order.) The other was a belief in rebirth in the Tuṣita Heaven, a prevalent trend after the unification of the Three Kingdoms.

The esoteric teaching that cannot be revealed to the uninitiated was popular just before the unification. Monk Myŏngnang returned from the T'ang in 635 and transmitted the secret incantation. In 671, he set up a secret platform to the south of Mount Nang and was reputedly able to sink the battleships of the invading T'ang forces. Monk Milbon healed the illness of Queen Sŏndŏk (632–647) and Kim Yangdo (*SGYS* 5:211–212). Healing of the sick, once the function of the shaman, was taken over by the Buddhist clergy.

Maitreya's Incarnation as a *Hwarang*
[From *Samguk yusa* 3:153–155]

The surname of King Chinhŭng, the twenty-fourth monarch of Silla, was Kim. His given name was Sammaekchong, or Simmaekchong. He ascended the throne in the sixth year, *kyŏngsin,* of Ta-t'ung [540]. In pursuance of the will of his uncle, King Pŏphŭng, he devotedly served the Buddha, erected monasteries, and issued certificates to monks and nuns. Endowed with grace, he respected the *hwarang* and made beautiful girls *wŏnhwa* (female leaders of the *hwarang*). His purport was to select persons of character and teach them filial piety, brotherly love, loyalty, and sincerity—the substance of governing the country.

At the time two *wŏnhwa*, Nammo and Kyojŏng (or Chunjŏng), were chosen, and their followers numbered three to four hundred. Being jealous of Nammo, Kyojŏng invited her to a party, made her drunk with wine, and led her to the banks of the North River, where she struck her dead with a stone and buried her. Unable to find her, Nammo's followers wept sadly and departed. One who knew of the crime then composed a song and had it sung by children. Thus Nammo's group went to the river, found her body in the midstream, and killed Kyojŏng.

Thereupon the king ordered the *wŏnhwa* abolished. After many years, he thought it best for the health of the country to establish the way of the *hwarang* and ordered a selection of virtuous youths from good families to be its members. At first, Knight Sŏrwŏn was made *hwarang* (*kuksŏn*)—this is the beginning of the *hwarang* institution. Thereafter a monument was erected in Myŏngju, and the king had the people refrain from evil and do good, respect their superiors, and be kind to their inferiors. Thus the five constant ways (goodness, righteousness, decorum, wisdom, and fidelity), the six arts (etiquette, music, archery, horsemanship, calligraphy, and mathematics), the three teachers, and the six ministers came into use.

During the reign of Chinji [576–579], the monk Chinja (or Chŏngja) of Hŭngnyun Monastery would make this plea before the image of Maitreya: "O Maitreya, please incarnate yourself as a *hwarang* so that I might be near you and serve you!" His kind sincerity and the fervor of his prayers increased day by day. One night he had a dream in which a monk told him, "If you go to Suwŏn Monastery in Ungch'ŏn (now Kongju), you will behold Maitreya." The stunned Chinja set out, bowing at every step throughout the whole ten days of his journey. Outside the monastery gate a handsome youth welcomed him with a smile and led him through a small gate into a guest room. Chinja went up, bowed, and said, "You don't know me. Why do you treat me so warmly?"

"I too am from the capital. I saw you coming, Master, and merely wished to refresh you," replied the youth. Then he went out of the gate and vanished.

Chinja thought this a coincidence and did not marvel at it. He told the monks about his dream and the purpose of his trip, adding, "If you don't mind, I'd like to wait for Maitreya at the last seat." The monks realized that they were being fooled, but sensing Chinja's sincerity, they said, "Go south and you'll find Mount Ch'ŏn, the traditional abode of the wise, where there have been many responses from the invisible. Why don't you go there?"

So Chinja reached the foot of the mountain, where a mountain god changed into an old man and welcomed him.

"What would you do here?" asked the god.

"I wish to behold Maitreya," Chinja replied.

"You already saw one outside the gate of Suwŏn Monastery. Why do you seek further?"

The stunned Chinja hurriedly returned to the monastery.

After a month, King Chinji heard the story and asked for the facts: "The boy is reported to have said that he was from the capital—and the sage doesn't lie. How is it that he does not visit the city?"

With his followers, Chinja sought the youth in the village and soon caught sight of a handsome youth strolling and amusing himself under a tree northeast of Yŏngmyo Monastery. Chinja approached him and said, "You're Maitreya. Where is your home, and what is your name?"

"My name is Miri, but I don't know my surname, because I lost my parents as a child," the youth replied.

Chinja then conducted the youth to the palace in a palanquin. The king respected and loved him and made him *kuksŏn*. He maintained harmony with other youths, and his decorum and elegant teaching were uncommon. After seven years of a brilliant career, he vanished.

Although Chinja was sunk in sorrow, he basked in Miri's favor. Continuing his pure transformation of the group, he cultivated the faith with sincerity. We do not know how he died. . . .

Now, the people call the *hwarang* "Maitreya Sŏnhwa" and a mediator is called *miri*—these are all vestiges of Chinja. PL

Myŏngnang, Founder of the Divine Seal School
[From *Samguk yusa* 5:215; 2:72]

According to the original record of Kŭmgwang Monastery, Master Myŏngnang was born in Silla and went to T'ang China to study Buddhism. On his return trip, he made a visit to the Dragon Palace at the request of the dragon of the sea, instructed it in esoteric doctrine, received as donation a thousand *yang* of gold, and, traveling underground, finally emerged from a well in his home garden. He then donated his house to be converted into a monastery and decorated the stupa and image with the gold given by the dragon king. The stupa and the image shone brilliantly. Hence the monastery was called Kŭmgwang (Golden Glow).

The master's taboo name was Myŏngnang; his polite name was Kugyuk; he was the son of the *sagan* Chaeryang. His mother was Lady

Namgan, also called Pŏpsŭng, daughter of the *sop'an* Kim Murim, the eldest sister of Chajang. Chaeryang had three sons—Great Masters Kukkyo, Ŭian, and, the youngest, Myŏngnang. His mother dreamed that she swallowed a blue pearl when she conceived him.

In the first year of Queen Sŏndŏk [632], Myŏngnang went to T'ang China and returned in the ninth year of Chen-kuan [635]. In the first year of Tsung-chang [668], the T'ang general Li Chi led a large army and, together with the Silla host, destroyed Koguryŏ. The T'ang army was then stationed in Paekche with the intention of destroying Silla as well. Knowing of the plan, Silla dispatched troops and beat back the enemy. Upon hearing of this, the angry T'ang emperor, Kao-tsung, ordered Hsüeh Pang to launch an attack. King Munmu of Silla, fearful of the invasion, asked Myŏngnang to use the mysteries of the esoteric school to repulse the Chinese. Thus he became the founder of the Sinin (Divine Seal) school.

At the time of the founding of the Koryŏ dynasty, pirates caused disturbances. Kwanghak and Taeyŏn, the heirs of Anhye and Nang-yung, were asked to devise a way to remove the evil and quell them, their art having been handed down from Myŏngnang, the ninth master in the line starting from Nāgārjuna. Wang Kŏn founded Hyŏnsŏng Monastery as the head monastery of the school.

[After the allied army of Silla and T'ang defeated Koguryŏ, the T'ang army remained in their garrisons and planned to attack Silla. At that time, *Kakkan* Kim Ch'ŏnjon recommended that Dharma Master Myŏngnang be consulted. The master who studied the secret dharma at the Dragon Palace advised the king to erect Sach'ŏnwang Monastery in Sinyu Forest, south of Mount Nang, and set up the Platform of the Path. But the T'ang army was approaching the Korean shores off Chŏngju, and the situation was urgent.

Myŏngnang then advised that the king set up a frame of the monastery with colored silk. The king did so, and had images of five dharma-protecting spirits made of grass, and ordered twelve famous monks versed in the esoteric art, headed by Myŏngnang, to design a mandala, a secret dharma. Then winds and waves arose, and the T'ang vessels were all sunk. When, in 671, the T'ang army of fifty thousand attempted another invasion, the same secret art was used to sink the Chinese vessels.](Summary of *SGYS* 2:71) PL

Rapprochement Between Buddhism and Shamanism

The Silla people believed that the holy mother—the mountain goddess and guardian of the country—lived on Mount West, or Mount Fairy Peach, west of the capital. She may have been a composite of a belief in the mountain god and a Taoist immortality cult. Thus Silla's Mount West was likened to a mountain where the Warrior Emperor of the Han received the peach of immortality from the Queen Mother of the West. Similar stories recount how Lady Unje, the queen of the second Silla king, became a guardian of Mount Unje in Yŏngil and how Pak Chesang's wife became a guardian of Ch'isul Pass. The fusion of the earth mother and Buddhism resulted in a belief in the Bodhisattva Sound Observer's presence on Mount Nak near T'ongch'ŏn in Kangwŏn, Korea's Mount Potalaka. Similarly, worship of Mount Odae evolved from a belief in Mañjuśrī fused with a popular belief in the five elements.

Holy Mother of Mount Fairy Peach
[From *Samguk yusa* 5:216–217]

During the reign of King Chinp'yŏng [579–632], a nun named Chihye who did many virtuous deeds wished to repair a hall for the Buddha at Anhŭng Monastery, but could not carry out her desire. A beautiful immortal fairy, her hair adorned with ornaments, appeared in the nun's dreams and consoled her: "I'm the holy goddess mother of Mount Fairy Peach (Mount West), and I am pleased that you would repair the Buddha hall. I offer you ten *kŭn* of gold. Take it from under my seat, decorate the three main honored images, and on the walls paint fifty-three Buddhas, six kinds of supernatural beings,[24] heavenly gods, and gods of the five mountains. On the tenth day of each month in spring and autumn, make it a rule to gather good men and women and hold a divination ceremony for all living beings."

Chihye awoke in amazement, went with her colleagues to the seat beneath the shrine dedicated to the goddess mother, dug up one hundred and sixty *yang* of gold, and carried out her plan—all according to the guidance of the holy mother. The evidence survives, but the ceremony was eventually abolished.

The holy mother, originally the daughter of a Chinese emperor, was named Saso. Early in her life she learned the art of the immortals and came to live in Korea, where she stayed for a long time. Her father, the emperor, tied a letter to the foot of a kite, instructing her to build her home wherever the bird perched. Upon reading the letter, Saso set the bird free, and it lighted on Mount Sŏndo, where she came to reside, becoming the mountain spirit. She stayed on the mountain called Sŏyŏn ("West Kite") a long time, protecting the country and performing many wonders. After the founding of Silla, she received one of the three sacrifices, superseding all mountain sacrifices.

King Kyŏngmyŏng, the fifty-fourth monarch, loved hawking. Once, while hunting on this mountain, he lost his hawk and offered prayers to the goddess and promised to enfeoff the hawk should it be found again. Suddenly the hawk returned and perched on the king's desk, whereupon he conferred on it the title of "great king."

When Saso first came to Chinhan, she gave birth to a holy man who became the first ruler of Silla—perhaps he was Hyŏkkŏse, who married Aryŏng. Therefore Chinhan was called Kyeryong, Kyerim— because the cock belongs to the west, and Paengma. Earlier, she had all the fairies weave silk and then dyed it red, made court robes of it, and gave these to her husband. Thus did the people know of her efficacy.

The *Historical Record of the Three Kingdoms* comments: "When Kim Pusik went to the Sung as envoy during the reign of Cheng-ho [1100–1125], he worshiped at the Yu-shen Hall, which enshrined the image of a fairy. The reception official Wang Pu asked, 'She is the goddess of your country. Did you know?' Long ago a Chinese princess drifted to the shores of Chinhan, where she gave birth to a son who became the founder of Korea. She herself became a guardian goddess and resides on Mount Sŏndo. This is her image." When Wang Hsiang, the Sung envoy, came to Korea and offered sacrifices to the holy mother of the east, the prayer read, "She gave birth to a sage who founded a state." Saso donated gold to make a Buddha image, lighted incense for the living beings, and initiated a religion. How could she be merely one who learned the art of longevity and became a prisoner in the boundless mist? PL

The Bodhisattva Sound Observer on Mount Nak
[From *Samguk yusa* 3:159–160]

Ages ago, Dharma Master Ŭisang, upon his return from T'ang China, heard that the abode of the dharma body of the "Great Compassion"[25] was to be found in a cave by the sea, and he called this place Naksan after Mount Potalaka in the Western Regions. The place was also called Small White Blossom after the abode of the true body of the white-clad mahāsattva.

On the seventh day of his purification, the master let his sitting mat float out on the morning tide. The eight kinds of supernatural beings[26] led him into the cave. He then looked up to the sky and worshiped the bodhisattva, and he was given a crystal rosary. The master received it, and as he withdrew, the dragon of the Eastern Sea offered him a fabulous jewel. After another seven days of abstinence, the master entered the cave and beheld the true features of the bodhisattva. The bodhisattva said, "On the mountain peak above my seat you will see a pair of bamboo plants growing. Build there a Buddha Hall." When the master emerged from the cave, two bamboo plants sprouted. There he built the main hall and enshrined the well-rounded and beautiful lifelike image of the bodhisattva,. . . named it Naksan Monastery, and deposited the rosary and jewel there.

Soon thereafter Dharma Master Wŏnhyo wished to make a pilgrimage to the cave. Upon his arrival at the southern outskirts, he saw a white-clad woman harvesting rice in the paddy. The master jokingly asked the woman to give him some rice, to which she replied that it was a lean year. As he went on under a bridge, he met another woman washing her menstrual napkin. When the master asked for drinking water, she scooped up unclean water and gave it to him. Wŏnhyo threw it away, scooped again, and drank. Then a blue bird in a pine tree called to him, "O monk"—but the woman was nowhere to be seen, except for a pair of sandals under the tree. Reaching the monastery, Wŏnhyo noticed under the seat of the Bodhisattva Sound Observer the same pair of sandals he had recently seen; only then did he realize that the woman he had met was the dharma body of the bodhisattva. His contemporaries called the tree the "Sound-Observer Pine." Wŏnhyo wished to enter the cave to behold the true form, but a storm forced him to depart before he could do so. PL

Fifty Thousand Dharma Bodies on Mount Odae
[From *Samguk yusa* 3:165–170]

According to an old mountain tradition, it was Dharma Master Chajang [fl. 636–645] who first called Mount Odae "the abode of the True Saints." In the tenth year of Chen-kuan [636], *pyŏngsin,* the master visited China in order to see the dharma body of Mañjuśrī on Mount Wu-t'ai. (The *Further Lives of Eminent Monks* gives the twelfth year [638], but we follow the *History of the Three Kingdoms.*)

Going first to the place of a stone image of Mañjuśrī by T'ai-ho Lake in China, Chajang worshiped humbly for seven days. On the seventh night, he had a dream in which the Great Sage conferred on him a verse in four feet. Awake, he could recite the verse from memory but did not understand the Sanskrit.

The following morning a strange monk appeared, dressed in a cassock of dark red gauze dotted with gold, and carrying a begging bowl and a relic of the Buddha's skull. Reaching Chajang's side, he asked him why he was sunk in melancholy. The master replied that he had received a verse but that since it was in Sanskrit, he could not interpret its meaning. The monk interpreted it as follows: "*Arapacana* means 'thoroughly to understand all dharmas'; *dṛṣṭikāya* means 'self-hood possesses nothing'; *Naṃgasiganaṃ* means 'one understands dharmahood in this way'; and *darśana* means 'forthwith one sees Rocana.' " He then gave the master his own cassock and other objects saying, "These were the appurtenances of our original teacher, the venerable Śākyamuni; guard them well. On Mount Odae, on the border of Myŏngju, northeast of your country, is the constant dwelling place of ten thousand Mañjuśrīs. Go there and visit it." When he had finished speaking, he vanished.

When Chajang was about to return to Silla, having looked everywhere for traces of the supernatural apparition, the dragon of T'ai-ho Lake appeared, begging for a meatless feast. When Chajang had presented the dragon with offerings for seven days, it at length declared to him, "The old monk who gave you the verse the other day was the real Mañjuśrī." The dragon earnestly besought Chajang to build a monastery and a stupa in Mañjuśrī's honor. All of this is recorded in full in a separate biography of Chajang.

In the seventeenth year of Chen-kuan [643], the master climbed Mount Odae to see the dharma body of Mañjuśrī, but a thick fog obscured his vision for three days, and he left with his wish unful-filled. He therefore returned to Wŏnnyŏng Monastery, where, it is said, he did in fact see Mañjuśrī. (This is also recorded in the separate biography.) The master then went to Kalbonch'o, now Chŏngam Monastery.

Years later, the ascetic Sinŭi, a disciple of Pŏmil, came to this mountain and lived in a cell in the master's old hermitage. After the death of Sinŭi, his cell became dilapidated, but the eminent monk Yuyŏn, from Suda Monastery, repaired it and lived there. It is the present Wŏlchŏng Monastery. . . .

(The following record of religious observances beneficial to the country is said to be the work of one Prince Poch'ŏn shortly before his death.)

Each peak of Mount Odae, which is of the same great mountain range as Mount Paektu, has a place of permanent abode of the dharma body of Mañjuśrī. There are green ones beneath the northern peak of the eastern terrace and at the tip of the southern foot of the northern terrace. Here you shall build a tabernacle for the Sound Observer, within which lodge a round image of the Sound Observer and ten thousand portraits of the Sound Observer against a green background. Have five virtuous members of your community read the *Diamond Scripture* in eight rolls, the *Perfection of Wisdom,* the *Scripture on Benevolent Kings,* and the hymn of praise to the thousand-armed Sound Observer by day. At night have them ceremonially intone confessions to the Sound Observer. This shall be called the Shrine of the Fully Rounded and All-Pervasive.

As to the red on the southern face of the southern terrace, you shall build a tabernacle for the Guardian of the Earth, wherein lodge a round image of the guardian and ten thousand portraits of the guardian, headed by eight great bodhisattvas, against a red background. Five virtuous persons are to read the *Guardian of the Earth Scripture* and the *Diamond Scripture* by day; at night they are to read a ceremonial confession based on the *Chan-ch'a (shan-o yeh-pao-ching).* This shall be called the Diamond Shrine.

As to the white on the southern face of the western terrace, you shall place a tabernacle for Amitābha, wherein you shall lodge round images of the Buddha of Infinite Life and ten thousand portraits of the One Arrived at Great Strength, headed by the Thus Come One of Infinite Life against a white background. Five virtuous persons are to read the *Lotus Blossom Scripture* in eight rolls by day and recite a ceremonial confession of Amita by night. This shall be called the Crystal Shrine.

As to the black at the southern face of the northern terrace, place a hall for the worthy one and in it enshrine a round image of Śākya and painted portraits of five hundred *arhats,* with Śākyamuni the Thus Come One at their head, against a black background. Five virtuous persons are to read the *Scripture of the Buddha's Recompense of Kindness* and the *Nirvana Scripture* by day and are to recite a ceremonial confession based on the latter by night. This shall be called the White Lotus Shrine.

As to the yellow, it is to be lodged in the Hall of Suchness on the central terrace. In it are to be lodged clay images of Mañjuśrī and Acala. Against the back wall are to be thirty-six portraits of emanations, headed by Vairocana, against a yellow background. Five virtuous persons are by day to read the *Flower Garland Scripture* and *Perfection of Wisdom* in six hundred rolls; at night they are to recite a ceremonial confession to Mañjuśrī. This shall be called the Flower Garland Shrine.

You shall also refashion Poch'ŏn Cell and call it Flower Treasure Monastery. Within it are to be lodged round images of the Vairocana trio and a complete Buddhist canon. Five virtuous persons are to store the scriptures by the long gate. By night they are to intone from memory the names of the gods from the *Flower Garland Scripture.* Every year hold a Flower Garland Convocation, which is to last one hundred days. The place is to be called the Shrine of the Dharma Wheel. The Flower Garland Monastery is to be the main convent of the shrine complex of Mount Odae. If you guard this tenaciously, commanding the fields of merit to be cultivated purely and preserving and fostering the incense fires, then the king of the realm will reign a thousand years, his people shall be secure and tranquil, the civil and the military shall be even and harmonious, and the hundred grains shall be plentiful. Furthermore, Munjugap Monastery, in the lower court, is to become the focal point of the shrine complex. Seven virtuous persons shall continuously, day and night, perform the rite of confession to the multitude of gods mentioned in the *Flower Garland Scripture.* If for the thirty-seven persons mentioned the food, clothing, and expenses are provided from the taxes of the eight provinces within Hasŏ *pu* and *to* (Kangnŭng), furnishing them with the four necessities, and if kings throughout the ages neither forget nor neglect to do these things, our wish shall be fulfilled. PL

The *Hwarang*

The origin of the *hwarang,* Silla's unique social group, may be traced to the "age set" organization of earlier times. Through that group's communal life and rites, young men learned the society's traditional values; through military arts, poetry, and music, they learned mutual understanding and friendship. Generally organized at the village or clan level, this basic social group maintained the fixed social structure. However, beginning in the middle of the fourth century, as Silla accelerated its development toward a state, the village or clan-based group became harder to maintain. Starting in the early sixth century, Silla began to expand its territory, and a transformation of the youth group became inevitable. Under the new conditions, the *hwarang,* now a semiofficial body at the national level, came into being as an organization dedicated to the nurturing of talent.

A *hwarang* group, comprising several hundred young men, was headed by a youth from the True Bone aristocracy and several monks. For a fixed period, they lived together to learn military arts and cultivate virtue. They also toured famous mountains and rivers to nurture love of their country, and they learned the beauty of order and harmony through poetry and music. Together they prayed for the country's peace and development. Monks serving as chaplains were entrusted with their religious education and taught them universalistic Buddhism and loyalty to the king.

Wŏngwang's "Five Commandments for Laymen" best illustrate the content of the *hwarang*'s education: serve the king with loyalty; tend parents with filial piety; treat friends with sincerity; never retreat from the battlefield; be discriminate about the taking of life (*SGSG* 45:425). Here courage required in the war for unification and the Buddhist concept of compassion were added to the Confucian virtues. Of these, loyalty and sincerity were considered fundamental. Some *hwarang* members went on to study the Confucian classics, the *Book of Rites,* and the *Tso Commentary.*

Willing to lay down his life for the country, the *hwarang* member vowed to serve it in times of need. Such spirit continued to inspire the youth as he came of age and began his career as a politician or soldier. With the firm bases of national morality and spirit established, the *hwarang* became a prime source of Silla's success in wars against its enemies.

After the unification of the Three Kingdoms by Silla military power was accomplished, however, the *hwarang* as a military organization went into decline. With the ensuing peace, Silla's people no longer felt the threat of war and the virile spirit once manifested by the *hwarang* disappeared. The *hwarang* subsequently came to be known more as a group specializing in poetry, music, and dance—not for moral cultivation but for enjoyment and "play."

Origins of the *Hwarang*
[From *Samguk sagi* 4:40]

The *wŏnhwa* ("original flower"; female leaders of the *hwarang*) was first presented at court in the thirty-seventh year [576] of King Chinhŭng.[27] At first the king and his officials were perplexed by the problem of finding a way to discover talented people. They wished to have people disport themselves in groups so that they could observe their behavior and thus elevate the talented among them to positions of service. Therefore two beautiful girls, Nammo and Chunjŏng, were selected, and a group of some three hundred people gathered around them. But the two girls competed with one another. In the end, Chunjŏng enticed Nammo to her home and, plying her with wine till she was drunk, threw her into a river. Chunjŏng was put to death. The group became discordant and dispersed.

Afterward, handsome youths were chosen instead. Faces made up and beautifully dressed, they were respected as *hwarang,* and men of various sorts gathered around them like clouds. The youths instructed one another in the Way and in righteousness, entertained one another with song and music, or went sightseeing to even the most distant mountains and rivers. Much can be learned of a man's character by watching him in these activities. Those who fared well were recommended to the court.

Kim Taemun, in his *Hwarang segi* (Annals of the Hwarang), remarks: "Henceforth able ministers and loyal subjects shall be chosen from them, and good generals and brave soldiers shall be born therefrom."

Ch'oe Ch'iwŏn [b. 857] in his preface to the *Nallang pi* (Inscription on the Monument of Knight Nan) says: "There is a wonderful and mysterious way in the country, called *p'ungnyu*. The origins of the institution are detailed in the history of the *hwarang*. In fact it embraces the Three Teachings and transforms myriad men. It is a tenet of the

Minister of Crime of Lu (Confucius) that one should be filial to one's parents and loyal to one's sovereign; it is the belief of the Keeper of Archives of Chou (Lao Tzu) that one should be at home in the act of inaction and practice the wordless doctrine; and it is the teaching of the Indian prince that one should avoid evil and do good deeds." Ling-hu Ch'eng[28] of T'ang, moreover, in the *Hsin-lo kuo-chi* (Record of Silla), states that "the *hwarang* were chosen from the handsome sons of the nobles, and their faces were made up, and they were dressed up. They were called *hwarang* and were respected and served by their countrymen." PL

Knight Chukchi

[From *Samguk yusa* 2:76–78]

During the reign of the thirty-second monarch Hyoso [692–702], there was one Tŭgo (or Tŭkkok) with the rank *kŭpkan* (Rank 9), who was a member of the band of Knight Chukchi (or Chungman or Chigwan). His name was duly registered in the *hwarang* roster, and he was attentive in his work, but then he failed to report for almost ten days. Knight Chukchi inquired after Tŭgo at his mother's. She replied, "My son has been appointed warehouse keeper of Pusan Fortress by *agan* (Rank 6) Iksŏn, the banner chief of Moryang district. He was called away so suddenly that he had no time to report to you, sir."

The knight said, "If your son had gone on private business, there would be no need to call on him, but since he went on an official mission I must go and entertain him." Taking a basket of cakes and a bottle of wine, he left with his servants and one hundred thirty-seven boys from his group.

Arriving at Pusan Fortress, he asked the gatekeeper where Tŭgo was. "Tŭgo is cultivating Iksŏn's demesne as usual," came the reply. The knight found him in the field where he fed him cakes and wine. He then asked Iksŏn to give Tŭgo leave but this request was refused. At the time a commissioner called Kanjin was delivering to the fortress thirty bags of rice he had collected as land rents from Nŭngjŏl of Ch'uhwa (Miryang) Prefecture. This Kanjin admired Knight Chukchi for his love of his young followers and despised Iksŏn's confusion and inflexibility. Kanjin offered the rice to Iksŏn in return for Tŭgo's release, but only when he offered the saddle of *saji* (Rank 13) Chinjŏl as well was Tŭgo allowed to leave. When they heard of this, the officials in charge of the *hwarang* sent a soldier to arrest Iksŏn and cleanse him of the impurity and unsightliness of his guilt. Iksŏn, however, had gone into hiding, so the soldiers arrested his eldest son instead and forced him to bathe in the palace pond in the midwinter cold. He froze to death.

Upon hearing this story, the king ordered all natives of Moryang village expelled from their offices in perpetuity and forbade even those of them that were monks to don a cassock or to enter the monastery. On the other hand, Kanjin's descendants were honored with the title of village chief. Although Dharma Master Wŏnch'ŭk was an eminent monk, he was not given a clerical post just because he was a native of Moryang.

Years before, when Lord Suljong was about to leave for his post as governor of Sakchu, he was given an escort of three thousand cavalrymen because armed rebels were abroad in the land. When his retinue arrived at Chukchi Pass, they saw a lay devotee repairing the road. The lord was impressed with the youth, and the youth was delighted with the lord's majestic air—it was an instance of mutual admiration. A month after taking office, both the lord and his wife had a dream in which the youth entered their room. Perplexed, the lord sent a messenger to inquire after the youth and learned that he had died a few days before. The governor ascertained from the report that the day of the youth's death was the same as that of his dream. "The youth might be reborn as my son," the lord said. He sent soldiers to bury the youth on the northern crest of Chukchi Pass and had a stone image of Maitreya erected before the grave. The lord's wife, who had conceived on the day she had her dream, gave birth to a son whom they named Chukchi. The child grew into the full bloom of his youth and, as vice-commander under Kim Yusin, unified the Three Hans, served as minister under four kings (Chindŏk, T'aejong, Munmu, and Sinmun), and brought peace to the country.

Earlier, Tŭgo had composed the following song in honor of Knight Chukchi:

> All men sorrow and lament
> Over the spring that is past;
> Your face once fair and bright,
> Where has it gone with deep furrows?

I must glimpse you
Even for an awesome moment.
My fervent mind cannot rest at night,
In the mugwort-rank hollow. PL

Kwanch'ang

[From *Samguk sagi* 47:437]

Kwanch'ang (or Kwanjang) was the son of General P'umil of Silla. His appearance was elegant, and he became a *hwarang* as a youth and was on intimate terms with others. At the age of sixteen he was already accomplished in horseback riding and archery. A certain commander (*taegam*) recommended him to King Muyŏl [654–661].

When, in the fifth year of Hsien-ch'ing, *kyŏngsin* [660], the king sent the troops and, together with a T'ang general, attacked Paekche, he made Kwanch'ang an adjunct general. When the two armies met on the plain of Hwangsan (now Nonsan), P'umil said to his son, "You are young, but you have spirit. Now is the time to render brilliant service and rise to wealth and honor. You must show dauntless courage."

"I shall," Kwanch'ang replied. Mounting his horse and couching his lance, he galloped into the enemy line and killed several of the foe. Outnumbered, he was taken a prisoner and brought to the Paekche general, Kyebaek. Kyebaek had Kwanch'ang's helmet removed. Kyebaek was greatly moved by the youth and valor of his captive and could not bring himself to kill him. He said with a sigh, "Silla has marvelous knights. Even a youth is like this—how much stronger must their soldiers be?" He then let Kwanch'ang return alive.

Upon returning, Kwanch'ang remarked, "Earlier when I attacked the enemy's position I could not behead the enemy general, nor capture their standard. This is my deepest regret. In my second attack I will be sure to succeed." He scooped up water from a well and drank; he then rushed upon the enemy line and fought desperately. Kyebaek caught him alive, beheaded him, and sent back the head, tied to the saddle of his horse.

P'umil took the head and, wiping the blood with his sleeve, said, "He saved his honor. Now that he has died for the king's cause, I have no regrets." The three armies were moved by this and strengthened their resolve. Beating drums and shouting war cries, they charged the enemy lines and utterly routed the Paekche forces.

King Muyŏl conferred the posthumous title of *kŭpch'an* (Rank 9) on Kwanch'ang and had him buried with full rites. Toward funeral expenses the king sent thirty rolls each of Chinese silk and cotton and one hundred sacks of grain. PL

Kim Hŭmun

[From *Samguk sagi* 47:437–438]

Kim Hŭmun was the eighth-generation descendant of King Naemul [356–402]; his father was Talbok, *chapch'an* (Rank 3). Whenever his comrades in Hwarang Munno's group mentioned the undying fame of a comrade who had perished in battle, Kim Hŭmun would shed tears of indignation, proclaim the valor of the fallen comrade, and spur himself on thereby. Monk Chŏnmil, one of the group, said, "Kim would not return alive if he were to go to the enemy lines."

In the sixth year of Yung-hui [655], King Muyŏl, angered by encroachments on the Silla frontier by Paekche and Koguryŏ, planned a retaliation and sent troops under Kim Hŭmun as Commander of the Nang Bannermen (*Nangdang taegam*). Battered by the wind, washed by the rain, Kim Hŭmun shared the joys and sorrows of his men. Arriving in Paekche territory, he pitched camp below Yangsan before attacking Choch'ŏn Fortress. Under cover of night Paekche people rushed to the Silla side and then at dawn climbed the ramparts. Startled, Silla's soldiers were thrown into confusion. Taking advantage of disorder, the Paekche soldiers made a sudden raid, sending a shower of arrows.

Astride his horse and with his lance in hand, Kim Hŭmun sat waiting for the enemy. *Taesa* Chŏnji advised, "Now that the enemy has started out in darkness we cannot see even an inch ahead. Even if you die in action, no one will know of it. Moreover, you are of nobility and a royal son-in-law. If you die at the hand of the enemy, it will be Paekche's pride but our disgrace."

Kim Hŭmun answered, "Once a man has resolved to die for his country, it matters little whether his fate is known or not. How could I seek only fame?"

Kim Hŭmun stood firmly rooted. The attendant holding his reins begged him to move back, but Kim Hŭmun brandished his sword and engaged the enemy. He killed several of them before he died. *Taegam* Yep'a and *Sogam* Chŏktŭk also died in action.

Hearing of the heroic death of Kim Hŭmun, *Pogi tangju* Poyongna said, "Although he was of noble origin and was powerful and lamented by people, Kim Hŭmun maintained his integrity to the end and died. As for me, no good will come of my living and no harm will come of my dying." He rushed to the enemy lines and died after killing several of the foe.

King Muyŏl lamented the deaths of these men and posthumously conferred the rank of *ilgilch'an* (Rank 7) on Kim Hŭmun and Yep'a and that of *taenaema* (Rank 10) on Poyongna and Chŏktŭk. The Silla people mourned their death in the "Song of Yangsan." PL

CHAPTER FOUR

Consolidation of the State

Unification of the Three Kingdoms

As Koguryŏ pressed hard upon Paekche and Silla, her enemies in the south, Silla turned to China for an alliance. Silla's envoy Kim Ch'unch'u obtained China's agreement that in the event the Silla-T'ang allied army won the war against Koguryŏ, the territory south of P'yŏngyang would belong to Silla. In 660, the combined Chinese and Silla forces destroyed Paekche. But after the conquest, the T'ang ignored the earlier agreement and set up five commanderies in Paekche. When Silla opposed this policy and executed pro-Chinese elements inside Silla, conflicts arose with T'ang China. But as long as Koguryŏ existed in the north, Silla avoided direct confrontation with the Chinese.

Although Koguryŏ repulsed the T'ang invasions, the continuous warfare dissipated its energy. Moreover, the Khitan and Moho tribes under Koguryŏ's control submitted to the Chinese, Koguryŏ's defense line in Liao-tung weakened, and the T'ang navy began to haunt the Yalu. After the fall of Paekche, the navy led by Su Ting-fang entered the Taedong River and laid siege to P'yŏngyang but without success. At this critical juncture, the Koguryŏ prime minister, Yŏn Kaesomun, died, his two sons feuded with each other, and his younger brother surrendered to Silla. Taking advantage of this internal discord, the T'ang army under Li Chi and the Silla army under Kim Inmun surrounded P'yŏngyang and reduced it in 668 after a fierce month-long battle.

With the fall of Koguryŏ, Silla and the T'ang openly collided. In 670, after the main Chinese forces had left Korea, Silla joined with the loyal forces of Paekche and Koguryŏ and attacked the Chinese army. Although the Chinese mobilized the Khitan and Moho tribes and the navy, they were compelled to withdraw after a number of battles. Finally, Silla was able to control the territory south of the Taedong River and Wŏnsan Bay and to unify the peninsula.

Account of the Silla-T'ang War
[From *Samguk sagi* 7:75–76]

In the second month of the fifteenth year of King Munmu [675], the T'ang general Liu Jen-kuei defeated the Silla army at the walled town of Ch'ilchung (Chŏksŏng) and returned home with his men. Then the emperor appointed Li Chin-hsing as Commissioner for Pacification of the East to govern the area. Thereafter the Silla king sent an envoy with tributes to beg for forgiveness, whereupon Emperor Kao-tsung forgave him and restored his office and title. Upon hearing the news on his way home from T'ang China, Kim Inmun went back and was enfeoffed as Duke of Lin-hai Commandery.

However, Silla took Paekche's territory as far as the southern borders of Koguryŏ and established provinces and districts of Silla.

At the news of the invasion of the T'ang army, together with Khitan and Moho soldiers, Silla mobilized its nine armies and waited.

In the ninth month, using the beheading of Kim Chinju, the father of P'unghun, a Silla student and imperial guard in T'ang China, as a pretext, the T'ang general Hsüeh Jen-kuei, with P'unghun as a guide, attacked the walled town of Paeksu. The Silla general Munhun and others met the attack and won the battle, beheading fourteen hundred of the enemy and taking forty war vessels. The Silla army also took a thousand war horses as Hsüeh raised his siege and fled.

On the twenty-ninth day of the ninth month, Li Chin-hsing stationed two hundred thousand men in Maech'o Walled Town (Yangju), but the Silla forces again routed them, capturing thirty thousand three hundred and eighty horses and weapons in the process. . . . Silla built a garrison along the Anbuk River (north of Tŏgwŏn) and built Ch'ŏlgwan wall (Tŏgwŏn).

The Moho attacked the walled town of Adal and plundered it; the Silla commander Sona was killed in action.

The T'ang army, together with Khitan and Moho soldiers, besieged the walled town of Ch'ilchung, but could not take it. The Silla official Yudong died in battle.

The Moho again besieged and reduced the walled town of Chŏng-mok; the magistrate T'algi led his people in a heroic resistance, but all of them died. Again, T'ang troops took the walled town of Sŏkhyŏn after a siege. Magistrates Sŏnbaek and Silmo and others died in battle.

The Silla forces won all their eighteen engagements with the T'ang, large and small alike, beheading six thousand and forty-seven of enemy troops and capturing two hundred war horses.

In the seventh month of the sixteenth year [676], the T'ang army attacked and took Torim Walled Town (T'ongch'ŏn); the magistrate Kŏsiji died in action.

In the eleventh month, the fleet of *Sach'an* (Rank 8) Sidŭk unsuccessfully fought the T'ang general Hsüeh in Kibŏlp'o (Changhang) in Soburi province (Puyŏ). Sidŭk finally won a victory, however, killing four thousand of the enemy in twenty-two engagements large and small. PL

The Life of Kim Yusin

[From *Samguk sagi* 41:394–43:406]

His lordship became a *hwarang* at the age of fifteen. His contemporaries, to a man, followed him as leader and styled him *Yonghwa hyangdo* ("Dragon Flower Disciple of Fragrance").

In the twenty-eighth year of Kŏnbok, of King Chinp'yŏng, *sinmi* [611], his lordship was seventeen. Seeing his country's border territory being invaded and attacked by Koguryŏ, Paekche, and the Moho, he was aroused in determination to defeat the brigands. Entering alone into a stone grotto in the Central Peaks where he purified himself, he then swore a pledge to heaven, saying: "Unprincipled enemies harass our lands like wolves and tigers—hardly a year is left in peace. I am but one insignificant subject, devoid of skill or strength, but determined to purge this calamity and unrest. If only heaven would look down and lend me a hand." There he remained for four days until suddenly an old man clad in rough garments came and said, "This is a frightful place filled with poisonous snakes and wild beasts. Why do you come here and stay by yourself, my noble youth?" He answered, "Where do you come from, my elder? May I know your esteemed name?" The old man said, "I don't live anywhere and come and go as fate directs. And it's hard to assign me a name."

When his lordship heard this he knew that this was no ordinary human. He bowed twice and then approached him saying, "I am a man of Silla. When I see my country's bitter enemies, my heart is pained and my head filled with aching—that is why I come here. My hope is to discover some solution. Humbly I beg you, my elder, to show compassion for my earnest sincerity and give me a formula." The old man was quiet and uttered not a word.

His lordship cried and sobbed and implored him again and again. After the sixth or seventh time, the old man spoke and said, "You are but a youth, yet determined to unite the Three Kingdoms. How brave!" Then, as he gave him a secret formula, he continued, "You mustn't pass this on recklessly. If it is used for improper purposes, it will turn disaster on you." Having thus spoken, he left and traveled for two *ri* or so. Although Yusin pursued him, he was nowhere in sight. There was only a light on the mountain top: a brilliance in all five colors.

In the twenty-ninth year of Kŏnbok [612], with the marauding neighbors squeezing even tighter, the stirring of his lordship's heroic spirit grew more intense. He took up his precious sword and went alone into a deep valley in the Yŏnbak Mountains where he burned incense and implored heaven in prayer and supplication. He swore the oath he had sworn in the Central Peaks, praying further that "the Keeper of Heaven send down a light and let a spirit descend into my precious sword." Then, after three days and nights, rays of light shone brightly from the Horn and the Void, and the sword appeared to quiver.

During the forty-sixth year of Kŏnbok, *kich'uk* [629], in autumn, the eighth month, the king sent *Ich'an* Imyŏngni, *P'ajinch'an* Yongch'un and Paengnyong, and the *Sop'an* Taein and Sŏhyŏn and others at the head of troops in an attack on Koguryŏ's Nangbi Fortress. The Koguryŏans sent out a counterforce and the situation turned against our men, with numerous deaths suffered and a breakdown in spirit to the point that none would fight on. Yusin was a Commander of the Central Banner at that time. He came forward to his father, stripped off his helmet and announced, "They've defeated us. But my life has been guided by loyalty and filial devotion, and I must be courageous

in the face of battle. We hear the saying, 'Shake a coat by its collar and
all the fur will fall smooth; lift up the headrope and the whole net will
open.' Can't I be the collar or headrope now?" Then he straddled his
horse, drew his sword, and leapt over a trench into the enemy's ranks
where he beheaded the general. He came back holding the head up
high, and when our army saw this, they struck out in attack to take
advantage of his victory. Over five thousand enemy men were killed
and beheaded, and a thousand were taken alive. The beasts inside the
fortress, too frightened to resist, all came out in surrender.

[*SGSG* 41:394] JJ

During Great King T'aejong's seventh year, *kyŏngsin* [660], in summer, the sixth month, the Great King and the Crown Prince Pŏmmin
moved out with a huge army to attack Paekche, setting camp at
Namch'ŏn. At the same time, the *P'ajinch'an* Kim Inmun, who had
gone to T'ang requesting troop support, came along with the T'ang
Great Generals Su Ting-fang and Liu Po-ying at the head of one
hundred thirty thousand troops, crossing the sea and landing at Tŏng-
mul Island. They had first sent an attendant Munch'ŏn on ahead to
announce their arrival; and with receipt of this news, the king ordered
the Crown Prince, Generals Yusin, Chinju, Ch'ŏnjon, and others to
take a hundred large vessels laden with troops to meet them. The
Crown Prince met General Su Ting-fang, and Ting-fang said to him,
"I'll go by the sea route and you, prince, go by land. We will meet at
the walls of Sabi, Paekche's capital, on the tenth of the seventh month."
When the Crown Prince reported this, the Great King led his generals
and warriors to an encampment at Sara. General Su Ting-fang and
Kim Inmun came into Ibŏlp'o by sea but ran aground and were unable
to proceed because of the thick coastal mud. Willow rush mats were
spread permitting the armies to land, and T'ang and Silla joined in
attack on Paekche. They destroyed her.

   Throughout that campaign, it was Yusin's merit that was greatest,
and when the emperor of T'ang heard of it, he sent an emissary to
praise and compliment him. General Su Ting-fang said to Yusin,
Inmun, and Yangdo, "My command allows me to exercise authority
as conditions dictate, so I will now present to you as maintenance
lands all of Paekche's territory that has been acquired, this as reward
for your merit. How would that be?" Yusin answered, "You came
with Heavenly Troops, Great General, to help realize our unworthy

prince's wish to avenge our small nation, and from our unworthy prince on down to all officials and people throughout the nation there is endless rejoicing. How could it be just for the three of us alone to enrich ourselves by accepting such a gift?" They did not accept it.

Once they had defeated Paekche, the men of T'ang camped on the Sabi hills and secretly planned to invade Silla. When our king learned of it, he summoned all officials together to discuss a strategy. Lord Tami put forward his opinion, saying: "Have our people disguise themselves as Paekche men—wear Paekche clothes and act as if they are going to rebel. The men of T'ang will surely strike at them, then we can use this as an excuse to fight and achieve our goal." Yusin said, "That idea is worth using. Let us follow that plan." But the king said, "The T'ang army has destroyed our enemy for us. If we turn about and fight them, would we have heaven's protection?" Yusin answered, "A dog fears his master, but if the master steps on its paw, the dog bites him. Why shouldn't one save himself when endangered? I beg that the Great King grant permission." But the men of T'ang, learning of our preparedness through spies, took the Paekche king, ninety-three officials, and twenty thousand soldiers as prisoners, and on the third day of the ninth month set sail from Sabi to return to T'ang. A group including Junior General Liu Jen-yüan was left behind to occupy the territory.

After Su Ting-fang had presented the prisoners, the Son of Heaven expressed words of commendation and indebtedness and then said, "Why didn't you follow through with an attack on Silla?" Ting-fang said, "The Silla sovereign is humane and loves his people, his officers serve their nation with loyalty, and those below serve those above as if they were their fathers or elder brothers. Even though it is a small country, one can't plot against them."

[SGSG 42:400–401] JJ

In the first year of Tsung-chang, *mujin* [668], the T'ang emperor appointed State Duke of Ying, Li Chi, to marshal a force to attack Koguryŏ. Aid was thus requested of us. Preparing to set out with troops in response, Great King Munmu ordered Hŭmsun and Inmun to serve as generals. Hŭmsun said in report to the king, "I fear we'll regret it if Yusin does not march out together with us." The king responded, "You three are our national treasures. Should you all go into enemy territory and some mishap occur that prevented your return, what then of the nation? My wish is to keep Yusin here to protect our nation. With him as imposing as a great wall we will be free from concern."

Hŭmsun was Yusin's younger brother and Inmun the son of his sister, so that they paid him great respect and never dared defy him. They reported to him then saying, "We, who are not equal to the task, are about to go with the Great King on an uncharted course and know not what to do. We are desirous of your counsel." He responded saying, "The general serves as shield and wall of the nation and as his prince's talons and fangs. It is in the midst of rocks and arrows that he determines victory or defeat. Only when he is in command of the Way of Heaven on high, of the figurations of the land below, and of the minds of men before him can he command success. Our nation survives today because of its loyalty and trust, while Paekche at this time by simply striking with our uprightness at their deviousness, but how infinitely more secure we are with the support of the august power of the Great State's brilliant Son of Heaven! Go now and strive your utmost. Don't fail your charge." The two bowed and said, "Your instructions have been respectfully received and will be carried into practice. We dare not slip or weaken."[1]

[*SGSG* 43:405–406] JJ

Confucian Political Thought

King Muyŏl, unifier of the Three Kingdoms, was not of the Holy Bone but of the True Bone class. He suppressed the revolts of Pidam and Alch'ŏn and emerged victorious. He took his wife not from the Pak clan, which had hitherto supplied queens, but from the Kim clan of Kaya origin. He also abandoned Buddhist names and adopted Chinese-style nomenclature. Thus he inaugurated the middle period of Silla ruled by his direct descendants until King Hyegong (765–779). This period was marked by the weakening of the aristocracy and the strengthening of royal authority. The *chipsabu* (state secretariat) became the principal administrative office, supplanting the *hwabaek* council. By the time of King Sinmun, the government consisted of six ministries. Local administration was also expanded to govern the conquered territory; King Sinmun set up nine prefectures and five subsidiary capitals. Likewise the army, consisting of nine banners (*sŏdang*) and ten garrisons (*chŏng*) stationed in provinces, defended the country. With the central and local administration firmly in place, Silla felt a strong need for an ideology such as Confucian political thought to buttress the country's administrative structure.

Posthumous Epithet for King Muyŏl
[From *Samguk sagi* 8:82]

In the spring of the twelfth year of King Sinmun [692], Emperor Chung-tsung [684–710] sent an envoy who orally communicated the emperor's edict: "As for our T'ai-tsung, the Cultured Emperor [626–649], his merit and virtue were matchless. Upon his death, therefore, he received the temple name of T'ai-tsung (Grand Ancestor). To accord the same temple name to your former king Kim Ch'unch'u [Muyŏl, 661–681] is to overstep the established norms. You should rename him at once."

After consulting his ministers, the king replied, "The posthumous epithet of our former king Kim Ch'unch'u happens to be the same as the temple name of T'ai-tsung, and so you order us to change it. How dare we not follow your command? Upon consideration, our former king too had in a high degree wise virtues. During his lifetime he obtained a good minister, Kim Yusin, cooperated with him in good administration, and unified Korea. His merit was indeed great. At the time of his death, therefore, our people, cherishing the dear memory of him, honored him with the name T'aejong, unaware that this was a violation of decorum. We have been appropriately chastened by your edict. I hope that Your Majesty's envoy will duly report our deliberations to Your Majesty."

No further edict on the subject was ever received. PL

King Munmu's Edict Concerning the Investiture of An Sŭng
[From *Samguk sagi* 6:65–66]

In the eighth month the king sent *Sach'an* Sumisan to enfeoff An Sŭng as king of Koguryŏ. The investiture read:

"On the first day of the eighth month, *sinch'uk*, of the first year of Hsien-heng, *kyŏngo* [21 August 670], the king of Silla sends an investiture to An Sŭng, the heir of Koguryŏ. Your progenitor, King Chungmo (Chumong) accumulated virtue in the north and performed meritorious deeds in the south. His majesty shook the Green Hill (Korea) and his benevolent teaching extended to Hsüan-t'u. Later, his heirs succeeded to the throne, and his direct and collateral lines were unbroken. The developed land extended to a thousand *ri,* and its history numbered some eight hundred years. But Yŏn Kaesomun's sons Namgŏn and Namsan struggled for power and caused domestic discord. Family and state were ruined, the royal ancestral shrine and the altars to the soil and the grain were destroyed, and the people were unsettled and had no one in whom to place their trust. Escaping all alone the dangers of the mountains and plains, you gave yourself up to your neighbor state Silla. The trials of your wandering recall those of Duke Wen of Chin,[2] and your resolve to revive the fallen state resembles that of Duke Hsüan of Wei.[3] The people must have a ruler, and Great Heaven must have one to entrust with the mandate.[4] You are the only true heir to the late king of Koguryŏ (Pojang). Who else but you should be in charge of ancestral sacrifices?

"I respectfully send my subject *Ilgilch'an* Kim Sumisan and others to proclaim your investitures and enfeoff you as king of Koguryŏ. I beg you to gather your scattered people, succeed to the old line, and enter into brotherly relations with us as a neighboring state. Be reverent, be reverent!

"I am dispatching herewith two thousand bags of nonglutinous rice, an armored horse, five bolts of pongee, ten rolls each of thin silk and fine hemp cloth, and fifteen *ch'ing* of floss silk. Please accept these gifts." PL

King Sinmun's Proclamation of His Accession
[From *Samguk sagi* 8:79–80]

On the eighth day of the eighth month of the first year of King Sinmun [25 September 681], *Sop'an* Kim Hŭmdol, *P'ajinch'an* Hŭng-wŏn, and *Taeach'an* Chingong and others were put to death for plotting treason.

Thirteenth day [30 September 681]: King Podŏk (An Sŭng) sent as envoy *Sohyŏng* Sudŏkkae to offer congratulations on suppression of the rebels.

Sixteenth day [3 October 681]: The king issued a proclamation: "To honor the meritorious is a worthy admonition of the former sages; to punish the criminal is the law of the former kings. With my own insignificant body and negligible virtue I have inherited a great undertaking. I have gone without meals, risen early, retired late. Together with my ministers I have wished to bring peace to the country. How could I have imagined that while I was in mourning a rebellion would arise in the capital? The rebel leaders, Hŭmdol, Hŭng-wŏn, and Chingong, obtained their positions not through talent but by royal favor. Being incapable of prudence and thrift, they plotted to aggrandize themselves by their iniquities. They insulted the officials and deceived those in high position and low. Each day gave new proof of their insatiable ambition, as they perpetrated various outrages, invited the wicked to their board, and associated with the petty officials in the palace. Misfortune spread within and without, and the evildoers banded together and set the date for their revolt. Luckily, I have relied on the help of heaven and earth from above and have received the help of my royal ancestors from below, and the plot of those who planned yet more grievous sins was brought to light. This indeed shows that they were abandoned by men and gods and were unacceptable to heaven and earth. Never before have there been more blatant violations of justice or injury to public mores. Therefore I assembled the troops, intending to do away with the disloyal ones. Some of these fled to the mountain valleys, while others surrendered in the palace courtyard. We hunted down the stragglers and wiped them out. In three or four days, the criminals were done with; there could have been no other outcome. I alarmed the officials because of this matter, and I cannot quiet my conscience morning or evening. Now that this evil band has been purged, no threat exists near or far. Quickly let the mustered soldiers and cavalry return and proclaim my wishes to the four quarters."

Twenty-eighth day [15 October 681]: The *Ich'an* Kungwan is put to death. The royal message reads: "The basis in serving one's master is loyalty, and the just cause of officialdom is constancy. The Minister of War, *Ich'an* Kungwan, rose to his position through the regular channels. But being unable to repair his own omissions, he could not do his part at court or devote his very life to the cause of the state. Instead he associated with the rebel Hŭmdol and others and kept his treasonous secrets for him. Kungwan had neither patriotic concern for the welfare of the country nor public spirit. How could he as minister recklessly confuse the laws of state? We will treat him as a common criminal as a warning to others like him. We will allow him and his one son by his legal wife to commit suicide. Let this proclamation be known far and near." PL

Confucian Learning

When an ideology was needed to manage the society and politics of Silla, King Sinmun established the National Academy and had scholars teach Confucianism and the classics. The establishment of institutions had already inspired interest in Confucian political thought, as evinced by the "Five Commandments for Laymen" and the "Record of the Oath Made in the Year *Imsin*." Thus in 636, before the foundation of the National Academy, Queen Chindŏk had appointed scholars to teach Chinese learning. With the establishment of the National Academy in 682, the core curriculum consisted of the *Analects* and the *Book of Filial Piety* and specialization in one of the following: the *Book of Songs*, the *Book of Changes*, the *Book of Documents*, the *Book of Rites*, the *Tso Commentary*, or the *Anthology of Refined Literature* (*Wen hsüan*). Students ranged in age from fifteen to thirty. In 788, a state examination system was instituted whereby students were classified into three classes. This system lasted only briefly, however, and never truly challenged the hereditary bone rank order.

The National Academy
[From *Samguk sagi* 38:366–367]

The National Academy belongs to the Ministry of Rites. Established in the second year of King Sinmun [682], the academy was called *Taehakkam* by King Kyŏngdŏk [742–765] but was again called *Kukhak* by King Hyegong [765–780]. There was one director, which King Kyŏngdŏk called *saŏp* but which King Hyegong renamed *kyŏng*. The director's rank was the same as that of other directors. Erudites and instructors were appointed in 651 as well as two holding the rank of *taesa*, who were called *chubu* by King Kyŏngdŏk but were again called *taesa* by King Hyegong. The ranks ranged from *saji* to *naema*. There were two erudites of history, and two more were added by King Hyegong.

The curriculum included the *Book of Changes*, the *Book of Documents*, the *Book of Songs* (*Mao shih*), the *Book of Rites* (*Li chi*), the *Spring and Autumn Annals*, the *Tso Commentary*, and the *Anthology of Refined Literature*. One erudite or instructor taught in each of the three areas of study: (1) the *Book of Rites*, the *Book of Songs*, the *Book of Changes*, the *Analects*, the *Book of Filial Piety*; (2) the *Spring and Autumn Annals*, the *Tso Commentary*, the *Book of Songs*, the *Analects*, the *Book of Filial Piety*; (3) the *Book of Documents*, the *Analects*, the *Book of Filial Piety*, and the *Anthology of Refined Literature*.

Students graduated in three ranks. Those proficient in the *Spring and Autumn Annals*, the *Tso Commentary*, the *Book of Rites*, and the *Anthology of Refined Literature*, as well as the *Analects* and the *Book of Filial Piety*, were assigned to the top rank. Those who had read the "Various Rites" (*Chü li*), the *Analects*, and the *Book of Filial Piety* were middle-ranking students. Those who had read the "Various Rites" and the *Book of Filial Piety* were ranked lowest. A student who was versed in the Five Classics, the Three Histories, and the various schools of Chinese philosophy was elevated a rank for employment. One erudite or instructor of mathematics was made to teach the *Chui ching*, the *San-k'ai*, the *Nine Chapters on the Art of Mathematics,* and the *Six Chapters on the Art of Mathematics*. The ranks of the students ranged from *taesa* to no rank, and their ages ranged from fifteen to thirty. The period of study was nine years. Simple, dull, and otherwise unpromising students were dismissed, but those who showed undoubted potential while still failing to complete the curriculum were allowed to remain beyond the standard nine-year period. Students were allowed to leave the academy only after attaining the rank of *taenaema* or *naema*. PL

Chinese Learning and the Growth of the Educated Class

Koguryŏ used Chinese script from early times. Under King Sosurim (371–384) a Chinese-style national university was established, and the learned class studied the Five Classics, histories, and the *Anthology of Refined Literature*. There were also private schools (*kyŏngdang*) that taught Chinese and archery. The representative example of writing from Koguryŏ is the inscription on the monument erected in honor of King Kwanggaet'o, which uses the Korean style of calligraphy. Paekche had erudites (*paksa*) of the Five Classics, medicine, and the calendar, and it was they who transmitted Chinese writing to Japan. An example of Paekche writing is the state paper King Kaero (455–475) sent to the Northern Wei in 472,[5] preserved in the *Wei shu*, and the monument of Sat'aek Chijŏk. Monuments erected at the sites of King Chinhŭng's tours of inspection show the mastery of written Chinese in Silla. Beginning with the time of King Chinhŭng Confucianism was actively studied, especially by monks.

Proficiency in Chinese enabled the compilation of national history in the Three Kingdoms: Yi Munjin condensed a history of one hundred chapters into five chapters in Koguryŏ (600); Kohŭng wrote history in Paekche (375), and, judging from the quotations in the *Nihon shoki,* other historical material also existed; Kŏch'ilbu (fl. 545–576) compiled history in Silla. The compilation of history in Paekche and Silla coincided with their territorial expansion and may be said to reflect their national consciousness.

When Confucian rule was proclaimed at the time of unification, studies in Chinese literature began to proliferate. Among the six writers famous at the time, Kangsu was known for his talent in drafting diplomatic papers. Then came Sŏl Ch'ong (c. 660–730), who used the *idu* transcription system to facilitate the reading of Chinese classics. With the emergence of Kim Taemun (fl. 704), the author of historical and geographical works, Silla no longer imitated Chinese models. Moreover, the number of students studying in China, officially or privately, increased, and among them were Kim Ungyŏng (fl. 821), Kim Kagi (d. 859), and Ch'oe Ch'iwŏn.

There were three styles in Chinese writing: the *hyangch'al* system used in the *hyangga* (see chapter 6); the simple style (as in "Record of an Oath Made in the Year *Imsin*") used by monks, village chiefs, and lower officials; and Buddhist Chinese. When the central authority declined in the latter part of Silla, the students going abroad consisted mainly of the sixth head-rank class. Among them were Wang Kŏin and Ch'oe Ch'iwŏn, who criticized the central government from the viewpoint of the learned class, and Ch'oe Ŏnwi (868–944) and Ch'oe Sŭngu (fl. 890–918), who aligned themselves with such local chiefs as Wang Kŏn and Kyŏnhwŏn (d. 936).

The Tombstone of King Muryŏng
[From *Chŭngbo Hanguk kŭmsŏk yumun,* no. 7]

The tombstone of King Muryŏng (501–523), discovered in Songsan-ri, Kongju, in 1971, consists of six lines comprising a total of fifty-two logographs.

"The Great General and Pacifier of the East,[6] King Sama (Muryŏng) of Paekche, died at the age of sixty-two on the seventh day, *imjin,* of the fifth month, *pyŏngsul,* of the fifth year, *kyemo* [5 June 523]. On the twelfth day, *kapsin,* of the eight month, *kyeyu,* of the *ŭlsa* year [14 September 525] he was laid to rest in a great tomb with due ceremony. We have recorded as in the left [to prove that the plot was purchased from the earth god]."[7] PL

Record of an Oath Made in the Year *Imsin*
[From *Chŭngbo Hanguk kŭmsŏk yumun,* no. 6]

On the sixteenth day of the sixth month of the year *imsin,* we two solemnly swear and record. We swear by heaven to conduct ourselves with perfect loyalty and not to commit any fault for a span of three years. We swear that if we act contrary to this oath, we will sin gravely against heaven. Especially when the country is unstable we swear to translate the oath into practice. Previously, on the twenty-second day of the seventh month of the year *sinmi,* we pledged ourselves to master the *Books of Songs,* the *Book of Documents,* the *Book of Rites,* and the *Tso Commentary* in the like period of three years. PL

Kangsu
[From *Samguk sagi* 46:428–429]

Kangsu [d. 692] was a man of the Saryang district in Chungwŏn Capital (now Ch'ungju). His father was *Naema* Sŏkch'e. Kangsu's mother conceived him after dreaming of a man with a horn on his head. When he was born, Kangsu had a piece of bone protruding from the rear of his skull. Sŏkch'e took his son to the acknowledged worthy of the day and asked, "What is the reason for his skull bone so shaped?"

"I have heard that Fu-hsi had the frame of a tiger," the worthy replied, "Nü-kua the body of a snake, Shen-nung the head of an ox, and Kao-yao the mouth of a horse. The wise and worthy are of the same kind, but their physiognomy differs from that of the ordinary. Your son also has a black mole on his head. According to the art of physiognomy, a black mole in the face is not good, but that on the head is not bad. This must be a marvelous sign."

Returning home, Sŏkch'e told his wife, "Your son is extraordinary.

If you rear him well, he will one day become a leading scholar, esteemed by all."

As an adult, Kangsu had taught himself to read, and he understood the meaning of what he had read. To test him Sŏkch'e asked, "Will you study the way of the Buddha or that of Confucius?"

Kangsu replied, "I have heard that Buddhism is a teaching that does not concern this world. Since I am a man of this world, how could I study Buddha's path? I wish to study of the way of Confucius."

"Do as you please," Sŏkch'e replied.

With a tutor Kangsu studied the *Book of Filial Piety,* the "Various Rites," the *Erh ya*—a lexical work comprising glosses on words in the classics, and the *Anthology of Refined Literature.* Though what he heard was mean and near at hand, what he attained was lofty and distant. Thus he became a giant among the learned of the day. At last he entered the officialdom, served in various posts, and he became famous.

Earlier Kangsu had had an illicit affair with the daughter of a metalworker and greatly loved the girl. When at the age of twenty his parents wished to arrange a marriage with a village woman of good bearing and conduct, Kangsu declined on the ground that he could not marry twice.

"You are well known and well thought of by all. Would it not be a pity to wed a woman of lowly birth?" his father replied angrily.

Kangsu bowed twice and replied, "To be poor and humble is not a thing to be ashamed of. What is shameful is to fail to put into practice what one has learned. The ancients say: 'The wife who has shared one's poverty must not be put aside in times of prosperity, and a friendship formed when one is poor and mean should not be forgotten later.' I cannot bear to abandon my love just because of her lowly origins."

When King Muyŏl ascended the throne [654], the T'ang envoy came with an edict that contained difficult passages. The king summoned Kangsu, who after one reading explained everything without hesitating or stumbling. Amazed and delighted, the king regretted having met him so late and asked his name. Kangsu replied, "Your subject is from Imna Kara (Tae Kaya) by origin, and his name is Chadu." The king said, "Judging from your skull bone, your are worthy to be called Master Strong-Head (Kangsu)." The king asked Kangsu to draft a memorial of thanks to the emperor. The memorial was well wrought and its import deep. Marveling all the more, the king no longer called his subject by his name Kangsu, but only by the name of "Mr. Im of Imna Kara."

Unconcerned about his livelihood, Kangsu was poor but serene. The king ordered an office to grant him one hundred bags of tax grain from Sinsŏng.

King Munmu said, "Kangsu accepted the responsibility of a scribe, conveying our wishes in letters to China, Koguryŏ, and Paekche, and succeeded in establishing friendly relations with neighboring countries. With military aid from T'ang China, our former king pacified Koguryŏ and Paekche. His military feats owe also to the help given by Kangsu's literary ability. Kangsu's achievements cannot be neglected." The king conferred on Kangsu the title of *sach'an* and increased his stipend to two hundred bags of tax grain annually. Kangsu died during the reign of King Sinmun [681–692]. The state provided funeral expenses and furnished an abundance of raiments, cloth, and other necessities. These the family offered to the Buddha.

When Kangsu's wife was about to return to her village because of a shortage of food, a minister heard of it and petitioned the throne to grant her a hundred bags of tax grain. She declined, saying, "As a humble person, I used to depend for food and clothing on my late husband and received many favors from the court. Now that I am alone, how dare I receive your kind present?" She then retired to her home village. PL

Sŏl Ch'ong

[From *Samguk sagi* 46:431–432]

Sŏl Ch'ong's grandfather, whose polite name was Ch'ongji, was Tamnal *naema*. Sŏl Ch'ong's father was Wŏnhyo, who once became a monk and studied Buddhist books but later returned to the laity, styling himself "Humble Householder."

Endowed with sagacity, Sŏl understood the Way from birth. He interpreted the Nine Classics in the vernacular and taught the young, and hence even today he is considered the foremost among the learned. He was an accomplished writer, but none of his works survives. Some of his inscriptions remain in the south, but with graphs missing, so that the meaning is unclear.

In the fifth month, from his high and bright hall, King Sinmun [681–692] spoke to Sŏl: "The rain has stopped, and warm winds have turned cool; delicacies and sad music are no match for intelligent discussion and interesting tales to dispel gloom. You must have heard many strange stories. Will you not tell me some?" Sŏl told the following story:

Your subject heard that long ago when the king of flowers, the peony, first came to this land, the people planted him in a fragrant garden and protected him with emerald curtains. In late spring he blossomed splendidly, excelling all other flowers in beauty. Thereupon all the lovely young flowers desired to have an audience and, fearing to miss the opportunity, hastened to his court from far and near.

Suddenly one shapely woman with a beautiful face and white teeth, freshly powdered and exquisitely dressed, stepped lithely out with a graceful gait and said, "I've walked upon the snow-white sands and, facing the sea clear as a mirror, have washed my body in the spring rain and refreshed myself in the clear breeze. I am called rose. Having heard of Your Majesty's excellent virtue, I desire to wait upon you inside the fragrant curtains. I beg Your Majesty to allow me the honor."

Then a white-haired man in cotton clothes and leather belt limped out and, leaning on a staff, said: "I live along the roadside on the outskirts of the capital. There I look upon broad green fields below and rely upon the scenery of rocky ranges above. I am called pasqueflower. I am aware that Your Majesty is well supplied from all sides. You dine on sumptuous delicacies and purify your mind with tea and wine. Yet your box lacks an elixir that will invigorate and a powerful drug to neutralize poison. It is said: 'Though you have silk and hemp, don't discard your grass and rushes. All go through vicissitudes of want.'[8] Would Your Majesty too take this to heart?"

Someone among the crowd asked, "Which will Your Majesty take?"

"The man has good claim upon my favor," the king of flowers answered. "But then such a beautiful lady is rare indeed. What shall I do?"

The old man stepped forward and said, "I came here to offer my service because I believed Your Majesty to be wise and moral. I see I was mistaken. Kings generally keep company with the treacherous and cunning. The righteous they avoid. Thus lived Mencius in obscurity, a man born out of his time, and Feng T'ang remained a petty official until his hair turned gray.[9] Since it has been so from ancient times, what is there for one to do?"

"I was in the wrong," the king said. "I was in the wrong."

Thereupon the king changed color and said, "Your allegory has a profound purport; write it down to serve as a mirror for future rulers." He then appointed Sŏl to a high position. PL

Nokchin
[From *Samguk sagi* 45:420–421]

The clan and polite names of Nokchin are uncertain, but he was the son of *Ilgilch'an* Subong. He first took office at the age of twenty-three, and after filling various court and provincial posts, he became Vice-Minister of State in the tenth year of King Hŏndŏk, *musul* [818].

In the fourteenth year, the king, being without an heir, appointed his younger brother Sujong as heir apparent and had him reside in Wŏlchi Palace. Thereupon *Kakkan* Ch'unggong became prime minister and presided in the administration hall over the selection of officials for service in the court and the provinces. After his withdrawal, Ch'unggong fell ill. The official physician took his pulse and said, "Your sickness is of the heart. You need dragon-tooth medicine."

Ch'unggong obtained a twenty-one-day leave. He closed his gate and would receive no guests. When Nokchin wished to see Ch'unggong, the gatekeeper refused him. Nokchin said, "I know that the minister refuses visitors because of his illness. But I should like to say a word to dispel his melancholy. I cannot withdraw without seeing him." In the end, the gatekeeper let Nokchin in.

To Ch'unggong Nokchin said, "I have heard that you are not well. Is this because you go to office early and retire late, exposed to the wind and the dew, and have impaired your circulation and injured your four limbs?"

"My ailment is not that bad," Ch'unggong replied. "I feel slightly dazed and cheerless."

"If so, your illness requires neither medicine nor needle; it can be dispelled by reasonable speech and lofty discussion. Would you listen to what I have to say?"

"You have not abandoned me, but rather you have honored me with your company. I beg to be allowed to hear you out, so that I might unburden my heart," replied Ch'unggong.

"When a carpenter builds a home," Nokchin said, "he uses hefty pieces of lumber for beams and pillars and smaller ones for rafters.

Only after crooked and straight pieces are placed in the right spots will you have a great house. Since olden times, has the wise government of a state ever been any different? If you place men of great talent in high positions and men of lesser talent in low positions, then from the six ministers and one hundred officials at court down to provincial governors and local magistrates, no position will be unfilled and none will be occupied by an unqualified person. There will be then perfect order high and low, and the wise and the incompetent will be kept apart. Only then will you achieve a royal rule. But it is not so today. Now favoritism undermines the public good, and offices are chosen for men. Even the unfit are awarded high positions if they are well linked; and even the capable are made to grovel in the ditch if they are in disfavor. Thus you are at a loss for a solution, and your ability to distinguish right from wrong is lessened. Thus the affairs of the state are muddled, and a statesman becomes weary and ill. If one is impeccable in the performance of his duties, the gate will be shut to bribery and special pleading. Promotion and demotion should depend on one's relative intelligence, and giving and taking should not depend on individual love or hatred. Like a scale one will be able to assess the gravity of the matter; like a plumb line one will be able to distinguish right from wrong. Then the laws and government will be worthy of trust and the nation will be at peace. You may then open the gate like Kung-sun Hung[10] and serve wine like Ts'ao Ts'an,[11] chatting cheerfully and enjoying yourself with old friends. How could you then worry about medicine, idle away your time, and discontinue your work?"

"I heard Nokchin's words which were like medicine and acupuncture needles combined. His method was by no means merely a matter of taking dragon-tooth medicine." Ch'unggong then recounted everything to the king.

The king said, "I have been your ruler, and you my prime minister. What a delight to have one who will admonish me honestly! You must report this to the heir apparent. Go to the Wŏlchi Palace!"

Upon listening to Ch'unggong, the heir apparent congratulated the king. "I have heard that if the ruler is bright, the subjects will be honest. This indeed is a praiseworthy matter," he said.

Later, when Hŏnch'ang, governor of Ungch'ŏn province, rebelled, the king took up arms to put down the revolt, and Nokchin served the king and distinguished himself. The king offered Nokchin the title of *taeach'an,* but he declined. PL

Ch'oe Ch'iwŏn
[From *Samguk sagi* 46:429–431]

Ch'oe Ch'iwŏn, whose polite name was Koun, was from the Saryang district of the capital of Silla. Since historical records have been destroyed, we know nothing of his genealogy. From his youth onward he was fine and astute and loved learning. When at the age of twelve [868], he went to board a ship to study in T'ang China, his father said to him, "If you cannot pass the examination in ten years, you are not a worthy son of mine. Go and study hard!" Once in China he studied diligently under a teacher.

In the first year of Ch'ien-fu, *kabo* [874], the examiner Pei Ts'an, vice-president of the Ministry of Rites, passed Ch'oe on his first attempt, and Ch'oe was appointed Chief of Personnel (or Comptroller) in Liao-shui county. After a periodic review of his work, he was made secretary and censor in attendance[12] and received a purple pouch with a golden fish tally. At that time the Huang Ch'ao rebellion broke out [874] and Kao P'ien [d. 887] was appointed Circuit Field Commander.[13] Kao appointed Ch'oe as his secretary, and the memorials, letters, and manifestos that Ch'oe wrote at that time are still extant.

At the age of twenty-eight Ch'oe wished to return home. Learning of his desire, Emperor Hui-tsung [873–888] sent him to Korea as envoy with an imperial edict in the first year of Kuang-ch'i [885]. He was then appointed Reader in Attendance,[14] Hallim Academician, Vice-Minister of War, and *Chi Sŏsŏgam*. Ch'oe had benefited greatly from his study in China. Upon returning to Korea he wished to realize his ideas, but these were decadent times, and, an object of suspicion and envy, he was not accepted. He then became the magistrate of Taesan prefecture.

In the second year of Ching-fu of Emperor Chao-tsung [893], Minister of Defense and *Napchŏng chŏlsa* Kim Ch'ohoe was drowned on his way to T'ang China, and the magistrate of Kansŏng prefecture, Kim Chun, was appointed as envoy to report the matter. Ch'oe, at that time magistrate of Pusŏng prefecture, was summoned by the king as the New Year Felicitation Envoy. But continued drought and rampant banditry prevented him from going. Ch'oe later went to China again as an envoy, but the year and month are uncertain. . . .

The monograph on literature in the *New History of the T'ang* says: "Ch'oe Ch'iwŏn has written a chapter of parallel prose and twenty chapters of his works called *Kyewŏn p'ilgyŏng*." A note reads: "Ch'oe

Ch'iwŏn is from Silla. He passed the examination for foreigners and served under Kao P'ien." Thus his name was well known in China. His works in thirty chapters are extant. . . .

King Hyŏnjong [1009–1031], mindful of Ch'oe's cooperation in the founder's undertaking and his essential contributions, conferred upon him the posthumous title of *naesaryŏng* [1020],[15] and in the fifth month of the second year of T'ai-p'ing, *imsul* [1023],[16] granted him the post-humous title of Marquis of Bright Culture. PL

Preface to the *Kyewŏn p'ilgyŏng chip*
[From *Ssu-pu ts'ung-k'an* ed.:1a–2a]

Your subject, Ch'oe Ch'iwŏn, the envoy who carried an imperial edict on his way home from Huai-nan and who as Inspector Under the Commander, Secretary, and Censor in Attendance was granted a pouch with the fish tally, presents to Your Majesty his miscellaneous poems, rhymeprose, memorials, and proposals in twenty-eight chapters, which comprise: modern-style verse, five pieces in one chapter; penta- and heptasyllabic modern-style verse, one hundred pieces in one chapter; miscellaneous poems and rhymeprose, thirty pieces in one chapter; *Chungsan pokkwe chip* in five chapters; *Kyewŏn p'ilgyŏng chip* in twenty chapters.

When at the age of twelve your subject was about to leave home and board a ship for China, his late father admonished him, "If you cannot obtain the *chin-shih* degree within ten years, then you are not worthy to be my son, and I shall tell people that I have no son. Study hard while you are in China." Your subject was bound by his father's strict injunction and studied earnestly, exerting himself to the utmost to fulfill his father's wishes. After six years his name was entered at the end of a roster of successful candidates. At that time he expressed feelings in song and wrote metaphorical verse. His rhymeprose and verse began to accumulate, but in a grown man such childish efforts could only inspire shame. After receiving the fish tally pouch, he put his writings aside. He then traveled to Lo-yang, the Eastern Capital, where he earned his livelihood by writing. Finally he compiled a three-volume anthology of five rhymeprose, one hundred poems, and thirty pieces of miscellaneous verse.

When he was appointed chief of personnel of Liao-shui county in Hsüan-chou, his stipend was large, his duties light, and each day his own to spend as he liked. He devoted every spare moment to study, and his writings, official and personal, numbered five chapters. To attain his aim he named his works *Pokkwe* ("Tilting One Basketful of Earth to Raise a Mound")[17] and added the place name Chungsan at the head of the work.

Later, he resigned his post to serve in Huai-nan as secretary to Field Commander Kao P'ien and was entrusted with drafting documents. He did his best to expedite military missives, which in four years had come to number over ten thousand. After repeated weeding only one or two tenths remained. Although it was like sifting sand for gold, it was perhaps a little better than doodling on the walls with a broken tile.[18] Thus was the twenty-chapter *Kyewŏn chip* (Cassia Grove Collection) compiled.

Your subject then lived through a rebellion and slept, ate, and drank in an armed encampment. Accordingly he titled his works *P'ilgyŏng* ("Plowing with a Writing Brush"), taking the words of Wang Shao[19] as a precedent. Although he has not realized his aspirations and is ashamed of his lowly position,[20] he has already plowed and weeded the fields of his mind[21] and cannot bear to discard the harvest. Earnestly hoping that they may reach Your Majesty's inspection, he respectfully presents twenty-eight chapters of poetry, rhymeprose, memorials, and memorials to express thanks for favors received (*chang*), together with the preface.

On the day of the first month of the sixth year of Chung-ho [886], the former Inspector Under the Commander, Secretary, and Censor in Attendance who was granted a pouch with a golden fish tally, your subject, Ch'oe Ch'iwŏn, submits to the throne. PL

Record of the Mañjuśrī Stupa at Haein Monastery
[From *Chŭngbo Hanguk kŭmsŏk yumun*, no. 61]

This stupa was erected as a memorial to those killed during the seven years of armed revolt that ravaged Silla around 895. According to the four record plates deposited in the stupa, it appears that the original plan was to erect similar stupas at four places: Haein Monastery, Unyang Terrace, Paeksŏng Mountain Monastery, and Mount Odae. The plan was not implemented, however, and only one was erected within the precincts of Haein Monastery. The record is carved on both sides of a dark tile plate 23 square centimeters big and 2.4 centimeters thick. The calligraphic style is that of Ou-yang Hsün.

The author of the record, Ch'oe Ch'iwŏn, says that the war and famine that raged during the Huang Ch'ao rebellion in China moved to Silla. In 888, Wŏnjong and Aeno rose in revolt in Sabŏl province (Sangju); in 890, Yanggil rose in Pugwŏn (Wŏnju); in 891, Kyŏnhwŏn called his state Later Paekche in Wansan; and in 893, Kungye marched to Asŭlla (Samch'ŏk) and established his power in the north the following year. Ch'oe Ch'iwŏn himself later retired to Haein Monastery to spend his remaining years there.

When the nineteenth ruler of T'ang China was about to be restored, the two calamities of war and famine ceased in the west but came to the east. With one misfortune following another, no place was unaffected. The bodies of those who had starved to death or fallen in action were scattered about the plain like stars. Out of intense grief, therefore, the venerable Hunjin of Haein Monastery bestowed the power of the leading master, called forth the hearts of the people, and had each donate a sheaf of rice. Together with others, the master built a three-story white stone stupa. The protection of the state generally forms the core of the Buddhist Path of the vow-wheel, whose special function is to save the souls of those who have died resentfully and violently. I record that the offering of sacrifice for their repose shall continue without end. The time I write is after the full moon in the seventh month of the second year of Ch'ien-ning [895]. PL

Taoism

Records are scarce on the subject of Taoism in the Three Kingdoms, but it appears that the aristocracy was attracted to its tenets. In his heptasyllabic quatrain sent to Yü Chung-wen, Ŭlchi Mundŏk cites a line from the *Lao Tzu*. The cult of immortality, as evinced in the murals of Koguryŏ tombs, merged with popular beliefs in prognostication. After the transfer of the capital to P'yŏngyang, Koguryŏ had close contacts with the Northern Wei and must have learned about Taoism. Upon entering diplomatic relations with the T'ang, Emperor Kao-tsu sent Taoist priests and images in 624, and in the following year Koguryŏ envoys were dispatched to China to study Buddhism and Taoism. In 643, at the request of Yŏn Kaesomun (d. 665), T'ai-tsung sent eight Taoist priests. Yŏn's promotion of Taoism was felt strongly by the Buddhist clergy: Monk Podŏk sought refuge in Paekche in 650.

We do not know when Taoism was first transmitted to Paekche, but it seems to have been quite early in the history of the kingdom. In its developmental stage, Paekche absorbed the civilization of Lo-lang and Tai-fang, the Chinese commanderies in the north, and later received the refined aristocratic culture of the southern dynasties in China. The earliest historical mention of Taoism in Paekche dates from the first year of King Kŭngusu (214). When the Paekche army was about to pursue the fleeing army of Koguryŏ, General Makkohae admonished Kŭngusu, then heir apparent, with a quotation from the *Lao Tzu* (chap. 46): "There is no disorder greater than not being content; there is no misfortune greater than being covetous. Hence in being content, one will always have enough." By the time of King Kŭngusu, the *Lao Tzu* and *Chuang Tzu* were widely read among the educated.

When a lake was dug in his palace, King Mu had an island built in the lake and called it Fang-chang (fairyland; a sacred mountain); Monk Kwallŭk, who went to Japan in 602, is said to have been a master of *tun-chia* (a method of prognostication and making oneself invisible). The inscription of Sat'aek Chijŏk (654) presented here is another indication of the understanding of Taoist philosophy among the aristocracy.

We do not know when Taoism was transmitted to Silla, either, but Taoist texts were known among the educated during the Three Kingdoms period. In his admonition to King Chinp'yŏng, who loved to hunt, Kim Hujik cited a passage from the *Lao Tzu* and the *Book of Documents*. Kim Inmun is said to have studied not only the Confucian classics but also the *Lao Tzu*, the *Chuang Tzu,* and Buddhist scriptures. The official transmission of the *Lao Tzu* is dated 738, when the T'ang envoy, Hsing Tao, presented King Hyosŏng with a copy, but inscriptions for the images at Kamsan Monastery (discovered in 1915), built by Kim Chisŏng (Kim Chijŏm in the inscription below) in 719, show the merging of Yogācāra philosophy and Taoism. Those who were disillusioned with the True Bone class, or had lost their struggles against it, lived in exile, voluntary or enforced, and espoused Taoist tenets. Kim Kagi died as a Taoist priest in T'ang China.

Yŏn Kaesomun (Koguryŏ)
[From *Samguk sagi* 49:448–450]

The clan name of Yŏn Kaesomun [d. 665] was Ch'ŏn. He seduced the people by claiming that he was born under water. He had an imposing presence and was broad-minded. Upon the death of his father, who held the rank of chief of the Eastern Province and chief minister (*taedaero*), the people stopped Kaesomun from inheriting the position because they hated his coldbloodedness. Thereupon Kaesomun kowtowed and apologized and begged to be allowed to take over the position, saying, "You may depose me if I fail. I will not complain." The people sympathized with Yŏn and permitted him to succeed to his father's post. Since Yŏn continued to be cruel and wicked, the chiefs had a private talk with the king, asking that Yŏn be put to death. The plan, however, leaked out.

Yŏn gathered the soldiers of his own province and pretended to review them. He also spread a banquet to the south of the walled city and invited the ministers to review his troops. As soon as the guests arrived, more than a hundred strong, Yŏn had them massacred. He then rushed to the palace, killed King Yŏngnyu, chopped the corpse into pieces, and threw the pieces into a ditch. He then set up the king's younger brother, Chang, as king and appointed himself as *mangniji*, which was tantamount to being both the Minister of War and Secretariat Director in T'ang China. He dictated to those far away and those nearby alike and conducted state affairs despotically. Possessing extreme dignity, he wore five knives; no one dared look at him. When he mounted or dismounted from his horse, he would make an aristocrat general prostrate himself as a stepping stone. When going out, he would march in rank and file, and a guide in front would shout and send the people scurrying out of the way. Thus the people suffered greatly. . . .

Yŏn reported to the king, "I have heard that in China the three ways of thought exist side by side, but in our country Taoism is unknown. I suggest that we send an envoy to T'ang China to obtain this learning for us." When the king sent a memorial to that effect, the T'ang court sent a Taoist adept, Shu-ta, with seven other envoys and a copy of *Tao-te ching* (The Way and Its Power). A Buddhist monastery was made into a Taoist temple. PL

Podŏk (Koguryŏ)
[From *Samguk yusa* 3:130–132]

According to the basic annals of Koguryŏ, toward the end of that kingdom [618–627] the Koguryŏ people strove to demonstrate their belief in Taoism.[22] Emperor Kao-tsu of the T'ang heard of this and sent a Taoist priest to Koguryŏ with the images of Lao Tzu to lecture on *The Way and Its Power*. King Yŏngnyu and his people attended the lecture—it was the seventh year of Wu-te [624]. The following year the king sent an envoy to the T'ang court to obtain books on Buddhism and Taoism, a wish the emperor granted.

Upon accession to the throne, King Pojang [642] wished to see Buddhism, Taoism, and Confucianism flourish in his country. At the time, his favorite minister, Yŏn Kaesomun, said, "Confucianism and Buddhism flourish now, but not Taoism. We should send a mission to China to seek knowledge of Taoism."

The Koguryŏ monk Podŏk of Pallyong Monastery (in Yonggang) lamented the danger to the country's fortunes if a conflict between Taoism and Buddhism arises and remonstrated with the king without success. By supernatural power he flew with his hermitage to Mount Kodae (or Kodal) in Wansan province (now Chŏnju)—it was in the sixth month of the first year of Yung-hui, *kyŏngsul* [650]. Soon thereafter, Koguryŏ was destroyed. It is said that the flying hermitage in Kyŏngbok Monastery is Podŏk's.

In the eighth year of Ta-an, *sinmi* [1092], the Chief of Clerics, Ŭich'ŏn, went to Podŏk's hermitage, bowed to his portrait, and composed a poem: "The teachings of universal nirvana were transmitted to Korea by him. . . . Alas, after he flew with his hermitage to Mount Kodae, Koguryŏ was on the verge of ruin." The postscript reads: "King Pojang of Koguryŏ was deluded by Taoism and abandoned Buddhism. Hence the master flew south with his hermitage and landed on Mount Kodae. Later, a guardian of the dharma appeared on Horse Ridge in Koguryŏ and said, 'Soon your country will be destroyed.' " This story is exactly like the one recorded in the national history, and the rest is in the original record and the lives of eminent monks. PL

Inscription on a Monument to Sat'aek Chijŏk (Paekche)

[From *Chŭngbo Hanguk kŭmsŏk yumun*, no. 11]

Here we present a translation of the inscription on a monument known as the Sat'aek Chijŏk Pi, erected in 654. Lines were drawn horizontally and vertically on the granite face of the monument to form squares in which logographs could be engraved in intaglio. Only four lines, fourteen graphs to a line, remain. Written in parallel prose and calligraphed in the manner of Ou-yang Hsün, its literary and calligraphic style manifests a refinement not yet attained in stone monuments of the same period in Silla. Sat'aek Chijŏk, a member of the Sa clan, one of the eight great clans in Paekche, held the rank of prime minister (*sangjwa-p'yŏng*). He retired from public life in 654. Reminiscing on the prime of his life and lamenting the approach of old age, he decided to espouse Buddhism. He had the main hall and the stupa built and ordered this monument erected to commemorate the occasion.

On the ninth day of the first month of the year *kabin* [1 February 654], Sat'aek Chijŏk of Naji Walled Town [Naeji-ri, Ŭnsan-myŏn, Puyŏ, South Ch'ungch'ŏng] laments the manner in which his days pass quickly and his months never return. He mined gold to build the main hall and chiseled jade to erect the jeweled reliquary. How imposing—its compassionate appearance emits a spiritual glow to dispel clouds. How lofty—its sad face bears sage brightness to. . . . PL

Inscription on an Image at Kamsan Monastery (Silla)

[From *Chōsen kinseki sōran* 1:36]

Among the sources indicating the spread of Taoism among the nobility are the inscriptions composed upon completion of the images of the Bodhisattva Maitreya and Amitābha the Thus Come One in Kamsan Monastery. Upon his retirement, Kim Chisŏng (or Kim Chijŏn, died c. 720), who held the rank of vice-minister of state (*chipsabu sirang*), had these two images cast to aid the souls of his parents. Upon retirement, the inscription says, Kim read the *Mahāyānasaṃgraha* (Compendium of Mahāyāna), the *Yogācārabhūmi* (Stages of Yoga Practice), the *Lao Tzu*, and the "Free and Easy Wandering" chapter from the *Chuang Tzu*. The two inscriptions at Kamsan are valuable sources for the study of Taoist thought in Silla. One of them, written by Sŏl Ch'ong to mark the casting of the image of the Thus Come One of Infinite Life, is given here.

Buddhism is everlasting in its nature, yet it manifested itself in early Chou. Śākyamuni comes and goes at will, yet he showed his form to Emperor Ming [58–75] of the Later Han in a dream. It began in the Western Regions and transmitted its lamp to the east. It then reached Silla. The Shadow of the Buddha Sun soon illuminated Korea; its scriptures crossed the P'ae River and made clear the Buddha's teaching. Monasteries rose up all jumbled together; stupas stood in rows. Silla resembled Śrāvastī and the Pure Land.

Chungach'an Kim Chijŏn was born in a blessed land and received the power of the stars. His nature was in harmony with the clouds and mist; his emotion befriended the mountains and waters. Equipped with outstanding ability, his name was known to his generation; carrying wise strategies in his heart, he assisted his time. He went to China as envoy, and the Son of Heaven bestowed on him the title of *shang-she feng-yü* (chief steward in the palace administration). Upon returning to Silla, he was granted the important post of minister of state (*chipsa sirang*). At age sixty-seven he withdrew and, shunning the world, lived in seclusion. He emulated the lofty magnanimity of the Four White Heads, declined glory, and nourished his nature. Like brothers Shu Kuang and his nephew Shu Shou,[23] he retired at an opportune time.

Looking up with respect to the true teaching of Asaṅga [fourth century], he read the *Stages of Yoga Practice* from time to time. In addition, he loved the dark and mysterious way of Chuang Tzu and read the "Free and Easy Wandering" chapter. He intended to repay his parents' love thereby, but it could not match the power of the Buddha. He wanted to repay the favor of his king, but it could not equal the primary cause of the Three Jewels: the Buddha, the Dharma, and the Order. PL

CHAPTER FIVE

The Rise of Buddhism

Around the time of the unification of the Three Kingdoms, the learned Silla monks Wŏnhyo, Wŏnch'ŭk, and Ŭisang began to study Buddhist philosophy and popularize the faith. The epochal development of Silla Buddhism at this time, almost a century after its introduction, was made possible by political and ideological factors that facilitated the study and understanding of Buddhist thought. Although Silla received Buddhism from Koguryŏ and Paekche, it may have come into direct contact with Chinese Buddhism when the Liang monk Yüan-piao arrived as an envoy.[1] Beginning with the time of King Chinhŭng (540–576), Silla monks studying abroad began to return home, bringing with them Buddhist images and scriptures. Thus toward the end of the seventh century, most scriptures translated into Chinese were known in Silla, as evinced by Wŏnhyo, who never went to China but was able to establish his own unique system of Buddhist philosophy based on translated scriptures.

Earlier Silla Buddhism may have leaned toward the ke-yi ("matching the meaning") technique used by translators of the Prajñā scriptures, but the influx of Mahāyāna texts enabled Silla to better understand the Great Vehicle—that is, the vehicle of the bodhisattva leading to Buddhahood. Although the doctrines of the Three Treatise school (as propagated in Koguryŏ) and the T'ien-t'ai school (as propagated in Paekche) were little known, the efforts of Wŏngwang (d. 640) and Chajang (fl. 636–645) enabled Silla monks to understand the tenets of the *Compendium of Mahāyāna* of the Consciousness-Only school and, later, those of Flower Garland metaphysics.[2]

The impetus for the development of Buddhist philosophy in Silla was the unification of the Three Kingdoms, which also entailed the absorption of Koguryŏ and Paekche Buddhism. Opposing the state's adoption of Taoism, the Koguryŏ monk Podŏk lectured on the *Nirvana Scripture* and finally moved to Wansan prefecture (now Chŏnju) in Paekche (650).[3] His eleven disciples built monasteries and lectured on the *Nirvana Scripture,* and Wŏnhyo and Ŭisang are said to have attended Podŏk's lecture. Wŏnhyo wrote a commentary on the text, and other commentaries followed—an indication of Koguryŏ influence on the formation of the Nirvana school in Silla. Likewise, the transmission of the Three Treatise school may have helped make Silla monks aware of the doctrinal differences between Mādhyamika and Vijñānavāda (or Yogācāra).

In China, Chih-i (538–597) established the T'ien-t'ai school; Hsüan-tsang (c. 596–664) translated the texts of the Consciousness-Only school that he had brought from India; and K'uei-chi (632–682) founded the idealistic Fa-hsiang ("dharma-characteristics") school. Thus the polemics between the Mādhyamika and Yogācāra schools were intensified—one upholding the truth of emptiness (*śūnyatā*) and the other expounding that everything exists in consciousness only. A new doctrinal system that could overcome these two opposing philosophies was Hua-yen (Flower Garland) metaphysics. As Silla pursued active diplomatic relations with the Sui and T'ang, trends in doctrinal studies in China were introduced and became the subject of inquiry for Silla monks. Mutual stimulation and development in T'ang and Silla testify to a close interaction between the two countries. Wŏnhyo, for example, wished to study and transmit the Consciousness-Only philosophy from Hsüan-tsang but remained in Silla all his life to develop his own system of Buddhist philosophy. Indeed, by abandoning his studies abroad he became the most original and prolific Buddhist philosopher in Korea and East Asia at that time. Wŏnhyo's accomplishments were transmitted to T'ang, where they stimulated the development of Hua-yen metaphysics—for example, Wŏnhyo's commentary on the *Awakening of Faith* inspired a similar work by Fa-tsang.[4] Conversely, T'ang developments in Consciousness-Only and Flower Garland philosophy influenced the formation of these schools in Silla, and Silla's contributions to the two schools were transmitted to T'ang (see Fa-tsang's letter to Ŭisang).[5]

With the development of royal authority in Silla came an awareness of the limits and contradictions of a Buddhism established and legitimized as a bulwark of the state. In its effort to consolidate power within and without, Silla used Buddhism to enhance the privilege and status of the ruling house and to foster enthusiasm for unification. Until unification occurred, Buddhism was regarded primarily not as a religion but as a political-religious ideology that furthered the secular objectives of the state, thereby the faith was deprived of its religious autonomy. With unification an accomplished fact, however, Silla Buddhism aspired to a new dimension: the abolition of conflict between the state's earthly objectives and the religion's otherworldly outlook, as well as the separation of church and state.

Meanwhile, in response to the consolidation of the administrative machinery after unification, Confucianism began to replace Buddhism as a political ideology. As Buddhism separated itself from politics, its political influence began to decline. The king was no longer a Buddha (as King Chinhŭng had been) but instead adopted a Chinese-style posthumous epithet. Similarly, the state sought Buddhism's aid not through eminent monks but through the Buddhist community.

Such Confucian scholars as Kangsu and Sŏl Ch'ong emerged to play a major role in importing Chinese civilization, drafting diplomatic papers, and functioning as political advisers, roles hitherto reserved for eminent monks. They also began to criticize a Buddhism that had forgotten its primary religious function, as the remarks attributed to Kangsu show. King Munmu, who wished to adopt Confucian political thought, banned contributions of land and money to monasteries in 664.[6] Aware of the contradiction inherent in upholding Buddhism with its magic and incantations as the state religion, he intended to curtail a drain on the kingdom's economic resources. In his attempts to point out a new direction for Buddhism, King Munmu ordered Ŭisang, who had just returned from China, to construct Pusŏk Monastery as the major place of worship for the Flower Garland school. In his will, he recommended Kyŏnghŭng, the master of the Consciousness-Only school, as national preceptor.

The outstanding questions around the time of unification, then, were the reconciliation of the tenets of the Mādhyamika and Yogācāra schools and a blending of the state's secular aims with the otherworldly goals of Buddhism. The solutions to these problems took the form of research into Buddhist doctrine and popularization of the faith.

Wŏnhyo's Buddhist Philosophy

Toward the end of the seventh century, Silla Buddhism made great strides in establishing a unique version of Buddhist philosophy through the efforts of Great Master Wŏnhyo (617–686). Posthumously honored as the "National Preceptor Who Harmonizes Disputes," he systematized different schools of Buddhism and established a basis on which the people of Silla might understand them. Wŏnhyo had no special teacher, nor did he travel to China. He read widely and interpreted every text he could find, regardless of its doctrinal affiliation. His works indicate the scope of his broad reading and acute comprehension of such Mahāyāna texts as the *Flower Garland,* the *Lotus,* the *Nirvana,* the *Vimalakīrti nirdeśa,* the *Great Perfection of Wisdom,* the *Explanation of Profound Mysteries,* the *Larger Sukhāvatīvyūha* (Pure Land), *Adamantine Absorption, Ta-chih-tu lun* (Great Perfection of Wisdom Treatise), the *Treatise on the Completion of Truth,* the *Treatise on the Completion of Consciousness-Only,* and the *Awakening of Faith.*

Focusing on the *Flower Garland Scripture* and the *Awakening of Faith,* Wŏnhyo was able to establish his unique universalistic and syncretic Buddhist philosophy, a harmonization of nature and characteristics. He traced various texts to their origins and periods of formation. His *Simmun hwajaeng non* (Treatise on Ten Approaches to the Reconciliation of Doctrinal Controversy) offers a logical basis for overcoming doctrinal inconsistencies and differences. Thus while Chih-i classified and rated the Buddha's teachings by periods, methods, and modes of doctrine, Wŏnhyo harmonized them and established their essential equality and unity.

Wŏnhyo's works were transmitted to China and Japan, where they exerted considerable influence. Known as the *Haedong so* (Korean Commentary), his commentary on the *Awakening of Faith,* which offers a theoretical system resolving the controversy between Mādhyamika and Yogācāra, is one of the three great commentaries on that text. His commentary on the *Adamantine Absorption Scripture,* which presents the practical theory of his Buddhism, was elevated to the status of *non* (treatise), indicating that the author was a bodhisattva, not a mortal man; his *Treatise on Ten Approaches,* together with *Ijangŭi* (Meaning of Two Obstructions), influenced Fa-tsang's *Wu-chiao chang* and was said to have been carried to India to be translated into Sanskrit. Chinese masters who were influenced by Wŏnhyo include Fa-tsang (643–712), Li T'ung-hsüan (635–730 or 646–740), and Ch'eng-kuan (738–839).[7] The Japanese monks Gyōnen (1240–1321) of the Flower Garland school (1240–1321) and Zenshu (723–797) and Jōtō (740–815) of the Fa-hsiang school were also influenced by him. Furthermore, Wŏnhyo visited Ŭisang at the Avalokiteśvara Cave on Mount Nak and discussed with him his *Ilsŭng pŏpkye to* (Diagram of the Dharmadhātu; 668), an indication that he maintained close ties with Ŭisang after the latter's return from China. Unlike Ŭisang, however, it was not Wŏnhyo's intent to found a school or nurture disciples. Hence he failed to form a school of his own, was accorded less esteem in Silla than in China, and had fewer disciples than Ŭisang. Only Ŭich'ŏn (1055–1101) was able to appreciate Wŏnhyo's contribution. Wŏnhyo's works were quoted by Silla monks but received no serious study—in sharp contrast to a host of later studies on Ŭisang's diagram.

Following are two biographies of Wŏnhyo as recorded in the *Lives of Eminent Monks Compiled During the Sung* (988) and the *Memorabilia of the Three Kingdoms* by Iryŏn. Iryŏn's account, which is more chronological and inclusive, begins with a statement of Wŏnhyo's family and native place. Then comes a recounting of stories known only in the local tradition; his birth, early years, and his exegesis on the *Flower Garland Scripture;* his proselytizing and his eccentric period; his commentary on the *Vajrasamādhi* (Adamantine Absorption Scripture); his death and funeral; and a eulogy. Iryŏn provides the following chronology: birth and early years (617–631); ordination and early vocation (c. 632–661); textual exegesis (c. 662–676); popularization of Buddhism (c. 677–684); return to scholarship (c. 685); and death (686). Tsan-ning's account in the *Lives of Eminent Monks* focuses on the recovery of the *Adamantine Absorption Scripture* from the repository of the Dragon King and Wŏnhyo's commentary on it. This tale draws on legends about the recovery of the Mahāyāna scriptures from the Dragon King by Nāgārjuna and on the dragon cult in Silla. The belief in the dragon as protector of the dharma was prevalent in Silla and is reflected in such stories as the founding of Hwangnyong (Yellow Dragon, or Imperial Dragon) Monastery and King Munmu's (661–681) vow that after his death he would be reborn as a sea dragon to protect Silla and Buddhism.

Wŏnhyo, perhaps the most seminal Buddhist thinker in Korea, contributed greatly to the development of a distinctively Korean style of Buddhist philosophy and practice. His range of scholarly endeavor spanned the whole of East Asian Buddhist materials, and some one hundred works are attributed to him. Wǒnhyo was a master of Chinese prose. The prefaces to his commentaries on various Mahāyāna scriptures are known for their concision and clarity, and he had a gift for summarizing the doctrine presented in various scriptures. Presented here are his introduction to *Exposition of the Adamantine Absorption Scripture, Arouse Your Mind and Practice!*, and the beginning section of his commentary on the *Awakening of Faith*, which greatly influenced Fa-tsang's commentary on the same text.

The Life of Wǒnhyo: Tsan-ning's Account

[From *Sung kao-seng chuan* 4:730a–b]

The clan name of the monk Wǒnhyo was Sǒl; he was from Sangju in Korea. When young, he graciously espoused the dharma. Following masters, he received instructions and toured the country without constancy. Valiantly he assaulted the encirclement of meaning and distinguished among the ranks of letters. Bold and militant, he never retreated once he had advanced. Versed in the three trainings,[8] his countrymen called him "a match for ten thousand." Such was his mastery of the principle and attainment of mystery.

Once, he wished to go to T'ang China with Dharma Master Ǔisang to study under Tripiṭaka Master Hsüan-tsang [596–664] at Tz'u-en Monastery, but his plans were not realized. He set his heart at ease and toured everywhere. But he acted defiantly, showing traces of unreasonable behavior. With lay religious folk he would enter taverns and brothels. Like Pao-chih of Liang [418–514], he carried a metal knife and an iron staff. At times he wrote commentaries and lectured on the *Flower Garland Scripture*. He would divert himself by playing the zither in a shrine, take lodging in a commoner's house, or sit and meditate in the mountains or by a river. He did as he pleased according to the occasion, without schedule or restriction.

At that time, the king held a great Assembly of the Hundred Seats to lecture on the *Scripture on Benevolent Kings,* and he sought eminent monks. Sangju recommended the reputed Wǒnhyo, but other monks disliked his personality and urged the king not to accept him. Wǒnhyo stayed only briefly.

Shortly thereafter, the queen had a tumor in her brain, and treatment by physicians was ineffective. The king, the prince, and their subjects offered prayers to mountains, rivers, and shrines everywhere. One shaman advised, "If a messenger is sent to China to obtain medicine, the queen will be cured." The king dispatched an envoy to T'ang to seek physicians. Suddenly, out of the boundless sea, an old man appeared. Riding on the waves, he jumped aboard the ship and intercepted the envoy. Journeying over the sea, the envoy and the old man reached a majestic and gorgeous palace. The envoy had an audience with the Dragon King, Yŏnghae, who said, "Your queen is the third daughter of the Green Emperor of the East. Since of old, our palace has had a copy of the *Adamantine Absorption Scripture*. A complete penetration of the two kinds of enlightenment shows the conduct of the bodhisattva. Now, taking the queen's illness as an ideal pretext, I wish to send this scripture with you. Take it to your country and propagate it." Thereupon the Dragon King brought out thirty loose sheets and bestowed them on the envoy. The Dragon King spoke again: "I fear there may be some interference from Māra during the voyage." Then he ordered an attendant to incise the lower abdomen of the envoy, put the papers in it, bandage the incision with waxed paper, and apply medicine. The abdomen was just as before. The Dragon King said, "Please command the holy man named Taean to put them in order, and ask Dharma Master Wŏnhyo to write a commentary and lecture and explicate it. Then the queen's illness is sure to be cured. Even the universal medicine *agada,* in the Himalayas, could not surpass this in efficacy." The Dragon King accompanied the envoy to the surface of the sea, where the envoy boarded his ship and returned home.

At that time the king heard the news and rejoiced. He first summoned the holy man Taean to bind and collate the scripture. Taean was an unfathomable person. Clad in unique garments, he would frequent the marketplaces and, beating the copper begging bowl, say straightly: "Taean, taean." Hence his name. To the king's order Taean replied, "Just bring the scripture here. I do not wish to enter the palace." Taean received the scripture and was able to arrange it into eight sections, all in accord with the intent of the Buddha. "Please send this to Wŏnhyo so that he can lecture on it, and not to anyone else," Taean said.

Wŏnhyo received the scripture in Sangju, his birthplace. He said to the messenger, "The essential doctrine of this scripture is the two kinds of enlightenment. Please prepare an ox cart and a table, and place the brush and inkstone between the horns." Wŏnhyo composed a commentary in five rolls, riding on the ox-drawn cart from start to finish.

The king requested that Wŏnhyo lecture on the scripture at Yellow Dragon Monastery on a chosen day. However, contemptuous men stole the new commentary. When this was reported to the king, he postponed the lecture for three days. Wŏnhyo wrote a second commentary, entitled *Yakso,* in three rolls. On the day of the lecture, the king, his subjects, the clergy, and the laity gathered like clouds in the Dharma Hall. Wŏnhyo's lecture was dignified, and it elucidated disputed points and could serve as a model. Sounds of praise and snapping fingers welled up into the sky. Wŏnhyo again said openly, "Yesterday, I did not take part when a hundred beams were gathered; but this morning we lay a single ridgepole, and I alone can do it." Famous and virtuous monks lowered their heads in shame and confessed and repented their misdeeds from the bottom of their hearts.

Formerly, Wŏnhyo displayed his traces without any constancy and converted the people in all manners. At times he would throw a food tray to save the masses or would spit out water from his mouth to quench a fire. He appeared and disappeared at several places, announcing his extinction in the six regions. His deeds recall those of Pei-tu of Chin and Pao-chih of Liang. His understanding of the fundamental nature of things was profound, illuminating every manifestation of it. His commentary has two editions, the extended and the shortened, both current in Korea, but only the shortened version was transmitted to China. Later, a learned translator changed the title to a "treatise." PL

The Life of Wŏnhyo: Iryŏn's Account
[From *Samguk yusa* 4:194–197]

The secular surname of the Holy Master Wŏnhyo [617–686], the holy monk, was Sŏl. . . . He was born under a *śāla* tree in Chestnut Valley, north of Pulchi village and south of Amnyang county. . . . The master's house was said to be to the valley's southwest. One day, as she was passing under the tree, the master's mother felt labor pains and gave birth to him. It was too late to return home, so she hung her husband's clothes on the tree and spent the night under it. That is why the tree is called the *śāla* and its unusually shaped fruit is known as the *śāla* chestnut.

An old record says that long ago an abbot gave his slave two chestnuts for supper. When the slave complained to an official about his meager rations, the official thought it strange and had the fruit brought to him. Upon inspection, he found that a single chestnut filled a wooden bowl. The official promptly decreed that subsequently only one chestnut should be given. It is from this story that Chestnut Valley got its name.

When the master became a monk, he turned his house into a monastery, calling it Ch'ogae. He built another monastery near the tree and named it Śāla. . . . The master's childhood name was Sŏdang, or Sindang. On the night he was conceived, his mother dreamed that a shooting star entered her bosom. At the moment of the master's birth, five-colored clouds hovered over the earth. This was in the thirty-ninth year of King Chinp'yŏng [617], the thirteenth year of Ta-yeh, *chŏngch'uk*. Wŏnhyo was a clever and versatile child who needed no teacher. *Further Lives of Eminent Monks* and the "Accounts of Conduct" describe the circumstances of his wanderings and the depth of his religious accomplishments, so I will omit them here and include only some curious anecdotes from our own sources.

While young, the master often had spring fever; once he walked through the streets singing: "Who'll lend me an axe without a handle?[9] I'd like to chisel away at the pillar that supports heaven." The people did not understand his cravings.

King Muyŏl heard of Wŏnhyo and said, "This monk wants to marry a noble lady and beget a wise son. If a sage is born the country will benefit greatly." At that time a widowed princess lived alone in the Jasper Palace. The king dispatched attendants to bring Wŏnhyo to the palace, but Wŏnhyo met them halfway, having already come down from Mount South as far as Mosquito Stream Bridge. There he deliberately fell into the stream and doused his clothes. The attendants took him to the palace, where he changed his clothes to dry them and spent the night. The princess conceived and gave birth to a son, called Sŏl Ch'ong. Clever and intelligent, Sŏl Ch'ong was versed in the classics and histories and became one of the Ten Worthies of Silla. He annotated in the Korean language [through the *idu* system of transcribing Korean words by Chinese graphs] the customs and names of things of China and Korea as well as the Six Classics and other literary works. His method of explication is continued by any scholar who wishes to elucidate the classics.

After breaking his vow and begetting Sŏl Ch'ong, Wŏnhyo put on lay clothes and dubbed himself a "Humble Householder." One day he met an actor who danced with a gourd mask, which struck him as uncanny. He made himself a gourd mask and called it "unhindered"[10] after a passage in the *Flower Garland Scripture,* which says that "All unhindered men leave birth and death through a single path," and then composed a song and sang it until many people knew it. He used to tour thousands of villages and myriads of hamlets singing and dancing to convert the people, so that even the poor and the ignorant soon knew the name of the Buddha and called on Amitābha in order to be reborn in his Pure Land. Such was his conversion of the masses. Wŏnhyo's native village was then renamed "Buddha Land" and his monastery was called Ch'ogae, or First Opening; he gave himself the name Wŏnhyo, which means "dawn" in Wŏnhyo's dialect but also indicates that it was Wŏnhyo who made the Buddha Sun shine brightly in Korea.

When he wrote commentaries on the *Flower Garland Scripture* in Punhwang Monastery, he stopped at the fourth chapter on the "Ten Transferences." As he was so busy with public affairs, he divided his body among the hundred pines;[11] so he was known as one in the first bodhisattva stage. Also, induced by a sea dragon, he received royal orders while traveling to write a commentary on the *Adamantine Absorption Scripture.* He placed his inkstone and brush on the two horns of the ox he rode, and soon the people called him Horn Rider. To this day "horn rider" symbolizes the subtle purport of the two enlightenments—original and actualized. Dharma Master Taean hurried to Wŏnhyo and pasted together the loose leaves of his commentary. Indeed, Taean was the one "who knew the sound and sang in harmony."

When Wŏnhyo died, his son, Sŏl Ch'ong, pulverized his remains and cast them into a lifelike image. This he enshrined in Punhwang Monastery, demonstrating his respect, love, and lifelong sorrow.

One day, as Sŏl bowed down, the image turned its head to look at him. Its head is still turned to one side. The site of Sŏl's house is said to be near a cave monastery where his father had once lived. PL

Introduction to *Exposition of the Adamantine Absorption Scripture*

[From *Taishō Tripiṭaka* 34:961a–963a]

Wŏnhyo's introduction to his *Exposition of the Adamantine Absorption Scripture,*[12] portions of which are translated here, is one of the principal statements of his ecumenical approach to Buddhist thought and practice. The *vajrasamādhi* (adamantine absorption) is a special type of meditative concentration that is said to catalyze the final experience of enlightenment. Just as adamant or diamond shatters all other minerals, so too the adamantine absorption destroys all forms of clinging, initiating the radical nonattachment that is nirvana. In this treatise, Wŏnhyo seeks to treat the *vajrasamādhi* as not only consummating all the progressive stages of the Buddhist path of religious training but as in fact subsuming those stages. He therefore uses this absorption as a tool for effecting his syncretic vision, especially with respect to Buddhist practice. There is, briefly, a fourfold structure to the explication of this scripture: a narration of its principal ideas, an analysis of its theme, an explanation of its title, and an explication of the meaning of passages in the text.

NARRATION OF ITS PRINCIPAL IDEAS

Now, the fountainhead of the one mind, which is distinct from existence and nonexistence, is independently pure. The sea of the three voidnesses,[13] which amalgamates absolute and mundane, is calm and clear. Calm and clear, it amalgamates duality and yet is not unitary. Independently pure, it is far from the extremes and yet is not located at the middle. It is not located at the middle and yet is far from the extremes: hence, a phenomenon that does not exist does not just abide in nonexistence; a characteristic that does not nonexist does not just abide in existence. It is not unitary, and yet it amalgamates duality: hence, its nonabsolute dharmas have not once been mundane; its nonmundane principle has not once been absolute. It amalgamates duality and yet is not unitary: hence, there are none of its absolute or mundane natures that have never been established; there are none of its tainted or pure characteristics with which it has not been furnished. It is far from the extremes and yet is not located at the middle; hence, there are none of the existing or nonexisting dharmas that do not function; there are none of their positive or negative aspects with which it is not equipped. Accordingly, while nothing is negated, there is nothing not negated; while nothing is established, there is nothing not established. This can be called the ultimate principle that is free from principles, the great thusness that is not thus. These are said to be the principal ideas of this scripture.

Thanks to this great thusness that is not thus, the explanatory statements of this scripture sublimely accord with the dharma realm. Because of its ultimate principle that is free from principles, its positions that are the topics of those explanations surpass the transcendental. Since there is nothing that it does not conquer, this scripture is entitled the *Adamantine Absorption*. As there is nothing that it does not include, it is also called the *Compendium of Mahāyāna Scripture*. As there are neither of these two aspects which are not subsumed under its positions that are of vast import, it is also entitled the *Fundamental Doctrine of Innumerable Meanings (Anantanirdeśasiddhānta)*. Now, only one of these titles has been adopted to place at the head of the scripture and, accordingly, it is called the *Adamantine Absorption Scripture*.

ANALYSIS OF THE THEME

The thematic essentials of this scripture have an analytic and synthetic aspect. From a synthetic standpoint, its essential point is the contemplation practice that has but a single taste. From an analytic standpoint, its fundamental doctrine involves ten types of approaches to dharma.

SYNTHETIC STANDPOINT

Contemplation practice: "Contemplation" means to penetrate into the true import of phenomenal objects and wisdom; "practice" means to encompass both cause and fruition. Fruition means that the five dharmas[14] are perfectly complete; cause means that one has fully mastered the six practices.[15] Wisdom is in fact the two enlightenments: original and actualized. Phenomenal objects are in fact the disappearance in tandem of both absolute and mundane. These disappear in tandem, and yet neither are extinguished; there are two enlightenments and yet both are unproduced. Practices that are unproduced arcanely harmonize with the signless. The signless dharmas correspondingly become the original inspiration. Since this inspiration is the original inspiration and yet is gainless, it does not waver from the edge of reality. Since this edge is the edge of reality and yet is distinct from nature, the true edge is also void. All the buddhas, the Thus

Come Ones, repose therein and all bodhisattvas enter it accordingly. Thus, reference is made to entering the womb of the Thus Come Ones. These are the principal ideas of the six chapters of this scripture.

In the approach to contemplation outlined in this scripture, there are six practices established—from initial resolute faith through equal enlightenment. When the six practices are completed, the ninth consciousness appears via an evolutionary process. The manifestation of this immaculate consciousness is the pure dharma realm. The other eight consciousnesses evolve into the four wisdoms.[16] Once these five dharmas are perfected, one is then furnished with the three bodies.[17] In this wise, cause and fruition are not separate from phenomenal objects and wisdom. Since phenomenal objects and wisdom are free from duality, there is only a single taste. Thus, the contemplation practice that has but a single taste is considered to be the theme of this scripture.

For this reason, there are none of the characteristics of the Mahāyāna teachings that are not included in this contemplation practice; there is nothing of this theme that has innumerable meanings that is not subsumed by this scripture. This is why it is said that its titles are not frivolously given. The single contemplation—the synthetic standpoint—has been explained in brief above.

ANALYTIC STANDPOINT
From an analytic standpoint, the themes of this scripture can be explained via ten approaches—that is to say, from an approach based on monads to an approach based on decades.

What is the approach based on monads? Within the one mind, one thought develops and conforms with the one reality. There is cultivation of one practice, entrance into the one vehicle, abiding in the one path, putting to use the one enlightenment, and awakening to the one taste.

What is the approach based on dyads? Not abiding on either of the two shores of samsara or nirvana, one accordingly abandons the two assemblies of ordinary people and Hīnayānists. Not grasping at the two kinds of selfhood, of person and dharmas, one accordingly leaves behind the two extremes of eternality and annihilationism. Penetrating to the twofold voidness of person and dharmas, one does not drop to the level of the two vehicles of śrāvakas and pratyekabuddhas. Assimilating both of the two truths, absolute and mundane, one does not turn away from the two accesses of principle and practice.

What is the approach based on triads? Taking refuge oneself with the three buddhas as above, one receives the three moral codes.[18] One conforms with the three great truths[19] and gains the three liberations,[20] the three levels of equal enlightenment,[21] and the three bodies of sublime enlightenment.[22] One accesses the three groups of voidness as above and annihilates the minds of the three existences.[23] What is the approach based on tetrads? One cultivates the four right efforts[24] and enters the four bases of supranormal powers.[25] Through the power of the four great conditions,[26] the four postures are constantly benefited. One transcends the four stages of meditative absorption and leaves far behind the four types of slander.[27] The four wisdoms flow out from its four vast grounds.

What is the approach based on pentads? With the arising of the five *skandhas*,[28] one comes into possession of fifty evils.[29] For this reason, while planting the five spiritual faculties[30] one can develop the five powers.[31] One wades through the sea of the five voidnesses,[32] topples the five levels,[33] gains the five pure dharmas, ferries across the beings of the five destinies,[34] and so on.

What are the approaches based on hextads, heptads, octads, enneads, and so forth? Perfecting the cultivation of the six perfections,[35] one forever abandons the six sense-bases.[36] Practicing the seven branches of enlightenment,[37] one annihilates the sevenfold matrix of meaning.[38] "Its sea of the eighth consciousness is limpid, and the flow of its ninth consciousness is pure."[39] From the ten faiths up through the ten stages, the hundreds of practices are completely accomplished and the myriads of meritorious qualities are fully perfected. In this wise, all of these approaches are the themes of this scripture. They all appear in the text of the scripture and will be explained in the commentary to that particular passage in the text.

Nevertheless, these latter nine approaches are all included in the approach based on monads, and the approach based on monads contains all nine; none are distinct from the contemplation of the single taste. Therefore, even if they are explained analytically, they do not add to the one; even if they are explained synthetically, they do not take away from the ten. Neither increase nor decrease is this scripture's thematic essential.

EXPLANATION OF THE TITLE

There are three different titles for this sūtra: *Compendium of Mahāyāna Scripture, Adamantine Absorption,* and *Fundamental Doctrine of Innumerable Meanings.* The first and last titles will be explained later. Now, however, I will first explain the middle title, because only this name appears at the head of the text.

This title has two elements. First, I will explain *vajra;* next, I will explicate *samādhi.* The first division on *vajra* is also in two subsections. First, I will explicate the denotation of the word itself; next, I will examine its overall significance.

EXPLICATION OF "VAJRA"

The word *vajra* (adamant) is a term that is used metaphorically: solidity is its substance; "to shatter by piercing" is its quality. *Vajrasamādhi* is also to be understood in this same manner: the edge of reality is its substance; its function is to pierce while shattering. The edge of reality is its substance because it realizes the principle and probes the fountainhead of the mind. As a later passage says, "It is the true concentration in which the dharma is realized."[40] That "its function is to pierce by shattering" has these two senses: first, it shatters all doubts; second, it pierces all concentrations. It shatters all doubts because it provides explanations that resolve doubts. As a later passage says, "It is certain to excise doubts and regrets."[41] "It pierces all concentrations" means that this concentration can bring into operation the functioning of all other *samādhis,* in the same way that polishing a precious gem can make it functional. As the *Great Perfection of Wisdom Scripture* says, "Why is it called *vajrasamādhi?* Because while abiding in this *samādhi,* one can shatter all *samādhis.*"[42] Its commentary says in explanation: "*Vajrasamādhi.* Just as there is nothing that adamant cannot bore through, so it is with this *samādhi:* there are no dharmas that it does not penetrate. It can bring into operation the functioning of all other *samādhis,* in the same way that only adamant can bore through amber, cornelian, and beryl."[43]

Explanation: This scripture says "shatter all *samādhis.*" "Shatter" means "pierce," as in the commentary, where it says "bore through" in explanation of the scripture's use of the word "shatter." Hence *vajrasamādhi* penetrates to the fact that all *samādhis* are devoid of own-nature, and it frees those *samādhis* from any sense of being ends in themselves. This is because it is free from impediments and thus is able to function optimally. The meaning of the title should be understood in this manner. . . .

EXPLICATION OF "SAMĀDHI"

The explanation of the term *samādhi* is in two subsections. First will be an explanation of the meaning of the term; second will be an analysis of different types of concentrations.

The explanation of an ancient master says, "In India it is called *samādhi;* here in China it is called correct consideration."[44] The following passages will be given in explanation of this statement.

It is said that when one is in a state of concentration, there is meticulous examination of the external sense spheres; hence, it is called correct consideration. As the *Treatise on the Stages of Yoga Practice* states, "*Samādhi* means that there is meticulous investigation of the external sense spheres; it involves one-pointedness of mind."[45]

QUESTION: Concentration perforce involves tranquillity, and tranquillity means that one is focused on a single point. Why then do you say there is meticulous examination? The functioning of examination perforce involves applied thought and imagination. How then can you say that concentration is examination?

RESPONSE: If you advocate that guarding one-pointedness is concentration, then concentration would even mean the one-pointedness of sloth and torpor. If correct examination is the same as thought and imagination, then examination conducted via perverse wisdom would not involve thought and imagination. It should be understood that examination is of two types. If examination refers to a faculty that is associated with both perverse and correct mental and verbal discrimination, then it involves both thought and imagination and is thus just discrimination. But if examination refers to a faculty that meticulously observes the external sense spheres, then it is precisely the functioning of concentration and is neither thought nor imagination. Concentration, on the other hand, applies both within discrimination and nondiscrimination; hence, it meticulously analyzes that thought and imagination.

Furthermore, one-pointedness is also of two types. If a person is one-pointed while being slothful, dull, and deluded, and he is not able to investigate carefully, then this is simply sloth and torpor. If a person is one-pointed while being neither torporific nor distracted, and he investigates meticulously, then this is called concentration. For this reason, investigation is different from sloth and torpor. Hence, it should be understood that one should not judge the difference between concentration and distraction based solely on the distinction between the one-pointedness of, or aberrations in, a particular thought process. Why is this? Although opinions that are hastily arrived at might develop rapidly, they still involve concentration; although a dull mind might abide for long periods on one object, it still involves distraction. Now, the reason that this adamantine absorption is said to be correct investigation is because it is neither correct nor incorrect; it is neither consideration nor nonconsideration. It is instead to be differentiated from discrimination and perverted thoughts. Furthermore, it is not the same as empty space or aphasia (*acittaka*). Therefore, correct consideration is the label we force upon it. The term *samādhi* can be explained briefly in this manner. . . .

The third section, on the explanation of the title, is now complete.

EXPLICATION OF THE TEXT

From this point on we consider the division of the text itself with appropriate explanations. . . . The main body of the scripture is in two principal divisions. Its first six chapters (chapters two through seven) each recount a particular aspect of contemplation practice. The final "Codes" chapter thoroughly removes all remaining sensations of doubt. There are six divisions in the section on the individual recounting of various aspects of contemplation practice: the "Signless Dharma" chapter elucidates the signless contemplation; the "Practice of Nonproduction" chapter illumines the practice of nonproduction; the "Inspiration of Original Enlightenment" chapter draws on the original enlightenment to inspire other beings; the "Approaching the Edge of Reality" chapter departs from illusion to approach reality; the "Voidness of the True Nature" chapter demonstrates that all practices derive from the voidness of the true nature; the "Tathāgatagarbha" chapter illumines the innumerable approaches through which to enter the womb of the Thus Come Ones. In this wise, the six aspects of contemplation practice are all covered.

Why is this the case? The beginningless churnings of all deluded thoughts ordinarily result from nothing more than the affliction of discrimination, which derives from clinging to signs. Now, wishing to reverse this churning in order to return to the fountainhead, one must first negate all these signs. It is for this reason that the scripture first explains the contemplation of the signless dharma.

But while all these signs may have been annihilated, if one conserves the mind that contemplates, then the mind that contemplates will continue to arise, and one will not experience original enlightenment. Consequently, one must annihilate the arising of the mind. Therefore, this second chapter of the main body of the text illumines the practice of nonproduction.

Once one's practice produces nothing, one then experiences original enlightenment. Drawing from this experience, one transforms beings and prompts them to gain the original inspiration. Hence, this third chapter elucidates the aspect of the inspiration of original enlightenment.

If, while relying on original enlightenment, one inspires sentient beings, then those sentient beings in fact can leave behind falsity and access reality. Therefore, the fourth chapter elucidates the approach to the edge of reality.

One's internal practice is in fact signless and unproduced. External proselytism is in fact the original inspiration's accessing of reality. In this wise, the two types of benefit (of oneself and others) are replete with the myriads of spiritual practices. These all derive from the true nature and all conform to true voidness. Consequently, the fifth chapter elucidates the voidness of the true nature.

Relying on this true nature, the myriads of spiritual practices are perfected. One accesses the tathāgatagarbha's fountainhead that has a single taste. Therefore, the sixth chapter illumines the tathāgatagarbha.

Since one has returned to the fountainhead of the mind, one then has nothing more to do. As there is nothing more to do, there is nothing that is not done. Hence, it is said that these six chapters incorporate all the Mahāyāna.

Furthermore, there is an alternative interpretation of these six chapters. The first chapter explains the dharma that is contemplated—dharma being the essence of the tathāgatagarbha of the one mind. The second chapter elucidates the practices that are the agents of contemplation—practices being the nondiscriminative contemplation that takes place on the six stages of practice. The third chapter, the "Inspiration of Original Enlightenment," illumines the arising-and-ceasing aspect of the one mind, while the fourth chapter, "Approaching the Edge of Reality," illumines the true-thusness aspect of the one mind. The fifth chapter, the "Voidness of the True Nature," negates both absolute and mundane without subverting the two truths. The sixth chapter, the "Tathāgatagarbha," completely assimilates all of these approaches and shows that they all have but a single taste.

In these two ways, the idea that these six approaches incorporate all the Mahāyāna is thus completed.

Furthermore, these six chapters can be grouped into three sections. The first two chapters incorporate the beginning and end of contemplation. The next two chapters cover the fundamentals and derivatives of proselytism. The final two chapters assimilate these causes so that the fruition is achieved. Furthermore, the first two chapters bring an end to signs and return to the origin. The middle two chapters produce practices from out of this origin. The final two chapters illumine both this return and this arising. In this way these two threefold divisions completely assimilate all the Mahāyāna.

Furthermore, these six chapters have only two sections. The demise of both signs and production are the "Inspiration of Original Enlightenment"; the edge of reality and true voidness are the "Tathāgatagarbha." Furthermore, the first division (from "Signless Dharma" to "Inspiration of Original Enlightenment") removes falsity and reveals the cause; the second division (from "Approaching the Edge of Reality" to "Tathāgatagarbha") reveals truth and perfects the fruition. In this wise, these twofold divisions also completely assimilate the Mahāyāna.

Furthermore, these six chapters have but a single taste. Why is that? Signs and production are devoid of nature. Original enlightenment is devoid of origin. The edge of reality leaves behind all limits. The true nature is also void. So how does one gain the nature of the tathāgatagarbha? As is explained below in the "Tathāgatagarbha" chapter: "The consciousnesses are perpetually calm and extinct; but that calm extinction is also calm and extinct."[46] The "Codes" chapter states: "The seventh consciousness and the five sensory consciousnesses are unproduced. The eighth and sixth consciousnesses are calm and extinct. The characteristic of the ninth consciousness is to be void and nonexistent."[47] In this wise, the one taste that is unascertainable is exactly the essential point of the theme of this scripture. It is merely because there is nothing to obtain that there is nothing that is not obtained. Therefore, as there are no approaches that are not opened through the scripture, it presents a theme that has innumerable meanings. RB

Arouse Your Mind and Practice!

[From *Hanguk pulgyo chŏnsŏ* 1:841a–c]

In addition to his exegetical writings, Wŏnhyo made a profound personal commitment to disseminating Buddhism among the people of Silla Korea. His Korean biographer, Iryŏn, tells us that Wŏnhyo "composed a song that circulated throughout the land. He used to . . . sing and dance his way through thousands of villages and myriads of hamlets, touring while proselytizing in song. He encouraged all classes of people to recognize the name 'buddha.' " Wŏnhyo's *Palsim suhaeng chang* (Arouse Your Mind and Practice!) is one of his few extant works that is clearly intended for proselytization. The peculiar phraseology of the text suggests that it may originally have been a Korean song recorded in *idu* ("clerical reading"), an early system of transcribing the vernacular language, and was subsequently converted into literary Chinese. Could this very text be Wŏnhyo's "song that circulated throughout the land"?

We do not know when the text was written. The translator has speculated elsewhere that Wŏnhyo probably spent the years between 662 and 676 writing commentaries and treatises before abandoning scholarship to travel around the Silla kingdom spreading the "good word" of Buddhism. Wŏnhyo's *Arouse Your Mind* probably dates from this proselytizing period, perhaps between 677 and 684. Whatever its linguistic pedigree and dating, *Arouse Your Mind* is Wŏnhyo's most edifying work and one of the strongest admonitions about the urgency of religious practice to be found in all of Buddhist literature. Even today it is among the first works read by Korean postulants who have just joined the Buddhist monastic community.

Now, all the buddhas adorn the palace of tranquil extinction, nirvana, because they have renounced desires and practiced austerities on the sea of numerous kalpas. All sentient beings whirl through the door of the burning house of samsara because they have not renounced craving and sensuality during lifetimes without measure. Though the heavenly mansions are unobstructed, few are those who go there; for people take the three poisons (greed, hatred, and delusion) as their family wealth. Though no one entices others to evil destinies, many are those who go there; for people consider the four snakes and the five desires to be precious to their deluded minds.

Who among human beings would not wish to enter the mountains and cultivate the path? But fettered by lust and desires, no one proceeds. But even though people do not return to mountain fastnesses to cultivate the mind, as far as they are able they should not abandon wholesome practices. Those who can abandon their own sensual pleasures will be venerated like saints. Those who practice what is difficult to practice will be revered like buddhas. Those who covet things join Mara's entourage, while those who give with love and compassion are the children of the King of Dharma himself.

High peaks and lofty crags are where the wise dwell. Green pines and deep valleys are where practitioners sojourn. When hungry, they eat tree fruits to satisfy their famished belly. When thirsty, they drink the flowing streams to quench their feeling of thirst. Though one feeds it with sweets and tenderly cares for it, this body is certain to decay. Though one softly clothes it and carefully protects it, this life force must come to an end. Thus the wise regard the grottoes and caves where echoes resound as a hall for recollecting the Buddha's name. They take the wild geese, plaintively calling, as their closest of friends. Though their knees bent in prostration are frozen like ice, they have no longing for warmth. Though their starving bellies feel as if cut by knives, they have no thoughts to search for food.

Suddenly a hundred years will be past; how then can we not practice? How much longer will this life last? Yet still we do not practice, but remain heedless. Those who leave behind the lusts within the mind are called mendicants. Those who do not long for the mundane are called those gone forth into homelessness. A practitioner entangled in the net of the six senses is a dog wearing elephant's hide. A person on the path who still longs for the world is a hedgehog entering a rat's den.

Although talented and wise, if a person dwells in the village, all the buddhas feel pity and sadness for him. Though a person does not practice the path, if he dwells in a mountain hut, all the saints are happy with him. Though talented and learned, if a person does not observe the precepts, it is like being directed to a treasure trove but not even starting out. Though practicing diligently, if a person has no wisdom, it is like one who wishes to go east but instead turns toward the west. The way of the wise is to prepare rice by steaming rice grains; the way of the ignorant is to prepare rice by steaming sand.

Everyone knows that eating food soothes the pangs of hunger, but no one knows that studying the dharma corrects the delusions of the mind. Practice and understanding that are both complete are like the two wheels of a cart. Benefiting oneself and benefiting others are like the two wings of a bird. If a person chants prayers when receiving rice gruel but does not understand the meaning, should he not be ashamed before the donors? If one chants when receiving rice but does not tumble to its import, should one not be ashamed before the sages and saints?

Humans despise maggots because they do not discriminate between clean and filthy; saints loathe the *śramaṇas* who do not differentiate between the pure and impure. The precepts are the skillful ladder for leaving behind the clamor of this world and climbing into the empty sky. Therefore, one who wishes to become a field of merit for others while breaking the precepts is like a bird with broken wings who tries to fly into the sky while bearing a tortoise on its back. A person who is not yet liberated from his own transgressions cannot redeem the transgressions of others. But how could one not cultivating the precepts still accept others' offerings?

There is no benefit in nourishing a useless body that does not practice. Despite clinging to this impermanent, evanescent life, it cannot be preserved. People who hope to achieve the virtue of dragons and elephants—that is, eminent monks—must be able to endure long suffering. Those who aspire to the Lion's Seat of the buddhas must forever turn their backs on desires and pleasures. A cultivator whose mind is pure will be praised by all the gods, while a person on the path who longs for sex will be abandoned by all the wholesome spirits.

The four great elements will suddenly disperse; they cannot be kept together for long. Today, alas, it is already dusk and we should have been practicing since dawn. The pleasures of the world will only bring suffering later, so how can we crave them? One attempt at forbearance conduces to long happiness, so how could we not cultivate? Craving among persons on the path is a disgrace to cultivators. Wealth among those gone forth into homelessness is mocked by the noble. Despite infinite admonitions, craving and clinging are not ended. Despite infinite resolutions, lust and clinging are not eradicated. Though the affairs of this world are limitless, we still cannot forsake worldly events. Though plans are endless, we still do not have a mind to stop them.

For todays without end, our days of doing evil have been rife. For tomorrows without end, our days of doing good have been few. For this years without end, we have not reduced the defilements. For next years without end, we have not progressed toward enlightenment.

Hours after hours continue to pass; swiftly the day and night are gone. Days after days continue to pass; swiftly the end of the month is gone. Months and months continue to pass; suddenly next year has arrived. Years after years continue to pass; unexpectedly we have arrived at the portal of death.

A broken cart cannot move; an old person cannot cultivate. Yet still we humans lie, lazy and indolent; still we humans sit, with minds distracted. How many lives have we not cultivated? Yet still we pass the day and night in vain. How many lives have we spent in our useless bodies? Yet still we do not cultivate in this lifetime either. This life must come to an end; but what of the next? Is this not urgent? Is this not urgent? RB

Commentary on the *Awakening of Faith*
[From *Hsü Tsang-ching* 71:310a–311a]

This treatise will be explained in three parts. The first reveals the essence of the doctrine; the second explains the title; the third clarifies the meaning of the sentences.

ON REVEALING THE ESSENCE OF THE DOCTRINE

The essence of the Great Vehicle is described as being completely empty and very mysterious. But, no matter how mysterious it may be,[48] how could it be anywhere but in the world of myriad phenomena? No matter how empty it may be, it is still present in the conversation of the people. Although it is not anywhere but in phenomena, none of the five eyes[49] can see its form. Although it is present in discourse, none of the four unlimited explanatory abilities[50] can describe its shape. One wants to call it great, but it enters the interiorless and nothing remains. One wants to call it infinitesimal, but it envelops the exteriorless without exhausting itself. One might say it is something, yet everything is empty because of it. One might say it is nothing, yet myriad things arise through it. I do not know how to describe it; therefore, I am compelled to call it the Great Vehicle.

Who indeed, unless one is Vimalakīrti[51] or the One-Glance Hero,[52] can discuss the Great Vehicle in the state of wordlessness; who can awaken deep faith in the state of no-thought? Because Bodhisattva Aśvaghoṣa had unconditioned great compassion, he was distressed over those people whose minds, moved by the wind of ignorance and delusion, are easily tossed about. He was grieved that the true nature of Original Enlightenment, which sleeps in a long dream, is difficult to awaken. Since Bodhisattva Aśvaghoṣa had the power of wisdom by which one regards others as his own body, he patiently wrote this treatise that expounds the deep meaning of the Thus Come One's profound scriptures. He wished to cause scholars who open this small treatise even for a moment to completely extract the meaning of *Tripiṭaka;* he wished to cause practitioners to permanently stop myriad illusory phenomena and finally return to the source of One Mind.

Although what is discussed in the treatise is vast, it may be summarized as follows. By revealing two aspects in One Mind,[53] it comprehensively includes the one hundred and eight jewels of the Mahāyāna teaching.[54] And by showing the essential purity in phenomenal impurity,[55] it completely synthesizes the subtle truth of *The Lion's Roar of Queen Śrīmālā Scripture*'s fifteen chapters.[56] The synthesis includes doctrines such as the *Scripture of the Great Nirvana*'s teaching of One Taste preached at Śāla Grove,[57] the *Lotus Scripture*'s[58] and the *Mahāyānabhisamaya Scripture*'s[59] teaching of Ultimate Result, stated in its doctrine of the three bodies of the Buddha,[60] the *Flower Garland Scripture*'s[61] and the *Ying-lo ching*'s[62] teaching of Profound Cause stated in its Four Stages doctrine, the *Larger Perfection of Wisdom Scripture*'s[63] and the *Great Collection Scripture*'s[64] broad and vast teaching of the Ultimate Path, and the teaching of the secret doctrine's mysterious gate expounded in the *Suryagarbha* and the *Candragarbha* chapters of the *Great Collection Scripture.* Only the *Awakening of Faith* penetrates the essence of all these scriptures. Therefore, the following sentence from the *Awakening of Faith* says, "Because this treatise aims at comprehensively embracing the limitless meaning of the Thus Come One's broad, great, and profound teaching, it must be written."

Such being the intent of this treatise, when unfolded, there are immeasurable and limitless meanings to be found in its doctrine; when sealed, the principle of two aspects in One Mind is found to be its essence. Within the two aspects are included myriad meanings without confusion. These limitless meanings are identical with One Mind and are completely amalgamated with it. Therefore, it unfolds and seals freely; it establishes and refutes without restrictions. Unfolding but not complicating; sealing but not narrowing; establishing but gaining nothing; refuting but losing nothing—this is Aśvaghoṣa's wonderful skill and the essence of the *Awakening of Faith.*

The meaning of this treatise is so profound, however, that interpreters hitherto have seldom presented its doctrine completely. Indeed, since all of them were attached to what they had learned, they distorted the meaning of the sentences. Not able to abandon their preconceptions, still they sought the meaning. Therefore, their interpretations do not come close to the author's intent. Some hoped to reach the source but got lost in the streams; some grasped the leaves but forgot the trunk; some cut the collar and patched it to the sleeves; some broke the branches and grafted them to the roots. Now I shall directly correlate the sentences of this treatise with appropriate parts of the scriptures in the hope that my commentary may provide information to people on the same path.

"On Revealing the Essence of the Doctrine" ends. SP

Ŭisang and the Flower Garland School

Ŭisang (625–702) won great acclaim as the founder of the Flower Garland school in Korea. Upon returning from his study under Chih-yen (602–668), Ŭisang expounded the school's philosophy and trained disciples. Unlike his colleague Fa-tsang (643–712), who systematized Flower Garland metaphysics, Ŭisang stressed practice and monastic life. His emphasis on practice is reflected not only in his diagram but also in the works of his disciples, who either summarized the essence of the scripture for the purpose of practice or elucidated the gate of contemplation and action to attain Buddhahood. (In addition, there are Kyunyŏ's commentary on the diagram and another by an unknown writer.) This emphasis seems to have slowed the development of Flower Garland metaphysics in Silla. When its doctrine was attacked by the Meditation school in late Silla and early Koryŏ, Kyunyŏ (923–973) was compelled to reexamine the early works on the Flower Garland school by Chih-yen, Fa-tsang, and Shen-hsiu (d. 706). Nevertheless, Ŭisang's disciples, at times numbering three thousand, included the "ten virtuous monks" and other eminent monks, such as Pŏmch'e and Tosin, whose efforts at exegesis helped develop the Flower Garland school as the most influential in Silla. The school's many monasteries include the famous Pusŏk Monastery (built in 676 at the order of King Munmu), as well as Hwaŏm and Haein monasteries (802).[65] Mount Nak, the school's holy place where Avalokiteśvara was believed to reside, and Mount Odae, where Mañjuśrī was said to reside, illustrate the contemporary cults of the two bodhisattvas. Ŭisang considered Mount Nak to be the holiest of places, and the Buddhist communities on Mount Odae had close connections with the ruling house during the unification and the political struggles that took place later in the capital. There were also religious societies on the mountain that, under state protection, lectured on scriptures, copied them, or repaired monasteries. The religious activities of these societies congregating around the Flower Garland school promoted its spread among the nobility.

The Flower Garland school teaches that principle or noumenon (ri/i) and phenomenon (sa), the two aspects of the dharma realm, are interfused without obstruction and that all phenomena are mutually identified with one another—the interpenetration and mutual identification of all the dharmas. Because every phenomenon is a manifestation of principle, one is the many and the many are the one. This all-inclusive system has everything leading to one point, the Buddha, and sees everything in the universe as a representation of the same supreme mind. This cosmology provides a spiritual background for both individual freedom and the harmony that must exist between the individual and the state and between the individual and the universe. At the time of unification, therefore, when Silla had to assimilate the aristocracy and loyalists of Koguryŏ and Paekche, Flower Garland metaphysics provided a unifying ideology that embraced subjugated states and peoples as well as a religious sanction for the centralized administration proceeding from the royal authority.

The Life of Ŭisang
[From *Samguk yusa* 4:194–197]

The surname of Dharma Master Ŭisang was Kim. His father was Han Sin. In the capital, at the age of twenty-nine, Ŭisang had his head shaved in Hwangbok Monastery and became a monk. Shortly afterwards, he decided to travel to China to gauge the extent of the transformations that the Buddha Dharma had brought about there. As it happened, he went with Wŏnhyo to Liao-tung [650] but was detained by the Koguryŏ guard as a spy. After spending dozens of days in confinement, he was set free to return home.

In the beginning of Yung-hui [650–655], Ŭisang sailed on the ship of the returning T'ang envoy, and so was able to visit China. At first he stopped at Yang-chou. There the governor of the prefecture, Liu Chi-jen, invited him to stay at the government offices and entertained him in grand style. Afterward Ŭisang went to Chih-hsiang Monastery on Mount Chung-nan and had an audience with Chih-yen [602–668].

The night before Ŭisang arrived, Chih-yen had a dream: A tall tree with luxuriant leaves shot out from Korea and covered China. In the top of the tree was the nest of a phoenix. Chih-yen climbed to the top and found a brightly glowing pearl that shone far and wide. After he had awakened, Chih-yen marveled and pondered over the dream. He sprinkled and swept his abode, and waited. Soon Ŭisang arrived. Chih-yen received his guest with special courtesy and addressed him calmly: "Last night, in a dream, I received an omen of your coming." Ŭisang was then allowed to become his disciple, and Chih-yen analyzed the wondrous teachings, even the most abstruse ones, of the *Flower Garland Scripture*. . . .

At that time T'ang Kao-tsung was planning to invade Silla, and the Silla officials Kim Hŭmsun (or Inmun), Yangdo, and others detained in the T'ang capital told Ŭisang to return home. He did so in the first year of Hsien-heng [670] and informed the Silla court of the danger. The great master of the Divine Seal school, Myŏngnang, was ordered to use his secret platform method to avert the invasion. Thus was Silla saved. In the first year of I-feng [676], Ŭisang returned to Mount T'aebaek and built Pusŏk Monastery in accordance with a royal command. There he preached Mahāyāna Buddhism and was rewarded for his prayers.

When Fa-tsang, a pupil of Chih-yen, sent a copy of the *T'an-hsüan chi* together with his personal letter to Ŭisang, Ŭisang ordered ten monasteries to study it. . . .

Ŭisang wrote the *Pŏpkye tosŏ in* (Diagram Seal of the Dharmadhātu) and the *Yakso* (Abridged Commentary), which encompass the essentials of the One Vehicle and are a touchstone for a thousand generations. Everyone made an effort to keep the purport of these works close to his heart. The *Diagram* was completed in the first year of Tsung-chang [668], the year Chih-yen died. . . . Ŭisang was thought to be a reincarnation of the Buddha. He had ten disciples. PL

Diagram of the Dharmadhātu According to the One Vehicle
[From *Taishō Tripiṭaka* 45:711a]

Based on the doctrinal essentials of the *Flower Garland Scripture* and the *Treatise on the Scripture Concerning the Ten Stages* (*Daśabhūmika sūtra śāstra*), this thirty-line heptasyllabic verse in two hundred and ten logographs begins with the logograph *pŏp* (dharma) at the center, goes through fifty-four meanderings, and ends at the logograph *pul* (Buddha).

First Ŭisang explains the meaning of the seal and analyzes its marks. The form of the seal expresses that three worlds—the material world, the world of sentient beings, and the world of perfectly enlightened wisdom—contained in Śākyamuni's teaching are produced from the ocean-seal *samādhi,* and the three worlds contain and exhaust all dharmas. He then interprets the seal's marks in three sections: the marks of the sentences, the marks of the logographs, and the meaning of the text. The one path of the seal expresses the one sound of the Thus Come One, the wonderfully skillful expedient means. Many meanderings in his expedient means show the differences in the capacities and desires of sentient beings and stand for the teachings of the three vehicles (*triyana*). The poem, however, has no beginning and end, because the Thus Come One's expedient means have no fixed method but correspond to the world of dharmas so that the ten worlds mutually correspond and are completely interfused. This is the round teaching of the one vehicle, the Flower Garland school. The four sides and four corners in the diagram manifest the four embracing virtues (almsgiving, kind words, conduct benefiting others, and adaptation to others) and the four immeasurables (benevolence, compassion, sympathetic joy, and impartiality). This shows the one vehicle by means of the three vehicles. The fact that the logographs at the center have a beginning and end shows that cause and effect are not equal from the standpoint of expedient means in practice. The unenlightened perceive a great distance between cause and effect; but from the standpoint of the dharma nature, cause and effect are simultaneous, and this is the essence of the Middle Path.

Ŭisang goes on to explain the structure and meaning of the diagram. Lines 1–18 concern the practice of benefiting self: enlightened reality (lines 1–4), conditioned origination (lines 5–6), the principle and function of *dhāraṇī* (lines 7–8), spatial containment of phenomena (lines 9–10), temporal containment of worlds and time periods (lines 11–14), mutual containedness of dharmas in terms of levels (lines 15–16), explanation of the meaning of the above (lines 17–18). Lines 19–22 concern the practice of benefiting others: ocean-seal explained (lines 19–20) and obtaining of benefit (lines 21–22). Lines 23–30 concern expedient means of practice (lines 23–36) and their benefits (lines 27–30).

In addition to Ŭisang's autocommentary (*T.* 45, 1887A), there are others: Ch'ewŏn ed., *Pŏpkye togi ch'ongsurok* in four chapters (*T.* 45, 1887B); Kyunyŏ, *Pŏpkye togi wŏnt'ong ki* in two chapters (lectured in 958); and Kim Sisŭp (1453–1493), *Tae-Hwaŏm ilsŭng pŏpkyedo chu* in one chapter (published in 1562). Also known as the "Diagram of the Dharma Nature" or the "Ocean-Seal Diagram," the "Diagram of Dharmadhātu" is dated the fifteenth day of the seventh month of 668 (27 August 668), three months before Chih-yen died. Asked why he did not record the name of the author, Ŭisang replied: "Because all dharmas produced by conditions do not have an author."

The dharma nature is perfectly interfused; it has no duality.
All dharmas are unmoving; by nature they are quiescent;
They have no names or characters; all distinctions are severed.
It is known through realization wisdom and not by any other
    means.
True nature is very profound and supremely fine.
It has no self-nature, but arises from causation.
It is the one in the all, the one in the many.
The one is the all, the many are the one.
A mote of dust contains the ten directions;
All the motes are thus.
The immeasurably distant cosmic age is the same as a single
    thought-moment,
A single thought-moment is the same as the immeasurably
    distant cosmic age.
Nine time periods and ten time periods are mutually identical;
They are not in confusion, but have been formed separately.
The first production of the thought of enlightenment is the same
    as true enlightenment.
Samsara and nirvana are always in harmony.
Noumenon and phenomenon are invisible and indistinct.
The ten Buddhas and Samantabhadra are the realm of great
    men.
Śākyamuni, in his ocean-seal meditation,
Constantly manifests inconceivable supernatural power—
A rain of jewels that benefits the living fills all space,
And all the living benefit according to their capacity.
Therefore the practitioner of conduct must return to the original
    source,
For he cannot attain it without ceasing false thoughts.
By expedient, unconditional means, he attains complete
    freedom,
Returns home, and obtains food according to his capacity.
With the inexhaustible treasure of *dhāraṇī,*
He adorns the dharma realm—a true palace of jewels.
Finally, seated on the throne of the Middle Way of Ultimate
    Reality,

From times long past he has not moved—hence his name is
Buddha. PL

Vow Made at the White Lotus Enlightenment Site
[From *Hanguk pulgyo chŏnsŏ* 2:9a]

We bow our heads in refuge. We contemplate the great perfect
mirror wisdom of the original teacher, the great saint He Who Observes the Sounds of the World. We also contemplate his disciples'
original enlightenment, which is the quiescence of the nature. . . .

We also contemplate all the inexhaustible major and minor marks[66]
of the original teacher, with which he is adorned like the moon
reflecting on the water, as well as the defiled bodily forms of his
disciples, the physical characteristics of which are like a flower in the
sky. The purity or impurity, suffering or pleasure, of their attendant
and primary karmic results are not the same. . . .[67]

Now, with these disciples' bodies, which are reflected in the mirror
of the Sound Observer, we take refuge with our lives and prostrate
ourselves before the great saint Sound Observer who is reflected in the
mirrors of his disciples. We make this sincere vow and hope to be
granted his sustaining power.

May it be that in every life, in every generation, we disciples will
honor the Sound Observer as the original teacher. Just as bodhisattvas
revere Maitreya, so will we revere the holy Sound Observer. His ten
vows, his six transferences, his thousand hands, his thousand eyes, his
great loving kindness, and his great compassion will find their equal
in all of us. Whether abandoning one body or receiving another,
whether being reborn in this realm or in another, we will follow him
to his place of residence like shadows following form. We listen
ceaselessly to the preaching of the dharma and assist in disseminating
its true message. We will universally prompt all the sentient beings of
the dharma realm to chant the Great Compassion Spell[68] and to recol-
lect the name of the bodhisattva. Together, we will enter the nature
sea of the *samādhi* of complete penetration.

We also vow that once this recompense is complete, we disciples
will personally receive the guidance of the great saint, which is like a
shining light, and will leave behind all fear and dread so that our
bodies and minds will be delighted and refreshed. In one moment, we
will then instantly take rebirth in the White Lotus Platform of the Path

and, together with all the bodhisattvas, listen to the true dharma and enter its flowing current. Thought after thought, our understanding will increase in clarity, and we will manifest the Thus Come One's great acceptance of the nonproduction of dharmas.

Completing this vow, we take refuge with our lives and prostrate ourselves before the Bodhisattva-Mahāsattva Sound Observer. RB

Fa-tsang's Letter to Ŭisang
[From *Wŏnjong mullyu* 22, in *Hsü Tsang-ching* 103:422a–b]

The monk of Ch'ung-fa Monastery in the Western Capital of T'ang, Fa-tsang, sends a letter to the attendant of the Buddha and dharma master of the great Flower Garland school in Silla.

More than twenty years have passed since we parted, but how could affection for you leave my mind? Between us lie ten thousand miles of smoke and clouds and a thousand folds of land and sea; it is clear we will not see each other again in this life. How can I express adequately how I cherish the memory of our friendship? Owing to the same causes and conditions in our former existence and the same karma in this life, we were fortunate; we immersed ourselves in the great scripture and received its profound meaning by special favor granted us by our late master.

I hear with even greater joy that you have, on your return to your native country, elucidated the *Flower Garland Scripture,* enhanced the unobstructed dependent origination in the dharma realm. Thus Indra's net is multimeshed and the kingdom of the Buddha is daily renewed; you have widely benefited the world. By this I know that after the extinction of the Thus Come One, it will be because of you that the Buddha Sun shines bright, that the dharma wheel turns again. You have made the dharma live for us. I, Fa-tsang, have made little progress and interceded even less for others. When I think of you and look on this scripture, I am ashamed that it was to me that our late master transmitted it. But, according to my duty, I cannot abandon what I have received. I only hope to be part of the future causes, direct and indirect, by relying on this karma.

Our teacher's discourses and commentaries, though rich in meaning, are terse in style and difficult for posterity to approach. Hence I have recorded his subtle sayings and mysterious purport, and have commented on their meaning. Dharma Master Sŭngjŏn has made a copy of my writing and will introduce it to your country upon his return to Silla. I beg you to scrutinize its good and bad points; I shall be happy if you would kindly revise it and enlighten me.

If we are reborn in the future, meet again in the Assembly of Vairocana Buddha, receive the boundlessly wonderful dharma, and practice the immeasurable vows of Samantabhadra, then evil karma will be overthrown in a day.

It is my earnest hope that you will not forget our friendship in the past and through all our future existence and that you will instruct me in the right path. I will inquire after your health either through a person or by letter whenever possible.

First month, twenty-eighth day [692].

With respectful salutation

Fa-tsang   PL

Wŏnch'ŭk and the Consciousness-Only School

While the Flower Garland school of Ŭisang emphasized practice, the Consciousness-Only (Wei-shih) school, which also flourished in unified Silla, stressed doctrinal studies. Here the pioneer was Wŏnch'ŭk (613–696), who studied the *Compendium of Mahāyāna* under Fach'ang and Seng-p'ien and later the Wei-shih doctrines under Hsüantsang. Because he lectured at Hsi-ming Monastery in Ch'ang-an, his disciples were known as the Hsi-ming school. When Wŏnch'ŭk gained public favor with his lectures on the *Treatise on the Completion of Consciousness-Only, Stages of Yoga Practice,* and *Explanation of Profound Mysteries Scripture,* K'uei-chi (632–682) stoutly opposed Wŏnch'ŭk's theory. This polemic might have given rise to "absurd" apocryphal stories attributed to both Wŏnch'ŭk and K'uei-chi.[69] Wŏnch'ŭk's philosophy was influenced by that of Paramārtha (499–569), while K'ueichi upheld only that of Dharmapāla (c. 530–561), rejecting all others as heterodox.

Wŏnch'ŭk's unprejudiced scholarship is exemplified by the fact that although he was well versed in Paramārtha's theories, he also accepted other Indian theories of the school; in his commentary on the *Explanation of Profound Mysteries,* he not only espoused Paramārtha's interpretations but also accorded respect to Hsüan-tsang as the "Tripiṭaka Master of Great T'ang." Indeed, the defamation campaign launched by the Kuei-ch'i group had no factual basis. Even so, Wŏnch'ŭk's doctrine, labeled unorthodox, gained little support in China. It was, however, introduced to Silla and the Tun-huang area. His commentary on the *Explanation of Profound Mysteries,* for example, was transmitted to Tun-huang by his disciple T'an-k'uang (Tamgwang; died c. 788) and was later translated into Tibetan by Chos-grub (Fa-ch'eng) and included in the Tibetan canon. Later, Chos-grub's translation of Wŏnch'ŭk's commentary was referred to by the scholarly reformist monk Tsongkhapa (1357–1419). Thus Wŏnch'ŭk's teachings were widely studied in the border area of Kan-chou and Tibet.[70]

Among Wŏnch'ŭk's disciples, Tojŭng (Tao-cheng) returned to Silla in 692 to spread the master's teachings,[71] while Sŭngjang (Sheng-chuang; fl. 703–713) remained in China to work on the translation of scriptures.[72] T'aehyŏn (or Taehyŏn; fl. 753–774), successor of Tojŭng, spread the teaching in Yongjang Monastery, on Mount South in Kyŏngju, and wrote a number of works.[73] Though a successor to Wŏnch'ŭk, T'aehyŏn did not hesitate to reject his master's interpretation or accept that of K'uei-chi; his nonsectarian attitude contrasts well with that of K'uei-chi's disciple Hui-chao. Followers of T'aehyŏn include Tunryun (or Toryun), Kyŏnghŭng, and Sungyŏng. Tunryun's commentary on the *Treatise on the Stages of Yoga Practice* by K'uei-chi is valuable for its quotations from the works on Consciousness-Only philosophy by Silla monks.[74] Kyŏnghŭng, who flourished under King Sinmun (681–692), wrote some two hundred and twenty rolls, second in quantity only to Wŏnhyo,[75] and Sungyŏng was a master of Hetuvidyā (science of cause and logical reasoning).[76] Another Silla scholar-monk who was well known in China was Sinbang;[77] as one of the four chief disciples of Hsüan-tsang, he took part in Hsüan-tsang's translation projects. With the doctrinal study of the Consciousness-Only philosophy was born the Pŏpsang (Fa-hsiang) school. Second in importance only to the Flower Garland school, it flourished until the end of Koryŏ. But because the school was too abstruse, did not accept the theory of dependent origination (*pratītya-samutpāda*) of the dharma realm, and denied that all sentient beings possess Buddhahood, it was not for the common people. PL

Sung Fu: Memorial Inscription to Wŏnch'ŭk

[From *Ta-Chou Hsi-ming ssu ku ta-te Yüan-ts'e (Wŏnch'ŭk) fa-shih fo she-li t'a-ming ping hsü*, in *Chin-shi ts'ui-pien* 146:34b–37a]

The dharma master's taboo name was Muna (Wen-ya); his soubriquet was Wŏnch'ŭk [613–696]. He was a descendant of a prince of the Silla kingdom. At the age of three he left home to be ordained as a novice; at fifteen he asked for his vocation and traveled to T'ang China, where initially he listened to the discourses of the two dharma masters Fa-ch'ang [567–646] and Seng-p'ien [568–642]. His natural astuteness was striking to the extreme. Although he might listen to several tens of millions of words, if his ears heard them only once his mind never forgot them. During the period of Chen-kuan [627–649][78] of the Civil Emperor T'ai-tsung, [Wŏnch'ŭk] was ordained as a monk and resided at Yüan-fa Monastery in Ch'ang-an. There he studied such works as the *Abhidharma* treatises, the *Tattvasiddhi* (Treatise on the Completion of Truth), the *Abhidharmakośa* (Treasury of Abhidharma), and the *Mahāvibhāṣā* (Great Exegesis of Abhidharma). There were no ancient or contemporary essays or commentaries that he did not understand completely. His fame and renown spread rapidly.

Just as the Tripiṭaka Master, the venerable Hsüan-tsang, was returning from India, Dharma Master Wŏnch'ŭk had a dream in which a Brahman gave him fruit until he was completely satisfied. The message conveyed by this dream was that his superior affinities would soon coalesce. The first time that the venerable Hsüan-tsang saw Wŏnch'ŭk, he was well disposed toward him without any ado, and he ordered that Wŏnch'ŭk be entrusted with such works as the *Treatise on the Stages of Yoga Practice* and the *Completion of Consciousness-Only Treatise,* as well as with the Mahāyāna and Hīnayāna scriptures and treatises Hsüan-tsang had translated. Wŏnch'ŭk's understanding of these texts was as clear as instinctual knowledge.

Later, Wŏnch'ŭk was summoned to become master of Hsi-ming Monastery. He wrote the commentary to the *Completion of Consciousness-Only Treatise* (*Sŏng yusingnon so*) in ten rolls, the commentary to the *Explanation of Profound Mysteries Scripture* in ten rolls, and the commentary to the *Scripture on Benevolent Kings* in three rolls, as well as commentaries on such texts as the *Diamond Scripture,* the *Kuan so-yüan yüan lun* (*Ālambanaparikṣā*; Treatise on Sense-Object Condition), the *Heart of the Perfection of Wisdom Scripture* (*Prajñāpāramitāhṛdaya sūtra*), and the *Scripture of Immeasurable Meanings* (*Wu-liang i ching*). He protected the secret canon of Buddhism and opened the eyes and ears of his contemporaries. Thus, he was one of those who assisted the venerable Hsüan-tsang in bringing about the eastward flow of the Buddhadharma and promoting greatly the infinite teachings.

It was the nature of the dharma master to take pleasure in mountains and streams. He sojourned at Yün-chi Monastery on Chung-nan Mountain. Furthermore, he lived in retreat at a single site over thirty *li* from the monastery, calming his ambition for eight years. His ordained disciples from Hsi-ming Monastery requested that he yield and return to the monastery, where he lectured on the *Completion of Consciousness-Only Treatise.*

At that time [c. 676], there was a Tripiṭaka Master from central India named Divakara [613–687] who had arrived in the capital. Upon imperial command, five senior monks were summoned and ordered to participate in the translation of such scriptures as the *Ghanavyūha sūtra* (*Ta-sheng mi-yen ching;* The Mahāyāna Dense Array Scripture). The dharma master was installed as their leader. Subsequently, Wŏn-ch'ŭk was summoned to enter the Eastern Capital to lecture and assist in Śikṣānanda's translation of the new *Flower Garland Scripture.* Before all the fascicles were completed, however, he passed away at Fo-shou-chi Monastery. It was the first year of Wan-sui-t'ung-t'ien of Empress Wu, seventh month, twenty-second day [25 August 696]. He was eighty-four years old. Therewith, on the twenty-fifth day of that month [28 August 696], he was cremated in a northern valley at Hsiang-shan Monastery in Lung-men and a white stupa was erected. At that time, his monk-disciples in the capital, such as Dharma Master Tz'u-shan, the abbot of Hsi-ming Monastery, Dharma Master Sŭng-jang [fl. 703–713], the master at Ta-ch'ien-fu Monastery, and others, were worried that this site would be unsuitable for paying respects to the master. Accordingly, at the funeral site on Hsiang Mountain they divided up the relics. One part they stored in a jeweled case and stone casket; the remainder they buried on the East Ridge at Feng-te Monastery on Chung-nan Mountain, a spot to which the dharma master had traveled long ago. Atop the funeral mound they erected a stupa, and at the base of the stupa they enshrined forty-nine relics.

But now the path to that site is completely unknown. The precipitous peaks are steep and sheer; the dense forests are close and impenetrable; the passes and thoroughfares are hidden and dangerous. The footprints of men seldom reach there. The isolation of the place buries his illustriousness and conceals his virtue. In just a few years, who will know the path to that site and go there to take refuge in him? For this reason, Dharma Master K'uang-yüeh of Lung-hsing Monastery's Benevolent Kings Cloister in T'ung-chou earnestly made an ambitious vow, and in the fifth year of Cheng-ho of the Great Sung dynasty, fourth month, eighth day [3 May 1115], he held a great offering ceremony at Feng-te Monastery. All of Wǒnch'ǔk's relics were reburied at Hsing-chiao Monastery to the left of the venerable Hsüan-tsang's stupa. There he built a new stupa in the style of the venerable K'uei-chi, with which it was one in form in every respect. Moreover, since the venerable K'uei-chi's stupa had become dilapidated, it was renovated with golden wheels and bejeweled bells. It rose up two stories high, as lofty as some magical creation. At its base, each wheel was ringed with wide ambulatories where votive images of the two masters were reverently installed to the left and right in worship of the venerable Hsüan-tsang. These were intended to prompt pilgrims to emulate them and give rise to faith. It is not known when these were completed. At the front of the stupa was constructed an oblatory basilica with six columns.

On the day of dedication, there was no time to search for someone proficient in composition, and so they begged me to outline straightaway the events surrounding the construction. I have appended to it this inscription:

The *pattra* leaves[79] of the scriptures came from the West;
their merit is great.
The teachings flowed to the Middle Region of China;
they are the eternal support.
The dharma experts have a refuge;
they meet in the realm of sincerity.
The fragrant mountains are remote and far off;
they shroud the hidden palace.
His prolific virtue was lofty and precipitous;
it preserves his numinous traces.
Later men will take refuge in him;
they will come from everywhere.
Those who have exceptional affinities
will obtain the power of his spiritual help.
His two-storied stupa is grandly erected;
K'uei-chi's was its model.
Therewith he worships the venerable Hsüan-tsang;

How utterly marvelous!
Chung-nan's appearance is lofty;
its peaks lean on heaven.
His prolific virtue was imposing;
his inscription is cut in stone.
Pilgrims will look up to him with reverence
for tens of millions of years. RB

Wŏnch'ŭk: Commentary on the *Explanation of Profound Mysteries Scripture*

[From *Hsü Tsang-ching* 34:291a–298a]

The *Sandhinirmocana sūtra* (Explanation of Profound Mysteries Scripture) is considered to be a seminal text of the Yogācāra school, for its doctrine of the three turnings of the dharma wheel justifies that school's claim of being the consummation of Mahāyāna Buddhism. The introduction to Wŏnch'ŭk's commentary to the text, portions of which are translated here, epitomizes the East Asian commentarial style and shows the author's familiarity with a wide range of Indian exegetical materials. The central issue explored in this selection is fundamental to the Indian Buddhist schools and their East Asian counterparts: defining the essential character of the Buddhist teachings. There were two basic propositions: First, following the Sautrāntika and Yogācāra schools, the teachings could be characterized as sound—an element that was considered to be part of the aggregate of matter. Second, following the Vaibhāṣika school of Abhidharma, the teachings could be considered a unique type of force that was dissociated from both mentality and materiality (*viprayuktasaṃskāra*)—that is, "word" (*nāmakāya*), the peculiar force that allows the meaning of a word to be comprehended. Through extensive citations of the various positions on this issue given in Indian philosophical treatises, Wŏnch'ŭk attempts to substantiate the position of his teacher, Hsüan-tsang, that both proposals are acceptable. Wŏnch'ŭk's treatment illustrates the communality of concerns important to the elites among Buddhist doctrinal exegetes, whether Korean, Chinese, or Indian in national origin, and it demonstrates that Korean Buddhism cannot be considered in isolation from pan-Asian developments.

CHAPTER ONE: PREFACE

To explicate this scripture, a division of four sections should be used: the promotion of the various teachings of Buddhism and the meaning of the title of this scripture; analysis of the essence and themes found in the scripture; an explanation of its place in the canon and its purposes; the actual explication of the text itself.

THE PROMOTION OF THE VARIOUS TEACHINGS OF BUDDHISM AND THE MEANING OF THE TITLE OF THIS SCRIPTURE

I have reflected on the fact that the true nature is extremely profound: while it transcends the varieties of images, it is itself still an image. The complete sound of the Buddha's voice is secretly arcane: while it disseminates all varieties of words, it is not itself a word. This complete sound, then, is just a word, and yet words are left behind. The true nature is not an image, and yet it is bound up with images. Although the principle is quiescent, it can be discussed. "This complete sound, then, is just a word, and yet words are left behind": this is because, although words are disseminated, there is no speech. For this reason, even though Vimalakīrti was silent as an expression of nonduality in the discussion that took place in his bedroom, that nonduality could still be discussed.[80] Similarly, when the three natures[81] were analyzed in the pure palace, the bodhisattva Maitreya explained the true and the mundane while actualizing both. The great being Nāgārjuna discussed emptiness and existence while refuting both. Nevertheless, actualization does not contradict refutation: thus the meaning of "consciousness-only" increases in clarity. Refutation does not contradict actualization: thus the purport of signlessness is thoroughly established. Being both empty and existent properly accomplishes the proposition of the two truths, mundane and absolute. Being neither existent nor empty correlates with the principle of the Middle Way. For this reason, we know that those who are deluded still cling to existence even while talking about emptiness. Those who are awakened thoroughly understand emptiness by analyzing existence. How could the ultimate fountainhead of the Buddhadharma be anything but this?

There are many ways to guide sentient beings to salvation; there is not just one entrance to the principle. For this reason, the King of Dharma, the Buddha, taught three turnings of the dharma wheel. First, for the benefit of those who aspire to the Disciple Vehicle, at the Deer Park in the kingdom of Banaras the Buddha inaugurated the causes and effects that result in either birth-and-death or nirvana. This is the first dharma wheel of the Four Noble Truths. Next, for the benefit of those who undertake the Bodhisattva Vehicle, at the sixteen assemblies, such as Vulture Peak Mountain and so forth, the Buddha proclaimed all the *Perfection of Wisdom* texts. This is the second dharma wheel of signlessness. Finally, for the benefit of those who undertake the All-Encompassing Vehicle, in such pure and defiled realms as the Lotus-Womb World and elsewhere, the Buddha proclaimed the *Explanation of Profound Mysteries* and other scriptures. This is the third dharma wheel of the Mahāyāna of definitive meaning. This is the meaning of the promotion of the teaching by the Thus Come One.[82]

The title of this text, *Explanation of Profound Mysteries Scripture,* is the comprehensive title of the entire text. "Chapter One: Preface" is the separate title of one of its chapters. *Hae* means "to explicate." *Sim* means "extremely deep." *Mil* means "secret." The themes of this scripture illuminate object, practice, and fruition's three types of un-equaledness.[83] Because it explicates such profound doctrines, it is entitled the *Explanation of Profound Mysteries Scripture.*

Sūtra is a Sanskrit word meaning "scripture." In the context of non-Buddhist literature, "scripture" means "enduring." The meaning of the teaching is constant and stable as it "continues on" from ancient times to the present: thus it is called "enduring."

Alternatively, *sūtra* is translated as "thread." The *Dharmaguptaka-vinaya* (The Four-Part Rule of Discipline) states: "A thread strings together flowers and ensures that they will not be dropped."[84] The Great T'ang Tripiṭaka Master Hsüan-tsang translated *"sūtra"* as *ch'i-ching,* which means "corresponding by tallying"—that is, tallying with the principles of the path and corresponding to the spiritual potentials of sentient beings. *"Sūtra"* also has two meanings: first, "to thread"; second, "to take up." "To thread" has the sense of the instructions of the Buddhas and bodhisattvas that respond to sentient beings; "to take up" refers to the sentient beings who are persuaded thereby. Because it includes both of these meanings, a *sūtra* is called a tallying-scripture.

Analyzing the name of this scripture, the two graphs "explanation" and "scripture" allude to the verbalization of the teaching: *abhidhāna.* The words "profound" and "mysteries" refer to the signification of that teaching: *abhidheya.* The title of this scripture was determined by referring to both the verbalization and the signification, for this is the scripture that gives an explanation of the profound mystery. For this reason, among the six types of analysis of Sanskrit compounds, this term *sandhinirmocana* is analyzed as a syntactic compound (*tatpuruṣasamāsa*).[85]

"Chapter One: Preface": "preface" means "causal precedent," for it brings up the causes leading to the preaching of the scripture itself. "Chapter" has the sense of either "typed by class" or "differentiated by class." This indicates that the doctrines that have already been heard and so forth are classified according to type, and the doctrines included in particular chapters differ from one another; such a section is then called a chapter. There are eight chapters in this one text. Because this chapter is at the very beginning, it is called "Chapter One." For this reason, it was called *Explanation of Profound Mysteries Scripture,* "Chapter One: Preface."

ANALYSIS OF THE ESSENCE AND THEMES FOUND IN THE SCRIPTURE

As far as the words "essence and themes" are concerned, "essence" is a general explanation for the essence of the verbalization of the teachings; the word "themes" indicates separately the signification of each of the teachings.

The Great T'ang Tripiṭaka Master Hsüan-tsang outlined five approaches for disclosing the essence of all the holy teachings:

1. Absorb the false and return to the true. This means that the words, sentences, and phonemes of the holy teachings,[86] as well as their sound, have suchness as their essence. For this reason, such scriptures as the *Explanations of Vimalakīrti Scripture* say: "So it is for all sentient beings; so it is for all dharmas."[87]

2. Absorb characteristics and return to consciousness. Briefly, there are two opinions regarding this. The first clarifies the meaning using the three functional divisions of the activity of perception. The self-essence ("self-corroborating function") is called consciousness. The two divisions of noesis and noema together are referred to as the characteristics. For this reason, the first fascicle of the *Treatise on the Completion of Consciousness-Only* says: "Transformation means that consciousness itself evolves into what appears as two divisions; this is because the divisions of noesis and noema both arise out of this self-corroboration."[88] Furthermore, the second fascicle says: "Although the characteristics into which consciousness is transformed are im-

measurable, the consciousnesses that are capable of transformation are of only three distinct types."[89] If one relies on this explanation and explicates this second approach, then characteristic means "appearance"; this is because noesis and noema are both the appearances of consciousness, which is itself the third self-essence division.

The second opinion clarifies the meaning using two divisions: the noetic components are said to be cognition itself, and the noematic component is taken as the characteristics. Therefore, the *Treatise on the Completion of Consciousness-Only* says: "Or, alternatively, the internal consciousness transforms into what seems to be external sense objects."[90] If one's explanation relies on this second opinion, then only the noematic component is meant by "characteristics." But these external characteristics are not separate from internal cognition: this is what is meant by "consciousness only." A comprehensive description of this idea would be: "The collections of words, sentences, and phonemes, as well as sound, are the appearances of consciousness, and for this reason they are called consciousness."[91]

3. Follow the real by means of conventional constructs. As is explained in the *Treatise on the Stages of Yoga Practice* and elsewhere, words are conventional constructs: sound is real.[92] Therefore, there is no autonomous word that is separate from sound and so forth. It is also explained that these previous approaches can each be subdivided into two distinct divisions. As far as the two divisions of the first approach are concerned, the first is the division that absorbs the false and returns to the true: this focuses on truth, not falsity. The second is the division that distinguishes between the true and the false: this focuses on falsity, not truth; for the four dharmas of words, sentences, phonemes, and sound are not suchness. As far as the two divisions of the second approach are concerned, the first is the division that absorbs characteristics to return to consciousness; this focuses only on consciousness, not characteristics. The second is the division that distinguishes between consciousness and characteristics. Now, relying on the explanation given in this land of China, the four dharmas of words, sentences, phonemes, and sound are only characteristics and not consciousness; this is because words, and so forth, are all included in the division of characteristics. As far as the two divisions of the last approach are concerned, the first is the division that follows the real by means of the conventional; this focuses only on the real, not the conventional. The second is the division that distinguishes between

the conventional and the real; this covers both the conventional and the real, for words, sentences, and phonemes are conventional constructs whereas sound is real.

4. The approach of determining the essence with respect to the three dharmas. "Three dharmas" refers to the approach to dharma of the three taxonomies: the aggregates (*skandha*), sense fields (*āyatana*), and elements (*dhātu*). Thus, the first chapter of the *Abhidharmasamuccayavyākhyā* (Commentary to the Compendium of Abhidharma) is entitled the "Three Dharmas Chapter."[93] Since the orthodox position of the exegetes of the Sarvāstivāda school considers sound to be the essence of the teachings, in these three taxonomies sound is included in the aggregate of form (*rūpaskandha*), the sense field of sound (*śabdāyatana*), and the element of sound (*śabdadhātu*). According to the Sautrāntika school, the two types of sound, conventional and real, are considered the essence of the teachings. From the standpoint of the five aggregates, sound is included in the form aggregate. From the standpoint of the sense fields and elements, sound is included in the sense field of sound and the sense field of dharmas (*dharmāyatana*), and in the sound element and the dharma element (*dharmadhātu*). This will be analyzed in detail in the next approach involving dharma listings.

Now, relying on the explanations given in the Mahāyāna, the four dharmas of sound, words, sentences, and phonemes are considered to be the essence. Among the five aggregates, these four dharmas are included in the two aggregates of form and forces (*saṃskāraskandha*); among the sense fields and the elements, these are included in the sense field of sound and the sense field of dharmas, as well as in the sound element and the dharma element. This is because the three dharmas of words, sentences, and phonemes are among the objects of the mind consciousness.

5. The approach that discloses the essence through listings of dharmas. This is subdivided into four separate approaches. First is disclosing the essence through listings of dharmas. Second is the existence or nonexistence of the fundamental thing and its appearances. Third is distinguishing the accumulated manifestations that pass through the mind. Fourth is analyzing whether sounds are the same or different.

As far as the phrase "disclosing the essence through listings of dharmas" is concerned, this means to analyze non-Buddhist teachings. The non-Buddhists of the Sāṃkhya school consider the principle of sound to be the essence of the twenty-five principles. According to

the Vaiśeṣika school, the property of sound is the essence. The non-
Buddhists of the Lokāyata school consider the four great elements of
earth, fire, air, and water to be the essence; this is because everything
has one of these elements for its nature. All the teachers of the Mī-
māṃsā schools take sound as the essence; this is because the sound of
the *Vedas* is permanent: it serves as the absolute measure and manifests
all dharmas.[94]

Turning now to the schools within Buddhism, we shall see that the
teachings vary. The Sarvāstivāda school has a total of seventy-five
dharmas, the meanings of which are as ordinarily explained. As far as
the essence of the teachings is concerned, however, two distinct theories are elucidated in the *Saṃyuktābhidharmahṛdaya* (Topical Heart of
Abhidharma) by Dharmatrāta [c. 300–350], in the *Abhidharmakośa-
bhāṣya* (Treasury of Abhidharma Treatise) by Vasubandhu [c. 400–
480], and in the *Mahāvibhāṣā* (Great Exegesis of Abhidharma) compiled by Kātyāyanīputra and others [c. A.D. 150]. The first is that the
Thus Come One's aggregation of dharma (the teachings of the Buddha) has the aggregate of form as its essence; and therewith this
essence is sound, because sound is included in the aggregate of form.
The other is that the aggregate of forces is the essence of the teachings,
because it includes the dissociated forces of words, sentences, and
phonemes. Because of these two different doctrines, the understanding of all the Buddhist masters of this world is not identical. There are
these three explanations:

1. The orthodox position is that the oral teachings themselves are
the essence. This is because sound is wholesome, while the dissociated
forces of words, sentences, and phonemes are indeterminate. For this
reason, the *Topical Heart of Abhidharma* says:

> Sūtra, Vinaya, and Abhidharma,
> These are called the mundane orthodox teachings,
> The thirty-seven limbs of enlightenment,
> These are called the orthodox teachings of ultimate meaning.[95]

The line-by-line exegesis adds: "The mundane orthodox teachings are
the orthodox teachings that are taught using words."[96]

2. The orthodox position is that the dissociated forces of words,
sentences, and phonemes are the essence. This is because they are the
agents that verbalize the meaning that is taught. For this reason, the
Jñānaprasthāna (Arousing of Knowledge Treatise) says: "QUESTION:

What is the nature of the twelve divisions of the scriptures? ANSWER: The collection of words, the collection of sentences, and the collection of phonemes, in that order."[97]

This is explained in detail there.

3. The orthodox position is that sound as well as the dissociated forces of words, sentences, and phonemes are all considered to be the essence. This view is an extension of the two positions explained previously. Now, if we turn to the first chapter of Hsüan-tsang's new translation of the *Treasury of Abhidharma Treatise,* we find that both of these explanations are outlined—that the essence is sound, or words, sentences, and phonemes; but, in either case, the analysis is the same.[98]

The third chapter of the *Nyāyānusāra* (Treatise That Accords with Reason)[99] narrates the theories of the two masters Dharmatrāta and Kātyāyanīputra; its account also parallels the description found in the *Treasury of Abhidharma Treatise;* and both are in the form of catechetical exchanges. That text, the *Treatise That Accords with Reason,* states: "Although words and teachings are differently named, the teachings include those words. If words and the teachings had separate essences, how would the teachings involve words? Some give this explanation: Basically, it is due to the fact that since there are words, it is then possible to say that there are teachings. For this reason, it would seem that the essence of the teachings is just words. Why is this? First, it is called the Buddha's teachings because the teachings' expression of the meaning accords with reality. Second, the teachings are words because words are the agents that express meaning. It is for these reasons that the essence of the Buddha's teachings is determined to be words. Words are placed at the head of the dissociated forces involving speech and therewith include the dissociated forces of sentences and phonemes."[100]

The third chapter of the *Abhidharmapiṭakaprakaraṇaśāsana* (Revelation of the Source of the Abhidharma Canon) gives the same explanation as the *Treatise That Accords with Reason.*[101] Tripiṭaka Master Hsüan-tsang's account says: "All the masters of the Western Region (Gandhāra) have handed down this explanation. Vasubandhu's *Treasury of Abhidharma Treatise* and Saṃghabhadra's *Treatise That Accords with Reason* both cover these two explanations, but each arrives at its own conclusion. How is this so? In the most basic sense that sound brings delight to beings, sound can be considered supreme. But if this question is considered from the standpoint of the importance of verbalizing the dharma, then words, sentences, and phonemes must be taken as supreme. Therefore, we know that while the contexts of these two explanations differ, both are permissible."[102] Hence, these two explanations are both correct.

Now, having examined in detail all the treatises, I will compare each of their positions on this question according to the statements in their texts. The idea of the *Treatise That Accords with Reason* takes the orthodox position to be that words, sentences, and phonemes are the essence of the teachings. As its conclusion states, "Therefore, the essence of the Buddha's teachings is definitely words."[103] Acknowledging this, the *Treasury of Abhidharma Treatise* arrives at the same position as the *Treatise That Accords with Reason*. Since the *Treasury of Abhidharma Treatise* neither refutes the view of the *Treatise That Accords with Reason* nor contradicts it, later masters were free to define their positions for themselves; the master of the *Treatise That Accords with Reason* was not shown to have been either superior or inferior.

The orthodox position of the Vaibhāṣika exegetes was that sound is the essence of the teachings. Fascicle 126 of the *Great Exegesis of Abhidharma* states:

QUESTION: "Thus, what is the essence of the Buddha's teachings? Is it language acts or the dissociated forces of words, and so on?"

ANSWER: "It should be explained in this way. Language acts are its essence."

QUESTION: "If this is the case, then how would statements made later be understood? If the Buddha's teachings are explained in this way, then what type of dharma would words be?"

ANSWER: "It is said that the collection of words, the collection of sentences, and the collection of phonemes should be listed in this order, arranged in this order, and connected in this order. . . . These latter items are intended to reveal the function of the Buddha's teachings; they are not intended to point out the self-essence of the Buddha's teachings. What is indicated by words, sentences, and phonemes that list, arrange, and connect is the function of the Buddha's teachings. Some, however, say that the essence of the Buddha's teachings is words, sentences, and phonemes."

QUESTION: "If this is the case, then how should the explanations in this passage be understood? As the *Arousing of Knowledge Treatise* says: 'What are the Buddha's teachings? They are the Buddha's words, addresses, and analyses, the sound of his voice, the range of his speech, his vocal activities, and his vocal expression. These are called the Buddha's teachings.' "[104]

ANSWER: "This explanation is based upon the successive operation of causes. It is like the principle of the successive birth of sons and grandsons in the world. That is to say, language gives rise to words, and words can express meaning. In an explanation of this type, language acts are the essence of the Buddha's teachings. This is because it is the Buddha's ideas as verbalized that are heard by others."[105]

A complete description of the meaning of the teachings would be done along these lines.

QUESTION: But how could the *Treatise That Accords with Reason* not be based on the explanations given in such texts as the *Great Exegesis of Abhidharma*? How would it not rely on the orthodox position of the exegetes of the Sarvāstivāda school?

ANSWER: For Saṃghabhadra, reason was honored as supreme. Therefore, this principle was established independently—that is, words, sentences, and phonemes represent the orthodox position.

EXPLANATION: Within the Sarvāstivāda school, the view that sound is the essence of the teachings is valid, because from the standpoint of the approach that gives listings of dharmas, only the single dharma of sound that belongs to the aggregate of form would be considered the essence. From the standpoint of the rival view that the dissociated forces of words, sentences, and phonemes are the essence, the three dharmas of words, and so on, would be considered the essence. If we were to attempt a synthesis of these two explanations, we would have to consider that these four dharmas together were the essence—that is, sound as well as words, and so on. The orthodox position of the Vaibhāṣika exegetes held that the one dharma of sound was the essence; this was also the standpoint of the Sautrāntikas, who considered sound the essence. Hence, fascicle 14 of the *Treatise That Accords with Reason* refutes the Sautrāntikas: "You should not explain that the collections of words, sentences, and phonemes have sound as their essence."[106] The first fascicle of the *Mahāyānasaṃgrahopanibandhana* (Commentary on the Compendium of Mahāyāna Treatise) by Asaṅga reaches the same conclusion. As that text says: "The view that the words of all the scriptures have language as their own-nature does not accord at all with reason. . . ."[107]

Briefly, there are four of positions on the signification of the teachings. First is the position which maintains falsity and hides truth. This is like the Sarvāstivādins and others who, although they preach the Four Noble Truths, do not advocate suchness. Second is the position that rejects falsity and maintains truth. This is like the teachers of the Sautrāntikas, who reject all false dharmas and maintain that the nature of dharmas is empty. Third is the position that rejects both falsity and truth. This is like Bhāvaviveka [c. 500–570] and others, who reject both conditioned and unconditioned dharmas. Fourth is the position that preserves both truth and falsity. This is like Dharmapāla [c. 530–561] and others, who preserve and establish such concepts as the two truths, the three natures, and so forth. Such concepts will be explained later where they appear in the text.

Alternatively, it is possible to assume that all of the themes covered in Buddhist texts are, briefly, of three types: (1) to analyze themes according to era; (2) to reveal themes by distinguishing texts; (3) to differentiate themes according to the fault they are intended to counteract.

Type 1: To analyze themes according to era. This also is of three types. First is the dharma wheel of the Four Noble Truths, which includes such texts as the four *āgamas*. Although this dharma wheel involves all sections of the canon, the Four Noble Truths are its theme.

Interlinear note: The Sanskrit word *āgama* is translated as *chŏn* ("transmitted"). Thus fascicle 85 of the *Treatise on the Stages of Yoga Practice* states: "When the Buddha was in the south of India, he instituted five *āgamas*. His disciples have progressively transmitted them down to the present; therefore, they are called *āgamas*." This means that apart from the standard four *āgamas* of the northern Hīnayāna schools, there was established separately an *āgama* scripture in one hundred sections. "The four *āgama* are: (1) discourses arranged according to theme (*Saṃyukta*); (2) medium-length discourses (*Madhyama*); (3) long discourses (*Dīrgha*); (4) progressively numbered discourses (*Ekottara*)." This is as is extensively explained in fascicle 85 of the *Treatise on the Stages of Yoga Practice*.[108]

Second is the [dharma wheel of the] signless Mahāyāna. This includes such texts as the *Perfection of Wisdom Scriptures,* which reject the imaginary nature. This type has signlessness for its theme.

Third is the dharma wheel of the Mahāyāna of definitive meaning. This includes texts like this *Explanation of Profound Mysteries Scripture.*

The themes it expounds include such doctrines as the three natures and so forth. These three types of the dharma wheels will be extensively treated in the second fascicle of this scripture.[109]

QUESTION: The theme of all the *Perfection of Wisdom Scriptures* is the clarification of signlessness. How can one distinguish whether the definitive meaning of this *Explanation of Profound Mysteries* is shallow or deep?

Bhāvaviveka explained that scriptures like the *Explanation of Profound Mysteries* analyze mundane things that can be apprehended; they are shallow, not deep. All the *Perfection of Wisdom* texts reveal the supramundane state that cannot be apprehended; they are the most profound of all scriptures.

Dharmapāla and others explained that what was taught during the two time periods of the Mahāyāna dispensation was the principle of signlessness, but this principle was neither shallow nor profound. The reason that the *Explanation of Profound Mysteries Scripture* was said to express the definitive meaning of Mahāyāna is that having classified all the scriptures from the standpoint of the doctrine of the three natures, this scripture was said to be of definitive meaning, for it revealed and explained the principle of signlessness, but this principle was neither shallow nor profound.

QUESTION: How can one know that all the *Perfection of Wisdom* texts belong to the second time period?

EXPLANATION: This meaning is explained in a note to the second fascicle of this scripture.[110]

Type 2: To reveal themes by distinguishing between texts. Although from the standpoint of time periods the themes covered in the teachings might be threefold, each of these time periods includes many texts of its own, and each of these texts is distinguished by the meanings it explains. In such texts as the *Lotus Scripture,* for instance, the one vehicle is the theme.[111] In such texts as the *Explanations of Vimalakīrti Scripture,* the inconceivable liberation is the theme.[112] In such texts as the *Nirvana Scripture,* the Buddha nature is the theme.[113] In such texts as the *Flower Garland Scripture,* the forty-two stages of contemplation practice of the sages and saints are the theme.[114]

In this one text, the *Explanation of Profound Mysteries Scripture,* the three types of unequaledness are the themes that comprise the signification of the teachings. First, the unequaledness of objects includes such things as the two truths, the three natures, and so on. The two truths are the comprehensive objects of the three vehicles. The three natures and other such principles are objects only for bodhisattvas. Second, the unequaledness of practices includes such things as calming and insight and the ten perfections. Calming and insight are the comprehensive practices for the three vehicles. The practice of the ten perfections is the approach to practice appropriate only to bodhisattvas. Third, unequaledness of the three fruitions refers to the fruitions of knowledge, forsaking, and the three bodies of a Buddha. Knowledge and forsaking are bodhi and nirvana; these are the comprehensive fruitions of the three vehicles. The three bodies are obtained only by bodhisattvas.

In this wise, the themes explained by various texts are all different and cannot all be narrated in detail.

Type 3: To differentiate themes according to the fault they are intended to counteract. Although the theme expressed is different in every text, each one explains one meaning. Still, all sentient beings are deluded in regard to the eighty-four thousand approaches to dharma, such as the aggregates, sense fields, and so on. Therefore, in all texts, each according to its own explanation, such dharmas as the aggregates, elements, and sense fields constitute the themes that comprise the signification of the teachings. Now, among the four themes of this *Explanations of Profound Mysteries Scripture,* the theme in which true and false are both preserved is given from the standpoint of analyzing themes according to era and has the definitive meaning as its theme; the theme that reveals themes by distinguishing between texts has the three types of unequaledness as the theme that comprises the signification of the teachings; the theme that differentiates themes according to the fault is intended to counteract the two truths, the three natures, and so on, as the themes that comprise the signification of the teachings. RB

The Life of Sungyŏng

[From *Sung kao-seng chuan* 4:728a]

Sungyŏng was another of the Korean disciples of Hsüan-tsang who drew the ire of K'uei-chi, the monk generally regarded as Hsüan-tsang's orthodox successor. The dispute that set K'uei-chi against Sungyŏng concerns the latter's charge that an inference used by Hsüan-tsang to

establish a key thesis concerning the nature of visual objects was falla-
cious. Sungyŏng criticizes Hsüan-tsang's reasoning in this syllogism
because it involves a fallacy in which two different, though equally
acceptable, reasons lead to contradictory conclusions. Hsüan-tsang asserts that the three elements of form, the sense faculty of the eye, and
visual consciousness are interrelated categories; therefore, visual objects
are not distinct from visual consciousness. Sungyŏng employs a different reason that is not ruled out by the form of Hsüan-tsang's syllogism
to prove the opposite conclusion—that form must be distinct from
visual consciousness because it is classified separately in the list of the
eighteen elements. Since Tsan-ning's account of this dispute is hope-
lessly addled, I have reconstructed it from K'uei-chi's earlier account.[115]

Monk Sungyŏng was from Nangnang (Lo-lang).[116] His clan was
Chinese, but his family's lineage was Korean; for this reason, it is
difficult to ascertain many details about his life. His multiple translations and his studies on the philosophy of language came naturally to
him; this was so even for his scholarship on logic. His comprehension
of the seminal research entrusted to him by Master Hsüan-tsang was
equaled by few Chinese monks. What else if not the power generated
in past lives could have brought about Sungyŏng's competent understanding?

He received via transmission Master Hsüan-tsang's inference[117] regarding the true doctrine of Consciousness-Only and ascertained that
it was an inference that contained the fallacy of an inferential mark
that is inconclusive in that it proves contradictory results.[118] During
the period of Ch'ien-feng [666–667], he tried to apprise Hsüan-tsang
of his position via an envoy on a tributary mission to T'ang, but by
that time Master Hsüan-tsang had been dead for nearly two years.

Hsüan-tsang's syllogism ran as follows:

Thesis: As one type of reality, what are commonly accepted as
visual forms are inseparable from visual consciousness.

Reason: Because they are not included within the category of vision
among the first three of the eighteenfold classification of perception[119]
accepted by us.

Example: Visual consciousness.[120]

It would seem here that the Tripiṭaka Master was constructing his
syllogism with great subtlety; it is not that his great wisdom was
unclear.

Sungyŏng constructed a contradictory thesis:

Thesis: As one type of reality, what are commonly accepted as
visual forms are quite distinct from visual consciousness.

Reason: Because they are not included within the category of visual consciousness among the first three of the eighteenfold classification of perception accepted by us.

Example: The faculty of vision.[121]

In this wise, he skillfully proved the converse idea.

At that time, Ta-sheng K'uei-chi [632–682] studied this syllogism and saw then what Sungyŏng had not understood. In the end, however, he had to accept that this was the view held by the provincial monks regarding cognition. He sighed, saying: "The fame of the Silla Dharma Master Sungyŏng moves T'ang and Tibet, and his scholarship covers both great and small points. His actions honor Kāśyapa by being solely devoted to cultivation of the ascetic practices. His mind emulates Bakkula by constantly seeking to be known for fewness of desires. Since he has mastered even Tangut (Hsi-hsia), his brilliance has spread among the Eastern Barbarians. His fame and virtue are daily renewed, and both ordained and lay bow to him respectfully. Although other ecclesiastical eminences are not few, these foreigners praise him as being extraordinary for showing that this inference of Hsüan-tsang's does result in the fallacy of allowing a contradictory thesis to be proved."[122] What Master K'uei-chi meant was that these provincials, with their agitated and keen wit, impudently assail Master Hsüan-tsang. Amidst this delusion, an opportunity will arise to vindicate the meaning of the Tripiṭaka Master. Alas, this did not prove to be so.

In his native country, Sungyŏng wrote a number of works. The perspective of those works that have also circulated in China is that of the definitive teachings of Mahāyāna of the Fa-hsiang (Dharmalakṣaṇa) school. After seeing the passage in the *Flower Garland Scripture* that "upon the initial activation of the thought of enlightenment Buddhahood is already achieved,"[123] he then ridiculed this scripture and would not have faith in it.

Others say that once he stretched out his arms and legs and ordered his disciples to support him and lower him to the ground. The ground then was rent asunder; Sungyŏng's body suddenly sank, and in that very body he fell into hell. Today there is still a pit over ten feet wide there, and the cavity is virtually bottomless. It is called Sungyŏng Naraka.[124] RB

The Life of T'aehyŏn
[From *Samguk yusa* 4:208–209]

The founder of the Yogācāra school, the venerable T'aehyŏn, resided in Yongjang Monastery on Mount South. There he would circumambulate the sixteen-foot stone image of Maitreya, whereupon the image would turn its face toward him. Wise, discriminate, and nimble, T'aehyŏn's decision was clear. Generally, the doctrine of the Fa-hsiang school was mysterious and profound and difficult to analyze. Hence the Chinese poet Po Chü-i [772–846] could not fathom it and said, "The doctrine of Dharmalakṣaṇa (which holds that all is mind in its ultimate truth) is too profound to be mastered, and the science of logical reasoning defies analysis." It was indeed difficult for the learned to study. But being well versed in all teachings, T'aehyŏn alone was able to detect errors and elucidate the subtle and arcane. Therefore Korean students all followed his teachings, and Chinese scholars took him as their model.

There was a drought in the twelfth year of T'ien-pao, *kyesa* [753], and King Kyŏngdŏk called the master to the palace and had him lecture on the *Golden Glow Scripture* and pray for rain. One day, at the observation of abstinence, the master opened his alms bowl, but the official was tardy in bringing the pure water and was scolded by his supervisor.

The official replied, "The palace well has dried up, and I was forced to go a good distance for water."

The master reprimanded, "Why then did you not tell me before?" At the day lecture, the master raised the censer silently in his hands, and cool water gushed forth from the well to the height of a flagpole, a full seventeen fathoms. The well was named the Well of Golden Glow.

The master styled himself the "monk of the green hills." PL

T'aehyŏn: Study Notes to the *Treatise on the Completion of Consciousness-Only*
[From *Hsü Tsang-ching* 80:1a–3a]

In this passage from the introduction to his commentary on the *Treatise on the Completion of Consciousness-Only*, T'aehyŏn examines the controversy between the Indian philosophical schools of Vijñaptimātratā-Yogācāra, as represented by Dharmapāla, and Svātantrika-Mādhyamika, as represented by Bhāvaviveka. Both differ on a variety of fundamental issues concerning absolute and phenomenal realities. As far as their positions on the phenomenal realm are concerned, Bhāvaviveka asserts that, from the standpoint of the absolute, all phenomena (the dharmas) are empty and illusory; Dharmapāla declares instead that all dharmas have an empty and nonempty aspect, both of which are equally valid from the standpoint of absolute truth. Concerning the absolute itself, Dharmapāla states that the absolute, suchness, is distinct from both existence and nonexistence; Bhāvaviveka argues that since the emptiness of phenomenal objects is itself suchness, the absolute is directly associated with the phenomenal world. Finally, Dharmapāla asserts the ultimate reality of consciousness, which is considered to exist in reality. By giving a positive description to ultimate reality, the Yogācārins thus accept the validity of positive descriptions of truth. Bhāvaviveka and the Mādhyamika school, however, assert that even positive concepts—such as the summum bonum of Buddhist spiritual culture, nirvana—can only be considered to exist from the standpoint of mundane truth; emptiness alone is ultimately real. Their ultimate position is therefore fundamentally negative. Finally, T'aehyŏn explores the different implications of this controversy as given by such Korean exegetes as Wŏnch'ŭk and Sungyŏng.

The outline of this treatise is divided into three sections: revelation of the doctrinal themes and disclosure of its essence; analysis of the name of the title; explanation of the meaning of the text.

As far as the revelation of the doctrinal themes is concerned, there are two positions. First, discussing the *Perfection of Wisdom,* Bhāvaviveka [c. 500–570] and others mention the concepts of compounded things, uncompounded things, mundane existence, and true emptiness. As is stated in a verse from Bhāvaviveka's *Karatalaratna* (Jewel in Hand Treatise):

> From the standpoint of the true nature, compounded things are
>   empty,
> Like an illusion, because they are produced through conditions,
> While uncompounded things are unreal,
> For they are nonarising, like sky flowers.[125]

Second, basing themselves on the *Explanation of Profound Mysteries Scripture,* Dharmapāla [c. 530–561] and others have said that the existence of all dharmas is both empty and nonempty.[126] As it is said in the *Madhyāntavibhāgakārikā* (Verses on the Middle and the Extremes):

Discrimination of what is unreal exists.
In regard to this the dichotomy of subject and object is
    nonexistent.
In unreal discrimination, there is only emptiness;
In regard to this dichotomy, there is only this unreal
    discrimination.[127]

Some explain that these two positions on the controversy over
the nature of true existence refer to such passages as are found in the
Exposition of the Scripture on the Buddha Stage (Buddhabhūmisūtropadeśa),
where it is explained that after one thousand years there will develop a
controversy in the Mahāyāna over emptiness and existence.[128] What is
this controversy? As far as compounded things are concerned, the
Treatise on the Completion of Consciousness-Only says: "Self and dharmas
do not exist; emptiness and consciousness do not nonexist. Leaving
behind existence and nonexistence, conform to the Middle Path."[129]
This refutes the imaginary nature of dharmas and maintains the remaining two natures of conditional dependency and perfection. The
Jewel in Hand Treatise says: "Just as the eye faculty is explained as
nonexistent in order to remove the defect of falling into the extreme
of annihilationism, so also is it explained as existent in order to remove
the defect of falling into the extreme of annihilationism. That is to
say, the eye faculty and so forth, which arise through the power of
cause and conditions, are included in the mundane truth and have an
own-nature that is existent. They are not the same as sky flowers,
which are completely devoid of any semblance of existence. It is
merely from the standpoint of the true nature that they are substanti-
ated as being empty."[130] This maintains the validity of the mundane
truth while ensuring that from the standpoint of the absolute truth all
dharmas are empty.

Furthermore, with reference to uncompounded things, the explanations of the two are not the same. Dharmapāla Bodhisattva opposed
Bhāvaviveka's position that the two emptinesses of self and dharmas
are identical to truth. As the *Treatise on the Completion of Consciousness-
Only* says: "The two emptinesses of self and dharmas[131] revealed
through the nature are not perfected reality. This is because the nature
of true suchness is separate from existence and separate from nonexistence."[132]

The Bodhisattva Bhāvaviveka countered the descriptions of the two
emptinesses given according to the position of Dharmapāla. As the

Jewel in Hand Treatise says: "That state which is merely devoid of all objectivity is proved to be true suchness."[133]

It is not merely in their disclosure of the essence that these two explanations are not the same; there is also considerable controversy as to whether the ultimate meaning is existent or nonexistent. As the *Treatise on the Completion of Consciousness-Only* states: "If this consciousness were nonexistent, there would then be no mundane truth. Rejecting the two truths is the perverse clinging to emptiness."[134] The *Jewel in Hand Treatise* says: "The Buddha explained that . . . nirvana exists from the standpoint of mundane truth. This is like the Buddha's explanation that there are apparitional beings. Since these are permitted to exist, this explanation is not faulted as being in violation of this proposition. It is from the standpoint of the true nature that the existence of the cessation resulting from intellectual comprehension is rejected."[135] This can be considered verification.

Wŏnch'ŭk and others relate that this was no controversy over the nature of real existence. They say there was no controversy whatsoever between the two teachers, because Bhāvaviveka does not accept that the absolute truth is nonexistence. As the *Jewel in Hand Treatise* says:

> The words "they do not exist," are merely intended to refute the claim that compounded things have a real nature. Once this function is expended, one does not then go on to refer to their nonexistence. Just as in worldly language the words "that is not white lustring" do not necessarily indicate the lustring is black.
>
> Furthermore, opposing this view, an opponent raises this difficulty. This was said by him: From the standpoint of the true nature, if the fact that all compounded things cannot be apprehended is your position, then you reject the existence of everything and fall into wrong views. In answer to this, our position is that "emptiness, lack of self-nature, and illusory revelation are synonymous." It is not that all things are rejected as nonexistent.[136]

For Dharmapāla, absolute truth also does not allow existence. As his *Ta-sheng kuang po lun shih-lun* (Exegesis to the Mahāyāna's Expanded Hundred Verses Treatise) states: "In the present, it is also not correct to claim that the absolute truth exists. This is because it arises from conditions, because it is like a magical illusion and so forth."[137] It also explains emptiness with the words: "It is a negative form of discourse, not a positive form. It is not merely the emptiness of existence; it is also the emptiness of emptiness."[138] This is discussed extensively there.

The Yogācārin who is rebutted by the *Jewel in Hand Treatise* is not Dharmapāla: he is the same Yogācārin whom Bodhisattva Dharmapāla rebuts in his *Exegesis to the Mahāyāna's Expanded Hundred Verses Treatise*. Hence this can be considered verification.

Master Sungyŏng [fl. 666–667] and others maintained that this was a controversy over nonexistence. They explained that these two descriptions might be conflicting in their expressions, but their meaning is identical. It is like disputing over the fact that the bottom of a stupa is broad while it narrows toward the top: it is only through accepting the one feature that the other feature is also possible. The position of Dharmapāla perforce brings up the imaginary nature of dharmas without indicating that it is separate from the four antinomical propositions.[139] This is because the natures of emptiness, existence, and so forth are all imaginary, and because these two natures have a sublime existence that is not completely nonexistent.

For this reason, this explanation is given: The two emptinesses of self and dharmas are not real. Emptiness, considered from one standpoint, is also nonexistent. This is because the elimination of the road of emptiness and existence is called true suchness. Bhāvaviveka Bodhisattva posited existence that was mundane, nonexistence that was separate from everything, and true nonexistence that distinguished everything. This is because the mundane is also nonexistent. The sublime nonexistence of the two natures of emptiness and existence cannot be apprehended. Hence if one only rejects existence, one can then gain nonexistence; but by also rejecting nonexistence, it is said that the state achieved cannot be apprehended.

"Unapprehensible" means that it is separate from the four antinomical propositions. This is because Asaṅga says in his *Po-jo lun:* "The four antinomical propositions are all associated with grasping at dharmas."[140] According to this logic, the words of Master Wŏnhyo [617–686] and others might be in conflict, but their ideas are identical. These differences in the words were designed so that disciples of dull faculties in the latter dharma-ending age will skillfully give rise to understanding through examination of this controversy.

Now I take the doctrinal themes of this treatise to be the three aspects of sense realm, manifestation, and fruition, which is the Middle Way of Consciousness-Only as narrated by Dharmapāla. And this treatise is included in the Bodhisattva *piṭaka* (in the twofold division of the canon), in the Abhidharma (in the threefold division of the canon), and among the expository scriptures (*upadeśasūtra* of the twelve divisions of the scriptures).[141] RB

Belief in the Pure Land

Early Buddhism in Silla, as noted earlier, was used by reigning monarchs as a political tool. The conversion effort by Wŏngwang and Chajang contributed to the establishment of unified Silla and a new moral system, but their audience was limited to the nobility in the capital. The sixteen-foot Śākyamunibuddha statue (574) and the nine-story stupa (645) in Hwangnyong Monastery (566–645) demonstrated the splendor of court Buddhism as a means of controlling society. The purpose of the Assembly of One Hundred Seats (*Paekkojwa hoe*) at Hwangnyong Monastery, where the *Scripture on Benevolent Kings* was recited and commented upon, was not so much to propagate the faith or convert the people but to pray for the Buddha's protection of the country and to enhance the ruler's prestige. Doctrinal development after the unification was too esoteric and abstract to serve the people as a guide to salvation. The form of Buddhism that fulfilled their needs was belief in the Pure Land and Avalokiteśvara ("He Who Observes the Sounds of the World").

Belief in the Pure Land of Maitreya was prevalent among the nobility during the Three Kingdoms period (some twenty images of Maitreya remain from this period), while belief in Amitāyus ("Infinite Life") was prevalent around the time of unification. The worship of Amitāyus was intended for the people, as only faith and devotion were deemed necessary to ensure that one would be reborn in the Sukhāvatī ("Happy Land"), where Amitābha ("Infinite Light"), or Amitāyus (Amita is a short form), dwells. Thus its appeal lay in its promise of salvation to all people regardless of class, wealth, sex, or age. Viewing this world as a sea of sorrow, it sought rebirth in the future.

Belief in the Sound Observer stressed that the bodhisattva's mercy would save people from suffering and calamity. The spread of Amitāyus worship fostered the worship of the Sound Observer, as believers sought not only rewards in this world but also deliverance and enlightenment in the future. Stories of miracles performed by the Sound Observer were joyfully transmitted from mouth to mouth. Faith in

Amitāyus and the Sound Observer was preached by monks who went among the people to proselytize. Unaided by the court or the nobility, they preached on the roadside or in the marketplace, making Buddhism a popular faith for the first time in Silla.

Monks active around the time of unification include Hyesuk, Hyegong, Taean, and Wŏnhyo. Hyesuk, who had formerly been a *hwarang* and lived in Chŏksŏn village in Angang, sliced the flesh from his thigh to admonish Lord Kudam for indulging in pleasures. He was summoned to court by King Chinp'yŏng (579–632), but he declined. Hyesuk built Amita Monastery for the people and taught them to utter Amita's name. The slave girl Ungmyŏn is said to have been transported to the Pure Land while invoking the name of Amita in the same monastery.[142] Hyegong, the son of an old maid, is said to have carried a basket, the common people's tool for earning their livelihood. Drinking, dancing, and singing were the expedient means he adopted to teach and convert people of inferior capacity. Hyegong was sought out by Wŏnhyo for consultation on doctrinal matters.[143] Taean, too, used unusual means to teach the people: he would beat on a copper bowl in the marketplace shouting "Taean, taean!" ("Great peace!"). He also shunned the privileged, as shown in Wŏnhyo's biography. Wŏnhyo was both a great scholar-monk and a friend of the people, respected by court and populace alike. He showed how one can practice one's faith so as to overcome the contradiction between *saṃvṛti-satya* (secular, relative truth) and *parmārtha-satya* (absolute truth). Leading a life different from that of the regular clergy, Wŏnhyo frequented the taverns or meditated in the wilderness. Some failed to understand his true intention, which was to mingle with the masses and indoctrinate them in the faith. Putting aside the distinction between absolute and relative truth, he would wander about striking a gourd inscribed with the word "unhindered." He also taught that rebirth in Amitāyus' Pure Land was easier than in Maitreya's Tuṣita Heaven—belief in the former, he claimed, was a faith for the common folk. PL

Monks Hyesuk and Hyegong
[From *Samguk yusa* 4:89–91]

Monk Hyesuk was formerly a member of the *hwarang* of Knight Hose. When Knight Hose resigned, Hyesuk returned to Chŏksŏn village for twenty years.

One day Lord Kudam, a *hwarang,* came to hunt in the suburb of Monk Hyesuk's hermitage. Hyesuk went out, held the lord's reins, and asked him if he might join him in the hunt. The lord agreed. Doffing his robe, Hyesuk ran this way and that side by side with the lord, who was pleased. The two then sat down to rest and roast game of which Hyesuk partook without aversion. "I have some delicious meat. May I serve it to you?" asked Hyesuk in front of the lord.

"Very well," replied the lord.

Rejecting a plea from onlookers, Hyesuk sliced a piece of flesh from his thigh and placed it on a tray, while his clothes dripped with blood.

"What are you doing?" the astonished lord asked.

Hyesuk replied, "I thought you a benevolent man whose compassion reached to other living things. Thus I followed you. Now I see that you indulge in butchering other living beings for your own pleasure. This can hardly be the way of a benevolent gentleman. You are not my kind." With these words, the master rose from his seat and departed.

Ashamed, the lord looked at Hyesuk's plate, which was still filled with meat. Marveling, he returned and told the story to the court. King Chinp'yŏng [579–632] sent a messenger to welcome the monk. Hyesuk purposely lay down on a woman's bed, and the messenger, thinking it unclean, turned back. But before he had gone seven or eight *ri* he encountered Hyesuk. When asked where he had been, the master replied, "I have been officiating at the seven-day abstinence offering in the capital. Now I am on my way home." The messenger reported the story, had a person locate the house of the patron, and found that the monk had indeed been there.

Shortly thereafter, Hyesuk died, and the villagers buried him to the east of Yi county. At the time a fellow villager, who was coming down from the west of the hill, met Hyesuk on the way and asked him where he was going. "I have lived here for a long time; now I would like to tour other places." After going about half a *ri* further, he mounted a cloud and vanished. Upon reaching the east of the hill, the traveler told the story to the mourners and dug up the grave, which yielded only one of Hyesuk's sandals.

Hyesuk's monastery is to the north of Angang county, where he lived. There also stands a stupa.

The childhood name of the monk Hyegong, the son of an old woman slave in the house of Lord Ch'ŏnjin, was Ujo. When the lord was about to die of boils, visitors filled the street. At the time Ujo was seven and asked his mother, "What has brought so many guests to this house?"

His mother replied, "Our master's illness is critical. How can you not know this?"

The boy replied, "I can cure him." The mother thought this strange and reported it to the lord, who sent a servant for the boy. The boy sat silently at the foot of the sick man's couch. In a short while his abscess burst, but the lord thought this a coincidence and took no special note of it.

As a youth, Ujo tamed the lord's falcon, thus earning his master's approval. The lord's younger brother was appointed to a provincial post and obtained from the lord a good falcon to take along with him. One night, however, the lord thought of his falcon and decided to send Ujo to bring it back early the next morning. Ujo divined his master's intent, brought the bird back, and presented it to the lord at dawn. Greatly astounded, the lord recalled the boy's wonderworking and realized that his power was unfathomable. Stepping down into the courtyard and bowing, he said, "Not knowing that a great sage was living in my house, I abused him with harsh words and rude acts. How can I atone for my sins? Henceforth please become my teacher and guide me."

His spiritual powers revealed, Ujo became a monk and changed his name to Hyegong. He lived in a small monastery, often drank wine like a madman, and sang and danced through the streets with a basket for carrying dirt slung over his shoulder. Hence he was called "the basket-carrying monk" and his monastery was known as Pugae ("Basket"). Since he would often descend into the monastery well and not emerge for two or three months, the well was named after him. Whenever he came out, an azure-clad boy would precede him, and his colleagues took this as a sign. His robe was never wet when he emerged.

Hyegong spent his later years at Hangsa Monastery ("Ganges' Sands," now Oŏ Monastery in Yŏngil). At the time, Wŏnhyo was compiling commentaries on scriptures and would consult Hyegong on doubtful points, or the two would amuse themselves with banter. . . .

Once, when the lord was picnicking in the mountains, he found the master's corpse mouldering and infested with maggots. After a long period of mourning the lord returned to the city to find the master drunk and singing and dancing. . . .

Myŏngnang, founder of the Divine Seal school, built Diamond Monastery and celebrated its completion attended by eminent monks. Only Hyegong was absent, but when Myŏngnang burned incense and prayed, Hyegong appeared. He came through a downpour, but his robe was not wet nor were his feet soiled with mud. He said, "You called me earnestly, so I am here."

Hyegong's miraculous traits were many. He breathed his last floating in midair, leaving behind innumerable relics. Once he glanced at the three treatises by Seng-chao [374–414] and observed, "These I wrote long ago." Hyegong was indeed a reincarnation of Seng-chao. PL

Ungmyŏn
[From *Samguk yusa* 5:217–219]

During the reign of King Kyŏngdŏk [742–765], a group of male devotees in Kangju set their minds on the Western Paradise, erected Amitābha Monastery on the border of Kangju, and prayed for ten thousand days. At that time a female slave, called Ungmyŏn, in the house of *Agan* Kwijin would follow her master to the middle courtyard and stand there chanting the name of Amitābha. Taking offense at this practice of Ungmyŏn, which was too exalted for her station, her master bade her pound two piculs of grain a night. She would finish her work in the early evening, go to the monastery, and call upon the name of Amitābha diligently day and night. She planted two poles, one to the left of the courtyard and one to the right, gouged holes in her hands, and passed a straw rope through them. This Ungmyŏn tied to the poles, and then moved her joined palms to the left and to the right in order to spur herself on.

Then a voice called to her, "Ungmyŏn, enter the main hall and invoke Amitābha." The worshipers then urged her to enter and devote herself to prayer as usual. Soon the sound of heavenly music was heard from the west, and the slave girl soared high through the roof beam and headed west to the outskirts of the town. There her mortal body fell away, and she changed into a true Buddha. Seated on a lotus and emitting brilliant rays of light, she slowly disappeared to the sound of music. The hole in the hall remains.

According to the lives of monks, Monk P'alchin, a reincarnation of the Sound Observer, formed a society of one thousand, which was divided into two groups—one called "Labor" and the other "Spiritual Cultivation." A supervisor among the first could not fulfill the commandments and was reborn as a cow at Pusŏk Monastery. While carrying the scriptures, the cow, through the power of these scriptures, was reincarnated as Ungmyŏn, a slave in the household of Kwijin. One day she went on an errand to Mount Haga, where in a dream she was stirred to aspire to enlightenment. The house of Kwijin was near Amitābha Monastery, which had been erected by Dharma Master Hyesuk. Whenever Kwijin went there to pray, Ungmyŏn followed him and invoked the name of Amitābha. . . . After nine years of devotion, on the twenty-first day of the first month of the fourteenth year, *ŭlmi* [8 February 755], during her worship she soared through the roof and reached Mount Sobaek, where she let fall one of her sandals. There she built Bodhi Monastery. Because she had shed her earthly form at the foot of the mountain, there she built the second Bodhi Monastery, calling the hall "Ungmyŏn's Ascension Hall." The hole in the roof is about ten arms' lengths wide, but a storm or thick snow could not wet the inside. Later, one of her followers covered the hole with a gilt stupa and recorded her miraculous deeds on it. Even today the tablet and stupa still stand.

After the departure of Ungmyŏn, Kwijin donated his house, where once a Buddha had lived, and made it into a monastery, named it Pŏbwang (Dharma King), and made offerings of fields and slaves. Long after, it fell into ruin and degenerated into a hill.

Great Master Hoegyŏng, together with *Sŭngsŏn* Yu Sŏk and *Sogyŏng* Yi Wŏnjang, made a vow to rebuild the monastery. The master, personally responsible for the construction, carried the lumber. In a dream an old man gave him one pair each of hemp and arrowroot sandals, led him to the old shrine, and taught him Buddhist doctrine. The master felled the trees and completed the construction in five years. More slaves were attached to the monastery, and it soon became famous in the southeast. Hoegyŏng was then called a reincarnation of Kwijin. PL

Kwangdŏk

[From *Samguk yusa* 5:219–220]

During the reign of King Munmu [661–681], the monks Kwangdŏk and Ŏmjang formed a warm friendship, vowing day and night that the first of them to attain the Promised Land would inform the other. Kwangdŏk retired to West Punhwang-ri and made sandals out of rushes to support his wife and children; Ŏmjang built a hermitage on South Peak and followed the plow.

One day, as the sun cast a crimson shadow and stillness settled on the pine grove, a voice spoke to Ŏmjang from outside: "I'm going to the West. Fare you well, but follow me soon." Going out, Ŏmjang heard heavenly music in the clouds and saw a bright light gathering below them. When he went to visit his friend the following morning, he learned that Kwangdŏk had died. Together with the widow he buried his friend's remains and then asked the widow, "Now that your husband is dead, will you live with me?"

The widow agreed. When Ŏmjang was about to embrace her at night, she warned, "Your seeking of the Western Paradise is like looking for a fish in a tree."

Startled, Ŏmjang asked, "You and Kwangdŏk were husband and wife. Why can you not be mine?"

The widow replied, "My late husband and I lived together for more than ten years, but he never shared his bed with me. Each night we knelt erect, invoked the name of Amitābha, and mastered the sixteen meditations expounded in the *Meditation on the Buddha Amitāyus Scripture*.[144] When the bright moon shone through the window, we sat cross-legged. Such was his devotion. Where else could he have gone but to the Pure Land? A journey of a thousand *ri* is determined by the first step. You are headed toward the east, not toward the west."

Overwhelmed with shame, Ŏmjang went to Dharma Master Wŏn-hyo, begging to be taught the essentials of faith. Wŏnhyo taught him the method of contemplation. Ŏmjang then cleansed himself, re-pented and cultivated meditation, and went to the Western Paradise.
. . .

Kwangdŏk's wife, the slave of Punhwang Monastery, was one of the nineteen bodies displayed by the Bodhisattva Sound Observer.[145] A poem by Kwangdŏk goes:

> O Moon,
> Go to the West, and
> Pray to Amitāyus
> And tell

That there is one who
Adores the judicial throne, and
Longs for the Pure Land,
Praying before him with folded hands.

Would he leave me out
When he fulfills the forty-eight vows? PL

Divination Ceremonies

As we have seen, monks were active in the Silla capital and the nearby countryside to bridge the gap between the classes and lead many to salvation. Then, from the middle of the eighth century on, monks began to arrive from distant provinces to convert the people. The representative figure is Chinp'yo (fl. 742–780), who was born in Kimje in North Chŏlla and used divination as a means of conversion. He emphasized the rules of prohibition and confession by divining good and evil deeds in the past, present, and future—his way of adapting Buddhism to indigenous beliefs and practices. Chinp'yo's method, originating with Wŏngwang, entailed throwing one hundred and eighty-nine bamboo sticks in the air and divining the relative merit or demerit of one's actions by observing how the sticks fell. Chinp'yo also taught people to believe in Maitreya and Kṣitigarbha (Guardian of the Earth), who vowed to deliver everybody from the suffering world. In Chinp'yo's system, Kṣitigarbha was an attendant of Maitreya; in Koryŏ he was worshiped independently and, together with the Sound Observer, became the bodhisattva closest to the people. Chinp'yo's teaching spread far and wide, extending to the Diamond Mountains; it was continued in the Koryŏ period by his disciples.

Chinp'yo
[From *Samguk yusa* 4:200–202]

The monk Chinp'yo was a native of Mangyŏng county in Wansan province (now Chŏnju); his father was Chinnaemal; his mother was Kilbo, surnamed Chŏng. At the age of twelve Chinp'yo became a monk, studying under the Dharma Master Sungje[146] of Kŭmsan Monastery. Once the master said, "Early in my life I studied under the T'ang Tripitaka Master Shan-tao [618–681] and then went to Mount Wu-t'ai, where I received the five commandments from the bodhisattva Mañjuśrī who appeared in response to my prayers."

Chinp'yo asked, "How long must one cultivate the way before receiving the commandments?"

"If you are sincere, you can receive them within a year," answered the master.

Chinp'yo then made pilgrimages to famous mountains and settled at Pursaŭi Monastery on Mount Sŏngye, where he worshiped the Buddha with perfect sincerity of body, mouth, and mind and performed the repentance rite of abandoning the body (*mangsinch'am*). [Three graphs are missing at this point.] He struck his forehead, the elbows, and the knees against a rock for seven nights, his knees and elbows broken and blood raining down on the rock, but there was no response. Resolved to cast off his body, he continued for seven more days. Then, at the time of the Dragon [7–9 A.M.], on the fifteenth day of the third month of the twenty-eighth year of K'ai-yüan, *kyŏngjin* [15 April 740],[147] the Guardian of the Earth Bodhisattva appeared to Chinp'yo and gave him the commandments. He was then twenty-three.

Wishing to behold Maitreya, Chinp'yo continued his practices and moved to Yŏngsan Monastery where he was diligent and courageous as before. At last Maitreya appeared to him, gave him a copy of the *Chan-ch'a shan-o ye-pao ching* (Scripture That Divines the Requital of Wholesome and Unwholesome Actions)[148] in two rolls and one hundred and eighty-nine divination sticks as fruits of his vigorous efforts, and said: "The eighth stick represents the newly obtained wondrous commandments; the ninth, all the prohibitions. These two sticks are my finger bones, while the others are made of sandalwood, signifying all depravity. These are rafts to ferry the suffering across to nirvana. Use them to spread the dharma and save the masses!"

Following Maitreya's instruction, Chinp'yo proceeded to Kŭmsan Monastery and set up a platform and taught the Buddha's truth. In its refinement and dignity, his platform was unparalleled in the period of the degenerate dharma.

After transforming the people by religion, when he arrived in Asŭlla province on his tour, the fish and turtles of the sea formed a bridge between the islands and led him to the underwater world, where he expounded dharma and gave commandments to those who dwelt there. This occurred on the fifteenth day of the second month of the eleventh year of T'ien-pao, *imjin* [5 March 752]. Another version gives the sixth year of Yüan-ho [811], which is erroneous.

King Kyŏngdŏk invited Chinp'yo to his palace, received from him the bodhisattva ordination, and gave him seventy-seven thousand bags of tax grain. The courtiers and the queen's family also received the commandments, donating five hundred rolls of silk and fifty ounces of gold. Chinp'yo distributed these donations to various mountain monasteries for the support of Buddhist services. His bones are now enshrined at Paryŏn Monastery, near the place where he had given the commandments to the fish and turtles.

His chief disciples included Yŏngsim, Pojong, Sinbang, Ch'ejin, Chinhae, Chinsŏn, and Sŏkch'ung, all of whom became the founders of monasteries. Chinp'yo transmitted the sticks to Yŏngsim, who resided on Mount Songni, as a worthy successor. His platform was different from that used for divination with six tops,[149] but was patterned on the original rules transmitted in the mountain. PL

Copying Scriptures

Buddhists copied scriptures to accumulate merit and pray for salvation. This act of devotion was popular in Silla times, but until recently the oldest example of a scripture copied by hand was part of the *Ta pao-chi ching* (*Ratnakūṭa sūtra*; *T.* 11, no. 310), written in gold on purple paper, dating from 1006. It consists of one roll and is preserved in Japan. But in 1979, two scrolls of the *Flower Garland Scripture* copied on white paper in black ink were discovered and designated a national treasure. One scroll comprises chapters 1–10; the other, chapters 41–50. Thus the copied scripture originally consisted of eight scrolls, each containing ten chapters of the new translation (695–699) of the *Flower Garland Scripture* by Śikṣānanda (652–710). Each scroll, consisting of thirty white papers joined together, is fourteen meters long and twenty-nine centimeters wide. In order to fit ten chapters into one scroll, each line consists of thirty-four instead of the usual seventeen logographs. The copyists used a number of new logographs current in Empress Wu's times. Written in *idu* transcription, the following is the postscript in fourteen lines that provides the dates, tells who made the vows to copy the scripture, and offers related rules and rites.

Postface to the *Flower Garland Scripture*
[Copied in 754–755]

The copying began on the first day of the eighth month of the thirteenth year of T'ien-pao, *kabo* [23 August 754], and was completed on the fourteenth day of the second month of the following year, *ŭlmi* [30 March 755].

One who made a vow to copy the scripture is Dharma Master Yŏngi of Hwangnyong Monastery. His purposes were to repay the love of his parents and to pray for all living beings in the dharma realm to attain the path of the Buddha.

The scripture is made as follows: First scented water is sprinkled around the roots of a paperbark mulberry tree to quicken its growth; the bark is then peeled and pounded to make paper with a clean surface. The copyists, the artisans who make the centerpiece of the scroll, and the painters who draw the images of buddhas and bodhisattvas all receive the bodhisattva ordination and observe abstinence. After relieving themselves, sleeping, eating, or drinking, they take a bath in scented water before returning to the work. Copyists are adorned with new pure garments, loose trousers, a coarse crown, and a deva crown. Two azure-clad boys sprinkle water on their heads and . . . azure-clad boys and musicians perform music. The processions to the copying site are headed by one who sprinkles scented water on their path, another who scatters flowers, a dharma master who carries a censer, and another dharma master who chants Buddhist verses. Each of the copyists carries incense and flowers and invokes the name of the Buddha as he progresses.

Upon reaching the site, all take refuge in the Three Jewels (the Buddha, the Dharma, and the Order), make three bows, and offer the *Flower Garland Scripture* and others to buddhas and bodhisattvas. Then they sit down and copy the scripture, make the centerpiece of the scroll, and paint the buddhas and bodhisattvas. Thus, azure-clad boys and musicians cleanse everything before a piece of relic is placed in the center.

Now I make a vow that the copied scripture will not break till the end of the future—even when a major chilicosm is destroyed by the three calamities, this scripture shall be intact as the void. If all living beings rely on this scripture, they shall witness the Buddha, listen to his dharma, worship the relic, aspire to enlightenment without backsliding, cultivate the vows of the Universally Worthy Bodhisattva, and achieve Buddhahood. [The names of nineteen persons follow: a papermaker, eleven copyists, two makers of the centerpiece, four painters, and the writer of the scripture's title.] PL

CHAPTER SIX

Poetry and Song

Even in ancient times, poetry and music played an important part in the daily lives of the Korean people. This love for song and dance impressed the ancient Chinese, as is attested by their early records. Little of the earliest flowering of Korean poetry has survived, however, owing to the unreliability of oral transmission and the lack of a unified writing system.

Broadly speaking, the word "*hyangga*" designates Korean songs as opposed to Chinese poetry (*si*), but the term specifically covers twenty-five extant poems produced from the seventh to the tenth centuries. (A collection of *hyangga* compiled by Monk Taegu during the reign of Queen Chinsŏng [887–897] is now lost.) In the absence of a native system of writing, the Koreans devised the *idu* system to provide particles and inflections for Chinese texts. However, in the *hyangga* the *hyangch'al* system is used to transcribe entire Korean sentences with Chinese logographs. Some graphs were used for their meaning (nouns); others transcribed verbs, particles, and inflections. While the *idu* is said to have been systematized by Sŏl Ch'ong, the creator of the *hyangch'al* system is not known.

The songs and music of the Three Kingdoms were closely allied to the religious life of people living in clan-tribal societies. Both songs and music were essential to such rites as the Puyŏ, Koguryŏ, and East Ye worship of heaven or during the sowing and harvest festivals in the south. Earlier songs, originating in shamanist chants, were sung during festivals and rites; they were transmitted orally and had a magic function. Later songs were more lyrical.

Seventeen of the twenty-five *hyangga* are Buddhist in inspiration and content, reflecting certain trends in Silla and early Koryŏ Buddhism. Belief in the Pure Land of Maitreya and Amitāyus is reflected in "Prayer to Amitāyus," "Song of Tuṣita Heaven" (760), and "Requiem"; belief in the Sound Observer is reflected in "Hymn to the Thousand-Eyed Sound Observer." Yŏngjae's "Meeting with Bandits" is perhaps the most difficult of all Silla poems, partly because four graphs are missing in the text and partly also because the poet's symbolic language is polysemous. A recent reading by Kim Wanjin goes: "I cannot see/ The mind's true nature./ The sun has set and birds return to roost./ As the moon rises, I go into the forest./ Even if the transgressing bandit stops me,/ Would I be frightened?/ You have listened to the dharma/ That scorns arms./ But my good deed is nothing/ Compared to the Buddha's might." I offer my own reading here until a more plausible one appears.

The selections also include poems in praise of Silla's elite corps of knights, the *hwarang,* poems with magical powers, and poems on the temporality of man. The "Song of Ch'ŏyong," of shamanist origin, is perhaps the most popular of all *hyangga.* That the dragon, the tutelary spirits of South Mountain, North Mountain, and the earth danced means that actors wearing such masks performed a shamanist exorcism. When the ruler was the chief shaman and bore the title *ch'a-ch'aung,* he was himself the officiator in the exorcism. During his tour of inspection, King Hŏngang perhaps saw performances of a popular dance preserved at Kaeunp'o and revived it; his purpose was to beseech the gods to quell the popular uprisings besetting his kingdom. The evil spirit that transformed itself into a man is symbolic of the corruption that destroyed the fabric of Silla society. Although the last two lines seem to indicate that the song accompanied a dramatic dance with two actors representing good and evil, the Ch'ŏyong dance performed at the temporary capital on Kanghwa Island during the Mongol invasion (1236) appears to be a solo dance. During the Chosŏn dynasty, the Ch'ŏyong dance, combined with the crane dance, became an important court pageant.

Master Yungch'ŏn: "Song of the Comet"

[From *Samguk yusa* 5:228]

When, during the reign of King Chinp'yŏng [579–632], three members of the *hwarang*, Kŏyŏl, Silch'ŏ (or Tolch'ŏ), and Podong were about to make an excursion to the Diamond Mountains, a comet violated Scorpius, a star in one of the twenty-eight lunar mansions. Filled with foreboding, the three were about to abandon their plans. Then Master Yungch'ŏn composed a poem [594], whereupon the uncanny comet disappeared and the Japanese troops withdrew, thus turning a misfortune into a blessing. The king was pleased and had the three youths go to the mountains. The song goes:

> There is a castle by the Eastern Sea
> Where once a mirage used to play.
> Japanese soldiers came,
> Torches were burnt in the forest.
>
> When Knights visited this mountain,
> The moon marked its westerly course,
> And a star was about to sweep a path,
> Someone said, "Look, there is a comet!"
>
> The moon has already departed.
> Now, where shall we look for the long-tailed star? PL

Master Ch'ungdam: "Statesmanship" and "Ode to Knight Kip'a"

[From *Samguk yusa* 2:79–81]

In the twenty-fourth year [765] of King Kyŏngdŏk, the gods of the five sacred mountains and three other mountains appeared from time to time and attended the king.

On the third day of the third month [28 March 765], the king mounted the tower in Kwijŏng Gate and asked his subjects to bring him an imposing monk. Just then an eminent monk was loitering on the road and was brought before the king. "He is not the one," the king said, and let him go. Another monk, dressed in a cassock, then came from the south carrying a tube of cherry wood on his back. Pleased, the king received him in the tower and looked into his tube, which contained utensils for the brewing of tea.

"What is your name?" asked the king.

"I am called Ch'ungdam."

"Where have you come from?" asked the king.

"It is my practice to offer tea to the World-Honored Maitreya at Samhwa Peak on Mount South on the third day of the third month and the ninth day of the ninth month. I am on my way from there now."

"Will you brew a cup of tea for me?" asked the king. Ch'ungdam offered a cup, which the king found to have an uncommon flavor and a rich bouquet.

"I have heard that your eulogy of Knight Kip'a has a noble intent. Is this true?" asked the king.

"Yes," replied the monk.

"Then compose a song of statesmanship."

The king praised Ch'ungdam's song and made him a royal preceptor, but the monk bowed twice and declined firmly. The song of statesmanship goes:

> The king is father,
> And his ministers are loving mothers.
> His subjects are foolish children;
> They only receive what love brings.
>
> Schooled in saving the masses,
> The king feeds and guides them.
> Then no one will desert this land—
> This is the way to govern a country.
>
> Peace and prosperity will prevail if each—
> King, minister, and subject—lives as he should.

His "Ode to Knight Kip'a" goes:

> The moon that pushes her way
> Through the thickets of clouds,
> Is she not pursuing
> The white clouds?
>
> Knight Kip'a once stood by the water,
> Reflecting his face in the blue.
> Henceforth I shall seek and gather
> Among pebbles the depth of his mind.

Knight, you are the towering pine
That scorns frost, ignores snow. PL

Master Wŏlmyŏng: "Song of Tuṣita Heaven" and "Requiem"
[From *Samguk yusa* 5:222–223]

On the first day of the fourth month of the nineteenth year of King Kyŏngdŏk, *kyŏngja* [20 April 760], two suns appeared in the sky and remained for ten days. The astrologer recommended, "Please invite a monk destined by karma to compose a song on the merit of scattering flowers." Thereupon an altar was erected at Chowŏn Hall, and the king went to Ch'ŏngyang Tower to await the coming of a monk. Just then Master Wŏlmyŏng came walking southward on the levee path. The king had a messenger bring the monk to him, and asked him to compose a song and prepare the platform. The master replied, "As a member of the *hwarang,* I know vernacular songs, but not Sanskrit verses." The king said, "Since you are the chosen one, compose the song in the vernacular."

Thereupon the master composed the "Song of Tuṣita Heaven":

O flowers strewn today
With a song. Since you attend
My honest mind's command,
You serve Maitreya!

The transcription reads, "On the Dragon Tower I sing a song of scattering flowers and send a petal to the blue cloud. In place of my sincere wish, go and welcome the Great Sage in the Tuṣita Heaven." People wrongly call it the "Song of Scattering Flowers" instead of the "Song of Tuṣita Heaven." The text of the real "Song of Scattering Flowers" is prolix and has been omitted. The calamity in the sky soon vanished.

The king granted the master a package of fine tea and a rosary of one hundred and eight crystal beads. Suddenly a handsome youth appeared from a small gate to the west of the palace, bearing the tea and the rosary. The master thought him a page of the queen; the king thought him a follower of Wŏlmyŏng; in fact, both were wrong. When the king sent a servant to follow the youth, he vanished into a stupa in the inner cloister, and the tea and rosary were found in front of the southern mural portraying Maitreya. The master's virtue and sincerity had reached the attention of the Buddha, and thus the whole country knew his name. Out of respect, the king further granted him a hundred rolls of silk in praise of his attainments.

Earlier, Wŏlmyŏng had had an abstinence ceremony performed in memory of his sister. When a sudden gust of wind blew the paper money away to the south, he composed a song:

> On the hard road of life and death
> That is near our land,
> You went, afraid,
> Without words.
>
> We know not where we go,
> Leaves blown, scattered,
> Though fallen from the same tree,
> By the first winds of autumn.
>
> Abide, Sister, perfect your ways,
> Until we meet in the Pure Land.

The master used to reside in Sach'ŏnwang Monastery and played the flute well. Once, when he was walking down the road past the gate in the moonlight playing his flute, the moon stopped in its path. The road was thereupon named Wŏlmyŏng-ni, and Wŏlmyŏng's fame spread far and wide.

Wŏlmyŏng was a disciple of Great Master Nŭngjun. Many people in Silla loved the *hyangga,* which was akin to the *shih* and *sung* and which often moved heaven, earth, and spirits. PL

Monk Yŏngjae: "Meeting with Bandits"
[From *Samguk yusa* 5:235]

The monk Yŏngjae was broad-minded and humorous and unattached to riches, and he excelled in vernacular poetry. Intending to spend his last days on South Peak in retirement, he was crossing the Taehyŏn Ridge when he met sixty thieves. The bandits drew their swords and threatened him; but he showed no fear and stated his name. Since the bandits had heard of his reputation as a poet, they asked him to compose an impromptu poem:

My mind that knew not its true self,
My mind that wandered in the dark and deep,
Now is started out for bodhi,
Now is awakened to light.

But on my way to the city of light,
I meet with a band of thieves.
Their swords glitter in the bushes—
Things-as-they-are and things-as-they-are-not.

Well, bandits and I both meditate on the dharma;
But is that sufficient for tomorrow?

Moved by the poem, the bandits presented him with two pieces of silk. The monk laughed and declined the gift. Since he knew riches were the root of evil, he said, he was about to abandon the world and live in the mountains. When the monk threw the silk to the ground with these words, the bandits threw away their swords and spears, shaved their heads, and remained on Mount Chiri all their lives. Yŏngjae was then ninety years old. This took place during the reign of King Wŏnsŏng [785–798]. PL

Ch'ŏyong: "Song of Ch'ŏyong"
[From *Samguk yusa* 2:88–89]

During the reign of the forty-ninth ruler of Silla, Hŏngang [875–886], homes with tile roofs stood in rows from the capital to the seas, with not a single thatched roof in sight. Music and song flowed in the streets day and night, and wind and rain came in due time throughout the seasons.

One day, the king went on a pleasure trip to Kaeunp'o (now Ulchu), and on his way back he stopped to rest on the beach. It was daytime, but black clouds arose suddenly, a dense fog closed in, and his men could not find the way. Inquiries were made, and an astrologer answered that this was due to the anger of the dragon of the Eastern Sea, which could be appeased only by prayers. As soon as the king ordered a monastery built nearby for the dragon, the fog lifted. The place was therefore named Kaeunp'o (Cloud Opening Cove). The dragon, pleased by the offering, appeared before the king with his seven sons, praised the king's virtues, and gave a musical performance. When the dragon returned to the sea, one of his sons did not accompany him but instead followed the king to the capital and helped him in state affairs. He called himself Ch'ŏyong. In order to keep him in the capital, the king gave him a beautiful woman for his wife and the title of *kŭpkan*. Seeing that she was beautiful, a demon of plague transformed himself into a man and attacked her in her room while Ch'ŏyong was away. But Ch'ŏyong returned and witnessed the scene. With calm he sang the following song and danced:

> Having caroused far into the night
> In the moonlit capital,
> I return home and in my bed,
> Behold, four legs.
>
> Two were mine;
> Whose are the other two?
> Two were mine;
> No, no, they are taken.

When Ch'ŏyong was about to leave the scene, the demon appeared in his true from, knelt before him, and said, "I admired your wife and now I have committed a grave crime. But you were not angry, and I am moved by your magnanimity. Henceforth, when I see even the picture of your face, I promise that I will not enter the house." Because of this, people pasted likenesses of Ch'ŏyong on their gates to protect themselves from evil spirits and to welcome happy events.

Upon returning to the capital, the king chose a scenic spot on the eastern slope of Mount Yŏngch'wi (the Numinous Eagle, Gṛdhrakūṭa) and erected a monastery called Manghae (Viewing the Sea)[1] for the dragon. When the king went to P'osŏk Pavilion, the spirit of South Mountain appeared before him and danced, but it was visible only to the king. . . . Again, during a royal visit to Diamond Pass, the spirit of North Mountain appeared before him and danced. . . . Also, at a banquet in the Tongnye Hall, the earth spirit appeared before him and danced. . . . The appearance of these spirits foretold the imminent fall of Silla; but the people misconstrued it as an auspicious sign and wallowed in pleasure. In the end, the country perished. PL

An Old Man: "Dedication"

[From *Samguk yusa* 2:78–79]

On his way to his new post as governor of Kangnŭng during the reign of King Sŏngdŏk [702–732], Lord Sunjŏng stopped to take his lunch by the shore. Behind him rose stony peaks that surrounded the sea like a screen. On peaks one thousand fathoms high, azaleas bloomed in full glory. The lord's wife, Lady Suro, asked, "Could anyone pluck those flowers and bring them to me?"

"These peaks are yet untrodden by men," her followers observed and refused.

An old man leading a cow happened to pass by and, hearing the lady's wishes, picked some flowers for her. We do not know his name.

After two days, the lord's party was again lunching at the Imhae Arbor, when the sea dragon suddenly emerged and kidnapped Suro to his underwater abode. The lord stamped his feet but could not devise any plan for her rescue. Again an old man appeared and said, "An old saying has it that many mouths can melt even iron. Even the sea monster is bound to be afraid of many mouths. Gather the people from the area, compose a song, and strike a hill with sticks. Then you will regain your wife."

The lord followed his advice, and the dragon reappeared and returned the lady. When the lord asked his wife about the bottom of the sea, she replied, "The food at the Palace of the Seven Jewels is delicious, fragrant, and clean, unlike our own." Her dress exuded a strange fragrance hitherto unknown in the world of men.

Being a peerless beauty, Suro would find herself snatched away by divine beings whenever she traveled through deep mountains and large lakes.

The song sung by the people goes: "O turtle, turtle, release Suro!/ How grave the sin of taking another's wife!/ If you go against our will,/ We'll catch you in a net and roast and eat you."

The old man's song at the time of dedicating the azaleas went:

> If you would let me leave
> The cow tethered to the brown rock,
> And feel no shame for me,
> I would pluck and dedicate the flower! PL

Great Master Kyunyŏ: Eleven Poems on the Ten Vows of the Universally Worthy Bodhisattva

[From *Kyunyŏ chŏn* 7, in *Korean Tripiṭaka* 47:260c–261b]

Great Master Kyunyŏ (b. 20 September 923; d. 19 July 973) was a learned monk-poet who singlehandedly revived the Flower Garland school in the tenth century. A voluminous commentator and a popularizer of Buddhism, he composed poems in the vernacular, taught them orally, and encouraged the congregation to chant and memorize them. (Some of his commentaries on Buddhist texts were also written in the vernacular before being translated into Chinese.) In his Chinese preface to the eleven devotional poems written in the *hyangch'al* system, Kyunyŏ explains his intention in using the vernacular:

"While the *sanoe* is a medium of popular entertainment, the practice of the vows is essential to the cultivation of the bodhisattva's practice. One must proceed therefore from the easy to the profound, from the near at hand to the distant. If one does not proceed according to the way of the world, one cannot lead men of inferior faculties. If one does not express oneself in common language, one cannot make known the path of universal causation. Thus I begin from the easily comprehensible and the near at hand and then lead people to the more difficult and profound teachings of Buddhism. I have written eleven poems on the model of the ten great vows. The poems may appear disgraceful in the eyes of the people; yet they may tally with the wishes of the many buddhas. My intent may be lost and my words awry, and my poems may not conform to the wonderful teachings of our saints, but I wish to convey these teachings through poetry to plant wholesome roots among the living. Thus even those who memorize these poems laughingly may lay a basis for their salvation, and those who chant them abusingly may benefit from them. I beg to make it known that it is a matter of indifference to me whether posterity denounces or praises my poems."

Ch'oe Haenggwi, the translator of Kyunyŏ's poems into Chinese in 967, praises the great master in these words: "As the teacher of three thousand disciples, Kyunyŏ's influence is second only to that of Varaprabha (Wonderful Light). As the master of eighty chapters of the *Flower Garland Scripture,* he was the head of his school and taught the masses to take refuge in the Three Jewels. As a great tree moistened by the rain of dharma, he benefited all living beings."

1. WORSHIPING AND HONORING THE BUDDHAS

I bow today before the Buddha,
Whom I draw with my mind's brush.

O this body and mind of mine,
Strive to reach the end of the dharma realm.

He who is in every mote of dust;
He who pervades every Buddha field;
He who fills the realm of dharma—
Would that I could serve him in the nine time periods.

Ah, idle body, mouth, and mind—
Approach him and be with him, unimpeded.

2. PRAISE OF THE THUS COME ONE

"Homage to the buddhas."
So speaks the tongue today.
O sea of inexhaustible eloquence—
Gush forth from a single thought.

We hail you, achiever of merit;
We praise you, Medicine King,
With your boundless ocean of excellence,
Who exist in dust and empty space.

Ah, would that my tongue could praise
An infinitesimal part of your virtue.

3. WIDE CULTIVATION AND THE MAKING OF OFFERINGS

Stirring the ashes and lighting the lamp
That burns at the altar, I pray
That the wick might become large as Mount Sumeru,
And the oil might become a sea.

This incense will reach beyond the realm of dharma.
This incense will honor all the buddhas
Who pervade the dharma realm
With many offerings.

Ah, offerings are many. But what will equal
The offering of the dharma?

4. REPENTANCE FOR SINS

I have lived in fancy and in vanity,
And strayed from the paths of light;
All my evil karma
Bars me from the realm of dharma.

With good deeds, words and thoughts
I will exert myself to keep my conduct pure.
Tell the buddhas of the ten directions
That today I have truly repented.

Ah, when the world of the living ends, my penance
Ends; so will all my evil deeds.

5. REJOICING IN THE MERIT OF OTHERS

The truth of dependent origination tells me
That illusion and enlightenment are one.
From the buddhas down to mortal men,
The other and myself are one.

Were I able to practice his virtues,
Were I able to master his ways,
I would rejoice in the merit of others;
I would rejoice in the good of others.

Ah, were I to follow in his footsteps,
How could the jealous mind be aroused?

6. ENTREATY FOR TURNING THE DHARMA WHEEL

To the majestic assembly of buddhas
In the dharma realm,
I fervently pray
For the sweet dharma rain.

Disperse the blight of affliction
Rooted deep in the soil of ignorance,
And wet the mind's fields of the living,
Where good grasses struggle to grow.

Ah, the mind is a moonlit autumn field
Ripe with the golden fruit of knowledge.

7. ENTREATY FOR THE BUDDHA TO LIVE IN THIS WORLD

Though the buddhas
Have fulfilled the purpose of their coming,
I will join my palms and pray
That they will still dwell with the living.

I have found a true friend
Whom I would follow night and day.
Have pity on those
Who have strayed from the Path.

Ah, were our minds but pure and clean,
His reflected image should shine there.

8. CONSTANT FOLLOWING OF THE TEACHING OF THE BUDDHAS

I would fervently follow the vows
That he cultivated in the past
And practiced with great hardship,
With arduous progress and with vigor.

When this body turns to dust,
Even at the hour of my death
I would joyfully fulfill the vows
Promulgated through time by all the buddhas.

O mind that cultivates the Path of Buddha:
Could you stray to another path?

9. CONSTANT HARMONY WITH THE LIVING

Śākyamuni takes the deluded as roots.
With his vows of great mercy,
He waters the fields of the mind,
That they might not wither.

I, who am one of the living,
Would live and die with him,
And serve and respect the living
Single-mindedly, without pause.

Ah, the day we attain his peace,
He, too, will rejoice in our progress.

10. TRANSFER OF MERIT

Would that all my merit
Might be passed on to others,
I would like to awaken them—
Those wandering in the sea of suffering.

When we attain the vast realm of dharma,
Removed karmas are jewels in dharmahood;
Since aeons ago
Bodhisattvas, too, have devoted their merit to others.

Ah, he whom I worship and I are one,
Of one body and one mind.

11. CONCLUSION

When the realm of the living runs out,
My vows, too, will have been acted out.
As the world of the living has no end,
Neither does the boundless ocean of his vows.

Since I strive and progress so,
Each way I tread is good—
These are the Vows of Samantabhadra
That the buddhas have fulfilled.

Ah, let us fathom Samantabhadra's zeal
And follow his single path. PL

CHAPTER SEVEN

Local Clans and the Rise of the Meditation School

During the final years of Silla (780–935), the administration was tailored not to the state but to the True Bone aristocracy to prevent its disintegration and internal strife. The king's role shrank to that of protector of his own clan's power. When the bone rank system ceased to be functional, the True Bone class became divided and powerful clans in the provinces rose to replace it. They built their economic base on international maritime trade or on the peasantry. In time, the course of history was determined by the composition and political character of such clans.

Silla Buddhism after the unification made great strides in the doctrinal studies pursued by Wŏnhyo, Ŭisang, and Wŏnch'ŭk. Wŏnhyo popularized Buddhism and spread it among the people. However, the more cultured circles gradually distanced themselves from such studies. The Meditation school, with its emphasis on individual attainment of truth, was able to overcome both the ideological tendency of doctrinal schools and the superstitious Buddhism that resulted from the combination with native shamanism. By allying themselves with Meditation school adherents, provincial clans were able to oppose the central aristocracy.

The middle period of Silla was ruled by the direct descendants of King Muyŏl (654–661). By the time of King Kyŏngdŏk (742–765), the aristocracy had risen in revolt. To deal with the crisis, the king attempted to initiate a political reform but without success. Under

King Hyegong (765–780), revolts again broke out. Indeed, the king was assassinated by collateral nobles who began to occupy the throne from the time of Sŏndŏk (780–785). One of the changes brought about by the aristocracy's revolt against the king's authoritarian rule was that the monarch no longer represented the aristocracy as a whole but only the group that installed him. With wealth of their own and private armies, members of the aristocracy now indulged in the struggle for power. Amidst this warring among the aristocracy and provincial rebellions, members of the sixth head rank groped for a solution. But lacking local support and an economic base, they could not emerge as leaders. Such roles were reserved for powerful local clans. Denied participation in politics, some local chiefs had turned to international trade, weakening the economic position of the central nobility. The typical example is Chang Pogo, who built a naval garrison of ten thousand men on Wan Island in 828 and controlled the Yellow Sea. Silla settlers (*Silla bang*), administered by Silla nationals, emerged on the Shantung peninsula and in the Kiangsu area. Chang also built the famous Dharma Blossom Cloister in Chih-shang village in Shantung as described in Ennin's *Diary*.

Other strong leaders, originally village chiefs, allied themselves with the peasantry and had the power to collect taxes and mobilize soldiers. Heavy taxation and famine also drove many to banditry, and chiefs such as Yanggil were powerful enough to develop their own administrations. The power base of Kungye, a subordinate of Yanggil, was built by bandits. Exploiting the anti-Silla sentiments in an area that once belonged to Koguryŏ, he founded Later Koguryŏ (T'aebong) but was unable to stop the plunder or to envision a better social structure. Indeed, he indulged in atrocities. By dealing a blow to Silla, however, Kungye helped to prepare Wang Kŏn's emergence as the founder of the Koryŏ dynasty. In the area of Paekche, Kyŏnhwŏn rose to found Later Paekche. Kyŏnhwŏn was a peasant-soldier who united the military, local clans, and pirates. Although he showed some skill in administration and diplomacy, he lacked any vision of a new society. By making a display of military might, he alienated the people and was destroyed. But by breaking down Silla's social iniquity, he too prepared the way for Wang Kŏn.

The Rise of Local Chiefs

Chang Pogo (d. 846) was a Korean adventurer and merchant prince whose name was once synonymous with the Korean maritime dominance in East Asia in the early ninth century. Son of a fisherman from Wan Island off the southwestern coast of the Korean peninsula, Chang Pogo migrated to T'ang China as a youth, and there he advanced to the position of captain in Hsü-chou in the lower Huai River valley. Returning to Korea in 828, he alerted the throne to the danger of Chinese piracy in the Yellow Sea, whereupon the king appointed him commissioner of Ch'ŏnghaejin, the military headquarters of Wan Island. There Chang raised a private navy, at times numbering ten thousand men, by which he controlled the ocean commerce between China, Korea, and Japan.

The ships engaged in this international trade were owned and manned by Chang, and Korean trading communities flourished along the southern coast of the Shantung peninsula and the lower reaches of the Huai. Some of these colonies, such as the famous Mount Ch'ih community overlooking the sea route between China and Korea, enjoyed extraterritorial privileges. These colonies often served as an intermediary between Chinese authorities and Japanese visitors; indeed, the Japanese pilgrim Ennin once addressed a letter to Chang asking for his assistance and shelter.

In 836 Chang was involved in a royal succession struggle. From the end of the eighth century on, the Silla court was beset by contention between the rising aristocracy and the authoritarian monarchy based on the bone rank system. Hence the throne, hitherto determined solely by bloodline, came to require political skill and military might. Often a contender, to bolster his claim, had to ally himself with local chiefs who were disillusioned nobles depending for their power on private soldiers recruited from serfs and vagrants. In 839 the son of the former king's rival ascended the throne as Sinmu.

History relates that Chang's downfall can be traced to his efforts to marry his daughter to the king. The marriage alliance had probably been promised by Sinmu during his protracted sojourn on Wan Island, but because of his untimely death Chang sought to force Sinmu's son to abide by the pledge. Chang's attempt in 845 to force the throne to adopt his daughter as royal consort irritated the central aristocracy, who frowned upon such an alliance as unsavory and potentially dangerous. Although Chang's death by assassination is traditionally placed in 846, it may have occurred a few years earlier. In 851 Ch'ŏnghaejin was abolished as a military base. Thus ended the maritime kingdom of Chang Pogo and with it Silla's brief maritime dominance in East Asia. What follows is a brief account concerning Chang Pogo in the *Historical Record of the Three Kingdoms.*

Chang Pogo
[From *Samguk sagi* 44:416–417]

Chang Pogo (or Kungbok or Kungp'a) was a man of Silla whose clan site and ancestors were unknown. He fought a good battle. He went to T'ang, where he became *Wu-ning-chün hsiao-chang,* and he was peerless in horsemanship and wielding a spear.

Upon his return to Silla, Chang had an audience with King Hŭng-dŏk. To the king he reported, "Everywhere in China they use our people as slaves. I beg Your Majesty to build headquarters at Ch'ŏnghae to prevent pirates from kidnapping our people and shipping them west."

Ch'ŏnghae, now Wan Island, was a strategic point on Silla's sea routes. The king gave Chang an army of ten thousand men and bade him pitch camp on the island [828]. Thereafter Silla people were no longer enslaved on the high seas. PL

Establishment of the Meditation School

The introduction of the Meditation school (Sŏn in Korean; Ch'an in Chinese; Zen in Japanese) to Silla is traced to Pŏmnang (c. 632–646), who returned to Silla in the latter half of the seventh century after studying with the Fourth Patriarch Tao-hsin (580–651). He transmitted the gradual teaching of the Northern school to his pupil Sinhaeng (d. 779). Robert Buswell suggests that Pŏmnang may have been the author of the *Adamantine Absorption Scripture.* Musang (680–762), a Silla monk, made seminal contributions to the school in China.[1]

The Life of Musang
[From *Li-tai fa-pao chi; T.* 51:184c–185a]

Said to be the third son of King Sŏngdŏk of Silla, Musang went to T'ang China in 728. There he was received by Emperor Hsüan-tsung and played an active part in the development of the Meditation school. In the area of Ch'eng-tu he practiced the meditation of Ch'u-chi (648–734), a disciple of Chih-shen (609–702), and became an abbot of Ching-chung Monastery. Musang was known for meditating on the name of Buddha and for his ascetic practices. He built a number of meditation centers and supervised the construction of Ta-sheng-tzu Monastery in Ch'eng-tu by order of Emperor Hsüan-tsung. Musang became the monastery's abbot upon its completion. His disciples include Wu-chu (714–774) and Ma-tsu (709–788). The biographical account presented here comes from *Record of the Dharma Jewel in Successive Generations.*

The secular surname of Dhyāna Master Musang of Ching-ch'üan Monastery in Ch'eng-tu, Chien-nan, was Kim; he was of the royal family. For generations his family lived in Korea. While he was still in his native country, his young sister, upon hearing that she was about to be given in marriage, cut her own face and vowed to become a nun. Upon seeing this, Musang said, "A woman is gentle and weak, but she has such a lofty determination. How can a man who is robust and strong be without aspiration?" At last he had his hair shaved and bade his parents farewell.

He sailed west and reached T'ang China. There, in order to search for a teacher and seek the Path, he made a tour of the country. He arrived at Te-shun Monastery in Tzu-chou and sought to pay his respects to Master T'ang (Ch'u-chi). The master was ill, however, and would not see Musang. Then Musang let his finger burn as a lamp and offered it to the master. Perceiving that Musang was an extraordinary person, the master allowed him to remain for two years. Then Musang lived on Mount T'ien-ku. Master T'ang sent one of his followers, Wang Huang, and secretly transmitted his cassock to Musang. "This robe was transmitted from the patriarch Bodhidharma; Empress Wu bestowed it on Master Chih-shen, who transmitted it to me. Today I entrust it to you." Thus Musang received the dharma succession and the robe.

At last he lived at the foot of a boulder on Mount T'ien-ku, wore cloth woven from grass, and ate moderately. When there was no food, he nibbled on earth. Even savage beasts were moved by this and protected him. Later, when Chang-ch'iu ta-fu begged him to unfold the principles of meditation, Musang lived in Ching-ch'üan Monastery for twenty years and taught the people the path of conversion.

On the fifteenth day of the fifth month of the first year of Pao-ying, Musang suddenly thought of Dhyāna Master Wu-chu on Mount Po-ya and said to his disciples, "I am ill. Gather together and come to see me."

"Why has Wu-chu not come?" Musang often asked his followers. "I'm old." He then quietly sent the artisan Tung Hsüan to Wu-chu, saying, "I will secretly send my robe and other garments as well as the seventeen requisites. Wu-chu should keep and cherish them. It is not yet the time for him to leave his mountain. After three or five years, when he learns that the times are peaceful, then he may come out. I entrust him with this from far off—I have settled an account."

On the nineteenth day of the fifth month of 762 [15 June 762], Musang instructed his disciples: "I am going to take a bath. Bring me a clean new cloth." At the time of the Rat [11 P.M.–1 A.M.], sitting in dignity, he breathed his last. . . .

In the twelfth and first month of every year, Musang, together with millions of mendicant monks and nuns, lay brothers and sisters, set up the Platform of the Path and preached the dharma from the pulpit. "First, softly invoke the name of the Buddha. With all your breath meditate on the Buddha. Then stop the voice and stop thinking," he taught them. "The absence of memory, the absence of thought, and the absence of delusion: the first is *śīla* (morality); the second, *samādhi* (concentration); and the third, *prajñā* (wisdom). These three phrases furnish absolute control over good and evil passions and influences."

Musang said again: "With the absence of thought, the mind is like a bright mirror that reflects all phenomena. The rise of thought is like the back of a mirror that cannot reflect anything."

He also said, "To know clearly birth and death—and to know them without interruption—is to see the Buddha. It is like a story of two men who went together to another country. Their father sent them a letter with instructions. One son obtained the letter, finished it, and followed his father's teachings without breaking the discipline. Another did the same, but he went against his father's teachings and committed many evil deeds. All living beings are like this. One who relies on the absence of thought is like an obedient son. One who is set on words is like a disobedient son. To use another parable, when one man was drunk and lying around, his mother went and called him, 'Let's go home.' But the drunken son was bewildered and railed against his own mother. Likewise, all living beings, drunk with ignorance, do not believe that by looking into their own nature they can become buddhas." PL

The Life of Tŏŭi
[From *Tsu-t'ang chi* 17:106b–c]

Tŏŭi (d. 825) played an important role in transmitting the Meditation school to Silla. The *Tsu-t'ang chi* (Collection from the Hall of Patriarchs) quotes the inscription on the monument erected in his honor at Chinjŏn Monastery, but the monument itself has been lost. Tŏŭi went to T'ang in 784 and received the doctrinal transmission from Chih-tsang (735–814) at K'ai-yüan Monastery in Hung-chou, Kiangsi. Then he sought Huai-hai (720–814) and returned home in 821. Thus Chih-tsang, one of the main disciples of Ma-tsu (709–788), played a role in the transmission of the Meditation school to Silla.

Tŏŭi's return marked a turning point in Silla Buddhism. Indeed, the Meditation school that Tŏŭi transmitted shook the foundations of the Doctrinal school. As contemporary Silla Buddhism either emphasized study of the scriptures or espoused a superstitious form of Buddhism mixed with native shamanism, the Meditation school, which questioned the true existence of man, could not be tolerated. Tŏŭi's teaching was denounced as devilish or fantastic, and he had to withdraw to Chinjŏn Monastery on Snow Mountain in Yangyang.

A stream of Meditation monks returning from China gradually helped establish the teaching. They then built monasteries in the deep mountains, and the so-called Nine Mountains came into being. The spread of the Meditation school was facilitated by the assistance it received from provincial chiefs. Most founders of the nine schools were provincially located. (Their ancestors may have been of the central aristocracy, but in their own generation, they were members of the local gentry.) They encouraged the establishment of Meditation centers, usually near their power bases. The Sŏngjusan school was set up with the help of Kim Hŭn, for example, who owned a large manor near Poryŏng, South Ch'ungch'ŏng. Thus the Meditation school became the faith of the powerful clans. Because Meditation stressed practice based on intuition, it appeared to some members to promote a warrior-like spirit: the possibility of sudden enlightenment was revolutionary and hopeful. Meditation monks in turn realized their need for the clan's financial aid and other forms of help during their confrontation with the Doctrinal schools.

According to the *Haedong ch'iltae rok* (Record of Seven Generations in Korea) quoted in the *Sŏnmun pojang nok* (1293), compiled by Ch'ŏnch'aek, Toǔi attempted to teach the "absence of thought and the absence of cultivation" and encouraged questions and answers that would lead to sudden awakening. Thus he adopted the tactics of the Southern school of Hung-chou and challenged the Flower Garland school, which represented the scholastic Buddhism of the day. The *Record of Seven Generations in Korea* is no longer extant, but it appears to have been a work on the Meditation school in Silla. Although Toǔi's exchange with Chief of Clerics Chiwǒn is an apologia stressing the superiority of the Meditation school over its rivals, it sheds light on the relationship between the Flower Garland school and the Meditation school at its beginning in Silla.

Dharma Master Wǒnjǒk of Chinjǒn Monastery on Snow Mountain (Sǒrak) was a successor to Chih-tsang [735–814]. He resided in Myǒngju. His taboo name was Toǔi, his clan name was Wang, and he was from Pukhan prefecture.

Before Toǔi's conception, his father saw a white rainbow entering his room, and his mother dreamed of sharing her bed with a monk. When the two awoke, fragrance filled the room. Startled, they said to each other, "This is an auspice that announces the birth of a holy child." After half a month, the wife conceived, and after thirty-nine weeks she gave birth to Toǔi. When Toǔi was about to be born, a monk carrying a staff appeared at the gate and said, "Please leave the womb (the caul and the placenta) of the newborn at the foot of the mountain by the river." The monk then disappeared. When the womb was buried there, a large deer appeared and watched over the place for a year. Passersby did not think of killing it. Because he left his household amid such wonders, Toǔi's Buddhist name was Myǒngjǒk (Bright Trace).

In the fifth year of Chien-chung, *chia-tzu* [784], Toǔi accompanied the Silla envoys Han Ch'anho and Kim Yanggong to T'ang China. Straightaway he went to Mount T'ien-t'ai and received miraculous responses from Mañjuśrī. In the void the sacred bell echoed, and in the woods wondrous birds flitted about. He received full ordination at Pao-t'an Monastery in Kuang-fu. When, at Ts'ao-ch'i, he was about to pay his respects to the patriarch, the gate opened of itself. When he left the gate after worship, the gate closed of itself. Then he went to K'ai-yüan Monastery in Hung-chou, Kiangsi, to visit Great Master Chih-tsang and study under him. His doubts were dispelled, and all hindrances were dissolved. The master felt as if he had found jade among stones, a pearl among oysters. He said to himself, "I will sincerely transmit the dharma to him. Who else is there but him?" He then had his disciple's name changed to Toŭi. Thereupon, as an ascetic practitioner, Toŭi went to visit Master Huai-hai [720–814] on Mount Pai-chang.

Master Chih-tsang used to say, "The meditation schools in Kiangsi are carried on by Silla monks." The rest is as the inscription records. PL

Toŭi: Questions and Answers with Chief of Clerics Chiwŏn

[From *Sŏnmun pojang nok* 2, in *Hsü Tsang-ching* 113:499a–b]

Chief of Clerics Chiwŏn asked National Preceptor Toŭi, "What other dharma realm is there besides the four dharma realms of the Flower Garland school? What other approach to dharma is there besides this progressive approach taught by fifty-five good friends? Except for the doctrine of this school, is there a separate path of meditation preached by the patriarch?"

Toŭi answered, "The four dharma realms you mention are the essence of the principle the school of patriarchs has brought up straightaway, and they dissolve like melting ice. Inside the fist of the True Principle the signs of the dharma realm cannot be found. One cannot see the signs of Mañjuśrī and Samantabhadra in the meditation of the patriarch's mind where originally there are no practice and wisdom. And the dharma gates of the fifty-five good friends are like foam on water. Such paths as the four forms of wisdom and enlightenment are like ore containing gold. Since it is mixed in indiscriminately, one cannot find it in the scriptural teachings. Therefore, when asked what is elucidated in the *Great Scripture Store* (*Tripiṭaka*), Master Kuei-tsung of T'ang merely raised his fist."

Chiwŏn asked again, "What is the purpose, then, of the principle and practice of the Doctrinal school, such as faith, understanding, practice, and realization? And what fruit of Buddhahood can one attain thereby?"

Toŭi answered, "Without thought and without cultivation, we understand the principle and nature by faith, understanding, practice, and realization. When the patriarch showed the dharma, he said, 'Buddhas and living beings cannot obtain it; the true nature of the Path can only be manifested straightaway.' Hence, in addition to the five doctrines, there is another transmission of the dharma, namely the patriarch's mind-seal transmission. The reason for the manifestation of the forms of the buddhas is for those who have difficulty in understanding the patriarch's True Principle. This is an expedient device of manifesting the body. Even if you desire to realize the transmission of the mind seal by reading scriptures for many years, you would not be able to do so even after many cosmic ages have passed."

Chiwŏn rose, bowed, and said, "Until now, I had only heard the Buddha's ornate teachings. The Buddha's mind-seal method cannot be obtained by a sideways glance." He then respectfully gave himself to Toŭi and had an audience with him. PL

Muyŏm: Treatise on the Tongueless Realm

[From *Sŏnmun pojang nok* 1, in *Hsü Tsang-ching* 113:495a–b]

Muyŏm (800–888) first studied the *Flower Garland Scripture* under the venerable Sŏkching at Pusŏk Monastery, the center of Silla's Doctrinal school. During his stay in T'ang China, Muyŏm realized the limitations of scriptural study and was converted to the Meditation school. He then studied under Ju-man, a disciple of Ma-tsu (709–788), at Fo-kuang Monastery; he continued his practice under Pao-ch'e, achieved awakening, and received a seal of certification. Sŏngjusan, the school of meditation Muyŏm founded upon his return to Silla, was the most active among the nine schools.

In his *Treatise on the Tongueless Realm*, Muyŏm characterizes the Doctrinal school as one that adapts itself to the capacity of believers, teaches by words, and cleanses impurity whereas the Meditation school transmits the right path, is tongueless, and is without cleansing and without impurity. The Doctrinal school he criticizes is the Flower Garland school, which teaches by expedient means. Originally an independent work, Muyŏm's treatise was included in the *Sŏnmun pojang nok* by Ch'ŏnch'aek. Elsewhere in the same work Ch'ŏnch'aek also quotes from the account of Muyŏm's deeds. Although the accuracy of the treatise's content is uncertain, it is mentioned in the histories of the Meditation school and the *Tsu-t'ang chi* (952).

QUESTION: What is the meaning of "tongued" and "tongueless"?

ANSWER: Yang-shan Hui-chi [803–887] said, "The tongued realm is the Buddha realm; it is the gate that responds to one's inward spring of movement (capacity). The tongueless realm is the school of meditation; it is the gate of the true transmission."

QUESTION: What is the gate that responds to one's inward spring of movement?

ANSWER: Friends that teach the dharma by raising the eyebrows or rolling eyeballs—all this is the gate that responds to one's inward spring of movement. Therefore it is tongued, to say nothing of words.

QUESTION: What is the tongueless realm?

ANSWER: It is he who has the capacity for meditation. In it there is neither teacher nor disciple.

QUESTION: If so, why did the ancients speak of a transmission from master to disciple?

ANSWER: Chang-ching [754–815] said, "If I were to use a comparison, it is like empty space whose character is without character. It has nonaction for its function. The Meditation school's transmission is like this—it has nontransmission for its transmission. Therefore, transmission is nontransmission."

QUESTION: The tongueless realm has neither one who converts nor one who is converted. In the scriptural doctrine, too, there is neither the converter nor converted in the Thus Come One's realization of mind. What, then, is the difference?

ANSWER: The ultimate of the scriptural gate is the ocean-seal meditation, which is the Thus Come One's realization of mind. The dharma seal that manifests in the three realms is never understood. Therefore it still has the traces of the three realms. The patriarchs who have continued the dharma are leisurely men of the Path, and no grass of purity or impurity grows in their minds—hence the mind does not go astray. Also, there is no trace of entrance or exit of the grass of the three realms. Herein lies the difference between the two schools. Purity is the dharma of true suchness and liberation; impurity is the dharma of birth, death, and defilement. For this reason the ancients said, "The source of the adept's mind is like deep water where the grasses of purity and impurity never grow." Furthermore, wearing the clothes of *samādhi* and *prajñā,* the student of the scripture first enters the fire of the burning lamp, which he considers to be the Buddha realm. Now he doffs the cloth of *samādhi* and *prajñā* and stands in the arcane land. Hence it still has traces. By its nature, the realm of the patriarch is free from liberation or bondage. One does not wear a single strand. It is therefore vastly different from the Buddha realm. PL

The Life of Sunji
[From *Tsu-t'ang chi* 20:124a]

The Meditation school has prided itself on being a "separate transmission outside the scriptural teachings" that rejects philosophical treatments of Buddhism in favor of direct personal experience. For this reason, verbal descriptions of Meditation teachings and techniques were generally considered inferior to nonverbal explanations. Sunji's sets of circle-symbols were one such attempt to describe various aspects of Meditation ideology and practice without taking recourse in verbalization. The use of circles as a teaching tool in the Meditation school seems to have begun with Nan-yang Hui-chung (d. 775), who transmitted a set of ninety-seven forms that apparently survived until Sunji's time but are no longer extant. Yang-shan Hui-chi (803–887), cofounder of the Kuei-yang school of Chinese Meditation and the teacher of Sunji, is said to have used circles and Chinese logographs in order to teach his students. Sunji's circle symbolism is apparently a further elaboration of these expedients used commonly in the Kuei-yang school. Perhaps the best known use of such circles is in the five rankings of Sunji's contemporary, Tung-shan Liang-chieh (807–869), cofounder of the Ts'ao-tung school. The explicit parallels between Flower Garland teachings and Sunji's explanations of the meanings of his circles—as well as his descriptions of the different levels of attainment of Buddhahood and his account of the reality limit that follow—exemplify the close associations between the doctrinal outlooks of the two schools, which are quite characteristic of Korean Buddhism. The following account is a narrative summary of the extensive presentation of Sunji's teachings found in the *Tsu-t'ang chi*.

The taboo name of the master of Sŏun Monastery on Mount Ogwan was Sunji. He was a disciple of Yang-shan Hui-chi of Mount Yang in Kiangsi. Sunji's secular name was Pak, and he was from the area of the Taedong River. . . . He entered Mount Ogwan to have his head shaved and received the full prohibitions on Mount Songji. . . .

Then, in the twelfth year of Ta-chung [858], Sunji made a vow to go to China and boarded a ship that was to take the Korean envoy to T'ang. During his voyage over myriad layers of billows, he was absorbed in meditation and never entertained any fear. Upon reaching the abode of Master Hui-chi, Sunji paid his respects to the master and expressed a wish to be his disciple. Laughing indulgently, Hui-chi said, "I wish this meeting could have taken place earlier. I already have something in view. Remain here." Sunji never left the master's side, and, like Yen Hui under Confucius or Mahākāśyapa in the presence of Śākyamuni, he consulted him about the mysteries of the school. Thus he won the esteem of his colleagues in meditation.

In the beginning of Ch'ien-fu [874–880], Queen Wǒnch'ang, the donor of Songak prefecture, and her son, Great King Wimu, gave alms to Yongǒm Monastery on Mount Ogwan, and Sunji went there to stay. Hence the name of the monastery was changed to Sǒun (Auspicious Cloud). PL

Summary of Sunji's Teachings
[From *Tsu-t'ang chi* 20:124a–125b]

EIGHT SYMBOLS IN FOUR SETS TO EXPLAIN THE NOUMENON

Master Sunji developed a series of eight symbols in four sets to guide his students in their realization of the noumenon.

A: IA. EMPTY CIRCLE: ◯

This is the sign of the absolute, "the nirvana which serves as a resort"; it is also called "the noumenal Buddha nature." Whether ordinary men or saints, all beings depend on this sign. Although the sign itself can never be differentiated, this is not to imply that delusion and enlightenment are the same; this is why there are ordinary men and saints. One who knows this sign is called a saint; one who is deluded in regards to it is called an ordinary person.

Once when the Buddhist patriarch Nāgārjuna was in southern India preaching the dharma, his body became like the orb of the moon. While the sound of his preaching could be heard from above where he had been sitting, no one could see his body. His disciple, Āryadeva, explained to the nonplussed congregation that this miracle was a way for his teacher to reveal the Buddha nature and show that the form of the signless absorption—the gate to enlightenment—was like the full moon. Before Āryadeva could finish his explanation, however, Nāgārjuna reappeared and spoke the following verse:

> My body appeared in the form of a full moon,
> In order to represent the essence of all the buddhas.
> Preaching the dharma does not involve this form,
> It is done through erudition, it is not sound.

If someone were to ask me about this sign of the full moon, I would answer him by adding the logograph for "ox" inside the circle.

1B. OX INSIDE THE CIRCLE: ⊕

This sign is known as "ox eating the grass of endurance." It is also called the sign of "seeing the nature and attaining Buddhahood." A scripture says, "In the Himalayan Mountains there is a kind of grass, called 'endurance,' which, if eaten by an ox, produces ghee."[2] It also says: "If a sentient being can hear and accept the teaching concerning the great extinction, he will see the Buddha nature."[3] In this simile, the grass refers to the dharma; the ox to a person who has the capacity to awaken suddenly; and the ghee to Buddha. Hence just as an ox who eats this grass will give ghee, so too will a person who comprehends this dharma achieve full enlightenment.

2A. THREE OXEN BENEATH THE CIRCLE: 犇

This sign is called "three vehicles in search of emptiness." Adherents of the three arhat, bodhisattva, and pratyekabuddha vehicles who hear about true emptiness may decide to go out in search of that emptiness, but they will never be able to discover it. For this reason, all three oxen are underneath the circle. If someone were to come and ask about the previous sign, I would reply with the sign of "the gradual seeing the nature and attaining Buddhahood."

2B. OX INSIDE THE CIRCLE: ⊕

This second sign of an ox inside the circle is also called "white ox in the open pasture." "Open pasture" refers to the Buddha stage and is also called "absolute emptiness"; "white ox" refers to the sublime wisdom of the dharma body. This is why there is a single ox inside the full circle.

QUESTION: Why is the sign with three oxen beneath the circle contrasted with the sign of an ox inside the circle that was used previously?

ANSWER: The sign of three oxen beneath the circle represents the three vehicles; one ox inside the circle represents the one vehicle of Buddhahood. This contrast is intended to demonstrate that the three vehicles afford provisional descriptions that aid in bringing about personal realization of reality, while the one vehicle is that realization itself.

QUESTION: You explained first that the ox inside the circle referred to the ox eating the grass of endurance. Why did you then say that it was sign of the white ox in the open pasture? Both are the exact same sign, so why should they be explained differently?

ANSWER: The explanations might be different, but the sign is the same. Although the sign might be identical, the speed at which seeing the nature is accomplished is not the same. This is why I use two different descriptions to explain the same sign.

QUESTION: Which of the two descriptions represents the swift attainment of enlightenment and which the slow attainment?

ANSWER: The ox eating the grass of endurance refers to the sudden vision of the true nature as explained in the *Flower Garland Scripture*; this is the swift attainment. The white ox in the open pasture refers to the process by which the three vehicles return to the one vehicle as explained in the *Lotus Scripture*; this is the slow attainment. Hence, although these two descriptions might be different, their principle is the same. Therefore, I have used the same sign to clarify that while the noumenal wisdom is not different, this does not mean that the process by which that wisdom is attained is absolutely identical.

3A. ONE OX ABOVE THE CIRCLE: 牛 / 〇

This sign is called "to cultivate cause[4] in accordance with the fruition." Why this name? While the attainment of Buddhahood might take place at the time of the inception of the bodhisattva path on the first abiding state of the arousal of the thought of enlightenment, this does not imply that one may dispense with the cultivation of all the Bodhisattva's practices. This is what the ancients meant by "walking in the footsteps of the Tathāgata." If a person were to come and ask about this sign, I would answer by placing the symbol for auspiciousness (*svastika*) inside the circle.

3B. *Svastika* INSIDE THE CIRCLE: ⊕

This is the sign for "cause is perfected and fruition complete."

QUESTION: Why do you reply with this sign when you were asked about the one in which the ox is above the circle?

ANSWER: The circle with an ox above is the sign for cultivating the cause in accordance with the fruition—that is, spiritual cultivation serves as the cause that results in the realization of the full circle. The *svastika* inside the circle is the sign for the cause being perfected and the fruition being complete—that is, the effect that is brought about through the completion of that cultivation.

4A. CIRCLE WITH OX UNDERNEATH: 牛̥

This sign is "seeking emptiness through diligent practice." This refers to the bodhisattva prior to the attainment of enlightenment. This is what is meant in the scriptures where it is said that over three incalculable aeons, a person cultivates the bodhisattva practices, enduring that which is difficult to endure, practicing that which is difficult to practice. He is unremitting in his search for the mind. If a person were to come and ask about this symbol, I would reply with the following sign.

4B. CIRCLE ENCLOSING A KING: ⊕

This is the sign of the "gradual realization of the reality limit." If a bodhisattva cultivates over an infinite number of aeons and destroys the hosts of demonic forces, he will then attain the true wisdom that is free from outflows, enter onto the Buddha stage, and will no longer be tormented by any of the habituations. This would be like a king who subdues all the hosts of brigands: the kingdom would then be peaceful and would never again be oppressed by spiteful bandits.

FOUR SYMBOLS IN TWO SETS TO NEGATE FALSITY AND REVEAL TRUTH

B: IA. MAN INSIDE THE CIRCLE, WITH OX ABOVE: 牛ⓧ

This is the sign of "abandoning the doctrine but retaining conceptual thinking." A person is able to attain liberation by depending on the doctrine of the one Buddha vehicle. While there is absolutely nothing wrong with this, because he has yet to understand his own noumenal wisdom, he remains completely dependent on the words of others. If someone came to ask about this sign, I would reply by removing the ox from the top of the circle enclosing a man.

IB. MAN INSIDE THE CIRCLE: Ⓐ

This is the sign of "cognize the root and return to the source." This sense here parallels the scriptural statement, "One turns one's spirit to abide in the cave of emptiness and subdues that which is difficult to control; freed from the bonds of the demonic forces, one sits aloof in the open pasture and realizes great extinction."[5]

QUESTION: Why have you removed the ox-logograph from the top of the sign but not the man from inside the circle?

ANSWER: The man inside the circle represents the noumenal wisdom. The ox above it is a symbol for conceptual understanding. Although a person might rely upon the teachings found in the canonical scriptures, if he has yet to display his own noumenal wisdom, his understanding will remain entirely conceptual in nature. When conceptual understanding no longer arises, then the noumenal wisdom appears. Hence, the ox has been removed, but the man is retained. Thus, the scriptures say to get rid of the disease, but not the cure.

QUESTION: Why do you not permit ordinary men to study the dharma while continuing to rely on the scriptural teachings?

ANSWER: If one has wisdom, what purpose is served by depending upon the scriptural teachings in the attempt to cognize the mind? But for an ordinary man, even relying on the teachings will do him no good.

QUESTION: Is there then any value in the canonical scriptures?

ANSWER: My previous statement was not intended to imply that one should not enter into awakening through relying on the teachings; it is wrong, however, to retain any conceptual understanding based on those teachings. It is for this reason that the Buddha criticized his disciple, Ānanda. For although Ānanda had memorized the sublime principles, as infinite as the sands of the Ganges, contained in the twelvefold division of the teachings of all the Thus Come Ones, this had only contributed to his conceptual proliferation. Therefore, you should know that conceptual understanding which is based on the teachings is worthless.

QUESTION: Why do the scriptural teachings say that one who hears the Buddha's teachings will perfect all of the holy fruitions, or that even a modicum of wholesome conduct will lead to Buddhahood?

ANSWER: A person of superior spiritual faculties may gain awakening through relying on the teachings and thus directly manifest the noumenal wisdom; he has absolute understanding. A person of inferior spiritual faculties, however, will not gain awakening even though he relies on the teachings; his conceptual understanding will be worthless. But if that inferior person continues to develop himself spiritually, who can say that in a later lifetime his practice will not prove to be beneficial to him? This is why the teachings make such statements.

2A. MAN INSIDE THE CIRCLE, WITH OX UNDERNEATH: 牛
This is the sign for "losing one's head and recognizing only one's shadow."[6] A person who does not understand that his own mind is both the Buddha and the Pure Land may believe that a Buddha's Pure Land is elsewhere than within himself; he may single-mindedly seek rebirth in that other Pure Land in order to see the Buddha and hear his dharma. Hence he diligently cultivates such Pure Land practices as reciting the name of the Buddha or recollecting the names and characteristics of the things in that Pure Land. This is what is represented by this symbol. As Pao-chih [418–514] said: "One who does not understand that mind is Buddha,/ Is truly like someone looking for a donkey while being mounted on a donkey."[7] I would answer one who comes to ask about this symbol by removing the ox from beneath the circle.

2B. MAN INSIDE THE CIRCLE: Ⓐ
This is the sign "turning one's back on one's shadow and recognizing one's head."

QUESTION: Why have you removed the ox-logograph from beneath the circle but retained the man?

ANSWER: A sentient being who has yet to give rise to true wisdom or penetrate to true emptiness may seek the Pure Land of the Buddha elsewhere than within his own mind and may desire to achieve rebirth in that external Pure Land in order to see the Buddha and hear his dharma. But if a sentient being traces the radiance emanating from his mind back to its source, thus giving rise to wisdom and penetrating to true emptiness, his own Buddha and his own Pure Land will then manifest in their totality, and he will never again need to seek the Pure Land and the Buddha apart from his own mind. Hence I did not remove the man that was inside the circle, but I did remove the ox underneath.

QUESTION: What does it mean to have a Buddha and a Pure Land in one's own mind?

ANSWER: If a sentient being gives rise to true wisdom and attains true emptiness, then that true wisdom would become the Buddha and that emptiness would become the Pure Land. Once this is experienced, you will know that nowhere else could one seek the Pure Land or the Buddha.

FIVE SYMBOLS IN FOUR SETS[8]

C: IA. HALF-CIRCLE: ▽

This is the symbol "lifting a box that is missing its lid." It is also called "half-moon waiting to become full." If a person were to come and ask about this symbol, I would reply by adding another half-moon on top of it, thus making a full circle. This would mean that the questioner lifts a box that is missing its lid, while the respondent takes the lid and places it on top of the box. Since both box and lid would then be present, the sign for full moon would be complete. The resulting full circle therefore represents the essence of all the buddhas.

IB. FULL CIRCLE: ○

This is the symbol "carrying a piece of jade and searching for the deed of ownership." If a person were to come and ask about this sign, I would answer by placing the logograph for "someone" inside the circle. This would mean that the questioner searches for the deed of ownership to a piece of jade he is carrying, and the respondent, once he certifies that it is the right piece of jade, places the document into his hand.

2. SOMEONE INSIDE THE CIRCLE: ⊘

This is the sign for "dropping a hook into the water and letting out the line." If a person were to come and ask me about this sign, I would answer him by appending the logograph "man" to the side of the logograph for "someone" inside the circle, yielding the logograph "Buddha." This would then mean that the questioner drops the hook into the water and lets out the line, and the respondent places a precious vessel on the line.

3. BUDDHA INSIDE THE CIRCLE: ⑭

This is the symbol "the precious vessel has been obtained." If a person were to come and ask me about this symbol, I would place the logograph for soil inside the circle.

4. SOIL INSIDE THE CIRCLE: ⊕

This is the sign for "purport of the arcane seal." It is also the sign "distantly transcending everything present before oneself." This symbol has no more associations with the scriptural teachings; it is like something that is right in front of your face and yet invisible. For this reason, the Third Patriarch Seng-ts'an [d. 606] said: "One iota of difference,/ And heaven and earth are rent asunder."[9] If a student in a later age whose spiritual potentiality is keen were to take up this sign, he would suddenly understand—like a chick pecking through its shell. At the same time, however, if a person who is dull and stupid were to study this doctrine, it would be hard for him to comprehend it—like a blind man trying to understand color.

THREE LEVELS OF THE ATTAINMENT OF BUDDHAHOOD

D: 1. ATTAINMENT OF BUDDHAHOOD THROUGH REALIZATION OF THE NOUMENON

Through the words of a meditation master, one traces the light of the mind back to its source and discovers that the fountainhead of one's mind is fundamentally devoid of everything. This type of attainment of Buddhahood is not a realization brought about through the gradual cultivation of the bodhisattvas' myriads of subsidiary practices; this is why it is called "attainment of Buddhahood through realization of the noumenon." For this reason, a scripture says: "The initial arousal of the thought of enlightenment is the attainment of perfect enlightenment."[10] As an ancient master also said: "The path to Buddhahood is not far off—it is nothing other than returning to the mind."

At this level of attainment, if it is said that the essential nature is completely devoid of even a single thing, this would imply that all three bodies of the Buddha—that is, one Buddha and two bodhisattvas—would have to be inherent therein.[11] Here the Buddha Vairocana represents the noumenon; the Bodhisattva Mañjuśrī symbolizes wisdom; and the Bodhisattva Samantabhadra portrays practice. Because these three all have the same essence, each of them must be present. As Li T'ung-hsüan [635–730] said: "All the Buddhas attained the bodhi of Buddhahood thanks to the two mahāsattvas Mañjuśrī and Samantabhadra."[12] He also said: "Mañjuśrī and Samantabhadra were the younger and elder brothers of all the buddhas."[13] The effort involved in attaining Buddhahood is symbolized by Mañjuśrī; hence the ancients said that Mañjuśrī was the mother of all the buddhas, for all buddhas attain bodhi through his wisdom.[14]

II. ATTAINMENT OF BUDDHAHOOD THROUGH COMPLETION OF THE INCUMBENT PRACTICES

After one has penetrated to the noumenon, one must then continue to cultivate the bodhisattva path in accordance with the practices and vows of Samantabhadra and to perfect both compassion and wisdom. This is why this level of attainment is called "attainment of Buddhahood through completion of the incumbent practices." An ancient master said that the place where you finally arrive in your practice is the same place from which you departed. Therefore, you should know that when your spiritual quest is completed, you return to your original place. This original spot is the noumenon. The noumenon that is realized at this level of attainment is no different from that achieved at the preceding level. Even though the noumenon is not separate from the practice, this second level of attainment involves a progression from cause (the cultivation of the path) to fruition (the attainment of Buddhahood), so it is given this name. Since this level involves the perfection of all the meritorious qualities inherent in the fruition of Buddhahood, it is achieved only through the practices of Samantabhadra.

This level of the attainment of Buddhahood also involves all three bodies of the Buddha. Because this level is concerned with the practices that result in the attainment of Buddhahood, the effort involved in bringing about this attainment is symbolized by Samantabhadra. It is for this reason that all of the bodhisattvas' myriads of subsidiary practices are referred to as "Samantabhadra." And because all the buddhas realize enlightenment through these myriads of practices, the ancients have said that Samantabhadra is the father of all the buddhas.

III. ATTAINMENT OF BUDDHAHOOD THROUGH MANIFESTING
ONESELF IN THE WORLD

After completing the prior two levels of the attainment of Buddhahood, then, for the benefit of all sentient beings, the adept displays
the eight stages in the achievement of Buddhahood that take place
during a bodhisattva's final life: descent from the Tuṣita Heaven;
entering the womb; residing in the womb; birth; leaving the household life; attaining enlightenment; turning the wheel of the dharma;
entering *parinirvāṇa*. These eight stages are actually illusory transformations; they do not really happen. This is why the scriptures say:
"The Thus Come Ones do not appear in the world and do not attain
nirvana; nevertheless, they do appear freely in the world through the
power of their original vow to attain Buddhahood."[15] The scriptures
also say: "Incalculable aeons have elapsed since my attainment of
Buddhahood."[16] Hence we know that, innumerable aeons in the past,
Śākyamuni the Thus Come One had already achieved the full enlightenment that is brought about through the completion of the bodhisattva practices; yet, for the benefit of all sentient beings, he displayed
this event of his initial attainment of Buddhahood.

A perusal of the scriptural teachings or an examination of the
records of ancient Meditation masters will show that any person's
attainment of Buddhahood always involves all three of these levels.
All buddhas, whether past or future, follow this same procedure, just
as people traveling the same road all follow along in the same ruts.

THREE TYPES OF ATTAINMENT OF THE REALITY LIMIT[17]

E: I. SUDDEN ATTAINMENT OF THE REALITY LIMIT

A sentient being who, since time immemorial, has yet to awaken
to the land of his self-nature continues to wander on in the three
realms, receiving retribution according to conditions. If he suddenly
meets a wise man who explains for him the true teaching and he
suddenly awakens to his nature, he then attains perfect enlightenment
without needing to progress through gradual stages of practice. For
this reason, this is called the "sudden attainment of the reality limit."

Although anyone may hear the dharma, not everyone will attain
enlightenment with equal speed. This is because people's faculties and
characters vary due to their different actions in previous lives. Hence

although everyone may hear the same teaching, one's realization will not be identical; it is not that there is any deficiency in the teachings that are preached by the wise.

This does not mean, however, that one should preach only to the wise and not to the dull. The wise are not originally enlightened; the dull are not internally deluded. Even though a sentient being whose faculties are dull hears the true teachings continuously, he will not come to understand his nature. But as soon as a sentient being whose faculties are keen hears those teachings, he will suddenly understand his nature and become wise. Hence there is no inherent difference between ordinary men and saints; there is merely a difference as to whether their faculties are sharp or dull. When the wise preach the dharma, it is not for the well-being of only one person. It is like a mother hen sitting on her eggs: all the eggs in the nest will hatch, but those that fall out will not. It is not fair to say that the mother hen discriminates between the eggs that remain in her nest and those that fall out; so whether an egg hatches or not has nothing to do with the hen but with whether the egg stays in the nest. It is the same with the dharma spoken by the wise: while they may preach their true teaching for the benefit of all sentient beings, only the clever will understand it suddenly; the dullards will not. But would that fact make it fair to say that the wise love only clever people and hate dullards? Hence whether one understands or not is entirely dependent upon one's faculties and character; it has nothing whatsoever to do with that dharma.

After a sentient being has heard this true teaching and has suddenly seen the land of the true nature, he must not remain complacent in that understanding. Rather, he must continue to practice both compassion and wisdom in order to bring benefit both to himself and to others. There are three aspects to this practice; each is correlated with the practices of Samantabhadra.

1. Bond-overcoming Samantabhadra: This is the practice after enlightenment. The adept must first free himself from the bonds of the habituations that continue to plague the person even after awakening to the mind. Thanks to his earlier enlightenment, however, the person is able to work on overcoming these habituations, while recognizing that they are ultimately illusory.

2. Bond-entering Samantabhadra: In this second stage of practice, the individual enters the world for the benefit of all sentient beings who have yet to be enlightened. Out of his great compassion, he attempts to save all beings from their suffering and bring them also to enlightenment. When both of these types of practice are consummated, it is called "equal enlightenment," the fifty-first stage of the path to Buddhahood, because both wisdom and compassion are completely perfected.

3. *After-fruition Samantabhadra:* This stage, in which all mental absorptions are cultivated, is the stage of "sublime enlightenment," the fifty-second and final stage of the bodhisattva path. Here a person clings neither to wisdom nor to compassion, and yet these appear spontaneously in all his actions. He does not remain fixed in any one status but appears at will in all situations in order to exhibit his great compassion for the benefit of all types of beings.

II. ATTAINMENT OF THE REALITY LIMIT THROUGH THE GRADUAL TEACHINGS

Since time immemorial, a sentient being has yet to awaken to the land of the nature and continues to wander on in samsara. He might hear the gradual teachings of the three vehicles and awaken to that dharma. Because of the calamities inherent in the three worlds, an adherent of one of these three vehicles might later come to hear the true teachings; his provisional understanding would then be transformed into sublime wisdom, and he would realize the reality limit. Hence this is called "attainment of the reality limit through the gradual teachings." For this reason, the ancients said that the three carts in front of the gate were the provisional vehicles, while the white ox in the open pasture was the reality limit.

Even though these two types of attainment are classified separately, they are not ultimately distinguishable. This is because, even though one may initially have fallen into the provisional understanding of the three vehicles, one need not remain forever bogged down in that understanding. Just as when hundreds of rivers return to the ocean they all lose their individual names, so it is when the three vehicles return to the one Buddha vehicle.

Even after a person has completed this type of attainment, however, this is not to imply that he should neglect the cultivation of all the incumbent practices. The person who attains the reality limit through the transformation of gradual practices is like the white ox in the open pasture: that ox continues to move around and does not stay only in the pasture. In the same way, despite his realization, that person continues to cultivate all of the bodhisattva practices in emulation of Samantabhadra. In this simile, the open pasture is the dharma that is realized—that is, the Buddha Vairocana. The white ox is the person who has realization—that is, Mañjuśrī. But because that white ox continues to move around and does not stay in that open pasture, it is also Samantabhadra.

III. GRADUAL REALIZATION OF THE REALITY LIMIT

There might be a sentient being who, since time immemorial, has yet to awaken to the land of the nature and continues to wander on in samsara, receiving the incumbent karmic retribution. Suddenly, he may hear the gradual teachings of the three vehicles and gradually give rise to faith and understanding. Following all the stages of the bodhisattva path for three incalculable aeons, he endures that which is difficult to endure, practices that which is difficult to practice, and finally brings an end to his delusion and achieves merit. At that point he finally achieves the nonoutflow wisdom and exposes the dharma body. Hence this is called "gradual realization of the reality limit."

Although this gradual attainment of the reality limit differs from the sudden approach discussed earlier, the two are ultimately identical–just as when rivers enter the sea, they all come to have the same taste of salt. As explained previously, after the sudden attainment of the reality limit one still performs all the incumbent practices of the bodhisattva—that is, the three types of Samantabhadra practice. One who follows the gradual attainment of the reality limit relies on the expedients of the gradual teachings and cultivates the bodhisattva practices over three incalculable aeons before he attains the nonoutflow wisdom and displays the dharma body. After this gradual attainment, one's practice still is dependent upon the stages and levels of the path; hence it is not the same as the practices that follow the sudden attainment of the reality limit. RB

The Life of Pŏmil
[From *Tsu-t'ang chi* 17:107a–c]

Great Master T'onghyo, from Sagul Mountain in Myŏngju,[18] was a successor to Yen-kuan Ch'i-an [750–842]. His dharma name was Pŏmil. His father,[19] Surwŏn, from the Kim clan of the Kyerim (Silla) aristocracy, served as the governor of Myŏngju. He was incorruptible, fair, and responsive to the sentiments of the commoners. He was magnanimous but firm in governing the people. The salutary climate of his rule is still noted in folk songs, and additional examples of his beneficent character are recounted in full in his official biography.

Pŏmil's mother, from the Mun clan, was part of a powerful family that had wielded influence for successive generations. The world considered her to be a "wifely paragon." When she conceived Pŏmil, she dreamed of a portent in which she caressed the sun; after thirteen months of pregnancy, she gave birth on the tenth day of the first month, in the year *kyŏngin,* the fifth year of Yüan-ho [17 February 810]. The infant was born with a remarkable appearance: his hair was curled in a topknot and he bore the unusual mark of a jewel on his crown.

When he turned fifteen, he vowed to leave the home life and asked his father and mother for permission to do so. Both of his parents consented, saying, "This salutary fruition of past conditions will not allow you to go back on your resolve. You must first emancipate us who have yet to be emancipated." Thereupon he bowed, taking leave of his parents, and left in search of a mountain site where he could enter the religious life.

When he turned twenty, he arrived in the capital Kyŏngju and received the complete precepts of a monk. He was perfect in his wholesome conduct and unremitting in his spiritual cultivation. He was a model of propriety for the gray-robed monks and a paragon for his religious companions.

In the middle of T'ai-ho [c. 830–833], he made a personal vow to travel to China. Accordingly, he came before the court and revealed his intentions to Lord Kim Ŭijong [fl. 843]. The lord praised his resolve and gave Pŏmil permission to travel together with him; he then requisitioned a ship, and together they sailed to T'ang.

In accordance with his earlier vow, he decided to go on pilgrimage around the country to seek out all the learned masters. He paid his respects to Great Master Yen-kuan Ch'i-an. The great master asked, "Whence have you come?"

Pŏmil replied, "I have come from Tongguk."

The great master proceeded to ask, "Did you come by land or by sea?"

He replied, "I did not tread on either route."

"Since you did not tread on either route, then how did you manage to get here?"

He responded, "What obstacle is there to the sun and moon appearing in the east or the west?"

The great master remarked, "You really are a Bodhisattva of the East."

Pŏmil questioned him, "How is Buddhahood achieved?"

The great master replied, "The religious path need not be cultivated; it merely involves not allowing yourself to become tainted and not holding to any view of there being either buddhas or bodhisattvas. The ordinary mind is the path."

Through these words, Pŏmil had a great awakening and was diligent in his practice for six more years.

Subsequently, the master visited Yüeh-shan (Wei-yen) [745–828]. Yüeh-shan asked, "Whence did you recently depart?"

Pŏmil replied, "I recently departed from Kiangsi."

Yüeh-shan asked, "What have you come to do?"

The master answered, "I have come to visit you, master."

Yüeh-shan said, "There is no road between these two places. So how are you going to visit?"

The master replied, "If you would advance one more step, you would find the student but wouldn't see yourself any more."

Yüeh-shan said, "How marvelous! How laudable! The fresh breeze blowing in from outside cools the desires and lusts of men. During your long pilgrimage, enter the abode of the emperor."

In the fourth year of Hui-ch'ang [844], monks were persecuted and temples destroyed; fleeing east, running west, there was no place to hide. Guided by the god of the river and escorted by the mountain spirit, Pŏmil eventually found a secluded place on Mount Shang where he stayed alone practicing meditation. He gathered fallen fruits to satisfy his hunger and drank handfuls of flowing spring water to quench his thirst. He became emaciated and wizened; his strength waned to the point that he did not dare to leave. After half a year had passed, he unexpectedly dreamed that a strange man told him, "You may go now."

Thereupon he impetuously planned his departure, but his strength was not yet up to it. In an instant, the mountain animals brought food to him in their mouths and laid it to the side of his seat. He ate the food, thankful for what he had received.

Later he vowed to travel to Shao-chou and pay his respects at the stupa of the Sixth Patriarch, Hui-neng [638–713]. Once he was within a thousand *li* of Ts'ao-ch'i Mountain, a fragrant cloud suddenly arose swirling in front of the shrine. A numinous crane flew down and sang from the top of the hall. The monks of the monastery were startled and marveled, "Such auspicious signs are truly remarkable. It must be an omen that a Ch'an master is coming to visit."

Finally, he decided to return to his homeland in order to disseminate the Buddhadharma. In the eighth month of *chŏngmyo*, the sixth year of Hui-ch'ang [14 September–12 October 847],[20] he again crossed the sea and returned to Kyerim. Aloofly, the light of his moon of morality glowed over the city of the black hare (the moon); brilliantly, the radiance of his gemlike ideas shone over the land of the green hills (the abode of the transcendents).

He sat in meditation on Paektal Mountain until the first month of the fifth year of Ta-chung [851] when Lord Kim, the governor of Myŏngju, invited him to reside at Kulsan Monastery. Once he had sat in the forest, over forty years elapsed. The arrayed pines were his cloister for practicing the religious life; the flat rocks served as his seat for cultivating meditation.

Someone asked Pŏmil, "What was the idea of the patriarchs?"

He replied, "Through six generations, it has yet to be lost."

He was asked again, "What does the monk's vocation involve?"

He answered, "Do not pursue the buddhas' rank. Do not emulate another's awakening."

Three kings performed special rites in absentia to express their reverence and decided to install him as a national preceptor: Great King Kyŏngmun in the twelfth year of Kan-t'ung, third month [25 March–23 April 871], Great King Hŏngang in the first year of Kuang-ming [880], and Great King Chŏnggang in the third year of Kuang-ch'i [887]. But each time they sent an envoy to escort him back to his new post in the capital, the great master remained stubborn in his refusal and absolutely declined to accede to the office.

On the last day of the fourth month of *kiyu*, the second year of Wen-te [2 June 889],[21] he abruptly summoned his disciples and said, "I am about to go elsewhere; I now must give my eternal farewell. None of you should allow yourselves to become distraught and grief-stricken, your thoughts trivialized by worldly emotions. Just cultivate your own minds; do not neglect the intent of this Meditation school."

Then, lying on his right side with one foot upon the other, he passed into extinction on the first day of the fifth month [3 June 889] at the upper master's room at Kulsan Monastery. He was eighty years old and had been a monk for sixty years. His funerary name was Great Master T'onghyo, and his stupa was called Yŏnhwi. RB

Geomancy

The belief in geomancy was associated not only with Confucian and Taoist thought but also with Buddhism. In the period of transition from the end of Silla to the beginning of Koryŏ, geomancy became aligned with the revolutionary Meditation school; belief in prognostication lore and texts served as a force for change. Essentially, the divination of terrain was an effort to determine how local currents of the cosmic breath affected human fortunes. Based on the location of mountains, water, and direction, the awareness of terrestrial conformation prevalent in earlier times became the foundation for the rise of geomancy. As time passed, geomancy accepted the yin/yang and five elements theories and adopted the Buddhist notion that "wholesome root produces wholesome fruit"—it was thought that the erection of monasteries and stupas could alter the geomantic situation. At times, allied with prognostication texts, such ideas acquired a revolutionary character. Thus geomancy, already known in the Three Kingdoms period, gained force with the adoption of a Buddhism that embraced native beliefs.

At first, the application of geomancy was restricted to the ruling classes in the capital who used it to enhance the ruler's authority or to choose sites for palaces and royal tombs. With the spread of the Meditation school to the provinces, however, it too was disseminated. Local clans who revolted against the central aristocracy used geomancy to rationalize the formation of their independent power. When the center of power moved from the aristocracy to provincial clan chiefs, these leaders singled out their power bases as centers of a new era. The area of Songak, for example, the base of Wang Kŏn, was known as an auspicious place worthy of being a capital. Although contenders for power did not leave records concerning their views on the subject, the phrase "an auspicious place of the Three Han," current among the Meditation centers, indicates that they too believed their bases to have been ideally chosen.

Ch'oe Yuch'ŏng: Stele Inscription at Jade Dragon Monastery

[From *Tong munsŏn* 117:18b–22b; *Chōsen kinseki sōran* 1:560–561]

Tosŏn, the geomancer and Meditation master, systematized contemporary theories on the subject, helping to lead popular sentiment away from Kyŏngju to the provinces. The shift of influence from Kyŏngju in the southeast to the middle of the peninsula was advantageous to Wang Kŏn, who rose from the Songak area to unify the later Three Kingdoms. Most historical materials on Tosŏn date from later times, but a comparatively reliable one is the inscription (1150) by Ch'oe Yuch'ŏng on a monument at Ongnyong (Jade Dragon) Monastery. The monument no longer stands, but the inscription is preserved in the *Tong munsŏn*. It consists of three parts: Tosŏn as a Meditation monk; the relationship between Tosŏn and geomantic thought; and the relationship between Tosŏn and Wang Kŏn.

In the fourth year after His Royal Highness Ŭijong succeeded to the throne, in the tenth month, *sinyu* day [9 November 1150], he commanded this subject, saying: "Considering that National Preceptor Sŏngak was flourishing and replete in his wisdom and virtue, and that his achievements on behalf of the state were most profound, the founder and exemplars of our royal line have repeatedly added to his honorary enfeoffment; thus it was that they brought veneration of the monarchy to repletion. Until now, however, these achievements have remained unchronicled, and on this account we feel ashamed. Our late sire Injong [1123–1146] has already commissioned you to compose an account: may you respectfully comply with this!" On hearing this I trembled with fear and, withdrawing, prepared the draft. Having obtained the relevant facts in some detail, I noted them down in proper order.

The master's taboo name was Tosŏn. His secular surname was Kim; he was a man of Yŏngam in Silla. The genealogy of his father and grandfather have faded from the record; some say that he was an illegitimate descendant of Great King T'aejong [654–661]. His mother, born Kang, dreamed that someone gave her a beautiful pearl and had her swallow it. Accordingly she became pregnant and for a full month abstained from strong-smelling vegetables and rank meats, devoting herself entirely to chanting the Buddha's name with scriptures in hand. When in due course she suckled and cared for the infant, he was incomparably superior to ordinary children. Even while laughing or crying as a babe in arms, his intention seemed to be to express his reverence and awe for the Buddha's vehicle. His mother and father, knowing that he was certain to become an instrument of the dharma, in their hearts assented to his leaving home. Versatile and precocious, he combined understanding with practice. Having had his hair shaved, he proceeded to Hwaŏm Monastery on Wŏryu Mountain where he read and practiced the scriptures of the Great Vehicle, penetrating the Great Meaning before a month had passed. The ineffable wisdom of Mañjuśrī and the mystic gate of Samantabhadra entered his mind [with nothing left over]. Students by the hundreds and thousands all submitted in astonishment, considering him to be divinely intelligent.

In the eighth year of King Munsŏng [846], at the age of twenty, he bethought himself: "A real man should be able to achieve tranquility by himself apart from the dharma. How can he do this while holding steadfastly to the letter of the dharma?" At that time Great Master Hyech'ŏl transmitted the secret seal to Sŏdang, Meditation Master Chijang, and opened a hall on Tongni Mountain. Many who were wandering in search of something better gravitated to him. And so Master Tosŏn lifted his robe at the dharma gate and asked to be accepted as a disciple. Great Preceptor Hyech'ŏl commended him for his intelligence and sagacity and welcomed him with utmost sincerity. All of what has been termed the unsaid saying and the dharmaless dharma was handed on to him as in the void, and in a vast serenity he achieved transcendent realization. At the age of twenty-three he received the full ordination at Ch'ŏndo Monastery. After Master Tosŏn had achieved revelation of the whole meaning, he wandered about with no settled abode. Treading through smoke and mist, he looked out over mountain springs; he looked for secluded places and sought out scenic beauty. But in so doing he never indulged in rest. Thus beneath Unbong Mountain he dug out a grotto for peaceful meditation, and before T'aebaek Cliff he wove rushes and sat in summer retreat. His name was everywhere heard, and all within the seas looked up to him in veneration. Those who were affected by his practice of the Path and the remaining evidences of his divine virtuosity are quite numerous; here we shall record only the most important ones.

On White Chicken Mountain in Hŭiyang county there is an ancient monastery called Jade Dragon. Stopping here after having wandered all around, the master loved the secluded beauty of the place and proceeded to repair and refurbish the halls. Then, with a start, he made a resolve to spend the rest of his days there. And indeed he sat quietly, forgetting to speak, for thirty-five years. At that time, students from all the four quarters converged upon him like clouds and adhered to him like shadows. Holding their towels and basins and presenting their staffs and sandals, those who became his disciples numbered several hundreds. Just as a single rain enriches all things however varied their motive power, so he with a piercing look made divine bestowals of enlightenment, and they who had gone to him empty went back filled up. King Hŏngang [875–885], out of respect for his lofty virtue, sent an emissary to extend welcome to him. At one meeting with him the king greatly rejoiced and kept him within the forbidden precincts, where he frequently opened and roused the king's heart with his mystic words and subtle discourse. But before long he took no delight in the royal amenities of the capital and earnestly requested that he might return to his home monastery.

Suddenly one day he summoned his disciples and said, "I am about to go. It was riding upon my conditioning that I came, and now that the condition has exhausted itself I shall depart. Why should you afflict yourselves with sorrow?" Having finished speaking, he lapsed into quiescence while seated in the lotus position. It was the tenth day of the third month of the first year of Kuang-hua of Great T'ang [898], the years of his life numbering seventy-two. His host of followers wailed and wept in both yearning and disbelief. Then they moved his sitting-place and erected a stupa on the hill north of the monastery, complying thereby with his testamentary command. When King Hyogong [897–911] heard of this, he sighed with grief and specially bestowed on him the posthumous title Meditation Master Yogong and named the stupa the Proven Sage's Lamp of Wisdom. His disciple Hongjŏk and others, fearing that their former master's deeds might go unrecorded, tearfully submitted a memorial begging that a chronicle be made. The king then commanded the Academician of Auspicious Writings Pak Inbŏm to write an inscription for the stele, but in the end it was never carved in stone.

Earlier, before the master had divined for the site of Ongnyong Monastery, he had set up a hut and stopped for rest on Bowl Hill of Chiri Mountain. One day a strange man paid a visit to his meditation seat and reported to the master saying, "For several hundred years I the disciple have lodged in obscurity beyond the phenomenal world. I am in predestined possession of a minor art, which I can proffer to you. If the venerable master will not look down upon my humble technique, I shall one day on the sandy seashore have something to confer upon him. This too is a method whereby the great bodhisattvas rescue the world and save all men." Then suddenly he disappeared. The master marveled at this. Later he went to the place agreed upon and indeed he met that very man. Bringing sand together to form configurations of harmony and antagonism, the man showed this; and when Tosŏn turned his head around to look, the man was no longer there. That place was in what is now Kurye county, which the local people call Sand Chart village. Thereafter the master, with a break-through of understanding, polished more than ever this knowledge of yin and yang and the five-phases techniques: occult secrets, however recondite, of golden tabernacle or jade cask were all as if imprinted in his heart.

Later on, the doctrine of Silla's rule gradually declined and there would soon be a sage who would receive the mandate and rise to preeminence. Accordingly, he made several trips to Songak prefec-ture. At that time our epochal progenitor Wang Yung was in the commandery building his residential villa. The master, passing his gate, said: "This place is fated to produce a king. But I'm not yet acquainted with the one who will initiate the process." It happened that an azure-clad servant boy heard this and went in to inform the epochal progenitor; the latter immediately ordered him to go out and welcome the master, who entered and conferred about the epochal progenitor's plans, making some changes in them. The master then said, "After two years you are certain to beget a noble son." There-upon he wrote one roll of text and sealed it securely. Presenting it to the epochal progenitor, he said: "This writing is to be proffered to the yet unborn lord. But you should present it to him only after the years have brought him to stalwart manhood." In this year Silla's king Hŏngang ascended the throne; it was the second year of Ch'ien-fu of the T'ang [874]. In the fourth year [877] our grand progenitor T'aejo was born in the earlier villa. Upon reaching manhood he obtained the writing and perused it, whereupon he knew that heaven's mandate had found in him its lodgement. He proceeded to exterminate the bandit rabble and undertook the creation of his realm. Respectfully mindful as he was of the spirits and the sages, how could it be that he ever had his mind set on conquering the world? As for the means whereby he eliminated chaos and turned the world back to rectitude, uplifting the people and prospering the region—granted that he re-stored the situation in which Heaven supported the virtuous and the people were embraced in humaneness—nonetheless, it was in the Source of Transformation that he inaugurated the holy era, and it was in Fate's hidden numbers that he fixed the fulfillment of his destiny. All these achievements have their origin in our master's instigation. One may indeed say that the preeminence and glory of his accomplishments were indeed as fully attested as this. It is only right that he be praised and posthumously exalted.

Therefore King Hyŏn [1010–1031] bestowed on him the title of Meditation Master, and to this Progenitor Suk [1096–1105] added the title of Royal Preceptor. And when it came to pass that our late holy sire Great King Konghyo [1123–1146] vastly exemplified the intent whereby the successive sage kings have commemorated achievements and rewarded virtue, he in turn advanced his enfeoffment to that of Precognizant National Preceptor. He then sent an emissary to announce the ceremony and conduct a ritual in the Portrait Hall of his original monastery. Our present sovereign Ŭijong [1147–1170] has further ordered that an account of the affair be carved in stone to perpetuate its transmission. How replete it is! There is nothing further to add by way of honors for Tosŏn. I have already tried to put the matter into words:

"When emperors and kings are about to rise, the spirit of their awesome numen blazes up, and this inevitably has the power to rouse and agitate beings. Therefore, those of lofty talent and unusual perception rise up as it were to the roll of drums and, whether before the action of the new ruler or after it, make their services available to him. In the case of the national preceptor's relationship with our grand progenitor his services were truly magnificent. For he had foreknowledge of events before the birth of the grand progenitor and brought his efficacy into play even after his body had perished. Their spirits matched in a mystic bond in a way that is beyond comprehension. Ah, the way of our holy master! His reaching to the outermost limit equaled that of the Buddha and patriarchs, and the significance that dwells in his achievements is like Chang Tzu-fang's reception of the writing or the prophecies of the divine monk Pao-chi. Moreover, he was a mate of the consummate master of numerology I-hsing. Many of the yin/yang theories the master transmitted in his writings are current in the world, and those who have later spoken about the principles of earth consider him to be their exemplar." MR

PART TWO

KORYŎ

Introduction

The Koryŏ kingdom (918–1392) developed out of the ruins of Silla. The process was slow, taking more than a decade and a half and ending in 936 when Koryŏ destroyed Later Paekche. Having accepted the formal surrender of the last Silla king the previous year, the dynastic founder, Wang Kŏn, established a state that lasted for nearly five hundred years before being succeeded by the Chosŏn kingdom (1392–1910). As the vital link between Silla and Chosŏn, Koryŏ inherited Silla's legitimacy and traditions and enriched this heritage before yielding the mandate of rule to Chosŏn.

Koryŏ history commonly is divided into three periods: aristocratic rule (918–1170); military rule (1170–1270), and Mongol domination (1270–1392). This division appropriately shows the changes in leadership and power. In this volume, however, Koryŏ is divided in half at the year 1170, the start of the military period. Certain themes appearing in the first half of the dynasty set the stage for subsequent development in the latter half. This periodization shows the inner coherence of Koryŏ while still making clear the differences that arose from the dramatic change in leadership and power structure that occurred in 1170.

During its first century, Koryŏ went through an intense period of development into a state. When Silla collapsed under mounting internal pressures, disintegration and chaos quickly set in, affording upstart regional figures opportunities to split Korea into rebel strongholds.

Wang Kŏn emerged as a powerful general under Kim Kungye in T'aebong in central Korea. In 918, he founded Koryŏ, overthrowing Kungye. Seventeen years later, the last Silla king formally acknowledged Wang Kŏn's hegemony by recognizing the new dynasty and peacefully transferring power to it. In 936, after militarily destroying the internally torn Later Paekche, Wang Kŏn became the unchallenged authority in the Korean peninsula.

Yet Koryŏ owed much to Silla. In Silla, birth determined one's social and political functions. Koryŏ was never able to escape totally from this rigid order, as the architects of Koryŏ were themselves mostly men from Silla aristocratic clans and some of the great clans would continue to dictate Koryŏ politics until the kingdom's collapse in the fourteenth century. Silla's religious beliefs also influenced Koryŏ thought. Buddhism, which had matured during the Silla period, continued to dominate Koryŏ society. The Buddhist hierarchy grew rich through its links with the court and great clans and influenced the life and thought of the kingdom. Indigenous shamanism merged with Buddhist beliefs as well as Taoism and folk cults, leaving indelible marks, particularly in the popular culture.

Chinese culture also contributed to Koryŏ's development. As Koryŏ's early kings searched for an effective system of government, they naturally turned to China's rich and varied experience and borrowed liberally from Chinese political thought and institutions, eventually affording Koryŏ a sophisticated system of administration. Koreans also adopted the Chinese system of official recruitment, which relied in good part on a state examination on skill in literary Chinese and the Confucian classics. The state examination became an important means to select civil officials of varied backgrounds, who in the latter half of the dynasty became an active check on the entrenched power of the aristocratic establishment.

Early Koryŏ, compared to Silla, was a much more mobile society that had greater resemblance to China both intellectually and politically. Koryŏ kings were generally well versed in Confucian thought while also devoted to Buddhism. Through its international contacts and internal maturity, Koryŏ achieved a level of sophistication that put it on a par with China, setting high standards in literature and art that became the envy of its world. Literary and artistic works of eleventh-century Koryŏ won the admiration of Chinese intellectuals for their refined style and erudition, for example, and the celadon produced in Koryŏ kilns has never been equaled to this day. Early

Koryŏ was a prosperous society that offered a degree of stability for both the rulers and the ruled.

Koryŏ was not, however, immune to foreign attack. Khitan and Jürchen tribes living to the north harassed Koryŏ from the start. The Khitan invaded Koryŏ on three separate occasions between 993 and 1018, forcing one Koryŏ king to flee his capital. When later challenged by the Jürchen, Koryŏ responded by building a long wall across its northern territory. But even with such fortifications, relations with the northern tribes remained tense and perilous. Through preemptive attacks and diplomatic appeasement, Koryŏ was able to keep frequently belligerent neighbors in the north in check until the massive onslaught of the Mongols in the thirteenth century.

The mid-twelfth century, which brought Koryŏ to the peak of its prosperity, also saw the dynasty in crisis. First, members of one of the kingdom's great clans, the Yi of Kyŏngwŏn, tried unsuccessfully to take control of the government. Less than a decade later, in 1135, a monk named Myoch'ŏng dared to challenge the power of the aristocratic establishment and even tried to establish a new dynasty with its capital at the site of modern P'yŏngyang. On both occasions the aristocratic elite establishment, calling on military officers, defeated these attempts, but the rebellions indicated growing political and societal unrest and tensions. In 1170 a group of disgruntled military officers who had been ostracized by members of the civilian elite revolted, enthroned a new king, and purged a large number of civilian aristocrats. The revolt commenced a century of military rule, as generals became the key figures in determining state policy.

In the middle of the military period a new danger threatened the dynasty: the Mongol invasions. By 1258, after nearly thirty years of resistance, the military ruler fell and a new civilian leadership ready to sue for peace emerged. The Mongols answered back by imposing a number of mechanisms of control upon Koryŏ. But with the eventual defeat of Yüan in China by the new Ming dynasty in 1368, Mongol domination over Koryŏ weakened. The end of the Mongols and the end of Koryŏ came nearly at the same time, as Neo-Confucian reformers, under the leadership of General Yi Sŏnggye, took control, instituting reforms and finally establishing the Chosŏn kingdom in 1392.

Despite the changes in its leadership, first with military rule and then with Mongol domination, Koryŏ remained a fairly stable, well-organized society. Although the literati officials had a more limited role in determining state policy in the latter half of the dynasty, the esteem for scholarship was undiminished. Much of Koryŏ's extant literature comes from the twelfth, thirteenth, and fourteenth centuries. The state examination, which had always been important, was maintained and even invigorated in the early fourteenth century. There is also evidence to suggest increased social mobility in late Koryŏ times. Nevertheless, great clans continued to dominate late Koryŏ life much as they had done earlier.

Although Buddhism remained the spiritual anchor of the kingdom, its thrust changed significantly. The Meditation school, which had spread in the closing days of the Silla kingdom, predominated in late Koryŏ society. With lavish donations and patronage from Koryŏ's leading families, meditation monasteries dotted the countryside. But this school was not the property of the elite alone. Because of its simple message, calling for meditation and relying on sudden enlightenment, the poor peasant and struggling merchant also found a source of inspiration in meditation.

Koryŏ, lodged between Silla and Chosŏn, is often overlooked in Korea's historical development. This is unfortunate because Koryŏ's legacy to contemporary Korea is impressive. Through the introduction of the civil service examination, it established merit as a criterion for government service. With its elaborate state apparatus, Koryŏ institutionalized government and made decisions in a rational manner. In Koryŏ, Buddhism expanded to become not only a religion of the aristocrats but a spiritual foundation for the entire society. In Koryŏ, as Koreans defended their land against invading troops, first from the north and then from Japanese pirates in the south, a sense and spirit of a people with a common heritage grew, heightening national consciousness. Koryŏ also produced priceless artistic and literary masterpieces. It was during the Koryŏ kingdom that the Western world first learned of Korea and began using the name Koryŏ for the country.

CHAPTER EIGHT

Early Koryŏ Political Structure

This chapter focuses on Koryŏ's political development through the early twelfth century, especially on the political foundations of the dynasty. King T'aejo (918–943) relied on both indigenous institutions and borrowed systems from China as he cautiously formed his new government. This structure was further strengthened by reforms launched by his successors, Kwangjong (949–975) and Sŏngjong (981–997) in particular. It was in the latter reign that Koryŏ's state organization clearly emerged through the efforts of Confucianized officials such as Ch'oe Sŭngno (927–989). Reform-minded officials like Ch'oe urged the implementation of Confucian practices that stressed proper moral conduct while trying to curtail Buddhist practices considered to be corrupting influences. Throughout the eleventh century, the political institutions were further refined as Koryŏ modified the dynastic structure through the successful transplantation of major Sung organizational forms.

While working on internal political stability, the dynasty also endeavored to normalize ties with the continental powers in the north. In response to shifting power, as first the Sung and then the Liao and Chin states emerged in succession, Koryŏ pursued a realistic foreign policy that sought a peaceful settlement of disputes through diplomacy while not shirking from military confrontation when necessary. The northern orientation thus set remained the basic direction of foreign relations for the rest of the Koryŏ period.

Founding of the Kingdom

Wang Kŏn, Koryŏ's dynastic founder, came from a locally prominent family in central Korea that joined the new leader of the region, Kim Kungye, in rebelling against Silla supremacy in the final days of the ninth century. Wang Kŏn rose quickly in Kungye's state of T'aebong, but as Kungye became more and more despotic in his rule, Wang Kŏn led disgruntled followers in a revolt and they founded Koryŏ in 918.

It was not until 936, however, that Wang Kŏn was able to gain full control of the peninsula, and until this was done, legitimacy was the foremost issue confronting him. When Silla's last king, Kim Pu (927–935), transferred his mandate to rule in 935, Wang Kŏn achieved the status and respectability necessary for his kingdom to gain dynastic legitimacy.

Wang Kŏn, also known by his posthumous title, T'aejo, spent the rest of his life consolidating political power in his reunified kingdom. The examples of his proclamations presented here attempt to justify his usurpation of the throne. They are cautious, reassuring statements promising that as the new ruler he will look for honest and able officials. He also declares that he will seek consensus by using the best traditions of both Silla and T'aebong (which first appeared as Later Koguryŏ).

Besides gaining acceptance for his leadership, Wang Kŏn wanted to assure his subjects of a well-managed government. In the edict he issued while visiting Yesan-jin in western central Korea, he poignantly displayed his concern about the capricious and unscrupulous way local leaders exercised power in his new kingdom and urged them to be disciplined and compassionate. The edict also reveals how hard he had labored to secure fair and just authority.

In the "Ten Injunctions," Wang Kŏn left his descendants clear instructions at the end of his reign to assure the success and continuation of the dynasty. This important document exerted a powerful influence throughout the remainder of the Koryŏ period. It was significant not only as Wang Kŏn's final statement, but also because of its wide-ranging advice covering Buddhism, geomancy, potential threats to dynastic security, and royal succession. The "Ten Injunctions" provide another view of early Koryŏ's intellectual climate.

Wang Kŏn's genealogy, which glorifies both his family inheritance and the forces that were to secure the dynasty, reaffirms the dynastic legitimacy. The earliest known publication of this genealogy dates from the twelfth century, and there is no reason to take literally his family's alleged aristocratic origins, links with T'ang China's imperial family, and sociopolitical prominence in central Koryŏ. The genealogy, rich in Buddhist, shamanistic, and geomantic references, is also revealing of certain mythological ideas prevailing in early Koryŏ.

Wang Kŏn: Enthronement Proclamation
[From *Koryŏ sa* 1:8b–9a]

On the fifteenth day, *pyŏngjin,* of the sixth month of T'aejo's first year [918],[1] Wang Kŏn was enthroned in the Hall of Statesmanship, calling the kingdom Koryŏ and taking the reign title Heaven's Bestowal (*ch'ŏnsu*). The king published a proclamation:

"The former lord Kungye gradually expanded the boundaries and eliminated bandits as Silla was collapsing like a pile of dirt. Even before the country was unified, however, his rule suddenly became tyrannical and cruel. He considered treacherous means to be the best and intimidation and insults to be necessary devices. Frequent corvée labor and heavy taxes exhausted the people, forcing them to abandon the land. Yet the palace was grand and imposing, and he ignored the established conventions. Endless public construction gave rise to popular resentment and criticism. He stole august titles to confer upon himself and killed his wife and children. Heaven and earth could not tolerate this. The deities and men all resented it. As his rule was collapsing, who would not take this to be a warning?

Owing to your hearty support, I became king. By joining together to correct laws, we can rejuvenate the country. Learning from past mistakes, we should look for solutions to problems in our immediate surroundings and recognize the mutual dependence of ruler and subject, realizing that our relations are like those of fish and water. The country will join in a celebration of the peace. I hope that people all over will know of my cherished intentions."

The ranking officials bowed in thanks and said: "At the time of the former ruler, we witnessed the gentle and good being harmed and the innocent being cruelly treated. The old and young wailed, harboring only resentment. Now, fortunately, under your enlightened rule, we can continue our lives. Why should we not exhaust ourselves to repay our indebtedness?" HK/ES

Formation of Government
[From *Koryŏ sa* 1:9b–11a]

On the twentieth day of the sixth month of T'aejo's first year [918], the king issued a proclamation that stated:

"In establishing government offices and assigning functions, it is most important to appoint men of ability. In making conventions beneficial and the people peaceful, the most urgent task is choosing the wise. Truly if there is no negligence, how could the government be out of control? I recall that, having undeservedly received the Heavenly Mandate and being about to manage the affairs of government, I was not at ease in accepting the responsibilities of the throne. I remember my fear of appointing the mediocre and pretentious. My greatest fear still is that I might not know clearly who the right people are, and therefore there may be many oversights in appointing them to appropriate offices. This leads me to worry that I may omit the wise, profoundly violating the process of selecting the right scholars. I worry about this all the time. If all officials of the central and local governments perform their duties properly, it will not only help in governing today but will be commended by later ages. Everyone in the country should know that I intend to be fair and just in giving fitting employment to the local gentry and in continuously testing and carefully selecting all officials.

"Accordingly, I appoint *Hanch'an* Kim Haengdo chancellor of the Department of the Chancellery (*Kwangp'yŏng sijung*) and *Hanch'an* Kŭmgang presiding minister of the Department of Ministries (*Naebong ryŏng*). . . . All these people are by character upright and fair and in managing business just and conscientious. They have all been meritorious in assisting me from the time I received the Heavenly Mandate and founded the dynasty.

"I also appoint *Alch'an* Im Chŏgyŏ executive of the Chancellery (*Kwangp'yŏng sirang*) and appoint former custodial executive of the Ministry of Pacification Forces (*Su sungunbu kyŏng*) Nŭngjun and executive of the Ministry of Storage (*Ch'angbu kyŏng*) Kwŏn Sik both executives of the Department of Ministries (*Naebong kyŏng*). . . . All these officials are well acquainted with the handling of government affairs, and, being honest and prudent, they have served the public diligently. They have been swift in making decisions and have always met the approval of the people.

"I appoint former chief officer of the Chancellery (*Kwangp'yŏng nangjung*) Kang Yunhaeng executive of the Department of Ministries; former assistant office chiefs of the Ministry of Pacification Forces (*Sungunbu nangjung*) *Hanch'an* Sin Il and Im Sik both office chiefs of the Chancellery. . . ."

Lower-ranking positions were also set up for all other offices, furnishing the needed number of government officials without exception. In general, the careful selection of outstanding talent at the inception of the dynasty made the administration of government affairs very just. HK/ES

Decree on Institutional Reform
[From *Koryŏ sa* 1:11b]

A royal decree stated, "I have heard that in reforming the nation's systems at an opportune time, one should correct errors thoroughly. In instructing the people and guiding their customs, orders must certainly be given prudently. The former lord Kungye changed the outmoded titles of Silla ranks and offices and those of provincial districts into a new system. Although the titles have been in use for many years, the people have not easily understood them, leading to confusion. From now on, we restore the Silla system and preserve those parts of Kungye's new system that are easily understood." HK/ES

Wang Kŏn: Edict at Yesan-jin
[From *Koryŏ sa* 2:6a–7b]

On the sixth day of the fifth month, summer, of T'aejo's seventeenth year [934], the king visited Yesan-jin and issued a proclamation:

"Recently, as Silla deteriorated politically, many bandits suddenly appeared, and people scattered in all directions, leaving skeletons exposed on the ground. Although the former lord Kungye had pacified contending factions and laid the foundation for the country, in his later years he brought harm to the people and endangered the kingdom. Succeeding at this perilous time, I founded this new country. How could it be my intention to burden the beleaguered peasants with corvée labor? But because the kingdom is still in its infancy I have allowed this to happen.

"Ignoring physical hardships, I have traveled all over the country inspecting the repairs of fortifications to protect my subjects from the harm caused by outlaws. Accordingly, the men have all gone to fight, and the women remain, carrying out the corvée labor. Nobody knows how many, unable to bear the hardship, have fled to the mountains or appealed to the government offices. If royal relatives and powerful families arrogantly and high-handedly repress the weak, how can I say that the people are not being harassed? How can I, only one person, call on house after house to see for myself? Accordingly, helpless peasants have no means to appeal and can only cry to heaven.

"You high-ranking officials who receive income from government stipends should know that I love my subjects as my own children, and you should look with pity on the people of your stipend villages. If you send uninformed retainers to your domains, they will only try to exact at will from the people as much as they can. How would you be able to know this? And sometimes, even when this is known, you do not forbid it. Even when the peasants see this and insist on appealing, officials, allowing their personal feelings to interfere, cause discontent to arise.

"As I have previously instructed on this matter, I want those who realized my concern to make further efforts and those who were not aware of it to increase their vigilance. Punish those who have disobeyed this command. Some have considered it advisable to hide their mistakes and do not report them. If this happens, how can I be aware of good and bad acts? If this is left unattended, who will care about integrity and correct his mistakes?

"You should adhere to my instructions and observe my order concerning rewards and punishments. Punishment should extend to the descendants of those who have committed crimes, regardless of their status. If merit is great and crimes are few, consider carefully the appropriate reward and punishment. And if their faults are not corrected, confiscate their stipends. Or forbid them to hold official rank for one year, or for two and three years, or for five and six years, or even for life.

"If their devotion to public service is great and without fault from beginning to end, provide them with rich stipends and honor during their lives, and after death let their families be known as illustrious families. Their posterity should receive privileged treatment and should be cited for their meritorious contributions. This shall be carried out not only for today but shall be transmitted forever afterward so that it will become a rule for all to observe.

"If one does not comply with an official summons as a result of a formal complaint by the people, then he must be summoned again and first be punished with ten strokes for his noncompliance. Then interrogate him regarding the crime for which he was summoned. If officials intentionally delay, calculate the number of days and account for the responsibility. Or if there are people who rely on power and influence, let their names be reported." HK/ES

Wang Kŏn: Ten Injunctions
[From *Koryŏ sa* 2:14b–17a]

In the fourth month, summer, of T'aejo's twenty-sixth year [943], the king went to the inner court, summoned *Taegwang* Pak Surhŭi, and personally gave him the injunctions, saying: "I have heard that when great Shun was cultivating at Li-shan he inherited the throne from Yao.[2] Emperor Kao-tsu of China rose from humble origins and founded the Han. I too have risen from humble origins and received undeserved support for the throne. In summer I did not shun the heat and in winter did not avoid the cold. After toiling, body and mind, for nineteen years, I united the Three Han (Later Three Kingdoms) and have held the throne for twenty-five years. Now I am old. I only fear that my successors will give way to their passions and greed and destroy the principle of government. This would be truly worrisome. I therefore wrote these injunctions to be passed on to later ages. They should be read morning and night and forever used as a mirror for reflection." His injunctions were as follows:[3]

"1. The success of every great undertaking of our state depends upon the favor and protection of Buddha. Therefore, the temples of both the Meditation and Doctrinal schools should be built and monks should be sent out to those temples to minister to Buddha. Later on, if villainous courtiers attain power and come to be influenced by the entreaties of bonzes, the temples of various schools will quarrel and struggle among themselves for gain. This ought to be prevented.

"2. Temples and monasteries were newly opened and built upon the sites chosen by Monk Tosŏn according to the principles of geomancy. He said: 'If temples and monasteries are indiscriminately built at locations not chosen by me, the terrestrial force and energy will be sapped and damaged, hastening the decline of the dynasty.' I am greatly concerned that the royal family, the aristocracy, and the courtiers all may build many temples and monasteries in the future in order to seek Buddha's blessings. In the last days of Silla many temples were capriciously built. As a result, the terrestrial force and energy were wasted and diminished, causing its demise. Vigilantly guard against this.

"3. In matters of royal succession, succession by the eldest legitimate royal issue should be the rule. But Yao of ancient China let Shun succeed him because his own son was unworthy. This was indeed putting the interests of the state ahead of one's personal feelings. Therefore, if the eldest son is not worthy of the crown, let the second eldest succeed to the throne. If the second eldest, too, is unworthy, choose the brother the people consider the best qualified for the throne.

"4. In the past we have always had a deep attachment for the ways of China and all of our institutions have been modeled upon those of T'ang. But our country occupies a different geographical location and our people's character is different from that of the Chinese. Hence, there is no reason to strain ourselves unreasonably to copy the Chinese way. Khitan is a nation of savage beasts, and its language and customs are also different. Its dress and institutions should never be copied.

"5. I achieved the great task of founding the dynasty with the help of the elements of mountain and river of our country. The Western Capital, P'yŏngyang, has the elements of water in its favor and is the source of the terrestrial force of our country. It is thus the veritable center of dynastic enterprises for ten thousand generations. Therefore, make a royal visit to the Western Capital four times a year—in the second, fifth, eighth, and eleventh months—and reside there a total of more than one hundred days. By this means secure peace and prosperity.

"6. I deem the two festivals of Yŏndŭng and P'algwan of great spiritual value and importance. The first is to worship Buddha. The second is to worship the spirit of heaven, the spirits of the five sacred and other major mountains and rivers, and the dragon god. At some future time, villainous courtiers may propose the abandonment or modification of these festivals. No change should be allowed.

"7. It is very difficult for the king to win over the people. For this reason, give heed to sincere criticism and banish those with slanderous tongues. If sincere criticisms are accepted, there will be virtuous and sagacious kings. Though sweet as honey, slanderous words should not be believed; then they will cease of their own accord. Make use of the people's labor with their convenience in mind; lighten the burden of corvée and taxation; learn the difficulties of agricultural production. Then it will be possible to win the hearts of the people and to bring peace and prosperity to the land. Men of yore said that under a tempting bait a fish hangs; under a generous reward an able general wins victory; under a drawn bow a bird dares not fly; and under a virtuous and benevolent rule a loyal people serves faithfully. If you administer rewards and punishments moderately, the interplay of yin and yang will be harmonious.

"8. The topographic features of the territory south of Kongju and beyond the Kongju River are all treacherous and disharmonious; its inhabitants are treacherous and disharmonious as well. For that reason, if they are allowed to participate in the affairs of state, to intermarry with the royal family, aristocracy, and royal relatives, and to take the power of the state, they might imperil the state or injure the royal safety—grudging the loss of their own state (which used to be the kingdom of Paekche) and being resentful of the unification.

Those who have been slaves or engaged in dishonorable trades will surrender to the powerful in order to evade prescribed services. And some of them will surely seek to offer their services to the noble families, to the palaces, or to the temples. They then will cause confusion and disorder in government and engage in treason through crafty words and treacherous machinations. They should never be allowed into government service, though they may no longer be slaves and outcasts.

"9. The salaries and allowances for the aristocracy and the bureaucracy have been set according to the needs of the state. They should not be increased or diminished. The classics say that salaries and allowances should be determined by the merits of those who receive them and should not be wasted for private gain. If the public treasury is wasted upon those without merit or upon one's relatives or friends, not only will the people come to resent and criticize such abuses, but those who enjoy salaries undeservedly will also not be able to enjoy them for long. Since our country shares borders with savage nations, always beware of the danger of their invasions. Treat the soldiers kindly and take good care of them; lighten their burden of forced labor; inspect them every autumn; give honors and promotions to the brave.

"10. In preserving a household or a state, one should always be on guard to avert mistakes. Read widely in the classics and in history; take the past as a warning for the present. The Duke of Chou was a great sage, yet he sought to admonish his nephew, King Ch'eng, with *Against Luxurious Ease (Wu-i)*. Post the contents of *Against Luxurious*

Ease on the wall and reflect upon them when entering and leaving the room." HP

The Foundation Legend of Koryŏ
[From *Koryŏ sa, segye:* 1a–8a]

HOGYŎNG

There was a man named Hogyŏng (Tigerish Effulgence) who, claiming to be the highest Holybone General, wandered down from Mount Paektu. Having reached the valley to the east of Mount Puso, he took a wife and settled there. He grew wealthy but had no children. An excellent archer, he made hunting his livelihood. One day, with nine of his fellow villagers, he was catching goshawks at Mount P'yŏngna when, the sun going down, they took shelter for the night in a cavern. Just then a tiger took a stand at the cavern's mouth and roared mightily. The ten men said to each other, "That tiger would like to devour us all. Let's try tossing our caps to him: the one whose cap he grabs will confront him." Accordingly they all tossed out their caps; the tiger grabbed that of Hogyŏng, who went forth to fight the tiger. But the tiger suddenly disappeared, and the cavern collapsed. Not one of the nine men inside was able to get out. Hogyŏng went back and told the people of P'yŏngna Commandery about it. They came to perform burial services for the nine, but first they offered a sacrifice to the spirit of the mountain. At that point the spirit appeared and said, "As a widow I hold sway over this mountain. Having now had the good fortune to encounter the Holybone General, I wish to marry him; as man and wife we shall together manage the spirit-government. I ask that you enfeoff him as great king of this mountain." Having finished speaking she vanished from sight, taking Hogyŏng with her. The people of the commandery accordingly enfeoffed Hogyŏng as great general and erected a shrine for offering sacrifice to him. They changed the name of the mountain to Nine Dragons because of the nine men who had together perished there. MR

KANGCH'UNG

Hogyŏng, not forgetting his old wife, came and joined with her often in dreams; they produced a son whom they called Kangch'ung.

Straight and awesome in physical appearance, Kangch'ung possessed talents and arts in abundance. He married Kuch'iŭi, the daughter of a wealthy man of Yŏngan village in the Western River. They settled on Cape Maga on Mount Ogwan. At that time there lived the *Kamgan* P'arwŏn, who was well versed in geomancy. Coming to Puso Commandery, which was to the north of Mount Puso, he observed that though the configuration of the mountain was superior, it was bare. Addressing himself to Kangch'ung he said, "If you will move the commandery seat south of the mountain and plant pine trees on it so that its rock formations are not exposed, the resulting auspices will be such that he who brings the Three Han together under his rule will come forth from here." Thereupon Kangch'ung, together with the people of the commandery, shifted the settlement south of the mountain and planted pine trees all over the mountain. Accordingly they changed the name of the commandery to Songak (Pine Hill). Kangch'ung finally became *sangsach'an*[4] of the commandery. Moreover, he made the villa at Cape Maga his hereditary holding, commuting to and from it. His family accumulated great wealth and produced two sons. MR

POYUK AND CHINŬI

The younger son, who was at first called Sonhosul, changed his name to Poyuk. Loving and benevolent by nature, he left home to practice the Way at Mount Chiri. On his return he settled on the north slope of Mount P'yŏngna, whence he further moved to Cape Maga. One day he had a dream in which, having climbed Kongnyŏng, he urinated facing southward. The urine inundated the mountains and rivers of the Three Han, which were thereby changed into a sea of silver. When he told his elder brother Ijegŏn about it the next day, Ijegŏn said, "You will certainly beget a heaven-supporting pillar!" and gave him his daughter Tŏkchu to be his wife. Poyuk then continued his life as a devotee on Cape Maga, where he built a retreat of wood. A Silla adept, seeing it, said, "If you continue to live here, you can be sure that a Great T'ang emperor will come and become your son-in-law."

Later Poyuk begat two daughters. The younger, named Chinŭi, was not only beautiful but also abundantly endowed with talent and wisdom. When she was just of marriageable age, her elder sister had a dream in which the elder sister had climbed to the top of Mount

Ogwan and urinated there, inundating the whole world. When she woke up and told Chinŭi about the dream, Chinŭi said, "Please let me buy it from you with my damask skirt." The elder sister having agreed to this, Chinŭi had her relate the dream again, while Chinŭi seized and embraced it three times. Immediately thereafter her body moved as if she had gotten what she wanted, and she was well content with herself.

When the August Theocrat of T'ang, Su-tsung [756–762] was in latent residence as heir apparent, he wanted to roam the mountains and rivers. In the spring of the twelfth year, *kyesa,* of Bright August's era of Heavenly Treasure [A.D. 753], he crossed the sea and arrived at the western estuary of the P'ae River. The tide being then at its ebb, the strand was muddy, so the attendant officers unloaded the boat's cargo of coins and spread them on the beach; then they were able to disembark upon the shore. Later that estuary was called Coin Estuary. Having finally reached Songak Commandery, Su-tsung climbed Kongnyŏng and, gazing southward, said. "This place is certain to become the capital of a state," whereupon one of his attendants said, "This is where the Eight Perfected Transcendants live." When Su-tsung reached the Yangja Cavern on Cape Maga, he put up for the night at Poyuk's residence. On seeing the two daughters he took delight in them and requested them to mend a tear in his robe. Poyuk, recognizing that this was a nobleman of the Middle Kingdom, observed to himself that his coming indeed matched the words spoken by the adept. Forthwith he ordered his elder daughter to respond to the nobleman's command, but she had hardly crossed the threshold when she suffered a nosebleed and went out again. He replaced her with Chinŭi, who then offered Su-tsung her pillow. After he had stayed for a month she became aware that she was pregnant. As he was about to leave, the nobleman said, "I am of the nobility of Great T'ang." And presenting her with bow and arrows, he said, "If you should give birth to a boy, give these to him." And indeed she bore a male child, whom she called Chakchegŏn. Later Poyuk was posthumously honored as Great King of Primal Virtue, Patriarch of the State; his daughter Chinŭi was honored as Queen Chŏnghwa (Chaste Harmony). MR

CHAKCHEGŎN

As a child Chakchegŏn showed intelligent perceptiveness and divine courage. At the age of five or six he inquired of his mother: "Who is my father?" To this she replied: "T'ang father." No doubt this was because she simply did not know what his name was. When he grew up, his talents embraced the six arts; his calligraphy and his archery were particularly superb. When he was sixteen, his mother gave him the bow and arrows that his father had given her. Overjoyed, Chakchegŏn let fly, hitting the mark a hundred times out of a hundred. People called him Divine Bow. Wishing to visit his father, he then took passage on a merchant vessel. When they had sailed out to the high seas, a cloudy vapor engulfed them, and the ship did not move for three days. The crew of the vessel, having cast a divination, said, "We should get rid of the Ko[gu]ryŏ man!" Chakchegŏn, bow and arrow in hand, cast himself into the sea, where, as it turned out, there was a large boulder on which he was able to stand. The mist then cleared, a favorable wind came up, and the ship went on its way as if flying through the air.

Suddenly there appeared before Chakchegŏn an old man who bowed and said, "I am the Dragon King of the Western Sea. Every afternoon Old Mr. Fox appears here, taking the form of the Thus Come One of Blazing Fullness. Descending from the void, he wraps the sun and moon, stars and planets, in a cloudy mist. Making music by blowing on a conch shell and beating a drum, he comes here and takes his seat on this boulder, where he proceeds to read the *Ongjong kyŏng* (Tumors and Swellings Scripture). He has given me a frightful headache! I have heard that you, sir, are a highly skilled archer; I beg you to rid me of this misery!" Chakchegŏn consented. When the time came, he heard music sounding in the midst of nowhere, and indeed there was someone coming from the northwest. Beset by doubt as to whether it might be the Buddha himself, Chakchegŏn dared not shoot. But the old man reappeared and said, "It really is Old Mr. Fox, have no more doubt about it!" Chakchegŏn then stroked his bow and fingered his arrows. Taking aim he let fly, and with the twang of his bowstring something fell to earth. Indeed, it was Old Mr. Fox himself.

Delighted, the old man welcomed Chakchegŏn into his palace, saying, "Thanks to you, sir, I've been rid of that plague. For this great favor I'd like to reward you. Do you plan to proceed westward into T'ang to visit your father? Or, enriched with the seven treasures, will you return to the east and offer them to your mother?'' Chakchegŏn said, ''What I really want is to rule over the Eastern Land, Korea.'' The old man said, ''Wait for the third Kŏn among your descendants, and your rule over the Eastern Land is certain. All else is only fate's decree!'' Hearing these words, Chakchegŏn knew that time's mandate had not yet come. He hesitated, and before he was able to reply, from behind his seat an old woman said in jest, ''Why don't you go back with his daughter as your wife?'' Chakchegŏn then awakened to his opportunity and made the request, whereupon the old man gave him his eldest daughter Chŏminŭi to be his wife. As Chakchegŏn was about to return bearing the seven treasures, the dragon daughter said to him, ''My father also has a willow staff and a pig. These are better than the seven treasures. Why not ask for them?'' Chakchegŏn then asked to give back the seven treasures in return for the willow staff and the pig. The old man said, ''These two things are my talismans, but dare I refuse any request of yours?'' And he added the pig to his gifts.

Thereupon they set sail in a lacquered boat bearing the seven treasures and the pig, and quickly made land on the rivershore in front of the cave of Ch'ang Mound. Yu Sanghŭi, Chŏngjo of Paekchu, and others, on hearing of this, said, ''Chakchegŏn has come with his bride, the dragon daughter of the Western Sea—truly an occasion for rejoicing.'' Leading the people of the four cities of Kaeju, Chŏngju, Yŏmju, and Paekchu, and of the three prefectures of Kanghwa, Kyodong, and Haŭn, they built the city wall of Yŏngan and laid out a place for them. No sooner had she arrived than the dragon daughter went to the mountain slope northwest of Kaeju, where she dug with a silver basin to get the water they needed. This is what we now know as the Great Well of Kaesŏng. After they had lived in Yŏngan for a year, the pig refused to go into its pen. So they said to the pig, ''If this is a place where we shouldn't live, we'll follow you wherever you go.'' The next morning the pig reached the southern slope of Songak, where he lay down. So they laid out a new villa there, right at the old villa of Kangch'ung. They lived there for more than thirty years, regularly going back and forth to Yŏngan.

One day the dragon daughter dug a well just outside the bedroom window of the new Songak villa; through this she went back and forth to the dragon palace of the Western Sea. This is the well to the north of the upper east wing of Kwangmyŏng Temple. She once made a pact with Chakchegŏn, saying, ''Whenever I go back to the dragon palace, be careful never to observe me; otherwise, I won't come back again!" One day Chakchegŏn secretly spied on her. What he saw was the dragon daughter with her small daughter, as they entered the well, being transformed into yellow dragons, while giving rise to a five-colored cloud. He marveled at this but dared not speak of it. When she came back the dragon daughter angrily said, "In the code of a married couple, keeping one's word is the highest value. Now that you have violated our pact, I can no longer live here." Thereupon she and her small daughter were transformed into dragons and went into the well never to return. In his later years Chakchegŏn lived in the Changgap Temple on Mount Songni, where he occupied himself with reading Buddhist texts until he died. Later he was honored posthumously as Esteemed Progenitor, Great King of Luminous Vigor; the dragon daughter was honored as Queen Wŏnch'ang. MR

YUNG

Wŏnch'ang produced four sons, the eldest of whom was called Yonggŏn, a name he later changed to Yung; his cognomen was Munmyŏng. He became Sejo (Epochal Progenitor). Imposing in appearance, with a beautiful beard and of vast capacity, he had a resolve to bring the Three Han under his control. Once in a dream he saw a beautiful woman and made a pact with her to form a family. Later, on the way from Songak to Yŏngan city, he met a woman on the road who looked just like the woman in the dream, so he married her. Because people did not know where she had come from, they called her "Lady Dream." According to some, she was given the surname Han because she was the mother of the Three Han. She became Queen Wisuk. Sejo lived for several years in the old villa at Songak and then undertook to build a new villa to the south of it; this is the foundation of the Yŏngyŏng Palace's Pongwŏn Hall. At that time Tosŏn, patriarchal master of Mount Tongni, having gone to T'ang where he obtained I-hsing's geomantic methods, came back and climbed Mount Paektu. When he reached Kongnyŏng and saw the new villa that Sejo had built, he said, "Why have you planted hemp in a place for planting millet?" These words uttered, he departed.

Lady Han heard what he had said and reported it to Sejo. Sejo, in such haste that he put his slippers on backwards, went in pursuit of him; no sooner had they seen each other than they were like old friends. Together they climbed Kongnyŏng and investigated the arteries of the mountains and rivers. On high they examined the patterns of heaven, and below they scrutinized the fateful turnings of the times. Tosŏn then said, "This system of earth conduits arises from Mount Paektu in the north; with water (the north) as its mother and wood (the east) as its trunk, it drops into this Hayagriva-guarded Bright Hall. You too are under the mandate of water; you should comply with the great destiny allotted to water and build a palace with six-times-six compartments. In this way you will respond exactly to the great destiny ordained by heaven and earth, and next year you will certainly produce a holy child, whom you should name Wang Kŏn." Accordingly he devised a seal of verification, inscribing the outside of it with these words: "A reverently offered scripture. Bowing a hundred times, I present this scripture to His Excellency the Lord Taewŏn, Ruler Who Will Unify the Three Han." The time was the fourth month of the third year of Ch'ien-fu [A.D. 876]. Sejo built a house in accordance with Tosŏn's words and dwelt therein. In this month Queen Wisuk became pregnant with the future T'aejo, Wang Kŏn.[5]   MR

Expansion of Confucian Polity I

Ch'oe Sŭngno (927–989), the son of a Silla aristocrat, met King T'aejo at the age of twelve and so impressed the king that the latter gave Ch'oe an academic appointment. Ch'oe Sŭngno remained aligned with the court, and by the time Sŏngjong (981–997) became king, Ch'oe was one of the kingdom's leading statesmen.

Alert to potential dangers confronting the dynasty and anxious to consolidate dynastic authority throughout the kingdom, Ch'oe presented an ambitious twenty-eight-point memorial on contemporary affairs. In the opening section, the first passage presented here, Ch'oe recounts how Wang Kŏn, with his confederation of great families, established Koryŏ. In reviewing the events of the dynasty's first five reigns, he emphasizes T'aejo's merit in founding and securing the dynasty. Through Ch'oe's numerous descriptions, T'aejo takes on the image of a superhero, a reputation worthy of a dynastic founder.

The subsequent reigns did not match the first. Hyejong, Koryŏ's second king, was racked by suspicions. His successor, Chŏngjong, while diligent, mistakenly tried to move the capital to P'yŏngyang. Ch'oe Sŭngno roundly condemns Koryŏ's fourth king, Kwangjong. Although Kwangjong started well, he quickly attracted mediocre followers. Ultimately, his reign gave way to ostentation and collapsed into purges that threatened the life of his own son as well as the dynasty. Kwangjong's son, Kyŏngjong, succeeded to the throne and brought a measure of stability, but he too relied on powerful figures who undermined the kingdom. To Ch'oe Sŭngno, the events of the first five reigns were powerful lessons that the new king, Sŏngjong, should study in order to avoid the mistakes of the past.

Having presented a chronology of the first five reigns, Ch'oe then offers a specific reform package. The original memorial, containing twenty-eight points, six of which have been lost, is here divided into two parts to facilitate comprehension. "On Current Affairs" is a broad discussion of contemporary abuses that demanded urgent attention. Ch'oe treats border relations and ties with China as well as the need for tighter internal governance. To Ch'oe, adherence to Confucian norms of frugality and social responsibility would resolve most dynastic woes. Ch'oe also wanted to see a new order imposed on Koryŏ, one that would place centrally appointed officials in the twelve regional provinces (*mok*).

"On Buddhism" presents Ch'oe's critique of contemporary Buddhism. Although he acknowledged the functions of Buddhism, Ch'oe, a committed Confucian, felt that too much reliance on Buddhist practices would undermine the good of society. Ch'oe was especially critical of past Buddhist extravagances and clearly warned that unless reform was pursued, the future of the dynasty was in peril. Ch'oe believed that Buddhism should be fostered to meet the spiritual needs of the people and Confucian ideology should hold sway in affairs of state.

Ch'oe Sŭngno: On the First Five Reigns
[From *Koryŏ sa* 93:2b–12a]

I grew up in the countryside and am by nature simple and unscholarly, but I have been fortunate to live at a propitious time and have long attended all the Koryŏ kings, often receiving special honors. Although I have no brilliant plans to correct the problems of the age, still, having some concerns, I have pledged to work for the country. I humbly think of the historian Wu Ching [670–749] of the K'ai-yüan period [713–742], who compiled and presented his work, *Chen-kuan cheng-yao* (Essentials of Government of the Chen-kuan Period), to encourage Emperor Hsüan-tsung to emulate the policies of Emperor

T'ai-tsung. Because of the similarities of the two periods, though in different countries, the successful policies of Emperor T'ai-tsung can be a model for us.

In my humble view, King T'aejo's founding of the dynasty and its passing on to posterity is the so-called ancestral merit. The successive kings' guarding of the throne can be called the successors' virtue. Although by establishing a dynasty a founder extends blessings to his descendants, not all the descendants succeed and prosper. They could not escape the vicissitudes of their age because in governing one has to distinguish between right and wrong, just as in affairs there is good and bad. Usually one is not as careful at the end as at the beginning; so one is led to difficulties as well as to crises, truly regrettable though this is.

Since King T'aejo's founding of the dynasty, all that I have come to know I still know by heart. I therefore wish to record all the policies of the last five reigns, tracing the marks left, good and bad, and that can guide Your Majesty's conduct of government through this presentation.

I reckon that when our T'aejo, Great Divine Holy King, ascended the throne, it was a time of chaos, manifesting the destiny that occurs once in a thousand years. That he could first suppress the unruly and destroy the evil was due to the hand lent by Kim Kungye, which heaven produced. Afterwards, as T'aejo received Heaven's Mandate, people recognized his sagely virtue and turned to him. Thereupon Silla destroyed itself and Koguryŏ rode the destiny of restoration. Binding itself to its own locality, Koryŏ built its palace at Songak. Calming the turbulent waves of the Liao River and the P'ae River and taking over the former Chinhan territory, Koryŏ united the new territory within nineteen years. Truly there is nothing more noble than this achievement or greater than this virtuous act.

As the Khitans share a border with us, normally we would have established friendly ties with them. But despite their pledge of peace with Parhae, they suddenly became suspicious and destroyed Parhae, disregarding their pledge. This is why, even when they sent envoys seeking peace, we refused the exchange with them. King T'aejo considered them too unscrupulous to establish friendly ties with them and even cast away the camels they presented, refusing to raise them. Such was his profound and farsighted policy, which prevented trouble and protected the state from danger.

As Parhae had already been destroyed by Khitan troops, its crown prince Tae Kwanghyŏn, seeing our country rise justly, led the remaining people of several tens of thousands of households, making haste day and night to get here. Deeply sympathizing with Tae, T'aejo generously welcomed him and conferred on him the royal surname Wang. He was registered in the royal genealogy and was allowed to offer sacrifices to the founding ancestor of his country. His ranking civilian and military officials and their underlings were all generously given official titles. Such were the king's policies in preserving a defeated state and enabling people from far away to submit.

Later Paekche's Kyŏnhwŏn, having an evil nature that nourished rebellion, killed the Silla king and oppressed the people. Hearing this, T'aejo wasted no time sending troops to punish the crime and finally restored order. Such was T'aejo; remembering his former king, restoring order, and halting a dangerous situation in this way.

From late Silla to the beginning of our dynasty, the people of the northeast frontier frequently suffered from the Jürchen horsemen who came to invade and rob. T'aejo himself decided to send a capable officer to guard the area—guarding it so effectively, in fact, that without a single weapon actually being used, the Jürchen came to surrender. After this, the area beyond the border became quiet, and the frontier was free of troubles. Such was his ability to recognize and employ capable men and to induce people in distant lands to come into close association.

Silla's leaders, feeling their fortunes exhausted and their numbers depleted, wished to surrender on their own. After declining the offer three times, T'aejo agreed to accept it. All of the hundred and ten fortresses lying east from Myŏngju to Hŭngye-bu, admiring T'aejo's benevolent virtue, took the opportunity to surrender. Such was his ability to use propriety to gain the submission of people.

Only in the southern pacification against Paekche was it necessary to use troops. On several occasions he deployed a great number of soldiers under the flags of command with his powerful troops in the line. Some of the enemy's men surrendered in battle; some, out of fear in the face of our might, capitulated. Thus, the enemy, even in combat, did not want to kill or injure anyone. It can therefore be said that the benevolent ruler has no enemies. After Kyŏnhwŏn himself had repeated evils for more than ten years, he was finally imprisoned by his own rebellious son. Escaping to us to avoid imprisonment, he asked for troops to kill his treacherous son. Hearing this, T'aejo generously welcomed him, showing proper courtesy. When he died,

T'aejo amply provided pecuniary assistance for the funeral. In this manner, his Way extended to both the dead and living and his righteousness embraced everything.

When pacifying Later Paekche, T'aejo entered its towns and provided relief, feeling pity for the impoverished peasants. He sincerely consoled them, ordering his various troops not to commit even the slightest offense. Moreover, even when the country was divided into north and south and between old and new for a long time, T'aejo treated them all alike with a persistence that saw no change from beginning to end. Such were his magnanimous virtue and simple generosity.

Even after unifying the country, he worked diligently on government affairs for eight years, treating China with respect and neighboring countries with propriety. Even in times of peace he was not lax. In meeting with people of inferior status, he was courteous, demonstrating his lofty virtue. He esteemed frugality, building his palace with no excess but only enough to withstand storms. He dressed in simple clothes adequate only to protect him from heat and cold. He held dear the wise and loved the good, giving up his own on behalf of others. A feeling of respect and politeness sprang from his natural disposition. Moreover, growing up among the peasants, he had experienced hardship and danger. Of the people's feelings there was nothing he could not discern. In everything, he could foretell peace and foresee danger. Because of this, his rewards and punishments were timely, and rights and wrongs could be distinguished. Such was his way of moral purpose, which gave him the dignity of an emperor.

When T'aejo knew a person, moreover, he did not overlook that person's talent, and through his management of people below him, he used their strength. In appointing the wise, T'aejo manifested trust; in eliminating evil, he had no doubt. Through his respect for Buddhism and his emphasis on Confucianism, T'aejo attained the excellent virtue of a ruler. His wise dynastic policies are thus worthy of being emulated.

Because it was still not long after the founding of the dynasty and the pacification, our dynasty was yet to be held shiningly in reverence. Our rituals and music, as well as our culture, still had many shortcomings; our government institutions and our official regulations were still not refined. T'aejo's sudden death therefore was a misfortune for the country. Truly heaven's unpredictability was regrettable.

As crown prince, King Hyejong resided in the Eastern Palace for a long time and often conducted state military affairs, respecting his teachers and receiving his advisers with propriety. Accordingly, he had a good reputation in the country, and when he first came to the throne, many people happily accepted him. At that time, some people slandered Chŏngjong and his brother, saying they planned treason. Hearing this, Hyejong did not respond and raised no questions. He became even kinder toward Chŏngjong and his brother, treating them as before. People admired his great magnanimity. In a little while, however, his virtuous rule was tarnished as he became unduly fearful for his personal safety, always surrounding himself with armed soldiers. In general, as his suspicions of people grew more severe, he lost much of the dignity of a king. Increasingly he became inclined to reward military officers, extending favors unequally so that all over the country resentment grew, and people began to harbor disaffection. Within a year of his enthronement, he suddenly fell ill and passed his remaining time in bed. Thereupon ranking officials and the erudite lost access to the king, and petty people from his local village always lingered in the royal sleeping quarters. As his sickness became more serious, Hyejong's anger and resentment daily grew worse. For three years the people did not see virtuous rule, and only the day of his death removed potential calamity. Is this not truly lamentable?

Before Chŏngjong became king, he had already enjoyed a good reputation. As Hyejong's illness grew worse, the state councillor Wang Kyu and others secretly concocted an intrigue, setting their eyes on the royal house. Chŏngjong early on realized this and secretly planned with loyal officers in the Western Capital (P'yŏngyang) to be ready for all eventualities. When internal unrest was about to break out, defending troops arrived in great numbers, and accordingly the evil plot did not succeed, and the wicked were all executed. Although this must have been due to a heavenly command, it was also planned by man, so how can it not be admirable!

For the last thirty-eight years, since Chŏngjong ascended the throne, the royal succession has not been broken. This is due to the actions taken by Chŏngjong. Having received the throne from his half-brother Hyejong, Chŏngjong unselfishly worked hard at governing day and night. Sometimes lighting a candle, he gave an audience to court officials; sometimes forgoing his meals, he made decisions on government affairs. Accordingly, in the early days of his reign, people all rejoiced in his success at governing. Because of his misplaced belief in geomantic prophesies, however, he decided to move the capital. As he was by nature resolute and unbending, he recklessly mobilized people for corvée, initiating public works and overworking laborers. Although it was the king's wish, popular sentiment did not accede, and resentment rose among the populace. Calamity quickly followed. He passed away before he could move the capital to P'yŏngyang. This is truly regrettable.

King Kwangjong, even in his childhood, had a remarkable appearance and an outstanding disposition. He received special care and love from his father King T'aejo. At King Chŏngjong's command on his deathbed, he inherited the throne, which was thus affectionately passed from older brother to younger brother. He treated those under him with much propriety, and he never lost his eye for judging people. He did not hold his royal relatives and high nobles too close, always restraining the mighty and powerful. He never neglected the humble and accorded favors to widows and orphans. For eight years after he ascended the throne, the government was clean and equitable, meting out no excessive rewards or punishments. From the time he employed Shuang Chi, he leaned heavily toward the literati, dispensing excessive favors and courtesy to them. Thereupon, even the untalented came forward, upsetting the order of seniority, and advanced quickly, becoming high ministers in less than two years. The king took pleasure in giving audiences day and night. As he neglected government affairs, important matters of state security were not attended to, but parties and banquets were held incessantly. Thereupon, mediocre people from north and south all competed to join in. Regardless of whether a person had knowledge or talent, the king treated all with special kindness and favor, so that even junior persons competed to advance, and the initial virtue of the king gradually disappeared.

Even though the Chinese system was valued, fine Chinese statutes were not adopted. Even though the king treated Chinese scholars with courtesy, he was not able to obtain the talents of China. As for the people, their provisions, the product of their blood and sweat, were increasingly expended to gain empty honors everywhere. As a result, the king did not regain his earlier concern and diligence for general state affairs even while meeting with his advisers. Their disgust deepened daily, therefore, as their discussions with the king on government affairs increasingly became blocked. No one dared to speak openly about the defects of the current policy.

Moreover, the king became excessive in his devotion to Buddhism and unduly valued Buddhists. Although regular observances of Buddhist fasting services were already numerous, many additional in-cense-burning prayers for special wishes were held. Prayers were merely offered to obtain blessings and longevity. Even though our financial means were limited, he tried to produce unlimited acts of merit. Taking his position as sovereign lightly, he sought to elevate the petty. His outings and banquets were all done with extreme ex-travagance. Not taking immediate hardship around him to be indica-tive of the future—peace to be wrought through Buddha's power—he did not seek to correct wrongs in carrying out his deeds. The court consequently was full of extraneous undertakings and regulations. In clothing and food, it was wantonly extravagant. In weighing the merits of public works, he disregarded proper timing; in devising clever undertakings, there was no resting. Even by a rough estimate, what he normally spent in one year was as much as T'aejo spent in ten.

In his later years, many innocent people were put to death. I fool-ishly believe that if Kwangjong had always been as respectful and frugal in his expenditures and as diligent in governing as he was early in his reign, how could he not have lived longer rather than having passed away at the age of fifty years! That he could not have been as good at the end as he was in the beginning was truly lamentable.

For sixteen years, moreover, from the eleventh year [960] to the twenty-sixth year [975] of Kwangjong's reign, the crafty and wicked competed to advance, and slanderous charges spread rampantly. True gentlemen were nowhere permitted, while small-minded persons achieved their goals. It even reached the point where children would rebel against their parents and slaves would talk back to their masters. Those in high and low positions grew distant in spirit; rulers and subjects lost their bonds of respect. Senior officials and seasoned gen-erals were killed in succession; close relatives of the royal family all perished. Hyejong's protection of his brothers and Chŏngjong's pres-ervation of the dynasty can be said to have been of great value when seen in terms of one's indebtedness and obligation. These two kings each had only one son, yet they were unable to protect their sons' lives. Not only were they unable to recompense their sons' virtue, but they also incurred their deep rancor. In his last years, Kwangjong also developed suspicion toward his only son. As a result, when his son Kyŏngjong was crown prince, he was not always without fear for his personal safety. Fortunately, however, he succeeded to the throne. Alas, how is it that at the beginning Kwangjong was so good and early gained an excellent reputation, but later he ceased to be good and came to this? This is truly lamentable.

As Kyŏngjong was born deep in the inner palace and grew up under the care of palace ladies, he had no opportunities to see and know of life outside the court. Yet by nature he was fortunately bright. Toward the end of Kwangjong's reign, he was able to clear himself of false charges and succeed to the throne. On becoming king, he had the slanderous documents from the preceding years burned and the innocent people who had been imprisoned for many years freed, thereby removing all the grievances and resentments so that the whole nation rejoiced.

Being imperfectly acquainted with the government, however, he relied entirely on influential and powerful people, letting harm reach royal relatives. Thus, omens of disaster first appeared. Although he later became aware of this, there was nowhere to pass the responsibility. Henceforth the king could not distinguish right from wrong, and his rewards and punishments lost consistency. Unable to uphold principles, he languished, and his rule in the end fell into sexual debauchery. Enjoying native music all day long, he never tired of gambling. As he was surrounded only by palace attendants and eunuchs, the words of virtuous men were not heard while those of small-minded people were sometimes heeded. Thus even if he had a splendid reputation at the beginning, he had no virtue at the end. This is not to say that there was no good beginning, only that it is difficult to conclude with a good ending. What loyal subjects and righteous men would not lament this? This is something that Your Majesty saw personally and knows.

Kyŏngjong also had something worthy of praise, however. When he first became sick but was not yet critically ill, he called Your Majesty to his sleeping quarters. Holding your hand, he instructed Your Majesty to take charge of the country's civil and military affairs. This was not only good fortune for the country but also a blessing for the people. We have had only two kings, Hyejong and Kyŏngjong, who inherited the throne as crown princes, and in those cases nobody harbored ambitions for the throne. But when there were no clear instructions, competition for the crown certainly would arise even between brothers. When Hyejong died after two years of illness, he left a son, Prince Hŭnghwa, who was still very young. Moreover, as Hyejong was incapable of passing on the throne to one of his various brothers, Chŏngjong himself sought and received the support of the ranking officials and succeeded to the throne. And when he approached death, he passed the throne to Kwangjong, safeguarding the dynasty. The last wills of Chŏngjong and Kyŏngjong were clear.

Earlier, when kings Hyejong, Chŏngjong, and Kwangjong succeeded each other, not everything in the new dynasty had been settled. As a result, half of the military and civil officials of the two capitals (Kaesŏng and P'yŏngyang) were killed or injured in succession disputes. Moreover, in the later part of Kwangjong's reign, disorder set in and slander flourished. Those implicated by laws frequently were innocent. As a result, meritorious officials and seasoned generals of many decades could not avoid death. When Kyŏngjong ascended the throne, there were only about forty former officials still alive. At that time, many others were also hurt; but as they were slanderous young outlaws, we need not pity them. The only exceptions were the two princes of Ch'ŏnan and Chinju, who were royal offspring. Kwangjong himself, overlooking the law, was generous to them. By Kyŏngjong's reign, although they could have been protectors of the dynasty, powerful officials unlawfully harmed them, putting them to death on false charges and making their spirits restless. How can this not be deplored for the sake of royal fidelity? That Kyŏngjong did not enjoy a long life was due largely to this calamity. Later generations should take this as a warning.

I humbly believe that, owing to the virtue of the ancient sages, Your Majesty has a new opportunity for restoration, as the glorious royal mandate has been passed on to Your Majesty due to the previous king's unselfish considerations. Accordingly, there is nothing within our borders that does not enjoy its existence and does not have a place to occupy. All are happy with each other while man and spirits congratulate each other. It is said that "heaven provides that in which the people participate." If Your Majesty truly follows King T'aejo's precedents, how would you be different from Hsüan-tsung's cherishing T'ai-tsung's old ways? Your Majesty, be selective, if you can, from the events of the last four reigns. It can be said that Hyejong upheld the principle of brotherly love, as his merit rests in having protected his close relatives. It can also be said that Chŏngjong exemplified the brilliance of strategy, as his early detection of a germinating rebellion allowed him to suppress disturbances in the palace, safeguard the dynasty, and preserve the crown to this day. Kwangjong's initial eight-year rule can be compared to the Three Ages of Hsia, Shang, and Chou; particularly noteworthy was his systemization of court ceremonies, but it might be said that the balance sheet of his achievement was evenly divided between the good and the bad. Kyŏngjong's freeing of thousands of unjustified prisoners of the preceding reign and his burning of the slanderous documents of many years may be considered the apex of generous leniency.

In general, this is the record of the four reigns. Your Majesty should put into practice selectively the good points and caution yourself on the bad by eliminating nonessential tasks and halting unbeneficial endeavors. Only by so doing will the ruler presiding above be at ease and the people below be joyful. By starting all efforts with goodwill, one may contemplate good results. If you are mindful of how you spend each day, your rest will be no idleness. Even if you are sufficiently noble to be a ruler, you should not esteem yourself too greatly. Even if you possess great talent and virtue, do not be arrogant. Through a feeling of sincere respect and through a continuous concern for the people, blessings will come by themselves, even when you do not seek them, and calamities will disappear by themselves, even if you do not pray to avert them by offering sacrifices. If you do so, how could Your Majesty's life not last for a long time and the dynasty cease only after one hundred generations? HK/ES

Ch'oe Sŭngno: On Current Affairs
[From Koryŏ sa 93:12a–b, 19b–22a]

Although I am not bright, I unworthily hold an important position in the government. I therefore desire to memorialize the throne with no thought of avoiding my duty, humbly record my thoughts on current affairs in not more than twenty-eight points and present them under separate cover in accordance with prescribed form.

It has been forty-seven years since our country united the Later Three Kingdoms. Our soldiers have yet to see peace, however, and military provisions are still in excessive demand. This is all because to the northwest there are many places to defend, as we border on barbarians. I hope Your Majesty will keep this fact in mind. Generally it was King T'aejo's intention to make Mahŏl Rapids a border, whereas it was the Chinese decision to make the stone wall on the banks of the Yalu River a border. I beg that between these two places Your Majesty in the future choose a more strategic location and establish a border for our territory. Then choose from among the local people those who are good at archery and riding and assign them to defend the area. Select from among them two or three as adjutant officers and put them in command so that the central army will be free from the task of defending the area in rotation and the cost of transporting military provisions will decline. . . .

Because soldiers in our dynasty's royal regiments during T'aejo's reign were charged with protecting the palace, their number was not large. King Kwangjong, believing slander, executed generals and ministers, creating suspicions himself, and then increased the number of soldiers. Selecting men of talent from the rural districts, he put them in the royal regiments and had them all quartered in the palace. Contemporaries considered this burdensome and useless. Although the number decreased slightly in Kyŏngjong's reign, there are still too many to this day. If Your Majesty will follow the precedents of T'aejo and retain only the strong and brave and dismiss the rest, the people will have nothing to lament and the country will have much to save.
. . .

Our T'aejo was sincere in his devotion to China, but he sent officials to affirm ties only once in several years. Nowadays envoys are sent frequently, not only for tributary visits but also because of trade. I fear that the Chinese may look upon this with disdain. Moreover, ships traveling back and forth frequently are shipwrecked, losing many lives. I ask that from now on we combine tribute missions with trade and strictly forbid all other contacts. . . .

The king, in governing the people, cannot visit them at home daily, and so he sends out magistrates to look into their welfare. After our T'aejo unified the country, he wished to set up provincial governments, but as it was still the formative age, many conditions were too unsettled for this. As I observe it now, the powerful local strongmen, under the pretext of public works, extort the people to the point that they can no longer endure it. I request that you establish provincial governments. And even if you cannot fill every office at once, first establish one provincial government for about ten *chu* and *hyŏn* and place two or three officials in each government to nourish and attend to the people. . . .

In Silla the clothing, shoes, and stockings of nobles, officials, and commoners each had its designated color. Nobles and officials in court wore formal clothing and shoes and held tablets, and when they were out of court, they wore what they wished. To differentiate the noble and humble and distinguish the high and low, commoners could not wear patterned clothing. In this way, even though official robes were not locally produced, the supply was adequate for the use of officials.

Since King T'aejo's time, we have worn clothes as we please regardless of social status. Even if one's rank is high, if his house is poor, he cannot afford an official robe. And if one is unemployed but has money, he can use silk gauze and elegant brocade. As for products in our country, there are few good items but many coarse goods. Even though none of the materials with designed patterns is locally produced, everybody wears them. I fear that the formal wear of the officials will not follow set regulations and will cause us embarrassment when we welcome officials from other countries. I ask that you command all officials to wear formal robes and shoes and to hold tablets at court meetings in accordance with Chinese and Silla conventions. In court presentations, have them wear socks and silk or leather shoes. Commoners should not be allowed to wear patterned silk but only plain silk fabrics. . . .

Although Chinese systems are good to follow, as the customs of each area have their own characteristics, it would be difficult to change every custom. As for the teachings of the classics on rites, music, poetry, and documents, as well as the ways of the ruler and subject and the father and son, we must fittingly follow China and reform our vulgar ways. In the rest of the systems, however, such as transport and clothing, we should follow our native traditions so that the ostentatious and frugal will be balanced. We need not be like China in everything.

The people who live on the various islands grew up in the middle of the sea because of crimes committed by their forefathers. But as their land produces little food, their livelihood is very difficult. And yet as the government agent presses demands for levies from time to time, he daily impoverishes them. I request that we adhere to the levies set for the mainland districts and equalize their tax burdens and corvée levies. . . .

According to the *Book of Changes,* "The sage influences the heart of the people, and consequently the world enjoys peace and harmony."[6] It is also stated in the *Analects,* "May not Shun be instanced as having governed efficiently without exertion? What did he do? He did nothing but gravely and reverently occupy his royal seat."[7] The sage can move heaven and man because he has the purest virtue and an unselfish mind. If Your Majesty maintains a humble spirit and is always respectful and courteous to your subjects, then who while in government would not exhaust mind and strength in exposing evil plots and who while in retirement would not think only of serving you? This is referred to as the ruler treating the subject with respect and the subject serving the ruler with loyalty. I hope that Your Majesty will always be singularly prudent and never arrogant and will be gentle in dealing with your subjects. Even though there are criminals, if you deliberate on their crimes in accordance with the law, you can expect great peace imminently.

Except for the court slaves doing labor in the palace, King T'aejo sent the rest to live outside to till land and pay taxes. In Kwangjong's reign, because his many Buddhist activities daily increased public construction works, he enlisted the slaves living outside to carry out the public works. As the funds appropriated for the palace were not sufficient to pay for all the expenses, the rice stored in the government warehouses was also diverted. Your Majesty has not yet been able to correct this abuse. Moreover, since the number of horses raised in the palace stable is considerable, the expense is extravagant, causing people to suffer. Should disturbances occur on the frontier, provisions will not be adequate. I ask Your Majesty, strictly following the systems established by T'aejo, to limit the number of horses and slaves in the palace and resettle the remainder outside the palace. . . .

According to the *Book of Rites,* "The hall of the Son of Heaven was ascended by nine steps; that of a prince by seven. . . ."[8] This has been the established practice. Recently, however, there has been no social distinction between the high and the low, and if a person has financial means, the first thing he does is build a house. Accordingly the powerful in all local administrative districts compete to build large houses exceeding the earlier standards. They not only exhaust the resources of their families but also cause harm to the people, resulting in excessive abuse. I humbly urge you to order officials of the Board of Rites to regulate house construction according to social status and to command all in the country to comply with this. Those who have already built in excess of these standards should be ordered to demolish the houses as a warning for the future. . . .

In earlier times, as China's virtue declined, its eight great families, Lüan, Hsi, Hsü, Yüan, Hu, Hsu, Ch'ing, and Pai, ended up as slaves. Although the descendants of the merit subjects of our dynastic founding should have received emoluments as stipulated each time royal commands have been issued, there are still some who have never received any rank and remain mixed among the slaves. As newly rising groups frequently insult them at will, discontent festers.

Ever since numerous court officials were purged in Kwangjong's last years, many descendants of the great families have been unable to continue their family lineages. I urge you to adhere to the often-issued royal commands and employ descendants of the merit subjects according to their rank. If you weigh the recipients of merit land grants in the year 940 and those officials who entered government service after the unification of the Later Three Kingdoms and confer upon them appropriate ranks and positions, this will mitigate past errors in regrettable charges and slights and avoid misfortune that could arise in the future. . . .

In winter and summer, the dynasty's prayer meetings and memorial services for former kings and queens have been practiced for a long time and are not something to be set aside. I urge you, however, to reduce other services that can be done away with. If they cannot be reduced, then observe them in accordance with the *yüeh-ling* of the *Book of Rites.*[9] This states that since the spirit of the fifth month connotes the struggle between yin and yang, resulting in distinction between life and death, the gentleman must purify his body and soul, confining himself to his living quarters, certainly moving around without haste, abstaining from music and women, and eating moderately. By so controlling desires, he puts his mind in order. All officials also cleanse their bodies and submit to the king no litigation to be heard, thus assisting the completion of yin.

Since the spirit of the eleventh month connotes the struggle between yin and yang, resulting in the destruction of all living things, the gentleman should purify his body and soul, confining himself to his living quarters, moving around without haste, dismissing music and women, forbidding addiction to lust, and putting the mind and body at peace. By so conducting everything in quiet, he waits for the stabilization of yin and yang. This then is a time to desist. Why? When it is very cold, people on corvée labor will suffer and food may be unclean. When it is extremely hot, one perspires profusely. Or one may kill many insects by mistake, making sacrificial offerings impure. What kind of virtuous merit can this bring? Moreover, even if today produces good things, tomorrow will not necessarily bring good rewards. This being the case, nothing is as good as improving government policies.

I request that you divide the twelve months of the year into two halves and, from the second to the fourth month and from the eighth to the tenth, devote half the time to government affairs and half to acts of religious piety. From the fifth to the seventh month, and from the eleventh to the first, exclude pious acts and concentrate only on government affairs. Everyday listen to government matters, and day and night assiduously deliberate on government policies. Every afternoon, in compliance with the four daily rituals of the gentleman,[10] refine government orders in the evening and look after health at night. In this way the seasonal conduct of the government will be orderly and Your Majesty will dwell in peace. This will also reduce the people's toils. How could all this not bring great religious merit?

The *Analects* state: "For a man to sacrifice to a spirit that does not belong to him is flattery."[11] The *Tso Commentary* states: "If a spirit is not your clan's, it will not receive sacrifices."[12] This is to say that offering sacrifices where one has no right to offer them brings no blessings. The services at our dynasty's ancestral temples and national altars still have many deviations that do not adhere to established rules. The services to the mountain peaks and the sacrifices to the constellations are vexing and excessive. It is said that sacrifices should not be done too frequently. If they are too frequent, they become burdensome. If they are burdensome, they become unrespectable. Although Your Majesty cleanses your heart in a most respectful way and certainly has no trace of laziness, if the sacrificial officials regard this as a routine affair, it becomes wearisome and is done without respect. How then will the spirits happily receive the service?

In ancient times, Emperor Wen of Han China had officials to conduct the sacrificial service with respect, but he did not lead them to pray. This detached view of the service can be called a great moral sense. If the spirits are unaware of the supplicant's needs, how can they extend blessings to him? If they are aware that these services are for self-gain and favors, as even a gentleman would have difficulty in responding to this, would the spirits not have even more difficulty? Furthermore, the expense of these services all come from the toil and blood of the people. It is my belief that if you ease the people's labor, you will win their hearts, and the blessings from this will certainly exceed those blessings gained from prayers. I hope Your Majesty will eliminate extraneous prayers and services and always preserve an attitude of humility and self-reproach toward heaven. In this way, calamity will of itself vanish and blessings appear.

The laws governing the free and the lowborn in our country have existed for a long time. When King T'aejo first founded the country, except for those officials who had originally had slaves, all other

officials who became slave owners had acquired them while in the
army, either by obtaining prisoners of war or through purchase.
T'aejo once wanted to free the slaves to be commoners, but being
concerned about agitating the feelings of the merit subjects, he followed a course of expediency. Since then, for the last sixty years, no
one has ever made an appeal. In Kwangjong's reign, the king began to
direct an investigation of slaves to determine their true status. All the
merit subjects resented the investigation, but none dared to remonstrate. Even when his queen Taemok urgently remonstrated, the king
did not heed. The lowborn and slaves gained their wishes and slighted
the nobles, and those who competed to lie and scheme against their
masters were numerous. Kwangjong himself created the causes for
calamity and was unable to stop it. By the end of his reign, many
innocent people had been killed, resulting in his great loss of virtue.

In early China when Hou Ching[13] encircled the palace in Liang, the
house slave of the high official Chu I[14] crossed over the palace wall
and surrendered to Hou Ching, who conferred on him the high title
of *i-tung* (*san-ssu*).[15] The slave, riding a horse and wearing a silk robe,
faced the palace and shouted, "After serving for fifty years, Chu I just
got the command of the central army, but I merely began to serve
King Hou and immediately received the highest title of *i-tung*." It is
said that the household slaves in the palace thereupon competed to
escape and surrender to Hou Ching and that the palace accordingly
fell. I hope that Your Majesty will carefully reflect on this earlier
incident and not allow the lowborn to put the noble to shame but will
follow the Golden Mean by separating slaves and masters. Generally
people who hold high office are reasonable and few commit illegali-
ties. How can people of low status, when they have insufficient wisdom and gloss over their wrongdoings, be made commoners? Although some royalty and nobles may have committed illegal acts
because of their influence, at present the government is clean as a
mirror with no pursuit of personal interest. [How can anyone transgress?] The misconduct of King Yu and King Li of Chou could not
conceal the virtue of King Hsüan and King P'ing, and although Queen
Lü of Han was unvirtuous, it did not tarnish the worthiness of Emperors Wen and Ching. Try to make important judgments with clarity
so as to have no future regret. There is no need to rekindle disputes
by reopening investigations of decisions that were made in earlier
times. HK/ES

Ch'oe Sŭngno: On Buddhism
[From *Koryŏ sa* 93:15b–19b]

I have heard that Your Majesty, in order to hold Buddhist merit rites, at times personally grinds tea and barley. Your Majesty's diligent labor troubles me deeply. Such practices started from Kwangjong's reign. Believing slanderous defamations, he had many innocent people killed. Misled by the Buddhist theory of just retribution and wishing to remove the consequences of past sins, he exacted provisions from the peasants to hold Buddhist services. He established Vairocana confessional rituals, held Buddhist maigre feasts on the polo fields, and set up Buddhist Festivals of Equal Bestowal of Wealth and Law on Land and Sea in Kwibŏp Monastery.

Every time there were service days to Buddha, he would always offer food to begging monks or give beggars rice cakes or fruit used for services in the palace. At dams built to retain fish in new ponds in Hyŏlgu and on Mount Mari and other sites, he would set up places to liberate the fish to gain Buddhist merit, and four times a year he would send officials to various temples in their jurisdictions to read Buddhist scriptures. He forbade the palace cook to slaughter livestock for meat dishes in the royal kitchen and instead had him buy meat at the market. He even commanded all his officials and the people, low and high, to offer contrition for their sins—indeed, those carrying grain, firewood, charcoal, fodder, beans, and other things on their backs on the roads for Buddhist offerings were countless. But what good would this do when he already believed the slanderous defamations and treated people like chaff, killing them, and piling up their corpses like a mountain?

The offerings at the Buddhist services were invariably provisions exacted from the people. At that time, children turned against their parents and slaves against their masters, and all sorts of criminals disguised as monks, many actually mingling with real monks, wandered around begging and came together to hold Buddhist services. What good would this do? Although Your Majesty's actions since ascending the throne are not like this, the matters you have troubled yourself with are without any benefit. I hope Your Majesty will rectify the regal polity and do nothing that is not of benefit. . . .

Your Majesty has given, as acts of charity, soybean sauce, wine, soybean paste, and soup to people on the road. I believe Your Majesty wants to imitate King Kwangjong's attempts to do away with evil karma by generously giving alms and gain good karma. This, however, is what is called "little favors do not prevail everywhere." If you make clear rewards and punishments and the reproval of vice and the promotion of good conduct, it will be sufficient to realize blessings. As trifling affairs (like the preceding) do not constitute the principle on which the ruler should govern, I beg you to stop this. . . .

Generally, for the money and grain of the Buddhist charity fund, monks of various temples send people to the local districts to manage their loans and collect their interest each year, causing trouble to the peasants. I ask you to forbid all of this and to transfer the money and grain to the manors of the temples. If the manor managers have tenants, place them likewise under the manors of the temples. This will lessen the people's distress. . . .

I respectfully see Your Majesty has sent a messenger to bring the monk Yǒch'ǒl of Mount Sagul into the palace. I believe that if Yǒch'ǒl were truly capable of bringing good fortune to people, since the place where he dwells is the possession of Your Majesty and since his everyday meals are also bestowed by Your Majesty, he would certainly want to return your favors daily by offering prayers for blessings. So why bother inviting him only to have him invoke blessings? In the past a certain Sǒnhoe, in order to evade corvée labor, left his home to become a monk and lived in the mountains. King Kwangjong respected him profoundly and extended all proprieties to him, but Sǒnhoe suddenly met an unexpected death on the road, and his corpse was left exposed and unattended there. If monks like him can incur personal misfortune, how in the world can you expect them to bring blessings to others? I request that you return Yǒch'ǒl to the mountain and avoid the ridicule that Sǒnhoe incurred. . . .

I have heard that monks, when traveling to the countryside, stay at government hostels and postal stations, chastising the local clerks and people for carelessness in their reception and provision of food. The clerks and people, fearing that the monks might be under royal orders, do not dare to speak out, which results in great abuses. From now on, please forbid monks to stop and stay at public facilities in order to end these abuses. . . .

In our country we hold the Buddhist Lantern ceremony in the spring and the Assembly of the Eight Prohibitions in the winter and enlist masses of people to help with these, putting them into corvée labor too frequently. I request that we limit these enlistments to lighten the people's labor. Moreover, we also construct many kinds of idols that are very expensive to make; then after presenting them once to the court, we casually destroy them. This practice has no meaning at all. Furthermore, idols are used in funerals. When the Khitans' Liao envoy came and saw these idols, considering them unlucky, he hid his face and passed by. I request that from now on you do not allow their use. . . .

As everyone following his own wishes builds temples in the name of sowing good to reap future reward, the number of temples has become excessive. In order to use monasteries as their own private residences, monks all over the country compete in building them. They urge the heads of the local districts to enlist people in corvée work, making their need for the labor more urgent than that for public projects, thereby troubling the people deeply. I request that you strictly forbid this practice to exempt the people from toil. . . .

The copying of Buddhist scriptures and the making of Buddhist figures are for the purpose of preserving them for a long time. How can one use treasured material for adornment and tempt a thief's mind? In the past, scriptures were all written on yellow paper scrolls, and sandalwood was used for the rollers. Statues were not made of gold, silver, bronze, or iron but only of stone, clay, and wood so no one would steal or destroy them. In late Silla the scriptures and statues were made using gold and silver and became outrageously extravagant, in the end causing Silla's demise. Merchants stole and destroyed Buddhist images, buying and selling them to make a living. To this day, there still persist remnants of these practices. I request that you strictly forbid this practice to get rid of the abuse. . . .

Although the worship of Buddhism is not bad, the merits of pious acts performed by kings, officials, and commoners are in fact not the same. Since what the commoner toils on comes from his own labor and what he spends comes from his own wealth, harm comes to no others. In the case of a king, however, it comes from the toil of the peasants and it spends the wealth of the people. Formerly Emperor Wu [502–550] of Liang China, with the dignity of an emperor, tried to cultivate the virtue of a common man, but the people deemed it not to be right. The ruler therefore should deeply contemplate the consequences of his actions and take the middle road in everything. Then abuses will not extend to the subjects.

I understand that fortune and misfortune and the noble and the humble are all endowed at birth and that they ought to be obediently accepted. Furthermore, the worshiper of the Buddha's teachings only sows seeds for the cause of life after death and has little benefit for the cause of this life. The essence of government clearly does not lie in this teaching.

Moreover, the Three Teachings (Buddhism, Confucianism, and Taoism) all have their own special qualities, and those who follow them should not get confused but keep them separate. Practitioners of Buddhism take spiritual cultivation as the basic principle. Practitioners of Confucianism take governing the nation as the basic principle. Spiritual cultivation is valuable for the afterlife, but governing the country is the task of the present. The present is here and the afterlife is extremely distant. How could it not be wrong to sacrifice the present for the distant?

A king should single-mindedly be unselfish so as to give relief to all universally. Why should he make unwilling people work and waste the savings in the warehouse in order to seek no benefits? Earlier in T'ang China, Emperor Te-tsung's [780–805] father-in-law, Wang Ching-hsien, and his son-in-law, Kao T'ien, made a gold and brass Buddhist statue to prolong the life of the emperor and presented it to him. Te-tsung said, "For me an artificially extracted pious merit means I have no pious merit." So he returned the Buddhist statue to the two men. This shows that even though the affection did not come to fruition, the emperor did have his subjects refrain from useless things like this. HK/ES

Expansion of Confucian Polity II

Sŏngjong's reign witnessed a rapid expansion of the authority of the central government throughout the kingdom. Confucian reforms were accompanied by much more subtle developments in Koryŏ society. Court procedures were refined as ceremony became a set part of official life. The first passage presented here, written in the fourteenth century by Yi Chehyŏn (1287–1367), describes the formal procedures used in meetings of the highest state council early in the dynasty and then goes on to deplore their subsequent decay. The Privy Council, composed of officials of the highest ranks of the Secretariat Chancellery and Security Council, met as needed and deliberated on important matters of state. The king made final decisions but only after carefully considering the Privy Council's recommendations, which were arrived at on the basis of unanimous consent. Precedent and regularized behavior were important in this Confucian order, as was consensual decision making. In this passage, Yi Chehyŏn shows how a formal atmosphere was created to allow adequate discussion and the rendering of a decision on which all members had pondered.

Good government was important not only in the highest echelons of authority but throughout the realm. King Hyŏnjong (1009–1031), who ascended the throne in the wake of the forced abdication of King Mokchong (997–1009) and under increasing military pressure from the Khitans, built on the earlier reforms by reorganizing the local government system. In 1018, on the eve of the third and most massive Khitan invasion, which Koryŏ resolutely crushed, he directed local officials to be more responsible in assuring good government and preventing possible corruption as part of his reorganization of local government.

Economic changes also affected early Koryŏ. Here too the court took the lead in bringing prosperity to the people, who were bearing the kingdom's mounting financial burdens. Mokchong, Sŏngjong's tragic successor, issued his proclamation on currency reform in 1002. This proclamation reveals the growing financial concerns of the government as its wartime expenditures were too inflationary to sustain a new coinage system modeled after the one in Sung China.

The three selections offered here, when studied together, provide clear evidence of a society that was developing sophistication in its management of government amid the increasing military threat from its northern neighbor, Liao of the Khitans.

Yi Chehyŏn: The Etiquette of Privy Council Meetings
[From *Yŏgong p'aesŏl* 1:10a–11b]

In Sinjong's reign [1197–1204] Ki Hongsu [1148–1210] and Ch'a Yaksong [d. 1204] became executives in the Royal Secretariat and sat in the joint meetings [of the Privy Council],[16] where Ch'a asked Ki how the peacocks were doing and Ki too queried Ch'a about the method of raising peonies. [Because of their insensitivity] they were ridiculed by their contemporaries.

[Earlier] Koryŏ set up the Privy Council and made the chancellor, executives of the Secretariat Chancellery, assistant executives in Political Affairs and Letters, and administrator of the Chancellery its superintendents, whereas officials in the Security Council below the superintendent became state councillors. When the nation had a serious decision to make, they all met, calling the meeting *hapchwa* [joint meeting]. The joint meeting, however, sometimes met only once a year, and at other times it did not meet for several years. Later, the Privy Council changed its name. . . . It was not until Koryŏ was placed under the suzerainty of the Mongols and began to have a great increase in urgent affairs of the state that the state councillors of the Chancellery and the Security Council met all the time.

According to the etiquette of Privy Council meetings, the ones who arrived early leave their seats and stand facing north. Those who arrived later then take their positions, and, standing in a row according to rank, they make an acknowledgment with their hands together in front of their chests. Then together they go to the front of their seats. There, facing south, they offer two light bows with their hands in front of their chests. Leaving their seats, facing north and bending low, they exchange greetings with each other. Then they again come to the front of their seats, and, facing south, they make two light bows. Next, leaving their seats, they face north and, standing in one line, they make an acknowledgment.

When officials in higher ranks than the administrator of the Chancellery arrive, all the state councillors of the Security Council step down to the courtyard, stand facing east with the most senior at the north end, and then lower their heads and hands. State councillors of the Chancellery take their positions at the head and standing in two rows, they then make an acknowledgment before proceeding into the hall. There they make a light bow and an acknowledgment and sit as described above. No welcoming protocol is repeated in the courtyard once a state councillor of the Chancellery takes his seat with the others.

Only when the prime minister arrives do the deputy prime minister and those below go down to the courtyard and, facing east with the most senior member to the north, welcome him. The prime minister, facing west, exchanges acknowledgments with them. After this, they all proceed up into the hall and offer light bows and then an acknowledgment as described above. When the prime minister sits in the east alone, which is called *kokchwa,* the deputy prime minister and others sit in a row on the opposite side. If the prime minister is not the chief state councillor (which was formerly the chancellor), he does not sit alone in the east, and the others do not go down to the courtyard to welcome him.

When the chief registrar announces the items on the agenda before them, everyone expresses a yes or no based on his opinion on the issues. The registrar moves back and forth among them and tries to bring the discussion to a consensus, and after consensus is reached, it is then implemented. This is called *ŭihap* (deliberating for a consensus). Aside from this, those present sit properly and say nothing. Looking solemn, they are truly respectful and stately.

Nowadays the state councillors of both the Chancellery and the Security Council have needlessly increased in number, and each has an official consultant to promote his interests. The superintendent of the Finance Commission improperly sits above the deputy prime minister, while the junior and senior commissioners sit above and below the minister of punishment. They come and go in a group, frequently making loud conversation and laughing. They show no restraint in talking about the personal matters of others and even about profiting from the gains and losses in rice and salt market prices. This may be compared to the dialogue on peacocks and peonies by Ki Hongsu and Ch'a Yaksong. Likewise this will pass. HK/ES

King Hyŏnjong: Six Instructions to Magistrates
[From *Koryŏ sa* 75:13a–b]

In the second month of Hyŏnjong's ninth year [1018], six points to be observed by the staffs of all provincial governments were newly issued:

One, inquire into the hardships of the people.

Two, examine the abilities of the local head clerks.

Three, detect thieves and the crafty.

Four, investigate the breaking of laws by the people.

Five, encourage filial and fraternal conduct as well as modesty and honesty among the people.

Six, investigate local clerks' loss of public funds. HK/ES

King Mokchong: Edict on Coinage
[From *Koryŏ sa* 79:10a–11a]

Since ancient times, a ruler's first duty has been to nurture the people. He would promote measures that enabled the people to be numerous and prosperous. For instance, he opened the three markets (enlarged, morning, and night) to benefit the people, and sometimes he used the two *shu* coins to help the economy.[17] All these measures enabled the people to live comfortably and caused their customs to be unpretentious yet rich. The court of my ancestor, looking back and following earlier conventions, promulgated decrees to have coins minted, and in just a few years they were able to fill a storehouse with cash strings, enabling the new coin currency to circulate. Accordingly, the senior officials were instructed to hold a special banquet to choose an auspicious day and put the coins into use. Since then, the coins have circulated without interruption. Having undeservingly inherited the dynasty's great undertaking, I faithfully continued the measures handed down by the earlier kings. In particular, I enacted strict rules for the use of coinage to facilitate business transactions.

However, the recent memorial of Chancellor Han Ŏngong states that if the people are to live in comfort and enjoy prosperity, one must follow ancient ways. Yet the continuous circulation of coins, while banning the use of coarse cloth as a medium for transactions, as was instituted by the court of the former king, has only disrupted the old conventions, bringing no benefits to the state but only complaints from the people. Knowing the sincerity of this frank appeal, how can I reject and not accept it? Accordingly, in order to get to the root of the problem, I have decided again to discontinue the use of coins. From now on, shops that sell such goods as tea, wine, and food shall continue the use of coins as they have before when engaging in transactions. In private exchanges, however, people may, at their discretion, trade in kind. HK/ES

Koryŏ's Foreign Relations

Foreign affairs remained a major concern for Koryŏ. Wang Kŏn had warned in his "Ten Injunctions" of potential problems with the Khitans to the north. This warning proved to be prophetic, for by the end of the tenth century, Khitan raids were creating a crisis in Koryŏ. The northern state of Parhae, overwhelmed by the Khitans, fell in the early tenth century (926). From their new base in Manchuria, the Khitans attacked northern China, took control of the area around modern Peking, and founded the Liao kingdom. At the same time Koryŏ was consolidating its control over the peninsula and pushing north. It was only a matter of time before the two would collide. The Khitans were just one of several powers to test Koryŏ's resolve. Later,

Koryŏ also had clashes with the Jürchens and their Chin dynasty while trying to maintain ties with Sung China and casual links with the Japanese.

Koreans were pragmatic, yet resolutely defending their national interests. Sŏ Hŭi (940–998), one of the dynasty's great statesmen, helped structure a foreign policy that did not compromise Korean interests. When confronted with exorbitant Khitan demands backed by armed force, Sŏ Hŭi negotiated boldly. In asserting Koryŏ's right to territory once occupied by the earlier Koguryŏ kingdom, he won a temporary respite from Khitan attacks.

Nearly one hundred years after Sŏ Hŭi, another Koryŏ statesman, Yun Kwan (d. 1111), faced a similar crisis, this one caused by the Jürchens. Khitan power had waned after the middle of the eleventh century and then collapsed before the Jürchens. The Jürchens followed the Khitan pattern and consolidated their power in Manchuria, attacked Sung China, and established the Chin dynasty, which controlled all of northern China by 1126. In contrast to Sŏ Hŭi, however, Yun Kwan proposed a much bolder policy of resistance. He led several expeditions to attack the Jürchens and established "Nine Forts" on Koryŏ's northeastern frontier to control the region.

Yet, throughout this period, Koryŏ's foreign relations still remained precarious. Kim Puŭi (d. 1136), a contemporary of Yun Kwan, for example, proposed a policy marked by caution. Anxious to avoid unnecessary conflict, Kim pragmatically suggested that tributary ties be established with Chin. The court wavered but ultimately normalized its contacts with Chin. Wary of its northern neighbors, the Koryŏ King Munjong (1046–1083) had earlier wanted to reestablish relations with Sung, but his counselors, anxious to avoid complications with the Khitans, had advised against such a policy. Ultimately Munjong did set up formal relations with China, but even in the absence of diplomatic exchanges, Koreans and Chinese had frequent commercial and cultural contacts throughout this period. Koreans openly embraced Sung China, if for no other reason than for its cultural benefits. That Koreans were comfortable with Chinese ideas and norms is readily apparent in many Koryŏ documents.

Sŏ Hŭi: Arguments on War

[From *Koryŏ sa chŏryo* 2:49b–52b]

In the winter, the tenth month of Sŏngjong's twelfth year [993], Chancellor Pak Yangyu was appointed commander of the Upper Army; the executive of the Royal Secretariat, Sŏ Hŭi, became commander of the Middle Army, and the executive of the Chancellery, Ch'oe Yang, became commander of the Lower Army. They were stationed in the Northern Frontier Provinces to defend against the Khitans. In the intercalary month, the king visited the Western Capital and then proceeded to Anbuk-pu, where he heard that armies led by Hsiao Sun-ning of the Khitans had attacked Pongsan-gun and captured the commander of our advance guard army, Reviewing Policy Adviser Yun Sŏan, and others. The king, unable to proceed any further, returned.

As Sŏ Hŭi led the army hoping to rescue Pongsan, Hsiao Sun-ning made an announcement that said: "Our great country has already taken the former territory of Koguryŏ. Now we have sent an expedition against you because your country invaded across the border." Moreover, he sent a letter that said: "As our great country is about to unify land on all four directions, we will exterminate those who have not submitted to us. You should promptly surrender to us without delay."

After seeing the letter, Hŭi returned and memorialized that there might be a possibility for peace. The king sent the investigating censor, Yi Mongjin, with a temporary appointment as deputy director of protocol to the Khitan camp to seek peace. Hsiao Sun-ning again sent a letter, saying: "The army of eight hundred thousand has just arrived. If you do not come out from the Taedong River and surrender, we will destroy you. The ruler and officials must all surrender swiftly before our army." Yi Mongjin went to the Khitan camp and asked the reason behind their invasion. Hsiao Sun-ning said: "Since your country does not take care of the people's needs, we solemnly execute heaven's punishment on its behalf. If you want to seek peace, you must come swiftly and surrender."

After Yi Mongjin's return, the king met with the ranking officials and discussed the matter. Some said that the king should return to the capital and order the highest officials to lead the soldiers and seek a surrender. Others advised giving the land north of the Western Capital

(P'yŏngyang) to the Khitans and drawing a line from Hwangju to P'aryŏng as the border.

King Sŏngjong decided to follow the proposal to cede the territory. He opened the granaries in the Western Capital and let the people help themselves to the rice. As there was still a lot of rice left over, the king, fearing that it would be used as provisions by the enemy, ordered that it be thrown into the Taedong River.

Sŏ Hŭi memorialized: "If provisions are sufficient, then a fortress can be defended and war can be won. Whether troops win or lose does not depend on their strength, but only on whether they can take advantage of rifts and move quickly. How can the rice be suddenly abandoned? Moreover, provisions are the sustenance of the people. Even if they may become the enemy's provisions, how could we wastefully throw them into the river? I fear this would not agree with heaven's wishes." The king, agreeing with Hŭi, then retracted his order.

Hŭi also sent a memorial that said: "From the Khitans' Eastern Capital to our Anbuk-pu there are several hundred *ri* of land that were all occupied by the Jürchens. King Kwangjong took this land and constructed fortresses at Kaju, Songsŏng, and other places. Now the Khitans have come with the clear intention of taking these two northern fortresses. Their vow to take the former Koguryŏ territory stems from their fear of us. It is not a good strategy therefore to cut off the land north of the Western Capital and give it to them, for as we see, their military strength is already too great. Moreover, the land north of Mount Samgak was former Koguryŏ territory. Should their insatiable greed demand it relentlessly, would we give it all to them? To relinquish our territory to the enemy would be an ultimate shame to us. It is my hope that Your Majesty will return to the capital and let us, your officers, wage one more battle. Even then, it will not be too late to discuss our peace offer. . . ."[18]

Having received no reply long after Yi Mongjin returned, Hsiao Sun-ning finally attacked Anyung-jin. Senior Colonel Tae Tosu and Junior Colonel Yu Pang together fought back and won the battle. After this battle Sun-ning dared not advance his troops again but sent messengers urging surrender. King Sŏngjong sent the Presenting Official of the Royal Archives, Chang Yŏng, to the Khitan camp as the emissary of peace contact. But Sun-ning said, "You ought to send a minister to the front to see me face to face." The king met with ranking officials and asked, "Who could go to the Khitan camp to repel the enemy through words and make a lasting contribution?" No one among the officials responded except Sŏ Hŭi, who said: "Although I am not bright, how dare I not follow your orders?" The king personally went out to the riverbank and, clasping Hŭi's hands, consoled him as he sent him off.

Sŏ Hŭi, taking the state letter with him, went to Hsiao Sun-ning's camp and insisted on the protocol for equals, refusing to bow to Sun-ning. Sun-ning thought Hui was extraordinary.

Sun-ning said to Hŭi, "Your country rose in Silla territory. Koguryŏ territory is in our possession. But you have encroached on it. Your country is connected to us by land, and yet you cross the sea to serve China. Because of this, our great country came to attack you. If you relinquish land to us and establish a tributary relationship, everything will be all right."

Hŭi replied, "That is not so. Our country is in fact former Koguryŏ, and that is why it is named Koryŏ and has a capital at P'yŏngyang. If you want to discuss territorial boundaries, the Eastern Capital of your country is within our borders. How can you call our move an encroachment? Moreover, the land on both sides of the Yalu River is also within our borders, but the Jürchens have now stolen it. Being obstinate and crafty, they shift and deceive, and they have obstructed the roads, making them more difficult to travel than the sea. That we cannot have a tributary relationship is because of the Jürchens. If you tell us to drive out the Jürchens, recover our former territory, construct fortresses, and open the roads, then how could we dare not to have relations? If you take my words to your emperor, how could he not accept them out of sympathy?" Hŭi's words and complexion were so patriotically indignant that Sun-ning knew he could not be forced. Accordingly, he reported this to the Khitan emperor, saying, "Koryŏ has already requested peace, so we ought to withdraw our troops."

Hŭi remained in the Khitan camp for seven days and then returned with ten camels, one hundred horses, one thousand sheep, and five hundred rolls of brocaded silk. King Sŏngjong was very pleased and went out to meet him on the bank of the river. The king at once was going to send Chancellor Pak Yangyu as an ambassador of goodwill to see the Khitan emperor. But Hŭi again memorialized: "I made an agreement with Sun-ning that we would exterminate the Jürchens and recover the former territory, and then we would open tributary relations. We now have only the territory south of the Yalu River. I suggest that it will not be too late to set up relations after we have acquired the land north of the river." The king said, "If we delay in sending a tributary mission for a long time, I fear there may be undesirable repercussions later." Finally Pak Yangyu was dispatched. HK/ES

Im Ŏn: Memorial on Victory at Yŏngju
[From *Koryŏ sa* 96:19b–22a]

Mencius said: "It is certain that a small country cannot contend with a great, and that a few cannot contend with many."[19] I have long merely recited these words, but now their meaning is clear to me. The Jürchens are inferior to our country in strength and size, but in reconnoitering our frontier in King Sukchong's tenth year [1105] they took advantage of our unguarded moment and attacked us, killing people and enslaving many others. King Sukchong, in indignation, marshaled troops to punish them in the name of justice, but regrettably, the king died before he could launch the attack.

The present king, Yejong, mourned for three years, but on completing his funeral obligations he said to his officials, "The Jürchens, who were once under Koguryŏ rule, lived in a community to the east of a spring on Mount Kaema. For many years, they brought tribute, and in return benefited profoundly from our ancestors' blessings. Then suddenly and unjustifiably they betrayed us, causing the deep indignation of my deceased father. I have heard the ancient saying that one who is filial will continue his father's goals to their satisfactory completion. Fortunately I have now completed three years of mourning. If I am to conduct state affairs properly, how can I not raise the banner of righteousness, vanquish the immoral, and erase the shame of my father?"

Thereupon he appointed Custodial Grand Instructor and Executive of the Royal Secretariat Yun Kwan to be grand marshal of the expeditionary force and appointed Administrator of the Security Council, Hallim Academician, and Royal Transmitter O Yŏnch'ong to be deputy marshal. They led three hundred thousand elite troops, taking complete responsibility for the pacification.

Lord Yun was heroic in waging the campaign. Once, in reminiscing about Kim Yusin the man,[20] he said: "[Silla General Kim] Yusin could freeze a river in the sixth month to cross it with entire armies. Such was his sincere determination. Can I be a person like that?" It is frequently said that divine influence also aided Lord Yun's determined efforts. Lord O, a man greatly respected by his contemporaries, was naturally cautious. In handling affairs, he always considered each matter three times. Thus in carrying out his well-planned strategy, he never failed.

Since the two lords had set their minds on this expedition, they became thrilled with inspiration upon hearing the royal command. Escorted by their troops, they marched eastward out of the palace. On the day they led their troops out, they donned their armor and helmets, and tears flowed down their cheeks even as they made their vows before the crowds. No one dared to disobey their orders. On entering enemy territory, the three armies became so greatly incited that one person became the equal of one hundred. They overcame their foes as easily as breaking down a rotten stump or wedging down bamboo. They beheaded more than six thousand. Laying down their bows and arrows, more than fifty thousand of the Jürchens surrendered at the front. One cannot estimate the number of the enemy who fled north in desperation, having lost their hope and fighting spirit. Alas, because of their stubbornness and foolishness, the Jürchens disregarded their strength and size and thus destroyed themselves in this manner.

Their territory covers three hundred *ri* square, reaching in the east to the Eastern Sea, in the northwest to Mount Kaema, and south to Changju and Chŏngju. But its mountains and rivers are beautiful and its land is fertile, so much so that our people could settle there. Since it was originally occupied by Koguryŏ, monuments and sites from that kingdom still remain. The territory that Koguryŏ had once lost is now recovered by the present king. How can this not be heaven's will?

Thereupon the king established six new garrison settlements. The first of these was the Hamju Greater Regional Command of the Chindong Army with the militia army consisting of nineteen hundred and forty-eight adult households. . . . Men selected for their proven talent as well as those capable of bearing the responsibility were assigned to placate the area. When the *Book of Songs* says, "Screens to all the states, diffusing their influence over the four quarters of the kingdom,"[21] this means to act as a fence for the dynasty. Therefore one will enjoy peace without the anxiety of paying attention to the capital.

Grand Marshal Yun Kwan said to me: "Earlier, the T'ang State Councillor and the Lord of Chin P'ei Tu [765–839] set out to pacify

West Huai. When it was pacified, his assistant, Han Yü [768–824], wrote an inscription to make known his activities. Therefore people of later times knew that the Emperor Hsien-tsung [806–821] had heroic and unequaled virtue, and they sang his praises. You have fortunately followed the events to this day and know the whole story in detail. How can you not record this and have the unprecedented great achievement of our dynasty perpetuated forever?" Receiving this instruction, I took up my brush and have recorded this.   HK/ES

Kim Puŭi: Relations with Chin
[From *Koryŏ sa* 97:3a–b]

The Jürchens, having recently defeated the Khitans, have sent emissaries to Koryŏ asking to establish fraternal ties. High officials have, however, vigorously objected to doing this to the point of wanting to behead the Chin envoy. Kim Puŭi alone submitted a memorial, stating: "In my humble view, Han China, in its relations with the Hsiung-nu, and T'ang China, in its relations with the Turks, sometimes called themselves subjects and sometimes sent princesses in marriage. Generally they did everything possible to establish friendly relations. Now Sung China and the Khitans have established relations accepting inferior and superior status respectively and have maintained harmony for a long time. The veneration of the Chinese emperor has made no enemies in the world; instead, barbarian countries submit and serve. This is called 'the sage using circumstances to facilitate the Way' and is an excellent policy to protect the nation completely. Earlier, during Sŏngjong's reign, we committed an error in guarding our frontier, hastening the intrusion of the Liao people. Truly this should be a lesson. I humbly hope that your august court will consider a long-range policy to preserve the state so there will be no regrets later."

The members of the State Council all sneered and rejected Kim's suggestions, and thus no reply was made to the Chin envoy.   HK/ES

Memorial on Relations with Sung
[From *Koryŏ sa* 8:11a–b]

The king wished to cut timber on Cheju and in Yŏngam and build large ships to be used to establish contacts with Sung China. The Royal Secretariat Chancellery memorialized the king: "The country has established friendly ties with the Khitans, and as a result the northern frontier has experienced no urgent alarms. The people are enjoying their lives. This is a good strategy to protect the country. Earlier, in 1010, the Khitans asked in an accusatory letter, 'To the east you have ties with the Jürchens, and to the west you have contacts with Sung China. What are you scheming to do?' And when Minister Yu Ch'am went as an envoy, the resident governor of the Eastern Capital of Liao inquired about Koryǒ's exchanging envoys with Sung, indicating the displeasure and suspicion of the Khitans. If this affair leaked out, certainly it would cause a split. Moreover, Cheju Island is barren, and the people are poor. They are able to make a living only through sea products and sailing. Last autumn, the government required them to cut timber, carry it across the ocean, and use it to build a new Buddhist temple. They overworked themselves to extremes. Now if we again cause a heavy burden, we fear it will provoke other incidents. Moreover, our country has for a long time enjoyed civilized ways, including rites and music. Merchant ships come and go continually, bringing precious goods daily. We do not rely on the Chinese government for trade. If we do not intend to break forever our ties with the Khitans, it is not wise to send envoys to Sung." HK/ES

CHAPTER NINE

Koryŏ Society

This chapter presents a glimpse of the people and society of the first half of the Koryŏ dynasty, as revealed in the surviving historical sources. The men of letters who were at the helm of Koryŏ's social order led lives centered on statecraft, scholarship, and literature. Their task was to apply learning to the benefit of society by becoming involved in governing. In theory, honest officials would run the government in a humane and judicious manner, assuring efficient rule. But Koryŏ, like every other society, had officials who abused their power and used their influence to intimidate the weak. Despite the infectious evils of their corruption, however, there were others who, on reaching the summit of success, chose a path that rejected power and influence in favor of tireless private efforts to improve the self and society. Some took the extreme route of rejecting all secular values and led reclusive lives devoted to spiritual salvation. For such men, Buddhism held an immense appeal.

Confucianism, which stressed adherence to proper human relations based on status, age, and sex, remained important to Koryŏ life. Loyalty and filial piety were especially singled out as essential to a strong state and stable family. Observance of Confucian principles was emphasized throughout the society, and women as well as men were lauded for their contributions to the observance. The Confucian emphasis on merit also blunted Koryŏ's indigenous preference for lineage. In contrast to Silla, social mobility was possible in Koryŏ;

indeed, the selections on social change in this chapter provide examples of people who advanced their social status in different periods of the dynasty. Nevertheless, slaves and other lowborn people were carefully watched and restricted in the roles they could play.

The Confucian Scholar

By the start of the eleventh century, the state-building process had been completed and Koryŏ entered a new phase of maturity. The success of Koryŏ's earlier kings made possible the emergence of a strong Confucian state that provided a high level of social stability and prosperity. Koryŏ was clearly one of the most sophisticated states of the age.

At the top of the Koryŏ social order were the civil aristocrats. As a class, the civil aristocrats monopolized the highest offices in the government, controlled extensive wealth, and dominated the educational institutions. The aristocrats led comfortable lives that increasingly centered on educational and literary pursuits.

Ch'oe Ch'ung (984–1068), living during this age, advanced the ideals of Confucian education by establishing an academy that became the model for all Korean centers of learning. To advance into the highest ranks of the civil government, a man often had to pass the state examination. The academies that Ch'oe Ch'ung and his disciples founded flourished, producing many successful civil examination candidates. As the initial passage tells, scholars balanced the time spent in rigorous preparation with relaxed occasions by holding poetry contests and elaborate banquets. The relationship between a teacher and his students had increasingly gained a Confucian overtone.

Ch'oe Cha (1188–1260), writing a century later, discussed several men who were in charge of the state examination and passed a number of their candidates. These successful candidates remained forever faithful to their examiners. The state examination played an important political and social role in Koryŏ.

Scholar-officials had numerous functions. These men frequently held political office and determined policy for both central and local areas. They also engaged in diverse cultural pursuits, many expressing themselves as accomplished poets and artists. The scholar often had a studio in which he could read, write, and practice calligraphy. "The

Four Treasures of the Studio," written by Yi Illo (1152–1220), provides a glimpse into this world of the scholar.

Ch'oe Ch'ung's Academy
[From *Koryŏ sa* 74:34a–35a]

In Munjong's reign, Ch'oe Ch'ung, the grand preceptor and secretary-general of the Royal Secretariat, gathered the young and instructed them diligently. His classes overflowed with students and others, and so he divided them into nine academies, calling them Celebrating the Sage (Aksŏng), the Great Mean (Taejung), Sagely Brightness (Sŏngmyŏng), Respecting Scholarly Endeavors (Kyŏngŏp), Creating the Way (Chodo), Following One's Nature (Solsŏng), Advancing Virtue (Chindŏk), Great Harmony (Taehwa), and Waiting for a Summons (Taebing). The students were called Lord Chancellor Ch'oe's Disciples. All children of high-ranking officials intending to sit for the state examination first joined his academies and studied under him. Every year in the hot summer months they rented monastic quarters and continued lessons. He selected instructors from among those who had passed the examination and were superior in scholarship and talent but did not hold government office. Their course of study included the nine Confucian classics and three Chinese histories.[1]

Occasionally scholars would visit, and, burning a candle to measure the time, they would compose rhymeprose and poetry. Listed in the order in which their poems ranked, they would enter as their names were called. Then, setting up a banquet, the young and the old would line up to the right and left and were presented wine and food. All acting with propriety and orderly in their relations, they sang and exchanged verses throughout the day. Everybody who watched thought it beautiful and admired it. From this time on, all those who sat for the examination had their names registered on the roster of the nine academies and were called Lord Chancellor Ch'oe's Disciples.

There also were eleven other Confucian scholars who brought their disciples together. The Disciples of Lord Hongmun were set up by Chancellor Chŏng Paegŏl; they were also called the Disciples of Lord Ungch'ŏn. Disciples of Lord Kwanghŏn was started by Assistant Executive of Political Affairs No Tan, Disciples of Namsan by Master of Sacrificial Wines Kim Sangbin, Disciples of Sŏwŏn by Senior Executive Kim Much'e, Disciples of Lord Munch'ung by Chancellor Ŭn Yun, Disciples of Lord Yangjin by Executive Kim Ŭijin or Office Chief Pak Myŏngbo, Disciples of Lord Chŏnggyŏng by Executive Hwang Yŏng, Disciples of Lord Ch'ungp'yŏng by Yu Kam, Disciples of Lord Chŏnghŏn by Chancellor Mun Chŏng, and Disciples of Executive Sŏ by Sŏ Sŏk. The founder of Disciples of Kwisan is unknown. These, together with Lord Chancellor Ch'oe's Disciples, were referred to as the twelve student assemblies, but Ch'oe Ch'ung's school was the most successful. HK/ES

Ch'oe Cha: Teachers and Disciples
[From *Pohan chip* 1:7a–b]

Examinees respect examiners of the state examination as sons would respect fathers. P'ei Hao[2] three times oversaw the T'ang state examination. His disciple Ma Yin-sun[3] supervised the examination once and took those who passed to greet P'ei. P'ei then composed a verse:

> Three times I supervised the examination,
> And I have reached the age of eighty.
> Now I meet my disciple's disciples.

In our own Koryŏ dynasty, when Academician Han Ŏnguk led his students to greet Lord Munsuk Ch'oe Yuch'ŏng [1095–1174], the latter composed a poem:

> How great an honor to have you all come and visit.
> Happy indeed am I to see my disciple's disciples.

Lord Yangsuk [Im Yu, 1150–1213] was the maternal uncle of three kings (Ŭijong, 1146–1170; Myŏngjong, 1170–1197; and Sinjong, 1197–1204) and held the position of first minister. His disciple Lord Munjŏng Cho [Ch'ung, 1171–1220], supervisor of sacrificial wines, supervised the state examination and took his successful examinees to the Office of Royal Edicts to greet Im. Yi Illo [1152–1220] composed a poem of congratulations:

> For ten years at the Secretariat Chancellery you have assisted the
>   promotion of peace.
> Four times you have single-handedly managed the state
>   examination.

The nation's new scholar has repaid his indebtedness to its
  former leading scholar.
Now the former disciple has himself obtained new disciples.

The first son of Lord Yangsuk, Executive Im Kyŏngsuk, oversaw the state examination four times, and among his successful examinees were more than ten persons who reached the highest official rank
in a matter of a few years, and among them were three former generals
and one junior colonel. This was previously unheard of. Royal Academician Yu Kyŏng supervised the qualifying examination only sixteen years after passing the examination himself. On the day after
announcing those who had passed, he went to pay his respects to the
former executive Im Kyŏngsuk, who, having reached seventy years,
had already retired as the grand preceptor. Among those who stood in
front of the stone steps to his porch were four nephews, two of whom
were state councillors in the Chancellery and the other two state
councillors in the Security Council. Also there were many cousins and
nephews who were ranking officials, along with those who had passed
the four examinations supervised by the executive. When Yu Kyŏng
led his disciples and bowed in the courtyard below, the executive sat
in the hall as musicians played. Those who watched all applauded in
admiration, even with tears in their eyes. Hallim Academician Im
Kyeil wrote a congratulatory poem:

> The state councillors bow deeply in your courtyard.
> Gathered before your gates are the great talents of the day.
> Seated you can see luxuriant branches of great peach and pear
>   trees burst forth.
> This rare and splendid event must be passed on forever to
>   succeeding generations. HK/ES

Yi Illo: The Four Treasures of the Studio
[From *P'ahan chip* 1b–2a]

Every scholar must possess the "four treasures" of the studio.
But of these, ink is the most difficult to make. In the capital, however,
as many treasures are gathered and are easy to obtain, people do not
consider them valuable. When I was sent out to be a magistrate in
Maengsŏng, I was instructed by the Greater Regional Military Command to prepare five thousand sticks of ink for the king and hasten to
present them in the spring. Quickly I went to Kongam village by

horse and urged the people to gather one hundred bushels of ashes of pine trees. Assembling good craftsmen, I personally supervised the work myself, finishing it in two months. My face and clothes were all the color of soot. I went to another place and with some effort cleaned myself and my clothes and returned to the town. Since then, whenever I see ink, even if only a little piece, I cannot regard it indifferently but value it dearly. The best quality paper, bamboo products, and silk produced like this are similarly valuable. An ancient said: "Li Shen,[4] in his 'Ode to Pity the Farmer,' wrote, 'who would know the toil that went into producing every grain of rice / in the rice bowl on the table?' Truly these are the words of a most humane person." HK/ES

Life of the Aristocrat

Aristocratic power in Koryŏ peaked in the early twelfth century. Two clans in particular, the Kims of Ansan and the Yis of Kyŏngwŏn, dominated court life. Through intermarriage with the royal family and extensive political and economic power, these lineages placed many of their clansmen in important dynastic offices. The Kyŏngwŏn Yi lineage makes an especially good study, for some of their clansmen controlled the kingdom for nearly three generations and ultimately tried twice to usurp the throne. Despite their later arrogance and occasional abuse of power, Kyŏngwŏn Yi clansmen were highly literate scholars schooled in the Confucian classics, as seen in the first selection presented here.

Yi Chagyŏm (d. 1126), one of the most powerful and despised civil officials in early Koryŏ, at the peak of his power had his grandson Injong on the throne, and two of his daughters were married to the monarch. Indicating the arrogance of power, the second selection portrays the decadence of Yi Chagyŏm's age. Symptomatic of the times, such arrogance was not limited to the leading Kyŏngwŏn Yi lineage, as other civil aristocrats increasingly abused their privileges too. Kim Tonjung (d. 1170), the son of Kim Pusik (1075–1151), of the prestigious Kim clan of Kyŏngju, epitomized the pursuit of ostentation and luxury as he expended great sums to build gardens and temples.

By Ŭijong's reign (1146–1170), many in the court were involved in bribery and other corrupt practices, as the final passage, "Courting of Royal Favor by Palace Attendants," details. These pieces are unusual in that they dramatically portray unrestrained corruption that may not have been the norm for Koryŏ society in general. Undoubtedly, however, such abuse of power ultimately contributed to the overthrow of Ŭijong and his civilian entourage and the start of the military period.

The Splendors of the Yi Clan of Kyŏngwŏn
[From *Pohan chip* 1:6a]

From early in the dynasty, the Yi clan of Kyŏngwŏn has produced great officials generation after generation. At the time of the Duke of Changhwa Yi Chayŏn [d. 1086], his son Ho became Count of Kyŏngwŏn, and three other sons, Chŏng, Ŭi, and An, all became state councillors. One of his daughters was none other than Queen Dowager Inye (Munjong's queen), and two other daughters became royal consorts. Chayŏn's younger brother, Chasang, who rose to become an executive of the Department of Ministries, had two sons, Ye and O, who became state councillors. Chayŏn's grandchildren all intermarried with the royal family and prospered as royal relatives. From ancient times to today, this may be unprecedented.

Earlier, when Ŭi was an official of the Policy Critics, there were some yin/yang practitioners who, insisting on geomancy, talked about each others' deficiencies. When the king asked about this, Ŭi responded: "Yin and yang principles are rooted in the *Book of Changes,* but the *Book of Changes* does not discuss the deficiencies of geomancy. Later irrational practitioners, incorrectly asserting this, wrote things that have confused the people. Besides, since geomancy is false and foolish, there is nothing in it worthy of acceptance." The king in his heart agreed with this.

The descendants of Chŏng, Ŭi, and O are now even more distinguished. Lord Changhwa, Yi Chayŏn, passing the state examination with highest honors, became a state councillor, and when he was in charge of the state examination, he selected many talented individuals. His disciples included Executive Ch'oe Sŏk, Executive Kim Yang-gam, Assistant Executive in Political Affairs Ch'oe Sahun, Pak Il-lyang, Academician Ch'oe T'aek, and Wi Cheman. HK/ES

The Decadence of Yi Chagyŏm and Kim Tonjung
[From *Koryŏ sa* 127:14b–15b, 98:20a–b]

Yi Chagyŏm [d. 1126] not only placed many of his clan members in important government positions but also sold official titles. His clique occupied many positions of responsibility, and he made himself a lord of the nation. In ceremony he was treated like a crown prince, and his birthday was called *insujŏl* (the day of benevolent longevity). All the congratulations offered to him were called *chŏn* (documents) as a special recognition. His many sons competed in building their mansions stretching from block to block and increased their power ever more. Bribes were openly made, and gifts were presented to him in abundance from all over, so much so that at any one time he had an excess of twenty or thirty thousand *kŭn* of rotten meat.[5] He forcibly took others' land and let his slaves seize other people's carts and horses to transport his goods. The helpless people destroyed their carts and sold their cows and horses. There was unrest in the streets.

Earlier, because Han Chŏng, executive of the Ministry of Civil Personnel, and Yi Wŏnŭng became estranged, Han Chŏng lost his position. The king specially erected a Buddhist temple at Injewŏn and made it a place to offer prayers. At that time, Wŏnŭng died, and Chŏng, reappointed to an office, offered prayers even more earnestly for good fortune. Kim Tonjung [d. 1170] and his brother Kim Tonsi [d. 1170] were at that time renovating Kwallan Temple, which was built by their father Pusik, and it was also said to be a place to pray for the good fortune of the king. The king said to Tonjung, Tonsi, and Chŏng, "I have heard that you gentlemen are trying to obtain blessings for me. I am very appreciative of this. I would like to go to see it soon." Because the mountain north of the temple had no trees or foliage, Kim Tonjung and the others mobilized the neighboring peasants to plant pine trees, white pines, cedar, and fir trees, exotic flowers, and rare grasses. They constructed a royal hall, decorating it in glittering and bright colors and using unusual stones in its steps. On the day the king visited the temple, Tonjung and the others held a banquet on the western terrace. The screens, tents, and dishes were quite luxurious, and the food was lavish. The king and the state councillors and courtiers completely enjoyed themselves. The king presented Tonjung and Tonsi each with three ingots of white gold and Chŏng with two ingots of white gold, and each also received ten bolts of silk cloth and seventy *kŭn* of Khitan silk thread. HK/ES

Courting of Royal Favor by Palace Attendants
[From *Koryŏ sa* 18:26a–b]

The left and right units of the palace attendants competed in presenting precious gifts to the king. The right unit then had many aristocratic youths in it. Invoking the royal prerogative through the eunuchs, they sought out many precious objects as well as calligraphy and paintings from public and private holdings. They also made ladders of satin and put various toys on them. Acting like foreigners offering tribute, they presented two blue and red parasols and two choice horses. The left unit, composed entirely of Confucian scholars, was unfamiliar with playing these games, and what it presented was not one-hundredth of that given by the right. Ashamed at being unable to equal them, they borrowed five fine horses and presented them to the king. The king received all these gifts and gave to the left unit ten *kŭn* of white silver and sixty-five *kŭn* of Khitan silk thread and to the right unit ten *kŭn* of white silver and ninety-five *kŭn* of Khitan silk thread. Later the left unit, unable to repay the debt, was daily pressed for it. Contemporaries laughed at them. HK/ES

The Scholar and Buddhism

The Koryŏ literati generally were of the Buddhist faith and saw no apparent contradiction in pursuing Buddhist beliefs along with Confucian practices. Confucianism addressed their societal concerns while Buddhism met their spiritual needs. The first selection, written by Kim Puch'ŏl (d. 1136) of the renowned Kyŏngju Kim lineage, discusses the scholar-official Yi Chahyŏn, who gave up his government posts to practice his faith more devoutly. Yi Chahyŏn was from the same clan as Yi Chagyŏm, and his life reveals that the aristocratic Kyŏngwŏn Yi clan also produced refined, disciplined individuals. Clearly there was an aesthetic side to the life of the Koryŏ official that was not always satisfied by active political involvement.

The second selection, "Hall of Helping People," presents another aspect in the life of the scholar-official devoted to Buddhism. Charity was an important component of Buddhist practices, and Ch'ae

Hongch'ŏl (1262–1340) established a foundation to assist people in need.

Kim Puch'ŏl: The Disciplined Life of Yi Chahyŏn
[From *Tong munsŏn* 64:27a–30b]

Mount Ch'ŏngp'yŏng of Ch'unju was formerly known as Mount Kyŏngun, and Mañjuśrī Hall formerly was Samantabhadra Hall. Earlier, the Ch'an Master Yung-hsien came to Silla from T'ang China. Later, eighteen years after Koryŏ's King T'aejo came to power, Silla's King Kyŏngsun turned over his territory to Koryŏ. This was the second year of Ch'ing-t'ai [935] according to the Later T'ang calendar. In the twenty-fourth year of King Kwangjong, which was the sixth year of K'ai-pao according to the Sung calendar [973], a meditation master began to visit Mount Kyŏngun and then erected a meditation cloister called Paegam. In the twenty-third year of Munjong's reign [1069], Lord Yi Ŭi, former senior policy adviser and commissioner of the Security Council, became the inspector of warehouses for the Ch'unju circuit. Cherishing the beautiful scenery of Mount Kyŏngun, he built a temple on the former site of Paegam Meditation Cloister and called it Pohyŏn Hall. This was the first year of Hsi-ning [1068] in the Sung calendar.[6] Later Master Hŭii [Yi Chahyŏn, 1061–1125] gave up his government positions and secluded himself here, and from then on robbers disappeared and tigers vanished from the area. And the name of the mountain was changed to Ch'ŏngp'yŏng. After having seen the Bodhisattva Mañjuśrī twice, he thought he should study the fundamentals of Buddha dharma, and therefore he changed the name of the hall to Mañjuśrī and renovated it.

Master Hŭii was Lord Yi Ŭi's oldest son. His name was Chahyŏn, and his courtesy name was Chinjŏng. His appearance was exceptional; his disposition was calm and dispassionate. In 1083 he passed the state examination (*chinsa* degree), and in 1089, when he was executive assistant in the Bureau of Music, he resigned his government post and withdrew from an active official life. While traveling about, he reached the Imjin River. Crossing it, he vowed to himself, "With this crossing I will never return to the capital." Although there was generally nothing he did not study, he researched deeply into Buddhist principles and especially liked Meditation teachings. He said to himself, "Once I read in the *Recorded Sayings of Hsüeh-feng I-ts'un* [822–908] the statement, 'When the truth is everywhere, why do you look for it in only one place?' Looking at these words, I suddenly realized their truth. From that time on, I understood and carried no doubts about the teachings of Buddha." After this, he traveled to all the famous mountains of Korea and visited the sites of the ancient sages.

Later when National Preceptor Hyejo was serving as the abbot at Hwaak Monastery on a neighboring mountain, he asked him about meditation doctrine. While living in the mountains, he ate only vegetables, wore a cassock, and took moderation and frugality to be his pleasures. Away from the monastery, in another place, he built a personal dwelling of more than ten structures such as hermitages, shrines, and pavilions. A shrine was called Munsŏng, the hermitages were named Kyŏngsŏng, Sŏndong, and Sigam, and each of the others had its own name. Every day he lived in them. Sometimes he sat by himself deep into the night without sleeping; sometimes he would sit on top of a rock for an entire day without moving; sometimes he would go into the hermitage Kyŏngsŏng for seven days without leaving. Once he said to one of his attendants, "Having read all of the *Tripiṭaka,* I looked through many other books. The *Suraṅgama Scripture* represents the Mind school of Meditation and clarifies the essential path. However, no students of Meditation read it. This is truly regrettable." Accordingly, he had his disciples study it, thus gradually increasing the number of those who read it.

Yejong [1105–1122] several times instructed his palace attendants to grant Master Hŭii royal gifts of tea, incense, and Buddhist paintings in large amounts and ordered him to come to the palace. But not wishing to abandon the vow made when he crossed the river, to the end Hŭii did not comply with this royal request. When the king went to the Southern Capital in 1117, he sent Master Hŭii's younger brother, Minister Yi Chadŏk, to ask Master Hŭii to come there. The king's summons was expressed in a poem:

> The passing of each day increases my desire to see you.
> Difficult though it is to override the will of a lofty sage,
> What would I do with my own heart's desire?

Master Hŭii sent a letter respectfully declining the invitation, but there was no way to change the king's earnest desire, and so in the eighth month of that year he went to the Southern Capital to pay his respects. The king said, "Although I have wanted to see you, a gentleman of high morality, for several years, I could not receive you in the manner of an ordinary subject." The king commanded him to come up to the throne and bow. The king responded with a bow. Then they sat, had tea, and talked quietly. Thereupon the king ordered him to remain at Ch'ŏngnyang Monastery on Mount Samgak for a while, and the king visited him, inquiring about meditation teaching. Master Hŭii in the end wrote and presented an essay titled "Simyo" (Fundamentals of the Mind) and then firmly asked to return to the mountains. The king gave him tea, incense, Buddhist utensils, and clothes, blessing his departure. On his leaving, the queen and princesses each presented him with clothing as gifts out of respect. In 1121 the minister Yi Chadŏk again received a royal instruction and went to the mountain to have Master Hŭii hold a special lecture on the *Surangama Scripture*. Scholars came from many places to listen to his lecture.

In 1122 the present king, Injong [1122–1146], ascended the throne and especially sent the courtier Yi Pongwŏn to ask kindly after Master Hŭii and give him royal gifts of tea, incense, and clothing. When Master Hŭii became slightly ill in 1125, the king sent palace attendants and a court physician to inquire into his illness and at the same time gave him tea, medicine, and the like. As Master Hŭii had already determined where he was to be buried, one day he told his disciples, "It seems I may not live for a long time. After I die, my disciple Chowŏn will succeed me at the monastery, and after Chowŏn, select those who practice the path and have them succeed one after another as the leader."

On the twenty-first day of the fourth month of that year, he again told his disciples, "Life is not constant. If there is life, there always is death. Please do not feel sad. Take comfort in nature's way." With these words, at the hour of the Monkey (3–5 P.M.), he died. Even facing death, his mind was clear. He talked and laughed as usual. At the time he died, an unusual fragrance filled the room and lasted for three days, gradually spreading into the mountain recesses. His body seemed as white as jade and had elasticity as in normal life. The twenty-three days of mourning were observed as he had willed. He had remained in the mountains for thirty-seven years, from 1089 to 1125. He was sixty-five years of age. In the autumn of 1130, the eighth month, he was given the posthumous title Lord Chillak (True Happiness). . . .

If we try to evaluate Master Hŭii's life, we must note that from ancient times there have been many gentlemen of high principle who have lived as recluses. Generally, lonely officials or unlucky people with no hope of advancing in life choose secluded lives. In the beginning they contentedly live in the wilderness, but in the end they fail to maintain their intentions, becoming troubled. Moreover, I have never before heard of a person from a powerful house related to the royal family who has been able to live his life in the wilderness. Master Hŭii, born to wealth and power, passed top in the state examination through his literary skill and entered government service with many advantages. Thus to him advancing to a ministerial position or becoming a general was as easy as picking up straw off the ground. He rejected wealth and power as one might discard a worn shoe. Thinking life was like a drifting cloud, he went into the mountains forever, never returning to the capital. Is this not strange indeed?

Moreover, Master Hŭii's family had for successive generations intermarried with the royal family, becoming one of the first families of Korea. Yet Master Hŭii alone, indifferent to worldly concerns, remained unaffected by worldly ambition. And yet with his virtue and personality so respected, how could men of wisdom help admiring him and at the same time regret his withdrawal from government? Even a peasant farming in the countryside, on hearing of the man's virtue, could not help liking and respecting him. Generally one rules people through loyalty and treats people with trust, and absolute sincerity will move people as well as spirits. Consequently, it is said that when he lived in the mountains, robbers disappeared and tigers vanished.

In the past, Liang Hung [first century A.D.] went to Mount Pa-ling, an act that may be considered fitting for a man of lofty character. Nevertheless, he was secretly accompanied by his wife Meng Kuang. P'ang Kung went and lived south of Mount Hsien and never returned to town life, but he openly took his family with him. How could Master Hŭii disregard his feelings for sensuality? How could he go and stay where there is no comfort? Being pure and noble, he unfailingly appreciated things that others did not. So lofty was his integrity that it could not be swayed by worldly power. A pleasant and pure wind always breezes through, enlivening man's motives and courage. As to gentlemen of high principle who have lived as recluses from the past to the present, truly it can be said that there has been only one. His disciple Chiwŏn came to me with a list of Master Hŭii's lifetime activities and asked me to write a tribute. His requests were so earnest that in the end I have written this tribute together with a detailed account of Master Hŭii's life story. The extraordinary beauty of Mount

Ch'ŏngp'yŏng's streams and ravines is indeed an exquisite spot in Korea. And waiting for a talented poet to describe this in the future, I have not referred to it here.   HK/ES

Hall of Helping People
[From *Koryŏ sa* 108:13a–b]

Ch'ae Hongch'ŏl was a meticulous man. He displayed talent in literary and artistic pursuits and was especially fond of Buddhism. North of his house he built a garden containing aromatic plants. He always supported meditation monks and also provided medicine to the poor. Many people in the country relied on them and called his garden the Hall of Helping People (Hwarindang). King Ch'ungsŏn once visited Ch'ae's garden and presented him with thirty *kŭn* of white gold. South of his home, he built a hall and called it Chunghwa (Moderation). At that time, he invited eight elder statesmen, including Prince Yŏngga Kwŏn Pu, to form the Kiyŏnghoe (Society of Distinguished Elders), and he composed "New Songs of Chahadong" (*Chahadong singok*). It is still included among musical notations.   HK/ES

The Family

Lineage was at the very core of Koryŏ's political order. Not only did the clan lineage enable great families to rise in society, but, as the following passages demonstrate, it determined one's status, whether aristocrat or slave. Accordingly, relations within the family were extremely important for the smooth functioning of this society, an attitude that was reinforced by Confucian ideology.

Of all the values Confucianism emphasizes, filial piety receives special attention. King Sŏngjong (981–997), Koryŏ's sixth monarch, in his rescript on filial piety, asked that filial subjects be recognized and rewarded. As the king indicated, to be filial at home meant to be loyal to the state. In short, filial behavior would help to secure the state and bring harmony to society.

Sound family relations are evident too in Ch'oe Nubaek's twelfth-century tomb inscription for his wife, Yŏm Kyŏngae. In this beautiful tribute, Ch'oe describes his deceased wife's humility and untiring devotion to him and his family. The woman's role in Koryŏ society is revealed to a limited degree through this eulogy. The description also provides a rewarding glimpse of social history, convincingly demonstrating that not all court officials lived lives of splendor.

King Sŏngjong: Rescript on Filial Piety
[From *Koryŏ sa* 3:17a–18b]

Generally in governing the country, one must first attend to what is fundamental. In doing so, nothing surpasses filial piety. This was exemplified by the Three August Sovereigns and the Five Emperors.[7] Filial piety is the order of myriad affairs and the core of all virtues. Accordingly, a Chinese emperor congratulated Yang Yin[8] for honoring his parents and built a gate to commemorate this in his home town. The emperor of Chin China commended the extreme filial piety of Wang Hsiang [185–269][9] by ordering his name recorded in histories.

As a child, I lost my father, and I may have grown up foolish and ignorant. Entrusted with the succession, I inherited the responsibility to protect the dynasty. Recalling my deceased grandfather, I grieve over the brevity of human life. Whenever I think of past times with my brothers, I feel even more fraternal affection. Accordingly, if we take the precepts from the six Confucian classics and rely for a ritual norm on the three ritual texts,[10] this will make the customs of a country return to the five filial virtues expected of rulers, feudal lords, officials, scholars, and peasants.

Recently I have dispatched officials to the six provinces to spread instructions to help the old and the weak who are starving and wandering, to rescue destitute widowers and orphans, and to look for and visit filial sons, obedient grandchildren, righteous husbands, and chaste women.

There was in Kurye-hyŏn, Chŏnju, a person named Son Sunhŭng. When his mother died of an illness, he painted a portrait of her and placed it on an altar. Once every three days he attended her grave, serving her as if she were living.

In Chibul station, Unje-hyŏn, a person named Ch'adal had three brothers, and together they supported their old mother. Ch'adal told his wife to attend his mother, but she was not diligent, and so he immediately divorced her. His two younger brothers also singleheartedly served their mother without even a thought of marrying.

The mother of Pak Kwangyŏm of Moran-ri in the Western Capital (P'yŏngyang) had been dead for seven days. Suddenly he saw some dried wood that seemed to be shaped like his mother. He carried it to his home and revered it with all propriety.

Consider the case of Hambu, the daughter of Nŭngsŏn, who lived in Nangsan-do, Namhae. When her father died from snakebite, she put his coffin in a bedroom for five months and served him as in normal times.

Chai, daughter of Chŏng Kangjun, a person living in Yŏnil-hyŏn, Kyŏngju, and the daughter of the Ch'oe family of Songhŭng ward in the capital both were widowed early but did not remarry. With filial care they attended their in-laws, rearing their children.

Chŏlch'ung-bu Subcolonel Cho Yŏng buried his mother in a garden at his house, holding memorial services for her in the morning and evening.

For Hambu and the seven men and women, erect celebratory gates in their villages and exempt them from the duties of corvée labor. For Ch'adal and his brothers, four in all, permit them to leave offshore islands and postal stations and then register them to live in the *chu* or *hyŏn* of their choice. To Sunhŭng and five others give official ranks in order to praise their filial ways. Send Royal Recording Secretary Kim Simŏn and others to them and give each of them one hundred *sŏk* of grain, two silver basins, and sixty-eight bolts of colored silk and cloth. Promote Cho Yŏng ten grades, conferring on him the concurrent titles of junior colonel of the Wiikpu, Honorary Censor, Senior Marshal, and Viscount, and grant him one set of official garb, thirty pieces of silver, and twenty bolts of silk.

The ruler is the sovereign of all the people, and the people are the subjects of the ruler. If there are good deeds, it is my blessing. If there are evil deeds, it is my worry. Illuminate action that respects parents so as to display the spirit of good customs. If humble, rural peasants diligently think about filial piety, how can government officials neglect serving their parents? Truly if one is filial at home, he will certainly be a loyal official for the state. All scholars and commoners, please take my words to heart. HK/ES

Ch'oe Nubaek: Tomb Inscription of Yŏm Kyŏngae

[From *Chōsen kinseki sōran* 1:357–359]

In 1146, on the twenty-eighth (*musul*) day of the first month, the wife of Hannam Ch'oe Nubaek, Lady Yŏm, duchess of Pongsŏng-hyŏn, died in her country house. Her coffin was placed in state in

Sunch'ŏn Hall, and on the eleventh (*imin*) day in the second month she was cremated north of the capital on the northwest ridge of Pakhyŏl. Her remains were interred temporarily east of the capital at Ch'ŏngnyang Temple, and three years later in 1148, *mujin,* on the seventeenth day of the eighth month, she was buried northeast of Inhyo Hall beside her deceased father's tomb. Ch'oe Nubaek composed the following tomb inscription.

Her name was Kyŏngae. She was the daughter of Yŏm Tŏkpang, junior executive of the Department of the Ministries and deputy director of palace storage. Her mother was Ŭiryŏng-gun Lady Sim. When she was twenty-five, she married me and subsequently gave birth to six children. The first boy is named Tanin, the second Tanwi, and the third Tanye. All have aspired in scholarship. The fourth son, Tanji, became a monk. One daughter, named Kwigang, married Ch'oe Kukpo, recording officer of the Awe-Inspiring Division. When Ch'oe died, she returned home. The second daughter, Sungang, is still young.

As a person, my wife was pure and modest. She was very literate and well understood moral obligations. In speech, appearance, skill, and conduct, she was superior to others. Before marriage she ably served her parents; after marriage she was extremely diligent in wifely ways. She was the first to perceive and carry out the wishes of elders, and with filial piety she nourished my now deceased mother. In good and bad fortune, in congratulations and condolences, she could share the feelings of immediate family members and in-laws. There was no one who did not praise her.

Earlier, I was sent out as a magistrate to P'aeju (in Chŏlla) and Chungwŏn (in Ch'ungch'ŏng). Without hesitation, crossing mountains and streams, she accompanied me all the way. And when I was involved in military matters, she endured hardship in our poor home and often made and sent military uniforms. And when I was a palace attendant, she used every means possible to supply delicacies to present to the king. How she followed me through all of these difficulties for twenty-three years I cannot entirely record.

Although my father died before we were married, she still offered sacrifices to him during the hot days of summer and on the cold memorial day of winter. She personally wove cloth, saving it little by little, and then made by hand a jacket or a pair of pants. Whenever it came to the day of sacrifice, she set up an altar and presented these as offerings. And when attending Buddhist services for the deceased, regardless of the number of people, she prepared stockings and presented them to the monks. This is what I most certainly cannot forget.

One day she said to me, "You are a man of letters. Mundane matters should not be important to you. I consider providing clothes and food for the family to be my task. Even though I repeatedly put forth effort to do this, it does not always come up to my expectations. Later on, even if I unfortunately die first and you attain more income, enabling you to do everything you wish, please remember me for trying to ward off poverty, not for my lack of talent." As she finished speaking, she released a vast sigh.

In the spring of 1145, *ŭlch'uk,* I advanced from supervising attendant in the Office of Heir Apparent to junior monitor, drafter of royal edicts and proclamations. My wife, showing her happiness in her face, said, "It seems we have almost seen the end of our poverty." I responded to her, "Being a policy critic is not a position to earn a rich stipend." My wife said, "If suddenly one day you are standing in the palace court with the king arguing over an issue, even if I am forced to wear a thorny wooden barrette and poor cotton skirts and carry heavy burdens in making our life, I will accept it willingly." These were not the words of an ordinary woman.

My wife fell ill in the ninth month of that year, and in the first month of 1146 her illness became acute and she died. What remorse I felt! In the summer of 1146 I advanced to junior reparationer (*usagan*) and then in the twelfth month to senior reparationer (*chwasagan*). In the spring of 1147 I was made general censor, and in the winter of that year I was demoted to assistant office chief in the Ministry of Rites. In the spring of 1148 I advanced to office chief of the Ministry of Rites and then became deputy magistrate of Ch'ŏngju. I continued to be promoted many times and successively received higher stipends. In looking at my family's present situation, however, it is not as good as in the days when my wife struggled to make ends meet. How could anyone say my wife did not have talent? When my wife was about to die, in leaving her last instructions to me and our children, all her words were reasonable and many were worth listening to.

When she died, her age was forty-seven. Her epitaph reads: "I, your husband, pledge not to forget you. That I am not yet buried together with you gives me great pain. The children will live in harmony and expect to be prosperous forever." HK/ES

Social Change

Only a small minority in Koryŏ enjoyed lives of luxury and wealth. Although most people lived lean, austere lives, Koryŏ society permitted a limited degree of mobility. For the intellectually able, there were always opportunities to advance, for example, through the state examination. Marriage presented a potential means of moving up the social ladder. The first selection describes the union between Wang Kŏn and Changhwa, one of his many wives. The daughter of a local personage, she met Wang Kŏn when he was a general serving T'aebong (901–918) under Kim Kungye (d. 918) and through a "miraculous conception" gave birth to Koryŏ's future second king. Legend mixes with history to provide a unique picture of social mobility in late Silla and early Koryŏ.

An Hyang (1243–1306) lived much later in the dynasty and came from the middle level of Koryŏ society. The short description offered here reveals the personal interaction between a hereditary local clerk and a centrally appointed official. Both had their own bases of power that could conflict but assured orderly dynastic rule when used effectively. Chŏng Kasin (d. 1298), the subject of the next selection, was another official who lacked an esteemed lineage. This anecdote clearly reveals the importance of one's lineage in establishing marriage ties even for those who were not members of the elite.

An excellent source for understanding twelfth-century Koryŏ is the *Kao-li t'u-ching* (Illustrated Account of Koryŏ) by Hsü Ching (1091–1153) of Sung. Hsü visited Koryŏ on a mission from China in 1123 and compiled this work describing Korea and the Koreans. In this particular passage, he briefly identifies the major social classes of Koryŏ for his Chinese readers and then gives a frank account of what he interprets to be Korean behavioral norms. Although Hsü's ethnocentrism is readily apparent in this and other passages, his work sheds precious light otherwise unavailable on aspects of Koryŏ life.

Queen Changhwa and the Dynastic Founder
[From *Koryŏ sa* 88:3a]

Queen Changhwa, Lady O, was from Naju. Her grandfather was Pudon, and her father was Prince Taryŏn. Her family had lived in Mokp'o for generations. Prince Taryŏn married village chief Yŏn-wi's daughter Tŏkkyo, and the future queen was born. Once Lady O dreamed a river dragon entering her womb. Surprised, she woke and told her parents, who both thought it strange.

Not long afterward, Wang Kŏn, as commander of [T'aebong] naval forces, set out for Naju. With his ships anchored at Mokp'o, he looked out above the water and saw a colored cloud moving. Coming closer, he saw it was Lady O doing her laundry. Wang Kŏn asked her to wait on him in his chambers. Because of her humble status, he did not want her to become pregnant, and so he ejaculated on the bed sheet. The queen absorbed it and became pregnant, giving birth in time to a son, who later became King Hyejong. As his face had many lines resembling those of a seat mat, contemporaries called him "The Lord of the Pleats." He sprinkled water on his bed and also took large bottles and filled them with water. He liked to wash his elbows with it. Truly he was the son of a dragon.

When the boy reached the age of seven, King T'aejo knew he possessed the virtue to be the successor but feared he could not succeed to the throne because of his mother's inferior origins. Therefore the king gave her an old chest containing a robe dyed in yellow. She showed it to Taegwan Pak Surhŭi. Contemplating [the meaning of] this, Surhŭi understood T'aejo's intentions and requested that the boy be installed as the crown prince. When the queen died, the posthumous title of Queen Changhwa was conferred upon her. HK/ES

The Career of An Hyang
[From Koryŏ sa 105:28a–b]

An Hyang's original name was Yu, and he was from Hŭngju. His father, Pu, was a local clerk with a degree in medicine but advanced to the post of deputy commissioner of the Security Council by the time he retired. As a boy, An Hyang enjoyed studying, and early in King Wŏnjong's reign he passed the state examination. . . . Once he went to Andong and ordered a local clerk to wash his feet. The clerk responded, "I am a local official. How can you disgrace me?" The clerk then plotted with a number of other local clerks to reproach An Hyang. An old clerk who had observed An's appearance came out and said, "I have seen many people. He will certainly become prominent. Do not take him lightly." HK/ES

The Career of Chŏng Kasin
[From *Koryŏ sa* 105:23b–24a]

Chŏng Kasin's courtesy name was Honji. His name originally was Hŭng. He was from Naju. His father, Songsu, passed the examination as a locally recommended candidate.[11] From birth, Kasin was precocious. Contemporaries especially commended his reading and writing. He went to the capital with the monk Ch'ŏngi. As he was poor and had no one else to rely on, he depended on Ch'ŏngi for food. Ch'ŏngi pitied him and sought to marry him into a rich family, but there were no interested parties except Deputy Director An Hongu, who consented. Even after the engagement was settled, Hongu still lamented, "Although I am of a poor scholarly family, how can I have as a son-in-law the son of a locally recommended candidate?" Not long afterward, Hongu died. As the family daily grew poorer, it permitted the marriage. Ch'ŏngi, taking Kasin's hand, went to Hongu's house. An old woman met them at the gate. With lighted kindling, they could see that it was just a small thatched house. Ch'ŏngi returned and said, crying, "Oh, how has the student Chŏng come to be like this!" HK/ES

Hsü Ching: The Life of the People
[From *Kao-li t'u-ching* 19:99]

Although the Koryŏ territory is not expansive, there are many people living there. Among the four classes of people, Confucian scholars are considered the highest. In that country it is considered shameful not to be able to read. There are many mountains and forests, but because there is not much flat land, their skill at farming has not developed as much as their craftsmanship. As the products of the countryside are all committed to the state, merchants do not travel widely. Only in the daytime do they go to city markets and exchange what they have for what they do not have. Although the people are prosperous, the favors they extend, however, are few. As they are lascivious, they love freely and value wealth. Men and women take marriage lightly and divorce easily. They do not follow proper ritual, which is deplorable. HK/ES

Peasants and Slaves

Koryŏ accepted the Confucian social differentiation into four classes: scholars, farmers, artisans, and merchants. At a still lower level were slaves and other menials. For them, upward mobility was difficult, if not impossible. They were the exploited underdogs of society whose labor helped pay for the extravagances of the elites.

Farmers, ranking second on the social ladder, produced the crops and paid the taxes in the kingdom, but impoverished peasants, as "The Burden of Corvée Labor" tells, were especially hard pressed. In fact, desperate social conditions like these ultimately contributed to the military coup of 1170 and to the accompanying social unrest.

Koryŏ enacted strict codes to limit the upward mobility of slaves. The rationale for this policy, undoubtedly influenced by Silla norms, is presented in the second selection. Although this memorial was written in 1300 in protest against the Mongol attempt to reform the slavery system in the Koryŏ kingdom, it describes events common to the entire dynastic period.

On occasion, slaves caused problems. In "Social Mobility of Slaves," the final passage presented here, the slave P'yŏngnyang, through his own hard work, became rich and bought his freedom. He then overstepped social boundaries, committed hideous crimes, and was punished. To the man of Koryŏ, the message was clear. Slaves, aside from being an indispensable source of labor, were inherently corrupt and must be suppressed. To the modern reader, this episode provides yet another insight into Koryŏ's social order.

The Burden of Corvée Labor
[From *Koryŏ sa* 18:31b]

Earlier, when building pavilions, each corvée worker brought his own food. One worker was too poor even to do that, so the other workers shared with him a spoonful of their own food. One day his wife came with food and said, "Please ask your friends to come and share it with you." The worker said, "Our family is poor. How did you prepare food? Did you have intimate relations with another man to get it, or did you steal it?" His wife replied, "My face is too ugly to be intimate with anyone, and I am too stupid to know how to steal. I simply cut my hair and sold it." Then she showed her head. The worker sobbed and could not eat. Those who heard this story were all deeply moved. HK/ES

Inheritance of Slave Status
[From *Koryŏ sa* 85:43b–44a]

In the past, our founding ancestor, setting down instructions to posterity on the question of inheritance, stated: "In general, the off-spring of the lowest class (*ch'ŏnnyu*) are of a different stock. Be sure not to allow the people of the lowest class to become emancipated. If they are permitted to become free, later they will certainly get government positions and gradually work into important offices, where they will plot rebellions against the state. If this admonition is ignored, the dynasty will be endangered."

Accordingly, the law of our country provides that only if there is no evidence of lowborn status for eight generations in one's official household registration may one receive a position in the government. As a rule, in the lowborn class, if either the father or mother is low, then the offspring is low. Even if the original owner of a lowborn person frees him, allowing him to achieve commoner status, the descendants of that freed individual must return to low status. If the owner has no heirs, the descendants of his freed lowborn belong to his clan. This is because they do not want to allow lowborns to achieve permanent commoner status.

Still there is fear that some may flee and escape their status, becoming commoners. Accordingly, even though we take preventive measures, many take advantage of the situation and become crafty. There is also fear that some, relying on power or merit, will dare to take the law into their own hands and plot rebellion against the state, but eventually they are destroyed. Although we know it is not easy to heed the founder's admonition, we still fear there is no way to check all disloyal feelings. HK/ES

Social Mobility of Slaves
[From *Koryŏ sa* 20:24b–25a]

P'yŏngnyang was exiled to a distant island. The house slave of Executive Kim Yŏnggwan,[12] he once lived in Kyŏnju. Through hard work at farming, he became rich. By sending bribes to rich and powerful people, he was manumitted from his low status, became a commoner (*yangmin*), and achieved the position of executive captain.[13] His wife was Deputy Director Wang Wŏnji's house slave. Wŏnji's house was poor, so he took his family and became dependent upon P'yŏngnyang. P'yŏngnyang treated him generously, urging him to return to the capital. Secretly with his wife's brothers, Inmu, Inbi, and others, they killed Wŏnji, his wife, and children on the road. He then felt happy that he had no master and would forever be able to be a commoner. P'yŏngnyang's son Yegyu was appointed lieutenant and was married to the daughter of Pak Yujin, superintendent of the P'algwan endowment. Inmu married the daughter of Instructor of Classics Pak Usŏk. People were highly indignant over this. Thereupon, the censorate arrested and interrogated them and banished P'yŏngnyang. It dismissed Yujin and Usŏk. Inmu, Inbi, and Yegyu all fled. HK/ES

CHAPTER TEN

Military Rule and Late Koryŏ Reform

The military coup of 1170 brought important political and social changes to Koryŏ. After rebellious officers seized power, military rule remained unstable until the rise of General Ch'oe Ch'ung-hŏn (1149–1219) in 1196. Under General Ch'oe and his immediate successor, there was a concerted effort to resolve the major social and political issues then confronting Koryŏ society. To strengthen control over the kingdom, the military leaders devised new institutional mechanisms to administer authority and recruit personnel as well as to support military force. They also continued to rely on civilian scholars to manage the government bureaucracy. Nevertheless, the start of the military period was accompanied by considerable domestic unrest as monks, peasants, and slaves rebelled, hoping to use the political instability triggered by the military revolt to redress their own grievances and to further their own interests. The power of the Ch'oe house rose as it demonstrated its mastery by quickly suppressing these uprisings.

By the middle of the thirteenth century, with the invasion of the Mongols, Koryŏ's military leaders faced a new challenge to their power. Although the military regime first met defeat by the Mongols in 1231, they continued resistance until 1259, when the Koryŏ court finally sued for peace following the fall of the Ch'oe house. Despite the peace, relations with the Mongols frequently remained adversarial as Koryŏ officials and monarchs sought to sustain Koryŏ's independent identity. As Mongol power waned, Koryŏ leaders pursued anti-Mongol policies with greater vigor, and in the last decades of the dynasty Neo-Confucian reformers came forward with sweeping reform proposals. Buddhism, which had closely associated itself with the old order, now came under attack as the reformers sought in their ideology a new framework for governance.

Establishment of Military Rule

The 1170 military coup d'état brought a distinct change to the Koryŏ kingdom as military officers vaulted into positions of power, crushing the traditional civilian leadership. Chŏng Chungbu (d. 1178), the mastermind of the coup, was a member of an old military family that had produced generals in preceding reigns. Unable to stomach any longer the insulting injustices being heaped upon military officials, he led a revolt. Joined by his subordinates, Yi Ŭibang and Yi Ko, in overthrowing the king, he attacked in particular those powerful officials and eunuchs who had belittled and discriminated against the military. In the purge that followed, Chŏng and his men did not kill all high-ranking civilians, as has often been claimed—indeed, they executed some military officials unsupportive of their cause, as well. Employing both civil and military officials who were not antagonistic toward the new leadership, Chŏng and his associates attempted to build a new order.

With the military takeover, however, political and social conditions rapidly deteriorated as generals contended among themselves for power. This situation did not begin to improve until 1196, when another general, Ch'oe Ch'unghŏn (1149–1219), successfully revolted and established a new order through which he dominated the kingdom until his death. Then his son U (also known as I; d. 1249), grandson Hang, and great-grandson Ŭi (d. 1258) in succession perpetuated the Ch'oe leadership until 1258.

But the Ch'oe house was not without its own internal power struggles, as Ch'unghŏn's brother Ch'ungsu vied for control. In the second selection, which describes this struggle, Ch'oe Ch'unghŏn is portrayed as a conservative sustainer of traditional morality. He realized that even though he possessed supreme military authority, it was unwise for his family to penetrate the highest lineages through a marriage tie with the royal family. He fought his brother Ch'ungsu over this issue, marking the first major power struggle after the establishment of his control.

Ch'oe Ch'unghŏn endeavored to build a strong and effective government. Shortly after seizing power, he presented a memorial (the third selection) delineating the fundamental faults of the previous rule and proposing ways to rectify the wrongs of the past. The memorial is a Confucian document chastising the king for allowing treacherous men to rule and for not being diligent in searching for honest officials. In it, Ch'oe also points out that abuses perpetrated by the Buddhist establishment and great families were the causes of the dynasty's woes. Through this call for reform and subsequent actions, he sought to revitalize the dynasty and its institutions with the goal of building a new, lasting order centered on Ch'oe authority.

The Ch'oe house inaugurated the privatization of government power through construction of its own political and military machines. It never denied the court's nominal authority; it simply overshadowed the court. The two principal organizations through which the Ch'oes handled government affairs were the Directorate General of Policy Formation (*Kyojŏng togam*) and the Personnel Authority (*Chŏngbang*). The Directorate General coordinated the enactment of decrees for the Ch'oe house. The Personnel Authority, described in the fourth selection, specifically concerned itself with civil personnel matters in the government under Ch'oe control. The men who held positions in the Personnel Authority formed a high-caliber group including a number of the learned scholars of the day, many of whom had passed the examination. These officials, while holding positions in the personnel administration of the Ch'oe, frequently held concurrent offices in the dynastic government structure, thereby enjoying stipends and land grants in addition to benefiting from Ch'oe largess.

A similar pattern emerged in the military sector. Ch'oe's private forces were already influential during the early years of Ch'oe rule, and this trend became all the more dramatic with the passage of time. At the core of Ch'oe's private forces was his Personal Security Force (*Tobang*), but this unit did not originate with Ch'oe. Rather, another strongman, Kyŏng Taesŭng (1154–1183), fearing for his life after seizing power, had institutionalized this special military detachment in 1181, and Ch'oe twenty years later further strengthened it. In addition to the Personal Security Force, which served as his personal bodyguard, Ch'oe and then his son U nurtured a large private army that eventually replaced the regular dynastic troops.

The Ch'oe house also perpetuated its power by building a strong financial base. From the start of his rule, Ch'oe sought to use the traditional land system as a means to pay the military and civilian personnel he used to strengthen his authority. He was also quick to abuse the traditional order for his personal gain. Throughout the period of military rule, the Ch'oe house remained the greatest land-owner in the kingdom with especially large estates in the southern provinces.

This trend continued even after the Ch'oe house was toppled by Kim Injun (d. 1268). Kim, a personal slave of the Ch'oes, tried to build a system following the pattern of his earlier masters. Although Kim's rule lasted only a few years, he too aggressively seized land wherever possible to build an economic base for his power. With the help of his sons and retainers, as shown in the final selection, he terrorized the countryside, amassing wealth and property, especially in the fertile southern regions of the kingdom.

The 1170 Military Coup
[From *Koryŏ sa* 128:2a–3b]

In Ŭijong's twenty-fourth year [1170] the king was attending a memorial service, and again he partied with his favorite civilian officials, exchanging poems and forgetting the time. The military escorts became especially hungry. When Chŏng Chungbu went out to relieve himself, Executive Captains Yi Ŭibang and Yi Ko of the Kyŏnyŏng Royal Regiment followed and talked to him in secret, saying, "Now the civilian officials are haughty, drunk, and full, but the military officials are hungry and troubled. How long can we endure this?" Chŏng Chungbu, who still resented having had his beard burned by Kim Tonjung, replied, "You are right," and thus they began to plot a coup.

Later, when the king went from Yŏnbok Pavilion to Hŭngwang Monastery, Chungbu said to Ŭibang and Ko, "Now is the time to act. If the king returns directly to the palace from the monastery, we will wait and endure; if he goes to Pohyŏn Hall, however, we cannot lose this opportunity."

On the next day, the king was going to Pohyŏn Hall, and in front of Five Gates, he called his attending officials to prepare wine. Feeling drunk, he said to the officials around him, "What a splendid spot!

Maybe it would be a good place for military training." He ordered his officers to hold boxing matches for the five armies.

Knowing that the military officers were disgruntled, the king wanted to soothe them with generous rewards. Han Noe, fearful that the officers were getting special favor, became very jealous. General Yi Soŭng, although an officer, was thin and weak in appearance. He was boxing with another man but lost and fled. Han Noe slapped him and pushed him down below the royal platform. The king and his officials applauded and laughed heartily. Im Chŏngsik and Yi Pokki cursed Yi Soŭng. Thereupon Chŏng Chungbu, Kim Kwangmi, Yang Suk, Chin Chun, and others looked at each other, blanching with rage. Chungbu rebuked Noe in a loud voice, exclaiming, "Even though Soŭng is a military officer, he is an official of third-grade rank. How can you heap so much disgrace on him?" The king took Chungbu's hand and soothed him. Yi Ko pulled out a knife and looked at Chungbu, whereupon Chungbu stopped him.

As the day was getting dark, the king and his entourage approached Pohyŏn Hall. Yi Ko and Yi Ŭibang went ahead with a false royal command to mobilize the Sungŭm troops. As soon as the king entered the gate and his high officials were about to retire, Yi Ko and others killed Im Chŏngsik and Yi Pokki at the gate with their own hands. Han Noe, relying on his close relationship to the eunuchs, hid inside the royal quarters under the king's bed. The king, greatly alarmed, sent his eunuch Wang Kwangch'wi to stop him. Chŏng Chungbu remarked, "The cause of this trouble is Han Noe, and he is still at the king's side. Please send him out to be executed." Palace attendant Pae Yunjae went before the king to report this. Noe, seizing the king's clothing, would not leave. Yi Ko threatened him with a knife, so Noe went outside, where he was immediately killed. Instruction Officer Kim Sokchae told Yi Ŭibang, "Ko dared to draw his knife in front of the king." With an angry look, Ŭibang scolded Sokchae, who did not reply.

Shortly afterward, Transmitter Yi Set'ong, Palace Attendant Yi Tangju, Censor of Miscellaneous Affairs Kim Kisin, Warden Yu Ikkyŏm, Director of Astrology Kim Chagi, Director of Astronomy Hŏ Chadan, and others, along with the accompanying civil officials, functionaries, and eunuchs, all met tragedy. Their corpses were piled as high as a mountain. Earlier, Chŏng Chungbu, Yi Ŭibang, and others had vowed, "Our group will bare our right shoulders and take off our caps; those who refuse will all be killed." Therefore the many military personnel who refused to take off their headgear were also killed. The king, in terror, wanting to soothe them, gave the various generals double-edged swords, whereupon the military officers became even more arrogant. HK/ES

The Struggle Between the Ch'oe Brothers
[From *Koryŏ sa* 129:9b–12a]

Earlier, the crown prince[1] married the daughter of Wang U, the Earl of Ch'anghwa.[2] Subsequently, Ch'oe Ch'ungsu wanted to marry his daughter to the crown prince and firmly requested this of the king. The king was not pleased. Ch'ungsu, disguising his intent, asked a court attendant, "The king has already sent away the crown prince's wife, hasn't he?" The attendant reported this to the king. The helpless king sent her away.

The princess, sobbing, could not control herself; the queen also cried. In the palace, everyone cried. Finally the princess left in disguise. Ch'ungsu at once set a date for a wedding and assembled artisans to prepare many bridal articles.

Hearing of this, Ch'unghŏn took some wine and went to Ch'ungsu's house, where they drank in leisure. When he felt intoxicated, Ch'unghŏn said, "I have heard that you want to present your daughter for marriage to the crown prince. Is it true?"

Ch'ungsu replied that it was true.

Ch'unghŏn tried to dissuade him, saying, "Now, brother, although our power can shake the country, our lineage was originally humble. If we have your daughter marry the crown prince, will we not be criticized? Moreover, between husband and wife there is mutual obligation. The crown prince has been married for several years, and now if one morning you separate them, how will they feel? As the ancients said, 'If the front carriage falls, the rear carriage should be on guard.' When Yi Ŭibang married his daughter to the crown prince, someone later killed him. Now you want to follow his precedent. Why?"

Ch'ungsu lay back with a big sigh. After a long while, he said, "Your words are correct. How dare I not follow them?"

Eventually Ch'ungsu dismissed the artisans. A little later, however, he changed his mind, saying, "When a man does something, he ought to determine it by himself!" He then reassembled the artisans, directing them as before. But his mother said to him, "When you had followed your brother's advice, I was really happy. Now why have you changed your mind?"

Ch'ungsu angrily said, "It is not what a woman should know." He pushed his mother with his hands, and she fell to the ground.

Hearing this, Ch'unghŏn said, "There is no greater crime than being unfilial. If he would disgrace his mother like this, what more would he do to me? Certainly I cannot reason with him with words. Tomorrow morning I will direct my followers to wait at Kwanghwa Gate and prevent him from marrying his daughter to the crown prince."

Someone reported this to Ch'ungsu, and Ch'ungsu said to his followers: "Even if someone wanted to stop me, who could dare to do anything to me? While my brother alone wishes to control me, he is relying on the support of his followers. Tomorrow morning I should sweep away all of his followers. So do your best."

Someone told this to Ch'unghŏn, who, in tears, addressed his followers, saying: "Ch'ungsu's wanting to marry his daughter to the crown prince is nothing but planning treason. Tomorrow morning he wants to sweep away my followers. Matters have become urgent. How shall we plan our strategy?" His followers responded, "Please consult with Pak Chinjae."

Ch'unghŏn at once summoned Pak Chinjae, Kim Yakchin, and No Sŏksung and told them. Chinjae said, "You two brothers are my maternal uncles. How can there be any difference in feelings? But the country's peace depends on this one event. To follow the younger brother is treason; to support the older brother is to follow the right course. Moreover, righteousness overrides personal relations. I, Yakchin, Sŏksung, and others should each lead our followers to aid you." Ch'unghŏn was very pleased.

At the third drum of the night, Ch'unghŏn led more than one thousand followers from Kodal Rise to Kwanghwa Gate and told the gate guard, "Ch'ungsu wants to cause a rebellion tomorrow morning. I am about to protect the dynasty. Take this message to the king."

When the guard reported this, the king was quite alarmed. He immediately commanded that the gates be opened to Ch'unghŏn and his followers. He then had them stationed on the polo field. He also took weapons from the armory and gave them to the palace guards to enable them to deal with the situation. Generals of the various central army divisions also came, eagerly leading their troops.

Upon hearing this, Ch'ungsu, in fear, addressed his followers:

"Because a younger brother was going to attack his older brother, this was called immoral. I will take my mother and go to the polo field to see my brother and beg for pardon. Each of you should leave on your own."

General O Sukpi, Chun Chonsim, Pak Chŏngbu, and others said, "We are your retainers because you have great potential to sway the world. Now if you, on the contrary, become a coward like this, it will mean the extermination of us and our clans. We ask you to fight to the end to decide the winner and loser."

Ch'ungsu agreed to this. At dawn, he led more than one thousand followers and camped at the crossroads. He pledged to his followers: "If you fight without fear of death and kill an opponent, his position will go to whoever killed him."

When Ch'ungsu's army heard that the various generals had all gone over to Ch'unghŏn, they deserted little by little, realizing that they had little aid coming. Thereupon, Ch'unghŏn went out from Kwanghwa Gate down toward the streets, while Ch'ungsu went toward the gate and up. They met and fought south of Hŭngguk Monastery. Pak Chinjae, Kim Yakchin, and No Sŏksung, each leading his followers, sent one group to Ihyŏn, one to Sahyŏn, and one to Kodal Rise. Coordinating their troop formations, they attacked the front and the rear. Armed with the great horned bows from the royal arsenal, archers fired arrows so that they fell like rain. Although Ch'ungsu's followers took the doors from nearby buildings to use as shields, they could not prevail and finally were badly routed.

Ch'ungsu said, "Today's defeat is heaven's will. If my brother occupies the area north of the Imjin River, then I will occupy the land south of the Imjin." At once, with O Sukpi, Chun Chonsim, and others, he ran quickly to Pojŏng Gate, cut down the gate guards, and went out. He crossed Changsŏ and went to Kŭmgang Monastery in P'ap'yŏng. The pursuers beheaded him and sent his head to the capital. Ch'unghŏn wept and told the pursuers, "I wanted only to capture him alive. Why did you kill him?" Then he sent men to bury him. HK/ ES

Ch'oe Ch'unghŏn: The Ten Injunctions
[From *Koryŏ sa* 129:4b–6b]

Ch'oe Ch'unghŏn and Ch'oe Ch'ungsu submitted a sealed memorial to the throne saying:

We humbly submit that the treacherous outlaw Yi Ŭimin's character was treasonous. He slighted his superiors, belittled those below him, and plotted against the throne. As a result, disaster prevailed, causing calamity for the people. Relying on Your Majesty's august power, we took to arms to exterminate him. We wish Your Majesty to reform the failures of the past and plan the future, emulating the just rules of King T'aejo (Wang Kŏn) so as to brighten and restore the nation. We solemnly present ten articles point by point.

Formerly King T'aejo united the Later Three Kingdoms and divined a location for a capital, which he established in Songak. At a propitious site, he built a great palace so his descendants could live there as rulers for myriad generations. Some time ago, the palace was burned and then rebuilt in a grand style. But because he believed in taboos, it was unoccupied for a long time. How does one know that one can rely simply on yin and yang? Your Majesty should, on an auspicious day, move into the palace and follow the eternal heavenly commands.

The number of government offices is based on a fixed number of stipends available. Lately there have been excesses in the number of positions of the Chancellery, the Security Council, and other agencies. Since the fixed number of stipends is insufficient, this has caused great difficulties. Your Majesty should take the old system as a standard, reduce the number of positions, and make appointments accordingly.

Under the system set up by the former king, all land except "public" land was granted to officials and people according to rank. Those in office, however, have become very greedy and have snatched both "public" and "private" land and held them indiscriminately without distinction. A single family's holdings of fertile land may extend across districts, causing the nation's taxes to decline and the military to wither. Your Majesty should instruct the agencies concerned to check official records and see that all illegally seized property is returned to its original owners.

Rents from "public" and "private" land all come from the people. If the people are destitute, how can sufficient rent be collected? The local officials are sometimes dishonest and corrupt; they only seek profits, thereby injuring the people. The slaves of powerful houses fight to collect land rents, making the people groan in anxiety and pain. Your Majesty should select good and able officials and appoint them to the provinces to prevent the powerful families from destroying the people's property.

The state dispatches officials to govern the two frontier districts and examine the five circuits, wishing merely to control local officials' treachery and alleviate the people's suffering. Now although the various circuit commissioners ought to investigate conditions in the provinces, they do not. Rather they demand exactions, and on the pretense of presenting them to the king, they burden public facilities with transporting them. Sometimes they even appropriate them for personal expenses. Your Majesty should forbid the various circuit officials to present tributes and make inspections their only duty.

Now few monks are mountain dwellers. Most loiter around the royal palace and even enter the royal sleeping quarters. Your Majesty, being enticed by Buddhism, has on each occasion willingly allowed them to do this. The monks already abuse Your Majesty's good graces and through their activities often tarnish Your Majesty's virtue. But Your Majesty has aided them by commanding the palace attendants to take charge of the Three Jewels—Buddha, Dharma, and Saṅgha—and to use grain as loans to collect interest from the people. The evils of this policy are not trivial. Your Majesty should expel the monks and keep them away from the palace and refuse interest on grain lent to the people.

Recently we have heard that many functionaries in the provinces are avaricious and that their behavior is shameless. The various circuit commissioners who are sent out do not question this. Sometimes even when people are honest, the commissioners do not recognize them. As they allow evil to continue and honesty to be of no benefit, how can one reprove vice and promote goodness? Your Majesty should order the two frontier district commissioners and the five circuit royal inspectors to examine the performance of local officials and then have them report their findings. Promote those who are able; reprimand those who are not.

Today court officials are neither frugal nor thrifty. They repair their homes and decorate their clothes and playthings with precious materials, thereby worshiping the exotic. Their customs have degenerated, and they soon will be in disarray. Your Majesty should admonish the bureaucracy by forbidding ostentation and luxury and promoting frugality.

In King T'aejo's day, temples were sited in accord with favorable and unfavorable features of geomancy, and this accordingly made the nation peaceful. In later times, generals, ranking officials, and unreliable monks, without examining the topographical conditions, built

Buddhist temples, calling them their prayer halls. Thus, injuring the earth's vital system, they often produced calamity. Your Majesty should make the officials in charge of yin/yang investigate and destroy immediately any additional temples besides those built by the dynasty and prevent yourself from becoming the target of ridicule for later generations.

The officials of the Chancellery and the censorate have the duty to remonstrate. If Your Majesty has any shortcomings, they should admonish regardless of the danger to themselves. Now everybody only thinks of flattering even with self-abasement and blindly agrees without discretion. Your Majesty should select the right men and have them speak out in court even to the point of subjecting Your Majesty to severe admonishment. HK/ES

Establishment of the Personnel Authority
[From *Yŏgong p'aesŏl* 1A:8b–9a]

The Ministry of Civil Personnel handled the appointment of civilian officials, while the Ministry of Military Personnel was in charge of selecting military officials. They prepared the personnel files, recording personal information like the date of entrance into the government service and degree of hardship of positions held, merits and demerits, and appraising ability. The Royal Secretariat drew up a list of who was to be promoted and demoted and reported to the king for approval. The Chancellery received royal decisions and implemented them. This was the law of the country, and it generally coincided with Chinese practices.

When Ch'oe Ch'unghŏn arbitrarily exercised power, deposing and installing kings at will, he resided in the government compounds and with his subordinates controlled the personnel files, deciding on appointment. Through his partisan royal transmitters, he presented the list of his choices to the king for approval. The king could do nothing but follow. Ch'oe Ch'unghŏn's son I, his grandson Hang, and Hang's son Ŭi, for four generations exercised power, making it an established practice. These partisan transmitters were called *chŏngsaek sŭngji* ("politically colored" transmitters). Among those, Ch'oe retainers who were third rank were called "politically colored" ministers. Those of fourth rank and below were called "politically colored" deputy directors. Below them, those who handled writing were called "politically colored" drafters of documents. The place where they met was called the Personnel Authority, which became the unofficial term for this office in the government circles.

Earlier, such famous literati as Executive Kŭm Ŭi (1153–1230), Prime Minister Kim Ch'ang (d. 1256), and Minister Pak Hwŏn (d. 1249) all advanced from these positions so that people of that time took this as honor; not one saw this as something to be ashamed of. When Lord Munjŏng, Yu Kyŏng (1211–1289), and Kim Injun (d. 1268) killed Ch'oe Ŭi and restored power to the court, they kept the Personnel Authority as it was and did not alter it. Important duties of the court have continued to be called under private labeling and held by powerful families as before. This is truly regrettable. HK/ES

Personal Security Force
[From *Koryŏ sa* 100:18a]

Military officials sometimes said: "Chancellor Chŏng Chungbu, upholding a great sense of justice, suppressed the civilians and elevated the authority of the military. Since he wiped out the indignation we had accumulated over the years, there was no one of greater merit. Now Kyŏng Taesŭng has suddenly killed four leaders—Chŏng Chungbu and three others. Who will punish him for this?"

In fear, Kyŏng Taesŭng gathered a suicide corps of some one hundred and ten people. Stationing them at his home to deal with any incident, he called them the Personal Security Force. Providing them big pillows and large blankets, he had them guard on alternating days. Sometimes he himself slept under the same blankets to show his commitment. HK/ES

Private Armies
[From *Koryŏ sa* 129:23a–b]

At this time they were about to send troops to defend against the Khitans. The bravest soldiers were all Ch'oe Ch'unghŏn's and U's retainers. Those in the government army were all thin and weak and useless.

Ch'oe Ch'unghŏn reviewed his private troops: From Chwagyŏng-ri to Ugyŏng-ri they formed several lines stretching two or three *ri*. Their lances held three or four silver vases to display to the people of the kingdom in order to recruit more soldiers. His son U's troops, stretching from Sŏni Bridge to Sungin Gate, hoisted banners and beat drums as they trained for battle. Anyone among his retainers who asked to join the government army to defend against the Khitans was at once banished to a distant island. HK/ES

The Estates of Kim Injun
[From *Koryŏ sa* 130:17a]

Kim Injun set up numerous estates and had his retainer Mun Sŏngju control those in Chŏlla and had retainer Chi Chun (d. 1268) control those in Ch'ungch'ŏng. They competed in extorting wealth by giving the peasants one peck (*tu*)[3] of rice seed for planting, for which they collected one bushel of rice at harvest. All his sons, imitating this, competed in assembling hoodlums and relied on their power to scize othcr pcoplc's property without restraint. The grievances against them were rampant. HK/ES

Civilians Under Military Rule

The Ch'oe house, while upholding its own military supremacy, took an interest in scholarship. The bounty of literature appearing during the military period revealed that there still was intellectual vitality in this age. Some of this literature is still extant today.

The first piece presented here explains the changes that had occurred during the military period as seen by Yi Chehyŏn (1287–1367), who lived nearly a century later. Yi Chehyŏn's description presents a rather bleak picture of the life of literati during the century of military control, reflecting an outlook that favored Confucian values over Buddhist practices.

Another writer whose life was typical of the literati of the time was Yi Illo (1152–1220), the author of "The Four Treasures of the Studio" (see chapter 9) and of the first literary miscellany in Korea, the *P'ahan chip* (Jottings to Break Up Idleness). Yi lived as a Buddhist monk through the early military period but returned to secular life after Ch'oe Ch'unghŏn's rise to power. Like a number of his friends, Yi passed the state examination, held official positions under Ch'oe rule, and indulged in literary pursuits. He associated closely with men of letters—O Sejae, Im Ch'un, Cho T'ong, Hwangbo Hang, Ham Sun, and Yi Tamji. They formed an exclusive group, enjoying wine and writing poetry, and calling themselves the Seven Worthies of the

Bamboo Grove, reminiscent of the earlier Chinese poets with the same name.

Two of Yi Illo's more renowned associates were O Sejae and Yi Kyubo (1168–1241). In particular, Yi Kyubo was the literary giant of the period, and more of his writings have survived than of any of his contemporaries. Active in public life, Yi Kyubo was an official for the Ch'oe house and composed many official documents. Some of his works have been preserved in the *Tongguk Yi sangguk chip* (Collected Works of Minister Yi of Korea). Two examples of Yi Kyubo's writings are translated here. One is a tribute to a close friend and teacher, O Sejae. Although O Sejae passed the state examination, a clear indication of his erudition, he never found a position in the Ch'oe government. Yi Kyubo's eulogy of O Sejae is rich in literary allusion, revealing Yi's full knowledge of the literary heritages of both China and Korea. The second piece samples a lighter subject and aptly demonstrates Yi's witty, airy style. Koreans to this day, when sharing good wine and reciting poems with friends, display wit and humor that retain the heritage of the past, and that is still an integral part of their social life. Yi describes his own experiences in a literary activity associated with wine, indicating that many segments of society— including the military dictator Ch'oe Ch'unghŏn—enjoyed this literati style of life.

Yi Chehyŏn: Education Under Military Rule
[From *Koryŏ sa* 110:22b–23a]

King Ch'ungsŏn [1308–1313] . . . asked: "It was said that in the past our country was the equal of China in literary pursuits, but now the scholars all study under Buddhist monks to become skilled in composition. Why is that?"

Yi Chehyŏn replied: "In the early period of the dynasty, King T'aejo wasted no time in building schools to foster talent. As soon as he went to the Western Capital, he ordered the talented Chŏngak to become a professor to teach the students of the six ministries. He granted silk to encourage learning and provided a government stipend to nourish them. One can see the earnestness of his commitment. From King Kwangjong's reign on, we fostered education even more, looking up to the National Academy in the capital and promoting rural schools in the countryside so that in all schools one could hear the recitation of poems and plucking of string instruments. This is why it was no exaggeration to say that literary pursuits in Korea equaled those in China.

"Unfortunately, a military revolt occurred in the last year of King Ŭijong's reign, and there was indiscriminate destruction of the good and the bad alike. Those escaping death fled deep into the mountains, where, shedding their rank and putting on Buddhist garments, they spent their remaining years. They were like the divine horse being freed of obligation or going off to a mountain to gain freedom.

"Since then, the state has gradually restored civilian rule, but those who desire to study have had no place to go. Therefore, they have all followed Buddhists to study. This is why I said that the idea of students learning from monks started from this period. Now if Your Majesty is attentive to this expansion of the schools, valuing the six arts[4] and making known the teaching of the five cardinal relations to explain the way of the former kings, who can turn his back on the true Confucian scholars and follow Buddhist monks?" HK/ES

Yi Kyubo: Eulogy on O Sejae, a Wasted Talent
[From *Tongguk Yi sangguk chip* 37:1a–2b]

O Sejae of Pogyang had the courtesy name of Tŏkchŏn. He was the grandson of O Hagin, a famous scholar of Koryŏ's middle period. For generations his family had been prominent for its Confucian scholarship. There were three brothers: Segong, Semun, and Sejae, the youngest. All were famous scholars of the day, and Sejae was the finest among them. His older brothers both felt that they could not equal him. Academician Yi Chisim allowed O Sejae to marry his daughter. Occasionally O Sejae was proud, peevish, and arrogant, but Lord Yi Chisim valued his talent and did not speak ill of him.

O Sejae poured his energy into studying the Six Classics and could recite from memory the *Book of Changes*. Of the remaining classics, although he never consciously tried to memorize them, he could still recite from memory by guessing his way through nearly half of them. Generally he was so familiar with the text that his words flowed out of his mouth effortlessly. Once, having copied the Six Classics, he said to someone: "To keep something in your mind, writing once is better than reading one hundred times." In writing, he emulated the styles of Han Yü [768–824] in prose and Tu Fu [712–770] in verse.[5] His writings were so famous that even the shepherds and errand boys knew his name.

When he was young, he was carefree and unconventionally unrestrained. In his later years, after he passed the state examination, he began to be more restrained and diligent, becoming a well-mannered gentleman. But he still was not accepted by society and remained blocked and unfulfilled. Once he wrote to Lord Cho and Lord Yu. His words were touching and sad, his intonation smooth and harmonious, truly bearing the style of an ancient. On reading what O Sejae had written, one could not hide his tears; nevertheless, O still could not get a recommendation. Such was the unsparing nature of the age.

Mr. O Sejae, realizing that he would never be hired, decided to go far away. The Eastern Capital (Kyŏngju) was the birthplace of his maternal grandfather, and he wanted to go there to retire. As the road to Kyŏngju was far and difficult to go by foot, he finally sought and obtained a position as a reader of sacrificial prayers for the commissioner of sacrificial offerings. As such, he rode on government station horses to Kyŏngju, where he remained, never returning to the capital. But in Kyŏngju, as well, there was no one able to help him, so in the end he died impoverished. On the day before he died, a friend, in a dream, saw Mr. O flying away on a white crane. The next day he went to visit him, but Mr. O, alas, had already been transformed into an immortal!

In ancient China, Ch'ü Yüan [c. 343–278 B.C.] and Chia I [c. 201–169 B.C.], though later abandoned, had earlier received royal patronage and enough help to expand their own potential considerably. The case of Li Po [701–762] is another example. And Tu Fu, although impoverished, also became vice-chief of a bureau. Only Mr. O died without a royal appointment. If it is heaven's will, how could heaven let a talented man be so unfortunate?

Earlier, before Mr. O went to Kyŏngju, he visited me at my estate to the west of the capital. He stayed there with me for twelve days, and we shared our innermost thoughts. At that time, I was eighteen and still unmarried; Mr. O was then fifty-three. I wanted to attend him in the manner that I usually treated my father's friends, but he was not willing to let me. Permitting a friendship that disregarded the differences in our ages, he said: "Men of the past, in discussing friendship, said that what mattered to them was only the quality of the ideas shared, not necessarily age. Although I am not as talented as Hsi K'ang [223–262], you can be like Juan Chi [210–263]."[6]

From this time on, while Mr. O and I shared our leisure, exchanging cups of wine and poems, he boasted of our friendship whenever he was together with famous people in large gatherings. Some would deride him, asking how an old scholar could have a young lad as a friend and make the lad conceited. Mr. O would abruptly reply, "It is not something you could understand." This was Mr. O's way of praising me, even though I had not yet distinguished myself. Although I spent a mere three years with him and was not able to take full advantage of his eternal wisdom, I nevertheless benefited greatly. In the past, when T'ao Ch'ien [365–427] died, his disciples personally gave him the posthumous epithet Master Ching-chieh (Quiet Integrity). Since from my early age I received more than a disciple can get, I personally gave Mr. O the epithet Hyŏnjŏng (Profoundly Quiet). HK/ES

Yi Kyubo and Impromptu Poems
[From *Tongguk Yi sangguk chip* 22:17a–18a]

The phrase "Calling a rhyme and writing quickly" means to have a person call a rhyme and then to have everyone compose a rhymed prose piece immediately. In the beginning, this was done only when close friends were intoxicated and had no other way to release their euphoria. Through poetry they raised their spirits to contribute to hearty laughter. It was not considered an acceptable practice, nor was it done in the presence of an honorable person. This game was first started by Ch'ŏnggyŏng Yi Tamji.

When I was young and carefree, I thought to myself: "If he can do it, why cannot I?" This is how I came to start since I frequently composed prose verses with Ch'ŏnggyŏng. By temperament I am basically hasty, however, and this is expressed in my fast writing. I compose in this style when I am especially inebriated. So there is no concern about how good or bad it is, only how fast I compose it. It is not only extremely cursive in writing but also abbreviated, so much so that the graphs appear incomplete. Accordingly, if there is no one around to write down what I compose word by word on a separate sheet of paper as I compose, later on even I cannot recognize what I have written. The quality of this style falls far behind when compared with things written at ordinary times. Therefore, with respect to syntax and style, there is little to look at. Accordingly, I may be called a sinner among poets.

At first, I did not expect that these fatuous games needed to be made known to the world. But when court officials and their noble relatives who had learned of them arranged special occasions for drinking and urged me to perform, once in a while I would unavoidably compose in this style. This has gradually come to resemble a sideshow performed by singers and actors, surrounded by audiences, who sometimes form a wall, making it even more laughable.

When I was about to stop this practice and never take it up again, State Councillor Ch'oe Ch'unghŏn so greatly praised it that this style became widespread among later practitioners. Although it seems worth watching at first, in fact it has no use and moreover loses its poetic style. If it gradually becomes an accepted practice, later generations may find in me an excuse to continue it. As these poems were composed while drunk, I have thrown away many and no longer remember them. HK/ES

Peasant and Slave Unrest

The military coup of 1170 and the subsequent turmoil in Koryŏ society unleashed political and social tensions and incited the impoverished peasantry and slaves. Indeed, two slaves, Mangi and Manjŏk, tried to take advantage of the turmoil to win their own freedom. Mangi's uprising started shortly after the 1170 coup amid the unsettled conditions sparked by the murder of King Ŭijong and the struggle for power among the generals. Manjŏk, several decades later in 1198, sought to foment a slave rebellion, believing the Ch'oe military leaders would be unable to suppress it. Manjŏk's capture and execution, however, and the quick defeat of the plot, revealed the ability of Ch'oe Ch'unghŏn to assert his authority and maintain his control over the kingdom. Thus even in the politically uncertain military period, many Koryŏ social norms remained intact.

The Slave Leader Mangi's Protest
[From Koryŏ sa 19:32a]

Mangi and others burned Honggyŏng Monastery, killed more than ten resident monks, and then forced the head monk to take a letter to the capital. The letter, in short, said: "After having already elevated our locality to a hyŏn (county) and appointed a magistrate to win over the people of the area, you have now turned around and again dispatched troops to subjugate us. You arrested my mother and

wife. What is the meaning of this? Even if I have to meet death under the knife's blade, I will never surrender and be a prisoner. Make no mistake, I will continue our struggle until I reach the capital."
HK/ES

Manjŏk's Slave Rebellion
[From *Koryŏ sa* 129:12a–13a]

In King Sinjong's first year [1198], private slave Manjŏk and six others, while collecting firewood on a northern mountain, gathered public and private slaves and plotted, saying, "Since the 1170 coup and the 1173 countercoup, the country has witnessed many high officials rising from slave status. How could these generals and ministers be different from us in origin? If one has an opportunity, anybody can make it. Why should we still toil and suffer under the whip?"

The slaves all agreed with this. They cut several thousand pieces of yellow paper and on each put the character *chŏng* (adult man) as their symbol. They pledged: "We will start from the hallways of Hŭngguk Monastery and go to the polo grounds. Once all are assembled and start to beat drums and yell, the eunuchs in the palace will certainly respond. The public slaves will take control of the palace by force, and we will stage an uprising inside the capital, first killing Ch'oe Ch'ung-hŏn and others. If each slave will kill his master and burn the slave registers, there will be no people of humble status in the country, and we can all become nobles, generals, and ministers."

On the date set to meet, their numbers did not exceed several hundred, so they feared they would not succeed and changed their plans, promising to meet at Poje Temple this time. All were ordered: "If the affair is not kept secret, then we will not succeed. Be careful not to reveal it." Sunjŏng, the slave of Doctor of Legal Studies Han Ch'ungyu, reported this incident to his master. Ch'ungyu told Ch'oe Ch'unghŏn, who seized Manjŏk and more than one hundred others and threw them into the river. Ch'ungyu was promoted to warder in the Royal Archives, and Sunjŏng was granted eighty *yang*[7] of white gold and manumitted to commoner status. Since the remaining gang could not all be executed, the king decreed that the matter be dropped. HK/ES

Relations with the Mongols

Koryŏ first encountered Mongol troops in the middle of Ch'oe Ch'unghŏn's rule. Wary from the beginning, Koryŏ soon learned of the terrifying power of this new enemy. After almost forty years of resistance, and with the kingdom in ruins, Koryŏ negotiated peace. The Mongols, taking the Chinese dynastic name of Yüan, dominated both Korea and China for nearly one hundred years and forced Koryŏ into a subordinate position.

Koryŏ experienced a gradual Mongolization of its aristocratic culture. The royal house, although still descendants of Wang Kŏn, was forced to intermarry with the Yüan imperial household, and Koryŏ princes spent much of their youth in the Yüan capital. The Eastern Expedition Field Headquarters (*Chŏngdong haengsŏng*), which the Mongols established in 1280 to subjugate Japan, became their major instrument to dominate Koryŏ.

When the Mongols first attacked Koryŏ in 1231, the Ch'oe leadership quickly met the challenge and stymied Mongol advances. Soon, however, Mongol attacks became much more threatening, throwing Koryŏ's leadership into crisis. The question was whether to surrender or to resist by fleeing to offshore islands. Yu Sŭngdan (1168–1232), realizing that it was the peasantry who paid the price of resistance, advised a negotiated peace. The Ch'oe leadership, in the hands of Ch'oe I (d. 1249), rejected this appeal and called for the evacuation of the Koryŏ capital, Kaesŏng, to Kanghwa Island.

Resistance to the Mongol invasion was energetic. Peasants across the country retreated to forts and fought. One of the greatest battles took place at Kuju in northern Korea, where a beleaguered town withstood months of Mongol attempts to destroy it. Under the leadership of Pak Sŏ, every Mongol siege tactic was effectively checked. Indeed, the people of Koryŏ resisted the Mongol war machine for as long and as effectively as any power in the world could. Slaves also helped in the struggle, as seen in the passage "Slave Armies and Mixed Special Patrol Troops." This selection is also of interest because of what it reveals about the tensions within Koryŏ towns and about the way malcontents used the Mongol attacks to redress domestic grievances.

The Mongol invasions finally ended with the Koryŏ court's capitulation. The dispute over the question of surrender ultimately brought about the fall of the Ch'oe house in 1258, leading to a restoration of the court's political authority. Mindful of the destruction inflicted by the Mongols, the civil leaders sued for peace in 1259, but they could not return to the capital until 1270, because of disaffected military leaders who resisted this move. The diehard Sam Pyŏlch'o troops carried their resistance from Kanghwa Island south to the islands of Chin and Cheju. The Sam Pyŏlch'o were destroyed in 1273, but their legacy of resistance to the Mongols has conferred on them a mantle of honor in the minds of Koreans.

Under Mongol domination, Koryŏ leaders were forced to spend years at the Yüan court and to explain every Koryŏ move. They endured Mongol rule but were anxious to avoid entangling their dynasty with Yüan ploys. The Mongols' grand design was the conquest of Japan, and they expected Korea to pay the bulk of the costs, both in manpower and provisions. Yi Changyong (1201–1272), the Koryŏ envoy to the Yüan court, repeatedly tried to blunt Mongol demands, placing Koryŏ interests above all other concerns, as seen in the fifth selection.

By the middle of the fourteenth century, Mongol power was eroding, and in 1368 the Ming dynasty rose in China. Korea responded to these events by increasing resistance to Mongol demands. Yi Chehyŏn (1287–1367), one of the period's major writers, used many means to circumvent Mongol policy, while King Kongmin (1351–1374) led the attack to eliminate Yüan interference.

Evacuation of the Capital
[From *Koryŏ sa* 102:6b–7a]

The Mongols invaded in great force, reaching the environs of the capital. Ch'oe I [d. 1249] met with the state councillors to discuss moving the capital to Kanghwa Island. Having had a long period of peace, the population of the capital had reached one hundred thousand households by this time, and dazzling houses of the rich lined the streets. Because the people felt attached to the land, they took the move hard. Fearing Ch'oe I, however, not one person dared to speak out except Yu Sŭngdan, who said: "It is right for a small nation to serve a great country. If we serve them with propriety and interact with trust, then why would they bother us? If we abandon the capital and the dynastic shrines and hide in the offshore island, even though we may forestall capture for months and years, it will cause people on our frontier and draftees at the front to be killed in war, and the old and weak will become enslaved as prisoners. This is not a great plan for the country." Ch'oe I did not listen. HK/ES

Resistance to the Mongol Invasion
[From *Koryŏ sa* 103:23a–26a]

Pak Sŏ was from Chukchu, and in 1231 he became military commissioner of the Northwestern Frontier District. The Mongol commander Sartaq swept over Ch'ŏlchu and reached Kuju. Pak Sŏ, as well as the general of Sakchu subcircuit, Kim Chungon, the general of Chŏngju subcircuit, Kim Kyŏngson, and the magistrates of Chŏngju, Sakchu, Wiju, and T'aeju, all leading troops, met at Kuju. Pak Sŏ had General Kim Chungon's troops defend the town on the east and west; Kyŏngson's army defended the south; the special patrol troops of the regional military command and the special patrol troops of Wiju and T'aeju, numbering more than two hundred and fifty men, defended three sides.

The Mongols encircled the town in several layers and attacked the west, south, and north gates day and night. The troops in the city went out at once and attacked them. The Mongol troops captured Wiju Deputy Commissioner Pak Munch'ang and ordered him to enter the town to persuade the defenders to surrender. Pak Sŏ beheaded him. The Mongols selected three hundred crack cavalrymen and attacked the north gate. Sŏ counterattacked and checked them.

The Mongols constructed wheeled observation towers as well as a great platform wrapped with cowhide in which they hid soldiers, using it to approach the base of the town walls to excavate a tunnel. Sŏ bored through the city walls and poured molten iron to burn the wheeled observation towers. The ground also collapsed, crushing more than thirty Mongols to death. Sŏ then burned rotten thatch to ignite the wooden platform, alarming the Mongols and causing them to scatter.

The Mongols suddenly attacked the south of the town with fifteen large catapults. Sŏ constructed platforms on the town walls, and, mounting catapults on them, he hurled stones and drove the attackers off. The Mongols also piled up faggots soaked with human fat and used them to attack the town with fire. When Sŏ tried to put them out by pouring water on them, the fire burned even more fiercely. Sŏ then had his men throw mud mixed with water to stop the fire. The

Mongols also ignited a cart loaded with grass to attack the gate tower. As Sŏ had prepared water reserves in the tower and poured these from the top of the tower onto the flames, the fire subsequently went out.

The Mongols encircled the town for thirty days and attacked it in every conceivable way. Sŏ, quickly responding to the changing situation, steadfastly defended the town. Unable to win, the Mongols retreated, and then, deploying troops regrouped from assaults on various northern frontier district towns, they attacked Kuju again. Lining up thirty catapults for the attack, they destroyed a fifty *kan* long corridor in the town wall.[8] As quickly as the walls were smashed, Pak Sŏ chained iron links across the holes and repaired them. The Mongols did not dare attack again.

Then when Sŏ went out fighting and won a great victory, the Mongols attacked Kuju again with a great catapult. But as Pak Sŏ too set catapults flinging rocks and killing the enemy in endless numbers, the Mongol troops retreated and camped in a wooded palisade in order to protect themselves.

Sartaq sent our interpreter Chi Ŭisim and Academic Clerk Kang Uch'ang with a dispatch from the Lord of Hŭian, Chŏng, to Kuju to persuade the defenders to surrender. Pak Sŏ did not listen. Although Sartaq again sent a man to persuade him, Sŏ stood firm and did not surrender. When the Mongols constructed scaling ladders and attacked the city, Sŏ counterattacked with a *taeup'o,* destroying everything and preventing the ladders from coming near. The *taeup'o* was a big weapon with large blades.

The next year, the king sent the administrator of the Military Commission of the Rear Army and Junior Policy Critic Ch'oe Imsu, as well as Investigating Censor Min Hŭi. They led the Mongols to a point outside the Kuju wall to order the town's surrender, saying: "We have already sent Chŏng, the Lord of Hŭian, to discuss peace with the Mongol troops, and our three armies have already surrendered. You may cease fighting and come out to surrender." They tried to persuade them four times, but Pak Sŏ would not surrender. Min Hŭi was exasperated at the firm refusal and wanted to draw his sword and stab himself. Ch'oe Imsu again ordered Sŏ to surrender, stressing that he was seriously violating the king's orders. Only then did he surrender.

Later the Mongol envoys wanted to kill Pak Sŏ because he had vigorously defended Kuju without surrendering. Ch'oe I told Sŏ, "There is no one who can compare with your loyalty to the country.

However, the words of the Mongol envoys are to be feared. You should consider this." Sŏ then retired to his hometown, Chukchu.

When the Mongols encircled Kuju, there was a Mongol general whose age was about seventy, and he went below the city wall and looked around at the fortress's ramparts and military weapons and sighed, saying: "Since my youth I have followed the army, and I am accustomed to seeing the cities of the world fought over and defended, but I have never seen anyone being attacked like this and to the end not surrendering. Certainly those military leaders in the city will later become distinguished generals and ministers of the state." Later Pak Sŏ in fact became executive of the Chancellery. HK/ES

Slave Armies and Mixed Special Patrol Troops
[From *Koryŏ sa* 103:37b–39a]

Earlier the deputy commissioner of Ch'ungju, U Chongju, frequently had disagreements with Superintendent Yu Hongik over records and documents, and their relations became strained. On hearing that the Mongol troops were about to invade, they discussed defending the fortress and again had differences. U Chongju, leading the *yangban* Special Patrol Troops, and Yu Hongik, leading the slave army and Mixed Special Patrol Troops, resented each other. When the Mongol troops arrived, Chongju and Hongik, along with the *yangban,* abandoned the town. The slave army and the Mixed Special Patrol Troops combined their strength and repulsed the Mongols.

When the Mongols retreated, Chongju and the others then returned to Ch'ungju and examined both government and private silver holdings. When the slave army claimed that the Mongol troops had looted them, local headman Kwangnip and others secretly plotted to kill the leader of the slave army. Those in the slave army knew this and said: "When the Mongols arrived, they all fled and did not resist. How can they now blame us and wish to kill us for what the Mongols stole? Why shouldn't we make a plan before they do?"

Gathering under the pretense of a burial, they blew a conch shell and assembled their members. First they went to the *yangban* ringleader's house and burned it. Then they searched out and killed all the powerful figures against whom they had grudges, sparing no one. Furthermore, they issued a command to all within the area saying, "Anyone who dares to hide these people will have his house destroyed." Thereupon those who hid others, even women and small children, were all punished. HK/ES

Rebellion of the Special Patrol Troops
[From *Koryŏ sa* 130:37b–40a]

Pae Chungson [d. 1273] advanced through many positions during King Wŏnjong's reign, reaching the rank of general. In 1270, when the court returned to the capital from Kanghwa Island, an official notice was posted to urge everyone to return by certain dates. When the Special Patrol Troops (*Sam pyŏlch'o*), in defiance, refused to comply, the king sent General Kim Chijŏ to Kanghwa to disband the troops and to seize the register of their names before returning. The Special Patrol Troops, fearful lest their names be made known to the Mongols, became increasingly rebellious.

Pae Chungson, with Training Officer of the Special Night Patrol Troops No Yŏnghŭi and others, revolted and appealed to the nation: "The Mongol soldiers are arriving in hordes and massacring the people. All those desiring to help the nation, meet at the polo field." In a short while, the people gathered in great numbers. Others, however, fled in all directions. Many drowned while fighting for boats to cross the river. The Special Patrol Troops blockaded the island and patrolled the river, calling out in loud voices, "All *yangban* who do not leave the boats should know they will all be killed." Everyone who heard this was afraid and disembarked.

As others desiring to go to the capital boarded boats, the rebels boarded skiffs and pursued, shooting at them. No one dared move. In the city, as people were terrified and scattered to hide in the forests and marshes, the wailing of women and children filled the streets. The rebels distributed weapons from the Kŭmgang warehouse to the soldiers and closed the city for defense. Pae Chungson and No Yŏnghŭi led the Special Patrol Troops to meet at the marketplace, where they compelled the Marquis of Sŭnghwa, On [d. 1271], to become king. They set up government offices with Grand General Yu Chonhyŏk and Senior Assistant Executive of the Department of Ministries Yi Sinson becoming senior and junior transmitters respectively.

Earlier, when the rebels had planned their revolt, General Yi Paekki [d. 1270] had refused to join. Thereupon they beheaded Paekki in the street along with the Uighurs whom the Mongols had sent. General

Hyŏn Munhyŏk's wife and Proctor Chŏng Mungam [d. 1270] and his wife all died. Assistant Executive in Political Affairs Ch'ae Chŏng [d. 1271], Deputy Commissioner of the Security Council Kim Yŏn and Recording Official of the Privy Council Kang Chiso escaped the rebellion, fleeing to Kyop'o. The rebels pursued but did not capture them. Many of the guards on Kanghwa Island fled to the mainland. The rebels, estimating that they were unable to defend the island, assembled ships and loaded them with valuables belonging to government offices and private individuals as well as with women and children and went south. Their ships, numbering more than one thousand, extended in an unbroken line from Kup'o to the Hangp'a River.

At that time, all the officials had gone out to welcome the king, but since their wives and children had all been seized by the rebels, the sound of their bitter weeping rent heaven and earth.

Former Drafting Adviser of the Royal Secretariat Yi Sukchin and Junior Colonel Yun Kilpo had gathered the slaves and attacked from behind the remaining rebels at Kup'o. After they beheaded five men, they arrived at Mount Purak, and there, facing the sea, they paraded the troops. Seeing this, the rebels fled in fear, thinking that the Mongol forces had arrived. Yi Sukchin, together with Office Chief Chŏn Munyun, sealed the official warehouse and had men guard it. The hoodlums could not steal any more.

The rebels occupied Chin Island and pillaged the local districts in the nearby areas. The king ordered Kim Panggyŏng [1212–1300] to go to pacify them. The next year Kim Panggyŏng, with the Mongol commander Hindu,[9] led three armies to attack and defeat the rebels, who abandoned the women and children and fled. The rebel leader Kim T'ongjŏng [d. 1272] led the remaining rebels to Cheju Island, where they hid.

Earlier, the retired Custodial Grand Master of Works Yi Po [d. 1272], Superintendent of the Bureau of Astronomical Observation An Pangyŏl [d. 1272], and Supreme General Chi Kyebang [d. 1272], as well as Grand General Kang Wibo, General Kim Chisuk, retired Grand General Song Suk, and Deputy Director Im Koeng, had all been captured by the rebels. When the rebels were defeated, they killed Yi Po and Chi Kyebang; but Kang Wibo, Kim Chisuk, Song Suk, and Im Koeng were able to escape and return to the court. Yi Sinson followed the rebels, wishing to go to Cheju, but on the way he turned back.

When the capital was returned to the mainland, An Pangyŏl sought an omen at King T'aejo's portrait in Pongŭn Temple and received a prophesy: "Half alive, half dead." He took this to mean the "dead" are the ones who will go to the mainland and the "alive" are the ones who will follow the Special Patrol Troops out to sea. So, he accompanied the rebels south and explained to them the prophecy: "The descendants of the dragon (Wang Kŏn) are exhausted after twelve generations. [King Wŏnjong was Wang Kŏn's twelfth-generation descendant.] The prophecy to go to the south and construct an imperial capital is presently being fulfilled." Consequently he became the rebels' chief plotter. When the rebels were defeated, he got away and was going to meet with Kim Panggyŏng, but the troops attacked and killed him.

Yu Chonhyŏk, based at Namhae-hyŏn, raided the coastal area. Hearing that the rebels had fled to Cheju, he took more than eighty vessels and followed them. Once having entered Cheju Island, the rebels constructed a double-walled fort, and roaming around, pillaging the local districts, and killing magistrates at that time, they upset the coastal area. The king sent the rebel leader Kim T'ongjŏng's nephew Kim Ch'an, O Injŏl, and others, six men altogether, to persuade them to surrender. Kim T'ongjŏng, however, detained Ch'an, his nephew, and killed the others.

In 1273 the king ordered Kim Panggyŏng to subdue the rebels. As Panggyŏng, with Hindu and others, attacked them, the rebels scattered, while Kim T'ongjŏng, leading more than seventy men, escaped into the mountains, where he hanged himself. Cheju thereupon was pacified. HK/ES

Yi Changyong's Defense of Koryŏ

[From *Koryŏ sa* 102:23b–27b]

In 1264 King Wŏnjong [1250–1274] was summoned to the Mongol court. The king had the state councillors deliberate this. Fearful of Mongol intentions, no one could make up his mind. Yi Changyong [1201–1272] alone said, "If the king heeds the summons, there will be peace; if not, this will produce new hostilities.". . . The deliberations then reached a decision and Yi Changyong was at last to accompany the king to the Mongol court.

At that time Wang Chun [1223–1283], the Lord of Yŏngnyŏng, was in Mongolia, and said: "Koryŏ has thirty-eight regiments, and with each regiment having one thousand men, the combined force should be thirty-eight thousand men. If you dispatch me, I certainly can bring them to the court for its use." The Mongol Prime Minister Shih summoned Yi Changyong to the Department of the Imperial Secretariat to inquire about this. Yi Changyong said: "The system under our dynastic founder was like that. But recently because of deaths caused by the ravages of war, what was supposedly one thousand men to a regiment is in fact not the case. As in your country's myriarch units, the numbers are not always exact. I request that Wang Chun and I return home and count the actual numbers. If what Chun says is correct, you may kill me. If what I say is correct, you kill Chun." Chun, who was standing beside him, did not dare to speak again.

Yi Changyong was also asked about the population of Koryǒ's local administrative districts. When he said he did not know, the Mongols said, "You are a state minister. How is it you do not know?" Changyong, pointing to a lattice window, said, "Prime Minister, how many openings are there in the window?" When the prime minister said he did not know, Changyong said, "The number of households in my country's local districts is the concern of a government office. Even though I am a state councillor, how can I know everything?" The prime minister was silent. . . .

The Mongol emperor sent an envoy to Koryǒ to conscript troops and ordered Yi Changyong to come to provide the number of conscripts available. When Changyong had an audience with the emperor, the emperor said: "I have ordered your country to dispatch soldiers to help wage war, but I have not heard clearly the number of soldiers in your country. This has been reported to me only in vague terms. When Wang Chun met with me, he reported, 'My country has forty thousand troops and a mixed force of ten thousand men.' Therefore, yesterday I commanded you, 'As your king cannot survive without an army, he may retain ten thousand soldiers to protect his country, but send forty thousand troops to help us fight.' You said, however, 'My country does not have fifty thousand soldiers. Wang Chun's words are not true. If Your Majesty does not believe me, check this out by sending an official, together with Wang Chun to count the actual number of soldiers we have. If in fact there are forty thousand soldiers, please punish me; but if not, please punish the one who made the false report.' If you had come and clearly reported the numbers of soldiers, why would I have to speak to you like this?" Finally he called Wang Chun and said, "You clarify this matter with Changyong."

Again the emperor instructed Changyong, saying: "You still must return to your country and quickly report the size of your army. If you do not, then I will send an expedition to your country. You may not know to which country I am going to send troops to attack. I intend to subdue only Sung and Japan. Now I see your country as part of our family. If your country has difficulties, how could I dare not to want to help? When I subjugate countries that are not paying allegiance to me, it is your country's duty to send troops to help me subdue them. It is your duty. Return and tell your king to build one thousand warships, [each of which] can carry three or four thousand *sŏk* of rice for provisions." Changyong replied: "How do I dare not to receive Your Majesty's command. However, if Your Majesty presses this on us, even if we have timbers to build boats, I fear there will not be enough time."

The emperor said: "It is not necessary for me to repeat the things that have happened since the time of the ancient three kings and five emperors in China, which you know well. I want to select an example closer to hand. Earlier at the time of the Emperor Genghis Khan, the king of Ho-hsi (west of the Yellow River), seeking peace, offered his daughter in marriage and said, 'If the emperor subjugates the Jürchens, I will become his right hand. If he subjugates the Moslems, I will become his left hand.' Afterward, when Genghis Khan was going to subjugate the Moslems, he demanded help in the subjugation. Ho-hsi to the end did not respond. The emperor attacked and destroyed them. You must also have heard this." Changyong replied: "Formerly my country had a force of forty thousand men. In the last thirty years, nearly all have died from war and pestilence. Although there are still units of hectorch and kilorch, these exist in name only." The emperor said: "You speak only of the dead. Hasn't anyone been born? Your country also has women. Why haven't there been any births? As you are old, you are fully versed in affairs. How can you explain these falsehoods?" Changyong replied: "In our country, owing to Your Majesty's gracious favor, there have been babies born and grown up since the withdrawal of the Mongol troops, but they are all young and weak and unfit to serve in the army." HK/ES

Yi Chehyŏn: Opposition to Yüan Policies
[From *Koryŏ sa* 110:23b–25b]

According to the *Doctrine of the Mean*, for all the states of the world, "there are nine standard rules, but the means by which they are carried into practice is singleness."[10] About dealing with vassals, it says, "to restore families whose line of succession has been broken, and to revive states that have been extinguished, to reduce to order, states that are in confusion, support those which are in peril; . . . to send them away after liberal treatment, and welcome their coming with small contributions."[11] A commentary said: "Make those without descendants continue their lineages, enfeoff states that have already perished, have the superior and inferior mutually at peace, have the great and small mutually support each other, then everybody will exhaust their loyalty and feudal domains will strive to protect the court." Formerly Duke Huan of Ch'i [d. 643 B.C.] had the marquis of Hsing move to Hsing, making it appear as if he were returning to his own land; the duke also reenfeoffed the state of Wei, making them forget their earlier demise. By bringing the feudal lords together to reestablish order in this way, the duke became the leader among the five hegemonic feudal rulers. When even a hegemonic feudal leader knows how to work at doing this, how much more would the emperor of a great state that rules the whole world know and follow such a principle?

I humbly submit that my country, from its founding by the Wang clan, has lasted more than four hundred years. We have submitted to Yüan, sending tribute every year. Since this has continued for more than one hundred years, our people have benefited profoundly, just as our contributions to Yüan have been plentiful.

In 1218 the surviving bastard Liao prince Chin-shan attacked, plundering the Chinese people and entering the islands in the east. As he continued to act recklessly, Genghis Khan sent marshals Qaji and Jalatai to suppress his plundering, but they encountered heavy snow, which made it difficult to get provisions through. Our King Kojong, however, ordered Cho Ch'ung [1170–1220] and Kim Ch'wiryŏ [d. 1234] to supply provisions and assist with weapons. They captured and killed the bandits with the speed of wedging up bamboo. Thereupon the two marshals and Cho Ch'ung vowed to be brothers and to remember this occasion forever.

When Emperor Shih-tsu [Kublai Khan, 1260–1294] returned from his conquest of South China, our King Wŏnjong, realizing that the Mongols had the Mandate of Heaven and popular support, traveled more than five thousand *ri* to have an audience with the emperor in the distant land of Liangch'u. Moreover, King Ch'ungnyŏl had personally never neglected having audiences with the emperor. At the time of the Mongol conquest of Japan, he not only did everything to supply weapons but was in the vanguard of the army. And at the time of the punitive expedition against the rebellious Yüan prince Qadan [d. 1292], the king assisted the Mongol government troops, killing rebel leaders and thereby assisting the emperor immeasurably. As a result, the emperor gave his princess in marriage to the king, thus strengthening our ties through marital relations. It is also due to Emperor Shih-tsu's rescript that the Koryŏ dynastic tombs and state shrines have been preserved in accordance with ancient customs.

Now I have heard that the imperial court intends to make Korea into a Yüan province by establishing a provincial government there. If this is true, even if we disregard Koryŏ's earlier contributions, what has become of Emperor Shih-tsu's rescript? In reading the provisions of the new imperial decree issued in the eleventh month of last year, I humbly find that by distinguishing right and wrong and establishing peace throughout the world, it purports to restore the wise policies of Emperor Shih-tsu's reign. What His Majesty has said in this decree is truly a blessing for the whole world, but how is it possible that only in the affairs of Koryŏ it has not upheld Emperor Shih-tsu's rescript? The Confucian instructions for posterity in the *Doctrine of the Mean* are no empty statement. According to this book: "The successors I will govern. Those destroyed I will raise. Those in chaos I will control. Those in danger I will pacify."[12] Now for no reason, Korea, a small country that has existed for more than four hundred years, will be extinguished one morning. Its state shrines will have no spirits to enshrine; its royal tombs will no longer have sacrifices. This certainly is not reasonable.

Furthermore, Koryŏ's land does not exceed one thousand *ri*. Its mountains, forests, streams, and marshes, which compose seven-tenths of its area, are useless land. The rent on the land is not sufficient to cover the cost of transporting it. The tax from the people does not meet the cost of official salaries. In terms of Yüan's court expenditures, it is a drop in the bucket. Moreover, Koryŏ is far away and the people are simple. Its language is not the same as China's, and its problems are very different from China's. I fear that if people hear about this decree, it will certainly cause apprehension, and it is not possible to go to every household to explain and put them at ease. Besides, we face the Japanese across the narrow strait of Korea, and when they hear what has been done to us, would they not take this to be a warning and use it to their advantage?

I humbly wish your excellency, keeping in mind how Emperor Shih-tsu remembered our merit and what the instructions in the *Doctrine of the Mean* said, will allow the state to be as a state should be and allow the people to be as they should be. By fostering their government and tax system, you will make Koryŏ your defender. This will sustain boundless happiness for us, and accordingly not only will the people of Koryŏ congratulate each other and praise your virtue, but the spirits of the dynastic ancestral tombs and the state shrines will cry in gratitude, though invisibly. HK/ES

King Kongmin's Appeal to Yüan
[From *Koryŏ sa* 39:12a–15a]

On the twelfth day of the tenth month of King Kongmin's fifth year [1356], the king sent Assistant Executive of Letters Yi Inbok [1308–1374] to Yüan to present a letter to the Yüan emperor. The letter said: "Recently the traitor Ki Ch'ŏl [d. 1356] and others, wishing to endanger the dynasty, have plotted to move armed forces. By relying solely on Your Imperial Majesty's virtue, we were able to prevent a calamity. But just as one seeing a house accidentally set afire finds himself too busy extinguishing the fire to report it right away, we, like a son who has escaped death after playing with weapons, have had difficulty in reporting it. Being ashamed of myself, I do not know what to do. Prostrate before you, I have received special favors. Even if I do my utmost, how could I sufficiently repay your kindness? As I already owe you unending favors, I dare state the nation's afflictions, hoping they will reach Your Majesty's ear.

"I keenly recall that when Emperor Shih-tsu set out to conquer Japan, he appointed our King Ch'ungnyŏl [1274–1308] as chief minister of the Eastern Expedition Field Headquarters and had the king recommend to his court officials for appointments in the headquarters. As the headquarters did not collect household taxes, it cannot be compared to other provincial governments. Subsequently Yüan established in succession the General Office of Pacification, the Office of Investigation, the Office of Confucian Studies, and the Office of

Medicine. Lately the officials of the Field Headquarters, conspiring with ladies and eunuchs of the court, obtain court orders at will and take power into their own hands.

"In my country there is a censorate and a Ministry of Punishments to hear litigation, administer punishments, and uphold justice. Yet officials of the headquarters, listening to people's reckless litigation, reexamine court legal documents already adjudicated by the offices concerned, turning right into wrong. Since no one can do anything about this, men resent them like wolves and tigers. Moreover, now there are officials in the headquarters who plot with traitors. I request that from now on I be authorized to recommend officials for appointment in all these offices so as not to repeat the previous mistakes and that entities like the Office of Investigation be abolished.

"When Emperor Shih-tsu set out to conquer Japan, he established myriarchs of the central, right, and left armies. Later he expanded the Patrol Army and placed myriarchs at Happ'o (Masan), Chŏlla, T'amna (Cheju), and Sŏgyŏng (the Western Capital, P'yŏngyang). These myriarchs have no troops under them, but carrying matching gold tallies for receiving orders, they boastfully proclaim imperial orders to entice ordinary people to enter falsely into these units. Moreover, they prevent the local districts from mobilizing them for other duties. This is indeed inadvisable. If we may be allowed to rely on the old system of Emperor Shih-tsu, we would beg you to abolish the additional five myriarchs and the General Office of Investigation, keeping only the original three myriarchs used in the pacification of Japan.

"The envoys from the Yüan court and officials dispatched by the various imperial offices, such as the administrations, courts, and bureaus (*fu, ssu, yüan*) as well as the directorates and offices (*chien, ssu*), are mostly people of my country. They do not endeavor to spread Your Majesty's virtuous ideas but seek rather to boast of themselves in their localities. Their own power becomes their passion as they seek always to repay obligations or take revenge, thereby insulting the state councillors and humiliating the country's ruler. They remain for years without returning to Yüan, taking more wives and concubines and committing every evil possible. Twice a year they offer special incense at various temples on Mount Kŭmgang, creating additional burdens for the people. By creating work, they go against Your Majesty's will to seek blessings for the people.

"As Korea has made defense preparations without cessation since the Japanese pirate raids, the commissioner of reinvestigation dispatched by the Yüan Security Council ought to be stopped, as should the officials sent by the Hsüan-hui, Tzu-cheng, and Chiang-tso halls, the Ta-fu and Li-yung directorates, the T'ai-p'u court,[13] and so on. Of the local products extracted by them, the ones that are appropriately needed should be clearly fixed in number and contributed by my country of its own will, so that burdens on the people of the various terminals on the routes will be lessened.

"Shuang-ch'eng (Yŏnghŭng) and San-sa (Pukch'ŏng) were originally within my country's borders. In 1258, in the former King Kojong's reign [1213–1259], Cho Hwi, T'ak Ch'ŏng, and others, fearing execution for crimes they had committed, enticed the Jürchens. Taking advantage of our inattentiveness, they killed officials and enslaved men and women. To this day, when elders discuss this incident, they cry and point at the ringleaders as their mortal enemies. Recently the traitors Ki Ch'ŏl, No Ch'aek [d. 1356], and Kwŏn Kyŏm, conniving with tribal chiefs, summoned those who had run away and incited them to rebel, promising to give assistance. Since then Ch'ŏl and others have already died, forcing many of his followers to go over to the fugitives. Therefore, we ordered an investigation. They have used troops to aid the fugitives, leaving us no choice but to dispatch troops in response. Their director-general, Cho Sosaeng, and chiliarch T'ak Togyŏng are currently in hiding, and I fear they will use this situation to cause trouble. Since the Yüan court regards all land within the borders of the empire as imperial land, why should you even argue about a small patch of barren soil? We humbly request that you return our former territory and allow us to establish border passes north of Ssangsŏng and Samsal. The Jürchens in the Nisŏng (Ch'angsŏng) area, staying in the mountains and the valleys, intrude over our borders to come and live. They bother the peasants, stealing their cows and horses, and give guidance to our fleeing criminals so that we cannot catch them. Indeed since Nisŏng is no different from Ssangsŏng and Samsal, we humbly request that you establish prohibitory regulations and prevent them from indiscriminately entering and plundering there as they did before.

"In our country from the time of the former kings on, children of royal concubines always became monks to clarify the distinction between the legitimate and illegitimate and to prevent them from longing for power. Now Ta-ssu Temür himself claims to be the son of King Ch'ungsŏn [1308–1313] by a concubine. Once he became a monk. But on growing up, he returned to secular life and fled to the

Mongol capital, enticing many reckless people in my country, fanning lies, and confusing and deluding people's minds. How can such a man bring the slightest benefit to the imperial court? I beg that you send this man and his partisans back to my country." HK/ES

Proclamation on Liao-Shen
[From *Koryŏ sa* 114:12a–13a]

This public notice, urging the Mongol royalists in Tung-ning to surrender, was posted on placards set up by the Koryŏ expeditionary forces sent to exterminate the Mongol forces there in 1370.

My country was founded in the time of Yao. King Wu of Chou [1122–255 B.C.] enfeoffed Chi Tzu (Kija) in Chosŏn and gave him land as far west as the Liao River, and for generations we protected the boundaries. After the Yüan dynasty unified China, it granted princesses in marriage to the Korean kings and set aside the land of Liao-shen (Liao-yang and Shen-yang) to cover part of their expenses and accordingly established a branch of the Eastern Expedition Field Headquarters there. Later on, when the Mongol emperors, having lost their thrones, fled far away, the leaders of Liao-Shen turned a deaf ear and refused to join them. Moreover, they did not conduct themselves properly with Koryŏ. In fact, they became sworn allies with the Koryŏ criminal Ch'i-sai-yin Temür (son of Ki Ch'ŏl) and gathered followers and oppressed the people. Their crime of disloyalty cannot be forgiven.

As we now mobilize our righteous troops to interrogate the criminal and others, they have rallied at Tung-ning, and, relying on their strength, they have defied orders. When our great army arrives there and indiscriminately destroys good and bad alike, it will be too late to repent. All people east of the Liao River, as well as major and minor chieftains within the borders of our country, should quickly come to the Koryŏ court to receive rank and stipends. If they do not appear, they should reflect upon what has happened at the Eastern Capital.[14] HK/ES

Late Koryŏ Reforms

Koryŏ leaders were divided among themselves on policy toward China in the waning days of the Yüan dynasty. Those who advocated a sharp break with Yüan eventually grew more vocal in their criticism of the Koryŏ order itself and ultimately moved to found a new dynasty, Chosŏn. Although these leaders were themselves products of the Koryŏ social order, their desire to reform society led them to the eventual overthrow of the dynasty. Ironically, King Kongmin (1351–1374), one of the first to understand his society's need for reform, was also instrumental in inaugurating the liberation from Mongol influence. As shown in the excerpt from the biography of Sin Ton (d. 1371), the king, with the help of his monk-adviser, launched a series of reforms that ultimately broke the control of the Mongol-backed elite. Although the reforms may have been necessary, they invoked harsh criticism from contemporaries and later Confucian historians, as seen in this biography written by later Chosŏn court historians (which, at least in parts, need not be taken literally).

In the next two selections, Yi Chehyŏn and Yi Saek (1328–1396), leading intellectuals of the period, present their strong arguments for urgent reforms. Both men entered the central bureaucracy through the civil service examination and distinguished themselves as able officials and scholars active not only in Koryŏ but also in Yüan. As forerunners of the Neo-Confucian reformers of late Koryŏ, they addressed themselves to the most serious economic and military issues facing the government.

Pak Ch'o (1367–1454) was a classics licentiate at the National Academy at the time of King Kongyang (1389–1392). His anti-Buddhist memorial was the most vehement of the various memorials attacking Buddhism at that time. The selection given here is considered to be the principal section of his memorial. Chŏng Tojŏn (d. 1398) wrote the twenty-chapter *Pulssi chappyŏn* (Discourses on Buddha) as a Neo-Confucian critique of various Buddhist doctrines such as the transmigration of souls, causation, human personality, and mercy. Two chapters considered to be among the book's most important—those on the transmigration of the soul and on the similarities and differences between Confucianism and Buddhism—are presented here.

The Reforms of King Kongmin and Sin Ton
[From *Koryŏ sa* 132:3a–7a]

Although King Kongmin [1351–1374] had been on the throne for a long time, he did not regard many of the state councillors as satisfactory. He thought that the aristocratic officials and great families were linked in personal cliques, mutually protecting each other. When newcomers first entered the government, they took on affectations and embellished their actions to gain fame. As they became noble and famous, ashamed that their origins were humble, they married into powerful families, entirely casting off their earlier intentions. As for Confucianists, they lacked backbone. But relating to each other as disciples, state examiners, or peers, they formed factions and engaged in favoritism. Since these three groups were all unsuitable for employment, the king had to obtain a man of independence who had abandoned the secular world and use him extensively to correct the abuses of the past.

When the king met Sin Ton [d. 1371], he saw that Sin Ton followed the Way and had few wants. Because Sin Ton was of humble origins and had no close associates, the king believed that if Sin Ton were appointed to handle important affairs of state, he would resolutely pursue them. Accordingly, the king finally decided to choose one among the monks and entrust him with state affairs.

The king asked Sin Ton to save the world by temporarily forgoing his priestly pursuits. Sin Ton pretended to be unwilling, which only strengthened the king's wishes. When the king strongly insisted, Sin Ton replied, "I once heard that the king and his ministers often give in to slander and act against each other. For the benefit of all concerned, I do not wish this to be the case." The king then wrote a pledge in his own hand stating, "May you help me and I help you by letting it be like this in life and death. I will not be misled by the words of others. May Buddha and heaven bear witness."

Thereafter they deliberated state affairs together. Within a month, however, vilifying the ministers, they dismissed Grand Chancellor Yi Kongsu [1308–1366], Chancellor Kyŏng Ch'ŏnhŭng, Superintendent of the Finance Commission Yi Susan, Executive of the Grand Chancellery Song Kyŏng, Deputy Commissioner of the Security Council Han Kongŭi, Assistant Executive in Letters Wŏn Songsu [1323–1366], Co-administrator of the Security Council Wang Chunggwi, and others. The state councillors, censors, and policy critics were all chosen by him, and the position of grand chancellor was for a long time left vacant until he himself filled it. Thereafter, he at last moved out of the palace and lived in a house owned by illustrious people. All the officials went to the house to discuss the affairs of state with him.

Sin Ton asked the king to establish the Directorate-General of the Regularization of Land and Slaves and made himself its superinten-dent. Throughout the country, placards bearing a proclamation an-nounced:

"Recently law and order have greatly deteriorated and graft has become common. The lands of the dynastic ancestral shrines, schools, granaries, temples, and salary stipends, as well as land for military appropriations and patrimonial land and people, have nearly all been taken by powerful families. Some lands that were determined to be returned to the original owners are still held up, and the people who have already been recognized to be commoners are still held as slaves. Among the clerks of the administrative districts (chu, hyŏn, and yŏk), the government slaves, and commoners who have escaped from the corvée, all have avoided detection and are hidden, greatly contributing to the establishment of great estates. All of this, harming the people and impoverishing the state, causes heaven to send down floods and droughts, as well as unending pestilence. Now we have established a directorate-general to investigate all of this. There should be no inter-rogation of those who admit their transgressions and reform them-selves within a fifteen-day limit in the capital or forty days in the countryside, but those who have passed the deadline and are found guilty will be subject to disciplinary action. Those who make false charges will also be tried."

When this proclamation came out, powerful households that had seized much land and many people returned them to their owners, causing joy throughout the country. Sin Ton appeared every other day at the directorate-general, where Yi Inim [d. 1388], Yi Ch'unbu [d. 1371], and all others made decisions as Sin Ton dictated. Out-wardly feigning concern for public justice and wishing to win over the people through displays of kindness, Sin Ton manumitted all lowborns and slaves who claimed to be commoners. Thereupon slaves rose against their masters and declared, "A sage has appeared."

When beautiful women came to make claims, Sin Ton would out-wardly show sympathy and entice them to his house, where he would seduce them. Their appeals would then certainly be redressed. Thereupon petitions from women increased, while officials ground their teeth in disgust.

Superintendent Chang Hae's house slave became a junior colonel. Upon meeting Hae, he offered a bow without dismounting from his horse. When Hae whipped him in anger, the slave made charges to Sin Ton, who then had Hae and his daughter imprisoned by the Patrol Army. Desiring to win people over with these small favors, Sin Ton assisted the wicked this way. As the officials met at Sin Ton's home, carriages and horses filled the streets, while the palace gates remained deserted. Those who understood the implications of this were chilled to their core. HK/ES

Yi Chehyŏn: Reform Proposals
[From *Koryŏ sa* 110:34a–37b]

Now Your Majesty, complying with the Yüan emperor's clear commands, has inherited the dynastic accomplishments of your ancestors at an age at which a crown prince customarily would enter school. Ascending in the wake of the former king's failures, how could you not be very careful, if only out of reverence and prudence?[15] As for the substance of reverence and prudence, there is nothing like cultivating virtue.

The important point in cultivating virtue is desiring to approach learning. Now as Master of Sacrifice Chŏn Sungmong has already been named royal tutor, select two wise Confucian scholars to lecture, together with Chŏn Sungmong, on the *Book of Filial Piety,* the *Analects, Mencius,* the *Great Learning,* and the *Doctrine of the Mean.* Learn the way of attaining knowledge through the investigation of affairs and things and rectifying the heart through a sincere mind. From among the children of officials, select ten who are honest, genuinely attentive, and fond of learning and propriety to assist Your Majesty as scholars-in-waiting. After mastering the Four Books, study in sequence the Six Classics so that arrogance, extravagance, lewdness, indolence, music, women, and venal officials will not reach your eyes and ears. When you achieve this and it becomes second nature, you will effortlessly realize virtue. This should be the most urgent priority at this time.

Since the correct relationship between ruler and subject is that they be as one, how could they not be closely bound to each other? At present the state councillors only get together when they have banquets, and without a special summons they do not have an audience. What kind of principle is this? Fittingly I request that when Your Majesty sits in your rest hall daily, discuss state affairs with the state councillors. Even if you have to divide your days to meet them, and even when there are no urgent matters, do not forgo this practice. Otherwise, I fear the great ministers will daily become distant, the eunuchs will daily get closer to you, and you will not be informed on the conditions of the people and the security of the dynasty.

The term Personnel Authority (*Chŏngbang*) is not from an ancient system but originated at the time of military rule. Accordingly, we ought to reform the Personnel Authority, returning its functions to the ministries of Civil Personnel and Military Affairs and establishing the Office of Merit Evaluation (*Kogongsa*) to record the careers of the officials and evaluate their ability. Every year in the sixth and twelfth months, upon receiving their ratings, investigate their personnel records, using them to determine personnel actions. If Your Majesty makes this a permanent policy, then you can curtail people seeking audience for special favors and close the gates to opportunists. If, on the other hand, you follow the current trends and do not restore the earlier institutions, I deeply fear that the likes of Yang Chang, Choryun, Pak Insu, and Ko Kyŏmji[16] will arise in the future, and the malicious manipulation of personnel rosters will not cease.

The Office of Falconry and the Office of the Inner Palace Carriage vex the people even more severely. Although an earlier decree was issued to abolish these offices, later, because of a move to delay its implementation, people everywhere were disappointed, reaching to the point of reprimanding a certain Ko Yongbo [d. 1362] for his coming out riding on horseback.[17] How can this not be embarrassing?

Generally if those granaries, such as Tŏngnyŏng and Pohŭng,[18] that are not part of the old granary system were radically reformed, the people forever would not disapprove Your Majesty's intention to extend relief diligently.

If you get the right people in the posts of prefect and magistrate, then the people will reap benefits. If you do not get the right men, then the people will be harmed. When a high-ranking official is demoted to a lower position, he becomes arrogant and inattentive to laws in his office. When those advanced in age get appointments, they are too feeble to perform their duties. Needless to say, one cannot say enough about those rustic rural gentry who begged for an audience and obtained a high post.[19] I request that, as in the ancient system, those officials who have yet to reach the court ranks (third to sixth grade) first be appointed as district magistrates. On reaching fourth grade, as in the regulation, they should be appointed provincial governors and have the royal inspectors evaluate their records before according them rewards and punishments. If unavoidable, give the so-called high officials, the aged, and those rural gentry who were recruited through a requested audience capital appointments but do not give them responsibilities close to the people in the provinces. If Your Majesty carries out this policy for twenty years, those who abandoned the land will all return and tax revenues will not be insufficient.

Gold, silver, and brocaded silks are not produced in our country. In the past, court officials used only plain satin, silks, and cotton for clothing, and for utensils they only used brass and earthenware. King Ch'ungsŏn once wanted to make a set of clothes, but on asking its cost, he discovered it was so expensive that he would not have it. King Ch'ungsuk once scolded the previous king, saying gold embroidered clothes and feathered hats were not the traditional ways of our ancestors. One can see that the country has been able to last more than four hundred years and preserve its dynastic state shrines only because we respected the virtue of frugality. Recently, extremely extravagant customs have brought hardship to the peasants' life and exhausted the state treasury. I request that the state councillors from now on use no brocaded silk for clothing or gold and jade for utensils. And those who ride horses in fine clothes should have no escort follow. If each task is done frugally, remonstrating those above and inspiring those below, the customs will return to their former state of decency.

Cloth that was harshly collected earlier as a tax should be returned to those who paid it. Yet I fear government officials will scheme to divert it so that the peasants will never receive its true benefits. Therefore, we should instruct the various concerned agencies to allocate it to next year's levies in order to eliminate the evils of having to borrow to pay taxes in advance. As the necessary documents have already been dispatched by the Temporary Field Headquarters, this should be enacted promptly.

Since the establishment of the three fiefs, the funds for the salaries of the officials have become insufficient. Generally speaking, if a nation's king enriches himself from funds set aside for officials to encourage honesty, how could he not be criticized by later generations? In reporting this situation to the two palaces, I humbly request that Your Majesty abolish the three fiefs and reallocate them to the Kwanghŭng granary to meet official salaries.

It has been nearly fifty years since the land in the capital province, except *choŏp* and *kubun*,[20] was all reallocated as land for official salaries. Recently, as most of the land has been seized and occupied by powerful families, the government in the meantime has often discussed radical reform. But because of frightening words deceptively used in reporting to Your Majesty, in the end this was never carried out. This is also why the ministers did not insist on the reform. If we carry out the reform, many people will rejoice, while in the end only a few dozen powerful families will not share this joy. Hence why do you hesitate and not boldly enact this?

From those who have owed taxes for a number of years in the local districts, even though the authorities use numerous ways to compel payment, no more than one-tenth of what is owed has been collected, all the while reaping only ill will. I hope that Your Majesty will completely exempt taxes owed prior to 1343. As for those destitute men and women who have been pawned and sold because of harsh taxes for the last several years, I request that Your Majesty instruct the commissioner of civil inspection and the provincial commissioner of inspection of the various circuits to issue proclamations allowing these people to come to the capital to report their status and use the government treasury to redeem them. Also order those who have purchased these people to report voluntarily. If they do not voluntarily report now, but do so late, do not pay them and forcibly return those bought or pawned to their parents, or sentence those who have been extreme in their negligence or deception. HK/ES

Yi Saek: Memorial on Current Affairs
[From *Koryŏ sa* 115:1a–4b]

Your Majesty's subject Saek [1328–1396], on mourning leave, here offers some ideas. I have heard that when the state enjoys peace, even the advice of its ministers carries little weight, while in a crisis even the words of an ordinary man are valued. Since I recklessly submit these daring thoughts despite my lowly commoner status, my crime of arrogance may not be pardoned. Since something insignificant can be transformed into what may be lofty and deep, a sage can find meaning even in the words of a lowly man. If Your Majesty would stoop to accept these trivial ideas, it may be a blessing for the dynasty and its ancestral shrines.

I have learned that the demarcation of right and wrong and the equalization of landholdings are the first tasks of governing people. Broadly speaking, the systems created and the regulations maintained by our dynastic ancestors left nothing uncovered, but after more than four hundred years have elapsed, how could there be no problems? This is especially so in the land system. Demarcation of right and wrong is unjust, as powerful families compete to amalgamate small landholdings, much like eagles nesting in pigeon coops. Even if the authorities, having considered all the conditions, determine ownership of a given tract of land on official land documents, if one claimant is powerful, the second finds himself helpless. Under the circumstances, even among the corrected land documents, how can there be no defect? The families that receive land, however, are all Your Majesty's subjects. Using surplus labor, they cultivate the lands of others. Thus one's loss is another's gain, which is like the people of Ch'u gaining a bow that another lost.

The only thing that is indispensable to the people is land. Although the peasants diligently work several *mu*[21] of land throughout the year to feed their families, it is still insufficient. When rent collectors arrive, however, if there is only one claimant to the land, it is not so bad. But sometimes there are three or four claimants, or even seven or eight. If their strength and influence are about the same, who will willingly yield? Thereupon if the rent paid is insufficient, the collectors call the unpaid portion a loan, making even more profit. How can one support parents and rear a family? The impoverishment of the peasant arises especially from this. Did not poem 192 in the *Book of Songs* say, "The rich may get through, but alas for the helpless and solitary."[22] When Your Majesty first ascended the throne, you considered the land system to be your foremost task and handed down benevolent decrees in succession, earnestly giving the matter close attention. It was glorious to see all the planning that had depth and foresight coming from Your Majesty's thought. It may be foolish, but I believe that if one wants fish, there is nothing like making a net. If you glue the stops, how can you then tune a lute? If you do not correct these laws, it will be difficult to eliminate their abuses.

I humbly implore you to use the principles established in the land and tax laws of 1313 as your basis. By referring to the corrected official documents, rectify those lands forcefully seized and survey newly reclaimed land. If you tax newly reclaimed land and reduce excessive land grants, state revenues will increase. If you adjudicate land that has been forcibly seized and pacify people who cultivate the land, then the people will obey with happiness. The happy obedience of the people and increases in tax collections are aims greatly sought by rulers. Your Majesty, why would you hesitate to pursue these goals? Some say, "It is difficult to seize a rich man's land abruptly, and after succeeding years of abuse, it is difficult to reform suddenly." This is true of an incapable ruler, but not what we would hope for from Your Majesty. The questions of how to implement the reform and how to refine it are things that advising ministers must certainly deliberate on, and a newcomer like me dares not discuss this. But whether to carry it out or not depends only on Your Majesty's will.

Recently Japanese pirates have invaded our borders, causing Your Majesty to worry day and night. The venerable and virtuous officials must have together planned a course of action aimed essentially at handling this problem. As I am in mourning (for my deceased father) and living by the seashore, however, I have on my own given a lot of thought to the problem. At present, there are only two strategies. One is to defend on land; the second is to attack on the ocean. Just as carts cannot cross rivers and boats cannot cross land, human nature is also like this. People of the north by nature can endure the cold, while people of the south by nature can endure the heat. People who live on land are not accustomed to water. Even before they set their feet on a boat, therefore, their minds become confused. When they run into wind and waves, they fall about on each other and look for a place to lie down. They cannot relax on boats, and even if they want to sit, work, advance, retreat, or fight valiantly with the enemy, it is all an ordeal for them.

I consider that if you defend on land, then enlist the people from the land, sharpen their weapons, place them at strategic locations, raise the morale of the troops, and sparingly use beacons to confuse the Japanese. This is something that the royal inspector and magistrates can adequately carry out. There is no need to use the inspecting high commissioner, who would humiliate the magistrate and drain expenses. As for the strategy of fighting on sea, our country is surrounded on three sides by water, and no fewer than one million people live on offshore islands. I believe handling boats and swimming are their special skills. These people do not farm but make their living from fishing and gathering salt. Recently, because of pirates, they have left their homes and lost their livelihood. Compared to the people living on the land, they hate the pirates ten times more. If you speedily send a detailed plan and summon those living by the water, offering them rewards, then you can get several thousand people in no time. If you use their great skills and have them fight against those whom they hate, how can they not be victorious? Moreover, if they kill the enemy and are rewarded, how can it not be more profitable than fishing and gathering salt? If you put them under the command of the police commissioner and have them always in boats at the ready, the local areas will benefit and the pirates can be defeated. These are the two main strategies to resist the invaders. If we simply guard the land and do not fight at sea, they will consider us cowards, and we will have no way to anticipate their raids. If we fight at sea but fail to guard the land, the enemy may come ashore at an unanticipated spot, causing considerable harm. Therefore, we defend the land to protect ourselves and fight at sea to overpower the enemy. If we follow this strategy, will we not accomplish both aims? HK/ES

Pak Ch'o: Anti-Buddhist Memorial
[From *Koryŏ sa* 120:34b–39a]

I, His Majesty's subject, have heard that it was after heaven and earth existed that the myriad things came into being; that it was after the myriad things existed that man and woman came into being; that it was after man and woman existed that husband and wife came into being; that it was after husband and wife existed that father and son came into being; that it was after father and son existed that king and minister came into being; that it was after king and minister existed that senior and junior came into being; and that it was after senior and junior existed that ritual and righteousness were established. This is the universal way of the world and the normal law of all times that cannot be disregarded even briefly. If it is abolished, heaven and earth will not tolerate its abandonment, the sun and moon will not shine, the ghosts and spirits will carry out executions jointly, and all the generations under heaven will concur with the joint beheading.

What kind of man is this Buddha who makes a son that should carry on the family line betray his father and sever the affection between father and son; who makes men resist the Son of Heaven and destroy the righteousness between lord and minister; who says that for men and women to live together is not the Way; who says that for men to plow and women to weave is not righteous, thus severing the way of generating life and blocking off the source of food and clothing; and who thinks that through his way he can transform all under heaven? If his way were really carried out, humanity would be finished in a hundred years. Heaven would carry on above and earth would bear below, but the only things to grow would be grasses and trees, birds and beasts, fishes and turtles, and dragons and snakes. How, finally, could the Way of the Three Bonds and the Five Relations endure?

This Buddha was originally a barbarian whose language was not like that of China, whose dress was weird, whose mouth did not speak of the kingly way of old, and whose body did not wear the sacerdotal clothing of the kings of old. He gave false revelations of three unhappy ways (to the hell of fire, of blood, and to the asipattra hell of swords) and incorrectly propounded the six ways of sentient existence, ultimately leading the foolish and ignorant to seek senilely for merit, fearing not the norms and carelessly violating the basic law. Furthermore, although life and death and longevity and brevity originate in nature, although power and fortune and punishment and virtue are linked with the ruler of men, and although poverty and wealth and nobility and baseness derive from accumulated merit, foolish deceiving monks all attribute these things to Buddha, thus stealing the authority of the ruler of men, treating arbitrarily the power of creation, dimming the eyes and ears of the people, plunging all under heaven into corruption, living in intoxication and dying in a dream without ever realizing it. Thus they build palaces and halls, which they serve; they decorate them with stone, wood, copper, and iron which they form; and they shave off the hair of commoner men and women whom they make reside there. Even though the Buddhists' palaces surpass the palaces and halls of Chieh of Hsia [trad. 2205–1766 B.C.], the beautiful palace and Deer Terrace of Chou of Shang [trad. 1766–1122 B.C.], the Chang-hua Terrace of King Ling of Ch'u [740–330 B.C.], and the A-p'ang palace of the First Emperor of Ch'in [221–209 B.C.], do they not all come from the resources of the people? How distressful! Who will correct this situation? It can only be set right after he who is above demonstrates propriety by cultivating himself with virtue and instructing those below and leads the people to know wherein the principle of heaven resides.

Generally speaking, since the late Silla our country has upheld the

Buddhist way, and stupas and shrines can be found throughout our villages. The doctrines of Buddha have spread widely, permeating our people's skins and penetrating their bones so that the doctrines can neither be dispelled by righteousness nor differentiated by discourse. When Koryŏ King T'aejo [918–943] reunited the country, he took severe measures against accumulated abuses and prohibited subsequent kings and ministers from privately establishing temples. Thereupon, Ch'oe Ŭng [898–932] urged him to abolish Buddhism, but T'aejo replied: "In late Silla, the doctrines of Buddhism penetrated the bones of the people. Everyone thinks that life and death, disaster and fortune, are all due to the Buddha. Now we have just reunited the country, and the people's minds are still unsettled. If we suddenly abolish Buddha, the people will be shocked."

Thereupon T'aejo drew up an admonition saying, "You must take a lesson from Silla, which carried out many Buddhist affairs yet perished." Thus was T'aejo's admonition to later generations profound and earnest. But kings and ministers over the ages were not able to realize the founder's testament and followed shabby precedent to build without cease so that now the abuses are even worse. How can the heart of those concerned about people's minds and public morals not ache?

The commentaries say: "If one man does not plow the fields, someone will go hungry; if one woman does not tend the silkworms, someone will go cold." These Buddhists eat without plowing and dress without tending silkworms. There is no way of knowing how many millions of them live and nourish themselves in comfort, and there is no way of knowing how many people have frozen and starved because of them. Even if they drink wind, imbibe dew, and live in bird nests out in the fields, one who is concerned about the state must drive them out. Furthermore, will there ever come a day when heaven and earth will accept these Buddhists who sit in fancy houses, eat fine food, and play idly while making obeisance to kings and parents? This is something we truly cannot live with.

How is it, then, that His Majesty, who has such qualities of intelligence, has been mesmerized by Buddhist prophecy and has been induced to travel south to visit, in all his royal dignity, Hoeam Temple, thereby singing the praises of the teachings that have no king and no father, raise up the customs of disloyalty and unfiliality, and damage our law of the Three Bonds and Five Relations. His Majesty's subject laments that His Majesty has not restored himself. On the birthday of the Queen Mother, moreover, His Majesty should have led his officials to wish her longevity, thereby displaying the flourishing virtue of His Majesty's restoration and filiality to his ministers and people. Instead, His Majesty followed the barbarian way, ignobly bowing to monks and making offerings to Buddha, thereby cutting off the hopes of the officials and people for a restoration. How can this be?

What is more, a case such as the corvée at the Yŏnbok Temple stupa and shrine, which steals people's labor and provokes people's resentment, causes cries of distress in both the capital and the countryside and diminishes the hopes of both the officials and the people. I, His Majesty's subject, cannot know, but are the timbers used in the construction being loaded by ghosts and transported by spirits, and are the materials coming down from heaven and gushing forth out of the earth? Searching for happiness in darkness will to the contrary cause distress in situations of brightness. His Majesty's subject thinks that if dust storms rise again while frost and hail strike repeatedly, monks cannot take up arms, nor can pagodas and shrines dispel starvation. Of old, Later Chou destroyed Buddhist scriptures and Buddhist statuary and rearmed its soldiers while Ch'i worshiped pagodas and shrines and neglected its administration of punishments; when they met in battle one morning, Later Chou triumphed and Ch'i perished. Thus we can know that Buddha cannot create fortune or misfortune in human affairs.

I, His Majesty's subject, respectfully think that His Majesty should follow the ways that flourished in the time of Yao and Shun and draw a lesson from the reasons why Ch'en, Ch'i, Liang, and Hsiao perished; that His Majesty should succeed to the intentions of the dynastic founder above and meet the simple hopes of us Confucianists below and return these Buddhists to their villages and use them to strengthen the military, levy corvée on their houses and increase the number of households, burn their books and cut off their roots forever, have the Military Supply Agency take charge of the lands given to them and meet military provisions, have the Directorate take charge of their slaves and divide them among the various agencies, have the Military Armament Agency receive the Buddhists' bronze statues and bronze implements and rearm the soldiers, have the Dignitary Reception Agency receive the Buddhists' dishes and implements and divide them among the various agencies. After this, if His Majesty teaches the people with ritual and righteousness and trains them with virtue, within a few years the people's minds will be settled and moral suasion will be carried out, granaries and warehouses will be full and the dynasty's finances will be sound. Then those who have turned their backs on father and ruler, damaged human ethics, and gone against the principle of heaven will eventually cast off their old pollution, display the conscience of morality, know the human ethics of father and son as well as ruler and minister, know the way of a husband being a husband and a wife being a wife. Men will plow fields and women will weave cloth, life will beget life, people will have full bellies and enjoy themselves, and government will flourish. It will be comparable to Hsia, Shang, and Chou and better than Han and T'ang. JD

Chŏng Tojŏn: Discourse on Buddhist Transmigration
[From *Sambong chip* 9:1a–3b]

It is because the creative process of the universe operates without stopping that humans and things produce and reproduce and are inexhaustible. Generally, the Great Ultimate's movement and quiet produce yin and yang, and the change and fusion of yin and yang give shape to the five elements. The true principle of the Great Ultimate and the essence of the yin and yang and the five elements mysteriously fuse and intertwine so that people and things produce and reproduce. Thus that which has already been produced is going and passes on while that which has not been produced is coming and continues, and there can be no stopping between them.

According to the Buddha, "Even though a person dies, his spirit does not perish and thus receives a new form." This gave rise to the doctrine of transmigration.

The *Book of Changes* says: "Find the beginning and return to the end and therefore know of death and life." It also says:"Essence and material force become things and unattached heavenly souls become changes."[23] Early Confucianists interpreted this to mean: "Even though the creative process of the universe produces and reproduces and is inexhaustible, where there is gathering so must there be dispersing, and where there is birth so must there be death. If you can find the beginning and know the gathering and birth, then you must know that later there will certainly be dispersal and death. If you can know that birth is obtained from the natural transformation of material force and that originally there is no spirit residing parasitically in the Great Void, then you can know that death is dispersal along with material force and that there is no reconstituted phenomenon that remains in some remote and dark place. Moreover, to say that 'Essence and material force become things, and unattached heavenly souls become changes' meant that after the material force of the yin and yang of the universe integrated to become people and things, the material force of the heavenly spirit returns to heaven while the material force of the earthly spirit returns to earth, thus leading to changes. To say that essence and material force become things is to say that essence and material force join to form things. Essence is earthly spirit and material force is heavenly spirit. To say that unattached heavenly spirits become changes meant that the earthly spirit and the heavenly spirit are dispersed and changed. The change spoken of here is not the change of transformation but the rotting of something solid, the perishing of something that exists, of something again not being."

Between heaven and earth is like a furnace so that even living things all melt and disappear. How can something that has already dispersed join again, and how can something that has gone come again? Examining now my own body, between one exhalation and one inhalation air leaves my body: this is called a breath. That which is exhaled is not inhaled again. Thus it can be seen that human breathing is also reproduction without end where that which is going passes on and that which is coming continues. Looking out and examining things, all grasses and trees have one material force passing from their roots through their trunks, branches, and leaves to their flowers and seeds. In the spring and summer the material force waxes so that leaves and flowers flourish while in the autumn and winter the material force wanes so that flowers and leaves wither and fall. But with the coming of the next spring and summer they once again flourish. This, however, does not mean that the previously fallen leaves are restored to their original state and have come back to life. Also, water that is drawn from the well each day for food is boiled away while that drawn for laundering is dried away by the sun so that there is no trace left. The water of the well flows forth continuously and has no end. This, however, does not mean that the previously drawn water has returned to its original place and come back to life. Also, in the growing of grains, ten *sŏk*[24] planted in the spring yield a hundred *sŏk* when harvested in the autumn, and the hundred becomes a thousand

and then ten thousand as the surplus multiplies. This shows that grains also produce and reproduce.

Let us look now at the Buddhist doctrine of the transmigration, which says that all things with blood and breath have a fixed number: even though they come and come and go and go, they neither increase nor decrease. If so, then the universe's creation of things is not as great as that of the farmer who profits from growing. Also if things with blood and breath are not born as humans, they must become birds and beasts, fishes and turtles, or insects; since the number is fixed, if this one increases, then that one must decrease, and if this one decreases, then that one must increase so that all cannot increase at the same time, nor can all decrease at the same time. But if we now observe, when the world waxes, humans flourish and so do birds and beasts, fishes and turtles, and insects; when the world wanes, humans decline and so do birds and beasts, fishes and turtles, and insects. This is because humans and the myriad things are all products of the material force of the universe. It is evident, therefore, that when material force is waxing, all flourish at the same time, and when material force is waning, all decline at the same time. Wrathful at how severely the Buddhist doctrine of transmigration has befuddled the world, I have obtained my doctrine by basing myself on the transformation of the universe in abstruse areas and by examining the production of humans and things in manifest areas, and I hope that persons of like mind will reflect upon this together.

Someone may ask: "Quoting the doctrine of the old Confucianists, you have interpreted the statement in the *Book of Changes* 'Unattached souls become changes'[25] to mean 'Earthly spirits and heavenly spirits separate, with heavenly spirits going up to heaven and earthly spirits coming down to earth.' This means that when a person dies, his heavenly spirit goes to heaven, and his earthly spirit returns to the earth. Isn't this what Buddha meant by saying 'Even though a person dies, his spirit does not perish?' " I will answer: "Of old, the fires of the four seasons were all obtained from wood. This is because fire originally resides within wood, and when wood heats, it produces fire. So does the heavenly spirit reside within the earthly spirit, and when the earthly spirit warms, it becomes the heavenly spirit. Thus it is said that when you rub wood, it gives forth fire and that when form is already produced, the soul gives forth knowledge. Form is the earthly spirit, and the soul is the heavenly spirit. Just as fire exists in affinity with wood, so do the earthly spirit and the heavenly spirit join to come into being. Just as when fire is burnt out, its smoke ascends to heaven and its ashes fall to earth, so when a human dies, his heavenly spirit ascends to heaven and his earthly spirit descends to earth. The smoke of fire is the heavenly spirit of humanity; the ashes of fire are the earthly spirit of humanity. Also, when a fire has died the smoke and the ashes do not join back together to become fire again, and after a human has died, his heavenly spirit and earthly spirit do not join back together to become a thing. Is this principle not evident?" JD

Chŏng Tojŏn: Discourse on Buddhism and Confucianism
[From *Sambong chip* 9:18a–21a]

Confucianists of old said: "In the ways of the Confucianists and the Buddhists, the terms are the same but the things they represent are different." Now, expanding on this, we say void (*hŏ*) and they say void, and we say tranquility (*chŏk*) and they say tranquility. Yet, our void, even though empty, exists while their void is empty and does not exist, and our tranquility, even though quiet, is felt while their tranquility is quiet and ceases to exist.

We speak of knowledge and action while they speak of enlightenment and self-cultivation. Our knowledge is being aware that the principle of the myriad things is embodied in our mind, and their enlightenment is realizing that the mind is originally empty and without anything; our action is behaving according to the principle of the myriad things without mistake or omission, and their self-cultivation is cutting off the myriad things so they will not accumulate in the mind.

We say that the mind embodies all principles while they say that the mind gives rise to all dharmas. Saying that the mind embodies all principles means that principle originally resides in the mind, that when the mind is fully quiescent and extremely tranquil, it embodies the essence of principle, and that when principle reaches action, it penetrated and is felt so that it carries out its function. Thus it is this of which it is said, "tranquil and not moving it feels and finally penetrates all the causes under heaven." The so-called giving rise to all dharmas means that there is originally no dharma in the mind and that dharmas come into being after encountering the outside world, that when the mind is fully quiescent there is nowhere where this mind resides, and that when it reaches action it accordingly encounters the outside world and comes into being. Thus it is said: "This mind comes into being in response to having no place to reside." (Per investigation this comes from the *Perfection of Wisdom Scripture*. It says that the response to having no place to reside has no inside or outside so that its center is vacant and without things and does not insert the sense of right and wrong in one's bosom. Thus the mind to which it gives rise is a mind having no place to reside, which responds to the outside and does not accumulate things. When Hsieh Liang-tso explained the *Analects,* he quoted this.) It is also said: "When the mind comes into being, all dharmas arise and when the mind perishes, all dharmas also perish." (Per investigation this comes from the *Awakening of Faith*.)

We say that principles are innate while they say that dharmas arise from cause and relations. How is it that the words are the same and the issues so different?

Regarding us, it is said that we interact with the myriad changes; regarding them, it is said that they submit in all things. The words seem similar. But the expression "interact with the myriad changes" means that the mind responds to things that present themselves and deals with them in the appropriate way, employing them without losing propriety. Sons must be employed to become filial, not undutiful, and high officials employed to be loyal, not traitorous. Regarding things, oxen are employed to plow and not to butt, horses to carry burdens and not to bite, and tigers and wolves to be caught in traps and not to harm people. Generally, each is dealt with according to its innate principles.

The Buddhists' so-called "submission in all things" means that in the case of sons, the filial is filial of himself and the undutiful is undutiful of himself; in the case of high officials, the loyal is loyal of himself and the traitorous is traitorous of himself; and in the case of oxen and horses, they plow and carry of themselves and butt and bite of themselves so that all we hear is that things become of themselves and that there is no place for our minds.

The Buddhists' learning is like this: even while themselves employing things, they say things are not being employed. Wouldn't it be strange, however, if when given a coin one did not know what to do with it? And why, then, did heaven make humans to be the essential spirit of the myriad things and give humans responsibility for their well-being?

The arguments are repetitions and have many beginnings, but the essence is that we believe that mind and principle are one while they believe that mind and principle are two, and they believe that the mind is empty and without principle while we believe that even though the mind is empty, it is endowed with the principles of myriad things. Therefore, it is said that we Confucians are one while the Buddhists are two, and we Confucians are continuation while the Buddhists are interruption. Since mind is one, how can there be similarities and differences between them and us? It is only a matter of whether people see things correctly or incorrectly.

Regarding the experiencing of the mind, the Buddhists say:

> Of the four components of the body,
> Which is the main?
> Of the six senses that lead us astray,
> Which is the essence?

(Per investigation, the four components of earth, water, fire, and wind come together to form the body but taken separately none is the original main component; the six senses[26] are light to the eye, sound to the ear, smell to the nose, taste to the mouth, and touch to the skin, but none taken separately is the original essence, just as something in a mirror is but really isn't.)

> Open your eyes in a dark land,
> All day you hear sound but see no form.

(Per investigation, when you illuminate function with intelligence, even though you open your eyes in a dark land, there is light within the darkness just as there is light in a mirror.)

Regarding the experience of the mind, these Buddhists say:

> If it exists, should there be traces?
> If it doesn't exist, how can it be?
> Only when it responds, interacting with things,
> Just seeing into the foundation.

(Per investigation, this is Chu Hsi's poetry.)

Regarding the experience of the mind, we Confucians say, furthermore: Can the mind of the Way have sound but no form? To the contrary, principle must be kept in the mind to interact with the foundation. If the scholar, in everyday life, goes to the places where the mind is manifested and studies them exhaustively, he will be able to see for himself the pluses and minuses and similarities and differences between us and them.

If I may repeat Master Chu Hsi's argument, even though the mind is master of the body, the spirit of its essence can manage the principle of all under heaven; even though principle is dispersed among the myriad things, the subtlety of its function in fact is not beyond the single mind of a man so that from the very beginning we cannot discuss what is in and what is out or what is fine and what is coarse. If, however, one does not know and does not keep the spirituality of his mind, things will be obscure and confused, and he will not be able to study the subtlety of all the principles. If one does not know and does not study the subtlety of all principles, he will be narrow and obstinate and unable to exhaust the completeness of his mind. Whether in theory or in reality, this is inevitable.

Thus the sage teaches to make people quietly know for themselves the spirituality of this mind, to dwell in propriety, dignity, and tranquility, and to know the fundamentals of study; to make people know the subtlety of all the principles and to study them when learning, asking, and reflecting so as to achieve the merit of the exhaustive mind and so that the huge and the minute take in each other and the active and the quiet foster each other; to make people not choose from the very beginning between the inside and the outside, between the fine and the coarse, to make people truly accumulate effort over a long time so that they widely understand the Way, whereupon they know that all is perfectly one and can say that there is no inside or outside, no fine or coarse.

Now, however, without fail people see this as shallow and incoherent and try to cover the form and hide the shadow while separately making an arcane, rapturous, tangled, and closed off doctrine, striving to have the learner place his mind outside of writing and speech and saying that "one can only obtain the Way like this." This only aggravates the imbalance, lewdness, deceitfulness, and escapism of Buddhism, and it is also wrong to try to use this to obfuscate the ancients' practical learning of illustrious virtue and renewing of the people. The words of Master Chu reiterate, discuss, and kindly illuminate this; the learner should immerse his mind there and gain this for himself. JD

CHAPTER ELEVEN

Buddhism: The Ch'ŏnt'ae and Chogye Schools

Buddhism, which first entered Korea in the Three Kingdoms period, remained a major religious and intellectual force in Koryŏ. It flourished at the start of the dynasty and then underwent several stages of reform in the middle period of the kingdom. Throughout the dynasty, Buddhism had close ties with the court as monarchs frequently allowed a son to enter the priesthood and sought advice on both political and religious problems from learned monks. Two major schools, Kyo (Doctrinal) and Sŏn (Meditation), dominated Buddhist thought although in the late eleventh century the royal monk Ŭich'ŏn (1055–1101) tried to fuse the practices of the two schools into the Ch'ŏnt'ae (T'ien-t'ai) school. Apart from its intellectual vigor, Buddhism thrived economically through its monasteries, some of which, like T'ongdo, held vast tracts of land. As in many powerful institutions, Buddhism became inevitably tainted by corruption and misuse of power, abuses that sometimes led to criticism of the monastic establishment.

Shortly after the rise of the military, Buddhism underwent a significant reform with the growth of the meditation-inspired Chogye school. The monk Chinul (1128–1210)—one of Koryŏ's most prolific Buddhist writers and profound thinkers—played an especially important role in this effort, calling for a new emphasis on the practice of meditation along with the study of texts. Ŭich'ŏn, writing a century earlier, had sought to compile the comments and interpretations of other Buddhist thinkers into a comprehensive compendium. This tradition of respect for printed scriptures was again dramatically demonstrated at the height of the Mongol invasions when the Koryŏ court, in its search for the Buddha's divine protection, supervised the recarving of more than eighty thousand woodblocks that were needed to publish the complete Buddhist canon, the *Tripiṭaka*.

Buddhism in Early Koryŏ

Buddhism first came to Korea during the Three Kingdoms period. Initially foreign monks propagated the faith on the peninsula, but as the indigenous states matured, Koreans traveled first to China and then to India in search of scriptures and greater understanding of the tenets of the faith. By the time of late Silla, Buddhism was an established, integral part of Korean culture. The religion was intellectually vital with two major schools—Kyo (Doctrinal) and Sŏn (Meditation)—providing different paths to Buddhist enlightenment.

The leading figures of late Silla and early Koryŏ allied themselves with Buddhist masters, often masters of the Meditation school. Through links with Buddhism, regional leaders could gain spiritual sustenance as well as potential economic ties to well-endowed monasteries and both practical and tactical knowledge useful in maintaining their autonomous power. While giving protection to the Buddhist clergy, each of the potential unifiers had monks to whom he turned for assistance. Wang Kŏn's family had close ties with several Meditation monasteries, and Wang Kŏn himself sought out Meditation monks coming from China for practical and political advice as well as for new religious learning. One such confidant was Yiŏm (870–936), who acted as his close adviser, frequently counseling him on pressing problems facing the infant dynasty. Nevertheless, Wang Kŏn valued the teachings of both the Doctrinal and Meditation schools and sought their unified support, as is evident in his "Ten Injunctions" (see chapter 8), which discuss the importance of assistance from both schools.

Kyunyŏ (923–973), an erudite monk of the Flower Garland school, was an adviser to King Kwangjong. Through liberal borrowing from the teachings of the Pŏpsang (Dharma Characteristics) school, Kyunyŏ furnished a religious ideology that helped Kwangjong to solidify his monarchical authority and to justify many of his high-handed political reforms. Kyunyŏ was also a poet, the author of a major portion of the *hyangga* surviving from early Koryŏ, and he used his literary skill to spread early Koryŏ Buddhist thought through the fusion of the Doctrinal tenets as expressed in the Flower Garland and Dharma Characteristics schools.

Ŭich'ŏn (1055–1101), a son of King Munjong (1046–1083), also sought to bridge the gulf between the Doctrinal and Meditation schools. Although, like Kyunyŏ, he belonged essentially to the Flower Garland school, Ŭich'ŏn was very critical of the former and tried to bring about the fusion of the Flower Garland and Dharma Characteristics schools. Trained in China first in the Flower Garland and then in the T'ien-t'ai schools, he eventually promoted the latter after his return to Koryŏ. In his exposition of the unity of the original nature (*sŏng*) and the phenomenal characteristic (*sang*), Ŭich'ŏn found the teaching of the Silla monk Wŏnhyo (617–686) especially important. Wŏnhyo, one of the seminal figures in the evolution of a uniquely Korean tradition of Buddhism, had expounded the unity of *sŏng* and *sang* earlier in his works. In stressing Wŏnhyo's theory, Ŭich'ŏn tries to restore his forerunner to what Ŭich'ŏn considered his rightful place as the "primate" of Korean Buddhism. In the eulogy presented here, Ŭich'ŏn notes the prominent syncretic tendencies in Wŏnhyo's thought, which inspired Ŭich'ŏn's own attempts to synthesize doctrinal study with meditation practice.

The principal thrust of Ŭich'ŏn's approach to Buddhism was the development of a system in which scholarship and meditation flourished in a symbiotic relationship. In his instructions to the disciple Ch'isu, Ŭich'ŏn laments the degenerate state of Buddhism in his country, which had failed to preserve a comprehensive program of spiritual training and engaged only in arguing over "opinionated theories." Ŭich'ŏn argues that such futile controversies should be abandoned and that scriptural study and meditation practice should be merged together into a comprehensive regimen of training. Only such a system would encourage students to use their doctrinal training not as a tool of disputation but "as a bright mirror to reflect their own minds."

Monk Yiŏm and King T'aejo
[From *Chōsen kinseki sōran* 1:127–128]

His Majesty Wang Kŏn had heard that the way of Great Master Chinch'ŏl was among the best in the world and that his reputation was spreading throughout Korea. Hoping to see him, His Majesty frequently sent out royal invitations asking the master to come to the court. The master, addressing the laity, said: "Living in this land, who would dare disobey the king's commands? One has no choice but to comply with a royal summons to become an adviser. I am about to go to the capital in compliance with the royal request to bring imperial dignity to the royal land." His Majesty, wishing to increase greatly the splendor of the dynasty, looked to the master for assistance. Consequently, he repaired T'aehŭng Temple and requested that the master stay there.

In the second month of the next year [924], His Majesty specially sent former Chancellor Kwŏn Yŏl and ranking official Pak Sumun to welcome the master at the Vairocana Cloister in the palace and earnestly asked him to become resident abbot there. He was obliged to accept. He had already actively promoted the religion when he held Buddhist offices outside the palace. Now he is accorded the honor of a teacher and esteemed for his pursuit of the law. It is like the time when the Indian monk Kāśyapa Mātaṅga [d. A.D. 73] first went to the Han emperor's palace and when K'ang Seng-hui first was honored by the King of Wu, riding in the royal chariot. At the display of a Sŏn dust whisk, the royal countenance showed signs of great pleasure, and the royal reverence accorded him nearly filled the palace. At this time, even as fish were happy in the water, there was no need to mention the great happiness in other respects.

At another time, the king, taking advantage of free time in the evening, quietly visited the Meditation cottage and said: "I, the disciple, would respectfully like to tell you my old wish directly. Now the enemies of the nation are increasingly behaving rather haughtily, and unfriendly neighboring countries invade one after another. This is just as when Ch'u and Han in China, opposing each other, could not decide who would be master. Now for nearly three years we have had two cruel enemies nearby who, despite our earnest desire to be friendly, have increasingly intensified their belligerence. I once took vows pledging to observe the teachings of Buddha and secretly developed a compassionate heart. But I fear I may bring destruction upon myself because of my leniency toward aggressors. Master, despite the great distance between us, you have come to transform the country, thus saving our inflamed land. Please make people see the light through your words of wisdom."

The master replied: "Generally, the Way rests in the heart and not in events. Buddha's law comes from the self and not from others. Moreover, the cultivation of an imperial ruler is different from that of an ordinary man. Even though a ruler may wage war, should he not have greater consideration for the people? A king makes the world his home, all the people his children. He does not kill innocent people but punishes the guilty, thus manifesting good conduct. This is called great assistance (*hongje*)."

The king, greatly moved, put his hands on his desk and said: "I have feared that the lay person may fall to hell because he has no way to know profound truth. As I listen to you, the master, however, it is like speaking with a heavenly being I have encountered."

Thereafter, the king saved criminals whose crimes deserved death and saved the people from suffering by not randomly waging war. This was the result of the master's teaching. HK/ES

Teachings of Great Master Kyunyŏ
[From *Kyunyŏ chŏn* 4, in *Korean Tripiṭaka* 47:260a]

Kyunyŏ was a follower of the Northern school. Toward the end of Silla at Haein Monastery on Mount Kaya, the Flower Garland school was divided into two branches under the leadership of Lords Kwanhye and Hŭirang. Kwanhye's branch was called the Southern school, while Hŭirang's was known as the Northern school. Kwanhye was the teacher of the chief rebel, Kyŏnhwŏn [d. 936], of Later Paekche, while Hŭirang was the teacher of the founder of Koryŏ, Wang Kŏn [918–943]. Both masters were trusted by their patrons and vowed to serve them. But since their convictions differed, how could their minds be one? This division even affected their followers, who opposed one another like fire and water. They even began to distinguish salty and sour tastes in the flavor of the dharma. It was difficult to eradicate these long-standing disputes.

Kyunyŏ, deploring this deep schism, tried to heal it and unite the two branches of thought. To this end he went with the abbot Inyu on a tour of famous mountains and monasteries, beat the drum of the dharma, raised the standard of the Buddha truth, and made all young believers follow him.

Master Hŭirang's commentary on some thirty topics in the Flower Garland school included the following: the same substance of the three teachings; emptiness and existence; exhaustible and inexhaustible; the provisional and the real; theories on the Lotus Treasury World (the *padmagarbha lokadhātu* of Vairocana); the creation of the world system; explication of the profound; sigh and nonsigh; absorbing the essence throughout three births comprising a past life of seeing and hearing Buddha truth; liberation in the present life and realization of life in Buddhahood; the transmission of office; the six characteristics of all dharmas;[1] following and settling in the real; the complete removal of the abstruse and small; the Tuṣita prince (Maitreya); the five types of attainment of Buddhahood; the characteristics of the division of buddhas according to their understanding and cultivation; efflux and property; turning one's mind away from the Lesser Vehicle; the six levels of the bodhisattva path; the eight assemblies;[2] the hundred and six cities; Sukhāvatī (Pure Land); the bodhi tree; nature origination; the five results; the four modes of reality;[3] wide cultivation and making offerings; and host and guest.

Because they came from diverse sources, Kyunyŏ thought, these writings must contain ambiguities. He therefore singled out the essential points and expunged the rest. He studied subtle meanings thoroughly to make them lucid, cited scriptures and treatises, and corrected all errors. Thus did he exhaustively study the holy writings.

When a state examination was instituted at Wangnyun Monastery to select monks [958], Kyunyŏ's correct path was made the orthodox norm and the others were considered collateral. How could the talented not follow this path? The most successful would become a royal preceptor or national preceptor, the lesser ones a great master or most virtuous man (*bhadanta*). Thus have many made their reputations and left their names behind. PL

Ŭich'ŏn: Eulogy to Great Master Wŏnhyo
[From *Hanguk pulgyo chŏnsŏ* 4:555a–b]

Now, on a certain day, month, and year, I, Ŭich'ŏn, a pilgrim *śramaṇa,* respectfully went with oblations of tea, fruit, and seasonable foods to make offerings to the Bodhisattva Wŏnhyo, the primate of Korea. I humbly mused that the principle is made manifest by means of the doctrine, and the path is disseminated by means of the person. But, as customs degenerate, the times become corrupted; then, as people become wayward, the path will vanish. Since the masters will each seal off the conventions of their own schools, their students too will come to cling to their views and learning. It will end up being like Tz'u-en's hundreds of volumes of exegesis, which only grasp at names and characteristics, or T'ai-ling's nine decades of preaching, which merely exalt noumenal contemplation.[4] Although their texts are said to comply with the standards of Buddhism, they were not perspicacious instructions.

Only our Korean bodhisattva comprehensively illuminated both nature and characteristics while arcanely merging past and present; only he resolved the points of contention of the hundred schools, gaining thereby the reputation of being the most eminent person of his generation. Moreover, his spiritual powers were unfathomable; his sublime functioning was difficult to imagine. Although he associated with the dust of the world, it did not soil his perfection; although he blended with its splendor, it did not affect his essence. For these reasons, his name resounds throughout China and India, and his compassionate proselytism reached to both the darkness and the light. It is certainly difficult to decide upon the amount of praise and acclaim he is due.

Early on, I availed myself of the blessings of heaven and soon came to admire the Buddha vehicle. I successively examined the learning of all previous philosophers, but none of it surpassed that of this saintly master. He anguished over errors in the subtle words of Buddhist scriptures; he grieved over the deterioration of the utmost path of the religion. He traveled far and wide among the famous mountain monasteries, seeking out neglected texts everywhere. Nowadays, it is fortunate that the old monasteries of Kyerim respect his form as if he were still alive: it is like meeting the first congregation on the ancient peak of Vulture Mountain.[5]

Thus, availing myself of these meager offerings, I presumptuously narrate this brief token of my respect in the sincere hope that his generous compassion might condescend to pass along the bright mirror of the Buddhist teachings. RB

Ŭich'ŏn: Instruction to the Disciple Ch'isu
[From *Hanguk pulgyo chŏnsŏ* 4:556a–c]

In order to indicate the primary and secondary aspects of both doctrine and meditation, I used to point out to my disciples that the attainment and elucidation of the ultimate characteristic were the ten mysteries,[6] while its transformation became the five teachings.[7] These words are not deceitful.

For superior doctrinal students who are equally intent upon the one

Buddha vehicle, who practice together the manifold practices of the bodhisattvas, whose great minds intent upon Buddhahood are unswayed; who have made vast vows for themselves, who hold in their hands Samantabhadra's vehicle of expedient means, and who roam leisurely in the realm of Vairocana, there is nothing better than initially to investigate phenomena exhaustively by means of the three contemplations[8] and the five teachings, and use this as the eye for entering the path. In fact, apart from this universal dharma, there is no other road via which to attain Buddhahood. Hence, at the climax of the provisional teachings, there are finally no realities. It is for this reason that my patriarch[9] used to say:

"I recall that even in the age of the right dharma the clear light was still hidden. It is fortunate indeed that during this semblance period one can still meet with arcane dissemination. . . . Now we reside at the end of the stupa and monastery period and are about to approach the period of contention. Even if one were to hear inconceivable scriptures, one would not be able to requite that good fortune even by pulverizing one's body. It is like coming upon a boat while one is drowning in the great sea, or riding a numinous crane while one is falling through the vast sky. How can my entire body convulsing with ecstasy ever reach this stage of rapture? Only the sages and saints can know how much I am moved and blessed."

Alas! Even though this patriarch lived during the stupa and monastery period of the semblance dharma age, he still uttered such eager exclamations. So now during this turbid age, right in the middle of the contention period of the degenerate age, how is it possible that one who is able to hear the complete and sudden teachings would not be moved and inspired? Be that as it may, our distance from the saints becomes ever farther; to add to this, we dwell in the hinterlands of Buddhism, our generation retains little of the orthodox religion, and those who train follow the heterodox. Accordingly, our religion seems now about to expire.

I constantly lament that, among the extant records that have been transmitted concerning all the previous generations of masters from Korea, there is no training outlined that is either detailed or comprehensive, and their opinionated theories are especially numerous. There is not one volume in a hundred that is fit to serve as a guide for future ignorant students. None of them uses the holy teaching as a bright mirror to reflect the student's own mind; relying upon their instructions, one would trifle away one's entire life, merely counting the treasures of others. These are what the present generation means by the erroneous writings of such masters as Kyunyŏ, Pomun, Chinp'a, and Yongyun. Their language is uncultured, and their meaning is not well communicated;[10] they embrangle the path of the patriarchs; they bedazzle and confuse later generations—at this there are no writings worse than these. Although I am insignificant and crass, it is my express determination to expose them through my words.

The reason for my concern is that when I was young I studied the *Flower Garland Scripture* and thoroughly examined Sudhana's determination to seek the dharma. Mañjuśrī instructed him: "Oh, son of good family! Approach and pay honor to all good advisers. This is the preliminary cause and condition for perfecting omniscience. For this reason, do not become lax in this endeavor."[11] The *Flower Garland Scripture* also says:

> If there should be any bodhisattva,
> Who is not repulsed by the sufferings of birth and death,
> He will then complete the path of Samantabhadra,
> There will be nothing that will be able to destroy him.[12]

Furthermore, Kuei-shan [780–841] said: "One seeking the path must nurture the dharma eye. The dharma eye cannot open by itself; one must seek a master in order to scratch open its lid." Whenever I reached this passage, I would shut the volume and breathe a long sigh, thinking to myself: "The doctrine established by the saints valued development in practice. That doctrine is not something that should merely be proclaimed by the mouth but ought, in fact, to be practiced by the body. How can practice be considered something as useless as a bitter gourd that is hung to one side and never eaten?"[13]

Unconcerned about my body, I inquired about the path and was intent on this endeavor. I was fortunate that, through past causes, I was able to pay successive visits to wise advisers. Finally, I received some cursory knowledge about doctrine and meditation during the lectures of the great Dharma Master Chin-shui. During that master's spare time from lectures and lessons, he used to admonish his disciples: "Although one who does not cultivate meditation and only imparts the scriptures might hear of the five pervasive causes and effects,[14] he does not, however, penetrate to the three levels of the qualities of the nature. Although one who does not transmit the scriptures and only cultivates meditation might awaken to the three major qualities of the nature, he cannot distinguish between the five pervasive causes and effects. This being the case, meditation cannot but be cultivated, and scriptures cannot but be transmitted."

The reason I am so concerned about both doctrine and meditation is because of my respect for these words. This is the very same idea as the statement of Ch'ing-liang [738–840]:

> If one does not mirror the square inch of mind,
> One futilely turns one's back on the numinosity of the nature.

For this reason, you should know that although one who transmits the *Flower Garland Scripture* but does not train in meditation methods might be called a "lecturer," I will not acknowledge it.

In recent times, while traveling among hundreds of cities, I satisfied my earlier determination to inquire about the dharma, and I now sit and read through various books. During that period, I observed that the present generation of doctrinal students studies the whole day through without knowing why. Some are lost in prejudiced heterodoxies; others are lost in the pursuit of fame and fortune; some are prideful; others are slothful; some were of two minds about their study.[15] Hence, even by the end of their lives, they will be unable to enter this path. RB

Buddhism and Koryŏ Society

Buddhism, the state religion in Koryŏ, was closely intertwined with secular affairs. Individuals turned to Buddhism for religious inspiration as did Christians in the West. They also generously gave to temples and shrines for the same reasons Europeans endowed churches. Like the church in the Middle Ages, the Buddhist establishment became rich through large landholdings and accumulated wealth.

When individuals chose to endow a temple, they often were concerned about its operation. The first selection is from the will of Ch'oe Chean (d. 1046), Ch'oe Sŭngno's grandson, who was trying to reestablish a monastery in the Kyŏngju area, the place of origin of his clan. Especially noteworthy is his concern that, despite his high position in the government and his family's influence, the monks should select their own abbot rather than having an outsider imposed on them.

Through generous donations such as that noted above, monasteries came to control vast holdings. T'ongdo Monastery in southeastern

Korea became one of Koryŏ's richest. The second entry, taken from a memorial stone inscription, provides just a glimpse into the large holdings that were under the control of this monastery.

Some monks used Buddhist devotion for their own ends. The final two selections are about charlatans who readily misled the simple with promises and fears. Using techniques and ideas that are not unfamiliar to us today, they asked only that the faithful believe. One even claimed that he was an incarnation of the Bodhisattva Maitreya and implied he would rescue the faithful, leading them to the Buddhist paradise. The monk Irŏm lived during the troubled years shortly after the military coup of 1170. Igŭm lived in the waning days of Koryŏ. Both appealed to lost souls searching for stability during periods of great uncertainty.

Ch'oe Chean: On Endowing a Buddhist Monastery
[From *Samguk yusa* 3:173–174]

I, Executive of the Royal Secretariat and Chancellery, Ch'oe Chean [d. 1046], benefactor of this temple, offer the following will.

Recently Ch'ŏllyong Monastery at Mount Kowi in the Eastern Capital (Kyŏngju) has fallen into disrepair. Especially desiring long life for the king and peace and prosperity for the people and nation, I, a lay follower of Buddha, having built a prayer hall with connecting hallways and living quarters with a kitchen and storage areas and having provided several stone and ceramic Buddhist images, will hold a ten-thousand-day Śākyamuni prayer meeting (*toryang*).

As these things have been donated for the benefit of the nation, it is also correct for the state to appoint an abbot. The monks of the services, however, are likely to be concerned with an abbot's changes. When we look at other examples of land donations to monasteries, we find the lands donated for adequate support are: two hundred *kyŏl*[16] to Chijang Temple at Mount Kong, twenty *kyŏl* to Tosan Temple at Mount Pibi, and ten *kyŏl* to each temple on the mountains surrounding the Western Capital. At each of these monasteries, candidates were selected on the basis of their observance of Buddhist commandments and their talent, not on the basis of where they were employed. Furthermore, it was made a rule to select them in a sequence determined on the basis of popular support by the monks of the temple.

I, a lay follower, was delighted when I learned of these customs and wish to have selected from among the monks of Ch'ŏllyong Temple a person who is of the most virtuous (*taedŏk*)[17] rank and possesses great virtue and talent, making him a pillar of the temple. Make such a person the abbot and have him hold services and maintain conduct for a long time. HK/ES

Landholdings of T'ongdo Monastery
[From *T'ongdosa chi*, pp. 24–30]

The mountains and streams providing the land base supporting T'ongdo Monastery are in an area of seventeen thousand *pu*[18] with stone posts totaling twelve in all.[19] To the east is a stone post at Hŭksŏk Peak. To the south are Sach'ŏn and P'och'ŏn peaks and a stone inscription stupa post. To the north is Tongŭl Mountain, where a stone post is placed. In the middle are Sŏngnae stream and Kwe stream, and each has a stele and a stone post. Within the area of these posts of four directions are, to the east, Choil Hall; to the west, Chajang Hall and Wŏlmyŏng Hall; to the south, Chŏgung Hall and Hoŭng Hall; and to the north, Paegun Hall and Koksŏng Hall. These are all halls attached to T'ongdo Monastery.

When the Vinaya Master Chajang first founded T'ongdo Monastery, he built a hermitage at Koksŏng Hall, and from there he oversaw the completion of the temple layout. Later, Koksŏng Monastery was named after one of his disciples, named Koksŏng, who lived and died there. Whenever Master Koksŏng sat in meditation, colored clouds covered the monastery and the fragrances of five incenses filled the valley. Because of this, its name was changed to Ungok Monastery and has remained the same ever since.

The area denoted by the posts in the four directions is divided into subwards with quarters for three thousand monks of the *taedŏk* rank. South is the subward of Mount Puch'ŏn, which has living quarters for one thousand monks of the *taedŏk* rank. To the north is Tongŭl Tea Village, where tea is produced and presented to the monastery. To this day, the spring water used for boiling the tea given to the monastery has not dried up. Later people considered it a village solely for tea production. Chajang's disciple Choil,[20] whenever he was free from lighting incense, went straight to the eastern peaks to examine closely the mountains and streams. He built a hut and set up a longevity post and lived there until he died. Later the hut was called Choil Hermitage. . . .

The land allotted to the caretakers of the posts in the four directions spread to the environs of Pukt'a (North Tea) village in the southeastern ward, and it also was on the boundary line of Kŏhwa-gun. Divided always into eastern and western groups, the three thousand monks of the *taedŏk* rank in the halls of east and west piled stones along large streams. Because of crimes committed in the ward, however, they were chased out and scattered. One thousand of them went to the southern boundary in Puch'ŏn ward and built hermitages in which to live. At dawn and dusk, they went back and forth to the monastery and, by worshiping with relics and cassocks, earnestly engaged in spiritual cultivation. One day, the flesh and bodies of five Buddhist mendicants, because of their worship of relics, ascended into heaven and flew toward the altar. Dropping skeletons in front of the temple's gate, they all disappeared. It is said that they were cremated. . . . Later people built a pavilion in front of the gate and called it Ch'iru Tower. . . .

Thus the twelve *pibo changsaeng* posts are: the two *changsaeng* posts of black wooden placards at the entrance to the ward in front of the gate; two stone *changsaeng* posts to the east at Hŭksŏk peak; in the middle, two stone *changsaeng* posts with steles at Sŏngnae stream and Kwe stream; in the south, two stone *changsaeng* posts at Sach'ŏn and P'och'ŏn peaks; to the west, one stone *changsaeng* post with stele at Taeryŏng hill; and one stone *changsaeng* post with stele to the south by the large stream. Stupas are divided in a row on the four boundaries, and each has ten caretakers who are supplied with land allocated to their position and land allocated to their households. These are all lands from within the area of the *changsaeng* posts in the four directions. The aforementioned stele and pagodas are all in a row within the *changsaeng* post area. There has never been any public or private landholding except that belonging to the monastery, which extends to the Ŭich'un district boundary. The rest of the information will not be recorded here, as it is actually all found in the original documents of the history of the monastery. HK/ES

The Monk Irŏm
[From *Koryŏ sa* 99:23b–24b]

A monk named Irŏm, who lived in Chŏnju, claimed he could make the blind see again and the dead live. King Myŏngjong [1170–1197] sent Palace Attendant Kŭm Kŭgŭi to receive him at the court. On the way, the monk wore a colorful scarf and rode a piebald horse, hiding his face with a silk fan. His escorts warded people off and protected him so they could not see him directly. When he stayed at Pohyŏn Hall, the people of the capital, high and low, young and old, competed to have an audience, emptying the village. All the sick, blind, deaf, crippled, dumb, and incurably diseased scattered about before him. The monk directed them with his fan.

Received at Ch'ŏnsu Monastery, he lived on the top floor of the south gate pavilion. State councillors and great ministers hastened to see him, while scholars and their wives competed to put their hair before him to have him walk on it. When the monk ordered them to chant to Amitābha, the chant was heard for ten *ri*. If they received even the smallest drop of the water with which he washed and bathed, it was like giving them one thousand pieces of gold. They all drank it and called it holy water, claiming it could cure all kinds of illnesses. Day and night, men and women mingled together, and illicit words spread. Although countless people shaved their heads to become followers, no one at that time admonished them to cease.

As King Myŏngjong gradually came to know of the monk's falseness, the monk was compelled to return home. Earlier, the monk had deceived the people, saying: "All laws stem from only one mind; if you diligently pray to Buddha and say, 'My illness is already cured,' then your illness will be cured. Never say, 'My illness has not yet been cured.'" From this, the blind said they already saw and the deaf said they already heard. This is why the people were so easily deceived. Executive of the Royal Secretariat Mun Kŭkkyŏm [1122–1189], wearing a disguise, came to pay his respects. Im Minbi [1122–1194] also bowed before his pavilion. HK/ES

Igŭm, the Self-Proclaimed Maitreya
[From *Koryŏ sa* 107:18a–19a]

In Kosŏng there was a wizard named Igŭm who called himself a Maitreya and bewitched the people, saying: "I can bring out Śākyamuni Buddha. All who pray and sacrifice to the gods, all who eat horse and cattle meat, and all who do not share their wealth among the people will die. If you do not believe me, by the third month, the sun and moon will not shine." He also said: "If I work at it, grass will grow blue flowers, trees will produce grain, and one seed can be harvested twice." Foolish people believed this and were afraid to be late in giving alms of rice, silk, or gold and silver. If horses or cattle died, they threw them out and did not eat them, and those with wealth gave it all to others.

He also said: "If I command the deities of the mountain and streams, then the Japanese pirates can be captured." The shamans respected and trusted him even more. Removing the shrines of the guardian deities of their areas, they treated Igŭm like a buddha, praying to him for blessings and fortune. Hoodlums followed and colluded with him, calling themselves disciples and feeding each other with lies. When he came, even magistrates sometimes welcomed him and had him stay in their official guest houses.

When Igŭm reached Ch'ŏngju, Kwŏn Hwa enticed him and his company, arresting and imprisoning five leaders and hastening to inform the court. The Privy Council sent instructions to all the circuits to capture and execute all his associates. Thereupon, when Superintendent Yang Wŏngyŏk, who believed and supported Igŭm's assertions, fled and went into hiding, he was searched out, whipped, and banished. He died on the way into exile. HK/ES

Resurgence of Buddhism

The military coup of 1170 signaled the beginning of a new order. The great aristocratic lineages lost their preeminence and ability to dictate all state matters, signifying a decline in their political and social power. The coup led to equally significant changes in Koryŏ's religious order as the Chogye sect of the Meditation school gradually emerged as the dominant spiritual voice in the kingdom.

During early Koryŏ, Kyo (Doctrinal) beliefs rather than Sŏn (Meditation) prescripts captured the imagination of the elite. By the start of the twelfth century, however, government officials and scholars alike, unhappy with the Doctrinal school's approach, reinvigorated the Meditation school. And by the end of the twelfth century, the highest military and civil authorities patronized Meditation monks and monasteries.

Yi Kyubo (1168–1241) described Ch'oe Ch'unghŏn's active support of Meditation in his "On a Trip to Ch'angbok Monastery." The military leader Ch'oe Ch'unghŏn not only rebuilt many Meditation monasteries but also sought out Meditation monks and sponsored religious meetings to propagate the faith. The Meditation school's simple spiritual message of finding truth and spirituality within the self undoubtedly appealed to Ch'oe Ch'unghŏn and other military leaders, but the Ch'oe house's patronage of Meditation practices was also a reaction to the earlier opposition to Ch'oe rule by monks of the Doctrinal school. Since the Doctrinal monasteries had been closely aligned with the former aristocratic forces before the military rose to power, they felt threatened by the new military leadership. And as the passage describing the clash between the monks and military rulers shows, the monasteries were dealt a crippling blow by Ch'oe Ch'unghŏn's well-organized and well-equipped forces.

The Meditation school, as it flourished in the second half of the dynasty, became the intellectual focus of many thinkers in Koryŏ. Scholars apparently did not neglect Confucian studies but often studied Confucianism in conjunction with Buddhism. In the third selection, Im Ch'un, one of the leading literary figures of the thirteenth century, describes this commingling of Buddhist and Confucian ideas. Since some of this religious expression took place in remote mountains, a description of one religious area, called Mount Sabul (Four Buddhas), is found in the fourth passage. As the region had been the center of considerable spiritual activity in the past, it was natural that under the Ch'oe house's rule, too, it continued to attract many new patrons.

Chinul (1158–1210), one of the leading masters of Meditation of this period, was mostly responsible for the Meditation school's phenomenal rise under military rule. A devotee of Meditation practices from his youth, Chinul, also known as the National Preceptor Pojo, called for the individual to empty the mind and free the self from the world of the senses. The final passage offered here was issued in 1190 upon the formal establishment of Chinul's Samādhi and Prajñā Community. The community sought to achieve enlightenment through worship, scriptural recitation, common work, and meditation. In this composition, Chinul explains the development of the Meditation community at Kŏjo Monastery and then its move to the Chogye region in southwestern Korea. The work served as both the compact of the community members and a call to others to develop the practices Chinul considered crucial to a successful Buddhist vocation.

Yi Kyubo: On a Trip to Ch'angbok Monastery
[From *Tongguk Yi sangguk chip* 25:8b–10a]

In general, adherence to the Way varies from time to time. Accordingly, Meditation practices became so invisible that they hung by a thread before our Lord Chingang [Ch'oe Ch'unghŏn] helped to restore Meditation by energetically building and maintaining it as one builds dikes destroyed by a raging flood. After this, the spring of Meditation overflowed, and the school's teachings became very popular everywhere.

In 1211 Lord Chingang obtained the old Ch'angbok Monastery southeast of the capital and renovated it. King Hŭijong [1204–1211] had ascended to the throne just two years earlier and wanted to hold a large Meditation meeting to explain the mind dharma. Before this, Lord Chingang heard that Pyŏngong,[21] the patriarch of the Meditation school, had secluded himself deep in the mountains to cultivate the divine within. The lord had earlier summoned the monk several times, but he did not come. The lord still wanted to persuade him with humble words. Someone said: "It has already been a long time since he went to the mountain and separated himself from humanity. I fear he probably will not change his mind and return." Lord Chingang laughingly said: "All buddhas and bodhisattvas carry the same intention of saving all sentient beings. How can one be so sparing of the dharma and not spread it? It is like a man accumulating vast wealth and not being able to dispose of it. Surely he would not be the one."

Later the king heard this and sent a man to persuade Pyŏngong cordially, and in the end he responded to the king's command and came, as Lord Chingang had predicted.

When Pyŏngong came, other high monks followed him. As they all organized themselves into a religious society and earnestly cultivated themselves; those who had cultivated themselves as highly as the monk Chingong all came,[22] responding to the summons. Without exception, the virtuous followers of the remaining sects too gathered like clouds. The popularity of Meditation assemblies had never been like this. In this assembly Pyŏngong became the patriarch and Chingong the deputy. They explained the *Lin-tsu t'an-ching* (Platform Scripture of the Sixth Patriarch) and the *Ching-shan yü-lu* (Recorded Sayings of Ta-hui),[23] and every night they discussed the meaning of emptiness, making it a regular event.

Thereupon, from those who followed the five Doctrinal schools to literati poets, all came to the assembly, requiring the holding of separate daily meetings, and mutually discussed the principles of its teaching. In the beginning, they all insisted on their own ideas, contradicting each other. Although they listened to the Meditation tenets, they did not take them to heart and seemed disappointed. Slowly they comprehended the Meditation tenets, gradually realizing their true meaning and attaining ultimate understanding. Thereupon, just as if after Mansan's Meditation slap, its meaning suddenly became definite and clear. Realizing the unequaled greatness of the Meditation teaching, they all asked to be disciples to seek further assistance.

Didn't Bodhidharma say: "The one thousand scriptures and ten thousand treatises clarify only the mind"? In the sudden enlightenment that comes through these words, what use will there be for doctrinal explanations? Great indeed is the way of meditation. It cannot be reached through knowledge and cannot be investigated by words. The essence of meditation is awakening to the mind. If one wants to awaken to the mind, it is through no-mind that one can awaken. The awakening that is no awakening is the true awakening. Awakening, then, is this very mind, and apart from this mind there is no Buddha. If one does not realize that there is a shining spiritual treasure that is commensurate with one's own province but seeks enlightenment from others, even though one searches for it the whole day long, one will only be wasting one's time in vain.

What the Buddha and patriarchs preached is not different from these tenets. Now with these tenets of the highest perfection, we satiate the gentry to the fullest extent, enabling them to understand the one, sublime, and true fount of the mind and extend the same benefit to many ordinary people.

If by a single blow of a meditation slap enlightenment is realized through ten thousand generations in Korea, then our country can indeed benefit forever. Almost twenty-eight days after the beginning of the assembly, we have finally come to its conclusion. The notable people attending the meeting are all listed below. HK/ES

Clash Between Monks and Military Rulers
[From *Koryŏ sa* 129:23b–24a]

In 1217 Ch'oe Ch'unghŏn and his son were at his house with their troops fully deployed and on alert. At that time, the Khitans were pressing near. Ch'unghŏn ordered all the officials to defend the city. He destroyed people's houses beneath the city wall and dug a moat. The monks of Hŭngwang, Hongwŏn, Kyŏngbok, Wangnyun, Anyang, and Suri monasteries, who were serving in the army, plotted to kill Ch'unghŏn. Pretending that they were retreating in defeat, they arrived at the Sŏnŭi Gate at daybreak and urgently announced, "The Khitan troops have already arrived." But the gatekeepers refused to admit them. The monks, beating their drums loudly, destroyed the gate lock and entered, killing five or six gatekeepers.

A certain junior colonel, Kim Tŏngmyŏng, used a yin-yang prophecy to flatter Ch'unghŏn and obtained the post of administrator in the Bureau of Astrology. The new calendar he presented changed old practices. The court astrologers and the censorial officials certainly knew this was not right, but fearing Ch'unghŏn, no one dared to speak. Moreover, Tŏngmyŏng several times raised corvée labor projects and exploited the resources of various monasteries. Therefore, the monks, who resented him, first destroyed his house and then proceeded toward Ch'unghŏn's house. Upon reaching the main thoroughfare, they were chased by the Patrol Army and fled to Sinch'ang Hall, and there they fought. Ch'unghŏn, however, sent his own house troops to attack in a pincers movement. When the monk leader was hit by a stray arrow and fell, his followers rushed to the Sŏnŭi Gate but found it closed. Unable to escape, they all scattered and ran. Ch'unghŏn's army pursued them, killing more than three hundred monks and capturing others. When interrogated, they revealed connections with the marshal of the Central Army, Chŏng Sukch'ŏm.

The next day, Ch'unghŏn closed the city gates and searched for the monks who had fled and killed them all. Just then, as a great rain fell, blood flowed like a river. They beheaded more than three hundred monks on the banks of Namgye stream. All together, they killed more than eight hundred people. The corpses piled up like a mountain, and the people were unable to pass for several months. HK/ES

Im Ch'un: Renovation of Sorim Monastery
[From *Sŏha chip* 5:8a–9a]

The way of the sage rises and falls with time and transforms the world. Therefore, in the past, Confucius, living at the time Chou was in decline, founded his teachings on humaneness and righteousness. Coming alternately to the times of Yang Tzu, Mo Tzu, the Yellow

Emperor, and Lao Tzu, strange sayings and weird practices appeared and spread in all directions. Their evil effects reached Ch'in and Han, leaving no place untouched and becoming unbearable to listen to.

Thereupon Buddhism entered China, purifying the land through the first principle of righteousness. Showing people and instructing them through the practice of compassion, it saved all living creatures and became the trend of the times. Therefore the Sixth Patriarch Hui-neng [638–713] considered Buddhism to be no different from the way of Confucius. He also said: "Buddhist scripture and the Confucian classics, used together, can show man the direction in which to go." Accordingly, even if unified and mixed, the teachings of Confucianism and Buddhism are the same in the end.

Thereupon, from Chin and Sung on, wise scholars have listened to these traditions and appreciated them. Even a great Confucian scholar of T'ang like Po Chü-i [772–846] believed deeply in Buddhism, personally practicing and studying it. In his old age, calling himself "the Buddhist Devotee of Hsiang-shan," he organized a religious society in the mountains and devoutly practiced Buddhism. His beliefs were truly sincere.

Now Chin Ling-i[24] of the Ch'ien-t'ang River in Chekiang has always worshiped Buddha and adored Po Chü-i. Always wishing to organize a fine Buddhist compact, wear Buddhist garments, and live there, he desired to transcend the sufferings of the secular world by following the path leading to enlightenment. How can it not be that "If you live by the Buddhadharma, then you will become part of the dharma"? HK/ES

Essay on Sabul Mountain
[From *Sinjŭng tongguk yŏji sŭngnam* 28:3a–b]

North of Sanyang there is a mountain called Sabul (Four Buddhas) or Kongdŏk (Merit and Virtue). To the east it connects to Chungnyŏng Pass, and to the south it leads to Hwajang. The mountain has a rock that is about one square *chang*,[25] and on its sides are carved the Buddhas of the Four Directions. It sits on a peak. Silla's King Chinp'yŏng [579–632], on a visit to the mountain, saw it and subsequently constructed at its side a monastery called Great Vehicle.

On the southwest side of the mountain there was a temple called White Lotus Society (Paengnyŏn-sa). Next to the temple garden there was a *mimyŏl* well and a platform where the monk Ŭisang [579–632] lectured on the Buddha dharma. A conical hemp cap and monk's staff were also there.

In 1242 Deputy Director Ch'oe Cha [1188–1260] became magistrate of Sangju and visited the monastery. He found in the old monastery hall the portraits of Wŏnhyo and Ŭisang, and the cap and staff were still there as before. About fifty paces outside the gate was a stone three *ch'ŏk* high, which tradition called the Kŭmho (Prohibit Tigers) stone. About twenty paces further was a spring where water bubbled out of a crack in the cliff. The evergreen and pine nut trees were green and dense. Below there was a flat rock that could seat thirty people. It was called Cool Spring Pavilion.

Lord Ch'oe commanded Lord Wang of the Ministry of Punishments to oversee construction and build a new Buddha's sanctum, an ancestral shrine, monks' quarters, and guest rooms as well as the Hŏbaek Tower. Below the Cool Spring Pavilion, he built a two-story bridge, calling it Sinch'ŏng Bridge. He requested the monk T'agyŏn from Mount Chogye to write an inscription and hang it. Because there is another White Lotus Society on Mount Mandŏk in Honam (Chŏlla), Paengnyŏn Society on Mount Kongdŏk east of the Naktong River is therefore called Eastern White Lotus to differentiate between the two. HK/ES

Chinul: The Compact of the Samādhi and Prajñā Community

[From *Hanguk pulgyo chŏnsŏ* 4:698a–b, 707a–c]

Reverently, I have heard:
A person who falls to the ground gets back up by using that very same ground. To try to get up without relying on that ground would be impossible.[26]

Sentient beings are those who are deluded in regard to the one mind and give rise to boundless defilements. Buddhas are those who have awakened to the one mind and have given rise to boundless sublime functions. Although there is a difference between delusion and awakening, essentially these both derive from the one mind. Hence to seek Buddhahood apart from the mind is impossible.

Since my youth, I have cast myself into the domain of the patriarchs of the Meditation school and have visited meditation halls everywhere. After investigating the teachings the Buddha and the patriarchs so compassionately bestowed on beings, I have found that they are primarily designed to make us bring to rest all conditioning, empty the mind, and then remain centered there quietly, without looking for anything outside. As it is stated in the *Flower Garland Scripture,* "If a person wants to comprehend the state of Buddhahood, he should purify his mind until it is just like empty space."[27] Whatever we see, hear, recite, or cultivate, we should recognize how difficult it is to come into contact with such things; examining these things using our own wisdom, we should practice according to what has been expounded. Then it can be said that we are cultivating the Buddha mind ourselves, are destined to complete the path to Buddhahood ourselves, and are sure to redeem personally the Buddha's kindness.

Nevertheless, when we examine the inclination of our conduct from dawn to dusk, we see that we rely on the Buddhadharma while adorning ourselves with the signs of self and person. Infatuated with the way of material welfare and submerged in the secular realm of wind and dust, we are not cultivating virtue but are only wasting food and clothing. Although we have left home, what merit does it have? How sad! We want to leave the triple world, but we do not practice freeing ourselves from sense objects. Our male body is used in vain, for we have not a man's will. From one standpoint we fail in the dharma's propagation; from another we are negligent in benefiting sentient beings; and between these two we turn our backs on our four benefactors.[28] This is certainly shameful! For a long time I have lamented these problems.

In the first month of *imin* [1182], I traveled to Poje Monastery in the capital for a convocation called to discuss meditation. One day I made a pact with more than ten fellow cultivators saying: "After the close of this convocation we will renounce fame and profit and stay in seclusion in the mountain forests. There, we will form a community designed to foster the constant training in *samādhi* (concentration) and *prajñā* (wisdom). Through worship of the Buddha, recitation of scriptures, and even through common work, we will each discharge the duties to which we are assigned and nourish the self-nature in all situations. We vow to pass our whole lives free of entanglements and to follow the higher pursuits of accomplished and true men. Wouldn't this be wonderful?". . . .

In the past, I have read Mahāyāna texts and carefully contemplated the explanations of those scriptures and treatises that belong to the

vehicle of the definitive teachings. I learned that there is not one
dharma that is not centered in the threefold training,[29] and there is not
a single buddha who did not rely on this threefold training to complete
the path. As the *Śūraṅgama Scripture* says: "All the Thus Come Ones
of the past have already completed this approach. All the bodhisattvas
of the present time each enter its perfect brightness. Students who will
cultivate in the future should rely on this very dharma."[30] Consequently, we should now make a special promise and a secret pledge to
cultivate the religious life. Then, looking to our true lineage, we will
not become discouraged. We will invigorate our bodies and minds
with *śīla, samādhi,* and *prajñā,* reducing defilements and reducing them
again.[31] Beside the riverbanks and at the foot of trees, let us constantly
nurture the sacred embryo. Let us roam about looking at the moonlight, listening in freedom to the sound of the rivers and torrents;
wandering at will in any direction, let us pass our time, as if we were
empty boats bobbing atop the waves. Like loosed birds soaring in the
sky, let us manifest our bodies throughout the universe. Immersing
the mysterious spirits of our minds in the dharma realm, let us respond to others according to their faculties, spontaneously and without stereotyping. This is exactly what I long for. If people who
cultivate the path give up fame to enter the mountains but do not
cultivate these practices and, instead, deceptively make a show of the
deportments to deceive faithful patrons, it is even worse than seeking
fame and gain, riches and position, or being addicted to wine and
women, dissolute in mind and body, and passing an entire life in vain.

All of those present who heard these words agreed with what was
said and swore, "On another day we will consummate this agreement,
live in seclusion in the forest, and be bound together as a community
that should be named for *samādhi* and *prajñā.*" In this manner the
pledge was put to writing and everyone's intentions were decided.
Later, due to unforeseen problems with the selection of an appropriate
site, everyone was scattered in all four directions. It has been almost
ten years now, and we still have not been able to fulfill our promise.

In the early spring of last year, *musin* [1188], the revered Meditation
monk, venerable Tŭkchae, who had also made the pledge, happened
to be staying at Kŏjo Monastery on Mount Kong. He had not forgotten the earlier vow concerning the formation of the Samādhi and
Prajñā Community, and he sent a letter to Pomun Monastery on
Mount Haga inviting me to join him. As he earnestly requested me a
second and a third time also, even though I had been dwelling in the

forest ravines keeping my stupidity and my utterly useless mind to myself, nevertheless, remembering our earlier agreement and moved by his honest sincerity, I chose this year's spring season to move my abode to that monastery and left together with the Meditation practitioner Hang. We invited those who had previously made the same vow to gather there with us. Some of them had died, others were sick, and still others were pursuing fame and profit and so were not able to join us. Finally, with the remaining group of three or four monks, we started this dharma assembly in fulfillment of our previous vow.

I humbly hope that men of high moral standards who have grown tired of world affairs—regardless of whether they are adherents of Meditation, the Doctrinal school, Confucianism, or Taoism—will abandon the dusty domain of this world, roam high above all things, and devote themselves earnestly to the path of inner cultivation, which is commensurate with this aim. Then, although they might have had no role previously in the formation of this project, I have allowed them to add their names at the end of the compact of this community. Although for some of them it may not be possible to train with us here in this assembly, they should constantly aim to gather together their thoughts and contemplate with insight and, in that manner, cultivate right causes together with us. Then it will be as the scripture says: "The wild mind that is brought to rest is *bodhi*. The sublime brightness of the nature's purity is not something that can be obtained from anyone else."[32] *Mañjuśrī's Gāthā* says:

> One thought of purity of mind is a *bodhimaṇḍa,*
> And is better than building seven-jeweled stupas as numerous as
>   the sands of the Ganges.
> Those jeweled stupas finally will be reduced to dust,
> But one thought of purity of mind produces right
>   enlightenment.[33]

Consequently, we know that although we are engulfed by the three calamities,[34] the operation of the nonoutflow cause which is produced by even temporary concentration of thought remains placid. And not only those who cultivate the mind will gain this benefit. Through this merit we pray that the king will live for ten thousand years; the prince will live for a thousand autumns; the world will be at peace; the dharma wheel will always turn; our teachers and parents during all the three time periods,[35] together with the lay supporters throughout the ten directions,[36] and all the beings born and dying in the dharma realm, will together be moistened by the dharma rain, will be eternally free from the sufferings and anxieties of the three evil bourns, will leap into the storehouse of great brightness, and will travel the ocean-like nature of *samādhi*. To the very limits of the future, may the dulling darkness be exposed, may the transmission of the lamp continue, and may its light never be extinguished. Would that not be merit that is forever one with the dharma nature? May those noble men who revel in the good keep this in mind and consider it carefully.

The time is the first year, *kyŏngsul,* of Ming-ch'ang, the last month of spring [1190]. Respectfully written by Moguja, who is living in seclusion on Mount Kong.

In the fifth year, *kyŏngsin,* of Ch'eng-an [1200], the community was moved from Mount Kong to Mount Chogye in the Kangnam region. In the vicinity, there was a monastery called Chŏnghye-sa (Samādhi and Prajñā Monastery). As this led to some confusion in names, a memorial was received from the court that changed our name from the Samādhi and Prajñā Community to the Meditation Cultivation Community (Susŏn-sa). Nevertheless, as this *Encouragement to Practice* had already been in circulation, the printing blocks were carved and the text printed and distributed under the old name. RB

Chinul and the Chogye School

Chinul spent much of his life explaining and discussing both Meditation and Flower Garland beliefs. His extensive writings show him to be one of Korea's greatest Buddhist thinkers. The first selection in this section is Chinul's abridgement of an important commentary to the *Flower Garland Scripture* by the Chinese exegete Li T'ung-hsüan (635–730). Chinul's own success in developing a synthesis between scholarship and meditation in Buddhism was to a large extent inspired by Li's innovative, practice-oriented interpretations of Buddhist doctrinal teachings. In his preface to these excerpts, Chinul provides an extensive autobiographical account of his own quandary concerning the connection between doctrine and practice. Scholars of the *Flower Garland Scripture* whom Chinul consulted claimed that the Meditation school focus on "seeing the nature of the mind" produced only introspective awareness, not the consummate, holistic knowledge of the "unimpeded interfusion of all phenomena," which they presumed to be the quintessence of Buddhism. This claim prompted Chinul to undertake a three-year study of the Buddhist canon to discover scriptural passages that would vindicate Meditation. He believed that he found such vindication in the *Flower Garland Scripture* and Li's commentary to that text. His reading suggested to him that the words of the Buddha were what matured into the doctrinal teachings of Buddhism, while the mind of the Buddha was what evolved into Meditation. Just as the words of the Buddha reflected what was in his mind, so too the doctrinal teachings of Buddhism reflected the mystical knowledge engendered through meditation. Hence Chinul discovered a basis for synthesizing the Flower Garland and Meditation schools into a comprehensive system of Buddhist thought and practice, one that would inspire all future generations of Korean Buddhists.

Fundamental to Chinul's syncretic vision was the basic unity he perceived between the descriptions of truth presented in Buddhist doctrine and the experience of that truth that occurs through meditation. Through a series of questions and answers in the selection from "Straight Talk on the True Mind," Chinul sought to prove that the variant accounts of the absolute in both Doctrinal and Meditation records can all be traced to a single concept: the true mind. The true mind for Chinul meant Buddhahood itself; but it also referred to that quality of sentience that is basic to all ordinary "sentient" beings as well. The true mind, therefore, serves as the matrix between the conventional reality of the ordinary world and the absolute truth of the dharma realm. In order to gain access to absolute truth, and thus enlightenment, Buddhist practitioners need only recognize the enlightenment inherent in their own minds. Faith—the wholehearted acceptance of the fact of their innate enlightenment—is the soteriological attribute that will allow students to relinquish their delusion that they are unenlightened. It is this peculiar kind of faith in Meditation—what Chinul termed "right faith in the patriarchal school"—that will reveal to all persons that they are originally buddhas.

In "Secrets on Cultivating the Mind," the most accessible of his accounts of the process of Meditation training, Chinul offers a summation of his key ideas and reiterates his lament that people "do not recognize that their own natures are the true buddhas." Chinul demands that practice begin with a sudden awakening, which reveals to the student that he is innately enlightened. This initial awakening occurs through tracing the light emanating from the fountainhead of his mind back to its enlightened source. But simply because the student understands that he is a buddha does not mean that he will be able to act as one, any more than a clever infant will be able to act as an intelligent adult. Even after awakening, the student must continue to control the full range of old habits, to which he will still be subject, as well as to cultivate the host of wholesome qualities that will enable him to express his understanding to others. Finally, when the student's understanding and conduct work in perfect unison, he will become a buddha in fact as well as principle. Chinul's soteriological program of sudden awakening/gradual cultivation was unique to the mature Buddhist schools of East Asia and helped to define the indigenous Korean tradition of Meditation.

Chinul's most influential disciple was the monk Hyesim (1178–1234). *Sŏnmun yŏmsong chip* is Hyesim's indigenous collection of *kongan* (public cases)—exchanges between enlightened Meditation masters and their disciples. Such exchanges were used as pedagogical material and eventually came to be used as themes for meditative contemplation. Anthologies of these exchanges began to be compiled in China during the tenth century and typically included the case itself, along with interlinear annotation, variant explanations of other masters, and verse exegeses. Hyesim's collection includes coverage of some 1,125 *kongan* (expanded posthumously by a disciple to 1,472 *kongan*) in thirty fascicles, making it one of the largest such anthologies compiled in East Asia.

The arrangement of *Sŏnmun yŏmsong chip* is unusual, however, in that the *kongan* are listed so as to follow the traditional Meditation lineage from the Buddha Śākyamuni through the twenty-eight Indian and six Chinese patriarchs down to the many masters of the mature Meditation school. It therefore functions as both a *kongan* anthology and a lineage record. Establishing this lineality of the Meditation transmission was important, given Meditation's putative antipathy toward the scriptural teachings of Buddhism. This elaborate pseudohistory sought to prove that contemporary Meditation masters derived their authority not from scripture but from a direct line of spiritual experience going back to the Buddha himself. Hence Meditation had no need for the scriptural teachings of Buddhism, but merely transmitted the mind of the Buddha down through the generations: whatever "words and letters" may be recorded in such anthologies as this were intended only as expedient means of passing on the "profound intent" of Meditation to posterity.

Touching on an idea broached in an earlier section, Hyesim also asserts in "Letter in Reply to Ch'oe Hongyun" the similarity between

Confucian and Buddhist beliefs. In this letter, Hyesim attempts to show the fundamental unity of Buddhism and Confucianism by distinguishing the variant functions of the two religions from their identical essence. While the terminology used in Buddhism and Confucianism may differ, the essence of the minds of Buddhists and Confucians is nonconceptual, unconditioned, and all-pervasive. Hence, by ignoring the outward trappings of these religions and penetrating to their fundamental core, the adept will realize his true self, which transcends all religious expression. Hyesim's essay leads even to a discussion of Taoism, pointing to the intellectual fervor of this age, which allowed scholars and monks to discourse actively across a broad range of ideas. RB

Chinul: Excerpts from the *Exposition of the Flower Garland Scripture:* Preface
[From *Hanguk pulgyo chŏnsŏ* 4:767a–768b]

In the autumn months of Ta-ting, *ŭlsa* [1185], as I began living in retreat on Mount Haga, I reflected constantly on the Meditation adage "Mind is Buddha."[37] I felt that if a person were not fortunate enough to meet with this approach, he would end up wasting many aeons in vain and would never reach the domain of sanctity.

I had always had doubts about the approach to entering into awakening of the Flower Garland teachings: what, finally, did it involve? Accordingly, I decided to question a lecturer on the *Flower Garland Scripture*. He replied: "You must contemplate the unimpeded interpenetration of all phenomena." He entreated me further: "If you merely contemplate your own mind and do not contemplate the unimpeded interfusion of all phenomena, you will never gain the perfect qualities of the fruition of Buddhahood."

I did not answer, but thought silently to myself: "If you use the mind to contemplate phenomena, those phenomena will become impediments, and you will have needlessly disturbed your own mind; when then would there be a resolution of this situation? But if the mind is brightened and your wisdom purified, then one hair and all the universe will be interfused, for there is, perforce, nothing that is outside the mind." I then retired into the mountains and sat reading through the *Tripiṭaka* in search of a passage that would confirm the mind doctrine of the Meditation school.

Three winters and summers passed before I came upon the simile about "one dust mote containing thousands of volumes of scriptures" in the *Ju-lai ch'u-hsien p'in* ("Appearance of the Thus Come Ones" chapter) of the *Flower Garland Scripture*. Later in the same passage the summation said: "The wisdom of the Thus Come Ones is just like this: it is complete in the bodies of all sentient beings. It is merely all these ordinary, foolish people who are not aware of it and do not recognize it."[38] I put the scripture volume on my head in reverence and, unwittingly, began to weep.

As I was still unclear about the initial access to faith that was appropriate for ordinary people of today, however, I reread the explanation of the Elder Li T'ung-hsüan [635–730] of the first level of the ten faiths in his *Hsin Hua-yen ching lun* (Exposition of the Flower Garland Scripture). It said: "Chief of Enlightenment Bodhisattva has three realizations. First, he realizes that his own body and mind are originally the dharma realm because they are immaculate, pure, and untainted. Second, he realizes that the discriminative nature of his own body and mind is originally free from the subject/object dichotomy and is originally the Buddha of Unmoving Wisdom. Third, he realizes that his own mind's sublime wisdom, which can distinguish the genuine from the distorted, is Mañjuśrī. He realizes these three things at the first level of faith and comes to be known as Chief of Enlightenment."[39]

It says elsewhere: "The difficulties a person encounters in entering into the ten faiths from the ordinary state are due to the fact that he completely accepts that he is an ordinary man; he is unwilling to accept that his own mind is the Buddha of Unmoving Wisdom."[40]

It also says: "The body is the reflection of wisdom. This world is the same. When wisdom is pure and its reflection clear, large and small merge with one another as in the realm of Indra's net."[41]

Thereupon, I set aside the volume and, breathing a long sigh, said: "What the World-Honored One said with his mouth are the teachings. What the patriarchs transmitted with their minds is Meditation.[42] The mouth of the Buddha and the minds of the patriarchs can certainly not be contradictory. How can students of both Meditation and Doctrinal schools not plumb the fundamental source but instead, complacent in their own training, wrongly foment disputes and waste their time?" From that time on, I have continued to build my mind of faith and have cultivated diligently without indolence; a number of years have already passed.

I say to men who are cultivating the mind that first, through the

path of the patriarchs, they should know the original sublimity of
their own minds and should not be bound by words and letters. Next,
through the text of Li T'ung-hsüan's *Exposition,* they should ascertain
that the essence and function of the mind are identical to the nature
and characteristics of the dharma realm. Then, the quality of the
unimpeded interpenetration between all phenomena and the merit of
the wisdom and compassion that have the same essence as that of all
the buddhas will not be beyond their capacity. Accordingly, whenever
there is time free from sitting meditation, I always explain this *Exposition* to my fellow trainees.

The text of the *Exposition* is awkward and inelegant, however,
while its content is extensive and broad in scope; it is difficult to
expound. Furthermore, the ideas it criticizes are not apprehensible by
those of ordinary capacity. Hence it has not been popular in the world.
Nevertheless, from the standpoint of sentient beings of great mental
capacity, its approach of entering into awakening through the complete and sudden teachings is unsurpassed as a mirror of the mind.

Accordingly, I committed all my energies and devoted myself to
my task; after offering incense and beseeching the Buddha's assistance,
I excerpted a summary of the important points in the forty chapters of
the *Exposition* and compiled it in three rolls. I charged my disciple, the
Meditation adept Ch'ungdam, with taking up a collection for the
enterprise of carving and printing the woodblocks so that the text
would be transmitted without interruption.

You who read these excerpts should put to rest all contentious
disputes and, allaying your concern with the body, contemplate on
your own until you attain in one thought-moment the nonproduction
of conditioned origination. Cutting yourselves free from the net of
views of the conventional teachings of the three vehicles, continue to
explain your understanding to others. Then you will receive benefits
for an eternity of aeons and will ensure that the lineage of the buddhas
and patriarchs will continue forever unbroken. How could this not be
the aspiration of great men?

The commentator's personal name was T'ung-hsüan; his surname
was Li. Some say that he was a descendant of the T'ang royal family;
others say that he was a native of Ts'ang-chou. It is impossible to
learn any details.

Chang T'ien-chüh's record says: "This elder was apparently a manifestation of Mañjuśrī or Samantabhadra. While the elder lived in the
world, a docile tiger carried the *Exposition* and numinous dragons

conjured up springs. During the daytime, heavenly maidens acted as his attendants; in the evenings, a glow from his teeth served in place of a lamp. These and other phenomena are all included among the subsidiary affairs of sages and saints and the eternal principles of spiritual response. What tradition calls 'the child conceived by the mother of cultivation' is similar to this. Now, summarizing these events, I have not written them all down."[43] RB

Chinul: Straight Talk on the True Mind
[From *Hanguk pulgyo chŏnsŏ* 4:715c–716b]

CHINUL'S PREFACE

QUESTION: Can the sublime path of the patriarchs be known?

CHINUL: Hasn't this already been explained by the ancients? "The path is not related to knowing or not knowing. Knowing is a false thought; not knowing is blankness. If you have truly penetrated to the realm that is free of doubt and as vast and spacious as the immensity of space, then how could you go to so much trouble to make such discriminations?"[44]

QUESTION: But does this mean that sentient beings do not benefit from the patriarchs' appearance in the world?

CHINUL: When the buddhas and patriarchs "showed their heads," they had no teachings to offer men. They only wanted sentient beings to see their original nature for themselves. The *Flower Garland Scripture* says: "You should know that all dharmas are the own-nature of the mind. The perfection of the wisdom body does not come from any other awakening."[45] For this reason, the buddhas and patriarchs didn't let people get snared in words and letters; they only wanted them to put deluded thought to rest and see the original mind. This is why when people entered Te-shan's room he struck them with his staff,[46] or when people entered Lin-chi's room he shouted.[47] We have all groped too long already for our heads;[48] why should we set up more words and language?

QUESTION: We have heard that in the past Aśvaghoṣa wrote the *Awakening of Faith*;[49] the Sixth Patriarch Hui-neng expounded the *Platform Scripture*;[50] and Huang-mei transmitted the *Perfection of Wisdom* texts;[51] these all were efforts involving a sequential approach for the sake of men. How can it be right that you alone have no expedients regarding the dharma?

CHINUL: At the summit of Mount Sumeru, ratiocination has been forbidden since long ago; but at the top of the second peak all the patriarchs have tolerated verbal understanding.[52]

QUESTION: Can we dare to pray that from the summit of this second peak you will bestow on us a few simple expedients?

CHINUL: Your words are correct. And yet the great path is mysterious and vast; it neither exists nor does not exist. The true mind is arcane and subtle; it is free from thought and abstraction. Hence even if people who haven't been able to enter into this state should peruse the teachings of five thousand volumes of the *Tripiṭaka,* it would not be enough. But if those who have perceived the true mind say merely one word in allusion to it, it is already surplus dharma. Today, without being apprehensive about my eyebrows,[53] I have respectfully written a few sections to shed light on the true mind, in the hope that they will serve as a basis and program for entering the path. This will do by way of introduction.

RIGHT FAITH IN THE TRUE MIND

CHINUL: In the *Flower Garland Scripture* we can read:

> Faith is the fountainhead of the path and the mother of all
> meritorious qualities.
> It nourishes all wholesome faculties.[54]

Also the Consciousness-Only texts say: "Faith is like a crystal that can purify cloudy water."[55] It is clear that faith is the vanguard in the development of the myriads of wholesome qualities. For this reason the Buddhist scriptures always begin with "Thus I heard . . . ," which is an expression intended to arouse faith.

QUESTION: What difference is there between faith in the Meditation and Doctrinal schools?

CHINUL: There are many kinds of differences. The Doctrinal schools encourage men and gods to have faith in the law of karmic cause and effect. Those who desire the pleasures that come from merit must have faith that the ten wholesome actions are the sublime cause and that human or deva rebirth is the pleasurable result. Those who feel drawn to the void-calmness of nirvana must have faith that its primary

cause is the understanding of the cause and conditions of arising and
ceasing and that its holy fruition is the understanding of the Four
Noble Truths: suffering, its origin, its extinction, and the path leading
to its extinction. Those who would delight in the fruition of Buddhahood should have faith that the practice of the six perfections over
three infinite aeons is its major cause and that *bodhi* and nirvana are its
right fruition.

Right faith in the patriarchal school of Meditation is different. It
does not believe in any conditioned causes or effects. Rather, it stresses
faith that oneself is originally a buddha; that all people possess the
impeccable self-nature; and that the sublime essence of nirvana is
complete in everyone. There is no need to search elsewhere, for since
time immemorial these have been innate in everyone. As the Third
Patriarch said:

> The mind is full like all of space,
> Without deficiency or excess.
> It is due primarily to grasping and rejection,
> That it is now not so.[56]

Chih-kung said:

> The signless body exists within the body which has signs,
> The road to the unborn is found along the road of ignorance.[57]

Yung-chia said:

> The true nature of ignorance is the Buddha nature.
> The void, phantom body is the dharma body.[58]

Hence we can know that sentient beings are originally buddhas.

Once we have given rise to right faith we must add understanding
to it. As Yung-ming [Yen-shou; 904–975] said: "To have faith but no
understanding increases ignorance; to have understanding but no faith
increases wrong views." Consequently, we know that once faith and
understanding are merged, entrance onto the path will be swift.

QUESTION: Is there any benefit that accrues solely from the initial
arousing of faith even though we are not yet able to enter the path?

CHINUL: The *Awakening of Faith* says: "If a person hears this
dharma without feeling fainthearted, it should be known that this man
will surely perpetuate the spiritual family of the Buddha and will
receive prediction of his future Buddhahood from all the buddhas.
Even if there were a man who could convert all the sentient beings

throughout the world systems of this trichiliocosm and induce them to practice the ten wholesome actions, it is not as good as a man who can rightly consider this dharma for a period the length of one meal. It is beyond analogy just how much it exceeds the previous merit."[59]

Furthermore, it is said in the *Perfection of Wisdom Scripture:* "And if they give rise to one thought of pure faith, the Thus Come One fully knows and sees this; through this faith, all of those sentient beings gain incalculable merit."[60] We know that if we want to travel for a thousand *ri* it is essential that the first step be right; if the first step is off, we will be off for the entire thousand *ri*. To enter the unconditioned kingdom, it is essential that our initial faith be right, for if that initial faith is wrong, we will move away from the myriads of wholesome actions. The Third Patriarch said:

> One iota of difference,
> And heaven and earth are rent asunder.[61]

This is the principle we are discussing here. RB

Chinul: Secrets on Cultivating the Mind
[From *Hanguk pulgyo chŏnsŏ* 4:708b–c, 709c–710a]

The triple world is blazing in defilement as if it were a house on fire.[62] How can you bear to tarry here and complacently undergo such long suffering? If you wish to avoid wandering on in samsara, there is no better way than to seek Buddhahood. If you want to become a buddha, you should understand that buddha is the mind; how can you search for the mind in the far distance? It is not outside the body. The physical body is a phantom, for it is subject to birth and death; the true mind is like space, for it neither ends nor changes. Therefore, it is said: "These hundred bones will crumble and return to fire and wind, but One Thing is eternally numinous and covers heaven and earth."[63]

It is tragic. People have been deluded for so long. They do not recognize that their own minds are the true buddhas. They do not recognize that their own natures are the true dharma. They want to search for the dharma, and yet they still go far away looking for holy ones. They want to search for the Buddha, and yet they will not observe their own minds. If they aspire to the path of Buddhahood while obstinately holding on to their feeling that the Buddha is outside the mind or that the dharma is outside the nature, then, even though they pass through aeons as numerous as dust motes, burning their bodies, charring their arms, crushing their bones, and exposing their marrow, or else writing scriptures with their own blood, never lying down to sleep, eating only one offering a day at the hour of the hare (5–7 A.M.), or even studying through the entire *Tripiṭaka* and cultivating all sorts of ascetic practices, it will all be like trying to make rice by boiling sand—it will only add to their tribulation.[64] If they would only understand their own minds, then, without searching, approaches to dharma as numerous as the sands of the Ganges and uncountable sublime meanings would all be understood. As the World-Honored One said: "I see that all sentient beings everywhere are endowed with a Thus Come One's wisdom and virtue."[65] He also said: "All the illusory guises in which sentient beings appear take shape in the sublime mind of the Thus Come One's complete enlightenment."[66] Consequently, you should know that outside of this mind there is no Buddhahood that can be attained. All the buddhas of the past were merely persons who understood their minds. All the sages and saints of the present are also just persons who have cultivated their minds. All future cultivators should rely on this dharma too.

I hope that all of you who cultivate the path will never search outside. The nature of the mind is unstained and is originally whole and complete in itself. If you will only leave behind false conditioning, you will be "such" like the Buddha.[67] . . .

QUESTION: You have said that this twofold approach of sudden awakening/gradual cultivation is the track followed by the thousands of saints. But if awakening is really sudden awakening, then what need is there for gradual cultivation? And if cultivation means gradual cultivation, then how can you talk about sudden awakening? We hope that you will expound on these two ideas of sudden and gradual some more and resolve our remaining doubts.

CHINUL: First, sudden awakening. When the ordinary man is deluded, he assumes that the four great elements are his body and the false thoughts are his mind. He does not know that his own nature is the true dharma body; he does not know that his own numinous awareness is the true Buddha. He looks for the Buddha outside of his mind. While he is thus wandering around aimlessly, the entrance to the road might by chance be pointed out by a wise adviser. If in one thought he traces back the light of his mind to its source and sees his own original nature, he would discover that the ground of this nature is innately free of defilement and that he himself is originally endowed with the nonoutflow wisdom nature, which is not a hair's breadth different from that of all the buddhas. Hence it is called sudden awakening.

Next, gradual cultivation. Although he has awakened to the fact that his original nature is no different from that of the buddhas, as the beginningless habit energies are extremely difficult to remove suddenly, he must continue to cultivate while relying on this awakening. Through this gradual permeation, his endeavors reach completion. He constantly nurtures the sacred embryo and, after a long time, becomes a saint. Hence it is called gradual cultivation.

This process can be compared to the maturation of a child. From the day of his birth, a baby is endowed with all the sense organs just like everyone else, but his strength is not yet fully developed. It is only after the passing of many months and years that he will finally become an adult. RB

Hyesim: Preface to Collection of the Meditation School's Explanatory Verses
[From *Hanguk pulgyo chŏnsŏ* 5:1a–b]

Now, since the time of Kāśyapa, the World-Honored One,[68] and continuing generation after generation, the light of the patriarchs' lamp has never been extinguished, and the secret entrustment of the Meditation school has been passed on consecutively; this is considered to be the orthodox transmission of Meditation. While this orthodox transmission and secret entrustment are not deficient in words and meanings, words and meanings are insufficient to reach them. Therefore, although the Meditation teachings are expounded, the patriarchs of Meditation do not establish words and letters: the mind is transmitted with the mind, and that is all.

Those who appreciate this matter of Meditation have contrived to record its traces. Entering it into records and documents, Meditation has been transmitted up to the present, but these coarse traces are certainly not worthy of honor. Nevertheless, such writings do not hinder one from following the flow to reach the fountainhead or relying on the branches to know the roots. Even though one who reaches the original fountainhead discusses the myriads of distinctions, he never misses the mark; but even if one who has not reached it excises all language and guards that fountainhead in silence, he is never unconfused. For this reason, venerable masters in all regions do not abandon words and letters and are not niggardly with their loving-

kindness and compassion. Whether through verification or maintenance, whether in succession or separately, whether in verse or in
song, they disseminate the profound intent of Meditation in order to
bequeath it to posterity. Thus, how could one who abandons these
teachings—but nevertheless wishes to open the correct eye of dharma,
perfect the arcane mechanism, enwrap the three worlds, and rescue
the four types of beings—possibly succeed?

Moreover, since its ancestor-saint (Wang Kŏn) united the Later
Three Kingdoms, our native dynasty of Koryŏ has used the path of
Meditation to extend the blessings of the kingdom. While wise discourse has suppressed neighboring troops, nothing is of more concern
than the booty of awakening to the source and discoursing on the
path. Hence, students who approach the Meditation school are like
thirsters longing for drink or starvers ruminating on food.

Receiving the compelling request of adherents, I reflected upon the
original intent of the patriarchs and saints so as to offer merit to the
kingdom and benefit to the Buddha's teachings. I then commanded
my disciple Chinhun and others to compile a total of eleven hundred
and twenty-five cases of ancient exchanges, together with the "finger-
ing verses" (yŏmsong)[69] and other spoken essentials of all the masters.
This has been recorded in thirty rolls in order to sustain the transmission of the lamp.

This I hope: May the wind of Yao and that of Meditation blow
forever. May the sun of Shun, together with the sun of the Buddha,
shine perpetually. May the seas be calm and the rivers clear. May the
season be peaceful and the year fruitful. May all things find their
rightful places. May every home be harmonious and enjoy perfect
freedom. May all trifling thoughts be devoted solely to this and nothing else.

I regret, however, that I have not yet been able to peruse completely the records of the words of all the houses of Meditation, and I
fear that there may be omissions. Those things that have not yet been
covered must wait for later sages. RB

Hyesim: Letter in Reply to Ch'oe Hongyun
[From Hanguk pulgyo chŏnsŏ 6:46c–47b]

In the past, I worked in the magistrature, but the magistrates
have now entered my religious society.[70] The magistrates are the
Buddhist Confucians, but I am a Confucian Buddhist. We have be-

come the guests and hosts of one another and call ourselves masters or
disciples. This has been the case since of old: it is not something that
has only now begun. If one acknowledges just their names, Buddhism
and Confucianism are dramatically different. If one knows their core,
Confucianism and Buddhism are without distinction.

Don't you see? Confucius said: "I have no idea [foregone conclu-
sions]; I have no 'I' [egotism]; I have no stability [obstinacy]; I have
no decisiveness [arbitrary predeterminations]."[71] Layman Wu-chin[72]
commenting upon this, said: "Now, if there is no idea, then there
must be a true idea preserving it. If there is no 'I,' then there must be
a true 'I' overseeing it. If there is no stability, then there must be a true
stability regulating it. If there is no decisiveness, then there must be a
true decisiveness maintaining it. The true idea requites the myriads of
transformations, but remains undisturbed. The true 'I' controls the
varieties of actions, but remains unagitated. The true stability appears
within birth and death, but remains unaffected. The true decisiveness
decides all types of intent, but remains unconfused. The saints and
sages live by this and die by this; they become poor and ignominious
by this. It might be considered 'white jade,' but if you prefer to call it
stone, that is all right. It might be considered 'pure gold,' but if you
prefer to call it lead, that is all right. They might be considered sages
and saints, but if you prefer to consider them malevolent demons, that
is all right."

Wu-chin's words really struck home. The so-called true idea, true
"I," true stability, and true decisiveness are all described according to
the exigencies of the moment; hence, while there may be four terms,
if they are discussed while probing their core, they are clearly without
any separate essence. Rather, every person's essence of mind, which is
free from thought (*munyŏm*), is not produced due to conditions, nor
does it arise based on the sense spheres; it is void but numinous,
quiescent but radiant; it unifies the myriads of phenomena and pervades all the ten directions; it continues through past and present,
neither excised nor extinguished—this is what it is. The Buddha said:
"Mahākāśyapa, I have permanently extinguished the consciousness
faculty, but the knowing awareness that is perfectly clear does not
depend upon mental states or thoughts." Is this not what Wu-chin
called the true idea? Forgetting the "I," one can achieve the great "I."
Is this not the true "I"? Even though your form be destroyed and your
life force brought to an end, how can this nature be destroyed or
extinguished? Is this not true stability? The saintly wisdom is perfectly

clear and deliberate. Is this not true decisiveness? The *Ch'i shih-chieh ching* (Origination of the World Scripture) says: "The Buddha said, 'I dispatched two saints to China to disseminate my religion. The first was Lao Tzu, who was the Bodhisattva Mahākāśyapa; the second was Confucius, who was the Bodhisattva Mānava.' "[73] According to this passage, the schools of Confucianism and Taoism have their source in Buddhism; while their conventions might be different, their core is identical.

Confucius said: "Shen! My Way has one thread that runs right through it."[74] He also said: "In the morning, hear the Way; in the evening, die content."[75] This so-called Way thus strings together the myriads of phenomena; it is that which is neither destroyed nor extinguished. Since he knew that the Way was neither destroyed nor extinguished, he confided: "In the evening, die content." I do not know what the prime minister thinks about this. If your faith is sufficient, then you will accord with the adage of the Great Master Ma-tsu: "Mind is Buddha, but it is neither mind nor Buddha."[76] Reflect carefully upon this all the time: this is the method leading to penetrating realization and penetrating awakening.   RB

Publication of the Tripiṭaka

The first orally redacted Buddhist canons are presumed to have been compiled in India shortly after the Buddha's death. The Chinese compiled their own manuscript canons early in the history of their own Buddhist tradition, and such canons were soon introduced into Korea. With the invention of xylographic printing techniques, a complete woodblock canon was carved in China during the tenth century, and the first Koryŏ canon, a similar project, was begun in 1011.

The Buddhist canons of East Asia were open collections, which permitted dramatic expansions in coverage when compared to their Indian counterparts. The monk Ŭich'ŏn (1055–1101) had the most liberal outlook toward the canon. Earlier Chinese Buddhist bibliographic cataloguers defined canonicity primarily in terms of translations of Indian materials. But Ŭich'ŏn believed that East Asian exegetes and authors also had made seminal contributions to Buddhist thought that warranted inclusion in the canon. Ŭich'ŏn feared that unless the canon were opened to such indigenous works, these were doomed to drop from circulation and would be lost to posterity.

To prevent such a fate, Uich'ŏn sent agents throughout East Asia to procure Buddhist texts by native authors. In 1090, he published his catalog of this collection, which listed some 1,010 titles in 4,740 rolls. Woodblocks for each of these texts were carved, and the collection was termed a *Supplement to the Canon (Sokchanggyŏng)*. Unfortunately, the woodblocks of the first Koryŏ canon and its supplement were burned during the Mongol invasion in 1231. While the main canon was recarved between 1236 and 1251, the *Supplement* was not. As Uich'ŏn had feared, most of the texts collected in his *Supplement* were lost to history; only his catalog of that collection has survived, the preface to which is translated in the first selection.

The Koryŏ government actively supported Buddhism, and the most dramatic expression of state-sponsored Buddhist activities was the printing of the *Tripiṭaka,* the Buddhist canon. Centuries earlier, Buddhist devotion and advances in printing had already been linked. With the recent discovery of a copy of a *dhāraṇī* scripture dating from before 751, Silla claims the oldest extant example of woodblock printing in the world.

A printing of the *Tripiṭaka* in woodblocks was undertaken on two separate occasions. The first blocks were started in 1011 in the midst of Khitan attacks. Koreans believed that the publication of the *Tripiṭaka* would invoke the divine protection of the Buddha, sparing Koryŏ from further attacks. This project lasted nearly seventy years. When the Mongols invaded in the thirteenth century, Koryŏ once again turned to aid from the Buddha with the second manufacture of the *Tripiṭaka* in woodblocks. The eighty-one thousand separate blocks completed at this time can still be seen at Haein Monastery in south central Korea.

This last production of the *Tripiṭaka,* in the middle of the Mongol invasions, attracted considerable attention. In the second passage, "Kojong's Rescript to Ch'oe Hang," King Kojong (1213–1259) discusses his indebtedness to the Ch'oe rulers for their support of this huge undertaking. The king was certain that the fruitful completion of the *Tripiṭaka* would bring blessings to the military rulers and peace to Koryŏ. In the third selection presented here, Yi Kyubo, reflecting on the significance of this project, believes that publishing the *Tripiṭaka* will guarantee the safety of the nation. The publication of the *Tripiṭaka* demonstrated the faith of the Koreans and their belief in the power of the Buddha to afford them divine protection. It is also another clear example of the technological sophistication of a people who could carry out such a mammoth project while fighting a terrible war. RB/HK

Ŭich'ŏn: Preface to a New Catalog of the Teachings of All the Schools
[From *Taegak kuksa munjip* 1:3a–4b]

Since the Yung-p'ing era [A.D. 58–75] of the Han, palm-leaf writings from India have continued to arrive in East Asia, and their translations have circulated—there has been no age during which such activities have not taken place. Down through the Chen-kuan era [627–649], there have been great collections made of scriptures and treatises. The teachings of the Western Saint (the Buddha) are still flourishing, and nothing can hinder them.

From Nieh Tao-chen[77] and Tao-an[78] to Ming-ch'üan[79] and the Vinaya Master Tao-hsüan,[80] bibliographers have each compiled catalogs such as the so-called *Chin-lu* (Chin Dynasty Catalog),[81] *Wei-lu* (Wei Dynasty Catalog),[82] and so forth. The same text might appear differently in the various catalogs, however, and an earlier entry might have a new title. There is much confusion about the text of a scripture, and whether it is authentic or spurious remains in doubt. A certain scripture might appear in two recensions, or a section or chapter might be entered in the catalogs as an "alternate translation" (*pyŏlbon*). Thus the forty or so experts were long confused.

During the K'ai-yüan era [713–741], a great Dharma Master, whose cognomen was Chih-sheng [669–740], finally corrected the mistakes and errors of previous catalogers, condensed the repetition, and compiled all his material into one book, entitled *K'ai-yüan Shih-chiao lu* (K'ai-yüan Catalog of the Buddhist Scriptures),[83] in a total of twenty rolls. This was the most seminal of all the catalogs, and critics have considered that it established the pedigree of the scriptural teachings. None was the equal of Chih-sheng's catalog, and none surpassed its achievement in preserving the bequeathed teachings of the Buddha.

While the *K'ai-yüan Catalog* includes scriptures and treatises translated from Indian languages but omits some of the tracts and commentaries of East Asian authors, I was concerned lest these latter have no chance of being disseminated. Hence, while adulating the venerable Chih-sheng's determination to protect the dharma, I have considered it my own duty to track down the traces of the teachings. For almost twenty years now, I have been diligent about this quest and have never abandoned it. I have put in order these new and old compositions, these illustrious treatises of all the schools, which I have recovered; unwilling to keep them private, today I publish them. Should there be other texts that might be found subsequently, I also want to continue to record them here. Ultimately, these compiled listings, as well as the cases and covers of the works included, together with the actual text of the *Tripiṭaka* collection itself, will be handed down without interruption throughout the future. Then my vow will be fulfilled. RB

Kojong's Rescript to Ch'oe Hang
[From *Koryŏ sa* 129:49b–50b]

Tan and Shih helped Chou; Hsiao and Ts'ao assisted Han.[84] The lord and subjects rely on each other. From the past to the present, it has been the same. Lord Chinyang Ch'oe I [d. 1249], from the time my late father ascended the throne until I became king, has protected the dynastic shrines, and together with his virtue he has helped me rule. Earlier, in 1231, when the generals in charge of border defense failed to protect the nation, allowing the Mongol troops to invade, with a remarkable plan he single-handedly made decisions, cutting off endless debates by high-ranking officials. Personally he helped the royal chariot, and through divination he selected a site for the new capital. In no time, palaces and government buildings were all built, the orders issued by the authorities were restored, and thus the government was revived.

The *Tripiṭaka,* however, which had been passed down and had warded off enemy troops, was completely destroyed by invading forces. Because the country experienced many problems, there was no time to make a new one, and so he separately established an office, and, using personal funds, he completed nearly half the woodblocks. We cannot forget his meritorious contributions that brought benefits to the nation.

Chancellor Hang [d. 1257], the rightful heir, inheriting his father's work, guided me, his lord, in checking difficulties. By providing funds and overseeing the work, he brought to a finish the *Tripiṭaka.* By holding Buddhist services in praise of Buddha's virtue,[85] he extended blessing all over the country. He set up battleships at strategic points in the waterways, and at Kanghwa he built a palace. Moreover in Kanghwa he has constructed an inner fortification so secure that the city is impregnable, making it reliable for ever.

However, I have been ill at ease for not setting up the dynastic shrine earlier when we first came to Kanghwa due to unsettled conditions. Command retainer Pak Sŏngsin to be supervisor of the corvée. Generally, as hundreds of expenses have all come from Ch'oe Hang's private funds, he has completed meritorious deeds in no time. As the system is in order, this is great meritorious service that is rare indeed. I greatly commend him and order the government to establish a new administrative district to enfeoff him with it. I also order the government to confer posthumously additional titles on his father and mother and to promote his two sons. And from Pak Sŏngsin to artisans, reward all according to rank. HK/ES

Yi Kyubo: Royal Prayer on the Occasion of the Production of the *Tripiṭaka*
[From *Tongguk Yi sangguk chip* 25:18b–20a]

I, King Kojong [1213–1259], together with the crown prince, dukes, lords, counts, state councillors, and civil and military officials, have respectfully cleansed our bodies and souls and pray to all the buddhas and bodhisattvas everywhere in the infinite void and from the Sakradevanam Indra to all the spirit-officials who protect the dharma in the thirty-three heavens.

Severe indeed is the calamity caused by the Tartars. The nature of their cruelty and vindictiveness is beyond description. With foolishness and stupidity greater than that of beasts, how could they know what is respected in this world and what is called the laws of Buddha? Because of this ignorance there was not a Buddhist image or Buddhist writing that they did not entirely destroy. Accordingly the woodblocks of the *Tripiṭaka* stored at Puin Monastery also were swept away without leaving a trace, alas! The achievements of many years were reduced to ashes in no time. It was the loss of a great national treasure! But if this can be endured by the various bodhisattvas and heavenly deities, what cannot be endured?

In examining ourselves, we, the disciples of Buddha, find that we were unwise and naive so that we did not have a plan of defense and our strength was incapable of protecting completely the teachings of Buddha, causing the loss of those great treasures. Truly this is because of our lack of merit and good conduct. Naturally we regret this. But the teachings of Buddha cannot themselves be destroyed. Only that which contains them can be destroyed. Whether the container gets destroyed or not is often a matter of chance. When it is destroyed, it should be reproduced. Moreover, as a state that worships Buddhist law, when we do not have this great treasure we certainly cannot be content with its loss. How can we hesitate over its reproduction on account of the enormity of such an undertaking? Now, together with the officials of the Privy Council and the rest of the civil and military officers, we have made this great vow and set up offices to take charge of this undertaking.

If we look at the first printing of the *Tripiṭaka* in the second year of King Hyŏnjong's reign [1011], the Khitans invaded with a large force, causing the king to flee south to avoid capture. When the Khitan troops occupied the capital and did not retreat, the king, together with ranking officials, made a truly great vow, promising to carve the *Tripiṭaka* in woodblocks. Thereupon, the Khitan troops withdrew of their own accord. Since there is only one true *Tripiṭaka,* the earlier and later carvings to produce it should be no different, just as the vows made by the kings and officials should also be the same. If the earlier undertaking succeeded in getting the Khitans to withdraw on their own, why would not the present undertaking accomplish the same with the Tartars now? It should depend only on the favor extended by the various buddhas of the many heavens.

As we are truly sincere in our prayer, we have nothing to be ashamed of before our ancestors. Therefore, we humbly pray that the various buddhas and sages in the thirty-three heavens receive our earnest prayers, extend to us divine power, cause the stubborn and vile barbarians to flee far away, and never again let them enter our territory. When the fighting ceases and peace prevails all over, may the queen dowager and crown prince enjoy long life forever and may Korea's good fortune last ten thousand years. Then we, your disciples, through our work will try to protect Buddhism even more and repay even a tiny proportion of our obligations. We pray with utmost sincerity and humbly hope you will answer these prayers. HK/ES

CHAPTER TWELVE

Popular Beliefs and Confucianists

Koryŏ was eclectic in its religious beliefs. Apart from Buddhism, native beliefs, geomancy, shamanism, Taoism, and Neo-Confucianism provided spiritual and intellectual sustenance. The native beliefs involved respect for the deities and guardians of the land. Throughout Koryŏ, people called upon these spirits to defend them against foreign invaders as well as against internal forces of destruction. Geomancy, the belief that topography can dictate one's fortunes, was also widely accepted, giving rise to the notion that undesirable disturbances to the natural environment could cause unrest. Many of these ideas blended with Buddhism and became an integral part of the Koryŏ religious world.

Taoism, originally a Chinese philosophy advocating freedom from man-made constraints and the pursuit of nature, became popular among various segments of society. To the government official, it offered an escape from the restrictive confinement of public life; to the peasant, it offered closer links with the natural order. Shamanism, the belief that spirits inhabit every object in the world and accordingly influence individual destiny, was yet another form of Koryŏ spiritual experience. Taken together, all of these practices influenced the lives of Koryŏ people, providing them with spiritual strength to confront the vicissitudes of life.

The growth of Neo-Confucianism in Sung China eventually influenced Koryŏ's Confucian heritage. With the growing distaste for

Buddhism and a desire for a more rigorous philosophical base for needed reform, scholars of late Koryŏ studied Neo-Confucian treatises on human nature and applied their new learning to societal reform, laying the philosophical foundation for the rise of the Chosŏn kingdom (1392–1910).

Native Beliefs

Aside from the state-sanctioned Confucianism and Buddhism, indigenous religious practices also functioned in an environment influenced by shamanism and geomancy. These native traditions had been expressed since Korea's earliest times through religion, art, music, and dance, and later many of these native impulses gradually found their way into Buddhism and divination theory. The test of any culture is its ability to blend outside influences with indigenous ways, and the people of Koryŏ successfully adapted Confucianism, Buddhism, Taoism, and geomancy—all originally external philosophies—to their indigenous beliefs.

Shamanistic beliefs held that spirits dwelled in natural objects such as old trees, rivers, rocks, and mountains, and that these spirits controlled everyone's destiny. If these spirits were properly treated and worshiped, they would bring peace and benefits to everyone. In the first selection in this section, Yi Chibaek urges a spiritual defense against the Khitan attacks at the end of the tenth century by appealing to the major native deities of the land. We find in his statement a clear sense of the need to preserve the Korean native traditions.

Such defenses of native spirits and ritualistic ceremonies pervaded the dynasty. King Ŭijong, mid-Koryŏ's controversial monarch who was condemned by later historians for contributing inexcusably to the causes of the military coup of 1170, called for the restitution of such ceremonies as the Assembly of the Eight Prohibitions (*p'algwan hoe*) in the second passage. The *p'algwan,* originally a Buddhist celebration, was later transformed into an annual national festival to commemorate vows made to local spirits and was held in the two capitals, Kaesŏng and P'yŏngyang, in the eleventh and tenth lunar months, respectively. There was a pervasive belief that such celebrations would help ensure dynastic security and nationwide prosperity. Especially handsome young men were selected to oversee the observance of native traditions, reminiscent of the *hwarang* movement of Silla. The final selection presented discusses Min Yŏn (1269–1335), who lived during the period of Mongol domination and was chosen to be a *kuksŏn* ("national immortal," the practitioner of native traditions).

Yi Chibaek: Memorial on Territorial Integrity
[From *Koryŏ sa* 94:3a–b]

Since our august ancestor's inception of the dynasty, we have preserved our sovereignty to this day. Now, without a single loyal official voicing objection, we rashly want to surrender land to the enemy. Is this not lamentable indeed? The ancients had a poem:

> A vast territory is disposed of in a casual manner.
> The civil and military officials of the two courts reproached
>   Ch'iao Chou.

Ch'iao Chou was a great minister of Shu in China who urged his young ruler to give up land to Wei, thus becoming the joke of eternity.

I propose that we bribe Hsiao Sun-ning with gold, silver, and other treasures to discover his real intentions. And rather than rashly cutting off land and handing it over to appease an enemy, is it not better to renew practice of the Lantern Festival, the Assembly of the Eight Prohibitions, and the Immortal Lad to elicit spiritual protection,[1] as was done under our former kings? Is this not a better way to preserve the state and achieve peace than to resort to the strange practices of others? If we are to do this, we ought first to report to our deities. As to whether there be war or peace, Your Majesty alone should decide. HK/ES

King Ŭijong: Rescript on Native Traditions
[From *Koryŏ sa* 18:36b–37a]

Uphold the way of the immortals. In Silla times, the way of the immortals was widely practiced so that the dragon and heavenly protectors of Buddhist law were pleased and the people were at peace. Therefore, from the time of the dynastic progenitor on, we have upheld these traditions. Recently, the Assembly of the Eight Prohibitions in the two capitals has daily deteriorated from its former scale and quality, resulting in the gradual decline of the inherited traditions. From now on, in holding the Assembly of the Eight Prohibitions, first select from the civil and military services those of means and designate them preservers of native traditions. By practicing old native traditions, keep the people and heaven both happy. HK/ES

Practitioners of Native Traditions
[From *Koryŏ sa* 108:2b]

In the nation's customs, the young always learned how to read from Buddhist monks. And among the young, one who had good appearance was called the Immortal Lad (*sŏllang*) and was held in reverence by both monks and laymen. Those assembled around him sometimes reached hundreds or thousands. These customs started from Silla times. When Min Yŏn[2] [1269–1308] was ten, he went to a Buddhist temple to study. He was by nature intelligent, and when he read books, he immediately understood their meaning. His eyebrows were like those in a painting; his appearance was graceful. Those who saw him all adored him. When King Ch'ungnyŏl [1274–1308] heard of him, the king summoned the boy to court, making him *kuksŏn* (the practitioner of native traditions). When he passed the state examination, he was appointed to the Eastern Palace of the crown prince. HK/ES

Geomancy

Geomantic theories were popularized in Koryŏ by the works of the Buddhist monk Tosŏn (827–898), who enhanced their appeal through an infusion of Buddhist ideas. His application of the Buddhist theory of causation to geomancy led Wang Kŏn to state in his "Ten Injunctions" that the topography of his power base, Songak (Kaesŏng), had unequivocally determined his dynastic success. Following his political unification of the Later Three Kingdoms in 936, he built the Hwaŏm monastery Kaet'ae (Exalted Beginning) to demonstrate his gratitude and gain further spiritual protection. He personally wrote the first selection presented here in appreciation of the divine protective powers of Buddha and the local mountain spirits, to which he attributed his success. Some of his political confidants, such as Ch'oe Ŭng (898–932), citing Confucian texts, criticized Wang Kŏn for his continuing reliance on Buddhist and native religious practices. But the king defended his stance on the grounds that the hard reality of the unsettled conditions of the time demanded these practices, which were close to the people of the land.

Believing that the strength of the dynasty was tied to the topographical powers of the land, Koryŏ formally set up four capitals: the central capital at Kaesŏng, the western capital at P'yŏngyang, the southern capital at Seoul, and the eastern capital at Kyŏngju. Kaesŏng was chosen because of its geomantic centrality in the kingdom, as well as because it was Wang Kŏn's political and economic power base. Subsequent attempts to move the capital, often rooted in the desire for political gain, were always foiled on the basis of geomancy. At the end of the eleventh century, Kim Wije urged that the southern capital (modern Seoul) be built and enhanced in stature to assure the continued success of the dynasty. In making this plea, Kim cited several sources, including the work of the monk Tosŏn, which had gained even greater respect by then than it had in the monk's own time.

The most dramatic and ultimately for the dynasty the most dangerous attempt to move the capital occurred in the 1130s when a nationalistic firebrand, the monk Myoch'ŏng (d. 1135), led a rebellion to establish the primacy of the western capital, P'yŏngyang. Myoch'ŏng was a charismatic monk who captured the attention of the troubled King Injong (1122–1146) and quickly gained the monarch's confidence. Taking advantage of an unsettled political scene that had led to the burning of the royal palace by Yi Chagyŏm (d. 1126) in 1126, the persuasive monk convinced many that the central capital, Kaesŏng, had lost its geomantic vigor. To resuscitate the dynasty it was imperative, according to Myoch'ŏng, to move the capital north. When blocked by the central aristocrats, Myoch'ŏng revolted, calling not only for a new capital but also for a new direction in foreign policy that would challenge the domination of China proper, then in the hands of the Chin dynasty.

In the end, the central aristocrats rallied to defeat the rebellious forces under Myoch'ŏng in P'yŏngyang, but as the monk first gathered strength, scholars fought him with ink and brush. The final passage, by Im Wan (Lin Wan in Chinese), a Chinese who had passed the examination in Koryŏ and served as an official at King Injong's court, cites natural calamities as a warning to the king not to listen to Myoch'ŏng. Calling on ideas first drafted by such prominent Confucian scholars as Han China's Tung Chung-shu (179–104? B.C.), Im appealed to logic to counter Myoch'ŏng's emotional demands. Im Wan also recalled Wang Kŏn's "Ten Injunctions" and the activities of

Munjong's reign (1046–1083) to support his request for King Injong's reform and the removal of Myoch'ŏng from the court.

King T'aejo's Reliance on Buddhism
[From *Pohan chip* 1:1b–2a]

In my lifetime, I have encountered many worrisome difficulties and was unable to overcome many of them. Soldiers encircled Hyŏndo Commandery;[3] disaster racked Chinhan.[4] People had nothing to rely on for their livelihood, and houses lacked protection. . . . I pledged before heaven to suppress great evil forces, to rescue the people from their misery so they can be free to farm and make handicrafts in their own villages. Relying first on the power of Buddha and then on the authority of Taoism, I have engaged through more than two decades in sea attacks and fiery battles, personally risking bombardment by arrows and stones. Advancing a thousand *ri* to the south or to the east, I used my weapons as pillows. In the autumn of 936, around Sungsŏn fortress, I faced the troops of Later Paekche. On hearing one battle cry, the cruel enemy collapsed. With the second beat of the war drum, the rebels melted like ice. Triumphant songs floated to heaven, joyful sounds shook the land. . . . Thieves in the rushes and outlaws in the countryside repented and, wishing to make a new start, thought of surrendering to me. My intentions being to seize the bad and eliminate evil, aid the weak and help the dependent, I have not committed the smallest transgression or injured even a blade of grass. . . . In order to respond to the sustenance accorded by the Holy Buddha, to repay the support of the mountain spirits, I especially commanded the government offices concerned to construct a lotus palace (Buddhist monastery) and to name the mountain on which it sits Ch'ŏnho (Heavenly Protection) and the monastery Kaet'ae. . . . May Buddha's authority provide protection and heaven's power sustain me.   HK/ES

King T'aejo and Confucian Advice
[From *Pohan chip* 1:1a–b]

When King T'aejo was still fighting to consolidate his newly founded kingdom, he resorted to the ideas of yin/yang and Buddhism.

Counselor Ch'oe Ŭng [898–932] remonstrated, saying: "The *Tso Commentary* says, 'At the time of disorder, cultivate letters to gain the hearts of man.'[5] Even during warfare, the ruler must cultivate civil virtues. I have yet to hear of anyone relying on Buddhism or yin/yang ideas to win the world."

The king said: "How could I not know it? Yet, the mountains and streams of our country are divine and extraordinary. Set in an out-of-the-way place, far removed from China, Koreans by nature love Buddha and spirits and expect blessings and prosperity. These days, war never ceases, and peace is never certain. Day and night, the peasants are troubled and are at a loss as to what to do. I only think of the hidden help of Buddha and the spirits as well as the divine response of the mountains and streams in the hope that they may yield results through my indulgences. How could this not be the great principle of ruling the country to win the people? After we settle these conflicts and live in peace and justice, then we can change our ways and enlighten the people." HK/ES

Kim Wije: On the Selection of a Site for the Capital
[From *Koryŏ sa* 122:1a–3b]

In 1096, Kim Wije became the executive assistant of royal insignia (*wiwisŭng tongjŏng*). At the end of Silla, there was a monk called Tosŏn who went to T'ang to learn from I-hsing[6] the methods of geomancy and then returned. He wrote a secret book to pass on his knowledge of the methods. Wije studied these methods and presented a memorial to the king requesting that the capital be moved to the southern capital, saying:

"The *Tosŏn ki* (Record of Tosŏn) said: 'In Koryŏ there are three capitals. Songak (Kaesŏng) is to be the central capital, Mongmyŏng-yang (Seoul) the southern capital, and P'yŏngyang the western capital. If in the eleventh, twelfth, first, and second months the king resides in the central capital, in the third, fourth, fifth, and sixth months the king resides in the southern capital, and in the seventh, eighth, ninth, and tenth months the king resides in the western capital, then the thirty-six states of the world will offer tribute.' The book also said: 'One hundred and sixty years after the establishment of the kingdom, it will have the capital at Mongmyŏngyang.' I suggest that now is the right time to move and build a new capital.

"I humbly recall Tosŏn's song 'Climbing a Mountain,' which goes:

After Kaesŏng declines, where shall one go?

For three cold winter months, there is P'yŏngyang, where the
  sun shines.
When later worthies tap a great well,
The fish dragons from the Han River can travel to the four seas.

"The sun comes out for three winter months means that during the
second month of the winter season, the sun appears to the southeast,
and Mongmyŏngyang lies southeast of the central capital. That is why
there is this saying.

"The song also says: 'The one at Songak will become the ruler of
Chinhan and Mahan. Alas, who would know when it will begin and
when it will end? Stems of flowers are delicate like leaves on branches.
Even with a pledge that it would last for one hundred years, why
would it not fall? Even if one wishes later to find the new power of
flowers to regenerate the dynasty, his going out and crossing the river
to the north will be in vain. But if the divine fish of the four seas
assemble in the Han River, the country and the people will be at peace
and prosperous.' Therefore, if a capital is established north of the Han
River, the dynasty will last forever; and as the nations of the world
will come with tribute, the royal family will prosper, truly making
this capital the site of the great hall of royal audience.

"The song also states: 'If wise scholars of later generations, recognizing man's life span, should not cross the Han River, it will produce
such a trend for ten thousand generations. If one crosses the river and
starts a royal capital, the site will be torn apart at the middle and
divided by the Han River.' . . .

"Also the *Sinji pisa* (Divine Records and Secret Verses) says: 'The
weight of a balance beam, the part of the beam where the holder is
tied, the beam itself or the chains (*puso*) that hold the weighing plate,
and the end of the beam all together symbolize the land of the five
virtues. If Paegagang is made to be a balance beam, then seventy states
will come in submission, bringing tribute with them. Through the
efforts of this auspicious site, it will protect the spirit. If you make the
beginning and end clear and are evenhanded throughout, the nation
will prosper and peace will prevail. If one abolishes the land of the
three edicts, the dynasty will decline.'

"This is using the scale to illustrate the three capitals. That is to say,
the part where a holder is tied is the head, the weight of the balance is
the tail, and the balance beam itself is the most essential point. Since
Songak is the chains that hold the plate, it is a simile for the scale.

Whereas the western capital is Paegagang, it is a simile for the head of the scale. As south of Mount Samgak (in Seoul) is the hill of the five virtues, it is a simile for the weight of the scale. As to the five virtues, at the center is Myŏnak (Plane Surface Peak), which is circular and symbolizes the power of the earth element. To the north is Kamak (Purple Peak), which is crooked and symbolizes the power of the water element. To the south is Kwanak (Cap Peak), which is sharply pointed and symbolizes the power of the fire element. To the east is Mount Namhaeng (Going South) in Yangju, which is straight and symbolizes the power of the wood element; to the west is Pugak (North Peak) in Suju, which is square and symbolizes the power of the metal element. These also coincide with the meaning of Tosŏn's three capitals. Our country today has central and western capitals but lacks a southern capital. I humbly hope that in the flat land south of Mount Samgak and north of Mount Mongmyŏk Your Majesty will build a capital and periodically visit there. As this is truly related to the future of the dynasty, I dare risk the taboo and present this."

Thereupon the diviner Mun Sang agreed and supported it.

In King Yejong's time [1105–1122], Ŭn Wŏnjung, using Tosŏn's explanations, also presented a memorial discussing this. HK/ES

Monk Myoch'ŏng's Use of Geomancy
[From *Koryŏ sa* 127:26b–29b]

Myoch'ŏng [d. 1135] was a monk in the Western Capital who later changed his name to Chŏngsin. In 1128, the diviner Paek Suhan [d. 1135], as honorary deputy director in the Office of Royal Lectures in the Western Capital, asked Myoch'ŏng to be his teacher. The two men used the secret art of yin/yang to delude the people. Chŏng Chisang [d. 1135] was also a person of the Western Capital who deeply believed their practices. He felt that the foundation of the main dynastic capital was already weakened as the palace had burned completely, leaving nothing, that the Western Capital had the royal essence, and that the king ought to move to P'yŏngyang, making it his main capital.

Then with the royal confidant and Office Chief of the Palace Attendants Kim An [d. 1135], they plotted, saying: "If we urge the king to move his chariot to the Western Capital and make it the main capital, we will become merit officials of the restoration. It will not only bring us wealth and prestige but also give our descendants endless blessings." Accordingly, they voiced this plan openly, congratulating each other.

Royal advisers Hong Isŏ and Yi Chungbu, and high officials Mun Kongin [d. 1137] and Im Kyŏngch'ŏng, agreed and collaborated with them. In time they memorialized: "Myoch'ŏng is a sage, and Paek Suhan is next after him in wisdom. As for the affairs of the state, we should first seek counsel from Myoch'ŏng and Paek Suhan on everything before acting. When what they request is granted, only then will the government conduct its affairs with success and the state be secure." They then asked that all the other officials cosign their approval. Executive Kim Pusik [1075–1151], Assistant Executive in Political Affairs Im Wŏnae [1089–1156], and Transmitter Yi Chijŏ [1092–1145] alone would not approve it and instead submitted a memorial. The king too had doubts, but because many people spoke strongly for Myoch'ŏng and Paek Suhan, he could not but believe them.

Thereupon Myoch'ŏng and others said to the king: "We, your subjects, saw in the topography of Imwŏn station in the Western Capital what practitioners of yin and yang call 'the power of great splendor.' If a palace is built and the court moves there, we can annex the whole world. The Chin kingdom will surrender, bringing tributary gifts, and the thirty-six states of the world will be your subjects."

The king finally made a trip to the Western Capital and ordered the accompanying state councillors, together with Myoch'ŏng and Paek Suhan, to divine the power of the topography at Imwŏn station. He commanded Kim An to build a palace, pressing the construction with great haste. At that time the weather was freezing cold, and the people were resentful and complained bitterly. When the new palace was completed in the seventh year of Injong [1129], the king again went to the Western Capital. Myoch'ŏng's followers sometimes presented petitions urging the king to declare Koryŏ's independence from Chin by assuming the imperial title and using the new reign title. At other times, they urged him to conclude an alliance with Liu-ch'i[7] to attack Chin from two opposite directions and destroy it. As those knowledgeable all thought this could not be done, Myoch'ŏng's followers grumbled but to no avail. The king in the end did not listen.

The king went to Kŏllyong Hall in the new palace to receive greetings from the officials. Myoch'ŏng, Paek Suhan, Chŏng Chisang, and others said: "Just when Your Majesty was to sit in the hall, we heard musical sounds in the air. How can this not be a good omen for Your Majesty's moving to the new palace?" Accordingly, they drafted a congratulatory memorial, asking the state councillors to approve. The state councillors refused, saying: "Although we are old, our ears are not deaf. We heard no music in the air. People can be fooled, but heaven cannot." Chŏng Chisang angrily retorted: "This is an unusual, propitious omen. It should be written down in history to be made known to later ages. But when high officials act like this, it is truly regrettable." The memorial in the end was not sent to the king.

The next year, when a stupa at Chunghŭng Monastery in the Western Capital burned, some asked Myoch'ŏng: "You asked the king to go to the Western Capital to ward off calamity. Why has there now been this great disaster?" Myoch'ŏng blushed in shame and could not answer. He bowed his head for a long time and then, raising his head, hit the desk with his fists and said: "If the king had remained in the main capital, this disaster would have been even greater. Because he came here, the disaster was confined outside, and His Majesty personally remains safe and well." Those who believed Myoch'ŏng said: "This explains it. How can one not believe him?"

In the following year, Kim An requested in a memorial: "The matters concerning the spheres of heaven, earth, and man ought to be transmitted in writing to the chamberlain to be made into three copies: one to be sent to the Royal Secretariat Chancellery, one to the Censorate, and one to the various offices concerned, and have the drafter of royal edicts direct each of them to comment and report to the king."

Myoch'ŏng also persuaded the king to construct a wall around Imwŏn Palace and set up eight shrines in the palace. The eight shrines were for: first, the truly virtuous Bodhisattva Mañjuśrī, the T'aebaek immortal of the nation-protecting Paektu peak; second, the truly virtuous Buddha Śākyamuni, the venerable Buddha of six supernatural powers of the dragon-encircled peak; third, . . . And he had portraits of the eight sages drawn. Kim An, Yi Chungbu, Chŏng Chisang, and others thought this to be in accord with the laws of the sages, as well as with the art of benefiting the state and prolonging the dynastic foundation. Kim An and others also petitioned to make offerings to the eight sages, while Chŏng Chisang composed a statement for the offerings that said: "Not to go fast and yet to be quick, not to act and yet to arrive, this is called the spirit of obtaining the absolute way. Even nothing is something; and real is nonreal. In general, this is the original form of Buddhism. Only the Heavenly Mandate can control all things; only earthly virtue can enable the king to rule over all.

Having divined the power of great splendor, we have constructed a new palace in the middle of P'yŏngyang. May we respect yin and yang and enshrine the eight immortals in the area, making the Paektu immortals and the immortals of Mount T'aebaek the first to be enshrined. May we consider divine virtue to be here with us; may we desire magical utilization to appear before our eyes; and may we see dazzling ultimate truth to be delivered. Although it is difficult to represent truly virtuous repose, for the true virtue may only belong to the buddhas, we direct the painting of the portraits with serenity, and, knocking on the front door, we pray." HK/ES

Im Wan: Memorial on Calamities
[From *Koryŏ sa* 98:33b–37b]

Once I have said it is not difficult to offer advice, but difficult to listen to it. But then it is more difficult to carry out the advice than to listen to it. Accordingly, it is said: "If in serving his ruler, a loyal official's words are earnest and direct, they will not enhance his employment but only endanger him. If his words are not earnest and direct, then they are insufficient to clarify the Way."

It may be said that during the reign of Han Emperor Wen [179–156 B.C.] the world was at peace. Even so, Chia I [201–169 B.C.] still spoke with great lamentations, weeping, and wailing as a warning. Recently there have been unusual portents in the heavens. It is a blessing of eternity that Your Majesty, fearing heaven's instructions in awe, has been led to listen to frank advice and send out a proclamation seeking counsel.

I once read writings of Tung Chung-shu [c. 179–104 B.C.] that said: "If a state is going to suffer the disaster of losing the Way, heaven first sends natural calamities in admonition. If on self-reflection the ruler still does not heed this, heaven then sends grotesque occurrences to alarm and instill fear. If he still does not understand the meaning of these occurrences, then injury and defeat are delivered. This is the expression of heaven's merciful love of the ruler and its desire to avert disaster. If a ruler's reign is not totally without the Way, then heaven would do its utmost to assist in bringing peace for him. The ruler's response to heaven's admonition is to work hard through concrete action; it cannot be anything else." The *Tso Commentary* said: "One should respond to heaven with substance (*sil*), not with words."[8] What constitutes substance is virtue (*tŏk*); what constitutes words (*mun*) is like today's Buddhist training place (*toryang*) and its religious ceremonies as well as Taoists' sacrificial offerings to nature. If the king cultivates virtue by responding to heaven, even though he does not wait for blessings, blessings by themselves will come. If he does not cultivate virtue, but depends on using empty words, he will not only reap no blessings, but he will defile heaven. The *Book of Documents* says: "Great heaven has no partial affections; it helps only the virtuous." It also says: "It is not millet that has the piercing fragrance; it is bright virtue."[9] As for what is virtue, where else can it be found but in the ruler's use of his mind and his conduct of affairs? Those who put their minds to good use and conducted affairs appropriately were: Yao, Shun, Yü; T'ang; and the first four rulers of the Chou dynasty, Wen, Wu, Ch'eng, and K'ang.[10] Accordingly, since everything they said and did met heaven's wishes, they were able to enjoy unlimited blessings. Those who did not put their minds to good use and did not conduct affairs appropriately were: the last rulers Chieh and Chou of the Hsia and Shang dynasties respectively; Kings Li and Yu, the tenth and twelfth monarchs of the Chou dynasty; and the first emperor of the Ch'in.[11] Accordingly, since everything they said and did violated heaven's wishes, and they could not protect even their own small selves, how could they rule the various states of the world? Moreover, as heaven and man are mutually far apart, no words can guide. Since blessings come from good acts and disaster comes from evil acts, it is like a shadow and an echo.

In the last few years, calamity has frequently appeared, and famine has come again and again. Lately white rainbows have pierced the sun, and in the first month there was rolling thunder that was especially strange. Such occurrences have never been heard of before. Don't they mean that Your Majesty is responding to heaven with words, not substance? Why are there so many strange happenings even though you continue to make sacrifices? As heaven always admonishes like this, it must be an expression of heaven's merciful love for Your Majesty. It is just like a parent who admonishes a child and earnestly wants to look after him and assure his peace. How can Your Majesty not respond to heaven diligently and with substance? Diligence with substance rests in reforming today's abuses. Reforming today's abuses only rests in honoring the injunctions of King T'aejo [918–943] and upholding the ancient statutes of King Munjong [1046–1083].

As for King T'aejo's injunctions, although I have not been able to hear their details, I humbly think the fact that the disorder of the time was settled, bringing peace and thereby establishing law and order, certainly must have required divine wisdom and clear planning. All this can be gathered by investigating what is recorded in national history. As Munjong's merit and legacy are not too distant in time, sometimes we can hear the words of elders and prominent people talking about him. When one hears their stories, one is so moved that one does not even notice one's own tears moistening one's collar. We see his personal conduct as frugal and his promoting the wise and talented. Titles were not bestowed on undeserving people, and authority was seldom delegated to those close to him. Those without merit, even if they were maternal relatives of the royal family, were not recklessly rewarded. Even individuals among those around him who enjoyed his affection were always punished if they committed crimes. Eunuchs and court attendants, selected from among those who were prudent and young, did not exceed some ten in number and were put in charge of cleaning. The palace attendants certainly were selected from among those who were meritorious and talented and did not exceed twenty-odd people. In their assigned tasks, all performed to the utmost of their ability. Unnecessary positions were reduced, and work was simplified. As expenses were reduced, the state became richer. Accordingly, the great granaries were filled with grains. Every household was sufficiently provided for, making the people satisfied. The period was thus called one of great peace, and this was because King Munjong was our dynasty's wise and sage ruler.

In recent times, everything has been entirely the opposite of King Munjong's time, and those managing state affairs are twice as numerous as before. As arrogance and extravagance increase daily, there is no sense of shame. Relying on power and using influence, officials extort and plunder. Because excessive levies and corvée labor have increased, people have become resentful. If Chia I could see the present situation, he would lament greatly, shedding tears and decrying conditions in bitter disappointment. For the sake of Your Majesty's plan, I propose that by taking responsibility and reflecting on yourself, you respond to heaven's warnings. This can be done by carrying out good government and the good laws of the illustrious dynastic ancestors. At present, if you were to carry out the laws of your royal ancestors, certainly it would not benefit the powerful nobles. Therefore, even though you have good government, what you enact in the morning will be changed at night, causing the laws to be in disarray. Truly this is not what Your Majesty intends by your hard work at improving your virtue. Only through Your Majesty's utmost manifestation of sincerity in your royal heart, by demanding the accountability of officials who assist the throne, and asking the deities for clarification, may you severely suppress those crafty people around you who are deceptive and scheming and finally eradicate the grotesque theories of supernatural, yin/yang explanations. By daily being cautious and working ceaselessly, let your great undertakings increasingly shine so as to make them an unending celebration for eternity.

Recently, grotesque theories of supernatural explanations have been extensively put forth by Myoch'ŏng. I believe Myoch'ŏng only deceives the king through his craftiness, and in this he is no different from Lin Ling-su of Sung China.[12] Ling-su, bearing heresy, bewildered the emperor. Gentry who sought quick advancement as officials, bent over to flatter him to gain honor and fame. Thereupon calamities frequently arose, yet the emperor did not apprehend their significance. In the end, Ling-su's wisdom was used up and his schemes were exhausted, leading to defeat and disorder. Even though Ling-su was executed, how did this help the situation? This is a story Your Majesty is already familiar with. How could anyone repeat the same blunders this story recounts? Yet Your Majesty favors and trusts Myoch'ŏng. Your attendants all around you and high officials all take turns in recommending and praising him as if he were a sage. He is so deeply rooted and well consolidated that he cannot easily be pulled out.

Beginning with the construction of T'aehwa Palace, people were overworked and agitated, resulting in their rising resentment. In the past year, when Your Majesty went on a trip, a disaster occurred at a Buddhist stupa. This year when Your Majesty went on a trip, shooting stars startled the horses, bringing disaster. These misfortunes have come in succession. Moreover, the original purpose in constructing this palace was to seek blessings. Now seven or eight years have passed, and there has not been one good omen; only calamities continue to arise. Why? Heaven's will is like the statement, "Treacherous people will bedevil the king. Even though they can cheat people, how can they cheat heaven?" The incidents of the past days are perhaps heaven's warnings to alert Your Majesty. Your Majesty, how can you cling to crafty officials and disregard heaven's will? I urge Your Majesty to wield your authority strongly, to behead Myoch'ŏng, to respond to heaven's warnings from above, and to console the hearts of the people below. This is the open expression of public opinion, not just the personal feelings of a foolish official. May Your Majesty look into this. HK/ES

Taoism and Shamanism

Taoism appealed to people's speculative instincts. Developed in China, Taoism and Confucianism came to Korea and spread gradually throughout the centuries of contact with China. Unlike Confucianism, Taoism put less emphasis on one's commitment to society, stressing instead human freedom and spiritual refinement. The Taoist search to transcend life led some practitioners to delve into quasi-scientific searches for elixirs and potions. Taoists eventually became associated with the free-spirited activities found in Korean native traditions as well as in Buddhism.

The first selection was written by Hsü Ching (1091–1153) of Sung China during his official trip to Koryŏ in the early twelfth century. He visited the kingdom at the end of the reign of King Yejong (1105–1122), a period of intellectual vigor. In describing Taoism's new popularity at this time, Hsü Ching provides a brief history of its growth in Korea. But he looks at it, as he does at all other events in Korea, from a sino-centric viewpoint, trying to show how Koryŏ differs from Sung China.

Shamanism is a native religious tradition practiced widely throughout Korea and northeastern Asia. Developed in close association with other native beliefs, including geomancy, shamanism maintains that natural objects are infused with a vital force and that shamans have the power to contact these spirits in nature and invoke them to bring blessings to the home, community, or country. To the uneducated peasant, the shaman was an important force in maintaining well-being; to the Confucian literati, however, the shaman was frequently a target of contemptuous suspicion and criticism.

The erudite Yi Kyubo (1168–1241) had little use for shamans. He thought that they lowered the cultural level of life and took advantage of superstitious peasants. An Hyang (1243–1306) echoed Yi Kyubo's thoughts. An, an important Confucian philosopher, confronted shaman disturbances and rid his district of their activities. To him and other scholars, shamans perpetuated superstition, which did much harm to the innocent but foolish peasantry.

There were, on the other hand, members of the officialdom who supported shamanism. King Injong (1122–1146), who listened for a time to Myoch'ŏng, was willing to allow the practice of shamanism. And some of his advisers, once their pockets were properly lined with bribes, petitioned to permit shamans to hold ritual sacrifices. Practitioners of shamanism, like certain Buddhist monks, claimed that their prayers had spared the nation disaster. "Enfeoffment of the Kŭmsŏng Mountain Deity" provides an example and also shows the close connection between mountain spirits and shamanism.

Superstition permeated the lives of ordinary people in Koryŏ. Fortunetellers, geomancers, and shamans were everyday fare, especially for the commoner. When Yi Chagyŏm (d. 1126) exiled Yi Yŏng (d. 1123), who subsequently died in anguish upon learning of the enslavement of his mother and children, Yi Yŏng became something of a folk hero, as the fifth selection reveals. One's burial site was significant according to geomancy, and this, of course, caused his son to rebury Yi Yŏng.

The interpretation of dreams was thought to be an important means of understanding what the future had in store. As the final selection reveals, dreams were believed to contain hidden messages that could predict significant events when interpreted by a skilled fortuneteller. Although commoners often wholeheartedly accepted irrational beliefs and superstitions, the Confucian literati, placing more faith in rational explanations, generally manifested skepticism—though there were always exceptions, as this case demonstrates.

Hsü Ching: History of Koryŏ Taoism
[From *Kao-li t'u-ching* 18:93]

Koryŏ is on the shores of the Eastern Sea, which must be situated not far from the Taoist mountains and the Islands of the Immortals. Its people would not have been unaware of the praise the Taoist teachings of longevity and immortality commanded. Earlier in China we had been too often engaged in military expeditions, and few tried to teach Taoism through the method of cleansing and nonaction. When T'ang rose, they honored the progenitor of the universe. Therefore, in the Wu-te period [618–626], Koguryŏ sent an envoy pleading that Taoist priests be sent to lecture on the five-thousand-word classic, the *Tao te ching,* and explain its profound and subtle meanings. T'ang Emperor Kao-tsu, since he was a sage ruler, was impressed and granted their petition. From then on, they started worshiping Taoism even more than Buddhism.

In the *keng-yin* year [1110] of the Ta-kuan era, the Emperor Hui-tsung of Sung China, caring for the distant land of Koryŏ, which wanted to hear about Taoism, sent envoys accompanied by two Taoist priests and had them instruct and guide selected Koreans well versed in the ways of religious teachings. King Yejong [1105–1122], a devout believer in religion, in the Cheng-ho era [1110–1117] started to construct Pogwŏn Taoist temple to receive more than ten eminently accomplished Taoist priests. The Taoist priests passed the day in the palace ancestral temple, however, and at night returned to their private chambers. Later, when the censors pointed this out, laws to restrict it were added. Some said that when King Yejong reigned over the country, he was constantly bent on supplying Taoists with books, wishing to replace Buddhism with Taoism. Although he never realized that goal, he seemed to have expected it to happen. HK/ES

An Hyang and the Shamans
[From *Koryŏ sa* 105:28b]

An Hyang . . . in the first year [1275] of King Ch'ungnyŏl's reign [1274–1308] was appointed administrative assistant in Sangju. At that time, there were three female shamans who were worshiping bewitching spirits and deluding the people. From Hapchu they went to different places. Upon their arrival, they cried out in the air. It was a mysterious shouting. Those who heard it ran and set up sacrifices. None dared to lag. Even the magistrate acted this way. When they reached Sangju, Hyang flogged and bound them. The shamans, claiming to speak the words of the spirits, enticed the people with threats of disaster and promises of blessings. As a result, the people of Sangju were all afraid. But Hyang was not moved. Several days later, when the shamans begged for pity, they were released. Their deluding of the people accordingly stopped. HK/ES

The Popularity of Shaman Customs
[From *Koryŏ sa* 16:16a–b]

The official astrologer memorialized: "Recently as shamanism has been widely practiced, its indecent sacrifices have increased daily. I request the king to instruct the offices concerned to expel all the shamans." The request was granted. Many shamans were grieved by this. They collected their valuables and exchanged them for more than one hundred silver vessels, using them to bribe powerful officials. The powerful officials thereupon memorialized: "Spirits being formless, we cannot know whether they are fake or real. To ban them completely is never advantageous." The king, agreeing with this argument, rescinded the earlier prohibition. HK/ES

Enfeoffment of the Kŭmsŏng Mountain Deity
[From *Koryŏ sa* 105:24a]

In the third year [1277] of King Ch'ungnyŏl, Chŏng Kasin [d. 1298] became a drafter of royal edicts in Pomun Hall. A person from Naju claimed that the deity of Kŭmsŏng Mountain came down to a shaman and said: "In the pacification of the last anti-Mongol resistance in the islands of Chin and Cheju, I truly had power. Why did they reward the military officers but not pay me a stipend? I must be enfeoffed as Lord Chŏngnyŏng (Settling the Peace)." Kasin was deluded by these words and ridiculously advised the king to enfeoff the spirit as Lord Chŏngnyŏng. Moreover, every year the town of Naju collected five *sŏk* of stipend rice and sent it to the shrine. HK/ES

Yi Yŏng's Corpse
[From *Koryŏ sa* 97:17a–b]

When Yi Chagyŏm killed Han Anin [d. 1122], Yi Yŏng, being Anin's brother-in-law, was implicated and banished to Chin Island. Someone said to Yŏng, "Your mother and sons are going to be made slaves." Yŏng said, "Reflecting on myself, as I have no cause for remorse, I have had no reason to bring death upon myself. So I have waited to this day. If because of me my old mother is made a slave, however, what am I living for?" Therefore he drank one *mal* of wine and died in anguish.[13] Contemporaries regretted his death. Yi Chagyŏm sent a conjurer to bury him on the side of the road. Cows and horses did not dare walk over the grave. When people who were gravely ill prayed there, they were cured. When Chagyŏm was ousted, Yŏng's son asked to change the burial site. When they dug it out, the corpse had not decomposed.   HK/ES

Unusual Dreams and Strange Effects
[From *Koryŏ sa* 88:27a–28a]

Queen Dowager Kongye, Lady Im [1109–1183], was the daughter of Secretary General of the Royal Secretariat Im Wŏnhu and granddaughter of Chancellor Yi Wi [1049–1133]. On the evening the queen was born, Yi Wi dreamed that a large yellow flag had been erected at his house's middle gate. The tail of the flag floated entwined in the tiles in the shape of a grampus tail on the roof line of Sŏngyŏng Hall.

When the queen was born, Wi especially cherished her, saying, "This girl should later enjoy Sŏngyŏng Hall." When she reached marriageable age, she was to wed Kim Chihyo, the son of Executive of the Royal Secretariat Chancellery Kim Ingyu. On the evening she was to be married, Chihyo came to her gate. As the queen suddenly became ill and was near death, however, he was sent back with apologies. A fortuneteller divining the illness said, "Do not worry. The nobility of this girl is undeniable. Certainly she will become the queen of the kingdom."

At that time, Yi Chagyŏm had already married two of his daughters to the king. When he heard these words, he resented them and immediately asked the king to demote Im Wŏnhu to mayor of Kaesŏng. After a year, an assistant to the mayor dreamed that the central beam of the magistrate's office cracked and made a great hole. A yellow dragon appeared in the hole and came out.

The next morning, the assistant put on his official robes and went to Wŏnhu to explain his dream. He congratulated Wŏnhu, saying, "Your family certainly will have an extraordinary celebration. You ought to know this."

King Injong once dreamed that he had five pecks of wild sesame (*im*) and three pecks of yellow sunflower. He told this to Ch'ŏk Chungyŏng, who said: "The sesame plant stands for the Im family. You will take for your queen a person with the Im surname. The number five is the happy omen that you will have five sons. Yellow stands for the emperor. Emperor and imperial ruler are the same. The sunflower (*k'uei*) means 'calculate,' which is the same as the principle by which a ruler examines his administration. The yellow sunflower means the ruler uses principle to examine his administration. It is the omen of a king ruling his country. The number three means that among your five sons, three will govern the country." The king had already dismissed Yi Chagyŏm's two daughters. In the fourth year [1126] of his reign he selected Lady Im to be his queen and called her Princess Yŏndŏk. HK/ES

Neo-Confucianism

Confucianism remained an important ideology of the state throughout the Koryŏ dynasty, but in the closing years of Koryŏ new interest grew in Neo-Confucianism, which had developed earlier in late T'ang and Sung China. Koryŏ literati, increasingly dissatisfied with the social and political life of late Koryŏ, needed fresh intellectual stimulation. Neo-Confucianism met that need with a resuscitation of basic Confucian ideals coupled with metaphysical speculations.

An Hyang (1243–1306) is traditionally credited with introducing Neo-Confucianism to Korea. An's first exposure to the ideas of Neo-Confucianism came in 1286 when he read the *Chu Tzu ch'üan-shu* (Complete Works of Chu Hsi) while staying in the Yüan capital as a member of a Koryŏ embassy to the Mongol court. Impressed by the ideas of Chu Hsi (1130–1200), An made a copy of the *Complete Works* and brought it back to Koryŏ. He subsequently devoted himself to reviving Confucian studies in Korea. As the first selection, taken from his biography in the *History of Koryŏ,* suggests, An's major contribution to the development of Neo-Confucianism in Korea came not from the originality of his thought but rather from his efforts to promote Confucian education and propagate the ideas of Chu Hsi. Nonetheless, it is important to note that when he cites social ethics in his discussion of Confucius's legacy, An introduces one of the major recurring themes of fourteenth-century Korean Neo-Confucianism.

Within a century after its introduction by An Hyang, Neo-Confucianism spread rapidly among the ranks of the officialdom and became the major focus of the curriculum in the highest academic institution. This is illustrated in the second selection, a biography of Yi Saek (1328–1396), one of the most prominent Neo-Confucianists of the fourteenth century.

Another prominent literatus, Chŏng Mongju (1337–1392), who

was lionized by Chosŏn dynasty Neo-Confucianists as the first great Korean Neo-Confucian metaphysician, also epitomized this new interest. Unfortunately, there is virtually nothing in his surviving writings to allow us to gauge the breadth and quality of his understanding of Neo-Confucian metaphysics. We can, however, see in Chŏng the emergence of some of the salient characteristics of late Koryŏ and early Chosŏn Neo-Confucianism. The third selection, drawn from Chŏng's biography in the *History of Koryŏ,* reveals two aspects of Neo-Confucianism that, while not unique to Korea, were much more emphasized there than in China, Japan, or Vietnam. One is anti-Buddhism, a central feature of Korean Neo-Confucianism from the late fourteenth century on; Chŏng's central role in launching the anti-Buddhism movement can be seen in his discourse on the evils of Buddhism. The other is the strong sense of moralistic righteousness which, while seen most clearly here in Chŏng T'ak's (1363–1423) memorial in defense of Kim Ch'o, was firmly fixed in the Korean Neo-Confucian mind by Chŏng Mongju's 1392 martyrdom in defense of the doomed Koryŏ dynasty.

Chŏng Tojŏn (d. 1398) was a central political figure in the change of dynasties between Koryŏ and Chosŏn; he was a major scholar of statecraft who did much to shape the institutions of the new dynasty, and at the same time also a seminal Nature and Principle thinker who began to develop a new philosophical dimension in Korean Neo-Confucianism through his rebuttals of Buddhism and Taoism. One of Chŏng's most significant writings was the three-part work *Simgi ip'yŏn* (Mind, Material Force, and Principle). In the first two parts of this work, mind (for Buddhism) and material force (for Taoism) criticize each other, leading to the climactic third part, where principle, representing Nature and Principle Neo-Confucianism, exposes (in Chŏng's view) the falseness in the underlying assumptions of both Buddhism and Taoism and presents Neo-Confucian principle as the only way that comprehends both mind and material force. The third part, entitled "Principle Admonishes Mind and Material Force," is reproduced here complete with introduction and annotations by Kwŏn Kŭn (1352–1409), Chŏng Tojŏn's contemporary.

The fourteenth-century Korean thinker who had the most sophisticated understanding of Neo-Confucian metaphysics was undoubtedly Kwŏn Kŭn, scion of one of the great aristocratic clans of late Koryŏ and great-grandson of Kwŏn Pu (1262–1346), who first published *Chuja sasŏ chipchu* (The Collected Commentaries of Chu Hsi) in Korea. Kwǒn Kǔn is the earliest Korean Neo-Confucianist to leave writings that show a comprehensive grasp of Nature and Principle metaphysics. His most representative work is the *Iphak tosǒl* (Diagrammatic Treatises for the Commencement of Learning), a book that has, in its most widely circulated editions, forty diagrams and explanations designed to help the beginner grasp the fundamentals of Nature and Principle learning. The selection presented here contains three diagrams and associated explanations; the first two deal with the fundamental ideas of Nature and Principle learning while the third uses a key Nature and Principle concept, mindfulness (*kyǒng*), to give fresh Neo-Confucian emphasis to a text on kingly duties that had been widely used throughout the Koryǒ dynasty.

An Hyang: The Introduction of Neo-Confucianism
[From *Koryǒ sa* 105:29b–31a]

An Hyang, concerned about the daily decline of schools, raised the issue in the Two Directorates,[14] where he said: "There is nothing in the duties of the state councillors that takes precedence over educating talent. The Fund for Nurturing Worthies is now exhausted,[15] and there is nothing to use to foster scholars. I request that all persons of the sixth grade and higher give one *kǔn* of silver and all persons of the seventh grade and lower give cloth according to their rank. These resources will go to the fund to be left as principal whose interest will be used as educational assistance money." The Two Directorates concurred. When the king heard of this, he gave money and grain from palace funds to help.

Commissioner of the Security Council Ko Se, referring to himself as a military man, did not want to pay. Addressing the various state councillors, An said: "The way of Confucius has bequeathed to eternity the standards whereby the official is loyal to his lord, the son filial to his father, and the younger brother respectful to his elder brother. Whose teachings are these? If one says, 'I am a military man; why should I be pressed to pay money for the fostering of your students?' he is disregarding Confucius. How can this be?" Upon hearing this, Ko was deeply embarrassed and paid immediately.

An Hyang also gave surplus funds to the erudite Kim Munjǒng and others and sent them to China to paint portraits of the ancient sages and the seventy masters as well as to bring back sacrificial implements, musical instruments, the Six Classics, the works of the various masters, and the Chinese histories. In addition, he recommended that retired Deputy Commissioner of the Security Council Yi San and Minister of Punishments Yi Chin [1244–1321] be appointed commissioners of the Directorate-General for Teaching Classics and Histories. With this, the number of persons studying the classics reached several hundred, including scholars from the palace schools, the Office of Palace Attendants, the Three Directorates, and the Five Funds as well as students from the seven government colleges and the twelve private academies.

There were some students who failed to treat their seniors with propriety. An was angry and intended to punish them. The students, however, apologized, whereupon An Hyang told them, "I look upon you students as my own children and grandchildren; how can you not grasp this old man's intentions?" An Hyang then took the students to his home, where he served them wine. The students said to each other, "Our master treats us with such sincerity. If we do not conform to his teachings, how can we become truly human?". . . .

An Hyang was solemn and composed, and everyone held him in awe. When he was in the Chancellery, he was skilled at planning and exercised good judgment so that his colleagues followed quietly and industriously without daring to argue. He always held the promotion of learning and the nurturing of worthies to be his duty. Even when he declined to serve and stayed at home, he never lost his concern for affairs. He enjoyed having guests and liked to give. His writing, clean and strong, was worth seeing. An Hyang also had the gift of perception; he saw Kim T'ae and Paek Wŏnhang when they were still young and said that they would someday surely become distinguished persons. On another occasion he summoned Yi Chehyŏn [1287–1367] and Yi I [b. 1287], who were of the same age and were both gaining names for themselves, and had them write rhymeprose and poetry (*fu* and *shih*). An then said that Yi Chehyŏn would become prominent and live long, but Yi I would die young; his prediction came true.

In his later years, An always hung up a portrait of Chu Hsi, whom he admired greatly. Eventually he himself took the pen name of Hoehŏn [after that of Chu Hsi]. Whenever he met potentially successful scholars, he encouraged them. In the sixth year [1319] of King Ch'ungsuk's reign, there was discussion about installing An in the National Shrine to Confucius. Some said, "Although An Hyang did suggest the establishment of educational assistance money, how can he be installed in the shrine for that?" Nonetheless, due to the strong urging of his student, Sin Ch'ŏn, An was eventually installed in the shrine. JD

The Spread of Neo-Confucianism
[From *Koryŏ sa* 115:10b–11a]

In the sixteenth year [1367] of King Kongmin, the National Confucian Academy (*Sŏnggyungwan*) was rebuilt, and Yi Saek [1328–1396] was appointed concurrently to be superintendent of the Capital District and supervisor of sacrificial rites in the National Academy. The number of classics licentiates (*saengwŏn*) was increased. Kim Kuyong [1338–1384], Chŏng Mongju [1337–1392], Pak Sangch'ung [1332–1375], Pak Ŭijung, and Yi Sungin [1349–1392], all scholars skilled in the classics, were given concurrent appointments as instructors in addition to the offices they held. Prior to this time, the number of students at the academy had been no more than a few dozen. But Yi Saek revised academic procedures and sat daily in Myŏngnyun Hall, where he divided the students on different Confucian classics and taught them. When the lecture was over, the students debated among themselves, forgetting their fatigue. Scholars gathered to share their perceptions and feelings. Thus began the rise of the Ch'eng-Chu school of Neo-Confucianism in Korea. JD/HK

Chŏng Mongju and the Development of Neo-Confucianism
[From *Koryŏ sa* 117:1b–12a]

Chŏng Mongju [1337–1392] was given concurrent appointments as an office chief in the Ministry of Rites and as a professor in the National Academy in the sixteenth year [1367] of King Kongmin. At the time, the only commentary on the classics to have reached Korea was the *Collected Commentaries of Chu Hsi*. Chŏng Mongju's discourses were superior and so far exceeded people's expectations that those who heard him were very suspicious. Later, when a copy of Hu Pingwen's [1250–1333] *Ssu-shu t'ung* (Encyclopedia of Four Classics) was obtained, it was found that there were no discrepancies between Hu's work and Chŏng's discourses. All the Confucianists were astonished. Yi Saek praised Chŏng highly, saying, "Even when speaking at random, Mongju says nothing that does not conform to principle," and exalted Chŏng as the founder of Neo-Confucianism in Korea. . . .

Once when King Kongyang [1389–1392] attended the royal lecture, Mongju said: "The way of the Confucian is the way of everyday routine affairs. The sameness of people in drinking, eating, and relations between men and women is where ultimate principle resides. The way of Yao and Shun was no more than this. Being correct in movement and quietness, and in speech and silence—that is the way of Yao and Shun. Even in the beginning it is not something extremely high or difficult to traverse. Such is not the case for the teachings of the Buddhists. They separate relatives and sever relations between men and women, sit alone in rocky caves, living as recluses and eating fruit, and have as their religion emptiness and annihilation. How can this be the regular way?" At the time, the king wanted to receive the monk Ch'anyŏng as a royal preceptor; thus Mongju gave a lecture covering this. The king, however, was mesmerized by Buddhism and did not listen. . . .

Kim Ch'o, a professor in the National Academy, presented a memorial disparaging Buddhism. The king was angry and wanted to have Ch'o executed. Chŏng T'ak, assistant office chief of the Ministry of Military Affairs, presented a memorial that said: "I hear that Your Majesty intends to execute Kim Ch'o, who rejected heterodoxy (Buddhism), for disparaging the established rites of former kings. I feel sorrow for Your Majesty on this issue. The *Book of Documents* says: 'Pay heed to the established rites of former kings and you will make no errors.'[16] The established rites of former kings refers to nothing more than the Three Bonds and Five Relations, all of which Buddha has gone against. It is not Kim Ch'o who is disparaging the established rites of former kings but rather Your Highness himself. I request that you pardon Kim Ch'o for his crime of wild forthrightness." The court spokesman and others, however, feared the king's wrath and dared not present the memorial.

Mongju and his colleagues then presented a memorial saying: "Trust is the great treasure of the ruler; the state is protected by the people, and the people are protected by trust. Recently Your Highness issued a proclamation calling for memorials and promising no punishment for those who spoke out. Thus everybody presented memorials exhaustively arguing the successes and failures of government and the joys and worries of the people. This has truly been a court without fear. There have also been some professors in the university and students who, in rejecting heresy, have presented memorials whose language has been imprudent, thereby desecrating the royal dignity.

The officials of the court cannot overcome their fear. We think that the rejection of Buddhism is a constant concern for Confucianists. From old, kings have not concerned themselves with this issue. Furthermore, with Your Majesty's great magnanimity, you could forgive these insignificant students. We entreat Your Majesty to bestow benevolence and pardon them all, thus demonstrating trust to the people." The king concurred, and Kim Ch'o and the others escaped punishment. JD

Chŏng Tojŏn: Philosophical Rebuttal of Buddhism and Taoism
[From *Sambong chip* 10:5b–9a]

Through the discussion of the following poems this essay will mainly argue for the correctness of the principle of righteousness of Confucianism and, by reasoning against Buddha and Lao Tzu, it tries to make the reader aware of their falseness. Principle (*li*) is the virtue (*te*) endowed upon the mind (*hsin*) and is the cause by which material force (*ch'i*) comes into being.

> Ah! Profound principle
> That exists before heaven and earth.
> Material force comes into being through the self,
> So is mind also given.

"Ah" is the expression of admiration. "Profound" is the ultimate clarity. This principle is pure and extremely good and originally has no adulteration. Thus one admires principle, saying, "Ah! Profound." "Self" is the self-appellation of principle. In the earlier sections, Chŏng Tojŏn [d. 1398] used the terms "self" and "I" for mind and material force. Here he uses the term "principle" as an indicator. Then, after expressing admiration for it, he calls it "self" in order to show that it is the way of impartiality without parallel in its nobility. It is not like Buddha or Lao Tzu, each maintaining his biased view and distinguishing on his own between self and other. This tells us that principle is the origin of both mind and material force. There is principle, and after that there is material force. After there is material force, the lightness and clarity of yang rise to become heaven and the heaviness and turbidity of yin sink to become earth. With this, the four seasons begin to flow and the myriad things come into being. Amidst this, human beings completely acquire the principle of heaven and earth and also completely acquire the material force of heaven and earth to become noble among the myriad things and become part of the heaven/earth/human triad.

The principle of heaven resides in humankind to become human nature while the material force of earth resides in humankind to become physical form. The mind combines principle and material force to become master of the body. Thus principle exists prior to heaven and earth and material force comes into being from principle, which is also received by the mind and becomes virtue.

> If there were only mind and no self,
> There would be only the race for worldly gain.
> If there were only material force and no self,
> There would be only a body of flesh and blood
> Moving like squirming insects
> And reverting to bird and beast.
> One different from that would be so rare!

"Squirming insects" appear to have no consciousness, and "so rare" means few. Chu Hsi [1130–1200] said: "A person whose consciousness and activity are like squirming insects is the same as a beast; a person of pure humanity, righteousness, propriety, and wisdom is different from beasts." This tells us that a human being is different from beasts because he has righteousness. If a human being has no righteousness, then his consciousness is no more than emotion, desire, and the selfishness of worldly gain while his activity is like a mass of squirming insects. Even though he may be called human, how far removed can he be from the birds and beasts? That is why when examining his mind and cultivating his material force, the Confucianist necessarily emphasizes righteousness.

The learning of Buddha and Lao Tzu worships purity and annihilation. Thus they necessarily strive to close off and eradicate even the greatness of moral duty and the beauty of ritual and music. The person who has no desire in his heart may be different from people who pursue worldly gain, but he does not know how to emphasize the impartiality of the principle of heaven so as to control the selfishness of desire. Therefore, in his daily speech and conduct, he always becomes trapped in worldly gain but does not himself know it.

Furthermore, there is nothing a human being desires more than life and nothing he hates more than death. Chŏng looks at this through the arguments of both Buddhists and Taoists. Buddha strove to escape death and birth, which means that he feared death. Lao Tzu strove for longevity, which means that he craved life. If this is not worldly gain, what is it? Furthermore, because they have no emphasis on righteousness, vacantly they acquire nothing, ignorantly they know nothing, and though their bodies may exist, they are nothing more than blood and flesh. Even though these four lines speak generally to the common man, they strike compellingly at the genuine ills of Buddhism and Taoism; let the reader look closely.

> Watching the crawling child,
> One's emotion is pity.
> That is why the Confucian
> Does not fear the rise of concern.

Mencius said: "Now when people suddenly see a young child about to fall in a well, they all have feelings of fear and pity."[17] He continued to say: "The feeling of commiseration is the beginning of humanity." This means that the feeling of compassion is inherent in our minds and reveals the error of the Buddhist elimination of thought and forgetting of emotion. As for humans being born with the life-creating mind of heaven and earth, this is what is called humanity. This principle is truly embodied in our minds. Therefore, that feeling of pity when we see a young child crawling into a well arises of itself and cannot be blocked. If one pursues this mind and expands it, his humanity will be inexhaustible, and he will be able to join and succor the whole world. Thus the Confucianist does not fear the rise of concern but only follows the natural manifestation of the principle of heaven. How could he be like the Buddhist, who fears the rise of feeling and concern and strives forcibly to eliminate them in order to return to annihilation?

> When it is time to die, they die,
> Their righteousness more important than their bodies.
> That is why the superior man
> Sacrifices himself to achieve humanity.

The Analects says: "The determined scholar and the humane man will not seek life at the expense of their humanity; they will sacrifice their bodies to achieve humanity."[18] This means that righteousness is important and life is unimportant, and it reveals the error of the Taoists' lusting after life by nurturing material (vital) force. Generally the superior man, having seen and acquired the genuine principle, cannot bear to save his life for even one day once it is rightly the time to die. Is his life or death important, or is his righteousness important? Therefore, when the Confucian must come to the aid of his lord or his father, he will sacrifice his body and his life racing to them. This is not like the Taoists who devote themselves to self-cultivation in their lust after life.

> In the thousand years since the Sage passed away,
> Learning has become fraudulent and language debased.
> People think of vital force as the Way,
> And of mind as religion.

"Debased" means confused. It tells that the arguments of heresy flourish because the time of the Sage is long gone and the learning of the Way is no longer clear. Therefore the Taoists do not know that material force is based in principle, and they use material force as their Way. The Buddhists do not know that principle is embodied in the mind, and they use mind as their religion. Both the Taoists and the Buddhists think of themselves as the ultimate in abstraction, but they do not know what incorporeality is and speak only in reference to that which is corporeal. They ensnare themselves in the shallow and common, the crooked and the skewed, but they do not know it.

> Living long without righteousness,
> A turtle or a snake indeed!
> Sitting and resting with eyes closed,
> A skeleton of soil and wood!

"Resting with eyes closed" means dozing. The first two lines rebuke Lao Tzu and the second two lines rebuke Buddha. That is, they signify the mind without self and the material force without self as discussed above. The previous section addressed itself generally to the common man, but this section speaks only to Lao Tzu and Buddha.

> The self resides in your mind,
> Making it clear and lucid.
> The self cultivates your material force,
> Bringing into being a strong, moving power.

Mencius said: "The self cultivates well my strong, moving power."[19] This tells of the merit of the learning of the sages in cultivating alternately both the internal and the external. If one keeps righteousness in his heart and nourishes it, he will eliminate the shroud of material desires, all will become lucid, and there will be no deviations in his great purposes. If one concentrates his righteousness while nourishing and expanding his material force, it will become the greatest and stoutest power, strong and moving, and coming into being by itself, filling up all between heaven and earth. The beginning and the end will join together and the internal and external will be cultivated alternately. This is why the learning of the Confucians is correct and is not like the biased learning of the Buddhists and the Taoists.

> The ancient sages had a lesson
> That the Way does not have two heights.
> Oh mind, oh material force!
> Respect and accept these words.

Quoting the following words from the *Book of Rites,* "Heaven does not have two suns and the earth does not have two kings,"[20] Hu Yüan [993–1059] said:[21] "The Way does not have two ultimates." He was striving to bring morality and study back to one. This means that the things discussed above are all based in the lessons left by the sages and worthies and not Chŏng Tojŏn's own personal words, that the height of the Way cannot be two, and that mind and material force cannot be compared to the Way. Therefore, at the end Chŏng has specially called out and warned mind and material force. In expounding so sincerely on this, Chŏng's purpose is extremely earnest. JD

Kwŏn Kŭn: Nature and Principle Metaphysics
[From *Iphak tosŏl* 1:1a–2b, 36a–b]

THE DIAGRAM OF UNITY IN THE NATURE OF HEAVEN AND HUMAN MIND

Chu Hsi said: "Heaven gives rise to the myriad things through yin and yang and the five elements, gives them form through material force, and also endows them with principle." Based on this, I have now drawn this diagram:

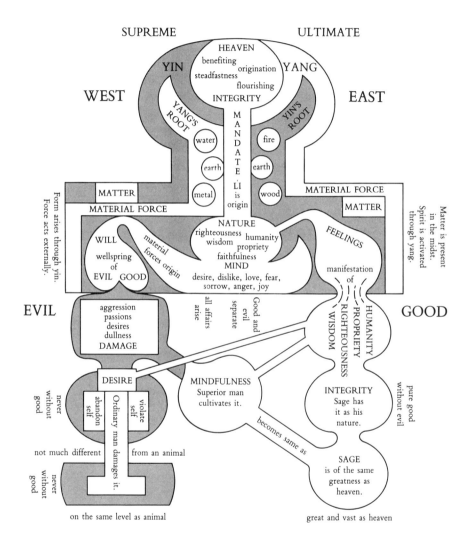

This diagram relies respectfully on Chou Tun-i's [1017–1073] diagram of the Supreme Ultimate and the explanation in Chu Hsi's *Chung-yung chang-chu* (Chapters and Sentences of the Mean). It deals with human mind and nature, illuminating the features of principle and material force, good and evil, and showing them to the learner. For this reason, it does not deal with the phenomena of the rise of the myriad things. In the coming into being of humans and creatures, they both share the same principle, but they differ in whether their material force is penetrating or congested, biased or straight. Those who obtain the straight and penetrating become humans, and those who obtain the biased and congested become creatures. Looking at the diagram, the area marked "integrity" obtains the most refined and most penetrating material force and becomes a sage. The area marked "mindfulness" obtains straight and penetrating material force and becomes an ordinary human. The area marked "desire" obtains biased and congested material force and becomes a creature. Below that are the fierce birds and beasts, while those that obtain even more biased and congested material force become grass and trees. Thus the phenomena of the rise of the myriad things are also contained therein.

As for the transforming activity of heaven and earth, production and reproduction are inexhaustible; that which is going rests while that which is coming replaces. Human and beast, grass and tree, the thousand forms and the ten thousand shapes—each has its own proper nature and destiny, and they all flow from within the one Supreme Ultimate. Although each of the myriad things has one principle, the myriad principles therefore flow from the same source. One piece of grass or one tree each has the one Supreme Ultimate, and there is no creature under heaven that lies outside the nature of humans. Thus the *Doctrine of the Mean* says that one who can fully develop his nature can fully develop the nature of other humans as well as that of creatures, and that he therefore can assist in the transforming and nourishing activities of heaven and earth.[22] How sublime!

THE DIAGRAM OF DETAILED EXPLANATION OF THE NATURE OF
HEAVEN AND HUMAN MIND

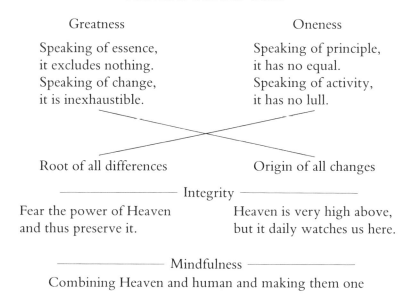

HEAVEN IS ONE AND GREAT

Greatness   Oneness

Speaking of essence,   Speaking of principle,
it excludes nothing.   it has no equal.
Speaking of change,   Speaking of activity,
it is inexhaustible.   it has no lull.

Root of all differences   Origin of all changes

—————————— Integrity ——————————

Fear the power of Heaven   Heaven is very high above,
and thus preserve it.   but it daily watches us here.

—————————— Mindfulness ——————————
Combining Heaven and human and making them one

To be human is to be humane. Humanity is the principle by which
heaven and earth produce creatures, and as a human acquires this and
is born, it becomes his mind. Therefore, the human being is the most
spiritual of the myriad things, and humanity is the greatest good.
Combined, these are called the Way. The sage is extremely sincere
and his way is like heaven; the superior man can cultivate his way
with seriousness. The common man is confused by greed and only
pursues evil. Therefore, although there is only one principle for humans, there are differences in good and evil in the stuff with which
humans are endowed and in the way they handle affairs. Thus the
logograph for human branches to give a warning. Only after one is
able to embody humanity, make complete the virtue of his mind, and
constantly maintain without fail the principle with which he is born,
can he be called human without being embarrassed and, by virtue of

that, be certain of having a long life. If not, he loses his inborn principle and is not human. Confucius said: "The humane person lives long." He also said: "The life of a human is uprightness; if one loses his uprightness and yet lives, his escape from death is merely good fortune." [1:1a–2b]

DILIGENCE

The word "diligence" warns against indolence and laziness by rulers of humans. Since ancient times, all the states under heaven flourished through the industriousness and frugality of their royal ancestors and fell through the indolence and laziness of their royal descendants. In ancient times, King Ch'eng [1122–1114 B.C.] of Chou took the throne while young. The Duke of Chou, concerned lest the young king become indolent and lazy, wrote this work to warn him. The Duke of Chou begins by making the king aware first of the difficulties of agriculture. From the time that the first Chou king founded the state with agriculture, it was passed down through the generations for over a thousand years, leading to King Wen's merit in nourishing the people and clearing land. The Chou kings all used industriousness, frugality, and diligence as their family law. Therefore the dynasty could prosper, leading to King Wu's possession of all under heaven. This is precisely what King Ch'eng needed to know first; furthermore, agriculture is the basis of human life.

When the people are busy in their fields, laboring hard all year to support their ruler and the ruler grows up deep within the inner palace, not knowing their hardships, not succoring the people, and indulging himself in arrogance, luxury, debauchery, and indolence while being impudent and licentious, then, at the least, the ruler will ruin his body and shorten his life, or, at the worst, he will lose his state and discontinue the sacrificial rites for his ancestors. Since this has been the disaster commonly suffered for generation after generation, it is the first thing that rulers should know. Therefore the Duke of Chou talked first of the difficulties of agriculture. After that, he cited the three ancestors of Yin who, fearing heaven and protecting the people, preserved the state for a long time; this was because he commended and admired them. Next he spoke of the later kings who were indolent and pleasure-seeking and were unable to live long; this was because he was warning and restraining King Ch'eng.

The Duke of Chou also spoke of Tan-fu, Wang-chi, and King Wen,[23] because he was emulating the royal ancestors' industriousness and frugality. Fearing the Mandate of Heaven above while protecting the people below; using the rise and fall of earlier times as a distant mirror while emulating close at hand the industriousness and frugality of the royal ancestors—this is the vision that a king succeeding to the throne should realize. The love of the Duke of Chou for his king was sincere and keen. Thus his words to his lord were detailed and complete, and he ended the work with the phrase, "the emperor himself is serious about virtue." "Serious" refers to the essentials of fearing heaven, protecting the people, using the past as a mirror, and emulating the ancestors; it is the true mind that has no indolence. The three ancestors of Yin were solemn, modest, respectful, and fearful, and one dared not disturb them. The fearfulness of Tan-fu and Wang-chi and the staunch modesty of King Wen were all seriousness. If one is serious, he is diligent and long-lived. If one is not serious, the result is the opposite. Afterward, King Ch'eng became the ruling king of Chou and reigned for thirty-seven years. Was this not because he had obtained the Duke of Chou's lessons? Can later rulers of men not be serious? [1:36a–b] JD

History

Korea's oldest extant history is the *Samguk sagi* (Historical Record of the Three Kingdoms), which was compiled by Kim Pusik (1075–1151) and others during Injong's reign (1122–1146). The *Historical Record of the Three Kingdoms* is an official court-sponsored history that reflects the Confucian values of its compilers. It was assembled to provide Koreans with a greater understanding of their own history and heritage; yet it is obvious that its compilers did not include all the facts and legends then known, particularly those that went against their ingrained moralistic view of history. For this omission they have often been criticized by modern historians.

Koryŏ's other great historical work is the *Samguk yusa* (Memorabilia of the Three Kingdoms). Written by the monk Iryŏn (1206–1289) during the devastating Mongol invasions, it presents many traditions and tales that were not included in the *Historical Record of the Three Kingdoms*. Reflecting its author's religious beliefs, the *Memora-*

bilia is replete with Buddhist themes. It is also interesting to note that Korea's mythical founder, Tangun, is described for the first time in this work.

The final selection in this section was written by Paek Munbo (d. 1374). Paek, a Confucian scholar writing in the last decades of the Koryŏ dynasty, presented a cyclical view of Korean history. Like Iryŏn, he dated the founding of Korea from Tangun's birth and attributed the chaos in late Koryŏ politics to the end of a long cycle. Regardless of their interpretations, each of these passages tells of the Koryŏ people's concern for their past and the importance of history to their lives.

Kim Pusik: On Presenting the *Historical Record of the Three Kingdoms* to the King
[From *Tong munsŏn* 44:12b–13b]

Your subject, Kim Pusik, wishes to report. All the states of the past established official historians to record events. Accordingly, Mencius said: "Such were *Sheng,* the annals of Chin; *T'ao-wu,* the annals of Chu; and the *Spring and Autumn Annals* of Lu."[24] The histories of Korea's Three Kingdoms are long, and their events should be set forth in an official record. Therefore, Your Majesty has ordered your subject to compile this book.

In looking at himself now, your subject sees many inadequacies and does not know what to do. . . . He humbly believes Your August Majesty is endowed with Yao's refined intelligence and perfected virtue as well as with Yü's diligence and frugality. In your leisure Your Majesty has read widely in histories of earlier ages and said: "Of today's scholars and high-ranking officials, there are those who are well versed and can discuss in detail the Five Classics and other philosophical treatises as well as the histories of Ch'in and Han, but as to the events of our country, they are utterly ignorant from beginning to end. This is truly lamentable. Moreover, because Silla, Koguryŏ, and Paekche were able to have formal relations with China from their beginnings to the unification wars [660–668], they were discussed in the biographical sections of Fan Yeh's *History of the Later Han Dynasty* and Sung Ch'i's *History of T'ang,* but these books are detailed on internal Chinese affairs and terse about foreign matters and did not record everything of historical significance. As for the ancient records of the Three Kingdoms, the writing is unrefined, and the recording of historical events is deficient. Accordingly, whether the ruler is good or evil, the subjects are loyal or treasonous, the country is at peace or in crisis, the people are orderly or rebellious, is not always exposed. To create a history that can serve as a guide, I ought to have a person who has three talents—intelligence, scholarship, and wisdom. This will lead to a work of outstanding quality to be handed down for eternity, shining like the sun and stars."

Your subject basically lacks these talents as well as profound knowledge. In his old age, your subject's mind has become daily more muddled. In reading books, once he closes them, he immediately forgets even though he tries hard not to. He writes with his brushes without vigor. Picking up sheets of paper, he finds it difficult to write anything down. Although his scholarship is shallow and the history of the earlier ages is vague, by exhausting his spirit and energy, your subject has barely been able to complete this volume. Yet, as this may be nothing worth viewing, it only causes him embarrassment. He humbly hopes Your August Majesty will understand this disorganized and abbreviated compilation and forgive the transgressions of this foolish work. Although it may not be good enough to be stored on a sacred mountain, may it not be set aside as merely a useless thing. Your subject's foolish thought is to have heaven's light shine down on it. HK/ES

Iryŏn: Preface to the *Memorabilia of the Three Kingdoms*
[From *Samguk yusa* 1:33]

Generally sages of the past enabled states to flourish through propriety and music and fostered learning through humaneness and righteousness. They did not talk about extraordinary forces and capricious spirits. Upon the imminent rise of a ruler, however, one receives an auspicious omen from heaven and a word of prophesy, and he has something with him that is different from others. Only then can he, riding the wave of great change, seize royal authority and complete the founding of a new government.

Accordingly, the Yellow River brought out the mystic diagram, and the Lo River gave forth writing, making possible the appearance of sages.[25] Similarly, a divine mother encircled by a rainbow gave birth to Fu-hsi, and a dragon touched Nü-t'eng, and she gave birth to the Fiery Lord.[26] Huang-o, while playing on Ch'iung-sang field, made love to a divine youth who called himself a son of the White Lord and then gave birth to Shao-hao.[27] Chien-ti swallowed an egg and gave birth to Hsieh;[28] Chiang-yüan followed footsteps and gave birth to Ch'i;[29] after a pregnancy of fourteen months, Yao was born; and a dragon made love with a great marsh and gave birth to the Lord of P'ei.[30]

How can one record everything since these events? If so, what is so strange about the mysterious birth of the founders of the Three Kingdoms? These wondrous tales will flow into this volume; this is the reason for its compilation. HK/ES

Paek Munbo: Explanation of Tangun's Significance
[From *Koryŏ sa* 112:14b–15a]

The Koryŏ dynasty has protected the nation for generations. In customs, ceremony, and music there are ancient ways that have been passed on. Unexpectedly the ravages of invaders have been frequent. Red Turban bandits have overtaken the capital, forcing the king to flee to the south.[31] How painful it is to mention this! Now in the aftermath of these disasters, the people have nothing to depend upon. We need to shower the people with generous benefits. Heaven works in a cyclical way, continuously going around and starting again. Seven hundred years is a minor cycle, and accumulating these to thirty-six hundred years makes a major cycle. Within these cycles, emperors and kings have periods of order and chaos and rise and fall. In Korea, it has already been thirty-six hundred years since the time of Tangun, the fruition of a major cycle. May Your Majesty fittingly follow the teachings of the sage rulers Yao and Shun and the Six Classics and not practice shortsighted measures. If you do this, heaven's pure protection will prevail, yin and yang will follow in orderly progression, and the dynasty's prosperity will extend for a long time. I wish Your Majesty to recall Yejong's establishment of the Pomun and Ch'ŏngyŏn pavilions and hold lectures on the sages' virtue to enlighten Your Majesty's scholarship. HK/ES

PART THREE

EARLY CHOSŎN

Introduction

Founded in 1392 by General Yi Sŏnggye (1335–1408; r. 1392–1398), the Chosŏn dynasty ruled Korea for more than five hundred years until 1910. Rising from an obscure military family that became prominent only during the last decades of the Koryŏ dynasty, Yi Sŏnggye became one of the most powerful and preeminent military figures following a series of successful exploits against the Red Turbans and the Japanese marauders that had harassed Korea. When ordered to invade China's northeastern region (Manchuria) to take advantage of the Yüan-Ming dynastic transition in China, Yi Sŏnggye instead turned his army against the Koryŏ court and staged a successful coup in 1388. Four years later, in 1392, supported by the Neo-Confucian scholar-officials, Yi Sŏnggye proclaimed himself king, thus formally inaugurating a new dynasty of his own.

Founding the Chosŏn dynasty was the work of an alliance based on a symbiotic relationship between a military strongman and a group of reform-minded Confucian intellectuals, such as Cho Chun (1346–1405) and Chŏng Tojŏn (d. 1398). The dynastic change from Koryŏ to the new dynasty was justified in the name of the Mencian concept of Heavenly Mandate as rationalized by the Neo-Confucian scholar-officials, who then went on to dominate the bureaucracy and set up the entire structure of government and society in the hope of realizing their Confucian ideals. This alliance in the end enabled the Confucian reformers to put their ideas into practice so that one of the architects of the new order, Chŏng Tojŏn, is said to have claimed that it was he, Chŏng, who used Yi Sŏnggye to realize his political goal.[1]

In order to make a clean break from Koryŏ, the new dynasty, with the approval of the Ming emperor of China, adopted the official dynastic name of Chosŏn (Morning Serenity) and moved its capital city from Kaesŏng to Hanyang (present Seoul) after carefully examining political, economic, military, and topographic as well as geomantic considerations. With its royal palaces and government office buildings, the new capital city was based on a well-laid-out plan and included main thoroughfares, living and shopping quarters, drainage canals as well as fortified walls surrounding the city.

After a shaky start caused by fratricidal succession struggles, the Chosŏn dynasty laid its firm foundation during the rule of its third king, T'aejong (1400–1418). By reorganizing various military groups into one single command under the king and restructuring the central government under the State Council (Ŭijŏngbu), King T'aejong eliminated potential threats to the court and placed the dynasty on a solid footing, thus preparing the way for the rule of his third son Sejong (1418–1450).

King Sejong was undoubtedly one of the great rulers in Korean history. A remarkable scholar in his own right and versatile in many fields—classics, literature, linguistics, and science, among others— King Sejong ushered in the golden age of creativity in Korea. Using the Hall of Worthies (Chiphyŏnjŏn) as a royal research institute, where he assembled the best minds and talents of the country, King Sejong introduced truly remarkable achievements in many fields. To give only a few notable examples, the new Korean alphabet, now known as hangŭl, was invented after many years of research; a number of books were published with improved printing techniques, including Yongbi ŏch'ŏn ka (Songs of Flying Dragons) written in hangŭl; many scientific instruments, such as rain gauges, automatic striking clepsydras, and devices for astronomical observation were invented or improved upon; a comprehensive inventory of music and musical instruments was made, with notation taken for all the existing music; and more scientific farming methods were introduced, such as improved seeds and fertilizer, more efficient use of irrigation, and a more equitable land tax system. Moreover, it was during Sejong's rule that Korea's northern boundary along the Yalu and Tumen rivers was secured firmly through his successful military campaigns and his policy of settling people in the border regions.

In 1455, the Chosŏn court once again went through a succession crisis as the ambitious Prince Suyang forcibly deposed his fifteen-year-old nephew, King Tanjong (1452–1455), and set himself up as King Sejo (1455–1468). The historical significance of Sejo's usurpation lies not so much in the bloodshed it produced as in the legacy it bequeathed to future generations of scholar-officials, raising the moral question whether usurpation might be justified and legitimated according to Confucian principles. This issue became an important contributing factor to the later split within the Confucian bureaucracy.

By the mid-fifteenth century, after long experimentation, the restructuring of the government was finalized with the publication of the *Kyŏngguk taejŏn* (National Code) in 1485, which prescribed the duties and functions of various offices. In assisting the king's rule, the State Council staffed by three High State Councillors was the highest deliberative organ. Execution and administration of state laws and policies were carried out by the Six Ministries (Personnel, Taxation, Rites, Military Affairs, Punishments, and Public Works). For local administration, the country was divided into eight provinces—Kyŏnggi, Ch'ungch'ŏng, Kyŏngsang, Chŏlla, Hwanghae, Kangwŏn, Yŏngan (Hamgyŏng), and P'yŏngan—which in turn were subdivided into counties of various sizes (*pu, mok, kun,* and *hyŏn*). Chosŏn Korea was a highly centralized state with all the officials of local administration appointed by the central government.

The creation of various mechanisms to check arbitrary exercise of power was a unique feature of the Chosŏn government. Although according to the *National Code* each of the three censorate offices— Office of the Inspector-General (*Sahŏnbu*), Office of the Censor-General (*Saganwŏn*), and Office of Special Advisers (*Hongmungwan*) —had different duties, they often worked together, and through their criticism and surveillance they represented a powerful check against arbitrary decision making or exercise of authority by a king or any other official. Moreover, there was a constant and persistent reminder to adhere strictly to the rigid Confucian principles inhibiting inappropriate behavior. And the ubiquitous presence of historians around the throne, taking notes of all the official transactions by the king and the officials for inclusion in the compilation of history for posterity, had the effect of obliging government officials to conform to Confucian norms.

One of the most firmly held beliefs under the Chosŏn dynasty was that the government must be staffed and run by men of virtue and talent. To recruit such men as government officials, the Chosŏn state depended largely on an examination system, which included civil, military, and technical examinations. Of these three, the civil service examinations carried far greater honor and prestige than the other two, as the civil officials exercised preponderant influence within the government. There were two tiers in the civil service examinations— the lower examination (*sokwa*) that offered *saengwŏn* or *chinsa* degrees and the higher examination (*taekwa*) that awarded the *munkwa* degree. Only the *munkwa* degree automatically qualified the recipient to serve in the civil bureaucracy, and thus it became the most coveted degree, sought by men of ambition and talent.

In addition, one could obtain a position within the bureaucracy through a protection appointment (*ŭm*), whereby family members of certain senior officials were allowed to become officials, or through a recommendation appointment (*ch'ŏngŏ*), whereby men of exceptional merit could be appointed through recommendation. But appointments through these routes carried far less honor and prestige during the Chosŏn dynasty.

The civil service examinations, conducted strictly on a competitive basis, tested candidates' knowledge of the Confucian classics as well as of history and literature. From time to time, the system was criticized on the ground that a competitive examination might not be the best way to select truly virtuous men. The system encountered its most serious challenge in 1519 when the idealistic Cho Kwangjo (1482– 1519) attempted to replace it with the recommendation examination. For want of a better substitute, however, the examination system remained the government's main channel of recruitment until 1894. Until recently, scholars believed that only men of *yangban* birth could take part in the civil service examinations; this view, however, is now being challenged by new evidence indicating that men of commoner origins were also allowed to take the examinations.[2]

In the Neo-Confucian state of Chosŏn, education was considered vitally important for promoting the ideals of the Confucian sages and preparing qualified students for the civil service examinations. Therefore, the Chosŏn dynasty maintained a well-structured educational system. In the capital city, the National Academy (*Sŏnggyungwan*) was organized and maintained; *saengwŏn* and *chinsa* degree holders as well as other selected students enrolled there. In addition to the Four Schools in the districts of Seoul, a county school called *hyanggyo* was established in every county to offer Confucian education to qualified students. All these schools were maintained by funds provided by the state and local governments; their students received stipends and other privileges, such as exemption from military and other duties.

As many students in these schools began to lose their enthusiasm for Confucian studies, concerned scholars in the countryside began to organize private academies called *sŏwŏn* to serve two objectives—to enshrine a favorite Confucian master of their choice and to pursue more serious Confucian scholarship. Founded by Chu Sebung (1495–1554) in 1543 while he served as the magistrate of P'unggi county in Kyŏngsang province, Paegundong (later changed to Sosu) Academy was the first private academy to receive a royal charter. Thereafter, private academies proliferated throughout the country and overtook county schools as centers of local education and scholarship. Organized at the initiative of local scholars, the private academies were usually well endowed financially through private contributions of land and slaves. When factional politics intensified during the seventeenth and eighteenth centuries, private academies often became involved as their scholars took sides in the disputes between the factions.

From its inception, the Chosŏn dynasty was governed by the ideals of Chu Hsi's Neo-Confucianism, the official ideology of the state. With a firm conviction that the fundamental principles of Neo-Confucianism are absolute and valid at all times and in all places, Chosŏn Neo-Confucianists zealously pursued policies promising the realization of the ideals of Confucian sages by remodeling the Chosŏn state and society to conform to Confucian norms. All other beliefs, customs, and traditions that did not comply with Confucian teachings were rejected as heretical.

Buddhism—the source of consolation and inspiration in Korea for many centuries—now came under severe restrictions as the Neo-Confucian state of Chosŏn rejected Buddhism as a heretical teaching and vigorously pursued a policy of persecution against Buddhist institutions. Although there were a few exceptions, such as kings Sejong and Sejo who privately maintained their faith in Buddhism, the followers of Buddhist belief had to practice their religion under extremely restricted conditions throughout the duration of the Chosŏn dynasty. Placed constantly in a defensive position, the Buddhist leaders thus spent much of their intellectual energy rationalizing and reconciling their teaching with the Neo-Confucian order.

Many of the indigenous traditions and customs suffered curtailment as well. As the Neo-Confucianists tried to establish all state and family rituals in strict conformity with Confucian rules, many traditional practices, such as wedding and funeral ceremonies, which had been rooted deeply in Buddhistic, shamanistic, and other native beliefs, were discouraged or prohibited. Nevertheless, despite the zeal exhibited by the Neo-Confucianists, the transformation of social mores and practices came only at a slow pace over a long period of time.

The Chosŏn dynasty maintained a relatively rigid social structure. *Yangban* were a privileged class whose status was determined largely by birth and Confucian education. The large majority of the people, however, were commoners (*yangin*), such as farmers and merchants, who bore most of the tax burden for the state. In between the *yangban* and the commoners was a small group, known as "the middle people" (*chungin*), who occupied mostly the technical and functionary positions within the government. At the bottom of the society were the lowborn, such as public and private slaves, whose status was determined by birth. Private slaves owned by individual families were sold and purchased as chattel.

The economy of the Chosŏn dynasty was predominantly agrarian, and land was the main source of revenue for the state and individuals. Determined not to repeat the chaotic land situation that plagued the last years of Koryŏ rule, the Chosŏn dynastic founders paid special attention to the equitable distribution of land and at the outset instituted a redistribution. Regarded as the fundamental source of life, agriculture was actively promoted by the state. With the introduction of the advanced Kiangnan technology from South China, wet-farming and rice transplantation methods were gradually adopted in the southern provinces during the fifteenth and sixteenth centuries.[3] These new technologies along with improved seeds and fertilizer eliminated fallow land and ultimately enabled farmers to reap two crops in one year from the same soil.

Commerce, on the other hand, was regarded by the Confucianists as a nonproductive occupation and thus was discouraged by the state. Merchants were viewed as parasitic—living on the sweat and labor of the farmers—and hence the government permitted only licensed merchants to set up shops in Seoul to cater to the needs of the government and the people. Despite the government's position, commercial activities gradually grew: in the countryside, certain localities began holding markets at periodic intervals, such as every five days, and bands of itinerant merchants began traveling from town to town to attend these markets. In general, however, the Neo-Confucian government of

Chosŏn scorned extravagance and stressed frugality and thrift in its approach to daily life.

In the traditional period, Korea maintained a special relationship with China that was largely characterized by *sadae* (respect for the senior state). As part of the East Asian Confucian world order in which China occupied the central position, the Chosŏn dynasty accepted a junior status to China and scrupulously observed the ritual practices of a tributary state. Ever since Korea had accepted Confucian norms as the way of conducting state affairs, it had no qualms about accepting China as the senior state. In terms of strategy, Korea was vitally important to China's own security and thus had never been permitted to fall into hostile hands. The configuration of power so favored China that Korea had no choice but to remain friendly. Moreover, the two East Asian countries had historically shared a mutual interest in security as both had faced the same threat, namely, the tribal groups in the north. Only a strong China could keep them in check and maintain peace in the region. Under these conditions, Korea simply could not afford to lose China's friendship, even if it meant accepting the status of a junior state. In the final analysis, Korea's *sadae* policy enabled it to maintain its independent nationhood free from interference—political, military, or otherwise—from China. Furthermore, Korea's practice of *sadae* diplomacy ensured almost limitless access to Chinese culture and civilization.

In addition, Korea also maintained a careful diplomacy toward Japan. Initially, the Chosŏn government's foremost concern had been the problem of Japanese marauders. Although their pillaging had been drastically reduced by the beginning of the dynasty, there were still occasional harassments from Japan. To eliminate these marauders once and for all, King Sejong launched a military expedition in 1419 against their base, the islands of Tsushima. Once Tsushima was subdued, the Japanese were allowed to engage in trade with Korea at three ports at and near present-day Pusan under strict supervision of the Korean government. Following the Hideyoshi invasion in 1592–1598, Korea maintained basically friendly relations with Tokugawa Japan in the name of *kyorin* (neighborly relations).

As the Chosŏn dynasty passed the first century mark, tensions within the Neo-Confucian bureaucracy flared up in the form of literati purges known as *sahwa*. These purges took place four times within the span of less than fifty years—in 1498, 1504, 1519, and 1545—and a number of officials were either executed or banished. As a result, the whole bureaucracy was paralyzed. The literati purges have been explained largely in terms of political, ideological, and economic conflicts between the so-called meritorious elites (*hungu*) and the Neo-Confucian literati (*sarim*). The meritorious elites were those officials who had gained power and wealth over a period of time largely on the basis of their proximity to the throne and their lineage, whereas the Neo-Confucian literati comprised a new breed of scholar-officials who rose through the government ranks inspired by the ideals of Neo-Confucianism as practiced by some of the Koryŏ loyalists who refused to bend their principles even when faced with death. Ideologically more firmly committed than the meritorious elites and unencumbered by vested interests, the Neo-Confucian literati criticized and remonstrated without hesitation whenever they felt the conduct of the kings and high officials did not meet the high standards of Neo-Confucian principles. Although the Neo-Confucian literati became the victims of these purges, their moralistic causes, such as the sagely rule championed by Cho Kwangjo (1482–1519), were upheld as just by later generations, and in the end their Neo-Confucian worldview prevailed among the scholar-officials of Chosŏn as the Neo-Confucian orthodoxy.

While the Neo-Confucian orthodoxy was widely accepted as the sole foundation of the state and society, the officialdom split into factions in the last decades of the sixteenth century. Divided initially into Easterners and Westerners over the appointment of an official to a key middle-ranking post within the Ministry of Personnel, the two factions were later subdivided further into Northerners and Southerners, and Old Doctrine and Young Doctrine, respectively. (The directional references are merely formal designations and have nothing to do with regional ties.) The politics of the Chosŏn court thereafter followed largely the competition for power among these factions, frequently involving important state policies, such as diplomatic relations with neighboring countries, the land tax and other revenue measures, and the rules governing various rites. The factional alignments may have followed the philosophical debate regarding the role of *i* (principle) versus *ki* (material force)—argued by the two greatest philosophers of Chosŏn, Yi Hwang (T'oegye, 1501–1570) and Yi I (Yulgok, 1536–1584)—in which the scholar-officials favored one side or the other.

The *i/ki* debate was easily the most important philosophical issue occupying the minds of Korean scholars during the Chosŏn dynasty.

The debate started when Ki Taesŭng (1527–1572) questioned Yi Hwang's position that "the Four Beginnings are the issuance of principle (*i*) and the Seven Feelings are the issuance of material force (*ki*)." The Four Beginnings refer to the Mencian concepts of humanity, righteousness, propriety, and wisdom, which are inherently good, whereas the Seven Feelings, joy, anger, sorrow, fear, love, hatred, and desire, are sometimes good and sometimes evil. The two philosophers then exchanged a series of letters debating the role of principle and material force in the functions of the Four Beginnings and the Seven Feelings. This celebrated debate between the two, also known as the Four-Seven Debate, ended with Ki Taesŭng agreeing basically with Yi Hwang after Yi modified his position somewhat.

Although the issue may have been settled between Yi Hwang and Ki Taesŭng, the controversy persisted among other scholars and was taken up anew by Yi I when he debated with his friend Sŏng Hon (1535–1598) and challenged Yi Hwang's position. In analyzing the functions of *i* and *ki*, Yi Hwang, as explained by the modern Korean scholar Ki-baik Lee, "stressed particularly the role of the formative or normative element, *i*, as the basis of the activity of *ki*; thus *i* comes to be seen as an existential force that masters or controls *ki*."[4] Thus, Yi Hwang emphasized the supremacy of *i* in the *i/ki* duality. Yi I, however, placed equal importance on both *i* and *ki* in the activation of the Four Beginnings and the Seven Feelings, but he came to be identified as emphasizing the supremacy of *ki*. The Four-Seven Debate thus became the most important philosophical issue of the Chosŏn dynasty.

The peace enjoyed by the Chosŏn dynasty for two centuries was abruptly shattered when Japan under Toyotomi Hideyoshi (1536–1598) launched an invasion against Korea in 1592. Long dominated by a civil bureaucracy that relied on Confucian civility in dealing with foreigners, the Chosŏn government was utterly unprepared for the crisis. Despite the gallant resistance offered by the Korean military, the capital city, Seoul, fell to the Japanese within three weeks, forcing King Sŏnjo (1567–1608) and his entourage to flee north toward the Chinese border. As the situation grew desperate, the Chosŏn government appealed to China for military assistance. To help Korea and to protect its own security, the Ming government sent a large number of troops to Korea and forced the Japanese to retreat southward. In the meantime, recovering from the shock of initial defeat, the Korean people organized militia units in various parts of the country to fight the invaders and inflicted significant damage upon the Japanese. At sea Korea maintained complete supremacy as the Korean navy, under the able command of Admiral Yi Sunsin (1545–1598), vanquished the Japanese navy using the iron-clad vessels known as "Turtle Ships." Though there was a short interlude, the war lasted six years until the death of Hideyoshi in 1598. It decimated the population and destroyed innumerable cultural and historic treasures.

Before Korea was able to recover from the devastation of the Japanese invasion, the Manchu invaded Korea twice, in 1627 and 1636. The 1636 invasion was particularly painful for Korea; as the Manchu troops stormed into Korea, King Injo (1623–1649) and his court sought refuge in the mountain fortress of Namhansan, located in the present southeastern suburb of Seoul, only to suffer ignominious defeat in the end. Consequently, the Korean king was obliged to perform kowtow to the Manchu conqueror and sue for peace. According to the terms of peace, Korea was to terminate its ties with Ming China and to accept the Manchu as the senior state. The Manchu then moved on to defeat Ming and established itself as the Ch'ing dynasty in China. Korea never forgot this humiliation at the hands of the Manchu, traditionally regarded as barbarians, and secretly held rancor in its dealings with Ch'ing for a long period of time—at one time even scheming to undertake a military retaliation against the Manchu.

Although the first half of the Chosŏn dynasty's rule witnessed a number of domestic conflicts and external threats, the Chosŏn state overcame them and maintained a remarkably stable political and social system. During this period, the Chosŏn dynasty attained a number of achievements. Particularly noteworthy is the spectacular success of King Sejong's rule; however, his successors were unable to match the standard of rulership Sejong had set. With respect to intellectual pursuits, although a greater emphasis was placed on conformity than on heterogeneity, the early Chosŏn dynasty nevertheless made significant advances in the scholarly pursuit of philosophical and metaphysical issues. In the arts and literature, a number of creative men and women have bequeathed us an array of impressive works. In the social and economic sectors, though the Chosŏn dynasty never enjoyed spectacular wealth, its people in general lived in reasonable security and comfort with adequate supplies of daily necessities. These are no small achievements for any preindustrialized state. YC

CHAPTER THIRTEEN

Founding the Chosŏn Dynasty

Founding the new dynasty of Chosŏn—replacing the Koryŏ dynasty that had ruled Korea for nearly five hundred years—was not an easy task for General Yi Sŏnggye. First he had to overcome the forces of opposition that had a vested interest in the Koryŏ court. This he accomplished with little bloodshed by means of a coup d'état. Imposing a new rule on the disaffected people, however, was an entirely different matter. Therefore, Yi Sŏnggye had to rely upon the Neo-Confucian literati to organize a new government and set up a new code of regulations for his fledgling state. Fortunately for him, he was able to attract a number of capable and reform-minded scholar-officials who were willing to work with him. With their help, Yi Sŏnggye justified the inauguration of the new dynasty in the name of the Mandate of Heaven.

Thus, the Chosŏn state embarked on its course toward realizing a Neo-Confucian society while rejecting or suppressing deeply rooted Buddhist beliefs and native traditions. To start anew, the dynastic founder decided to shift the capital from Songdo (now Kaesŏng). After careful considerations of several alternative sites, Hanyang (present-day Seoul) was chosen as the new capital, which then was developed in accord with careful city planning.

Upon his ascension to the throne on the seventeenth of the seventh month in 1392, King T'aejo issued decrees covering a variety of administrative issues, to make appointments throughout the top bureaucracy, and to report the founding of the new dynasty to the Ming emperor. On the twenty-eighth, he issued what may be called his "founding edict," asserting his legitimacy, claiming the loyalty of his officials, and setting forth the means and rationale for action in several key areas of government.   DC

King T'aejo: Founding Edict
[From *T'aejo sillok* 1:43a–45a]

The king issued the following edict to all the officials . . . and the people:

The king announces:

It is heaven which created all the people of the earth, who ordained their rulers, heaven which nurtured them to share life with each other, and heaven which governed them so as to enjoy peace with one another. There have been both good and bad rulers, and there have been times when people followed their rulers willingly and other times when they turned against them. Some have been blessed with the Mandate of Heaven and others have lost it. This is a principle that has remained constant.

On the sixteenth of the seventh month of the twenty-fifth year in the reign of the Hung-wu Emperor [1392], the Privy Council (*To-p'yŏngŭisasa*) and all ranks of officials together urged me to take the throne, saying: "After King Kongmin died leaving no legitimate heir . . . the doom of the Koryŏ dynasty was sealed. . . . Although King Kongyang [1389–1392] was empowered temporarily to take charge of state affairs, he was confused and broke the law, causing many people to rebel and even his own relatives to turn against him, and he was incapable of preserving and protecting the ancestral shrines and institutions. How could anyone restore what heaven has abandoned? The ancestral shrines and institutions should only be entrusted to one who is worthy, and the throne must not be left vacant for long. People's minds are all looking up to your meritorious achievements and virtue, and you should accept the throne to rectify the situation, thereby satisfying the people's desire."

Fearful that I lack both virtue and capacity to assume the awesome responsibilities, I declined the offer of the throne repeatedly. But I am told that the people's wishes are such that heaven's will is clearly manifested in them and that no one should refuse the wishes of the people, for to do so is to act contrary to the will of heaven. Because the people insisted so steadfastly, I yielded finally to their will and ascended the throne. . . . Now that we are at the threshold of a new beginning, I must show abundant grace, and I hereby announce the following policies for the benefit of the people. . . .

As for the civil and the military examinations, I will not abandon one in favor of the other. Let more students be chosen for the National Academy in the capital and the county schools in order to promote scholarship and train men of talent. The original purpose of the examination system was to recruit men of talent for the state. With the practice of calling the examiners "masters" and the candidates "disciples," the system of impartial selection has been replaced by a system of private favors. This does not accord with the original purpose of the law. From now on, the registrar of the National Confucian Academy in the capital and the governors of each province will select those students in their schools who are bright in the classics and of good character; they will certify their age, clan, and three ancestors and record the classics they mastered; and then they will send them to the director of the National Academy. The students will then be examined on their knowledge of the classics, and those who did well on the Four Books and the Five Classics as well as the *Tzu-chih t'ung-chien* (Comprehensive Mirror for Aid in Government) will be ranked according to the degree of their mastery. Those who pass this first stage of the examination will be sent to the Ministry of Rites for the second stage, where they will be tested on their ability to compose documentary prose (*p'yo*), memorials (*chang*), and rhymeprose (*kobu*). They will then be examined at the final stage on problem essays (*ch'aengmun*). Of those who are successful in all three stages of examination, thirty-three men will be selected. They will then be forwarded to the Ministry of Personnel for appointment to an office according to their abilities. . . .

The Military Training Administration will be in charge of instruction in military matters. Candidates will be instructed in the seven military classics as well as marksmanship and horsemanship, and they will then be ranked according to their mastery of the classics and their skill as marksmen and horsemen. Thirty-three finalists will be awarded the military degree in the manner of awarding the civil examination degree. Their names then will be sent to the Ministry of War for official appointment.

The cardinal rituals of our state are the rites of capping, marriage, funerals, and ancestor worship. In order for human relations to be harmonized and customs to be rectified, let the Ministry of Rites carefully research the classics and codes, deliberate on past practices, and then establish regulations for the rituals.

We cannot overemphasize the importance of the magistrates, whose duties involve direct dealing with the people. The Privy Council, the Censorate, and the Six Ministries will recommend those whom they know to be just, fair, upright, and capable of appointments as magistrates. After thirty months in office, those whose records are outstanding will be promoted. If any fail to live up to expectations, those who recommended them will bear the blame.

Because of the importance of morals and customs, we should encourage loyal ministers, filial sons, righteous husbands, and faithful wives. Let local officials seek out such people and recommend them for preferential treatment and further advancement and for memorial arches to commemorate their virtuous deeds.

The king should place importance on extending sympathy and providing relief to aged widowers and widows, orphans, and the childless. All local officials should assist those who are hungry and destitute within their jurisdiction and should give them exemption from corvée duties . . . .

Toward the end of Koryŏ, there was no unified system of criminal justice. The Ministry of Punishments, the constabulary, and the detention halls all meted out punishments on their own. These were not always appropriate. Henceforth the Ministry of Punishments will be in charge of the criminal code, litigation, and criminal investigations and punishments. The constabulary, on the other hand, will be in charge of patrolling, catching thieves, and maintaining order. At present, when the Ministry of Punishments renders judgment in a case, the culprit is invariably stripped of his writ of appointment and forced to resign his post, even if the offense is only punishable by flogging, and guilt is attached to his descendants. This is not the way the sage-kings meant it to be. DC

Admonition to the New King
[From *T'aejo sillok* 1:40a–42b]

The Office of the Inspector-General was one of two main bodies (the other was the Office of the Censor-General) whose functions included remonstrating with the king and pronouncing on morals in general and abuse of public office in particular. The Inspector-General was a high-ranking official (Rank 2B), sometimes even a member of the State Council. This document is an admonition to the new king to avoid the evil practices of the past by setting up new procedures. A key element is the repeated concern over the appointment of good men to office, reflecting the early Chosŏn dynasty's critiques of government in the late Koryŏ period. Notable too are the numerous allusions to the Chinese classics, which give authority and legitimacy to the ideas being expressed. DC

Once again the Inspector-General memorialized the throne:

Your Majesty, responding to the call of heaven, has accepted the mandate and has now ascended the throne. In the *Book of Documents* it is written: "God dwelling in the great heavens has changed his decree in favor of his eldest son and this great dynasty of Yin. Our king has received that decree. Unbounded is the happiness connected with it, and unbounded is the anxiety. Oh! How can he be other than reverent?"[1]

Reverence is the heart's controlling force and the basis of all things. Thus, whether on such important occasions as serving and offering sacrifices to heaven or in such small matters as rising, dwelling, eating, and resting, one should never turn away from piety for even a moment. The reason for the rise of King T'ang is that from early morning until late at night he was filled with awe and wonder, uplifting and reverencing the Heavenly Way. The reason for the fall of Kings Chieh and Chou is that they lost virtue and ruled by force and neglected the way of reverence. This one word, "reverence," is the source of good government for all rulers. Throughout history, all rule and misrule, and all the rises and falls, have emanated from it. What Your Majesty does from this day forward is the foundation that will be passed down to future generations; likewise, today's actions will determine whether heaven decrees good or bad fortune for the future. Thus it is our earnest wish that Your Majesty think constantly as if you were with the Lord of Heaven and act as if the Lord of Heaven were present, even in moments of idleness. In dealing with matters of state, you should be even more prudent in your thinking. If you do this, the reverence in your heart will be sufficient to move heaven, and you will be able to realize the ideal rule.

With this memorial we undertake respectfully to enumerate certain things you should do. We sincerely hope that you will adopt and implement them so that the model of this generation can be emulated by myriad generations.

First, establish rules and laws. One who wishes to rule his state well should not be concerned about safety and peril; rather, he should be concerned with whether the rules and laws are properly established. . . .

Second is an unambiguous system of rewards and punishments. The power to grant rewards and mete out punishments is part of the great authority of the ruler. Even Yao and Shun could not have ruled had they not rewarded men of merit or punished those who did wrong. If you give rewards and punishments fairly, the path of merit will be clearly revealed to all, and the people will have no grounds to criticize you. . . . Third is the cleaving to superior men and distancing yourself from inferior men. Truly it is necessary to distinguish between superior men and inferior men. The superior man is one who is honest and holds to principle, not relying on others, who knows how to act with utmost loyalty when in office and how to counsel the sovereign in his weakness when not in office, who is open and fair-minded; who is concerned about the ancestral shrines and institutions and not about himself. The inferior man is one who is wicked and sycophantic; who curries favor to gain acceptance; who usurps authority and abuses it; who claims credit for the accomplishments of others and ingratiates himself with servile flattery; who is concerned solely with his selfish interests without heeding others' opinions. Superior men are hard to find and easy to lose, inferior men are easy to find and hard to get rid of. . . . In the *Book of Documents* it is written: "In your employment of men of worth, let none come between you and them; put away evil without hesitation."[2] We beseech Your Majesty to appoint men in whom you truly discern wisdom despite their minor faults and to shun those in whom you truly discern empty flattery despite their merits.

Fourth is the willingness to accept remonstrance. In the classics it is written: "The Son of Heaven who has seven remonstrance officials will not lose the empire though he himself is without the Tao; the feudal lord who has five remonstrance officials will not lose his state even though he himself is without the Tao." This is an adage for all generations. For the minister does not remonstrate with his sovereign for profit; rather he does it for the good of the state. The sovereign's majesty is like thunder; his power is as weighty as iron. Is it an easy thing for the minister to brave the thunder and bear the heavy weight to offer his sovereign words as if to cure his ailments? And yet the difference between accepting and rejecting such advice can mean the

difference between good fortune and disaster, between profit and loss
for the state. Therefore, the ruler must always guide and seek remonstrance, accepting it with equanimity. . . . As it is written in the *Book
of Documents:* "He listened to expostulation and did not resist," and
"If the sovereign follows remonstrance, he becomes like the sage."[3]
We beseech the king to take these words to heart.

Fifth is rooting out slanderous talk. The sage-emperor Shun said:
"I abominate slanderous speakers and destroyers of right ways, who
agitate and alarm my people."[4] Is it not dreadful that people become
so easily confused by slander that even such a sage as Shun was
concerned with it? Slanderers and flatterers employ all means to implicate innocent persons, using criminal charges in order to confuse the
sovereign. . . . If you discern wickedness with wisdom, then deceitfulness cannot escape and slandering will be rooted out.

Sixth is to beware of indolence and dissoluteness. In the *Book of
Documents* it is written: "Let not the emperor set to the rulers of states
an example of indolence or dissoluteness."[5] The harm that indolence
and dissoluteness inflict upon virtue is not confined to one thing. The
desire to be in repose in the palace, to feast on fine food, to enjoy the
ministrations of your queen and palace women, the pleasures of the
hunt, raising dogs and horses, and to amuse yourself with flowers and
plants: all these things harm men's disposition and dissipate their will.
Therefore, one must exercise caution. For indeed, the Mandate of
Heaven is a transient thing; it is a help to one who has virtue, but . . .
even one moment's lapse into indolence and dissoluteness will be
noticed by heaven. It is indeed to be feared.

Seventh is respect for frugality and economy. King Yü of Hsia
demonstrated his virtue by building his palace low and being frugal in
clothing. Emperor Wen of Han displayed his exemplary attitude by
being thrifty in the use of money and having his clothes made of black
silk. Even though they were noble enough to become Sons of Heaven
and rich and powerful enough to become rulers of all under heaven,
they were yet frugal and sparing. How much less should the sovereign
be careless in his expenditure in Korea, whose land is squeezed between the mountains and the sea and whose population and taxes are
not numerous! . . .

Eighth is the shunning of eunuchs. The problem of eunuchs is an
old one. . . .

Ninth is the weeding out of unqualified Buddhist clergy. Buddhism
is a practice of barbarians. It first came into China during the Yung-

p'ing era of the Han [A.D. 58–76] and then was passed on to Korea, where its practice became even more widespread. . . . Originally, the dharma taught ways to cleanse the heart and lessen men's desire; those who followed its teaching even ran away and hid themselves in caves, eating only vegetables and drinking only water in an effort to discipline themselves. Now, however, they mingle with ordinary people using high-sounding words and professing high ideals, bedazzling even scholars and intimidating simple folk with talk of retribution for sin, fostering wasteful habits among the people and encouraging them to forsake their proper occupations. . . . Indeed, nothing is more likely to destroy the state and sicken the people than this. We beseech Your Majesty to round up these Buddhist clerics and examine them carefully on their doctrine and practice. Those who truly know the doctrine and truly practice virtue should be allowed to teach; all the others should be made to grow out their hair and return to their former occupations.

Tenth is the regulation of access to the palace. The establishment of the palace is meant to enhance the sovereign's power and to define clearly the boundary between the inner and outer courts. With the qualities endowed by heaven, Your Majesty has transformed your house into a new state. Your former associates, your relatives, and people relying on the influence of others move in and out of the palace; yet guards will not dare question them. We are afraid that this will give rise to increasing requests for favors and to slander, causing antagonism between the inner and outer courts and confusion in government and justice. We beseech Your Majesty to order the gate guards to prohibit the unauthorized entry of anyone without official position, and especially to spurn shamans who practice women's magic and those who cunningly flatter.

Your ministers believe that trust is the sovereign's greatest asset— for the state is protected by the people, and the people are protected by trust. For this reason, the sage would sooner have done without an army and food to eat, than to have done without trust, and that is a profound lesson for later generations and our time as well. If Your Majesty does not employ trust in establishing the rules and laws and in making clear distinctions between rewards and punishments, the rules and laws will surely decline, and the system of rewards and punishment will inevitably disintegrate. If you do not act with trust in attracting superior men and spurning inferior men, the superior will easily become estranged from you, and the inferior will easily find their way into your company. If you do not act with trust in hearing remonstrance and in trying to root out slander, you will find that good advice seems unpleasant to the ear while flattering words will come to influence your decisions. If you do not act with trust in warning against indolence and dissoluteness and in respecting frugality and economy, you will be unable to achieve your good intentions and to ward off treacherous flattery. . . . If you do not keep trust in mind as you purge the eunuchs and weed out unqualified monks, those you have already purged will find ways to advance themselves again, and those not yet purged will find ways to stay. And if you do not keep trust in mind while regulating access to the palace, there will be no way to stop unscrupulous people from trading on their connections in order to gain entry. We beseech Your Majesty to keep this trust unwaveringly and firmly, to enforce these points as faithfully as the seasons follow one another, never forsaking the mandate granted you by heaven above to help you, nor the desires of the officials and the people to have you lead them as their king, so that unbounded peace will prevail for myriad generations.   DC

Moving to the New Capital
[From *T'aejo sillok* 6:11a–13a]

Choosing a new location for the capital was an important symbolic step for the new dynasty. The decadence of the final years of Koryŏ encouraged thoughts of a fresh start in a new city, despite the great effort and inconvenience that would attend such a move. Many things had to be taken into account in siting the new city. It had to be defensible, for example, yet accessible by water and road so that officials could travel and tax commodities could be carried in and out. The lay of the land was important, too, though T'aejo's officials differed in their respect for the laws of geomancy. The Chinese classics had to be consulted in order to determine precedents for moving the capital. And beneath it all were practical considerations of officials who apparently did not want to leave Songdo, the metropolitan center of Korea, for the undeveloped valley of Hanyang (present-day Seoul).

Among the several sites considered, two were given intensive study: the valley south of Mount Kyeryong, northwest of today's Taejŏn, in southern Ch'ungch'ŏng province, and the valley between the southern spurs of Mount Muak, just west of the site eventually chosen (known today for the location of Yonsei and Ehwa universities.) The excerpt translated here describes the final choice, beginning with arguments solicited by the king from his officials concerning the merits of the Muak valley site.   DC

In considering whether to establish the capital here, he had first ordered his officials to scout out the area. Now he ordered each one separately to express an opinion to him about whether it was worth moving the capital to the Muak site.

The Director of Treasury Chŏng Tojŏn said: "This place lies in the center of the country and the transport is good, but unfortunately it lies in one small valley, and there is not enough room for the palace within the city, and no place to set up markets or ancestral temples outside, and thus it is not a suitable place for the king to reside. Your minister is not learned in yin/yang theory, and since most people nowadays cannot argue such issues without using yin/yang theory, perhaps your minister's opinion is not worth hearing. But as Mencius said: 'A man spends his youth in learning the principles of right government, and being grown up to vigor, he wishes to put them into practice. . . .'[6] Thus I beg to speak of what I have learned from experience. King Ch'eng of Chou [1115–1078 B.C.] established his capital at Chia-ju, and his posterity continued for thirty generations and eight hundred years. Four hundred forty-nine years after the rise of the Chou house, in the time of King P'ing, of the eleventh generation, the capital was moved to Lo-yang proper. The Ch'in established their capital on the site used by the Western Chou, and in the time of King Nan, of the thirtieth generation of Chou, the kingdom was lost and the Ch'in rose in its place. One sees by this that the fate of Chou, which lasted eight hundred years through thirty generations, was not a thing that rested on geography. . . . Other examples in Chinese history demonstrate that it is people who determine whether a state is ruled wisely or foolishly; it is not a thing that depends on geography. . . .

"Since the Three Kingdoms period in our country, our capitals have been Kyerim [Kyŏngju] in the east, Wansan [Chŏnju] in the south, and P'yŏngyang in the north, while in the center there is Songgyŏng [Songdo or Kaesŏng]. Kyerim and Wansan are located in isolated corners of the country, in places too remote for the effective conduct of royal business. P'yŏngyang is too near the northern frontier, and your minister believes it, too, is unsuitable for a capital.

"Your Majesty's rule follows that of the collapsed former dynasty. Because the people's livelihood has not yet recovered and the foundation of the state has not yet been consolidated, it would be better that you first pacify the people and allow them to rest so that they can regain strength. You should select a suitable site for the capital in accordance with the heavenly signs and people's wishes and should wait for a proper time to move. In this way, all will be safe while your dynasty's rule over Chosŏn will be everlasting along with the descendants of your ministers.

"Those who discuss geomancy nowadays are drawing on the experiences of earlier people rather than on their own, just as your minister's words are based on the experiences of earlier people. How, then, can one believe in geomancers and reject the wisdom of Confucian scholars? Your minister's fervent hope is that Your Majesty will deeply ponder this problem, put the people's welfare first, and only then try divination to determine a new capital, so as to avoid misfortunes."

The Royal Secretary Yi Chik [1362–1431] said: "I have carefully studied the geography texts on the matter of founding states and establishing capitals and have found that they generally recommend the location of capitals and palaces where myriad streams and thousands of hills merge and where there are stately mountains and great rivers. This means the place where the vital forces of nature converge and where water transport is convenient. . . . Our own country's legendary prophecies point to the area south of Mount Samgak, to the banks of the Han River, and also to Musan [Mount Muak]. They all seem to indicate this locale. In general, choosing a site and moving the capital is an exceedingly important task, not something to be decided by one or two people but rather something to be done in keeping with the will of heaven and the wishes of the people. It is written in the *Book of Documents:* 'If . . . the tortoise, the milfoil, the nobles and officers, and the common people all consent to a course,'[7] there can be no other way but to follow it. Whether or not to move the capital depends on time and destiny. How could your minister argue it lightly? Your Majesty should decide by reading the heavenly will and the people's mind, and in this way you are going along with heaven. But even so, I think that the Muak valley site is too narrow."

Disturbed that so many of his ministers had spoken in opposition to moving the capital, the king said: "I will return to Songdo and decide the matter in the Office of Taoist Rites." He then set out for the southern capital Hansŏng. The next day the king inspected the ancient palace sites of the southern capital and observed the configurations of the mountains. He then asked Yun Sindal and his other companions:

"What about this place?"

Yun replied: "Within the borders of our land, Songdo is the best spot of all, but this is next best. However, it has one regrettable feature: the northwest corner is too low, so the spring water dries up too readily."

The king was pleased and said: "How can there be no deficiencies even in Songdo? As I see the terrain of this place, it seems like a fit location for a royal capital. What is more, it is accessible by water, it is centrally located, and it will also be a convenient place for the people."

The king then spoke to the Royal Preceptor Chach'o, asking: "What do you think?"

Chach'o answered: "There are heights and scenic beauty on all sides here, and the center is level. It is a good place for fortifications and also for a capital. Still, you should consider the opinions of many people before you decide."

The king then ordered his ministers to discuss it, and they returned with a consensus: "If you are determined to move the capital, then this is a good place to move it to."

Ha Yun [1347–1416] alone dissented, saying: "The mountains seem well configured, but from the standpoint of geomancy it cannot be considered good."

Then the king, acting on the advice of his ministers, decided on Hanyang as the capital.   DC

CHAPTER FOURTEEN

Political Thought in Early Chosŏn

The founders of Chosŏn were fully committed to Sung Neo-Confucianism as their guiding creed and endeavored to transform Korea into a Confucian state in which the Ch'eng-Chu tradition would be properly preserved. For the scholar-officials of early Chosŏn, Neo-Confucianism was above all a political philosophy that, grounded in the sociopolitical models of China's antiquity, provided them with reliable and efficient patterns for reforming state and society. They spoke of Neo-Confucianism as "substantial learning" (*sirhak*) that provided not only a new political vision but also answers to the most pressing problems of their time.

Korean Neo-Confucianism recognized the *Ta hsüeh* (Great Learning), the small treatise that Chu Hsi (1130–1200) had selected as one of the Four Books—the basic text that outlined a systematic and pragmatic program for moral education as well as political action. The fundamental purpose of scholarship now was to recreate the ideal political order as exemplified by China's sage-rulers, Yao and Shun, and the founders of the Hsia, Shang, and Chou. This connection between scholarship and good rule developed in the course of time into an idealistic imperative of great intensity that ran like a thread through all political thought of early Chosŏn. MD

Ruling the New Dynasty

Cho Chun: On T'aejo's Accession to the Throne
[From *Tong munsŏn* 40:25b–26b]

Cho Chun (1346–1405) was one of Yi Sŏnggye's first supporters and a principal architect of Chosŏn Korea. In this memorial (1392) Cho Chun recalls the initial years of this collaboration and praises Yi Sŏnggye for achievements to which he himself had contributed significantly, most notably the land reforms. In the untranslated second part of this memorial Cho Chun reviews the political events of the final years of Koryŏ and depicts Yi Sŏnggye's seizure of power as a historical necessity comparable to the dynastic changes of ancient China that were manifestations of heaven's shifting mandate. He thus embedded Yi Sŏnggye's ascendance to power in an ideological context that lent the new dynasty legitimacy and authority. MD

Your minister Chun reports. Your servant first held military functions in the service of the former dynasty. Midway I suffered bad luck, closed the door, and read books, intending to finish my life in this way. When I first saw Your Majesty while you were still a concealed dragon, not yet in power, it was as if I had met an old acquaintance. Heaven made me meet you! In the first month of the year *mujin* [1388] you and General Ch'oe Yŏng [1316–1388] wiped out the villains Yŏm Hŭngbang [d. 1388] and Im Kyŏnmi [d. 1388] who had poisoned the people's life for fifteen years, and your virtue of having destroyed them settled in the people's mind. When Ch'oe Yŏng, lacking learning, plotted with the illegitimate ruler King U to attack Liao-tung and led an army across the Yalu, Your Majesty righteously turned around the flag and averted disaster for the people of the Three Han [Korea]. Your merit of having brought about peace settled in the land.

At the time you made me Inspector-General, there was nothing your servant knew that he could not say and nothing you said that was not followed. You activated the disrupted social relations and spread the just way. You elevated the superior and good and chased out the wicked. You relieved the people of their burdens, achieved good relations with China, and, by expelling the false ruler Sin Ch'ang, restored the Wang house. The Son of Heaven, the Chinese emperor, rejoiced at this and sent an envoy to encourage you, for your merit of having restored the dynasty became known across the world. When you made me Inspector-General, you generously inaugurated the great peace for myriad generations and announced this to the gods in heaven. You repelled the slander of the wicked and withstood the anger of the influential. You reformed the evils of private land that had accumulated over the years and saved the living from their precarious situation. You provided enough food for the soldiers in difficult times and used them to build ships and fortresses. The military's prestige was thereby heightened and canals and roads opened. The calamity of the Japanese marauders under which the Three Han had suffered for forty years came to an end in one morning. You established rank land (*kwajŏn*) in Kyŏnggi, the capital province, to compensate the scholar-officials; you established military land (*kunjŏn*) in prefectures and magistratures to nourish officers and soldiers. Even local clerks and ferryboat attendants were given land.

As the land had a permanent system and the state established laws, each one had his fixed share and did not deprive the other. When monopolization of land ceased, the fields and houses of the myriad people were secure. Taxes and levies were light. Orphans and widows had enough to dress and to eat. As salaries were sufficient, modesty and a sense of propriety prevailed; as the storehouses were filled, state expenditures were defrayed.   MD

Kwŏn Kŭn: On Royal Action
[From *T'aejong sillok* 1:4b–7b]

Kwŏn Kŭn (1352–1409) was one of the spiritual founders of Chosŏn Korea. In his treatises and commentaries on the Chinese classics he laid out the basic concepts of Neo-Confucianism and illuminated their relevance for the political as well as the social life of the new dynasty. He emphasized the importance of Confucian learning for activating people's moral nature, a process of self-realization that was to culminate in the development of the proper human relationships between ruler and subject, father and son, elder and younger. One of Kwŏn Kŭn's favorite texts was the *Great Learning,* in which he found an outline for social and political action.

This memorial (1401) was written after a fire in Such'ang Palace, the royal home of the last Koryŏ kings in which Yi Sŏnggye had held his enthronement ceremony. Because this fire was interpreted as a warning of heaven to King T'aejong's young rule (1400–1418), Kwŏn Kŭn pointed out six matters to which the king should pay special attention: loyalty to King T'aejo (1392–1398), administration of state affairs, treatment of officials, attendance of royal lectures, rewarding of loyalty, and performance of state rituals. Kwŏn Kŭn advocated in particular the rehabilitation of his teacher, Chŏng Mongju (1337–1392), who had died as a Koryŏ loyalist. MD

ON TREATING COURT OFFICIALS

Although the distinction of ruler and minister is ceremonially strict, their relationship must be emotionally intimate. In olden times, the ruler was intimate and close to his high ministers, and he met face to face with his court officials. Every day he spent long hours with his ministers and officials, but the time during which he was close to eunuchs and concubines was short. Therefore slander and wickedness had no way to advance, and deception could not arise. The relationship between ruler and minister was based on mutual confidence, and the feelings between high and low were not concealed. Consequently the ruler was able to examine the hearts of the loyal and the wicked, and the minister was able to do his best to communicate his inner feelings to his ruler.

Rulers of later generations lived hidden in their palaces, and the ministers they received at court bowed perfunctorily and then retired. Since the feelings of ruler and ministers did not at all match, the wicked and the false deceived their ruler and took pleasure in concealing from him the gains and losses outside the palace and the interests and urgent concerns of the people. Because the rulers foolishly did not learn about these concerns, disaster resulted. This is a calamity common to present times as well!

Your servant wishes that from now on Your Majesty would regularly sit in court and receive your ministers in audience all through the day. You should grant an audience to all officials who depart and take leave or come from outside the court, regardless of their rank. If you use warm words to console them and clear questions to draw them out, all your officials will have grateful hearts, and you will learn all about the affairs of the people. Will the profit not be great? MD

ON ATTENDING ROYAL LECTURES

The way of emperors and kings is made bright through scholarship, and the rule of emperors and kings is extensive due to scholarship. From antiquity, those kings who were good even established royal lectures in order to investigate the learning of the sages. Although Your Majesty, since ascending the throne, has instituted royal lectures, the days on which the lectures are not held are numerous. Your Majesty is by natural disposition talented and bright, and your scholarship is refined and broad. When Confucian scholars come to lecture, can they possibly elucidate anything for you? Nevertheless, when you attend the royal lectures, you fix your attention on them, and in your mind their meaning is clear and manifest. There is indeed a difference between the time you are at ease and inactive and the time when you listen to the many matters of government. Is it not through this that the learning of the sages makes progress? . . .

Your servant respectfully wishes that, regardless of the brilliance of your natural talents or the inadequacy of the Confucian scholars, Your Majesty would daily attend the royal lectures and, with unprejudiced mind and humble determination, diligently pursue the studies. May you not stop the lectures for one single day! On a day that you stop them for whatever reasons, it is nevertheless proper to receive the lecturers, to inform them directly, and then to dismiss them. MD

ON REWARDING LOYALTY

Since antiquity, rulers have certainly rewarded scholars of integrity and righteousness as a means to secure the social fabric for myriad generations. When a king upholds righteousness and founds a dynasty, he rewards those who support him and punishes those who do not. This is indeed proper. If the time comes that the great undertaking, the founding of a new dynasty, is completed and secure, it is necessary to reward even those officials who remained loyal to the previous dynasty—the dead with posthumous titles, the living with appointments. Moreover, awarding them additional honors will encourage the integrity of officials of later generations. This is a principle common to both ancient times and the present.

Now, in response to fate, our state has founded a new dynasty, and three sage-kings have succeeded each other. The civil realm is at peace, but the law of rewarding integrity and purity has yet to be established. Is this not an omission? In my view, Chŏng Mongju of the former dynasty, as a poor scholar, received T'aejo's special favor of recommendation and thus advanced to high office. Was his heart unwilling to repay T'aejo such favors? With the brilliance of his talents and knowledge was he unaware of the direction in which the Heavenly Mandate and the hearts of the people went? Did he not know that the house of Wang was doomed? Did he not know that his safety was at stake? Even so he concentrated his mind on what he was doing and did not swerve from his integrity. Therefore he suffered death. This is what is called "even in great emergencies not being deprived of one's principles." Chŏng Mongju died in Koryŏ. Is it utterly impossible to honor him posthumously today? MD

New Government

With his broad erudition and energetic character, Chŏng Tojŏn was a prime mover in the founding process of the new dynasty. In his philosophical works he outlined the Confucian point of view and aggressively turned against Buddhism. He put an end to the Confucians' traditional tolerance of the Buddhist creed and advanced philosophical arguments against it. He also paid close attention to renewing and tightening the governmental structure. Inspired by the *Chou li* (Rites of Chou), Chŏng Tojŏn wrote the *Chosŏn kyŏngguk chŏn* (Administrative Codes of Chosŏn) in which he drafted the constitutional outline of the new dynasty. Although he emphasized the ruler's pivotal position in the governing process, he equally envisaged a strong standing for the *ch'ongjae* (prime minister), whose major task was to assist the king at the head of a well-organized administration. He also recognized the importance of the censorial agencies for checking the king as well as for supervising the officialdom. Chŏng Tojŏn's major concern, however, was the building of a government that would function through benevolence rather than force. In this sense he followed the Mencian tradition that eschewed coercion and espoused virtue as the sole means for winning the people's hearts. Chŏng Tojŏn's ideas exerted a lasting influence on the legislative process during the dynasty's first century. MD

Chŏng Tojŏn: On Rectifying the Throne
[From *Sambong chip* 7:1a–2a]

The *Book of Changes* says: "The great treasure of the sage is called 'seat.' The great virtue of heaven and earth is called 'giving and maintaining life.' Whereby is this seat preserved? By humanity."[1] The Son of Heaven enjoys the tribute of the world, and the local lords enjoy the tribute of their localities. They all are at the pinnacle of wealth and social prestige. The worthy and able devote themselves to wisdom; the brave and the courageous devote themselves to strength. The people hurry to fulfill their particular duties and follow only the ruler's orders. Hereby he has attained the throne. If this is not a great treasure, what is it then?

Heaven and earth concentrate on nothing other than nurturing the ten thousand things. The material force (*ki*) of this one source is all-pervasive, and the ten thousand things receive this force for their growth: thick things and thin ones, high things and low ones, each takes its own form and has its own particular nature. Therefore it is said: heaven and earth make the creation of things their principal concern. The so-called principal concern of creating things is nothing other than the great virtue of heaven and earth.

The throne of the ruler is indeed eminent and dignified. The world, however, is extremely wide and the ten thousand people are extremely numerous. If one ruler did not win their minds, great anxiety would exist. The common people are extremely weak, but it is not possible to coerce them with power; they are extremely ignorant, but it is not possible to trick them with wisdom. If the ruler wins their minds, they submit themselves to him. If he does not win their minds, they leave him. Between their leaving or following him there is no room for a single hair, no room for a compromise.

But winning their minds is done neither by abusing them with self-interest nor by seeking fame by going against the Way. It is done solely by humanity. If the ruler were to make the principal concern with which heaven and earth create all things his own concern, and were to conduct a government "which cannot bear to see the suffering of the people"[2] so that the people in the four parts of the world were all happy and looked up to him as to father and mother, then he would forever enjoy the pleasure of peace and wealth, of respect and honor, and the danger of disorder and upheaval would not exist. Is it thus not appropriate to preserve the throne with humanity?

Your Majesty obeys heaven and complies with the people, and you have quickly rectified the throne. You know that humanity is the sum of mind and virtue and that love is what humanity brings forth. Thus, to rectify the mind in order to embody it in humanity, to extend love in order to reach the people, this is the essence and the proper working of humanity. Who then would not have confidence that you preserve the throne and transmit it to thousands of generations? MD

Chŏng Tojŏn: On the Prime Minister
[From *Sambong chip* 7:5a–6a]

The administrative department is the domain of the prime minister. As the functionaries, et cetera, are all subject to the prime minister, administering the educational department also is one of the prime minister's duties.[3] If the prime minister gets the right men, the Six Ministries are well run, and the hundred offices are well regulated. Therefore it is said: "The ruler's task consists in settling for one chief minister." This points to the prime minister.

Above, he assists the king; below, he guides the officials and controls all the people. His task is indeed great! Furthermore, the abilities of rulers differ: some are dull, and some bright; some are strong, and some weak. The prime minister goes along with the ruler's goodness, but corrects his badness; he presents him with the feasible, but withholds from him the wrong. By so doing, he enables the ruler to enter the realm of the Great Mean. Therefore he is called "assistant"; this means that he supports and assists.

All the officials have different tasks, and the people have different occupations. The prime minister treats them fairly so that each does not lose what is proper for him; he treats them impartially so that all gain their proper place. Therefore he is called "chief minister"; this means that he rules and directs.

Only the prime minister knows about the services of the royal consorts and concubines, the duties of the eunuchs, the enjoyments of carriages and horses, of dress and ornaments, the provision of food and drink within the confines of the royal palace. He is an important minister. He is the one the ruler faces with decorum, yet he personally attends to the minutest matters. Is this not trivial? No! The royal consorts, the concubines, and the eunuchs are actually ready for the royal summons. But if the prime minister does not watch over them, they might deceive the king with wickedness and flattery. The carriages and horses, the dress and ornaments, the food and drink are actually for the provision of the royal person. But if the prime minister does not economize, there might be luxurious and lavish expenditures. Therefore the earlier kings established laws and entrusted them all to the prime minister who uses them for regulating and restraining. Their concern was far-reaching!

Because of the ruler's elevated position, it is difficult for his ministers to look up to him and correct him. It is impossible for them to restrain him with their power of wisdom; it is equally impossible to contest with him with their tongue. The only way open to them is to accumulate their own sincerity and to move him thereby and to correct themselves and to rectify him thereby.

It is also difficult for the prime minister alone to control all the many officials and the people. It is impossible for him to instruct them by holding their ears for attention; it is equally impossible to teach them house to house. The only way is to recognize the wise and the stupid and then to promote the former and keep the latter away so that every affair is taken care of and every official is under control. If all the matters are distinguished and taken care of according to their feasibility, things find their right place and the people are at peace.

The great Confucian of the Sung, Chen Te-hsiu [1178–1235], discussed the task of the prime minister and said: "He corrects himself and rectifies the ruler; he knows the people and tends the affairs." How excellent are these words! In my opinion, the perfection of self and the rectification of the ruler are the foundation of politics, and knowing the people and administering the affairs are the mechanism of politics. Therefore I have discussed this topic here. MD

Chŏng Tojŏn: On Censors and Inspectors
[From *Sambong chip* 10:4a–b]

The censor should put authority first and impeachment second. Why? Because even if the one who has authority does not speak all day long, the people fear him and submit themselves to him. The one who lacks authority, however, displays the hundred statutes every day, but the people do not fear him. Strong purpose and straightforward conduct are commonly not familiar to the human mind. If the censor wanted to purge officials and rectify the country with the power of censorship alone, the principles of society would not develop; on the contrary, fear and slander would arise first. . . .

The inspector reprimands people, but he also must reprimand himself. To reprimand others is not difficult; to reprimand oneself, however, is difficult. As for the secret inspector reprimanding others, those generals and ministers and high officials who are not the right persons, those officials and functionaries who do not fulfill their duties, those in the world who destroy the law and disrupt society, slander others, and hide their wickedness—the inspector has to reprimand them all. Does this mean that the inspector alone is without reprimand? If in his position there are things he does not know, or knowing them does not articulate them, or articulating them does not put them into action, or not putting them into action does not dispute them: this is what the superior man regards as evil, while the inferior man regards it as lucky. This is what the inspector must reprimand. Even if he does not reprimand himself, the world will reprimand him. Only the one who does not find it difficult to reprimand himself can reprimand others; thus he can fulfill his duty. MD

The Kingly Way

A prominent scholar-official of the mid-fifteenth century, Yang Sŏngji (1415–1482) outlined for teen-age King Tanjong (1452–1455) the essentials of kingly rule. Like his predecessors, Yang Sŏngji emphasized the close correlation between the king's moral stature and the stability and success of his rule. For striking a healthy balance between these two, the selection of capable officials was a king's foremost task. He needed the scholar-officials for his own enlightenment—the pursuit of "right learning" (chŏnghak) required their instruction and explanations. But he needed them equally for carrying the message of kingly rule beyond the palace walls. The scholar-officials were thus not only the king's teachers but also the most effective propagandists of the kingly way among the people at large. MD

Yang Sŏngji: Discussion on the Kingly Way
[From *Nulchae chip* 1:22b–24a]

Your servant observes that Your Majesty has at your youthful age taken over a great and difficult heritage. The ancestral charge is indeed heavy, and the expectations of the people are indeed great. The Heavenly Mandate is difficult to fathom, however, and the people's minds are not constant. If one single thought lacks seriousness, this may cause numerous matters to go wrong. If one single matter is not handled with prudence, this may cause boundless disaster. This is exactly what the *Book of Documents* means by the "unbounded happiness . . . and unbounded [. . .] anxiety"[4] of receiving the Heavenly Mandate.

Your servant has heard that there are three essentials a ruler keeps in mind: humanity, understanding, and resoluteness. Humanity means loving and nourishing the people. Understanding means differentiating between good and bad. Resoluteness means keeping inferior men at a distance. There are also three essentials for governing a country: to employ right men, to heed admonitions, and to reward and punish. If one employs the right men, all matters are regulated. If one heeds admonitions, everything good accumulates. If one is trustworthy in rewarding and stern in punishing, the good are encouraged and the bad take warning. And the whole world will exert itself. Ah! Heaven has created the people, but it cannot rule them by itself. Therefore it has entrusted them to the ruler. The ruler cares for the people, but he cannot rule them alone. Therefore he commits them to officials.

Now, in the capital the State Council supervises the hundred officials and the Six Ministries manage all matters. It is proper to charge those in high positions with supporting and nourishing the royal virtue and those in low positions with aiding and fostering the people's livelihood. For selecting officials, it is necessary to choose the proper men; for collecting taxes and levies, it is necessary to have equal standards; for rites and education, it is necessary to cultivate understanding; for the military administration, it is necessary to motivate to action; for punishments, it is necessary to be impartial and forgiving; for works and repairs, it is necessary to be careful and economical. In all matters of the various offices, it is necessary to be diligent and cautious.

Outside the capital, the governors administer localities, and the local magistrates are in charge of counties. The governor investigates the sufferings of the people and checks the greediness and cruelty of local magistrates. He encourages agriculture in order to enrich the people's livelihood and promotes schools in order to rectify their customs. When assigning corvée labor, he takes care to be impartial and equitable; when deciding prison sentences, he is determined to be sincere and honest. He promotes what is profitable and does away with what is harmful. It is his task to preserve and care for the people.

The provincial military commanders control separate areas. Each fortification and river station must have adjoining land, and it is necessary to train the soldiers well and make them courageous, to make the weapons and equipment strong and sharp, to maintain the fortresses and embankments well and in good repair, and to keep sufficient provisions. The training must be diligent and the patrolling alert. The commander's task is the rearing of troops and the defense of the country.

The Royal Secretariat is the king's mouthpiece, and the censorial agencies are the ears and eyes of the state. The Royal Secretariat issues the royal orders and handles all important matters. The Office of the Censor-General amends deficiencies of the royal orders and corrects omissions. The Office of the Inspector-General screens all offices and scrutinizes the gains or failures of the court and the good or bad actions of the officials. This is its responsibility.

Your Majesty should also put your mind to right learning for making clear the source from which right rule comes forth. You should keep close to the right men for the benefit of your enlightenment. You should engage high officials and widen the channel of memorials. You should act with care every single day and be concerned at the beginning about the end. With high and low you should be in mutual harmony and with capital and countryside in cooperation to maintain forever the peaceful rule of the dynastic ancestors. If, however, among the officials there are flatterers and pleasers, fickle men and those who curry favor, greedy and extorting men, and those who turn their back on the public good and concentrate on private gain, the state has strict laws and should punish them without mercy. Chao Ts'o [d. 154 B.C.] of the Han dynasty said: "It is in every man's nature that he desires long life. The Three Kings therefore let people live and did not injure them. It is in every man's nature that he desires riches. The Three Kings therefore let people have enough and did not make them poor. It is in every man's nature that he desires leisure. The Three Kings therefore let people spare their energy and did not exhaust them."[5]

If Your Majesty pays special attention to these three thoughts, the state as well as the people will indeed be fortunate! MD

The Way of Principle

At the end of the dynasty's first century, the founders' Confucian vision of a perfect government under a virtuous ruler still remained unfulfilled. Indeed, the century had witnessed Sejo's (1455–1468) usurpation of the throne and Yŏnsangun's (1494–1506) contemptuous and arbitrary rule. The Confucian officialdom itself had lost much of its initial enthusiasm and was bogged down in sterile book learning. Only a relatively small number of scholar-officials continued to pursue the Neo-Confucian dream. Collectively, they became known as the

Neo-Confucian literati (*sarim*). One of them was Cho Kwangjo (1482–1519) who became the recognized leader of an ideological and political restoration movement that centered on the embodiment of the Way (*to*) in government. Emphasizing the value of scholarship for an enlightened rule, one of Cho's principal concerns was the cultivation of personal virtue as the mainspring of a ruler's transformatory influence (*hwa*). Ruler and scholar were therefore interdependent, and only the ruler's judicious use of the scholar-officials could result in the recreation of government on the pattern of Yao and Shun, the idealized legendary rulers in China. Cho Kwangjo and his followers espoused these views from the vantage point of the censorial agencies, but, as before, such ideological pressure in the end proved counterproductive. Cho Kwangjo became the most prominent victim of the literati purge of 1519. His legacy, however, continued to shine throughout the sixteenth century. MD

Cho Kwangjo: On Problems of the Time
[From *Chŏngam chip* 3:12b–14b]

Of old it has been said: Extreme sincerity affects the spirits. It has also been said: Without sincerity there are no things. If the ruler's treatment of his officials and the officials' service to their ruler are determined by sincerity, the governmental process can be expected to become perfect.

Our country is narrow and small. If the ruler utters one single word, everyone in the eight provinces hears it without delay. Thus, the ruler should be respectful toward his high ministers, show consideration toward all officials, encourage the artisans to come, and treat the people like his children. The only thing he worries about in his treatment of officials and his love for the people is that he might not be sincere enough. He is not concerned about the difficulty of transforming them. Indeed, the ruling way gradually deteriorated in later generations, and antiquity could not be restored because among the rulers of the later generations there was none whose sincerity equaled that of the rulers of antiquity.

Today some say: We want to restore the ruling way of antiquity. But all they do is change the old statutes at random. This is because their knowledge is mediocre, and they only talk about what they see. Recently, the spirit of the scholars has been on the rise, and the orientation of the people is also gradually improving. I wish Your

Majesty would daily increase the "watchfulness over yourself"[6] and sincerely realize the efforts that eventually lead to the investigation of things and the extension of knowledge. If you do not err from this course from beginning to end, the transformational process of ruling can reach completion. If, on the contrary, you let the way of the world deteriorate daily so that in the end it will be irreparable, the way of the people will return to the stage of wild animals.

Even though it cannot be easily said that today the rule of the Three Dynasties can be restored, is there really no way at all to achieve this? If you first nourish your own virtue and apply it to the management of state affairs, all people will submit themselves in sincerity, and, without anyone expecting it, the transformation will occur all by itself. If one does not cultivate one's virtue, but merely polishes up governmental affairs, of what profit would this be? It is necessary to enrich one's virtue so that all transformation will come forth from one's illustrious virtue, and then the people below will naturally and infinitely be attracted and moved by it. Furthermore, it is not sufficient merely to fold one's arms and preserve one's virtue. It is imperative to stir up and stimulate the people with rites, music, punishments, and administrative measures, and to set up the proper facilities. It is proper to arouse enthusiasm for anything that can be accomplished and then to do it with energy.

In our country at the time of King Sejong [1418–1450], rites, music, literature, institutions, and implementations were similar to those of the Chou period. But in the first years of the deposed King Yŏnsangun [1494–1506], King Sŏngjong's [1469–1494] coffin had not been long in the memorial chamber when matters in the palace were already deplorable and not one person was able to preserve its integrity. Therefore the scholar-officials all lost their determination and finally were bewildered and confused, but nobody came to their rescue. Because the virtue and benevolence of the dynastic founders were abundant and rich and had penetrated the people's minds, after Your Majesty ascended the throne the people's minds were about to turn toward goodness. Old habits and corrupt customs, however, are difficult to reform all at once. If at this very moment the scholars' mores are not rectified, the people's livelihood is not enriched, and an indestructible basis for many future generations is not established, what will the royal descendants take as a model? Why is it that from ancient times the one who wished to rule was not able to rule well? It is because there were inferior men who took pleasure in slandering others and starting trouble. Your servant says that if Your Majesty's learning is daily progressing toward higher knowledge and brighter insights and you treat your high ministers with greater sincerity, they will not dare make wild statements in front of you and will certainly devote themselves completely to the affairs of the state. If the affairs of the state are not handled by Your Majesty's high ministers, high and low will oppose each other and not find harmony, and good rule will not be achieved. MD

Cho Kwangjo: On the Superior Man and the Inferior Man
[From *Chungjong sillok* 32:66a–b]

The ruler's entire mind must be brilliantly clear before he is able to recognize the wicked and the upright among men. Since even among inferior men there are some who resemble superior men, there are certain to be inferior men among the officials. If one observes their words and actions, one naturally recognizes whether they are worthy or not. If the ruler, however, does not make an effort to investigate matters and extend his knowledge, he may take a superior man for an inferior man or an inferior man for a superior man. Furthermore, when an inferior man attacks a superior man, he may point at him and call him an inferior man. Or someone may say that a man's words and actions are incongruous, or that he is fishing for fame. A ruler cannot but closely observe such cliquish scholars. Even when a superior man who fears that an inferior man might attain his purpose argues back and forth about the inferior man's motives, perhaps during a royal lecture, if the ruler does not like goodness with a sincere mind, he will not listen and make use of the superior man's words. On the contrary, he will be misled by the inferior man and doubt the superior man. In fact, the superior man and the inferior man are as incompatible as ice and charcoal. The inferior man is bent on destroying the superior man, but in the end he does not preserve himself. The inferior man can indeed be called stupid! Of old it has been said: If someone wishes to blame another, is he concerned about the lack of a pretext? If the inferior man plots against the superior man, does he not adduce any pretext?

In our country, since the time of the deposed King Yŏnsangun, the scholars' mores have not been correct. Although nowadays some issues are debated, there are still too many foolish words. This is indeed frightening. Now the ruler should clearly differentiate their kind. If there are wicked men who speak up, he should call them wicked. He should evaluate them and call them either right or wrong. If the judgment of right and wrong emanates from the ruler, the scholars' mores will naturally turn toward what is correct. MD

On Sage Learning

Yi Hwang: Memorial on Six Points
[From *T'oegye chŏnso* 6:42a–46b]

Yi Hwang (1501–1570) did not have a brilliant political career in the central government, but his influence on the political thinking at court, exercised from the deep countryside, was nevertheless considerable. In 1568, during his last sojourn in the capital before his death, he submitted the *Mujin yukcho so* (Memorial on Six Points Presented in 1568) to King Sŏnjo (1567–1608). This document is one of the most powerful political statements of the Chosŏn dynasty. After reading it, Sŏnjo exclaimed: "These six points are indeed the wise legacy of antiquity, but equally the most urgent matters of our days."[7]

The first two points deal with problems that had become acute because Sŏnjo, at the age of fifteen, had been chosen to succeed his uncle Myŏngjong (1545–1567) who died without leaving an heir. They include correct continuation of the royal line, close relations with the two dowager-regents, and guarding against slander. The theme of the third point, here translated in its entirety, is sage learning (*sŏnghak*) as the basis of good rule. The fourth point elucidates the development of the Way (*to*) from antiquity to early Chosŏn, warns against heterodox teachings (Buddhism), and entreats the young king to give the Way a permanent abode in Korea. In the fifth point Yi Hwang emphasizes the importance of trustworthy high officials and the censorial agencies. The last point shows the close connection between recognizing the will of heaven and the kingly way. MD

THIRD: BY ESTEEMING SAGE LEARNING,
THE BASIS OF GOOD RULE IS BUILT.

Your servant has heard that the essential method of the mind, which is part of the learning of the emperors and kings, originated from the Great Shun's order to Yü that said: "The mind of man is restless; its affinity for the right way is small. Be discriminating, be single-minded, that you may sincerely hold fast to the Mean."[8]

Shun entrusted the world to Yü with the wish that he should pacify it. Among the words with which he addressed him, none were more urgent than those on government. But Shun's injunctions and admonitions to Yü did not go beyond these words because he realized that learning and perfect virtue constitute the great foundation of ruling while discrimination and single-mindedness are the great law of scholarship. If the great foundation of ruling is established with the great law of scholarship, all governments of the world will emanate from this. Because the plans of the sages of antiquity are like this, even your ignorant servant understands that sage learning is the basis of perfect rule and presumptuously addresses Your Majesty on this subject.

Even so, Shun's words only spoke of insecurity and smallness without giving the reason for insecurity and smallness; they only instructed the ruler to be discriminating and single-minded without indicating the method of being discriminating and single-minded. For men of later generations who wanted, on the basis of these words, to know the method exactly and put it into practice, it was very difficult. Therefore several sages followed one upon the other, and with Confucius the method became well established. This was the "investigation of things" and the "perfection of knowledge," the "sincerity of the will" and the "rectification of the mind" of the *Great Learning* and the "understanding of good" and the "sincerity with oneself" of the *Doctrine of the Mean.* Thereafter various Confucians successively emerged until Chu Hsi. His theories, which were indeed brilliant, were embodied in his commentaries and queries to the *Great Learning* and to the *Doctrine of the Mean.* If we now concentrate on these two books and pursue the learning of true knowledge and practice, it is like seeing the sun in the sky upon opening one's eyes, or like walking on the wide path simply by placing one's foot on it.

Regrettably, however, there are few rulers in this world who aspire to this learning. And among those who do aspire to it and are able to make a beginning, few reach the end. Ah! This is the reason why this learning has not been transmitted and government is not like of old. Yet, there is hope that it will become like this!

In my opinion, Your Majesty's august and sage disposition is a heavenly gift, and your deep and bright learning progresses daily. None of your Confucian ministers and lecturers is without deep admiration and praise. Thus, owing to Your Majesty's disposition and aspiration to this learning, one can say that you have made a beginning with the method of extending knowledge and the effort of acting in earnestness. But in your servant's uninformed opinion, you may not be able to suddenly gain the ability of knowledge and action with this beginning alone. Your servant begs to speak first about the extension of knowledge.

From the nearness of our own nature and appearance and daily applied human relationships to the myriad things of heaven and earth and vicissitudes of past and present, everything has in itself the principle of absolute thusness and the norm of absolute oughtness. This is what is called the Mean of what exists by itself through nature. Therefore, scholarship must be extensive, inquiry accurate, thinking careful, and judgment enlightened. These are the four elements of the extension of knowledge, and among them careful thinking is the most important. What is thinking? It means to search for it in the mind and to obtain it through experience. If one can experience it in the mind and clearly differentiate its principle, if one wishes the inner workings of good and bad and the judgment of righteousness and profit, of right and wrong, to be completely exact and free of error, then it is possible to know truly and without doubt the so-called reason for insecurity and smallness and the method of being discriminating and single-minded.

Because Your Majesty has already made a beginning in the study of these four elements and set out on this course, your servant hopes that, on the basis of this beginning, you will make an even more sustained effort. The procedure and the items of your study should be based on the details pointed out in Chu Hsi's queries. You should make seriousness your priority and investigate all matters as to their normative state and the reason why they may deviate from that state. You should ponder this deeply, turn it over in your mind, thoroughly internalize it, and finally reach the ultimate limits of these four elements. If you make such great efforts over a long period of time, one morning, without your realizing it, all problems will dissipate and be solved and complete penetration will be reached. Then at last you will understand the meaning of "substance and functions have one source, and there is no gap between the manifest and the hidden."[9] Neither confused by restlessness and smallness nor bewildered by discrimination and single-mindedness, you will hold fast to the Mean: this is what is called true knowledge.

Your servant wishes also to speak about earnest action. To make the will sincere is to investigate thoroughly the subtle, even the reality of a single hair. To rectify one's mind is to investigate motion and rest, even the correctness of one single matter. Cultivating your personal life, don't get trapped in partiality. Regulating the family, don't err in one-sidedness. Be alert and fearful; be watchful when alone. Strengthen your determination without resting. These are the elements of earnest action, and among them mind and will are the most important. The mind is the heavenly ruler, and the will comes forth from it. If one first makes sincere what comes forth, this sincerity will be sufficient to stop the ten thousand errors. If one rectifies the heavenly ruler, that is, the mind, the whole body will follow its orders, and its movements will all have reality.

Your Majesty has already made a beginning and a start in regard to these various efforts. Your servant hopes that, on the basis of this start, you will make an even more sincere effort. For rules and guidance you should follow the instructions that these two books, *Great Learning* and *Doctrine of the Mean,* hand down and make seriousness your priority. If at all times and everywhere, in all your thoughts, you are guided by them and remain cautious in all your affairs, the manifold desires will be washed away from the mind, and the five relationships and all actions will be polished to their very best. Even when eating or resting or receiving guests, be submerged in righteousness and principle; in restraining your anger and curbing your selfish desires, in correcting your faults and changing to the better, be striving for sincerity and single-mindedness. Being wide and great, high and bright, do not deviate from rites and laws. Forming three with heaven and earth and assisting the transforming and nourishing process of heaven and earth, ordering and adjusting the great relations of mankind,[10] all come forth from "not being embarrassed in the dark inner room."[11] If you thus make a sincere effort over a long period of time, you will naturally become thoroughly familiar with righteousness and humanity, and even if you wanted to abandon them, you could not do so. Suddenly, without being aware of it, you will enter the realm of equilibrium and harmony of the sages and worthies.

If the success of practice reaches this point, the Way will be accomplished and virtue established. Moreover, the foundation of ruling will exist herein: the rules of selecting men will surely not be extraneous, and worthies will naturally appear in great numbers; their achievements will be brilliant and make the world prosperous and peaceful and will lead the people to humanity and longevity. There will be nothing difficult about this.

Someone says: The learning of emperors and kings is not the same as the learning of scholars and students. This refers only to adhering to textual meaning and laboring over compilation. Making seriousness the basis, investigating the principles of all things in order to extend knowledge, and examining oneself in order to practice it: these are the essentials of making the method of mind subtle and transmitting the learning of the Way. Is there in this respect a difference between emperors and kings and ordinary men?

True knowledge and practice are like the two wheels of a cart: it is not possible to have one missing. They are like the two legs of a man: they need each other to move ahead. Therefore Master Ch'eng said: There is none who extends his knowledge and does not abide in seriousness. Chu Hsi said: If in personal action there is no effort, there is no place for investigating principle. If one thus speaks of the efforts of knowledge and action together, they are each other's beginning and end. If one speaks of them separately, each has its own beginning and end. Ah! If there is no beginning, there is certainly no end. If there is no end, of what use is the beginning? Furthermore, the learning of the ruler most often has a beginning, but no end. At first he is diligent, but later on negligent; at first he is serious, but later on dissolute. With an unsteady mind he vacillates between doing and stopping and finally ends up despising virtue and ruining the state. What is the reason for this?

The reason is that, being restless, the human mind is easily trapped by desires and finds it difficult to return to principle; the reason is that, being small, the affinity for the Way is only for an instant open to principle and then gets closed up by desires. Now, suppose one wishes to make what is easily trapped, that is, the human mind, repel the desires so that they cannot arise, and what is for an instant open to principle continue without a moment's interruption, in order to fulfill the teachings of holding fast to the Mean the emperors and kings have transmitted. How can this be done if not by the effort of being discriminating and single-minded? Fu Yüeh said: In learning, make the aspirations modest, and from beginning to end, think of learning, and your virtue will be polished without your being aware of it. Confucius said: "He knows the utmost point to be reached, and reaches it, thus showing himself in accord with the first springs of things; he knows the end to be rested in, and rests in it, thus preserving his righteousness in accordance with that end."[12]

If you pay attention to this, it will indeed be fortunate! MD

Yi I: Memorial in Ten Thousand Words
[From *Yulgok chŏnsŏ* 5:10b–39a]

Yi I (1536–1584), who with his older contemporary, Yi Hwang, dominated the field of Neo-Confucian philosophy in the sixteenth century, did not exhaust his efforts in speculative thinking. He paid equally close attention to the practical problems of his time, and his pronouncements on political, economic, and social issues were widely respected. He did not tire of repeating his fundamental insight according to which the health and stability of the state rested solely on the peasantry, and he therefore termed the strengthening of the peasants' livelihood the most urgent task of his time.

The *Memorial in Ten Thousand Words* (1574), of which some key passages are translated here, is only one of several important political documents Yi I submitted to King Sŏnjo. It combines Neo-Confucian instruction on kingly rule and popular indoctrination with practical advice on economic, military, and administrative matters. Most significantly, Yi I called for flexibility in policy planning and legislation and thus distinctly distanced himself from timeworn legal conservatism. For him, too, the basic program of internal cultivation and its application to politics, outlined in the *Great Learning,* remained the foundation of all moral and, by extension, political action. MD

What is called timeliness means being flexible in accordance with time to establish laws and to save the people. Master Ch'eng, when discussing the *Book of Changes,* said: To know time and to recognize the timely circumstances are the great method of learning the *Book of Changes*. He also said: Changes according to time is the constant rule. In general, laws are established according to a particular time; as times change, the laws do not remain the same. Shun followed upon Yao, and appropriately everything remained unchanged, yet he divided the nine provinces into twelve. Yü followed upon Shun, and appropriately everything remained unchanged, yet he changed the twelve provinces back to nine. Was this because sages like to make changes? They did so only in accordance with their time. Therefore Master Ch'eng said: As Yao, Shun, and Yü followed upon each other, it is only natural that there were slight differences in their culture and disposition. Later, from Hsia and Shang on, the small changes between the new dynasties cannot be enumerated one by one. To mention only the major ones: the people of Hsia esteemed loyalty. Because loyalty became corrupted, the founder of Shang saved it with simplicity. Because simplicity became corrupted, the founder of Chou saved it with refinement. Because refinement became corrupted beyond repair, thereafter the world deteriorated and fell into disorder and entered the era of strong Ch'in.[13] Because Ch'in was violent and cruel, it burnt the *Book of Songs* and the *Book of Documents* and then perished. The Han rose and took Ch'in's abuses as a mirror. . . .

For several thousand years, the marks through the ages of political order and disorder were generally like this. Those governments that, in accordance with their time, were good in saving the people from abuses were only the Three Dynasties. After the Three Dynasties those that did so were indeed few, and even they did not fully realize the Way. In general, what can be changed in accordance with a particular time are the laws and institutions. Unchangeable, however, in ancient as well as in present times, are the kingly way, humane government, the three bonds that exist between ruler and minister, father and son, and husband and wife, and the five constants of humanity, righteousness, propriety, wisdom, and faithfulness. In later generations when mastery of the Way was no longer skilled, the unchangeable was at times changed, and the changeable was at times adhered to. For this reason the days of political order were generally few whereas the days of disorder were generally numerous.

Speaking of our eastern region, Korea, there is no textual evidence of Chi Tzu's Eight Rules,[14] and when at the time of the Three Kingdoms disturbances broke out, the government policies were obliterated. The five hundred years of the former dynasty, Koryŏ, were darkened by the wind and rain of political crises. Arriving at our dynasty, King T'aejo started the dynastic fortunes. King Sejong preserved and advanced them and first used the *Kyŏngje yukchŏn* (Six Codes of Governance). Under King Sŏngjong the *National Code* was published, and thereafter, in accordance with time, laws were established and called the *Supplementary Code*. Because sage-king followed upon sage-king, there was appropriately nothing that was not the same; the one used the *Six Codes of Governance,* the other the *National Code.* That these were augmented by the *Supplementary Code* was but an adjustment to the time.

At the beginning of the dynasty, the officials were free to submit their opinions. Institutions were created, but people did not regard them as strange nor was the execution of law interrupted. The people were thus able to rest easy. In contrast, Yŏnsangun was wild and unruly and his expenditures lavish. He changed the tribute laws of the dynastic founders and was daily intent on harming the people and benefiting the royal house. When King Chungjong brought about a restoration, the government should have been made as before, but during the first years those in charge of the state were only ignorant merit subjects. Thereupon the worthies of the year *kimyo* [1519] wanted action, but they were falsely accused and destroyed. This was followed by the purge of the year *ŭlsa* [1545], which was even more cruel than the one of 1519. From then on the Neo-Confucian literati lost heart and regarded an unobtrusive life as good luck. Since they did not dare speak up on state affairs, cunning and powerful groups acted according to their own will and without scruples. What was profitable to them they preserved as old laws; what stood in their way they abolished with new laws. They were solely intent on fleecing the people and fattening themselves. They went so far that the state was daily more hard pressed and the national foundation daily more weakened. Was there anyone who thought about this matter, even if only for an instant? . . . [13b–15b]

Now I present the essentials of cultivating self and pacifying the people as strategies of praying for heaven's eternal mandate. There are four principles of self-cultivation: first, to arouse Your Majesty's aspiration to the hope of returning to the prosperity of the Three Dynasties; second, to encourage Your Majesty's scholarship so that it completes the effort of making the will sincere and rectifying the mind; third, to do away with one-sided selfishness in order to restore the full measure of complete equity; fourth, to keep close to the worthies in order to receive the benefit of their assistance.

There are five principles for pacifying the people: first, to open one's sincere mind in order to obtain the sympathy of all subordinates; second, to revise the tribute plan in order to abolish the hardship of coercion and extortion; third, to uphold frugality in order to reverse the trend of extravagance; fourth, to change the selection of slaves for service in the capital in order to relieve the unhappy lot of the public and private slaves; fifth, to revise the military administration in order to strengthen internal as well as external security.

When I speak of arousing Your Majesty's aspiration to the hope of returning to the prosperity of the Three Dynasties, my meaning is as follows. Of old, Ch'eng Ch'ien said to Duke Ching of Ch'i: "They were men. I am also a man. Why should I stand in awe of them?"[15] "They" meant the sages and worthies. If with the qualifications of a Duke Ching one makes strenuous efforts to strengthen oneself, it is possible to become like the sages and worthies. Therefore Ch'eng

Ch'ien spoke like this. When Mencius talked to King Hui of Liang and King Hsüan of Ch'i, he discussed nothing else but the kingly way and also encouraged humane government. If with the qualifications of a King Hui of Liang and a King Hsüan of Ch'i they were capable of practicing the kingly way and effectuating humane government, they can indeed be equated with the founders of the Three Dynasties. Therefore Mencius spoke like this. Do you think he liked big words and did not measure their actual effects?

Now I see that Your Majesty's qualifications are impressive: your humanity sufficient to protect the people, your intelligence sufficient to discern cunning, your resoluteness sufficient to decide on sanctions. But Your Majesty's aspiration to become a sage is not firm, and your sincerity to seek right rule is not genuine. Assuming that you cannot reach the level of earlier kings, you withdraw and refer to your own smallness, giving no thought to advancement and development. I do not know what you have experienced to make you like this. . . . If you make a genuine effort toward self-cultivation and put your sincere mind to pacifying the people, you will be able to find worthies and rule with them, you will be able to correct the abuses and salvage the situation. With a strong aspiration, can there be defeat? Master Ch'eng once said: In ruling a country, to arrive at praying to heaven for a long mandate; in nourishing oneself, to arrive at longevity; in learning, to arrive at sagehood. As to these three things, human effort clearly can bring about such transformation, yet people do not do it. How true are these words! From of old one has never heard of someone who really made an effort and failed to see real results! [24b–25b] MD

CHAPTER FIFTEEN

Culture

Once the dynastic foundation was consolidated, the Chosŏn state attained brilliant achievements in many fields. Respect for education and scholarship was a hallmark of the dynasty. There were many incentives for talented young men to pursue careers in scholarship and government service, as scholars and officials were accorded the highest prestige in Chosŏn society. In 1420 King Sejong organized the Hall of Worthies, where selected scholar-officials were assigned to devote their time to scholarly research. From these studies came a number of important publications on the classics, history, geography, linguistics, law, music, agriculture, astronomy, and medicine. Most significant, however, was the invention of the Korean alphabet in 1443.

The early phase of the Chosŏn dynasty was also characterized by brilliant achievements in science and technology. A number of scientific instruments—sundials, clepsydras, armillary spheres, rain gauges—were invented and refined. Moreover, a strong emphasis on the practical application of knowledge to the needs of daily life led to the publication of several manuals for farming as well as medical treatises and compendia of herbal remedies for various diseases. The highly sophisticated advances in book printing developed in Korea at this time easily accommodated these publications.

Invention of the Korean Alphabet

The invention of the Korean alphabet, called *chŏngŭm* (Correct Sounds), is the crowning achievement of the Chosŏn dynasty. Prior to devising its own writing system, Korea had used Chinese graphs for transcription. But because the Korean language is totally different from Chinese, there were many problems in the use of Chinese graphs in a Korean setting. It was to amend this situation that King Sejong (1418–1450) assembled a group of scholars to devise scripts suitable for the Korean language. Under the personal leadership of the king, after many years of painstaking studies, a phonetic alphabet was finally created in 1443. To assure the practicability and wide usage of the newly devised alphabet, King Sejong published a eulogy cycle called *Yongbi ŏch'ŏn ka* (Songs of Flying Dragons) and the translation of a Chinese classic, among other works, using the new script before it was formally proclaimed in 1446.

When the new writing system was officially published, it was called *Hunmin chŏngŭm* (Correct Sounds to Instruct the People). Consisting of twenty-eight letters—seventeen consonants and eleven vowels— the Korean alphabet is wholly phonetic and capable of transcribing almost any sound. Hailed by modern linguists as one of the most scientific writing systems in the world, the script is extremely simple and very easy to learn. In the twentieth century, this alphabet has been called *hangŭl* (Great Letters).

In publishing the *Hunmin chŏngŭm* in 1446, King Sejong wrote a preface explaining his motivation for devising the new writing system, which was followed by a detailed explanation of how the alphabet worked. Chŏng Inji, an official who assisted the king in the invention of the alphabet, then wrote a postscript. Translated here are King Sejong's preface and Chŏng Inji's postscript. YC

King Sejong: Preface to *Hunmin chŏngŭm*
[From *Hunmin chŏngŭm* 1a]

The sounds of our language differ from those of Chinese and are not easily communicated by using Chinese graphs. Many among the ignorant, therefore, though they wish to express their sentiments in writing, have been unable to communicate. Considering this situation with compassion, I have newly devised twenty-eight letters. I wish only that the people will learn them easily and use them conveniently in their daily life. YC

Chŏng Inji: Postscript to *Hunmin chŏngŭm*
[From *Hungmin chŏngŭm haerye* 26b–29b]

Just as there are enunciations that are natural to heaven and earth, there must also be writing that is natural to heaven and earth. It is for this reason that the ancients devised letters corresponding to enunciations so as to convey the situations and sentiments of myriad things and to record the ways of heaven, earth, and men so that they cannot be changed by later generations.

Yet climates and soils in the four corners of the world are different, and enunciations and material force are likewise diverse. In general, the languages of different countries have their own enunciations but lack their own letters, so they borrowed the Chinese graphs to communicate their needs. This is, however, like trying to fit a square handle into a round hole. How could it possibly achieve its objective satisfactorily? How could there not be difficulties? It is, therefore, important that each region should follow the practices that are convenient to its people and that no one should be compelled to follow one writing system alone.

Although our country's rituals, music, and literature are comparable to those of China, our speech and language are not the same as China's. Those who studied books in Chinese were concerned about the difficulty of understanding their meaning and purport; those who administered the penal system were troubled by the difficulty in communicating the complexity of its legal texts. In the old days, Sŏl Ch'ong [c. 660–730] of Silla first devised the writing system known as *idu,* which has been used by our government and people to this day. But all the graphs were borrowed from Chinese, and frequently there arise problems and difficulties. Not only is *idu* vulgar and baseless, but as a means of linguistic communication, it cannot transmit one meaning in ten thousand cases.

In the winter of the year *kyehae* [1443], His Majesty, the king, created twenty-eight letters of the Correct Sounds and provided examples in outline demonstrating their meanings. His Majesty then named these letters *Hunmin chŏngŭm.* Resembling pictographs, these letters imitate the shapes of the old seal characters. Based on enunciation, their sounds correspond to the Seven Modes in music. These letters embrace the principles of heaven, earth, and men as well as the mysteries of yin and yang, and there is nothing they cannot express. With these twenty-eight letters, infinite turns and changes may be explained; they are simple and yet contain all the essence; they are refined and yet easily communicable. Therefore, a clever man can learn them in one morning while a dull man may take ten days to study them. If we use these letters to explain books, it will be easier to comprehend their meanings. If we use these letters in administering litigations, it will be easier to ascertain the facts of a case. As for rhymes, one can easily distinguish voiced and voiceless consonants; as for music and songs, twelve semitones can be easily blended. They can be used whatever and wherever the occasion may be. Even the sounds of wind, the cries of cranes, the crowing of roosters, and the barking of dogs can all be transcribed in writing.

Consequently, we were commanded to provide more detailed explanations for all the people to understand. This servant, therefore, along with his other ministers—Ch'oe Hang, Fourth Grade official; Pak P'aengnyŏn, Junior Fifth Grade official; Sin Sukchu, Junior Fifth Grade official; Sŏng Sammun, Sixth Grade official, all in the Hall of Worthies; Kang Hŭian, Sixth Grade official in the Royal House Administration; Yi Kae, acting Junior Fourth Grade official; and Yi Sŏllo, acting Junior Fourth Grade official in the Hall of Worthies—have prepared all the explanations and various examples to illustrate the general outline of the new writing system so that any reader can learn it without a teacher. The subtlety of its profound sources and deep meanings, however, is beyond the scope of our ability to demonstrate fully.

As we humbly reflect, our king, being a heaven-endowed sage, has instituted various systems and institutions that excel those established by a hundred other kings. As for the making of the Correct Sounds, it is not something that has been transmitted from our ancestors but has been achieved by nature. There is nothing in the Correct Sounds that is not based on the ultimate principle; there is no bias such as one finds in the things made by men. Although our country has existed in the eastern corner of the world for a long period of time, not until today has the great wisdom of cultivating a new enlightenment and completing its task been realized. YC

Ch'oe Malli: Opposition to the Korean Alphabet
[From *Sejong sillok* 103:19b–22a]

Although the invention of the Korean alphabet was hailed as a great achievement of the sagely rule of King Sejong, there was a group of scholar-officials, led by Ch'oe Malli (fl. 1419–1444), who strongly opposed the use of Korea's own script. They believed that Korea had long emulated Chinese ideas and institutions and that adoption of Korea's own writing system would make it impossible to identify Korean civilization with that of China. The following text is the memorial submitted by Ch'oe Malli offering his reasons against the use of the Korean alphabet. Y C

Twentieth day of the second month of the year [1444]. Ch'oe Malli, First Counselor in the Hall of Worthies, and his associates offered the following memorial: We humbly believe that the invention of the Korean script is a work of divine creation unparalleled in history. There are, however, some questionable issues we wish to raise for Your Majesty's consideration.

1. Ever since the founding of the dynasty, our court has pursued the policy of respecting the senior state with utmost sincerity and has consistently tried to follow the Chinese system of government. As we share with China at present the same writing and the same institutions, we are startled to learn of the invention of the Korean script. Some claim that the Korean script is based on old writings and is not a new alphabet at all. Although the letter shapes are similar to the old seal letters, the use of letters for phonetic value violates ancient practice and has no valid ground. If this becomes known to China and anyone argues against it, it would disgrace our policy of respecting China.

2. Although winds and soils vary from region to region, there has been no separate writing system for local dialects. Only such peoples as the Mongolians, Tanguts, Jürchens, Japanese, and Tibetans have their own writings. But this is a matter that involves the barbarians and is unworthy of our concern. It has been said that the barbarians are transformed only by means of adopting the Chinese ways; we have never heard of the Chinese ways being transformed by the barbarians. Historically, China has always regarded our country as the state that has maintained the virtuous customs bequeathed by the sage-king Kija and has viewed our literature, rituals, and music as similar to its own. Now, however, our country is devising a Korean script

separately in order to discard the Chinese, and thus we are willingly being reduced to the status of barbarians. This is like abandoning the fragrance of storax in favor of the obnoxious odor of mantis. Is this not a great embarrassment to the enlightened civilization?

3. Although the *idu* writing devised by Sŏl Ch'ong of Silla is vulgar and rustic, it uses the graphs widely used in China as auxiliaries to our tongue, and hence the graphs are not different from the Chinese. Therefore, even the clerks and the servants sincerely want to study the Chinese graphs. At first they read several books to acquire a rough understanding of the Chinese graphs; only then are they able to use the *idu*. Those who use the *idu* must depend upon the Chinese graphs to communicate their ideas, and a number of people become literate through the use of the *idu* writing. Therefore, the *idu* is a useful aid in stimulating learning. . . . If the Korean script is widely used, the cleric officials will study it exclusively and neglect scholarly literature. . . . If they discover that knowledge of the twenty-[eight] letter Korean script is sufficient for them to advance in their official careers, why would they go through agony and pain to study the principles of Neo-Confucianism? If such a situation lasts several decades, then surely the people who understand the Chinese graphs would be reduced to a very small number. Perhaps they could manage their clerical affairs using the Korean script, but if they do not know the writings of the sages, they will become ignorant and unable to distinguish right from wrong. . . . This Korean script is nothing more than a novelty. It is harmful to learning and useless to the government. No matter how one looks at it, one cannot find any good in it. . . .

His Majesty, having read the memorial, responded to Ch'oe Malli and his associates as follows: You said that the use of letters for phonetic value violates the old practices. Is not the *idu* of Sŏl Ch'ong also based on alien sounds? Is not the main objective of devising the *idu* to make it useful to the people? If it is useful to the people, is not this new Korean script also useful to the people? You and your associates believe the work of Sŏl Ch'ong to be good, yet you reject the work of your sovereign. Why? What do you know about the book of rhymes? Do you know how many vowels there are in the Four Tones and Seven Sounds? If I do not correct the book of rhymes now, who is going to do it? YC

Education and Scholarship

Education was one of the principal areas emphasized by the Chosŏn dynasty. Indeed, the Neo-Confucian state of Chosŏn held an almost religious belief that the ideals of Neo-Confucianism could be realized only through education. Thus, from its very beginning, the Chosŏn dynasty set up a well-planned nationwide school system to offer the Confucian education to qualified students. In the capital city of Seoul, a district school was organized in four of the five districts; local schools called *hyanggyo* were established in every county throughout the country; for higher education, the National Academy (*Sŏnggyungwan*) was organized in the capital. Usually well endowed by the state, these schools became the center for training future leaders of the government, as all the candidates for the state civil service examinations were drawn from them.

From the mid-sixteenth century on, moreover, private academies, called *sŏwŏn,* were organized in the countryside at the initiative of local scholars and in time became important centers of Confucian scholarship in Korea. The private academies were usually endowed richly through private donations, and they also received a royal charter from the king in the form of a name plaque along with a generous grant of books, land, and servants from the government.

The Office of Special Advisers (*Hongmungwan*) was a unique institution in Korea. Originally organized in 1420 by King Sejong as a royal research institute called *Chiphyŏnjŏn* (Hall of Worthies), it was reorganized by King Sejo into the *Hongmungwan* in 1463. Assigned to provide advisory services on all matters dealing with the Confucian classics and literature, this office maintained a library within the palace and offered the royal lecture (*kyŏngyŏn*) for the king. Thus, its officials carried the highest prestige and honor.

Chosŏn kyŏngguk chŏn (Administrative Code of Chosŏn) by Chŏng Tojŏn served as the basic code for the Chosŏn dynasty since its foundation in 1392. The article dealing with the establishment of schools, translated here, describes the structure of the national educational system as envisioned by the dynasty's foremost architect. The description of the National Academy is taken from the *Sinjŭng Tongguk yŏji sŭngnam* (Revised and Augmented Gazetteer of Korea), which was published in 1530. The White Cloud Grotto Academy, organized in 1543 by Chu Sebung, was Korea's first private academy. Fashioned after the renowned White Deer Grotto Academy of Sung China, this academy, later renamed the Sosu Academy, became the model for hundreds of private academies that subsequently sprang up throughout the country. The description of its foundation is taken from an account given in the *Myŏngjong sillok* (Veritable Records of King Myŏngjong).

Chŏng Tojŏn: Establishment of Schools
[From *Chosŏn kyŏngguk chŏn* in *Sambong chip* 7:30b]

Schools are the center of teaching and transformation, where the cardinal principles of human relations are further illustrated and men of talent receive training. At the times of the Three Dynasties in ancient China, the laws regarding schools were well prepared. Since the Ch'in and the Han dynasties, despite certain shortcomings in the educational system, there have been few who did not see that schooling was important and that the vigor or decline of the schools was the key to the success or failure of the government. All these characteristics are applicable to the present situation also. Our state has established the National Academy to teach the sons and brothers of the nobility and the officials as well as men of superior talent among the people. The state has also established district schools in the capital city where instructors are assigned to teach young students. Extending this law to districts, towns, big counties, and counties, local schools have been organized where teachers have been assigned to instruct students. In addition, schools for military affairs, law, mathematics, medicine, and foreign languages have been established, and appropriate instructors have been assigned to teach the students enrolled there. In these ways, our educational system has achieved great success. YC

National Academy
[From *Sinjŭng Tongguk yŏji sŭngnam* 2:10a–b]

The National Academy, located in the eastern section of Sung-gyo district of the capital, is charged with the mission of instructing the Confucian students. The Hall of Illustrating the Cardinal Principles stands north of the Confucian Shrine; to the east of the shrine is the library, and to the north is the Office of Sacrificial Offerings. A thick grove of pine trees grows in luxuriant green to the immediate north of the academy, and within the grove stands the Arbor of Green

Pine. Under the jurisdiction of the academy are the Office of Registration and the four schools of Seoul: the Central District School, the Eastern District School, the Southern District School, and the Western District School. . . .

Sŏng Kan (1427–1456) wrote the following essay of eulogy for the Hall of Illustrating the Cardinal Principles: Our King T'aejo established the National Academy in his inaugural year in the northeastern section of the capital. At the same time, he laid out meticulously the plans for its management, future direction, site and buildings, and organization, so that there might be nothing that is lacking. Within the academy, the shrine is located in the south, being flanked by temples on both right and left, and the former sages and the former national masters are enshrined in the shrine and the temples respectively. The Office of Registration is situated at the east end of the academy; the food preparation building is south of the Registration Office, and the dining hall is south of the food preparation building. North of the shrine extend two long corridors leading to an elevated platform that is flanked by rooms on the right and left sides. At the center of the platform stands a hall where teachers and students gather for lectures and study: the Hall of Illustrating the Cardinal Principles. All the structures in the academy are constructed with dignity and nobility.

At daybreak each morning, with the beating of a drum, the headmaster along with the instructors of the academy assemble the students in the courtyard. After making a bow to the instructors, the students enter the hall where lectures and discussions on the classics take place. They study, deliberate, counsel, and assist one another to reach a full understanding of the relationships between ruler and minister, father and son, husband and wife, elder brother and younger brother, and friend and friend. For days and months, together they work and rest as one body to train themselves until they become new men. It is from these students that the future loyal ministers and the future filial sons are produced in prolific number to serve the state and their families. Indeed, never before in the history of our country have we witnessed such a splendid success in nurturing loyal officials and filial sons as we see now. Some people object that since the sage's teachings are many, there is no reason why this hall alone should be called the Hall of Illustrating the Cardinal Principles. To them I say: The relationships between ruler and minister, father and son, husband and wife, elder brother and younger brother, and friend and friend are rooted in the heavenly principle, and hence they are unchanging and everlasting. How can there be any teaching more important than this? YC

White Cloud Grotto Academy
[From *Myŏngjong sillok* 10:6a–b]

Tenth day of the first month of the year [1550]. Chief State Councillor Yi Ki, Second State Councillor Sim Yŏnwŏn [1491–1558], Third State Councillor Sang Chin [1493–1564], Minister of Rites Yun Kae [1494–1566], and Deputy Minister of Rites Sŏ Ko offered the following proposal:

White Cloud Grotto Academy in P'unggi was founded by the incumbent governor of Hwanghae, Chu Sebung, when he was serving as the magistrate of P'unggi [1543]. It is located in the same village where An Yu [1243–1306] once resided. All the rules and regulations governing the academy have been modeled after those of the White Deer Grotto Academy of the Great Master Chu Hsi. The academic setup, the library, and the land and food and other supplies have all been richly endowed so that men of talent can further cultivate their potential. Yi Hwang [1501–1570] petitioned the king to grant a charter in the form of a name plaque as well as books, land, and servants. The king granted the charter with the name plaque, books, and two or three additional items, and these grants have encouraged Confucian scholars in the countryside to pursue their scholarship with greater zeal. As for land, the endowment arranged by Chu Sebung is sufficient for the academy to sustain itself, and there are adequate numbers of servants. In order for the Confucian scholars to pursue their scholarship, it is essential that they do so in surroundings of peace and quiet. If the provincial governor or the county magistrate, wishing to exalt their study, prescribes restrictive rules for these scholars, it will deprive them of their freedom and divert them from the proper way of cultivation. There should be no interference from outside. YC

Office of Special Advisers
[From *Sinjŭng Tongguk yŏji sŭngnam* 2:9a–10a]

The Office of Special Advisers is located to the west of the Office of the Royal Secretariat and was formerly called the Hall of Worthies. It also maintains a library. It has an office south of the Military

Command Headquarters within Ch'angdŏk Palace and another to the east of the Office of the Royal Secretariat within Ch'anggyŏng Palace. It has the duty to maintain books for the court and is also entrusted with conducting royal lectures and literary counseling. . . .

During the reign of King Sejo [1455–1468], Yang Sŏngji offered the following advice: I have learned that books and records were kept in the past either in well-known mountains or in restricted buildings in order to safeguard them from any loss and to ensure their permanent transmission to posterity. The practice of safekeeping books started during the time of King Sukchong [1095–1105] of the previous dynasty. One of these collections has books stamped with: "The Royal Collection in the Year of *Sinsa* [A.D. 1101] of the Fourteenth Ruler of the Koryŏ State," "The Ascension Year of Chien-chung Ching-kuo of Great Sung [1101]," and "The Ninth Year of Chien-t'ung of Great Liao [1109]"; another collection is stamped with "The Royal Collection of the Koryŏ State." Although it has been three hundred and sixty-three years since the time of King Sukchong's reign, these stamps look as if they were stamped yesterday, and the books are readily available to us for reference. Many of the ten thousand volumes now preserved in the royal collection date from the Sukchong era. It is therefore humbly proposed that we write on the reverse side of each book, in formal characters, "The Royal Collection in the Year of *Kyemi* [1463] of the Sixth Ruler of the Chosŏn State and the Seventh Year T'ien-shun [1463] of Great Ming," and on the front side, "The Royal Collection of the Chosŏn State" in seal characters. In this way, these books may be known to posterity for myriad generations. It is also recommended that the collection of these books be placed under the supervision of the Office of Special Advisers, to be staffed with a director and deputy director, who will in turn hold the concurrent posts of Office of Royal Decrees, and that the Office of Special Advisers be charged with loaning and collecting all the books.

King Sejo adopted the proposal and ordered the library collection placed in the small structure, which then was named the *Hongmungwan,* next to the Hall of the Crown Prince. . . . In the tenth year of His Majesty's rule [1479], the present building was constructed to house the Office of Special Advisers and its library. Y C

The Recruitment Examinations

The Chosŏn dynasty relied mainly on recruitment examinations to select officials to serve in the government. There were three types of examinations—the civil, the military, and the technical—and of these the civil examination was the most important and carried the highest prestige. The civil examination in turn consisted of the lower civil examination, which awarded the graduates either the *saengwŏn* degree for the classics or the *chinsa* degree for literary writings, and the higher civil examination for the *munkwa* degree, which qualified the holder to serve in the government as an official. Normally, all candidates in the civil examinations had to go through three stages of rigorous testing—demonstrating their knowledge in the classics, history, and literature—before the successful candidates were finally selected. For ambitious young men, to become a successful candidate in the higher civil examination was the most coveted honor, and many devoted considerable time and energy to preparing themselves for such an honor.

Two accounts of the examination scene are given here: one, by Sŏng Hyŏn (1439–1504), describes how the examination was conducted; the other, by Yu Hŭich'un (1513–1577), relates his own experience as an examiner. YC

Sŏng Hyŏn: On the Civil Service Examination
[From *Yongjae ch'onghwa* (Koryŏ taehakkyo ed., 1963), pp. 391–392]

The recruitment examination under the previous dynasty was conducted under the supervision of only two men, the Chief Examination Officer and the Deputy Examination Officer. Because these officials had been appointed in advance, prior to the examination, there were deficiencies in the way it was conducted leading to the criticism that the successful candidates tended to have been drawn from influential families or from immature scholars. Although the present dynasty continued these deficiencies at the beginning, King Sejong introduced drastic reforms in the examination system.

According to the new system, the Ministry of Personnel at first makes a list of the qualified examiners and presents it to the king, who will in turn select and appoint the examination officers from the list just before the examination. Once appointed, the examination officers go to their respective examination sites. The officials of the Three Offices in charge of registrations assemble all the candidates, and at daybreak each candidate's name is called, one after another, to lead them into the fenced-in examination ground. The inspection officers, standing at the entrance, search each candidate's clothes and writing brush container. If anyone is caught carrying books or notes, he is handed over to arresting officers. If he is arrested before entering the examination site, he is barred for one triennial examination; if he is arrested inside the examination site, he is suspended for two triennial examinations.

Just before sunrise, the examination officers appear on the large platform and take seats under torchlight. Their august appearances resemble those of immortals. The officials of the Three Offices then enter the examination ground, arrange the proper seating of the candidates, and leave. At sunrise, the examination questions are posted. At noon, the examination papers are collected and stamped and then returned to the candidates for further work. . . . As the sun begins to set, with the beating of a drum, the candidates present their papers to the collection officers, who in turn hand them over to the registration officers. These officers then record the matching numbers on both ends of the examination papers and cut them apart—one part has the name of the candidate now concealed, and the other contains the candidate's answers to the examination questions. The officials responsible for concealing the candidates' identity retire to a separate room carrying with them the portions of the papers with the concealed names. To prevent recognition of candidates' handwriting, the recording officials have the copyists rewrite the candidates' answers in red ink. When the rewriting is finished, the collating officer reads the originals to the assistant collating officer, who checks the copied version to make sure it is accurate. When all these things have been done, the copied versions of the examination papers are given to the readers. Only after these papers have been graded and their rankings decided upon are the officials responsible for concealing the names of candidates allowed to identify the authors of the examination papers.

Moreover, the candidates must go through the oral examination on the classics . . . in three different stages—the preliminary, the middle, and the final. At the end, the points scored at each stage are added up. All the examination processes are supervised not just by one man but by many, and the evaluation of the candidates is conducted not just by one man but by many. Indeed, there is nothing in the state system that is more judicious than the recruitment examination. YC

Yu Hŭich'un: Diary of an Examiner
[From *Miam ilgi ch'o* (Chōsenshi henshūkai ed.) 3:310–312]

Eighteenth day of the eleventh month in the year [1572]. I was nominated as a possible candidate for the examination officers. . . . In the evening, I received the formal appointment as an examiner for the second examination site, so I went to the Office of Palace Keepers where I was joined by Pak Ch'ungwŏn [1507–1581] and Min Kimun [1511–1574], who were also appointed as officers for the second examination site. At the beginning of the second night watch, the forty-five examination officers of the five examination sites, along with the military examination officers, had an audience with the king, who graciously bestowed wine upon us. We left the guest house, and when we reached the National Academy, it was already the fourth quarter of the second night watch. Sixth State Councillor Pak Ch'ungwŏn was the senior examination officer and therefore sat at the north end of the room; I, Yu Hŭich'un, sat at the east side as the second senior examination officer; Inspector-General Hŏ Yŏp [1517–1580] and Fifth Minister Without Portfolio Min Kimun sat on the west; Chief Ordinance Officer Yi Kŏ, Third Inspector Sin Chŏm, Personnel Section Chief Chŏng T'ak [1526–1605], Rites Section Chief Yu Taesu [1546–1586], and Military Section Chief Hong Hŏn sat on the south. We then discussed the formulation of the examination question. As they all asked me to draft a question, I moved into a comfortable room nearby where I prepared a question.

We requested the administrative staff to provide sufficient heat for the candidates during the examination. We also asked the Four Offices to let the candidates enter the examination site at the first quarter of the fourth night watch. I asked Chŏng T'ak to prepare another set of questions.

Nineteenth day. Clear weather. Today is the day for the preliminary segment of the special examination. I got up at the fourth night watch, and by the end of the watch all the examination officials had assembled in the big hall to decide on the final question. The question I had prepared was: "How should the high ministers assist the young ruler in governing the state?" Section Chief Chŏng drafted: "Discuss

Chu Hsi's inquiries into confusion arising from the disarrangement of tablets in the *Great Learning* and various different views that have developed subsequently." Both Hŏ and Min preferred Chŏng's question, and I agreed. With a minor modification, the examination question was finally ready. At daybreak, the number of the candidates taking part in the examination totaled fourteen hundred and seven. . . .

Twentieth day. Clear weather. After the morning assembly, we urged expediting the copying of the examination papers to ensure anonymity. We evaluated thirteen rolls of examination papers, which means we read one hundred and thirty pieces of essays today. Of these, we chose seven as successful essays, and one of them may be considered for the top honor.

Twenty-first day. Clear weather. . . . We evaluated two hundred essays in twenty rolls, and when we returned to our quarters, it was already the third quarter of the second night watch. Today we selected twelve essays as successful.

Twenty-second day. Cloudy weather. We read examination papers until the second quarter of the second night watch, evaluating two hundred and forty essays, of which eleven were selected. We all agreed that we should be able to finish by the twenty-fifth day and that the final announcement of the successful candidates may be made on the twenty-sixth.

Twenty-third day. Clear weather. We worked from the fifth night watch till the third quarter of the second night watch on the examination papers, reading two hundred and eighty essays, of which we chose nine. . . .

Twenty-fourth day. Clear weather. We rose early as usual to read the examination papers, going over three hundred and fifty essays. We finished the evaluation today; final announcement of the results can be made tomorrow. . . .

Twenty-fifth day. Clear weather. We all got up before daybreak and met at the chamber of the senior examination officer to decide upon which paper should win the top honor. . . . After sunrise, we moved into the Hall of Illustrating the Cardinal Principles to identify the authors of the two hundred successful essays in the presence of the anonymity officers and others. We then had the examination registration officers and three other officials write up the names of the successful candidates for the preliminary examination for announcement. When this was all done, dusk was descending. Nine examination officers went to the palace . . . to present the list of the successful candidates to His Majesty. The officers of the first examination site of the capital city also accompanied us in the audience. His Majesty graciously presented us with wine. When we returned to our quarters, it was the first night watch. YC

Compilation of History

Few states in world history, it may be said, were as conscious of history as the Chosŏn dynasty. Continuing the long tradition of historical writing in Korea, the Chosŏn dynasty sponsored the compilation of a number of historical works and expended a prodigious amount of energy to produce and preserve historical records.

For historical record keeping, court diarists called *hallim* were appointed to take note of all the activities around the throne, and no official business could be conducted by the king without the presence of a court diarist. Appointed from the cream of the recent graduates of the civil service examination, the court diarists strove to live up to the ideal of "straight brush" without fear or favor in recording the activities of the court. After the death of each king, these records as well as the documents of various offices within the central government were assembled for the purpose of compiling the annals called *sillok* (Veritable Record). Thus, we have the *sillok* for the rule of every king of the Chosŏn dynasty. To safeguard the historical records, the Chosŏn dynasty maintained four separate archives in remote mountainous areas in addition to the central archive in Seoul. Aware that their actions and speeches were being recorded for posterity, the Chosŏn dynasty rulers and their officials often found themselves in a defensive position.

There were two types of historical works: official and private. The official histories were compiled under the auspices of the state; the private histories were written by individual scholars in a private capacity. Both the *Koryŏ sa* (History of Koryŏ) and the *Tongguk t'onggam* (Comprehensive Mirror of the Eastern Kingdom), whose introductory remarks are translated here, belong to the former category.

The project of compiling the official history of the Koryŏ dynasty in the tradition of China's official dynastic history was started within a few months of the founding of the Chosŏn dynasty in 1392, but it was not completed until 1451 after having undergone several major revisions. Because of its extensive use of primary sources, the *History of Koryŏ* is by far the most important history of the Koryŏ dynasty. The *Comprehensive Mirror of the Eastern Kingdom,* on the other hand, is a general history of Korea from antiquity to the fall of Koryŏ. Published in 1484, the book was perhaps the most widely read book on Korean history among Korean scholars and officials. Because the Chosŏn dynasty was a Neo-Confucian state, the editorial outlook of both the *History of Koryŏ* and the *Comprehensive Mirror of the Eastern Kingdom* strongly reflect the Confucian worldview. That is, history, in addition to recording what happened, also had to provide moral lessons for future generations by praising good deeds and condemning evil acts.

Translated here are the dedication written by Chŏng Inji for the *History of Koryŏ* and the preface by Yi Kŭkton (1435–1503) for the *Comprehensive Mirror of the Eastern Kingdom.*

Chŏng Inji: Dedication of the *Koryŏ sa*
[From *Koryŏ sa, chŏn* 1a–4b]

It is said that when one makes a new ax handle, he examines an old one as a model and that when one builds a new carriage, he uses an old carriage as a model. This is so that we can learn lessons from the past. Because the rise and fall of various states in history likewise offers lessons of encouragement and warning for the future, we have compiled the *History of Koryŏ* and hereby present it to Your Majesty for your perusal.

The Wang clan rose at the beginning from the state of T'aebong, compelled Silla to surrender, eliminated Later Paekche, and reunited the Three Han under the rule of one family. The new dynasty then turned against Liao, established a respectful relationship with T'ang, maintained deference toward China, and secured our land of Korea. The new government of Koryŏ introduced reforms by eliminating vexing and exploitative rules and regulations and laid the foundation of the state on a grandiose scale. With the institution of the recruitment examination system under King Kwangjong [949–975], Confucian studies began to flourish. With the adoption of various new institutions under King Sŏngjong [981–997], the governing structure of the state was perfected. During the reign of King Mokchong [997–1009], failures in the government led to the decline in the fortune of the state. But under King Hyŏnjong [1009–1031], the country was revitalized, and the state institutions regained stability. King Munjong

[1046–1083] ruled the country in great peace and stability, allowing the people to enjoy prosperity and economic abundance.

Unfortunately, however, the succeeding rulers became lax and confused in their rule, giving rise to powerful individuals who abused their power and even attempted to usurp the sacred throne with the military strength they commanded. Such a situation developed at first during the reign of King Injong [1122–1146], but it was during the days of King Ŭijong [1146–1170] that an outright rebellion against the ruler took place. Thereafter, evil men seized power in succession and replaced the king at will as if he were a pawn while the country became the victim of invasion by a powerful enemy, the Mongols, in which people were mowed down like grass. King Wŏnjong [1259–1274] was able to restore order from the crisis of lawlessness and barely managed to preserve the ancestral institutions of the state. King Ch'ungnyŏl [1274–1308], however, surrounded himself with his favorites and sycophants and indulged in feasts and sensual pleasures, leading to the rise of conflict with his own son. From the rule of King Ch'ungsuk [1313–1339] until that of King Kongmin [1351–1374], abnormal natural phenomena and disturbances occurred frequently, bringing about a serious decline in the fortunes of the state. The foundation of the state deteriorated further under the pretenders U [1374–1388] and Ch'ang [1388–1389], until the dynastic fortune finally fell to the true ruler, T'aejo. Our great King T'aejo [1392–1398], with his heaven-endowed courage and sagacity, renewed and expanded his virtue and achievements, pacified the country with his military might, brought peace and tranquility to the people, and ascended the throne, thereby inaugurating the new dynasty in response to the new mandate.

King T'aejo believed that even though the dynastic fortune and institutions were in ruin, the history of Koryŏ ought not to be obliterated, and hence he ordered the historians to compile its history in an annalistic style following the format of the *Comprehensive Mirror for Aid in Government*. To carry out this wish, King T'aejong in turn entrusted his ministers to work on the task of compilation; although a number of scholars were engaged in the project, the work remained unfinished during T'aejong's rule. Continuing the achievements of his predecessors, King Sejong actively promoted literary works and reestablished the History Office because he believed that the compilation of history requires exhaustive preparation. The work produced, however, still contained inaccurate information and omissions in chronology and narration; moreover, the annalistic format, unlike that of "annals, biography, table, and treatise," was not well suited to give complete and full narrative accounts. King Sejong then ordered this humble minister, who lacks sagacity, to take charge of compiling the history once again.

The guidelines for compiling the history follow those of Ssu-ma Ch'ien [c. 145–85 B.C.]. On every issue related to the basic principles, we consulted with His Majesty and abided by his final decision. We avoided the use of the term *pongi* (basic annals) and called it instead *sega* (ruling family) in order to demonstrate our respect for the principle of rectification of names. We downgraded the Sin family members by including them in the biography section to show our harsh condemnation for usurpation. We recorded the loyal and the deceitful officials as well as the evil and the upright individuals under separate categories; we entered various institutions and cultures under their respective classification. We also clarified those parts of the annals of reigns that were confusing and established verifiable chronologies. We traced historical events as fully and clearly as possible and made sure that those aspects that lacked sufficient information were supplemented with additional data. But, alas, King Sejong passed away before the work was ready for print. . . .

Your Majesty, . . . concerned that the history of the former dynasty was still unfinished, ordered this humble servant to take charge of completing the task. Your servant, Chŏng Inji, and other officials respectfully accepted your command although we are deficient in ability and went over all the writings of individual authors and the records of all the archives and offices. After three years of exhaustive effort, we have been able to complete the entire history of Koryŏ. Only by probing into the past can we be sure of achieving the impartiality of historical writings; only by exhibiting the illustrious mirror of history can we ensure that the consequences of good and evil acts shall not be forgotten by posterity.

The *History of Koryŏ* that we have compiled consists of one hundred and thirty-nine chapters—forty-six chapters on the ruling families, thirty-nine chapters of treatises, two chapters of tables, fifty chapters of biographies, and two chapters of table of contents. Your servant, Chŏng Inji, hereby submits with trepidation the completed draft history along with this letter of dedication. YC

Yi Kŭkton: Preface to the *Tongguk t'onggam*

[From *Tongguk t'onggam* (Chosŏn kwangmunhoe ed., 1911), sŏ, pp. 1–4]

The books of the classics contain the Way and the books of history record events. The classics, as revised and compiled by Confucius, have provided lessons for myriad generations. Moreover, many history books have been written since the times of Ssu-ma Ch'ien and Pan Ku, as each generation thereafter produced historical works, and there are far too many to list them all. A scholar may devote a full ten years and still fail to read them all. If this is the case, how much more difficult would it be for a ruler to find time to read them, as he is pressed daily with myriad affairs of state? The former upright Minister Ssu-ma of Sung China, having assembled a multitude of historical and other books, selected their essentials and compiled the *Comprehensive Mirror for Aid in Government,* covering the period from the decline of Chou to the end of Five Dynasties. Since then this work has truly become the model for all historians. Based on this book, Master Chu Hsi in turn compiled the *T'ung-chien kang-mu* (Abridged Essentials). Written in simple language with clear elucidation, *Abridged Essentials* makes it easier to discern what to guard against and how to distinguish omens. These works accord with the solemn objectives of the *Spring and Autumn Annals.* All writers since then have abided by the standard set by these two great masters.

In ancient times, our country was ruled in succession by Tangun, Kija, and Three Han; however, there are no verifiable records for these periods. Only since the time of the Three Kingdoms do we begin to have some recorded national histories; even then, these records were often carelessly compiled and contain unreliable stories. Thereafter, many authors compiled histories in succession, and thus there are several types of histories, such as complete histories, summarized histories, and abridged histories. Unfortunately, these works contain the defects of earlier works. The Koryŏ dynasty, having reunited the Later Three Kingdoms, ruled for nearly five hundred years under thirty-three rulers. Although it has dynastic histories, these works are inconsistent, their descriptions being at times too complex or too simplified. Unavoidably, they are inadequate.

In our own Chosŏn dynasty, King T'aejo, having inaugurated the new state in response to the mandate, widely collected old books and records to preserve them. Three successive rulers continued to promote literary scholarship and established an office to compile the history of the Koryŏ dynasty. Thus, we now have historical works, such as a complete history and abridged histories, of the previous dynasty. With these histories, the void in our historical scholarship is gradually being filled. King Sejo [1455–1468], himself a naturally endowed scholar of sagely learning and mindful of the classics and history, expressed his view at one time that although there are several types of history, that there is no "comprehensive mirror" covering the overall history of our country that is comparable to the *Comprehensive Mirror for Aid in Government.* He then ordered the literary ministers to work on such a history. Unfortunately, this project was not completed during his rule. Your Majesty, having succeeded to the great throne and wishing to continue the plan of the previous ruler, has commanded your servants, Sŏ Kŏjŏng, the Lord of Talsŏng, . . . to compile and present the *Comprehensive Mirror of the Eastern Kingdom.* . . .

In compiling the *Comprehensive Mirror of the Eastern Kingdom,* we examined all the available historical works since the times of the Three Kingdoms as well as various works on Chinese history. We then decided to follow the format of "annals and narratives." We also took the guidelines of the *Comprehensive Mirror for Aid in Government* as our guide and have eliminated those that are confusing and trivial while preserving the important and essential ones. The period of rivalry among the Three Kingdoms is classified as the Three Kingdoms era, the period of the Unified Silla as the Silla era, Koryŏ as the Koryŏ era, and the period before the Three Han as the External era. We have tried to narrate in a straightforward manner the unity and disunity of national strength, the good and weak points in national fortunes, the beneficial and evil rules of kings, and the successful and failed administrations in governing the state for fourteen hundred years. We have been particularly strict in emphasizing the rectification of names, in respecting loyalty and uprightness, in condemning rebels, and in punishing evil and deceitful men in the hope that these will provide lessons for the encouragement and admonition of posterity. Wherever the critiques of former scholars are available, we have included them. We have also added our own unworthy views here and there, even though we are fully aware that our opinions do not merit being placed alongside those of former scholars.

It is believed that the ancient sage-king Kija implemented the teachings of eight articles based on the grand plan of government. Although there must have been historians who recorded the commendable words and deeds at that time, all the records of this period have been lost and none has survived. The records of the Three Kingdoms, on the other hand, tend to be inadequate and absurd, while those of Koryŏ are skimpy and confusing. Even with the assistance of the able Pan Ku and Ssu-ma Ch'ien, it would be difficult to compile an acceptable literary composition. And how could we, who lack talent and knowledge, produce a work that will meet the expectations of Your Majesty? Despite our limited ability, we have compiled the *Comprehensive Mirror of the Eastern Kingdom* in fifty-seven chapters and hereby present it to Your Majesty. As Your Majesty reads this in your leisure hours, we hope that the past history of peace and chaos and the rise and fall of various states will become the constant admonitions of today. If Your Majesty were to exert himself toward the splendid virtue of inquiring into the past, it would indeed be of no small assistance in attaining an exemplary rule. YC

Printing Books

The invention of movable metallic type can be regarded as one of Korea's most significant contributions to world civilization. Having learned from China the technique of book printing by means of woodblocks, Korea became the first country in the world to develop movable metallic type, dating back as early as the beginning of the thirteenth century. Continuing this tradition, the Chosŏn dynasty frequently undertook book printing projects, constantly improving and refining the technique of typesetting. A recent study has verified the casting of as many as twenty-one different species of type during the fifteenth century alone.[1] The various types cast in Korea are usually identified by the year in which they were cast. For the Confucian state of Chosŏn, book printing was important not only for promoting scholarship but also for striving to realize the ideals of good government. The three accounts translated here indicate the extent of painstaking effort the early Chosŏn state expended in the matter of book printing. YC

Sŏng Hyŏn: On Printing
[From *Yongjae ch'onghwa* (Koryŏ taehakkyo ed., 1963), pp. 456–457]

In the year 1403, King T'aejong remarked to the courtiers around him: "In order to govern the country well, it is essential that books be read widely. But because our country is located east of China beyond the sea, not many books from China are readily available. Moreover, woodblock prints are easily defaced, and it is impossible to print all the books in the world by using woodblock prints. It is my desire to cast copper type so that we can print as many books as possible and have them made available widely. This will truly bring infinite benefit to us." In the end, the king was successful in having copper type cast with the graphs modeled after those of the *Old Commentary on the Book of Songs* and the *Tso Commentary,* and this is how the typecasting foundry became established in our country. This type is now called *chŏnghae* [1407] type.[2]

But because this *chŏnghae* type was bulky and irregularly shaped, King Sejong had new type cast in the year of *kyŏngja* [1420], and thus it is called *kyŏngja* type. This new type is smaller and has a more regular shape, and all the available books have been printed with it. In the year of *kabin* [1434], more type was cast using the calligraphy of Wei-shan[3] as a model. This type is a little bigger than *kyŏngja* type, and its graphs have an extremely fine appearance. King Sejong also ordered King Sejo, who was then Prince Suyang, to write Chu Hsi's *Kang-mu* in big graphs and had copper type cast using Sejo's calligraphy as a model. Using this type, *Kang-mu* was printed and is now known as the *hunŭi* edition.

In the year of *imsin* [1452], King Munjong smelted the *kyŏngja* type to recast it into *imsin* type, whose characters were modeled after the calligraphy of Prince Anp'yŏng. In the year *ŭrhae* [1455], King Sejo smelted the *imsin* type to recast it as *ŭrhae* type, whose characters followed the calligraphy of Kang Hŭian. This type is being used now. Thereafter, in the year of *ŭryu* [1465], using Chŏng Nanjong's calligraphy, King Sejo cast the *ŭryu* types to print the *Yüan-chüeh ching* (Perfect Enlightenment Scripture), but the characters of this print are irregular. In the year *sinmyo* [1471], King Sŏngjong cast the *sinmyo* type, selecting logographs from the works of Wang An-shih and Ou-yang Hsiu; this type is smaller than *kyŏngja* type and has great refinement. King Sŏngjong also cast the *kyech'uk* [1493] type using the logographs of the new edition of *Kang-mu,* which he obtained from China.

The process of typecasting is as follows. First, logographs are engraved on *hwangyang* wood;[4] then flat print plates are prepared with soft clay collected from the seashore where seaweeds grow. And then the wooden graphs are pressed against the clay to produce impressions of the graphs. Both print plates are placed together and molten copper is poured through a hole to flow downward, filling the indentations until each graph is formed. The graphs are then removed and refined. The person who engraves on wood is called the engraver, and the person who casts is called the casting artisan. The finished graphs are stored in boxes, and the person responsible for storing type is called the typekeeper. These men were selected from the young servants working in the government. A person who reads manuscript is called the manuscript reader. These people are all literate. The typekeeper lines up the needed graphs on the manuscript papers and then places them on a plate called the upper plate. The graph leveling artisan fills in all the empty spaces between type on the upper plate with bamboo and torn cloth, and tightens it so that the type cannot be moved. The plate is then handed over to the printing artisan to print. The entire process of printing is supervised by members of the Office of Editorial Review selected from among graduates of the civil service examination.

At first, no one knew how to tighten up the type on a printing plate, and beeswax was used to fix type on the plate. As a result each logograph had an awl-like tail, as in the *kyŏngja* type. Only after the technique of filling empty space with bamboo was developed was there no longer a need to use wax. Boundless indeed is the ingenuity of men's intelligence. YC

On the Typecasting Foundry
[From *Sejong sillok* 11:15b–16a]

An entry on the twenty-fourth day of the third month of the year [1421]: His Majesty King Sejong granted one hundred and twenty bottles of wine to the Typecasting Foundry. To print books, type used to be placed on copper plates, molten beeswax would be poured on the plates to solidify the type alignments, and thereafter a print was made. This required an excessive amount of beeswax and allowed printing of only a few sheets a day. Whereupon His Majesty personally directed the work and ordered Second Minister of Public Works Yi Ch'ŏn [1376–1451] and former Deputy Mayor Nam Kŭp [fl. 1421] to improve the casting of copper plates to match the shape of the type. With this improvement, the type remained firmly on the plates without using beeswax, and the print became more square and correct. It also allowed the printing of several dozen sheets in a day. Mindful of the Typecasting Foundry's hard and meritorious work, His Majesty granted wine and food on several occasions. His Majesty then ordered them to print *Abridged Essentials* and asked the Hall of Worthies to attach an errata. This work lasted from the winter of the year *kyŏngja* [1420] until the summer of the year *imin* [1422] before it was completed. YC

Pyŏn Kyeryang: Postscript to the Typecasting
[From *Tong munsŏn* 103:18b–19a]

In the spring, second month of the year [1402], His Majesty King T'aejong remarked to his courtiers: "In order to govern the country well, it is essential that books be read widely. . . . But because our country is located east of China beyond the sea, not many books from China are readily available. . . . It is my desire to cast copper type so that we can print as many books as possible and have them made available widely." The king then granted a fund from the palace and ordered Yi Chik and several other officials to supervise the work. . . . On the ninth day of the same month, the typecasting began; within several months, the pieces of cast type of the Chinese logographs numbered several hundred thousand. His Majesty's sagacious policy for cultural works . . . will lead to the printing of books in tens of thousands of volumes, and these books will be transmitted to posterity for thousands of generations. . . . YC

Science and Technology

The early Chosŏn dynasty achieved great success in science and technology. The moving force behind this development was King Sejong, who, equipped with personal knowledge, initiated a number of scientific programs to improve and refine the observation and measurement of various natural phenomena. The king was particularly interested in astronomical matters. Seasonal changes, times of sunrise and sunset, rainfall and drought—all were vitally important for a country whose economy was almost totally dependent upon agriculture. Thus, we have elaborate armillary spheres charting constellations, refined rain gauges, and various sundials and clepsydras (water clocks) designed with great scientific sophistication, all made during the reign of King Sejong. Particularly noteworthy is the construction in the year 1434 of an instrument that announced the hours automatically: the *chagyŏngnu* (automatic striking clepsydra). Devised and constructed by a former slave, Chang Yŏngsil (d. 1455), this automatic clepsydra was installed on the grounds of the royal palace to tell the time twenty-four hours a day. (The main parts of a replica of this instrument made in 1536 are still preserved in Seoul.) The *Veritable Records of King Sejong* records in detail how this clepsydra operated and offers other information on the development of science and technology. YC

The Automatic Striking Clepsydra
[From *Sejong sillok* 65:1a–3a]

On the first day of the seventh month [1434],[5] the new clepsydra was put into operation. The king had decided that the old clepsydra was not accurate enough and had ordered casting of metal parts for a new one, with four water-delivering dragon-mouthed vessels of different sizes. There were two inflow dragon-ornamented vessels, one for the double-hours and one for the night-watches, each 11.2 feet long and 1.8 feet in diameter, having two indicator-rods 10.2 feet long.

The surfaces of the rods were divided into the twelve double-hours, each with eight intervals and the extra fractions at the beginnings and mid-points of the double-hours to make up a total equivalent to 100 intervals, each interval comprising twelve fractions.

The night rods formerly numbered twenty-one, and were troublesome for the attendants to use in the night-watches. In conformity with the Shou-shih calendar's day/night apportionment increases-and-decreases, two fortnightly seasons were now served by one rod, there being thus altogether twelve rods in the case of a nonstriking clepsydra. When tested they agreed with the Simplified Instrument without the slightest discrepancy.

The king was also worried that the officials in charge of time announcements could not avoid mistakes, so he ordered Chang Yŏngsil of the Palace Guard to construct wooden jacks that would announce the time automatically without human agency.

The construction was as follows:

First he erected a pavilion with three pillars (*ying*). Between the eastern pair two stories were built. On the upper story stood three immortals as announcers, sounding double-hours by a bell, night-watches by a drum, and divisions of night-watches by a gong. On the story below the middle was placed a horizontal wheel having twelve immortals round its circumference. Each immortal was carried on an iron rod upon which it could move up and down and had a placard to announce one of the double-hours in turn. . . .

[The text then goes on to describe the design of the mechanism for these movements in detail, a part of which reads as follows:]

Thus as the water trickles down into the left-hand inflow vessel, the indicator-rod floats upward corresponding to the passage of the double-hours, and it opens the latches of the holes in the left bronze rack, so that the small bronze balls fall one after the other and find their way into the 4.5–foot-long bronze tube. Falling through its holes, they operate the release mechanisms so that the large iron balls fall too and enter the left-hand short tube suspended under the upper story. As they fall they operate the mechanical spoon, the other end of which transmits a motion from within the top of the accompanying tube to impel the elbow of the double-hour-announcing immortal to sound the bell.

The watches' and divisions' actions are similar, but the night-watch initial balls run into the central suspended short tube to fall and operate the spoon mechanism, which from within the top of the left-hand round pillar impels the elbow of the night-watch-announcing immortal to sound the drum. Then the balls turn into the night-watch divisions tube to operate the initial-division mechanism, which from within the top of the right-hand round pillar impels the elbow of the division-announcing immortal to sound the gong; then they stop. . . .

All the mechanisms are hidden so that they cannot be seen; the only things visible are the fully dressed immortals. . . .

The king ordered Kim Pin [d. 1455] to make an inscription for it, the preface of which said: Among the policies of emperors and kings, none has been more important than the unification of times and seasons. The methods used for the study of these matters have been the armillary sphere, the celestial globe, the sundial, and the clepsydra. Without the sphere and the globe, there could be no study of the motions of the heavens and earth; without the sundial and clepsydra there could be no measure of the divisions between the days and nights. Over a thousand years, at the correct moment each one will start without any error. This can be achieved only if no neglect is permitted in the summation of the smallest differences in gnomon shadow length. Therefore all through time the sages have followed the heavens in their government; none has failed to respect this.

Now, His Majesty's servants, having in mind his profound respect for the Emperor Yao, and imitating the example of the Great Shun . . ., have constructed this new clepsydral apparatus in order to equalize the sundial and the intervals; it is set up in the western part of the palace. . . .

As each hour comes round, the jackwork immortals of the clepsydra respond with the appropriate time-signals. Consulting the celestial globe and the armillary sphere, people find that the time-signals correspond to the movement of the heavens without the slightest mistake. It is really as if the gods and spirits were in charge of it. No one seeing it does not heave a sigh and aver that we Koreans certainly had nothing like this in former times. . . .

Having received the command, I, [Kim] Pin, have written this for future generations and humbly present the inscription, which says: Yin and yang follow each other, day and night alternately come round. . . . The sundial and clepsydra have long been made, but from the time of the legendary sage-emperor Huang-ti on there have been different methods, and only we Easterners have developed and extended the different designs. . . .[6]

Kim Ton: Instruments to Measure Days and Nights
[From *Sejong sillok* 77:7a]

At the beginning of the year [1437], King Sejong had ordered the construction of instruments to measure the days and nights. . . . The king commissioned Kim Ton [1385–1440] to make an inscription, the preface of which said:

The making of celestial globes and armillary spheres is a high and ancient practice. From the emperors Yao and Shun down to the Han and T'ang dynasties there was no one who did not regard it as a most important thing. The literature about it is to be found in the classics and histories, but as we are far removed from ancient times, the methods have not been handed down in great detail. Now His Majesty reverently took the work of these sages as the capstone of the achievements of antiquity. While resting from the myriad concerns of his duties, he turned his attention to the principles of astronomy and uranographic models. Accordingly, what were of old called armillary spheres, celestial globes, gnomons, simplified instruments, automatic striking clepsydras, small simplified instruments, hemispherical scaphe sundials, horizontal sundials, and plummet sundials, all these instruments have been made without one missing. Such is His Majesty's respect for heavenly knowledge and for the exploitation of earthly things.[7]

King Sejong and Scientific Instruments
[From *Sejong sillok* 77:10b–11a]

In the spring of the *muo* year [1438] the authorities concerned asked that a record should be made of the previous several years' instrument-making activity from beginning to end for the information of posterity. So they discussed their views with your servant, and I was ordered to write the account that precedes this summary about all these affairs. As far as I can see, they were all based on Kuo Shou-ching's Shou-shih calendar of 1280, which depends on the fundamental measurement of the heavens carried out by means of the armillary sphere and the celestial globe. . . .

Now His Majesty, in his sage wisdom and his profound respect for heaven, while resting from the myriad concerns of his duties, considered that the calendar was not as perfect as it ought to be, and ordered that it should be further studied and better established. Disturbed that measurements were not as accurate as they could be, he ordered that new instruments be constructed. How could Yao or Shun themselves have done any better? The instruments thus ordered were not only one or two, but quite a number, so that the results could be compared with each other. Such a wealth of equipment has never previously been recorded. All these His Majesty is intimately acquainted with, and even Kuo Shou-ching of the Yüan could have offered nothing better. After the Shou-shih calendar had been corrected, observational instruments were made to follow the seasons of the heavens above and to be of service to the works of the people below.

His Majesty's sense of responsibility in the exploitation of the works of nature is of the highest, as is also his benevolence in the high valuation of agriculture. We Easterners have not seen anything as fine as these instruments before. Like the high tower of the observatory itself, they will be passed down for time without end.[8]

Invention and Use of Rain Gauges

Because traditional Korea was a predominantly agrarian society, people's livelihood depended largely on the land and the state's main source of revenue was the land tax. As the success or failure of the harvest depended heavily on the amount of rainfall, it was important for the state to keep a correct assessment of this amount. Based on a long tradition of science and technology, an instrument to measure accurately the amount of rainfall was invented in 1442 under the reign of King Sejong. Modern scientists marvel at the rain gauge perfected during Sejong's rule, as it is almost identical to the instruments that are currently in use. The government's effort to establish uniformity in gauging and reporting the amount of rainfall throughout the country is also impressive.

Measuring the Amount of Rainfall
[From *Sejong sillok* 93:22a–22b]

On the eighteenth day of the eighth month of the year [1441], the Ministry of Taxation reported to the king that the provincial governors are required, according to the existing laws, to report the amount of rainfall in their provinces. But because soils are sometimes dry and sometimes soaked, the exact amount of rainfall is not easy to determine. Therefore, the Office of Astronomy has been requested to make a pedestal upon which to place a cast-iron vessel, whose measurements are two *ch'ŏk* [42.5 cm] in depth and eight *ch'on* [17.0 cm] in diameter, to receive rainfall. Then officers from the Office of Astronomy can report the amount of rainfall more accurately using this vessel.

Also, a slab of stone should be placed at the bottom of the water west of the Majŏn Bridge and two support stones holding a wooden pole in between should then be erected upon this stone and tied together with iron chains. The wooden pole then is engraved with gradations of *ch'ŏk* [feet], *ch'on* [inches], and *pun* [tenths of inches]. Then officials from the Ministry of Taxation can report the amount of rainfall by reading the depth of water from the pole.

In addition, a marker with *ch'ŏk, ch'on,* and *pun* gradations should be erected upon a rock on the bank of the Han River, and the ferry master should measure the depth of water and report it to the Ministry of Taxation.

At the same time, the county officials in the provinces should be instructed to make ceramic or tile vessels modeled after the cast-iron vessel of the capital city, and to place them in the yard of their offices. The magistrate then can report the amount of rainfall to the provincial governor, who will in turn report the same to His Majesty. The king approved these proposals and ordered them implemented. YC

Regulations for Gauging Rainfall
[From *Sejong sillok* 96:7a–b]

Eighth day of the fifth month in the year [1442]. The Ministry of Taxation submitted the following regulations on measuring the amount of rainfall:

1. In the capital city, a vessel 1.5 *ch'ŏk* [31.9 cm] in length and 7 *ch'on* [14.9 cm] in diameter shall be cast in iron, and it will be called *ch'ŭgugi* (rain gauge). The rain gauge will be placed on a pedestal at the Office of Astronomy, and after each rainfall the officials from the Office of Astronomy shall measure the depth of the water using the standard ruler and shall record it along with the date and time of rainfall as well as the weather conditions. The Office of Astronomy shall keep a file of these records and report to the throne as necessary.

2. One iron rain gauge and one standard ruler shall be sent to each province so that replicas of these are made either in ceramic or in tile to be distributed to all counties. The rain gauge shall then be placed on a pedestal in the courtyard of the county office. Each county shall also make a copy of the standard ruler with bamboo or wood. Using this, each magistrate shall personally measure the amount of rainfall after each rain and record it along with the date and time. The magistrate shall report to the king the amount of rainfall as necessary and keep a file for future reference. The king approved the new regulations. YC

Compilation of Medical Books

Korea has a long tradition of compiling and publishing medical books. The Chosŏn dynasty, from its beginning, devoted considerable time and energy to compiling and publishing a number of medical works in order to bring the latest information on remedies to the people. Conducting exhaustive research into all the available medical books, including those published in China, and undertaking comprehensive collections of the native prescriptions and herbs that had proven effective, the Chosŏn government spared no effort to publish the collections of medical remedies. In 1393, King T'aejo dispatched medical instructors to every province to train medical specialists; in 1397, *Hyangyak chesaeng chipsŏng pang* (Collection of Native Prescriptions to Save Life) was published. During his brilliant reign, King Sejong sponsored the compilation and publication of a comprehensive medical book entitled *Hyangyak chipsŏng pang* (Compilation of Native Korean Prescriptions). Completed in 1433 after two years of exhaustive research, this work explains some 959 different diagnoses and gives prescriptions for 10,706 different remedies, its material being classified into various specialties such as internal and external medicine and ophthalmology. In addition, the book also covered 1,476 different techniques of acupuncture. In preparing this book, special effort was made to collect remedies that had proven effective in Korean experience. With the compilation of this work, the study of medical science in Korea reached a new milestone. In 1445, King Sejong published another medical work, *Ŭibang yuch'wi* (Classified Collection of Medical Prescriptions), a medical encyclopedia. Then, after the Japanese invasion of 1592–1598, a monumental work entitled *Tongŭi pogam* (Exemplars of Korean Medicine) was compiled by Hŏ Chun (d. 1615) and published in 1610. Widely admired for its usefulness, it was published in China and Japan as well.

Translated here is the preface to *Compilation of Native Korean Prescriptions* written by Kwŏn Ch'ae (1399–1438) and published in 1433. Noteworthy in this preface is the emphasis on finding proper medicine and remedies based on Korean experiences in the compilation of this collection. YC

Kwŏn Ch'ae: Preface to *Compilation of Native Korean Prescriptions*
[From *Sejong sillok* 60:39b–40a]

Eleventh day of the sixth month of the year [1433]. The *Compilation of Native Korean Prescriptions* has just been completed. Following the royal command, Kwŏn Ch'ae wrote the preface as follows: Since the times of the legendary rulers of Shen-nung and Huang-ti in China, there have been medical officers who looked after the illnesses of myriad people. In diagnosing illness and dispensing medicines, the doctor gives remedies appropriate to the nature of each individual case and does not depend solely on one method for all cases. The people in regions separated by one hundred *ri* do not have the same social customs, just as the areas separated by one thousand *ri* do not have the same wind. Just as the plants and trees have favorite places to grow, so do the people have favorites in food and drink, according to their customs. Because of this, the ancient sages at first learned the nature of various plants and respected the characteristics unique to the regions in governing the state.

Situated by heaven in the eastern corner of the world, our country is endowed with abundant resources in both mountains and sea, sufficient to nurture its people, and is blessed with rich supplies of herbal medicinal materials, sufficient to treat those who are sick. There is nothing that is lacking. Yet, from ancient times, the study of medicine in our country has failed to flourish: the people often did not collect herbs at appropriate times, therefore, and sought them from far places rather than from nearby areas. When they became ill, people invariably sought medicine from China that was hard to obtain. Such unpreparedness is like seeking three-year-old moxa to treat a seven-year-old disease. If the right medicine cannot be obtained, there is no way to treat the disease. Frequently, there are cases in which an elderly person among the common people is able to treat a particular illness with a certain herb with an extraordinary success, and this is because both soil and medicine are well suited to the disease. Just as people will not hesitate to travel one thousand *ri* in order to seek a treatment to restore a crooked finger, they will go anywhere to seek treatment of their diseases if the correct treatment is available within the country.

Previously, Minister Kwŏn Chunghwa [1322–1408] compiled *Hyangyak kani pang* (Simple Prescriptions for Folk Medicine) based on the data he had collected. This he later revised after he and Cho

Chun [1346–1405], the Lord of P'yŏngyang, ordered the medical officers to conduct further research on prescriptions, adopted additional prescriptions found to be effective among Koreans, and classified them into various categories. After its publication, it has become easier to obtain medicines and to treat patients for the relief from diseases. There are still only a few books of remedies published in China, however, and many of China's medical terms are different from those of Korea. Thus, those who practice medicine deplored this situation as deficient. Mindful of this, His Majesty commanded the selected medical officials to accompany every diplomatic mission dispatched to the Chinese capital for the purpose of seeking out medical books. His Majesty even wrote a special memorial to the Chinese emperor asking him to permit Korean officials to check with the Chinese Bureau of Medicine to examine and correct the names of herbs. Then, in the fall of the year [1431], His Majesty ordered Yu Hyot'ong [fl. 1408–1431], Second Counselor in the Hall of Worthies; No Chungnyc [fl. 1423], Director of the Office of Medicine; Pak Yundŏk, Deputy Director of the Office of Medicine; and others to collect more prescriptions of folk medicine, to conduct further research into the written works, and to classify all the collected prescriptions into systematic categories. It has taken more than a year to complete this work. As a result, we now have 959 different diagnoses explained, as compared to the 338 we had previously, and 10,706 different prescriptions prescribed, as compared to 2,803 previously. In addition, 1,476 prescriptions of acupuncture, the list of native-grown herb plants, and the methods of medicine preparations are included in the appendix. Completed in eighty-five chapters, the work has been presented to His Majesty under the title of *Compilation of Native Korean Prescriptions*. As the book is being prepared for printing for wide circulation, His Majesty has commanded this servant, Kwŏn Ch'ae, to prepare a preface.

In the humble opinion of this servant, nothing is more important than humanity in the kingly way, and humanity, being ultimately great, is of many different kinds. Now, His Majesty is totally committed to the greatness of the kingly way in order to realize virtuous rule in government, and his benevolent rule is fully demonstrated in this project of compiling and publishing a book of medicine for the purpose of promoting the people's welfare. In the past, there were rulers who personally prepared medicine for the benefit of individual patients, receiving accolades from posterity. The compilation of a medical book for wide dissemination, however, brings benefit to millions of people for thousands of generations, and the extent of the benevolence it bestows is great and diverse. From now on, those who suffer from illness may take medicines according to the prescriptions explained in this book to regain their health. And if that allows them to enjoy the normal lifespan given by nature, is not this the result of the benevolent rule of our ruler, who is totally committed to humanity? YC

CHAPTER SIXTEEN

Social Life

The establishment of the new dynasty in 1392 ushered in an era of social reform that led to a fundamental restructuring of Korean society. Champions of the Confucian way and vigorous opponents of Buddhism, the scholar-officials surrounding the dynastic founders envisaged a new sociopolitical order rooted in Confucian moral principles. Theirs was an idealistic program that favored the formation of a controlled political elite. Inspired by the models they found in Chinese classical literature, the Confucian legislators laid the groundwork from which the highly structured patrilineal descent groups characteristic of Chosŏn society eventually emerged. New standards of ritual behavior and thinking were to provide the elite with values relevant to private as well as to public life. Their platform of ritual action was the *Chu Tzu chia-li* (Family Rites of Chu Hsi), the most authoritative ritual manual of the Chosŏn period.

The reforms, although propagated through moral incentives as well as legal sanctions, were slow in taking root, and the dynasty's first two centuries were a distinct transition period. Traditional institutions and beliefs resisted change and were therefore not reformed "in one morning." The acculturation process went through several stages. The first is illustrated by the documents that are presented here. MD

Confucian Protests Against Buddhism

The Confucians' rise to power was accompanied by the persecution of Buddhism. Mismanagement by the Buddhists was held responsible for the economic and spiritual demise of Koryŏ. According
to the Confucians, Buddhism lacked the pragmatic standards necessary for social control and economic prosperity. The first measures
against Buddhism taken at the beginning of the dynasty were moti-
vated by economic and military considerations and therefore directed
at the institutional foundation of the Buddhist monasteries. The contest for control of the spiritual-religious realm, however, was more
difficult because the early kings and the people at large continued to
adhere to traditional Buddhist customs and ceremonies. Even King
Sejong's attitude toward the religious past was ambivalent, and he
opposed "sudden changes." Typically, then, warning voices and bold
proposals came from the Hall of Worthies (*Chiphyŏnjŏn*)—a research
institution founded in 1420 and staffed with young and energetic
Confucian scholars—and from activist circles at the National Academy. By exposing the defects and inadequacies of Buddhism as a
religion and as an institution, the Confucians were able to propagate,
in contrast, the qualities of Confucianism. MD

Yun Hoe: On the Harmfulness of Buddhism
[From *Sejong sillok* 23:27a–b]

Yun Hoe [1380–1436], Deputy Director of the Hall of Worthies,
and others submitted the following memorial [in 1424]: We consider
the harm of the Buddhists to be prevalent still. Since the Han period
the reverence for Buddha has been increasingly fervent, yet neither
happiness nor profit has been gained. This is recorded in the historical
books, which Your Majesty has certainly perused thoroughly. Must
you therefore wait for your ministers to tell you? . . .

We think that of all the heterodox teachings, Buddhism is the
worst. The Buddhists live alone with their barbaric customs, apart
from the common productive population; yet they cause the people to
be destitute and to steal. What is worse than their crimes? Beasts and
birds that damage grain are certainly chased away because they harm
the people. Yet even though beasts and birds eat the people's food,
they are nevertheless useful to the people. The Buddhists, however,

sit around and eat, and there has not yet been a visible profit. No rain falls now—it is a year of drought. The public granaries are empty, and as to the livelihood of our people, neither life nor death is guaranteed. And yet the food these Buddhists eat is the same in good years as well as bad. One sees only the people starving, never a monk. One sees only the people dying of starvation, never a monk. They are reckless in daily deceiving and betraying the people. We are indeed concerned about it, and in the past many superior men earnestly pointed out their harm. MD

Sin Ch'ŏjung: On the Deceitfulness of Buddhism
[From *Sejong sillok* 23:30a–32b]

Sin Ch'ŏjung, a licentiate at the National Academy, and one hundred and one others went to the palace and tendered the following memorial [in 1424]:

Your servants have carefully read the Explanatory Notes of the *Book of Changes* that say: "Heaven and earth existing, all material things then got their existence. All material things having existence, afterward there came male and female. From the existence of male and female there came afterward husband and wife. From husband and wife there came father and son. From father and son there came ruler and minister. From ruler and minister there came high and low. When the distinction of high and low had existence, afterward came the arrangements of propriety and righteousness."[1] This is the universal way of the world and the constant rule of ancient and present times— something we cannot depart from for even a moment. If we abandon it, no disorder will be greater than this.

Those Buddhists, what kind of people are they? As eldest sons they turn against their fathers; as husbands they oppose the Son of Heaven. They break off the relationship between father and son and destroy the obligation between ruler and subject. They regard the living together of man and woman as immoral and a man's plowing and a woman's weaving as useless. They abrogate the basis of reproduction and stop the sources of dress and food. They do not speak of the right ways of the early kings and do not submit themselves to their laws. They falsely propagate the "three ways" and make an empty demonstration of the "six methods."[2] They mislead the common people's eyes and ears and destroy the principles of their minds. . . . We think that life and death are determined by fate and that good fortune and bad fortune arise by themselves. Certainly they can neither be attained nor avoided by sheer luck. The ignorant monks falsely state, however, that life and death, good fortune and bad fortune, all originate from Buddha! . . .

We observe that Your Majesty takes as a model that through which T'ang, Yü, and the Three Dynasties emerged and takes as a warning that through which Ch'i, Liang, Ch'en, and Sui were ruined. Above, you continue the legacy of your ancestors; below, you aid the expectations of us Confucians. If those monks were forced to return to their home villages; if they were treated as men fit to join the military; if they were made to settle down in order to increase the households; if we burnt their books in order to destroy their roots and branches; if their fields were requisitioned in order to supply military rations; if their slaves were given to the government in order to distribute them among the offices; if their bronze statues and bells were entrusted to the Offices of Supply in order to mint copper cash; if the utensils they use were handed over to a ceremonial office in order to prepare them for official use; if the woodblocks they cut for their scriptures were collected and reused for printing Confucian books; if each of those bald heads who is over sixty and no longer of use was returned to his relatives in order to preserve his remaining strength; if within the capital the temples of each sect were divided up among the offices without buildings; if the temples outside the capital were all torn down in order to build postal stations and school buildings; if for funerals the *Family Rites of Chu Hsi* were exclusively relied upon, and offenders were severely punished in order to warn the others; if at last those upholding the old, ingrained customs were taught propriety and righteousness and nourished with morality—then, in a few years, the human mind would be corrected and the heavenly principles clear, the households would increase, and the number of soldiers would be complete. Those who had earlier turned their back upon ruler and father would then know the necessity of loyalty and filial piety; those who had earlier idled around would then know the necessity of farming. Would there be a single man who does not change, a man who places himself outside rites and laws? This is an opportunity for renewing Your Majesty's transforming influence! MD

The Role of Rites

In their effort to transform Korean society into a Confucian society, the Confucians never tired of pointing out the fundamental role of the four rites (*sarye*)—capping, wedding, funeral, and ancestor worship—in this transformatory process. To the Confucian, rites were not an imposition upon human nature. Rather, they activated what was good in a person and thus formed the human mind. If properly observed, they determined the relationships within the domestic sphere and stabilized the social foundation of the public realm. The peace and prosperity of a state were thus guaranteed in proportion to the purity of its ritual life. MD

Sŏng Hyŏn: The Fundamental Role of Rites
[From *Hŏhaektang chip* 10.12a–13b]

Rites must be cultivated. If they are not cultivated, the human mind is unstable, laws and orders are numerous, and the way of good rule cannot emerge. It is comparable to curing a man's sickness: if one tried to remedy it hastily in one morning with poisonous medicine, would his constitution not also be harmed? One should first provide the taste of the five grains; thereafter his body naturally regains vitality, and the sickness disappears.

In ancient times the states that cultivated the rites well were Yü[3] and Chou. Po-i was in charge of the rites, Hou-chi was in charge of music, and Hsüeh observed the five orders of human relationships. Hereby they all cultivated the rites and therefore accomplished a rule of harmony and peace. The Duke of Chou [d. 1094 B.C.] regulated the rites and played music. The evidence that he cultivated the rites is contained in the *Rites of Chou* and the *Book of Etiquette and Ceremonies*. Therefore Kings Ch'eng and K'ang succeeded the rules of Kings Wu and Wen and thereby accomplished their excellence. They put human feelings at ease by following that whereby human feelings are naturally at ease; they made the customs effective by following that whereby the customs are naturally effective. They induced good and warded off evil; they were imbued with humanity and righteousness. Due to the simplicity of their cultivation of the rites, their performance was easy; and because their rule was not rushed, it lasted long.

What was the method by which they cultivated the rites? If a man lives idly and does not have instruction, he is insolent and disorderly and differs but slightly from wild animals. Therefore the sages have made the rites as guidelines so that the one who overshoots them retrenches and adapts himself, and the one who falls short desires to reach them. When a man grows up and is capped, he reaches adulthood. The sages, fearing it might look hasty and ill-prepared, have made the rite of divining the date and the names of the guests, the rite of adding the three things,[4] and the rite of the libation; hereby they cultivated the proper rites. The wedding is the great desire of men; it is the match by which two surnames are joined. Fearing that it might look intimate and be lacking the proper separation of the sexes, the sages have made the rites of betrothal (*napch'ae*), of asking the name of the bride's mother (*munmyŏng*), of divining the bride's qualities (*napkil*), and of sending the wedding gifts (*napp'ye*); hereby they cultivated the proper rites. The funeral is the final act by which a man is sent off, and a son devotes all his mind to it. Fearing that he might be negligent and incomplete, the sages have made for the son the rites of drinking water and eating gruel, of weeping and mourning; hereby they cultivated the proper rites. Ancestor worship is the communication with the spirit of the deceased. It is the means by which the son pays his gratitude to his parents. Fearing that there might be distance and forgetfulness, the sages have made the rites of presenting offerings and libations to the soul of the deceased; hereby they cultivated the proper rites. People communicate with each other, and visitors come. Therefore the sages have made the rites of entertaining the guests and presenting gifts; hereby they cultivated the proper rites. People get together and feast. Therefore the sages have made the rites of bowing and yielding and exchanging the wine cups. . . .

Rulers and subjects cultivate loyalty and righteousness. Fathers and sons cultivate filial piety and love. Brothers cultivate friendship and brotherliness. Senior and junior cultivate guidance and respectfulness. Teacher and friend cultivate sincerity and faithfulness. In all these cases cultivation of the rites has its proper methods, and people rely upon them to live. If cultivation loses the right methods, profit and desire are able to upset the rites; depravity and excesses are able to destroy the rites; violence and rudeness are able to ruin the rites; coercion and force are able to impair the rites so that the people of this world all wear angry looks like tigers and leopards caught in a cage. Such harm cannot be described!

Liu Hsiang [77–6 B.C.] of Han wrote: The main task of rites is nourishing the people. If there is an excess, it should be in nourishing the people. An excess of punishments may lead to death or injury. Yet the officials ask that laws and orders be established. They are determined to kill rather than to nourish people. Rites are the mainstay of good rule, and punishment is an instrument for supplementing good rule. To rule a country with rites is like bringing up people with food and drinking. To keep people in check with punishments is like driving out sickness with poisonous medicine. MD

Funerary and Ancestral Rites

Buddhist and shamanist beliefs and ceremonies that had prevailed in Koryŏ continued to dominate the cult of the dead at the beginning of the Chosŏn dynasty. The Confucians tried to counteract these overwhelming traditions by demanding that the focus of ancestral rituals be shifted away from the Buddhist temple and shaman altar to the *kamyo* or *sadang* (domestic shrine). This necessitated an architectural addition to the Korean house, an innovation not easily accomplished. More important, the institution of domestic shrines introduced an entirely new rhythm into the daily life of Koreans because the continued presence of the ancestors required regular offerings and frequent communication. These ritual tasks were entrusted to the eldest male member of the household. He became the chief officiant for the ancestors who were his direct lineal forbears. The ancestral shrine in the Confucian model, then, concentrated exclusively on the male descent line, and the participants at the seasonal offerings were all patrilineally related. Women, the ritual practitioners of the past, were excluded from this male domain. The establishment of domestic shrines and the institutionalization of Confucian-style ancestor worship were instrumental in introducing the patrilineal concept into Korean society. MD

Yi Chi: On the Establishment of Domestic Shrines
[From *T'aejong sillok* 2:21b–22a]

Inspector-General Yi Chi [d. 1414] and others memorialize [in 1401]:

The law concerning domestic shrines must be strict. Those in antiquity who served their parents well extended their filiality to them while the parents were alive, and after they died, they looked after them even better than during their lifetime and served them as if they were still alive. As long as they lived they never became negligent. This is the meaning of not regarding the parents as dead.[5] Buddhist theories about quick transformation of the dead circulate, and thus sons are misled by such false theories. When their parents die, they entrust them to Buddha in the hope they will live on in heaven. After taking off mourning garb, they regard their parents as vanished and do not serve them in the domestic shrine. In recent years, therefore, the state has been concerned about the daily deterioration of customs, and every time Your Majesty issued an edict, you gave priority to the order to establish domestic shrines, wishing the people's virtue to return to wholesomeness. That nobody has yet willingly complied is due to the strength and persistence of the Buddhists' false theories, and there may also be some who do not yet know how to establish domestic shrines.

In our opinion the royal capital is the source of the civilizing influence and the mainstay of good government. If the scholar-officials are ordered to establish shrines first, and the order reaches the rest of society later, would there be noncompliance? Moreover, quarters are cramped within the city walls, and thus it may be difficult to establish shrines. Instead, for convenience, a wooden box may be used to store the spirit tablets in a clean room. Outside the capital, a domestic shrine should provisionally be built at the east side of the government office in each prefecture and district. If those appointed magistrates are eldest sons, they should take the spirit tablets to the place of their appointment; if they are not eldest sons, they should use paper tablets in the district shrines and perform the rites. Whether inside or outside the capital, those in charge of the rites in the domestic shrine should rise at dawn daily, burn incense, and bow twice, and when they go in or out of the house, they should announce this in the domestic shrine. If the ancestral rites follow the *Family Rites* completely in order to give an example to those below, this influence will naturally reach the people without special encouragement. Even those who have not yet established shrines will from then on become active. In the capital this building of shrines should start from the first month of next year [1402], in the provinces from the second month. Those who do not comply will be investigated by the censorial offices, dismissed from office, and later reported to the king. MD

Reform of Funerary Practices
[From *Sejong sillok* 76:15b–16a]

The royal edict to the Department of Punishments [in 1437] reads as follows:

The people of our country follow in their mortuary and ancestral rites the bad customs of Koryŏ. Although prohibitions were put into the *Six Codes of Governance,* the authorities are unable to investigate the violations, and the old practices are thus still observed. We are a long way from correcting them. Nowadays people of high and low social status commonly compete with each other in upholding wanton ceremonies; they respect and trust shamans and dissipate fortunes. Some mourners visit shaman houses where music is played and the spirit of the dead is feasted. Others go to Buddhist temples and have a service held for the repose of the soul. Still others serve wine and food on the burial day, and host and guests console each other. All strive to outdo one another in lavishness and extravagance. The rich are boastful; the poor make strenuous efforts. They call in guests and friends, and men and women mix freely. Only when the costs of entertainment are excessive do they rejoice in their hearts and get praise from their neighbors. Because this has become a custom, they do not restrain themselves. Once they have a bad harvest, they come close to starvation. This is indeed something to worry about because the people's livelihood consequently deteriorates, and the quality of the customs is bound up with this.

From now on the playing of music, the gathering of guests, and the performance of wanton ceremonies for the spirits as well as visits of mourners to shaman houses to feast the spirit of the dead, or the invitation of guests to pray for the soul's repose, and the serving of wine on funeral days must be clearly and sternly prohibited by the censorial offices in the capital and by the local authorities in the province. If there are offenders, host and guests will be held equally responsible. MD

The Position of Women

The Confucians' emphasis on the patrilineal descent line had serious consequences for the women's relationship to men and their position in society. In Koryŏ, it had not been uncommon for an upper-class man to have several wives who were not subject to any social ranking order. In the patrilineal society the Confucians envisioned, however, only one woman, the primary wife, could qualify to become the mother of her husband's lineal heir. Any other women the husband might have were therefore of lesser importance, and the differentiation between main wives and concubines (*ch'ŏch'ŏp*) became one of the sharpest as well as most tragic social dividing lines in Korean society.

The union between husband and wife was regarded as the foundation of human morality and the mainspring of the socialization process that extended from the relationship between father and son to that between ruler and subject. The main wife was in charge of the domestic sphere (*nae*), while the husband's domain was the public sphere (*oe*). Peace and stability of the family were a precondition for peace and prosperity of the state. Women, although inferior members of society, nevertheless carried the responsibility of providing the government with loyal and capable men. MD

On Differentiating Between Main Wife and Concubine
[From *T'aejong sillok* 25:13a–b]

The Office of the Inspector-General memorializes [in 1413] as follows:

Husband and wife are the mainstay of human morality, and the differentiation between main wife and concubine may not be blurred. For this reason the sage Confucius compiled the *Spring and Autumn Annals:* "Duke Hui of Lu made Chung Tzu his wife, and the king by heaven's grace sent presents for the funerals of Duke Hui and Chung Tzu. Duke Hsi made Ch'en Feng his wife, and the king sent presents for her funeral."[6] Hereby Confucius clarified the differentiation between main wife and concubine as the constant rule for all generations, one that should not be destroyed by the selfish desires of one period. Embodying the great principles of the one hundred kings of the Spring and Autumn period, King T'aejo accentuated the boundary between main wife and concubine of the scholar-officials and instituted the law of conferring ranks and land on main wives. The distinction between main wife and concubine has thus become clear and the root of human morality straight.

At the end of the former dynasty, the influence of propriety and morality was not pervasive and the relationship between husband and wife deteriorated. The members of the officialdom followed their own desires and inclinations: some who had a wife married a second wife; others made their concubine their main wife. This has consequently become the source of today's disputes between main wives and concubines. . . .

We have carefully examined the Ming code, which reads: The one who makes a concubine his main wife while the latter is alive is to be punished with ninety strokes of the heavy bamboo, and the situation must be rectified. Someone who already has a main wife and still gets another one is also to be punished with ninety strokes, and they must separate. We have already tried to differentiate between main wife and concubine by means of the marriage arrangements. Those alive who have made a concubine their main wife, or have taken another wife while they already have a main wife, should be punished according to the law. Those who have died so that neither rectification nor separation is possible, we wish to treat according to the foregoing example in the *Spring and Autumn Annals*. If the first wife is made the main wife upon whom a rank and land are conferred, the influence of the sage emerges, and the differentiation between main wife and concubine will indeed become clear. This was granted by the king. MD

On Treating the Main Wife
[From *Sejong sillok* 30:20a–b]

[In 1425] the Office of the Inspector-General demands the punishment of Yi Chungwi who maltreated his wife.

The king says: Of old, Confucius and Tzu-ssu both expelled their wives without mentioning any reason. The early Confucians regarded them nevertheless as loyal and honest. Now an ordinary man maltreats his wife because of temporary anger or a trivial matter, and all the authorities accuse him of disrupting the relationship between husband and wife. What does such a small and trivial matter amount to in the entirety of government?

The Second Inspector Chŏng Yŏn answers: The maltreatment of a main wife and the discord between brothers must be investigated and punished. There have been clear orders. Now Yi Chungwi does not look after his wife and always lives in the house of his concubine. It is clear that the sequence of primary and secondary wife has been lost. It is not possible to consider this a trivial matter and leave it untreated.

We ask that the prohibitions be made clear in order to rectify human relationships.

The king says: If we leave such a case untreated, there will be no warning for the future, and this will certainly lead people to throw off all restraint. Nevertheless, this trivial case cannot be investigated. But prohibitions must be firm. Each of you should state how he would settle such a matter.

Inspector-General Ko Yakhae [1377–1443] says: If there is a ranking order of main wife and concubine, the domestic way is straight. If it gets lost, the domestic way is in disorder. If somebody treats his concubine preferentially and does not look after his main wife, he should be punished according to the law.

Minister of Personnel Hŏ Cho [1369–1439] says: The woman manages the interior of the house; the man manages the exterior. If someone allows his concubine to become the mistress of his household and to dominate his house, not only does the social ranking break down but this also leads to discord among the brothers and estrangement among the slaves. How is it possible to manage a house under such circumstances? It is absolutely necessary to punish the crime of such fellows.

Royal Secretary Kwak Chonjung says: If someone loves his concubine and estranges his main wife, his property is generally transferred entirely to the concubine's house, leaving the main wife poor and destitute and causing mutual resentment. It is proper to punish such a man severely.

The king agrees and orders to proceed according to the law so that it is made known. MD

Ch'oe Hang: On Remedying the Wedding Rite
[From *T'aehŏjŏng munjip,* "Kiyŏng hoegi," 2.1:30a–37b]

During Koryŏ, the customary form of marital residence was uxorilocal —that is, the husband moved into his wife's house. In the eyes of the Confucians this was an objectionable living arrangement because it upset the natural order of male preceding female. The early legislators therefore demanded the reform of the wedding ceremony, which, according to the *Family Rites,* came to a climax when the bridegroom personally inducted the bride into his own house (*ch'inyŏng*). Tradition proved especially persistent, however, in the native wedding customs, and no Confucian-style wedding ceremony was performed in an upper-

class house during the fifteenth century. In this document Ch'oe Hang
(1409–1474) encourages a reluctant King Sejong to initiate corrective
measures as part of his overall reform policies.

Your servant has respectfully read your policy plan that states
that the wedding rite is not easy to change all of a sudden. From this
your servant recognizes Your Majesty's sincerity to reform this custom and to restore the old ways.

Your servant says: That heaven precedes earth is the principle of
hard and soft. That the wife obeys her husband is the principle of yin
and yang. Therefore the man makes taking the reins his talent and
leads, and the woman makes obedience her task and follows behind.
This is the constant principle of heaven and earth and the universal
rule of former and present times. If, then, the wedding rite is not
correct and the meaning of leading and following not clear, how will
the three relationships be correct and the five social constants be in
order? . . .

Our Great Korea was in ancient times praised for holding up the
rites, and sages and spiritual men succeeded each other. . . . Even
with the wedding rite there was nothing wrong, and the families
observed the rite of the bridegroom meeting his bride. The wedding
customs had the air of "the peach tree is young and elegant; this young
lady is going to her future home."[7] How come the abuses of the
former dynasty have not been checked and Koryŏ customs continue
unchanged? . . . The man enters the woman's house and thereby
confuses the meaning of husband and wife. Yang obeys yin and
thereby opposes the principle of heaven and earth. Is there not a
deficiency in the codes of this well-ruled time? . . .

Your servant wishes that Your Majesty would not say that old local
customs cannot be changed all of sudden and that what makes human
feelings at ease cannot be restored to the state of antiquity. The rites
are the means by which the unregulated of the people is regulated; the
government is the means by which the unordered of the people is
ordered. If you enforce over a long period of time strict measures
against the wrongs in the decadent women's quarters, people will
themselves recognize the quality of the rite and will no longer dare
conduct weddings in violation of the proper rites. Should we then be
concerned that the error of the bridegroom proceeding to the bride's
house and living there as son-in-law cannot be reformed? MD

Prohibition Against Remarriage of Women
[From *Sŏngjong sillok* 82:9b–20a]

Marriage was largely an affair between "two surnames," and, as far as the wife was concerned, it lasted beyond her husband's death. Confucian ideology stressed the woman's devotion to one husband, and this emphasis on the exclusive nature of the marital relationship provided Confucian legislators with the arguments they needed to prohibit the remarriage of women, a custom prevalent during Koryŏ. The lost version of the *National Code* of 1469 apparently barred the sons and grandsons of thrice-married women from advancing into the higher officialdom. The debate of 1477 makes clear that the majority of the discussants, here represented by Chŏng Ch'angson (1402–1487) and Kim Yŏngyu (1418–1494), was in favor of keeping the restriction to third and not extending it to second marriages. King Sŏngjong (1469–1494), who was especially concerned with improving upper-class mores, sided with the minority opinion, here represented by Im Wŏnjun (1423–1500). How sensitive the issue was is documented by the fact that the *National Code* of 1485 did not directly outlaw remarriage but provided that the sons and grandsons of remarried women would not be eligible for civil or military office and would be barred from taking the lower and higher civil service examinations. The ideological and legal implications thus, in fact, made remarriage for a woman impossible. MD

[In 1477] the king orders the members of the highest officialdom to discuss the prohibition against the remarriage of women.

Chief State Councillor Chŏng Ch'angson and others say: If a woman of an honorable house loses her husband at a young age and swears to preserve her chastity until her death, this is very good indeed. If this cannot be done, a woman, driven by hunger and cold, may easily give up her intention to remain unmarried. In case we completely prohibit remarriage by law, punish the offender, and even implicate her sons and grandsons, we will, on the contrary, harm the customs. This would not be a small mistake. Except that we record, as before, women who marry three times, could we not leave this matter alone?
. . .

Inspector-General Kim Yŏngyu and others say: In our country, the houses of the scholar-officials have been upholding propriety and morality for generations, and their loyalty and faithfulness have never been impaired. This is attested in historical works. Recently, however, the great social safeguards have become somewhat lax, and there are cases like the one of Yi Sim's wife, born Cho, who married Yi on her own initiative. Her bad reputation has been spreading, and if such behavior is not strictly checked, women of lower status may take Sim's wife's example as a pretext not to maintain faithfulness any longer. Could we then overcome our distress about the destruction of propriety and mores?

But now, according to the *National Code* [1469], thrice-married women are listed together with licentious women, and their sons and grandsons are barred from the examinations and cannot receive posts in the censorial and administrative offices. Twice-married women are not mentioned. Generally, statutes are based on fundamental law, and propriety is connected with human feelings. For a woman of a poor and lowly house who on neither side has supportive relatives, it is difficult to keep her chastity when she becomes widowed in early years. If her parents or relatives decide that she should marry for a second time, this does not harm propriety. . . . We think that the law of the *National Code* according to which the sons and grandsons of thrice-married women do not receive high office should be strictly enforced and that Yi Sim's wife, born Cho, should be severely punished. If we clearly point out what is good and what is bad, morality and mores will naturally become correct even if we do not make a new law concerning remarriage, and widows will understand this as a warning. . . .

Sixth State Councillor Im Wŏnjun and others argue: In the past Master Ch'eng I said: "Women remarry only because people of later generations are afraid of freezing and starving to death. But to lose one's integrity is a very serious matter. To starve to death, however, is a very small matter." Chang Heng-ch'ü said: "If a man takes someone who has lost her integrity to be his own match, it means he himself has lost his integrity."[8]

Thus, a marriage once concluded cannot be changed within a lifetime: this is a woman's principle. If she marries a second husband, how is this different from birds and beasts? In case the customs disregard integrity and morality, even those whose property is abundant and who do not have to be concerned about freezing and starving will all marry again. Moreover, a state without strict prohibitions will cause the sons and grandsons of those who lost their integrity to hold important office. Such a practice will then turn into a custom that nobody will consider strange. Under such circumstances there will be women who, even without a master of ceremonies, will obtain a husband on their own initiative. If this is not prohibited, where will it lead? From now on remarriage must be strictly prohibited. A woman who in disregard of the law remarries should be punished for having lost her manners, and her sons and grandsons should also be barred from office in order to encourage integrity and morality. . . .

Royal edict to the Ministry of Rites: The *Book of Rites* says: "Faithfulness is the virtue of a wife. Once married to her husband, she does not change it during her lifetime."[9] Therefore there is the morality of the "three obediences" (*samjong*),[10] and no rite would ever violate one of these. Because the ways of this world are daily deteriorating, womanly virtue is no longer upright, and upper-class women no longer care for propriety and morality. Some violate their feelings because of their parents; some follow a husband on their own initiative. They thus destroy not only their own family traditions, but in fact also defile the Confucian teachings. If we do not take stern countermeasures, it will be difficult to stop such licentious behavior.

From now on, in order to correct the customs, the sons and grandsons of twice-married women will no longer be listed as members of the upper class. MD

Ŏ Sukkwŏn: Critique of Discrimination Against Secondary Sons
[From *P'aegwan chapki* 2:88]

The distinction between main wife and concubine (*ch'ŏch'ŏp*), instituted at the beginning of the dynasty, had grave consequences for the social status of the concubine's sons (*sŏŏl*). As far as the main descent line was concerned, they were superfluous members, and, because their mothers usually belonged to the lower strata of society, they were socially despised as well. Historically, the origin of barring them from the examinations and the higher officialdom had been attributed to Sŏ Sŏn's (1367–1433) personal initiative, but it is clear that the structural constraints of strictly lineal considerations caused this social imbalance. Ŏ Sukkwŏn, himself a secondary son, lived under these restrictions in the first half of the sixteenth century. MD

It is not an old law of our country that the descendants of secondary sons are not allowed to take the civil service examinations and enter the bureaucracy. According to the *Six Codes of Governance,* in the thirteenth year of Yung-lo [1415] Royal Secretary Sŏ Sŏn and others urged the king not to admit the sons and grandsons of secondary sons to high office in order to differentiate between primary and secondary sons (*chŏksŏ*). Thus, while before 1415 secondary sons had been admitted to high office, after 1415 they were only allowed to take the examinations but not to enter the ranks of the regular elite. Since the compilation of the *National Code,* when the barring of secondary sons from office was added for the first time, one hundred years have not yet passed. Between heaven and earth and outside the nine divisions of China there are far more than a hundred territorially based countries, yet such a law has never been heard of. Besides, even local clerks and sailors, the basest of occupations, are admitted to the civil examinations. Speaking of their paternal and maternal lines, local clerks and sailors do first of all not even have a verifiable place of origin, and they may have intermarried with nomads and fugitives. Who can thus make out whether they are good or base? For the sole reason that secondary sons—even when they are the sons of high officials—do not have a proper maternal line, they are barred from office for generations. Even if they have outstanding talents and usable skills, in the end they bow their heads in frustration and die in the countryside. Is it not regrettable that they are valued less than local clerks and sailors? MD

Propagation of Confucian Values

The conduct of a ritually pure life was the privilege of the upper class whose members possessed the necessary learning as well as the economic means to enact the intricate prescriptions of the ritual manuals. They were frequently admonished to set an example with their proper behavior that could be emulated by the lower social classes. In addition, books like the *Samgang haengsil to* (Illustrated Conduct of the Three Bonds) were distributed to inculcate in the minds of the uneducated the fundamental Confucian virtues of loyalty, filial piety, and chastity. For easy comprehension the Chinese text was augmented with a Korean rendering, enriched with pictures for each story. Because of its didactic value this book was printed in many versions throughout the dynasty and was undoubtedly instrumental in propagating basic Confucian values among the common people. MD

Kwŏn Ch'ae: Preface to *Illustrated Conduct of the Three Bonds*

[From *Tong munsŏn* 93:19–21]

Among the five great principles of this world the Three Bonds stand at the very head; in fact the great law of arranging the moral imperatives is the principal source of all human transformation. If one searches for it in antiquity, one finds that it was the foremost task of emperors and kings: Emperor Shun carefully elaborated upon the five human relationships; Prince T'ang first polished the social principles; and the house of Chou regarded the five teachings as important for the people and recommended those who mastered the three standards.

In the summer of the year *sinhae* of Hsüan-te [1431], our King Sejong said to his closest ministers: "The Three Dynasties all ruled by illuminating human relationships. In later generations their teachings deteriorated, and the people were no longer friendly to each other. The great social relationships between ruler and subject, father and son, and husband and wife were no longer considered as innate qualities, and they became steadily more tenuous. There were many, however, with outstanding behavior and great integrity who were not misled by customary practices, but caught the people's attention with their exemplary behavior. I wish to have the most prominent ones selected, their pictures drawn, and their stories compiled and distributed inside and outside the capital so that all the ignorant husbands and wives, by looking at them with sympathy, may be easily stimulated to proper behavior. This, then, will also be a method to transform the people and improve the customs." Thereupon he charged the first counselor of the Hall of Worthies, Sŏl Sun [d. 1435], with the compilation.

Sŏl Sun surveyed all such stories recorded in old and new books in China as well as in Korea and selected the most noteworthy ten from among one hundred for each category of filial sons, loyal subjects, and chaste women. He first put in their pictures and then recorded their stories and even added some poems. As to filial sons, he respectfully copied the poem about filial sons and obedient grandsons that Emperor T'ai-tsung had personally written and also perused the eulogies of the famous Confucian, Yi Chehyŏn [1287–1367], from the *Hyohaeng nok* (Record of Filial Behavior), which my great-great-grandfather, Kwŏn Pu [1262–1346], had compiled. The remaining eulogies he assigned to current high officials. He also made current civil offi-

cials write poems on loyal subjects and chaste women. As soon as the
work was finished, the king gave it the title *Illustrated Conduct of the
Three Bonds* and ordered the Printing Office to prepare the blocks for
its continuous transmission. Then he ordered me to write a preface.

I think that the moral imperatives concerning rulers, fathers, and
spouses as well as the way of loyalty, filial piety, and chastity are
properties bestowed by heaven upon all people alike. They have been
present from the beginning of heaven and earth and will not disappear
until the end of heaven and earth. It is thus not so that Yao and Shun
were men of humanity because they received more of these properties
than others or that Chieh and Chou were brutal because they received
less. But at the time of the early kings the five relationships were
observed, and the people were peaceful and friendly and lived well.
After the Three Dynasties the well-ordered days diminished steadily,
and unruly fellows succeeded each other in the world. This was entirely dependent on the leadership quality of the rulers.

Now with his divine faculties, His Majesty fulfills the way of ruler
and teacher. His achievements are complete and his rule secure, and
the ten thousand items of government are all well settled. Thus he
makes the fostering of the human imperatives and the maintenance of
the proper ruling of the world his principles. He leaves nothing connected with the teachings of the sages unstudied and unconsidered; he
makes them clearly his moral guidelines. His instructions to the people
come forth to the highest degree from his personal enacting and
internalization of these teachings. But out of his concern that this way
of motivating the people is still deficient, he has made this book and
distributed it widely among the people so that everyone—the wise
and the stupid, the noble and the base, small children and women—is
able to look at it with pleasure and listen to it studiously. By looking
at the pictures one can imagine the appearance; by reciting the poems
one can experience the emotions of the exemplary personalities described in the work. There will be none who does not desire and
admire them and receive admonition and encouragement so that he
will develop his innate goodness and fulfill his tasks in life. Although
comparable to the early emperors' and kings' esteem and propagation
of the cardinal virtues, His Majesty's method is even more thorough.
Hereby the people's customs will be transformed, and the way of
ruling will be enriched. The families will have filial and obedient sons
and the state loyal subjects. The songs of Nan-kai and Po-hua describing filial sons and those of Han-kuang and Ju-fen[11] will spread even to

the narrow alleys. The excellence of kingly influence will certainly not be inferior to what is described in Chou-nan and Shao-nan, and the evidence of kingly rule will be transmitted to ten thousand generations. The superior men of later times will emulate the royal example even more and never fail to preserve and respect it. Will this not be splendid? MD

Sŏ Kŏjŏng: Preface to the Genealogy of the Andong Kwŏn
[From *Andong Kwŏnssi sebo sŏ* 1a–2b]

With the emergence of the concept of patrilineal descent, it became important to be able to document the main as well as the collateral lines of kin that derived their origin from a common apical ancestor. Written genealogies (*chokpo*), while proliferating from the seventeenth century, began to be compiled as early as the fifteenth century. The genealogy of the Andong Kwŏn, dated 1476, is one of the first extant examples. Although often only putative, the origin of such prominent descent groups was frequently traced as far back as Silla times. Such written genealogies were, and still are, impressive evidence of lineage consciousness, and only someone with a certified lineage background could hope to maintain a position of prominence in the political, social, and economic life of the country. The preface to the Andong Kwŏn genealogy was written by Sŏ Kŏjŏng (1420–1488), a prominent official and literary figure.

The Kwŏn originally belonged to the Kim, a descent group of Silla. Toward the end of Silla, when a certain Kim Haeng was prefect of Koch'ang-gun, Kyŏnhwŏn [d. 936] invaded Silla, killed the king, and abused the queen. Koryŏ T'aejo [918–943] came to their rescue and was locked in battle with Kyŏnhwŏn. [In 930] Haeng persuaded the people and said: "Because propriety demands that we do not live under the same sky as Kyŏnhwŏn, let's rally around Wang and wipe out his grievance!" Thereupon they submitted themselves to him. Koryŏ T'aejo said: "Haeng has capably and brilliantly adapted himself to the circumstances (*kwŏn*)." And he bestowed the surname Kwŏn upon him, gave him the title of Great Teacher, and made Koch'ang-gun his estate and elevated it to Andong-bu. Haeng begot Inhaeng who advanced to the office of *nangjung* (Rank 5). Inhaeng begot Ch'aek who at his own request became local administrator of that place. . . . The Kwŏn thus became *hyangni* (local administrators) from Ch'aek on, but because they returned to obscurity they did not prosper for seven generations. With Sup'yŏng they again began to rise, and sons and grandsons proliferated. Munjŏng [Kwŏn Pu, 1262–1346] for the first time reached prominence and prosperity, and Suhong's descendant, Munt'an [Kwŏn Hangong, d. 1349], also regained high status and prestige. Thereafter, the Kwŏn split into two great descent lines, and the family members who today stand at court, clad in cap and gown and ceremonially adorned, number several thousands. They all derive from these two lines. My maternal grandfather, Kwŏn Kŭn [1352–1409] is also Munjŏng's great-grandson. My maternal uncle, Kwŏn Che [1387–1445] for the first time compiled a brief genealogy, and his son, Kwŏn Nam [1416–1465], continued his father's intention and, by widely collecting material and visiting far and wide, he greatly augmented it, but it was not yet complete. With my kinsmen, Pak Wŏnch'ang and Ch'oe Howŏn, I again intensified the search, filled up lacunae, corrected mistakes, and arranged everything in three volumes of genealogical tables.

This genealogy is detailed from Munjŏng and Munt'an on, but sketchy before them. This is because we have recorded what is known and omitted what is not known in an effort to transmit only reliable facts to future generations. When it was finished, it was printed in Andong by Yun Ho, the governor of Kyŏngsang province.

I think that in ancient times there was a "clan law" according to which the clan members were arranged in the chao-mu order[12] and differentiated on the basis of branch lines so that even one hundred generations of descendants could be identified. After the clan law deteriorated, the genealogical records came into use. To make a genealogy it is necessary to trace the clan back to its very origins and record in detail its developments, to differentiate clearly the various branches, and to specify close and remote relatives. This is also adequate to express mutual respect and harmonious feelings among the clan members and to regulate the human principles. . . .

In Korea, however, there was of old neither clan law nor genealogy; even big families and great descent groups did not have family records. Thus, after several generations the names of the ancestors in the four ascending generations were lost, and their descendants consequently became estranged from each other, looking at one another like strangers in the street. Do they wait until after the mourning obligations are over and kinship has ended to become distant and remote? Would it not be difficult then to wish to stimulate filial and brotherly behavior among them and to achieve mutual courteousness?

For this reason Kwŏn Che and Kwŏn Nam tirelessly compiled the genealogy, and I made an effort to bring their intention to completion.

Since Kwŏn Haeng first was enfeoffed, six hundred years have passed. His descendants are proliferating, and the tradition of reciting the *Book of Documents* and the *Book of Songs* had long been uninterrupted. Only if the roots are deep are the branches luxuriant in growth; only if the source is distant is the stream long: this is a compelling principle.

Alas! Since antiquity the famous clans and prominent descendants have been quite numerous. Who of those in high office and brilliant positions were not looked up to and respected? Why, then, have they, after only a few generations, declined and disappeared? It is because the foundation of the earlier generations was not firm, and the descendants lost it by sudden arrogance and extravagance.

The Kwŏn have maintained their house over generations with honesty and have made loyalty and filiality their central concern. Could it be that the descendants are not mindful of the efforts with which their ancestors have built up their house? Could it be that they do not think about the way to continue it? The *Book of Rites* says: "The human way consists of recognizing one's relatives. If the relatives are recognized, the ancestors are honored. If the ancestors are honored, the line of descent is respected. If the line of descent is respected, the kin is in harmony." [13] If it is possible to begin with "recognizing one's relatives" and to extend this to the nine generations of the family, would there be any deficiency in the way of nurturing the basis and consolidating the branches? Poem 235 in the *Book of Songs* says: "Ever think of your ancestor, cultivating your virtue." [14] With this I would like to admonish again the descendants of the Kwŏn. MD

Sin Sukchu: "House Rules"
[From *Pohanjae chip* 13:1a–4b]

Confucian society functioned through the proper observance of the rites (*ye*). Their practice started with the cultivation of the moral potential of the individual and extended to those with whom the individual interacted most closely: his family and relatives. House rules (*kahun*) were aimed at smoothing the relationships within a kin group and spreading a civilizing influence even into the domestic sphere of the house, the women's quarters. They constituted an idealized code of conduct based on the assumption that people have to be constantly encouraged to strive for moral perfection. If the principal members of the family were to observe the rules of proper conduct, it was reasoned, even the domestic slaves could be persuaded to lead moral lives. Prepared by Sin Sukchu (1417–1475) in 1468, "House Rules" preached moral integrity and economic austerity and linked the harmony in the domestic sphere directly to peace and stability in the public realm. These "House Rules," then, contained the essence of the moral capabilities of the Confucian society, which, if properly developed, were the mainstay of the Confucian state. MD

RULE ONE: MAKE THE MIND DISCERNING

Man's mind does not have constancy. If it is trained, it exists; if it is neglected, it vanishes. If the mind does not exist, one looks but does not see; one listens but does not hear. How much more is it like this in the discernment of right and wrong? . . . The mind is the prime minister of the body. In the eye's relationship to color, it is the mind that sees. In the ear's relationship to sound, it is the mind that hears. All the members of the body depend on the mind for functioning. This is why it is the prime minister of the whole body. Therefore, if one wishes to straighten out the members of the body, one should straighten out the mind first.

RULE TWO: BE CIRCUMSPECT IN BEHAVIOR

If the body is not trained, it is not possible to regulate the house. Why do I say this? If in serving my father I do not exert myself to be filial, my son will do to me as I have done to my father. If in serving my elder brother I am not respectful, my younger brother will do to me as I have done to my elder brother. Therefore, only if I make myself stand on faultless ground will everyone among father and son, elder brother and younger brother, husband and wife, be equally correct. This can be extended to the relationship between ruler and subject and between friends.

RULE THREE: BE STUDIOUS

One who has narrow ears and eyes can never have a wide mind. For widening eyes and ears nothing is better than reading books. The ways of the sages and worthies are laid out in books. If, once the determination is firm, one progresses step by step and with great care, in the course of time one naturally gets results. The essential of learning lies in gathering up the dissipated mind. If the mind is concentrated, it is naturally brilliant and circumspect, and its understanding is more than sufficient. It is not possible to advance in scholarship without a settled mind. The essence of gathering up one's mind lies solely in seriousness.

For a human being, not to study is exactly like facing a wall. If what has been studied is not vigorously practiced, it is of no use to read even ten thousand volumes. Therefore, when reading the books of sages and worthies, one should search for their minds and incorporate them one by one in oneself.

RULE FOUR: ON MANAGING A HOUSEHOLD

Under present customs father and son and brothers rarely live under one roof. As they establish their own households, each keeps his own slaves, and gradually they become estranged from each other and are no longer on friendly terms. As father and elder brother, one should be patient and forbearing, generous and humane, and not petty and small. As son and younger brother, one should leave the unimportant and think of the important, advance sincerity and be mutually sympathetic, filial, and friendly.

The harm of extravagance is greater than a natural disaster. If a house declines, it is usually because of overspending. Therefore frugality is the first principle in managing a household. This does not mean one should be stingy and avaricious. If the needs of the house are met—the living fed and the dead sent off properly, the needy supported, and emergencies relieved—is this not enough of prosperity?

We and our relatives derive from the same source and split up into branches. Seen from our ancestors, we are all alike. If we are able to establish households thanks to the accumulated good and the extra blessings of our ancestors, we have to be mindful of aiding the poor and sympathizing with the orphans in order to counterbalance the blessings of our ancestors. . . .

RULE FIVE: ON HOLDING OFFICE

As a high official, one cannot rule independently; one must rely on one's subordinates. The way to treat a subordinate is to extend sincerity in order to employ him. In case of doubt, don't employ him.

If employed, don't doubt him. If a man knows that he is doubted, he certainly does not dare to do his best. . . . A high official thus should not have doubts about his subordinates. Once he has a doubtful mind, he cannot but be a bad administrator.

RULE SIX: ON INSTRUCTING WOMEN

The wife is the mate of the master of the house and has the domestic management in her hands. The rise and fall of a house depends on her. Usually people know how to instruct their sons, but do not know how to instruct their daughters. This is misguided.

A wife is loyal and pure, self-controlled, flexible and obedient, and serving others. She minds exclusively the domestic realm and does not concern herself with public affairs.

Above, she serves her parents-in-law; if she is not sincere and respectful, she cannot fulfill her filial loyalty. Below, she treats the slave servants well; if she is not kind and benevolent, she is not able to win their hearts. Only if she is sincere and respectful in serving her superiors and kind and benevolent in treating her subordinates is there complete affection between husband and wife.

Generally, she should also be accomplished in female tasks. If she herself is not diligent, she lacks the capacity to lead her subordinates. MD

CHAPTER SEVENTEEN

Economy

Like most preindustrial societies, the Chosŏn dynasty was predominantly an agrarian state, and land was its main source of wealth and revenue. Thus, the primary emphasis of the state economy was on agriculture. After the drastic land reform of 1390 based on the principle of an equitable redistribution, a great deal of effort was put into increasing the land's productivity. Advanced agrarian methods were introduced from China, and various experiments were conducted, leading to the publication of several manuals of farming. With the use of improved seeds, fertilizer, and irrigation, there was a significant increase in food production in early Chosŏn.

While the Neo-Confucian state of Chosŏn regarded agriculture as the root of all wealth, it treated commerce as an unproductive branch that existed at the expense of farming. Initially, commerce was limited strictly to licensed merchants; but the need to exchange goods for daily life gave rise to periodic markets in rural areas. The government's attempts to circulate paper currency early in the Chosŏn period were not successful, as people continued to use cloth as a medium of exchange. (The use of coins was not accepted widely until after the seventeenth century.) Believing the resources of wealth to be limited, Chosŏn society placed a great deal of emphasis on frugality in expenditure by both the state and individuals.

The Land System

An equitable distribution of land to all tillers was the ideal of good government in traditional Korea. The disintegration of the land system in the latter period of the Koryŏ dynasty (918–1392) was a main contributing factor to its demise. As the state control over land weakened, the land system in late Koryŏ became chaotic. Ownership of land became concentrated in the hands of powerful families and Buddhist temples and monasteries, forcing more and more people to leave the land, exposing them to desperate straits. It was under this situation in 1390 that General Yi Sŏnggye, after dramatically burning all the existing land registration records, carried out a drastic land reform. A member of Yi Sŏnggye's brain trust in founding the new Chosŏn dynasty, Chŏng Tojŏn was one of the masterminds of the 1390 land reform. In the essay translated here, Chŏng Tojŏn depicts the chaotic land system of late Koryŏ (at least partly to justify the reform he helped institute) and offers some basic ideas shaping the new land system, which the Chosŏn dynasty continued to maintain. YC

Chŏng Tojŏn: On Land
[From *Sambong chip* 13:14b–16a]

In ancient times, all the land belonged to the state, and the state then granted land to the people; thus, all the land that the people cultivated had been given them by the state. There was no one who did not receive land, and there was no one who did not cultivate land. Therefore, there was no excessive differentiation between the rich and the poor and between the strong and the weak. Because all the produce from the land went to the state, the state was prosperous. But as the land system began to disintegrate, powerful individuals acquired more and more land. While the land of the rich extended far and wide, the poor had no land even to stand on. The poor thus were forced to lease land from the rich to till. Even though they worked hard and diligently all year round, they still did not have enough to eat. The rich, however, did not cultivate their land and remained idle. Instead, they hired men to work their land and collected more than half of the yield. The government took no measures to alleviate the plight of the poor and did nothing to bring benefit to the state. Thus, both the people and the state became increasingly poor. It was this situation that gave rise to the theories of limited land and equal land. These theories are, however, no more than makeshift measures. The best land policy is for the state to grant land to the people to cultivate. . . .

According to the land system of the Koryŏ dynasty, there were lands for royal descendants, government officials in active service, merit subjects, graduates of the civil service examinations, soldiers, and nonactive officials. They maintained their living by collecting rent from these lands. The people who worked the land were allowed to reclaim new land for their ownership, and the government did not intervene. Those who commanded considerable manpower extensively reclaimed new land; those who were weak and lacked manpower were obliged to submit to the powerful in order to lease land from them. After cultivation, the harvest was divided, half going to the landowner and half to the tillers. This was how there came to be two consumers for every tiller. The rich thus became richer and the poor poorer until the poor became unable to support themselves and were eventually forced to abandon their land and become vagabonds. It was these people who turned to petty occupations and, in extreme cases, even became thieves and bandits. Alas, how can one describe the evil effects of all this? . . .

His Majesty King T'aejo had personally witnessed the evil effects of this chaotic land situation while he was still a private person and was determined to abolish the private land system as one of his future missions. He believed that all the land in the country should revert to the state and should then be given to the people based on careful account, in order to revive the rectified land system of ancient times. But the old families and the powerful lineage groups, realizing that His Majesty's plan would work against their interests, slandered and obstructed the plan with all the power at their command. Because of their obstructions, the people were unable to gain the benefits of this reform. It was indeed lamentable! His Majesty, however, together with two or three like-minded ministers, investigated the laws of the former dynasties, deliberated about what would be good for the present situation, and surveyed and measured all the land in the country in terms of *kyŏl*.[1] [His Majesty then instituted the land reform in the year 1390.] He established court land, military provision land for state use, and office land for civil and military officials. Also, off-duty military men residing in the capital as guards for the royal court, widows remaining faithful to their deceased husbands, government

workers in the local magistracies, postal station workers, and river
ferry workers, as well as commoners and artisans performing public
duties, have all been granted land. Although the distribution of land
to the people may not have reached the standard set by the ancient
sages, the new land law has restored equity and balance. Compared to
the evil system of the former dynasty, the new land reform has
brought infinite improvement. YC

Promotion of Agriculture

Fifteenth-century Korea witnessed a dramatic increase in food
production as a result of technological advances in agriculture. First,
the fallow system whereby certain portions of land are periodically
kept uncultivated was gradually replaced by a new system of continuous cultivation. This more intensive use of land was made possible
largely by the introduction of improved organic fertilizers developed
in post-Sung southern China. The second change involved shifting
from dry farming to wet farming in rice cultivation. Wet farming at
this time involved direct seeding of rice in wet land. The transplantation system that is used presently in Korea was gradually adopted in
the three southern provinces during the fifteenth and sixteenth centuries. For this kind of wet farming, it is essential to secure sufficient
water. Largely to meet the demands of these changes, King Sejong
ordered the compilation of a farm manual, *Nongsa chiksŏl* (Straight
Talk on Farming), which was printed for wide distribution in 1429.
Designed to increase productivity, the manual emphasizes four points:
the appropriate timing of sowing, the effective use of fertilizers, the
need for weeding, and the autumn plowing. As stated in the preface
to the manual, the information contained in the book was obtained
from actual experimentation carried out by veteran farmers in various
regions as well as from various manuals published in Korea and China.
The manual provided the practical information and ideas that were
suitable to local climate and soil conditions. The preface, translated
here, describes the nature of the book and its objectives. YC

Chŏng Ch'o: Preface to *Straight Talk on Farming*
[From *Sejong sillok* 44:16b]

His Majesty ordered Commissioner Chŏng Ch'o [d. 1434] and other officials to compile *Straight Talk on Farming*. Its preface reads as follows:

Farmers are the roots of all the nations in the world. Since ancient times, all sage-kings have emphasized the importance of farming. When Emperor Shun organized nine officials and twelve magistrates, he placed the greatest importance on the appropriate timing essential for food production. Without farming, it is truly impossible to provide for sacrificial rites and the resources needed to nourish life. Our own King T'aejong at one time ordered the Confucian ministers to select the most useful parts of the old agrarian manuals and to add commentaries in the vernacular script. He then had these printed and distributed widely so that the people would work diligently for agriculture. Continuing the illustrious work of King T'aejong, His Majesty King Sejong has shown particular concern for the people's welfare.

Because climate and soil in different regions are not the same, each area should have its own way of sowing and cultivating, as is appropriate to the region, and they cannot all conform to the old manuals. His Majesty therefore ordered the governors of all the provinces to seek out and interview experienced farmers in various prefectures and counties and to collect information on farming that is based on experiments actually conducted in the region. His Majesty then ordered this subject, Chŏng Ch'o, to add detailed explanations. I and Pyŏn Hyomun [b. 1396], Assistant Director in the Office of Royal Genealogy, studied the information carefully to avoid duplication, selected what is important, and compiled it in one book. We then named it *Straight Talk on Farming*.

In compiling the book, we tried to make it as clear and brief as possible and did not include anything that is not related to farming, so that people even in the remote mountains and fields can easily understand it. The book is now in the hands of the Office of Printing and will soon be distributed everywhere. It is hoped that this book will guide the people to an enriched life so that every household will be well provided for and every individual well supplied. YC

King Sejong: Edict for the Promotion of Agriculture
[From *Sejong sillok* 105:25a–26b]

If Korea has ever produced a sage-king, Sejong certainly came closest to that ideal. In addition to his brilliant achievements in language, literature, science, and technology, the king vigorously promoted agriculture throughout his thirty-two-year reign. Subscribing to the idea that people had to be well fed and clothed before they could be taught to follow the sage's way, the king persistently pursued the goal of abundant food production. In 1429, as we have seen, he published a farm manual. A few years later, in 1437, the king personally conducted an experiment in which he planted two *hop* of millet (a *hop* is one-tenth of a pint) to produce one picul (*sŏk*), leading him to conclude that human effort could overcome adversity in nature.[2] He also set up an astronomical observatory to observe celestial phenomena. He then had his officials devise highly refined rain gauges, which he distributed throughout the country, to ensure accurate reporting of the amount of rainfall. Then in 1444, the king issued the Edict for the Promotion of Agriculture. As the direct responsibility for overseeing the farmers was in the hand of magistrates, the edict was addressed largely to these officials, outlining what the king expected of them in their dealings with farmers. Noteworthy is King Sejong's strong belief that the effects of natural disaster, such as those caused by drought, could be averted by human effort. The edict reads as follows.

The people are the root of the state, and food is an indispensable necessity of the people. Because all food and clothing are produced by the farmers, our government must give them foremost priority. As the mandate for the people's livelihood depends on the farmers, we should spare no effort and do our utmost to serve them. If those in high positions do not lead them with sincere minds, how can we expect the people to work diligently to produce the basic necessities that will enable the continuation of life? In ancient times, Emperor Shen-nung introduced plow and plowshares for the benefit of all people, and Emperor Shao-hao instituted nine officers to take charge of agriculture; by doing so, these saintly rulers established the proper way to benefit myriad lives in accordance with heavenly will. . . . When King T'aejo, responding to the call of destiny, inaugurated our dynasty, he first rectified the land system to relieve the people of misery and allow them to enjoy the benefits of agriculture. The ways by which he tried to promote agriculture have been incorporated into laws. King T'aejong, continuing the task, redoubled the efforts to promote agriculture. Apprehensive that the people might not be well informed about the proper ways of sowing and reaping, King T'ae-jong ordered his officials to translate the books on farming into the vernacular script and to publish and transmit them widely.

I sincerely wish to continue the works of our forefathers. . . . I believe that agricultural matters should be entrusted to those officials who are in intimate contact with the people. I have therefore taken extra care in selecting these officials and have personally encouraged them to carry on their duties diligently. Moreover, based on experiments conducted at various localities, *Straight Talk on Farming* was compiled in such a way that every farmer could easily understand it. Everything useful to farmers is explained in the manual after careful research. It is my wish that everyone exert his utmost so that no land is left idle. When people fail to store grain, one crop failure will suddenly bring starvation. In such a situation, how can one blame officials for not having followed my instructions faithfully? This is what I fear most.

As I examined the sagacious magistrates of the past, I found they were able to achieve good works and bring benefit to the people only through diligence and hard work. . . . In general, men need to be aroused to work hard; when not aroused, they tend to be indolent. One former sage said: "Only if the lowest officials have their mind set on loving people will the people be saved." Indeed, how appropriate this statement is to the governors and magistrates of today, as the joys and sorrows of the people are wholly dependent upon them! If the magistrates truly possess a sense of commiseration for the people, how can they fail to attain the level of earlier men?

In general, farm families who start early also harvest early, and those who put in more effort reap more. Therefore, the key to agrarian administration lies in not missing the appropriate time and in not depriving the people of their energies. All grains have a proper time for sowing; if one misses the time, one can never recover for the whole year. As a man has only one body, his energy cannot be divided; if the government takes people's labor away, how can we exhort them to work hard on the land? If men do all they can, even when nature is unfortunate, we can still defend against a disaster. The fallow land method used by I Yin of Shang and the land rotation system used by Chao Kuo of Han are good examples. Our recent experiment in the year *chŏngsa* [1437], conducted on land behind the palace, has shown that we can avert disaster from drought by means of the maximum use of manpower, as the land produced an abundant crop in spite of bad weather. This experiment has proved clearly that natural misfortune can be overcome by human effort.

In an ancient record, it is said: "People's lives depend on diligence; where there is diligence, there is no poverty." In the *Book of Documents*, it is said: "You are like the husbandman who yields himself to ease, and is not strong to toil and to labor on his acres, who in such a case cannot have either rice or millet."[3] From these we learn that it is better to overwork than to be idle and lose the harvest. During the season of *mangjong*,[4] manpower is short; but as long as we do not miss the proper time to plant rice, even if it may not be early enough, we can still anticipate a harvest in the fall. The *mangjong* is an important signpost of the sowing season; the sowing must not be later than this or we will lose our crops. On the other hand, this does not necessarily mean that we must always wait for *mangjong* for sowing. The manual for agriculture suggests that in general it is desirable to plant early. The magistrates of today, however, mired in old customs, often do not act even when the proper time for sowing is with us, insisting on waiting until *mangjong*. Thus, they fail to take action on land litigations and delay in loaning seeds and grains, resulting in the loss of a season. In some cases a magistrate reports to a provincial governor and the governor merely transfers the report to the Ministry of Taxation, only to be forwarded to the State Council, which in turn follows a formal procedure to present it to the throne. While these exchanges are taking place, the *mangjong* season may have passed already. In some cases magistrates, ignorant of the appropriate time for plowing and sowing, are concerned only with the duties of exhorting and leading the farmers to plant seeds prematurely, which results in the death of the seeds, thus bringing the farmers to ruin. In other cases magistrates, truly not knowing the proper season, become careless in their calculations, thus losing the opportunity for sowing. How can these examples accord with the wishes of those who love and care for the people and share their woes?

All the officials in my government should embody my entrusted wishes in their duties. They should observe faithfully the ancestral laws for enriching the well-being of the people, should emulate the rules practiced by the former sage officials for promoting agriculture, should investigate widely what may be good for the climate and soil of the region, and should consult the agrarian manual to prepare in advance so as not to be either too early for sowing or too late. Moreover, no one should impose corvée duties upon the farmers that will deprive them of their time. Instead, everyone should devote his mind and effort to guide the people into attending to agriculture. If the people work diligently in agriculture and also serve their parents and support their wives and children, my people will enjoy long lives, and the foundation of our state will be further strengthened. If the needs of all the households and individuals are sufficiently met, the principle of propriety and modesty will prevail, and the people will all enjoy harmony, abundance, and happiness. YC

King Munjong: Edict on Irrigation Works
[From *Munjong sillok* 10:24b–26a]

As the eldest son of King Sejong, King Munjong had received a good education and training for Confucian rulership before he succeeded his father in 1450. He remained on the throne for only a little over two years, however, as he died in 1452 at the age of thirty-eight. As the fifth monarch of the Chosŏn dynasty, Munjong continued the brilliant achievements of his father. The progress in agriculture during the fifteenth century necessitated a greater and more efficient use of water. Since the ancient period, reservoirs had been constructed at higher elevations by damming water from mountains and hills, thus allowing a controlled flow of water to farmland below. These reservoirs alone, however, were not sufficient to meet the increasing demands of fifteenth-century agriculture. Thus, there were a number of attempts to devise new methods of irrigation. Both Kings T'aejong and Sejong attempted a wider use of water mills, for example, borrowing ideas from China and Japan, but water mills proved ill suited to Korea's terrain and soil conditions. A new method, however, was more successful and eventually became widely used throughout the country. This method involved drawing water from a river by constructing embankments. For land at higher elevations, the embankment was made at an upper river flow; for lower land, the embankment was constructed along the river to divert small channels of the flow. This irrigation method later came to be called *po*. Although the southern provinces had developed an efficient system of irrigation, the northwestern regions lagged behind. So when a drought struck the two northwestern provinces of Hwanghae and P'yŏngan in 1451, King Munjong issued the following edict emphasizing that human effort can avert natural disasters.

His Majesty personally composed the following edict for the governors of Hwanghae and P'yŏngan provinces. It reads:
I hear that various means of irrigation are used widely in China and that much of their success is due mainly to the use of water mills. I

also hear that the state of Japan takes advantage of irrigation to the extent that a small-scale flood or drought rarely causes farmers to lose their crops, and hence the people have a constant and sufficient supply of food. Our country too has constructed from ancient times river dikes to contain water, but still there are places where the advantages of water control are not available. Therefore, when there is a flood or drought, people lose their homes and are forced to flee. Troubled by this, the former kings have established ways to construct water mills. But as the soil of our country is arid, it cannot carry water, and hence the water mills have not produced the expected advantages. As I reflect, there are myriad lives flourishing in the universe, and rain moistens while the sun dries; all these phenomena are meticulous and orderly. And yet, as the universe is vast, there must be something that displeases heaven, causing flood and drought, which are beyond man's control. Heaven also lends assistance to men, but all things will succeed only after men do their best in planting, nourishing, and assisting. Only if we do our best, exhausting all the means available before awaiting heaven's response, can we then expect favors from heaven.

As I considered the intent of the former kings in the construction of water mills, and as I contemplated day and night the ways to save those people in the northern provinces who have been the victims of this year's misfortune, I came to the conclusion that nothing is more urgent than the work on river embankments and other irrigation. Some may say that because our country has a long history, the people in the past must have constructed irrigation systems in all the areas that could be irrigated, and therefore there must be no more room for new irrigation works. Based on recent experience, in which the river embankments constructed in Kyŏnggi province were all destroyed by water, wasting all the labor that was invested, some may insist that no advantages will come from the construction of new irrigation works.

I, however, disagree with this thinking. If we accept the notion that all that can be done has been done by men in the past and that hence there is no room for new considerations, how can there be cotton in our country, which was introduced not long ago, and how can we have the benefit of refined gun powder, which was not developed until the year *ŭlch'uk* [1445]? There have been many other similar developments in recent years. If we had followed these people, we would not be enjoying the benefit of these things. As for the experience in Kyŏnggi province, which brought no benefit, the blame lies in the failure of men not doing all that possibly could have been done.

How could it be a crime on the part of the river dikes? Controlling water has been difficult since ancient times. During the time of Emperor Yao, if Kun had been punished for his failure in spite of many achievements, and if Emperor Yü the Great,[5] had not been reappointed to office, it would not have been possible for people in the world to appreciate grain foods.

At present, we must discuss the amount of manpower needed and the feasibility of water that can be utilized and then determine the benefits and loss that may follow the construction of an irrigation system. The solidity of irrigation dikes will depend entirely upon the work of men. If we are talking about things that can be placed anywhere without causing great harm, we can simply follow the old practices, and there is no need to amend them. On matters dealing with farming, however, we cannot relax. In the case of the three southern provinces, there is abundant wet land and a tradition of hard working, so we can say that there is no need to make any changes. In P'yŏngan and Hwanghae provinces, however, there has been a series of disasters in recent years, forcing more than half of the region's population to abandon their homes. It is most urgent that we now find ways to save this situation. We must not delay. In farming in general, flood is harmful to dry land and dry weather is harmful to wet land. Although we can do little against the ravages of floods, we can prevent the damages of drought by collecting water in reservoirs, using river dikes. The reason for the extreme famines in P'yŏngan and Hwanghae provinces in the years *pyŏngin* [1446] and *chŏngmyo* [1447] was the dearth of wet land in the region. This year, again there was a loss of grain in the same two provinces, but the damage in the wet land area has not been too severe. This is why I am so eager to construct river embankments and to increase wet land.

I, therefore, wanted to select one or two officials, who are diligent, intelligent, and generous, and entrust them with the duties of the waterworks. They would go around the countryside in spring and autumn to encourage the people in their farming and sericulture, explain earnestly the advantages of wet-land cultivation, and, following the wishes of the people, construct river embankments and reservoirs and reclaim the land where water is available. Although these newly cultivated lands may not bear fruit abundantly in the first years, the harvest will double within several years. If people become encouraged by this and reclaim many new wet lands, they will receive a full exemption of land tax in the first two years. Furthermore, they will have to pay only half of the land tax in the third and fourth years, and only after the fifth year will they be required to bear the full land tax. This will also be an effective way of relieving the people's hunger.

This was my original idea. But when I consulted with the ministers, they all said there is no need to send such officials; instead, they counseled that I should issue a royal edict to the governors of these provinces urging them to promote the reclamation of wet land. As I reflected, the people are presently preoccupied with many things just as the ministers have argued. If I send out officials to start new projects, the short-sighted people, unable to foresee long-term bene-fits, may be stirred up and become resentful. I have therefore decided to withhold this matter.

But as I examined the situation carefully, I observed that there is a large amount of area with water, and yet the people are unwilling to reclaim it for wet land. You, governors, knowing this situation, should make the villagers understand my intention and guide them in realiz-ing the advantages of wet land. Then there will be some who recog-nize the advantages and will in turn lead other people so that they too may respond favorably. After meeting and discussing this with the people, you should reclaim as much wet land as possible, either by means of spring water or by constructing river embankments. If you carry out these works without harming or causing resentment among the people, you can build a firm and solid irrigation system. You should take advantage of the terrain by soaking the areas where pos-sible and by collecting water where possible. You must carry out this work without causing discord among the people. Some say that the rivers in P'yŏngan province are too rough and too large to dam. You should take notice of all such views and do your best to prepare for the irrigation works. After carefully investigating whether or not the works are feasible and whether or not the people favor them, you should submit a report to me. YC

Wealth and Commerce

Kim Sisŭp (1435–1493) was enshrined as one of "the six loyal subjects" for his refusal to serve under King Sejo (1455–1468), who usurped the throne of his fifteen-year-old nephew, King Tanjong (1453–1455), and for his support of the causes of the ousted Tanjong. Spending most of his life as a wandering monk, Kim Sisŭp wrote many works on a variety of subjects ranging from philosophy and political and social thought to fiction. Though a devoted Buddhist, he was also well versed in Confucianism, as his writings on government and society demonstrate. In the following passage, Kim Sisŭp emphasizes the Confucian concept of humanity, quoting passages from the *Great Learning*. YC

Kim Sisŭp: On Producing Wealth
[From *Maewŏltang chip* 20:15b–16b]

Since ancient times, people everywhere have striven to seek what they should not seek, namely, short-term profits. It is always easy to seek short-term profits, but doing so will surely lead to failure in the end. There is, however, one thing that everyone ought to seek—that is, to work for the righteousness of myriad generations. And yet we do not practice this because we are blinded by selfish profit. If we seek righteousness, it is certain that success will be attained. Although it is difficult to save those who seek profit from failure, it is also difficult to prevent the success of those who pursue righteousness. Following the way of failure may bring pleasure to one's mind at the beginning, but in the end it will never completely fulfill what one wishes. Following the way of success, on the other hand, may seem irrelevant and impractical at the beginning, but in the end it will achieve its desired goal. This is because wealth gained by harsh taxation is the same as wealth obtained by forcibly taking away goods belonging to others. People will resent this, and therefore its failure is inevitable. Wealth earned by humanitarian rule, on the other hand, comes from one's heart, and what comes from the heart expands and refills with greater substance. Therefore, humanity becomes more widely shared and its success cannot be prevented. Success or failure depends on whether one chooses righteousness or profit at the beginning when the difference between good and evil is minuscule. Even the minutest error in one's thinking will lead one astray for thousands of miles. One must indeed be extremely cautious. In order to be cautious, one must take this into consideration and scrutinize one's own mind.

How can there be anyone who does not wish to increase his wealth? If the ruler becomes mindful of this and extends this wish to the people, the people in turn will become mindful of his wishes and will serve him with respect. How can anyone not wish to seek his own profit? If the ruler becomes mindful of this and extends this wish to the people, the people in turn will become mindful of his wish and will work for his profit. If I treat him with virtue, he will treat me with sincerity. If I treat him with cruelty, he will treat me with malice. It is only natural that virtue is reciprocated with sincerity and cruelty with malice; this is only natural. If the ruler becomes truly capable of discerning this principle, he then can be said to be well prepared for the way of producing wealth.

To explain this further, it is said in the *Great Learning*: "There is a great course also for the production of wealth. Let the producers be many and the consumers be few. Let there be activity in the production, and economy in the expenditure. Then the wealth will always be sufficient."[6] These four ideas can be attained only by means of humanity. When the people are treated with humanity, they will dwell in contentment and security and will actively pursue their occupations; therefore, there will be few idle consumers and many producers. When the ministers are treated with humanity, they will willingly do their utmost while the wicked and the deceitful will retreat, being ashamed of themselves. Therefore, there will be few who steal in office and who eat the bread of idleness, and there will also be fewer consumers. When the people are ruled with humanity, there will be no unnecessary public works or forced mobilization of labor; therefore, people will not be deprived of their time, and they will be active in production. If all things are considered with humanity, all use of money, grain, and articles will be based on necessity, and consumption will be in accordance with revenue; therefore, there will be economy in expenditure. It is a truism that there is a limit to the wealth and goods that the world can produce; therefore, one must never waste. If we do not curb abuses, such as burning forests to hunt birds and draining ponds to catch fish, all will be exhausted and nothing will be available. Likewise, it is wrong for the ruler to compel people to engage in forced labor and unnecessary activities that will result in diminished wealth. If the ruler strives to produce wealth by means of humanity and to economize by means of righteousness, the people's savings and accumulations will be my savings and accumulations, and my treasury will be the people's treasury, and the people in high and low places will assist each other, and the root and the branches will support each other. There will be no fear of shortage nor any apprehension of resentment. This situation will then lead to the so-called state of abundant surplus, in which there will be sufficient supplies for the people as well as for the state. YC

Yi I: On Economy

[From *Yulgok chŏnsŏ 23:49b–51a*]

In addition to being known as one of the Chosŏn dynasty's two greatest philosophers of Neo-Confucianism, Yi I (Yulgok, 1536–1584) was a highly respected statesman who enjoyed a distinguished career as a government official. Among his many works on government and individual ethics, *Sŏnghak chibyo* (Essentials of the Sages' Learning) was one of the most popular writings, read widely by scholars and officials. Written for the king in 1575 as a guide for sagely rule, *Essentials of the Sages' Learning* offers Yi's views on how a ruler should conduct himself and administer the government. In it Yi quotes from former sages as well as adding his own comments and ideas. In the seventh chapter, dealing with economy, Yi emphasizes the importance of economizing in order to protect the country's wealth and promote the well-being of the people.

Economy in my humble opinion means showing respect for virtue, whereas extravagance is a great evil. If one is economical, his heart is never dissolute, and his mind is at ease with anything that may occur. If one is extravagant, his mind will always seek external things and will never be satisfied, not even for one day. Consider a family whose ancestors have built up a fortune through industry and hard work. If its descendants preserve it with economy, the family inheritance will be transmitted for many generations without diminution. If, however, there is one person who is inclined to extravagance, he will indulge himself in pleasure, and the wealth that has been accumulated over the years will be squandered away overnight. Although the success or failure of one family will affect only a small number of people, a state involves all aspects of the accumulated achievements of the ancestors, in a magnitude that cannot be compared with one family's fortune. There is nothing in the state's treasury that is not produced by the toil and sweat of the people. How dare one carelessly indulge himself in extravagance and dissipate this precious wealth, causing distress among the people and bringing ruin to the achievements of our forefathers?

The former kings of this country ruled the state by means of economy for many generations and their expenditures were always based on revenues; therefore, the country was affluent and the storehouses were full of surplus. But since the time of Yŏnsangun [1494–1506], the expenditures in the palace have increased extravagantly, disregarding the practices of former rulers. Since then, the court has followed undesirable customs and has so far failed to reform itself. Therefore, the state's expenditures have increased daily. There are at present no unusual luxurious customs being practiced in the palace and no unessential public work projects being carried out within the country; yet the annual revenues cannot support the annual expenditures and the savings accrued under many former kings will be exhausted in the future. If a famine strikes or a war breaks out, we will be utterly helpless. Is this not truly deplorable?

The costumes being used in the palace now, which were reformed at the beginning of the dynasty, no longer demonstrate economy. Thus, the ordinary people too have developed a luxurious lifestyle; they dress themselves in colorful costumes, indulge in rich viands and sumptuous fare, and try to outdo each other in luxury. Even the bedding of the lowly actors and singing girls is all made of silk. As there is no regulation governing the relationship between the upper and the lower people and as waste abounds, people's morality has become lax and their livelihood progressively more difficult. If there is no reform from above, the state will lose its reason for existence. The way to correct this cannot be found in the ordinary rules. Instead, the reform must come from above, with the heart of Emperor Yao, who lived in a house thatched with reeds and used earthen steps. The queen and the court ladies must emulate the Empress Ma of Later Han, who always dressed herself in costumes made of coarse cloth, and must economize by reducing the palace expenditures. If the economizing starts in the palace and the families of scholar-officials become impressed by these practices and accept them, economizing will then spread to the people. Only then can we expect the old detrimental practices to be reformed, the precious wealth to be saved, and people's wealth to grow. As Wu-chu in the Spring and Autumn era said: "If selfish interest prevails and flourishes, it is difficult for virtue and righteousness to grow. If virtue and righteousness are not practiced, the people nearby will rise against the government, and the people in the distance will further be alienated." I humbly beseech Your Majesty to ponder this matter seriously.   YC

Yu Paeksun: On Commerce

[From *T'aejong sillok* 20:24a–b]

The Chosŏn dynasty government in general followed the Confucian notion of discouraging commerce. Believing agriculture to be the sole creator of wealth, the Chosŏn Confucianists treated commerce as a nonproductive occupation and regarded merchants as a parasitic element living at the expense of the farmers. The following passage is part of a memorial submitted by Censor-General Yu Paeksun in 1410.

It has been said that farming is the root of government. It has also been said that when too many people pursue the petty occupation of commerce, farming is at the mercy of the marketplace. With sweat and strain, farmers' work is hard and arduous; the more land they cultivate, the greater their hardship. Merchants, on the other hand, merely exchange cheap goods with precious items, thereby gaining twofold profit. Instead of toiling, merchants lead a life of ease and pleasure. It is no wonder therefore that the number of farmers diminishes and that of merchants increases daily. Since one farmer who works on the land feeds ten people, how can the state possibly become affluent and the people have sufficient food if this situation continues? It is requested that from now on all merchants should be required to register with the magistrate office in the capital or in the county where they reside and that, following the ancient practice of taxing idle people, they be required to carry a transit permit to be issued only after they pay two piculs (*sŏk*) of rice for each peddling trip. Anyone who engages in commerce without proper authorization should be reported to the government, whereupon all the merchant's goods would be confiscated—half going to the government and the other half to the person reporting the unauthorized merchant. In this way, we can realize the goal of promoting agriculture and discouraging commerce. YC

Circulation of Currency

As the use of currency as a medium of exchange has obvious advantages over other media, in 1401 King T'aejong enacted a law to promote the use of paper money. The people in general, however, were reluctant to use the government-issued paper currency, as they had long been accustomed to the use of *osŭngp'o* (five-ply cloth) as a medium of exchange. This practice created serious problems. At first, the government prohibited the use of *osŭngp'o* in an attempt to encourage the sole use of paper currency. When this measure failed, the government allowed the concurrent use of paper currency and *osŭngp'o*. When this did not work either, King Sejong minted copper coins for circulation in 1424. But the copper coin was not accepted by the public either. Thereafter, for about one hundred years until the early sixteenth century, the Chosŏn government tried to circulate paper currency without success. Cloth and grain were the more popular media of exchange until the early seventeenth century, when a further growth in commerce gave rise to the general acceptance of metallic coins. The following passages from the *Veritable Records* suggest the motivation for pushing for the circulation of paper and metallic currency and the problems it created.

Nineteenth day of the fourth month [in 1401]. Inspector-General Yu Kwan [1346–1433] and other officials offered a memorial requesting the circulation of cloth money. His Majesty, however, did not approve. The memorial reads as follows: The Office of Currency Management was established to manage all matters related to the paper currency. This currency is issued by the government without any limit, but the use of cloth as a medium of exchange, a practice started by the people, is causing problems. We believe that the use of paper currency in place of cloth will bring benefit to the state and be more convenient for the people. But as our country is circumspect in serving the senior state, China, is it permissible that we carry out such a measure without approval?

Because the use of cloth as a medium of exchange has a long history in our country, it is requested that currency be made of cloth in accordance with the currency law. The regular "five-ply cloth" can be used by dying it light blue. Its length and width should be three *ch'ŏk* [roughly three feet] with both the top and bottom ends stitched up and a picture drawn on the four corners. In addition, the seals of the Office of Currency Management, the Office of Land Management, and the Office of Grain Management should be affixed in the inner space, and it should have letters that read "Currency of Korea." This currency can be circulated within the borders of our country.

We can also make two-*ch'ŏk* and one-*ch'ŏk* denominations in the same way as the three-*ch'ŏk* currency. We then draw three strokes on the three-*ch'ŏk* denomination and make it worth three *tu* of unhulled rice; we can draw two strokes on two-*ch'ŏk* denomination and make it buy two *tu*. People then can distinguish the value of the currency by the number of strokes marked on the money, and they can trade hundreds of goods at various prices.

[From *T'aejong sillok* 1:25b] YC

Twenty-first day of the tenth month [in 1401]. The Office of the Inspector-General submitted a memorial requesting abolition of the Office of Currency Management. His Majesty disapproved it. The memorial in summary reads as follows: "Our country has not used paper currency before. People are accustomed to using cloth money and do not like to use paper currency. It is requested that we stop making paper currency and dismiss the officials in the Office of Currency Management."

His Majesty T'aejong summoned Inspector-General Yi Chi [d. 1414] and Third Inspector Pak Ko and stated: "I am always pleased to receive advice that is meant to benefit the people, such as you have submitted. It is, however, my intention to promote the use of paper currency because it is convenient to use. And yet you are opposing it on the grounds that the practice may become known to our senior state. The paper currency will be used only within our borders; even if the senior state does find out, what blame can they find in it?" Pak Ko replied: "How can I, your subject, dare offer opinions that may go against the interest of the people? What the people value are rice and cloth only. In order to promote the use of paper currency, Your Majesty prohibited the use of *osŭngp'o* and has also exchanged all the tribute cloth from Kyŏngsang and Chŏlla provinces with rice. These measures have caused incalculable damage to the people. I do not know of any way to produce wealth by means of using paper currency. How can the state possibly have sufficient wealth to spend?" The king stated: "What you are saying is reasonable. Even so, if we continue to use paper currency for a long time, it will be widely accepted in the end. If it becomes clear that the use of paper currency harms the people, I will amend it without waiting for your words." His Majesty then ordered Director Pak Sŏngmyŏng [1370–1406] to bestow a feast for Yi Chi and Pak Ko.

[From *T'aejong sillok* 2:15b–16a] YC

Twenty-fourth day of the tenth month [in 1402]. The Office of the Inspector-General and Office of the Censor-General offered a joint memorial as follows: Since ancient times, the rulers have enacted laws and created institutions based always upon the needs of the people. Emulating the Chinese system, our country printed paper currency in order to make it a valuable item for both public and private use. It is thought that the paper currency will not only bring unlimited advantages to the state but also be convenient to carry and store. When this law was first enacted, all the court officials believed it to be a good law that would enrich the nation and the people. Since the circulation of paper currency, we have seen that the government opened its grain storage to allow people to trade, thus demonstrating its trust in the people, and also exchanged the *osŭngp'o* that the people had saved. The government then mutilated this *osŭngp'o* in order to remove any doubt over the intent of the currency, thus manifesting the severity of the law.

But as our people's customs and products are different from those in China, they have no trust in the paper money and regard it as useless. As their worry and doubt increase daily, the price of commodities has been rising with no end in sight. The more strictly the government enforces the currency law, the cheaper the value of the paper currency becomes. How long can this situation continue without serious problems? Now that the new crop is already on the market, the price of grain is supposed to go down; yet indigent people are unable to purchase even one *tu* of rice with one sheet of paper currency. Hard-pressed with hunger, their resentment is rising in the extreme, for which we cannot help being concerned. Confucius said that man's heart is the rice paddies of the sages, from which the proper way of government originates. Thus, Lu Chih of T'ang said: "The key to the state lies in winning the support of the people's heart." At present, the use of paper currency is causing deep resentment as it brings the people no benefit. That it is rejected by the people is manifestly clear. Although the use of paper currency was regarded as a good law in the beginning, it has created serious problems in its implementation. How can we hesitate to revise it? It is humbly requested that Your Majesty look into the heart of the people and order the concerned officials to revise this law. Your action on this matter will truly benefit the people. If the law cannot be changed forthwith, please allow the *osŭngp'o* to be used along with the paper currency, just as it is written on the paper money. It is important that we listen to what the people prefer, that we do not force laws upon them, and that we follow their heart.

The king instructed the State Council to discuss this memorial. In the meeting of the Three Offices, the officials were divided on the use of paper currency, but the majority at the same time favored restoration of the use of cloth money.

[From *T'aejong sillok* 4:14a–b] YC

Twenty-seventh day of the tenth month [in 1410]. His Majesty reiterated his intention to enforce the paper currency law and instructed the State Council as follows: I hear that people are not willing to use paper currency in the marketplace and refuse to open their shops. I hear also that many of them are planning to engage in commercial activity in the countryside using cloth. If this is true, it will be difficult to promote the wider use of paper currency. If the miscellaneous tribute taxes are collected in the form of paper currency, then the merchants and the ordinary people will have no choice but to use the paper currency. Let this rule be implemented immediately.

[From *T'aejong sillok* 20:23b–24a] YC

Twelfth day of the twelfth month [in 1422]. The value of the paper currency has diminished; one must pay three sheets of the currency to purchase one pint of rice. Thus, few people are using the paper currency to exchange goods. Although anyone who uses items other than paper currency to exchange goods is punished by confiscation of his household, those who are quietly breaking this law are mostly poor people in the countryside, and no wealthy merchant has ever been charged. As the value of paper money has not improved, there arose a proposal to use metallic coins as currency.

[From *Sejong sillok* 18:20b] YC

Sixteenth day of the ninth month [in 1423]. There was a discussion whether or not metallic currency should be minted. When the paper currency was first introduced, one sheet of paper money could buy one peck of rice and thirty sheets were worth one bolt of cotton cloth. But the value of paper currency has now been greatly diminished, and one sheet of paper money can buy only one-tenth of a peck of rice, and more than a hundred sheets are needed to buy a bolt of cotton cloth. Thus, a joint conference of the State Council and the Six Ministries was held to discuss the question of minting metallic currency to be circulated along with the paper. The Ministry of Taxation then offered a memorial: "Copper coins have been used historically in China. It is requested that in minting coins the weight of ten coins should be made equal to one *yang,* following the standard used by K'ai-yüan coins of T'ang, that each coin should carry an engraving of 'Currency of Korea,' . . . that the Office of Currency Management should handle all matters related to coinage, and that any private individual who mints unauthorized coins should be punished in accordance with the law." His Majesty approved the proposal.

[From Sejong sillok 21:17a–b]   YC

Twenty-sixth day of the second month [in 1426]. Director Pyŏn Kyeryang stated the following before His Majesty: The intent of new laws is to bring people's hearts together and to sustain the national polity so as to secure long-lasting rule and safety for the state. If the implementation of new laws brings resentment and discord among people, it will cause disharmony in natural phenomena in the form of various and endless disasters. In implementing laws, one must never move in a rush; instead, one must move prudently to gain long-term effectiveness. No matter how good a new law may be, if one does not follow a prudent course in implementing it, it cannot be successfully enforced. Master Ch'eng of Sung said: "Since ancient times, no one has ever succeeded in establishing a government by trying to impose laws that were opposed by the people." These are truly appropriate words. As a new law of metallic currency has now been formulated, its main purpose is to facilitate the benefit of the people. And yet it contains certain provisions that are excessively hard to implement, and these should be seriously considered. People must not go without food even for a day; yet famines in recent years have made it doubly difficult to obtain food. And now the new law requires all trade to be transacted with metallic currency. The people, however, are accustomed to the old practices and are not willing to use coins. In buying and selling, they do not wish to be paid in coins; they would rather use what they possess to exchange goods in private. Thus, there will be a number of people who will violate the law. A family may consist of one or two, or three or four, or even five to seven members. Yet, if one of them should violate the law, it calls for confiscation of the entire family's property, thus forcing the whole family to starve. This provision is not appropriate. . . . It is humbly requested that the people be allowed to trade either in coins or in goods as they please, so that they can maintain their existence, and that only the payment for redemptions and for government purchases be made in copper currency. If this proposal is accepted, the metallic currency law will be preserved, the people's hearts will be united, and chaotic natural phenomena will disappear.

His Majesty replied: I can see good intentions in your statement. But formulating a new law is meant to demonstrate the government's trust in the people, and how can we amend a law according to people's likes and dislikes? If the metallic currency law is applied only to the government and is not enforced among the people, this is not the way to demonstrate trust in the people. . . . As for the law on metallic currency, we must either do away with it or enforce it. If we are to enforce it, we should not try to amend the law each time there is a dispute.

[From *Sejong sillok* 31:19b–20a] YC

Precious Metals

Early Chosŏn Korea discouraged the use of gold and silver— partly because of Confucian asceticism and partly to avoid Chinese demand for the precious metals. In the year 1542, however, the thirty-seventh year of King Chungjong, the official Japanese envoy brought eighty thousand *yang* (taels) of silver and asked to trade, causing a lengthy controversy at court. At issue was how to reconcile the Confucian purists' insistence that the precious metal had no practical use in daily life with the need to maintain friendly relations with the Japanese. In the end a compromise was reached: a portion of the Japanese silver could be traded. Then there arose disagreement between the Koreans and Japanese over the price of silver as measured against cotton cloth, the main medium of exchange in lieu of currency in Korea at the time and also a trade item coveted by the Japanese.

Twentieth day of the fourth month [in 1542]. Chief State Councillor Yun Ŭnbo [1468–1544] and other ministers offered the following memorial: If we allow a trade of the total amount of eighty thousand *yang* of the Japanese silver as part of the official trade, it will result in a drastic rise in the price of many other commodities. The entire stock of cotton cloth stored presently in Kyŏngsang province will be the equivalent price for it, but even then it will not be easy to supply them sufficiently. If we are to supply them with the stock stored in the capital city, there will be a host of problems in transporting it. It is respectfully requested that the Board of Taxation calculate the price and trade an appropriate amount as official trade and that the remainder be allowed to be traded by private merchants. . . .

[From *Chungjong sillok* 98:13b] YC

Twenty-fourth day of the fourth month [in 1542]. The Office of Censor-General offered the following memorial: In the name of the communication mission, the Japanese envoy brought silver amounting to eighty-thousand *yang* and asked us to trade for it. Although silver is a precious item, people cannot eat or dress with it, and in reality it is of no use. In our country, cotton cloth is widely used and all the people depend on it for their living. To exchange what people depend upon for an item of no practical use will give the Japanese an advantage at our expense. This is extremely undesirable. There is no precedent for the Japanese envoy bringing silver to our country. If we allow this trade now, they will gain an easy profit and will in future bring twice the present amount. Once this silver trade is open, it will be difficult to comply with the limitless wishes of the Japanese. If they are rejected at the beginning, even though they will be disappointed, their anger will be superficial. On the other hand, if the trade is allowed and their wishes are frustrated at some future date because we cannot comply with their demands, their anger will be profound and the harm will be great. Therefore, exchanging silver as part of the official trade should not be permitted. Since allowing private trade by ordinary people would violate existing laws prohibiting silver trade, this too should not be permitted. It is requested that, to prevent further problems in the future, there should be no trade for the silver.

[From *Chungjong sillok* 98:15a–b]   YC

Twenty-second day of the fifth intercalary month [in 1542]. Following the insistent demands of the Japanese envoy to trade silver, His Majesty called the meeting of the former and incumbent members of the State Council and the Ministers of the Six Boards for consultation. Yun Ŭnbo and other ministers proposed: We have discussed among ourselves the issue of trading the Japanese silver. We should divide the silver into three parts; a third of it should be traded as part of the official trade, and the other two-thirds should be traded in private trade. As to the price of silver, the appropriate office should be instructed to determine it. . . . Yi Ŏnjŏk [1491–1553] then made the following proposal: A king should not value things that are brought from afar; he should value only virtue. The rare treasures of gold and silver are not urgently needed for the people's life or for their food or clothing. In principle, they ought to be rejected and should never be accepted. The price of silver in our country is extremely cheap. They will offer the silver to us as a precious item; if we buy it as a cheap item, they will surely be disappointed and might even be angry. Since the silver has already been brought into the capital, we should not reject all of it. Instead, we should allow them to trade only twenty or thirty thousand *yang* at a very high price as a way of mollifying their desire; the remainder of the silver should be turned down with appropriate excuses. This idea seems to be a good way of handling it. The king agreed to accept Yi Ŏnjŏk's suggestion.

[From *Chungjong sillok* 98:4a] YC

Twenty-fourth day of the fifth intercalary month [in 1542]. The joint memorial by the State Council and the Ministry of Rites reads: Upon being informed of the decision to permit a trade of twenty thousand *yang*, the Japanese envoy has requested to trade two-thirds of the silver. . . . The Minister of Rites, however, replied that the court decision cannot be amended. . . .

[From *Chungjong sillok* 98:50a] YC

Ninth day of the sixth month [in 1542]. The king issued the following instruction: Because many Japanese have recently brought silver and we have allowed a large amount of it to be traded, there should be no shortage in the supply of silver. Because there has been a great deal of difficulty among the people in mining silver at Tanch'ŏn, I hereby order a halt to the mining for five years. Anyone who engages in illicit mining will be punished severely according to the law.

[From *Chungjong sillok* 98:51b] YC

Tenth day of the sixth month [in 1542]. Yun Ŭnbo and other officials stated: The price of commodities fluctuates. Recently the law prohibiting silver trade has been very stringent; even when the Japanese from different islands brought silver, the people were not willing to trade it. Because of this situation, the price of silver is extremely cheap. To obtain one *p'il*[7] of cotton cloth, they pay two *yang* of silver. This is what the Japanese envoy has seen and heard. We are, however, offering him a discount to trade two *p'il* of cotton cloth for three *yang* of silver. . . .

[From *Chungjong sillok* 98:52a] YC

Eighteenth day of the sixth month [in 1542]. The Japanese envoy insisted on trading silver at the 1538 price, when four *p'il* equaled one *yang*. Whereupon, Yun Ŭnbo and other officials stated as follows: All articles that are sold and bought are commodities, and all commodities must involve negotiation on price, which may be high or low depending on the time. The price of silver was dear formerly but is cheap at present. Unlike copper and iron, the silver price fluctuates, and this is well known.[8]

[From *Chungjong sillok* 98:55b]   YC

Development of Rural Markets

Commercial activities under the Chosŏn dynasty were carried out largely by licensed merchants under government supervision. Toward the end of the fifteenth century, however, a new phenomenon began to develop that was eventually to have a far-reaching impact upon the economy and society. This was the rise of *changmun* markets (later *sijang*) at various population centers in all the provinces. Apparently originating in the southwestern province of Chŏlla as a meeting place to exchange goods in times of famine or other economic distress, *changmun* gradually became a popular site for private commercial activities. Fearful that commerce would drain people from farming, the Chosŏn government attempted to suppress the growth of these markets. The government effort, however, was in vain. Once the people began to realize their convenience and usefulness, they flocked to the markets, which were established in virtually every town throughout the country and held regularly at certain periodic intervals, such as every five days. These periodic markets became important centers not only for economic but also for social activities in the rural areas, even down to the present day. The following translations, selected from the *Veritable Records,* offer a picture of the debates within the government on the growth of the markets during their formative years.

Twenty-seventh day of the seventh month [in 1472]. The Minister of Taxation offered the following memorial: In response to reports that many profit-seeking people gather together at what are now called *changmun* in Muan and other counties of Chŏlla province, causing a number of problems for the people, Your Majesty asked the concerned officials to discuss this matter and make a recommendation as to whether these markets should be done away with or allowed to continue. When this minister communicated with the governor of Chŏlla province, Kim Chigyŏng [1419–1485], on this issue, he reported that a large number of people assemble on roadsides in many different counties to open a marketplace twice every month, and that although people trade at the marketplace to obtain what they do not have for what they have, they are abandoning the root of agriculture to seek the branch of commerce. This is causing the price of commodities to rise, thus inflicting a great deal of damage. The governor also reported that he has already instructed all the county magistrates to prohibit markets. It is therefore recommended that Your Majesty issue a further order to the governor to strictly forbid holding markets. His Majesty approved.

[From *Sŏngjong sillok* 20:16a] YC

Eleventh day of the second month [in 1473]. Sin Sukchu [1417–1475], former Chief State Councillor, offered his views on currency and markets: There is a reason for currency not being used widely in our country. With the exception of the capital city, there are no shops in our country. So even if one had money, how could it be used? If we wish the currency to be widely used, we must first consider the fundamental factors; otherwise, the currency law will only cause turmoil among the people. There is only one way to promote a wider use of currency, and that is to open markets and shops in various provinces where people can trade goods with each other. When they trade, they will consider the distances they have to travel and the value of various goods before the transactions. For these transactions, currency will become a necessity, and for the circulation of currency, shops and markets are necessary. In establishing shops and markets, we will not be successful if we do not follow the people's wish.

In the year *kyŏngin* [1470] when there was a famine, a large number of people gathered in Chŏlla province to open shops and markets, and they called these *changmun*. The people managed to survive the famine only because of these markets. This was truly a good opportunity to develop markets in the countryside. But when the Minister of Taxation sought opinions of the county magistrates on this matter, all the magistrates, without considering the possible beneficial or harmful effects, wanted to prohibit markets simply on the ground that they had never existed in the past. This is a deplorable attitude of blindly following the old practices. Only Magistrate Yi Yŏnggyŏn [fl. 1470] of Naju requested that we do not prohibit markets. But in the end, the Minister of Taxation decided to prohibit them, and thus we have lost forever a golden opportunity to develop markets. This is indeed regrettable.

In my humble opinion, a program must follow the hearts of the people if it is to succeed. Because the people in the southern province have had the experience of supporting themselves by means of exchanging goods in the marketplace, I recommend that we permit people to establish shops and markets in the administrative and population centers in the provinces.

[From *Sŏngjong sillok* 27:4a–b] YC

Twenty-first day of the third month [in 1529]. At the morning lecture before His Majesty, First Minister Without Portfolio Nam Kon [1471–1527] stated the following: Markets (also called village markets) have now been established in all the provinces. When I was serving as governor of Chŏlla, I tried strictly to prohibit this. But now the number of markets has greatly increased, and the number of people attending them has reached the tens of thousands. All are people who neglect farming, thus causing great harm to food production.

Pak Sumun, Expositor in the Office of Special Advisers, stated: The development of marketplaces has begun only in recent years; on market day, multitudes of men and women prepare wine and food to sell for profit. Nothing is more harmful to farming than these developments.

His Majesty stated: Some people say that the market system has beneficial effects. But ultimately it supports commerce at the expense of farming.

[From *Chungjong sillok* 38:57b–58a] YC

Twenty-seventh day of the ninth month [in 1547]. Yi Hwang, Expositor in the Office of Special Advisers, stated at the morning lecture session before His Majesty: Markets at various localities are causing many people to seek commerce, and the number of robbers and thieves has also increased. For these reasons, the government had prohibited the markets. But as we are severely afflicted by a bad famine at present, the people have to rely upon markets to trade goods in order to support themselves. If we prohibit markets, how can the people sustain their lives? . . . When there were famines before, no prohibition against markets existed and the people were allowed to help one another to obtain relief. For this years's famine, however, there is a total prohibition against markets, and as a result the people are suffering greatly. I recommend that we do not prohibit markets.

[From *Myŏngjong sillok* 6:28a] YC

CHAPTER EIGHTEEN

Thought

Neo-Confucianism is the name given by Western scholars to a Confucian revival movement that began about A.D. 1000 in China. After centuries of Buddhist and Taoist predominance, a new Confucian movement creatively synthesized traditional Confucian social and moral concerns with a new metaphysics and spirituality that rivaled the sophistication of the Buddhists and Taoists. Neo-Confucianism subsequently became the predominant intellectual and spiritual tradition throughout East Asia. The first and "orthodox" school of Neo-Confucian thought was that of the great synthesizer, Chu Hsi (1130–1200); the second major school was that of Wang Yang-ming (1472–1529), which at times overshadowed Chu Hsi's school in China and Japan. One of the distinctive characteristics of Korea was its consistent and almost exclusive development of the Chu Hsi tradition.

Introduced to the Korean peninsula toward the end of the Koryŏ dynasty, Neo-Confucianism played a central role in the political, intellectual, and spiritual life of the subsequent Chosŏn dynasty. The selections that follow, arranged chronologically, are taken from the works of outstanding Neo-Confucians of the first half of the Chosŏn dynasty. They are intended to introduce various facets of what this rich and complex tradition meant to Koreans. We begin with selections that illustrate the broad outlines of the Neo-Confucian worldview, then consider the practical spiritual concerns inherent in the seemingly theoretical philosophy, and conclude with important texts related to the most central and formative controversy in Korea's Neo-Confucian intellectual history: the Four-Seven Debate. MK

Kwŏn Kŭn (1352–1409)

Kwŏn Kŭn's *Iphak tosŏl* (Diagrammatic Treatises for the Commencement of Learning) is the earliest extant Korean exposition of Neo-Confucian thought. When it was written in 1390, the Neo-Confucian movement had been gradually gaining strength on the Korean peninsula for over seven decades. Indeed, in just two years the Koryŏ dynasty would be replaced by the Chosŏn dynasty, the only East Asian regime officially founded under Neo-Confucian auspices. The two sections selected from the *Diagrammatic Treatises* reflect the appropriation of the new learning at this early stage.

Diagrammatic Treatises: Explanation of the First Diagram
[From *Iphak tosŏl* 1:1b–2a]

This first selection is from the text that accompanies the first and most important of Kwŏn's diagrams, entitled "Heaven and Man, Mind and Nature, Are Conjoined as One." The diagram and text are intended as a synthetic presentation of the content of two of the most important works by early Chinese Neo-Confucians, Chou Tun-i's *Diagram of the Supreme Ultimate,* and Chu Hsi's *Commentary on the Great Learning.* The former is the cornerstone of Neo-Confucian metaphysics; the latter presents the essential path of learning or self-cultivation in terms of a metaphysically based structure of the inner life. The scope of this ambitious synthesis illustrates the broad and accurate grasp of this complex system even at this very early date. Its concern with the system of the inner life of the mind and nature foreshadows what was to become the hallmark of Korean Neo-Confucian thought in later centuries. At the same time, there is no hint of awareness of the pitfalls and complex issues hidden in the neat and orderly explanation of unity and diversification, perfection and graded imperfection, we find here. MK

In the diagram at the right I have respectfully followed the explanations found in Master Chou Tun-i's *Diagram of the Supreme Ultimate* and Master Chu Hsi's *Commentary on the Great Learning* regarding man's mind-and-heart and his nature in order to clarify for students the distinction between principle and material force and between good and evil. Therefore it does not directly include a representation of the transformative production of the myriad creatures.

Nonetheless, in the coming into being of humans and other creatures, this principle is the same although their material force has the differences of being penetrating or blocked up, partial or integral. The recipient of integral and penetrating material force becomes a human being; the recipient of partial and blocked up material force becomes a lesser creature. If we look at this diagram, the circle labeled "integrity" is the case of one who has received the most refined and penetrating material force and so is a sage; the circle labeled "mindfulness" is one who has received integral and penetrating material force and is an ordinary man; the circle labeled "desire" is one who receives partial and blocked-up material force and is like a subhuman creature; beneath it is the level of animals. Those who receive even more partial and blocked-up material force become grass and trees. In this respect a representation of the transformative production of the myriad creatures is likewise included here.

Indeed in the inexhaustible transformation and productive activity of heaven and earth, the past ones rest and the coming ones continue the process. Human beings and beasts, plants and trees, have myriad shapes and forms, each with its own correct nature and mandate, all flowing forth from the midst of the single Supreme Ultimate. And there is nothing in the world outside the compass of this nature; therefore the *Doctrine of the Mean* says: "It is only he who is possessed of the most complete sincerity that can exist under heaven, who can give its full development to his nature. Able to give its full development to his own nature, he can do the same to the nature of other men. Able to give its full development to the natures of creatures and things, he can assist the transforming and nourishing powers of heaven and earth."[1] Ah! This is indeed the ultimate! MK

Diagrammatic Treatises: Life After Death?
[From *Iphak tosŏl* 1:22b–23b]

The second passage is taken from a section of the *Diagrammatic Treatises* that deals with questions from beginning students. The student is fictional, but his questions represent matters that concern many. The matter at hand—the question of personal survival after death—must have been particularly troubling. Centuries of Buddhism had deeply impressed the belief in reincarnation on the Korean mind, but the Neo-Confucian view reflected in this passage seems to have little place for life after death. At the same time, great effort was being made to introduce orthodox Confucian ancestor rituals to Korean society. In his response to the obvious question, Kwŏn displays a typical Neo-Confucian philosophical point of view. The less educated probably continued to think in terms of spirits, but the more deeply one comprehended Neo-Confucian thought and its implications the more one would be moved toward the kind of attitude presented here.

In other passages the term *ki* (*ch'i*) has been translated as the conventional "material force." Here, however, it is left untranslated because the intellectual force of the discussion depends somewhat on reading the term with its rich historical ambiguity. In technical philosophy it is "material force," the stuff of all existence. In more common parlance it is "vital force," "life force," or "vital spirit," the concrete animating principle that is the life of one's body and also the physical life transmitted from parents to children and so on down through the generations. In a real way, the life and "spirit" of one's ancestors still course through one's veins, and through rites one's whole psyche can be attuned to the life and spirit that continue in one's own existence. MK

A student asked: Chu Hsi in the sixteenth and seventeenth chapters of his *Questions on the Doctrine of the Mean* is extremely critical of the assertion that one does not perish but survives—which is not something we Confucians can rightly say. In this view, after one has died the forces of yin and yang are dispersed and the subtle spirit, the yang soul, and the yin soul have no further existence. As for what is called "sacrificing and nurturing the spirits," what is there to nurture?

My reply: It is difficult to say. In the coming into being of humans and other creatures, they begin with *ki* condensing and taking concrete form, and they end with *ki* dispersing and the form dissolving. Human beings and animals and plants are all the same. In the transforming activity of heaven and earth, the past ones rest and the coming ones continue the process; it is not that the *ki*, which has already withdrawn, returns again as the vital expansive *ki*. Therefore at the end when yin and yang have separated, the yang soul rises upward and the yin soul descends, and one's *ki* entirely disperses. It is not that there is some subtle animating principle that coheres and does not die, but, like the "imperishable ones" spoken of by the Taoists, remains in some boundless realm.

But this *ki*, though it belongs to heaven and earth, is also entirely founded upon the bodies of my ancestors and passed on to me; so although my ancestors have already passed away, their *ki* is in me and has never ceased. It is similar to the way the fruits of plants and trees are endowed with the wholeness of their *ki*. Although the roots and trunk may rot and dry up, the seeds in the fruit all produce according to their kind: from the roots and trunk to the fruit's seeds and its product, the *ki* has never been cut off. But if the fruit rots, the *ki* has been cut off, and it will produce no further. Thus man regards being without posterity as the greatest calamity, for with this the ancestors' *ki* is cut off, and there cannot be further sacrifice.

The *ki* of my person is the *ki* of my ancestors. Therefore if I bring the greatest sincerity and reverence to sacrificing to them, there is a spiritual interaction and arousing of our *ki,* and in this there is that which is nurtured. The existence of the *ki* is the existence of the spirit; the approach of sincerity is the same as the approach of the spirit. . . . The spirits of my ancestors, then, are not outside but within my own person. Thus one can understand what is meant by the statement that "spiritual beings enter into all things, and there is nothing without them."[2] And the way I maintain my body must be reverent, and the requiting of my ancestors must be sincere. MK

Sŏ Kyŏngdŏk (1489–1546)

During the first century of the Chosŏn dynasty, Neo-Confucianism developed in Korea along two distinct lines. One group was actively involved in government service; these worked mainly to transform the political and social institutions of Korea in the light of ideal Confucian models. The second group stayed in the countryside, avoiding the turmoil of the court and devoting themselves to study, self-cultivation, and teaching.

Sŏ Kyŏngdŏk, better known by his pen name, Hwadam, represented the second group. He endured poverty in order to live an undisturbed life of study and teaching. His thought bears the mark of the early period of wide-open investigation and speculation before Neo-Confucian thought had taken on an orthodox, public face in Korea. He is famous for elaborating a philosophy that is an emphatic monism of *ki* (*ch'i*), material force—a pronounced contrast to the dualism of *i* (*li*) and *ki* characteristic of the school of Chu Hsi, the orthodoxy of both China and Korea. Sŏ Kyŏngdŏk took great pride in his independence and originality, but historians note a marked similarity between his ideas and those of the early Chinese Neo-Confucian Chang Tsai (1020–1077). Although only a slender volume of Sŏ's writing has survived, he is generally considered one of the three outstanding thinkers of the Chosŏn dynasty. The two brief pieces that follow illustrate the character of his ideas. MK

The Theory of the Great Void
[From *Hwadam chip* 2:14b–15a]

The Great Void is empty and yet not empty. The void is identical with material force. The void is inexhaustible and all-embracing; material force is likewise inexhaustible and all-embracing. If it is called the void, how can it be called material force? When the void is in repose, it is the substance of material force. Coagulation and disintegration are its functions. If one knows that the void is not really empty, one cannot call it nonbeing. Lao Tzu says: "Being is born from nonbeing."[3] He did not know that the void is identical with material force. It is also said: "The void can produce material force."[4] This is not so. If one says that the void produces material force, then there would exist no material force before it was produced, and the void would be something dead. If material force did not already exist, from what could it be produced? Material force has no beginning and no birth. Not having a beginning, how can it end? Not having birth, how can it become extinct? Lao Tzu speaks of nothingness, the Buddhists speak of annihilation. This is because they do not know the source of principle and material force. How could they know the Tao? MK

Discussion on Life and Death, Ghosts and Spirits
[From *Hwadam chip* 2:15a–16a]

The theories of Masters Ch'eng I and Ch'eng Hao, Chang Tsai, and Chu Hsi seem to give a full account of such matters as life and death, ghosts (negative spiritual forces) and spirits (positive spiritual forces). Nevertheless they have not yet thoroughly explained the full reason why these things are as they are. They all give quotations without enlarging upon them and let other scholars understand these for themselves. This is the reason why their juniors know only one part of their theories but not the other and why they hand down a rough outline but do not understand the subtleties of the whole picture. I wish to make a selection from the subtle ideas of the three masters in order to set up a clear-cut discussion sufficient to dispel long-existing points of doubt.

Ch'eng Hao has said that life and death, men and ghosts, are one thing and yet two, two things and yet one. This gets to the bottom of the problem. I likewise am of the opinion that life and death, men and ghosts, are just a coagulation or disintegration of material force and nothing else. Although there is coagulation and disintegration, there is no being and nonbeing—such is the fundamental substance of material force. The clear uniformity and pure emptiness of material force entirely fill the all-embracing void. A large-scale coagulation forms heaven and earth; small-scale coagulations form all creatures and things. It all depends on the relative strength, duration, and speed of the energy of the coagulation or disintegration. Because of the quantitative coagulation and disintegration in the Great Void there are differences in size in creation. If even the material force of slight objects like a blade of grass or a tree will never entirely disintegrate, how much less will that be so in the case of the human mind and consciousness, a great and durable coagulation! In the course of time, however, man's outward form and spiritual component manifest that they disintegrate and seem to disappear into nothingness.

This point has yet to be realized by anybody. Even among the pupils of the three masters, none was able to reach this ultimate conclusion. They just gathered up the dregs of their masters' teachings and turned them into their own theories. The translucent uniformity and pure emptiness of material force originate at the beginning of the Great Void's moving and giving rise to yang, quiescing and giving rise to yin. When the gradual intensification of its coagulation has reached its saturation point, it becomes heaven and earth and us men. The disintegration of man is just the disintegration of his outward form and spiritual component; the translucent uniformity and pure emptiness of the coagulation actually never disintegrate, but dissolve into the translucent uniformity and pure emptiness of the Great Void and are identical with the one material force. As for the coagulation and disintegration of consciousness, it is only a matter of relative duration and speed. Even if the disintegration is very fast it is a matter of days or months, as in the case of the most insignificant entities.

But what does it mean to say one's material force in the end also does not disintegrate? Since material force in its translucent uniformity and pure emptiness never had a beginning, it never has an end. This is why principle and material force are utterly mysterious. If scholars could apply themselves and reach this point, they would for the first time fully perceive the incompletely transmitted subtle meaning of the thousand sages. Though the material force of a piece of incense or a candle seems to disintegrate before our eyes, its remaining material force in the end never disintegrates. How could one speak of complete annihilation? MK

Yi Ŏnjŏk (1491–1553)

Neo-Confucian thought, however speculative it may sound, had as its essential rationale the grounding of a practical system of moral and spiritual self-cultivation. In the early Chosŏn dynasty, however, development was not necessarily even; before a common and "orthodox" consensus on the interpretation of basic concepts was formed, there was room for a misconstruing of certain ideas in a way that led in the direction of quietistic Buddhist forms of self-cultivation. Neo-Confucians spoke of the mind as having two basic conditions: that of being active and that of being quiescent. Self-cultivation addressed to the latter condition amounted to a kind of meditation practice often referred to as "quiet sitting." This condition, understood as the mind-and-heart being in serene union with the Supreme Ultimate or the Tao, the inner nature of all things, could easily be construed as superior to the active involvements of everyday life.

One must understand that the "Supreme Ultimate" or "Tao" in the Neo-Confucian context refers to the fundamental inner pattern that existed precisely as a guide to inform and direct *activity*. When the full purport of the theoretical framework is grasped, it is clear that there is no place for meditative quiet to become an end in itself or to be given preference over active moral cultivation. A famous series of letters by Yi Ŏnjŏk to Cho Hanbo (Manggidang) attacked his quietistic orientation and explained the orthodox meaning of "the Supreme Ultimate and Ultimateless." These letters mark the coming to maturity of Chosŏn Neo-Confucianism in these matters. MK

Third Letter to Manggidang
[From *Hoejae chip* 5:17b–19b]

Although your letter says you have not been mired in theories regarding trance for years, it seems that your old habituation in these matters has not yet been put off. Therefore your discussion is excessive regarding the most extreme and mysterious aspects of moral principle, but it is deficient when it comes to the essential practice of thoroughly embodying the Tao in personal conduct. You present vast and empty themes that have nothing to do with practical down-to-earth lessons in what is proper. This I cannot bring myself to accept.

I have heard that Master Chu Hsi has said: "The Tao is the principles or patterns we should follow in dealing with everyday affairs; these are all present in our mind-and-heart as the characteristics of our nature. There is no creature that does not have this pattern and no time when it is not so."[5] From ancient times to the present the discussion of the substance of the Tao comes to this, and it cannot be more perfectly presented.

I would like to explicate this a bit further. The Tao in its Great Origin proceeds from heaven and spreads to the Three Ultimates, heaven, earth, and man. In all the universe there is nowhere one can go where there is no ongoing activity of this Tao; there is not a creature that does not embody this Tao. As for the form it takes in man, the greater elements are the primary relationships between ruler and subject, father and son, husband and wife, elder and younger; the lesser elements are the appropriate measure regarding activity and quiet, food and rest, coming forward to serve in office or retiring, rising and declining. This goes to the extent that each case of speaking or keeping silent, each frown or smile, has its own proper norm. One cannot part from it for the slightest moment or deviate from it by a hair's breadth. There is nothing that is not the wondrousness of this principle. . . .

If one sees it as diversified in its varied functioning, it seems so complexly and minutely divided that one could hardly grasp its essential points; it has such myriad forms and types that it seems one could never make a unity. Nevertheless the original substance by which this is so is nothing but the undivided Heavenly Mandate, which constitutes our nature and is present in our mind-and-heart. When the feelings of joy and anger, sorrow and pleasure, have not yet been aroused, the perfect genuineness of our mind-and-heart is quiet and unmoved: this is what is described as the wonder of the Ultimateless (or "Ultimate of Nonbeing"), and the Great Foundation of the universe consists in this. Therefore one should always apply oneself to preserving and nurturing it so that the Great Foundation may be established and serve as the master of our interaction with others and the myriad changing developments of life. Then what issues from the aroused mind-and-heart will be perfectly measured, and one will have attained to being right whenever one acts.

Nevertheless at the moment of the subtle incipient activation of the mind-and-heart there is the conflict of heavenly principle and selfish human desire, and a hair's breadth of carelessness interrupting the process may result in an error of a thousand miles. At this point one must bring even greater mindfulness and caution to bear! . . . In the terms Chang Nan-hsien [1133–1180] used to describe this, one must preserve one's inborn good nature in quiescence in order to nurture the foundation of activity; one must exercise discernment in activity so that it will manifest what was preserved in quiescence; only then will nothing escape.

If one deals with things in this way, there will not be the slightest interruption in the constant clarity of the mind-and-heart, and it will not be beclouded by selfish desire for things. Then the establishment of the Great Foundation will daily become more firm, and, furthermore, at the subtle incipience of interaction in response to things there will not be a bit of selfish desire mixed in. As a result, one's response will be a pure manifestation of moral principle. From one's individual mind-and-heart and one's own person to the handling of the countless affairs and things of the world, there will be nothing inappropriate and in carrying out one's activities there will never be a transgression. . . .

In your letter . . . there are certainly elements that deal with the practice of self-cultivation in times of quiet. But if you set aside the need to devote oneself to study and leave out the practice of personally experiencing what is meant by moral principle and exercising discernment and reflection, then that amounts to not treating the matter of the practice of self-cultivation in one's activity. Therefore your description of how to apply oneself to the pursuit of the Tao is grand and distant, not concrete and real, and inevitably slips into theories of empty void such as are found in heretical schools. MK

Yi Hwang (1501–1570)

The Four-Seven Debate is easily the most famous philosophical controversy in Korea's history. In many respects it set a distinctive agenda for the following centuries of Neo-Confucian thinkers on the peninsula. The first round of the debate took place from 1559 to 1566 in lengthy letters between Yi Hwang (T'oegye) and his young friend Ki Taesŭng (Kobong). Then in the next generation the position finally abandoned by Ki was taken up by Yi I (Yulgok) and further developed in debate with his friend Sŏng Hon. Yi Hwang and Yi I, generally considered the two greatest thinkers of the Chosŏn dynasty, thus became the protagonists for opposing positions. Loyalties to these two and their contrasting orientations constituted the major intellectual divide through the remaining three centuries of the Chosŏn dynasty.

In Neo-Confucian thought, principle and material force describe not only the constitution of the universe but also the constitution of every individual being. Thus they also have an important role in describing the inner life of the psyche. Principle constitutes the inborn normative pattern of our nature, informing our activity as we respond to things around us. Material force concretizes, particularizes, energizes, and also, by its relative degree of purity or turbidity, limits or distorts the otherwise perfect goodness of our "original nature." Thus Neo-Confucians speak not only of our original nature (principle with its inherent perfection) but also of the "physical nature"—that is, principle as limited by the imperfection of the material force that constitutes our concrete psychophysical being.

Mencius, in discussing the goodness of human nature, mentions four feelings, the Four Beginnings, as the inherently good tendencies that constitute our nature. The *Doctrine of the Mean* mentions seven feelings[6] in a context that indicates they are sometimes good, sometimes evil. These are respectively the "four" and the "seven" of the Four-Seven Debate. Against the background of terminology differentiating original nature and physical nature in terms of principle and material force, the issue raised here is whether one can in a similar manner distinguish these two sets of feelings. Is the difference real or nominal? From the real composite of principle and material can there be a different way in which these feelings issue, or are all feelings absolutely identical? Do the Four Beginnings mentioned by Mencius (and hence the original nature) have a distinctive existential status?

The parallel debate over Mencius in China would be whether the human mind-and-heart is to be identified with principle or with principle and material force. This issue produced the major split of Chinese Neo-Confucian history—that between the "orthodox" school of Chu Hsi and the school of Wang Yang-ming. The Koreans, at a time when the Yang-ming school had grown to overshadow that of Chu Hsi in China, developed through the Four-Seven Debate an approach to the issue that was premised on the Chu Hsi position and posed the question on a new and more subtle level. This amounted to a bypass of the Wang Yang-ming position, which never established a significant following in Korea. The absence of Wang and the exclusive devotion to Chu Hsi are commonly considered distinctive characteristics of Korean Neo-Confucianism. It should also be evident, however, that to this distinctiveness one must also add the unique Korean development of the Mencian problem within the framework elaborated by Chu Hsi.

The document that really began the Four-Seven Debate in earnest was Yi Hwang's famous "twelve-paragraph letter." In correcting a work by another scholar, Yi had happened to state that "The Four Beginnings are the issuance of principle; the Seven Feelings are the issuance of material force." He amended this slightly in response to the objections of a young contemporary, Ki Taesŭng, but Ki only pressed further his critique of this distinction. Yi responded with this letter, the first full explication and argument for his position. MK

Twelve-Paragraph Letter
[From *Sa-ch'il i-ki wangbok sŏ* 1:3a–6b]

PARAGRAPH ONE

As for the argumentation regarding nature and feelings, the pronouncements and explanations of former Confucians have been precise. But when it comes to speaking of the Four Beginnings and the Seven Feelings, they only lump them together as "feelings"; I have not yet seen an explanation that differentiates them in terms of principle and material force.

PARAGRAPH TWO

Formerly, when Mr. Chŏng made his diagram, it included the thesis that the Four Beginnings issue from principle and the Seven Feelings from material force. My opinion was that the dichotomy was too stark and would lead to controversy. Therefore I emended the expressions "pure goodness," "combined with material force," and so on, for I wanted to support him in working it out clearly. It's not that I thought there was no problem in his expression.

PARAGRAPH FOUR

Indeed, the Four Beginnings are feelings, and the Seven Feelings are also feelings. Both are equally feelings, so why is there a distinct terminology of the Four and the Seven? The reason is what your letter describes as "the point of view from which they are spoken of being not the same." For principle and material force are fundamentally and mutually necessary as substance and are interdependent as function; there definitely can never be principle without material force or material force without principle. Nevertheless, if the perspective from which they are spoken of is not the same, then it is also true that one cannot but distinguish them. From ancient times sages and wise men have discussed them as two. How has it ever been necessary to fuse them together as a single thing and not speak of them as distinct?

PARAGRAPH FIVE

And if we were to discuss the matter in terms of just the single word *nature*, Tzu-ssu refers to the nature that is the Heavenly Mandate and Mencius refers to the nature that is the good nature.[7] To what, we may ask, do these two uses of the word "nature" refer? Could it be anything other than a matter of approaching the composite endowment of principle and material force and pointing to this as the aspect of principle in its original condition as endowed by heaven? Since the point of reference is principle, not material force, it therefore can be described as purely good and without evil—that is all. If due to the fact that principle and material force are inseparable one therefore wanted to include material force in the explanation, it would already be other than the nature's original condition.

Indeed, Tzu-ssu and Mencius have a penetrating view of the substance of the Tao in its integral wholeness, and they set up their propositions from that point of view; but that does not mean they are aware of just the one side and not the other. It is really due to the fact that if one speaks of the nature as mixed with material force, then one cannot see the original goodness of the nature. It was only in later times, after the appearance of the Ch'eng brothers, Chang Tsai, and other thinkers, that a thesis regarding the physical nature finally became unavoidable. That likewise was not just a case of creating differences out of a fondness for complexity. Since what they were referring to concerned the condition posterior to being endowed with material force and being born, then it was also not practicable to refer to it without distinguishing it from the original nature. Therefore I recklessly ventured that the distinction of the Four Beginnings and Seven Feelings in the case of the feelings was similar to the difference between the original nature and the physical nature in the case of the nature. If that is so, since it is considered permissible to distinguish between principle and material force in speaking of the nature, why should it suddenly become impermissible to distinguish between principle and material force when it comes to speaking of the feelings?

PARAGRAPH SIX

From whence do the feelings of commiseration, shame and dislike for evil, yielding and deference, and right and wrong issue? They issue from the nature which is comprised of humanity, righteousness, propriety, and wisdom. And from whence do feelings of joy, anger, sorrow, fear, love, hatred, and desire issue? They are occasioned by circumstantial conditions when external things contact one's form and cause an internal movement. As for the issuance of the Four Beginnings, since Mencius has already referred to them in terms of the mind-and-heart, and since the mind-and-heart is the combination of principle and material force, then why do we say that what is referred to in speaking of them has principle as its focus? That is because the nature comprised of humanity, righteousness, propriety, and wisdom exists in its pure condition within us, and these four are the commencements of its active manifestation. As for the issuance of the Seven Feelings, Master Chu says they originally have a standard of what they ought to be, so it's not that they are without principle. But then how is it that what is referred to in speaking of them is a matter of material force? When external things arrive, that which is most susceptible to stimulus and the first to move is our physical form, and the Seven Feelings are its outgrowth. It does not make sense to say that they are within us as pure principle but at the moment they issue they are mixed with material force, or that what is externally aroused is physical form but its issuance is the original substance of principle.

The Four Beginnings are all good. Therefore it is said, "Without these four dispositions, one is no longer human."[8] And it is also said, "As for the feelings, it is possible for them to be good."[9] In the case of the Seven Feelings, then, good and evil are not yet fixed. Therefore when we have them but are not able to exercise discernment, the mind-and-heart will not attain its proper condition. And only after they have issued with proper measure can they be called harmonious.

From this perspective, then, although neither of the two is separable from principle and material force, on the basis of their point of origin reference to each has its distinctive focus and emphasis. Thus, there is no reason why we cannot say the one is a matter of principle and the other a matter of material force.

I have carefully examined your letter. You have profound insight into the interdependence and inseparability of principle and material force and are very forceful in advocating this kind of explanation. Therefore you look to the fact that there never has been material force without principle or principle without material force and say that the Four Beginnings and Seven Feelings do not mean something different. Although this is almost correct, if you compare it with what the sages and worthies meant, I fear there is still some discrepancy. . . .

PARAGRAPH NINE

I beg leave to go over the matter using the words of the sages and worthies in order to clarify the essential truth of what I have been saying.

In antiquity, Confucius proposed that the continuation of the Tao in one's own person is good and that which fulfills the Tao is the nature,[10] and Master Chou had his thesis regarding the Ultimateless and the Supreme Ultimate. Both approach the interdependent pair, principle and material force, and single out and speak exclusively of principle. Confucius spoke of the nature by which human beings are similar at birth but become dissimilar through practice and habituation; Mencius spoke of the nature with respect to the ears, eyes, mouth, and nose.[11] This is all a matter of approaching principle and

material force in their mutual complementarity and selectively referring only to the material force aspect. How are these four cases anything but a matter of approaching what is similar and understanding
that there are also differences?

In Tzu-ssu's discussion of equilibrium and harmony, he mentioned
pleasure, anger, sorrow, and joy but did not mention the Four Beginnings; in Master Ch'eng's *Treatise on What Yen Hui Loved to Learn,* he
mentioned pleasure, anger, sorrow, fear, love, dislike, and desire but
did not mention the Four Beginnings.[12] These approach principle and
material force in their interdependence and speak without discriminating between them. Are not these two cases a matter of approaching
what is different and seeing that there are similarities?

PARAGRAPH TEN

But now your approach to the argument is quite different from
this. You like sameness and hate difference; you take pleasure in the
undifferentiated whole and dislike analytical distinctions. You do not
seek the point of origin of the Four Beginnings and Seven Feelings;
rather, you generalize in terms of their combining principle and material force and including both good and evil with a strong conviction
that speaking of them in a differential mode is not permissible. In the
course of your argument, although you say that principle is weak and
material force strong, that principle has no concrete sign but material
force is physically in evidence, when it comes to the conclusion, you
regard the natural manifestation of material force as the fundamental
substance of principle. If one follows this line of thought, it leads to
thinking of principle and material force as one thing with nothing that
distinguishes them. Recently Lo Cheng-an has advanced the thesis
that principle and material force are not two things and has gone so
far as to consider Master Chu's explanation as wrong. Being a common sort of person, I have not yet been able to understand what he is
getting at (not to say that the intent of your letter seems similar).

PARAGRAPH ELEVEN

And after your letter has already said that Tzu-ssu and Mencius
do not speak from the same point of view, and further that you
consider the Four Beginnings as singled out from the other feelings,
then on the contrary you say that the Four Beginnings and Seven

Feelings have different referents. Is this not close to contradicting oneself? Indeed, to pursue learning while disliking distinctions and concentrating on explanations that fit everything into a unity was characterized by the ancients as "a hawk gobbling dates whole"; this approach is highly problematic. And if one goes on like this, without even being aware of it, one may ineluctably slip into the abuse of discussing the nature in terms of material force and fall into the calamity of thinking of human desires as heavenly principle. How could this be allowed!

PARAGRAPH TWELVE

When I received your letter, I wanted to express my thoughts, foolish though they are, but I could not venture to view my opinion as necessarily correct and beyond question, and so for a long time I have not put it forth. But recently I have found a passage in the *Chu Tzu yü-lei,* the last section of his discussion of Mencius' Four Beginnings, that directly discusses this matter. His explanation is as follows: "The Four Beginnings, these are the issuance of principle; the Seven Feelings, these are the issuance of material force."[13] Have not the ancients said, "Do not venture to confide in yourself, but confide in your teacher"? Master Chu is the one I take as my teacher, and likewise he has been revered as teacher by sages past and present throughout the world. Having obtained his explanation, I can finally have confidence that my own ignorant opinion did not involve any great misunderstanding; and Chŏng's initial explanation likewise had no problem and seems not to need revision. And so I have ventured to give this rough description of my notions in order to request your instruction on the matter. What do you think? If one considers that although the thrust is as stated, when it comes to the verbal expression there might be an imprecision that departs from the truth. Then wouldn't it be better to use the old explanations of former Confucians? If so, I suggest that we substitute Master Chu's original explanation and remove ours; then everything would be proper. What do you think? MK

The Four-Seven Debate

The pivotal point of the Four-Seven Debate involved a basic distinction in the way the two sets of feelings arise, a matter Yi Hwang introduced especially in the sixth paragraph of his *Twelve-Paragraph Letter*. The following selection is composed of passages that argue this matter, excerpted from the exchange of correspondence between Ki Taesŭng and Yi Hwang. In the course of this exchange Yi Hwang hit upon the formula that became the hallmark of his thought: "In the case of the Four Beginnings, principle issues them and material force follows it; in the case of the Seven Feelings, material force issues them and principle mounts it." MK

Ki Taesŭng: Response to the Sixth Paragraph
[From *Sa-ch'il i-ki wangbok sŏ* 1:14a–18b]

GENERAL RESPONSE

I would suggest that these paragraphs are a superb discussion of the character of the Four Beginnings and Seven Feelings. Truly this is the most important part of the entire treatise. However, since it draws too sharp a distinction between principle and material force, what is spoken of as a matter of material force is no longer referred to in terms of the mixture of principle and material force but rather refers exclusively to material force. As a result the whole thesis inclines to one side. Now I beg your leave to first discuss the fact that the Seven Feelings are not exclusively a matter of material force; after that we can try to comprehend the matter paragraph by paragraph.

The *Doctrine of the Mean* remarks: "Before the feelings of pleasure, anger, sorrow, and joy are aroused, it is called equilibrium. When these feelings are aroused and each and all attain perfect measure, it is called harmony. Equilibrium is the great foundation of the world; harmony is its universal path."[14]

Master Chu's *Commentary* says: "Pleasure, anger, sorrow, and joy are feelings. The condition before they are aroused is the nature. Since one's nature is not leaning toward one side, it is called 'equilibrium.' When feelings are aroused and each and every one attains perfect measure, that is the proper condition of the feelings; since there is neither excessiveness nor deviation, it is called 'harmony.' The 'great foundation' refers to the nature as conferred by heaven. All the world's principles derive from this; it is the substance of the Way. The 'universal path' refers to that which follows the nature, insofar as it is what all under heaven past and present follow; it is the function of the Way. This refers to the proper character of the nature and the feelings in order to elucidate the meaning of the statement that we cannot (for a moment) separate from the Way.''

The *Questions On the Doctrine of the Mean* comments: ''Actually the myriad principles are all inherent in the nature conferred by heaven. Pleasure, anger, sorrow, and joy, each has its proper place. Before they are aroused, they reside within in an undifferentiated manner. Since there is no one-sidedness or deviation, it is called 'equilibrium.' When they are aroused and assume their proper place, since there is no excessiveness or deviation, it is called 'harmony.' It is called 'equilibrium' to signify the proper character of the nature, the substance of the Way. Since it embraces all the principles of heaven and earth and all creatures, it is called 'the great foundation of the world.' It is called 'harmony' to manifest the proper condition of the feelings, the function of the Way. Since it is what people and things past and present all follow, it is called 'the universal path of the world.' Indeed, the nature conferred by heaven is perfectly genuine and supremely good, and that which is inherent in the human mind-and-heart in terms of the completeness of its substance and function in all cases is originally like this. Sageliness and stupidity neither add to nor subtract from this.''[15]

In the miscellaneous commentaries of the *Chang-chü,* there is a passage of Mr. Li of Yen-p'ing [Li T'ung, 1088–1158] that says: ''The condition before one is aroused is called 'equilibrium.' It is the nature. When the feelings are aroused and are perfectly measured, it is called 'harmony.' If they do not attain perfect measure, then there is disharmony. The difference between harmony and disharmony is perceived only after the mind is aroused; this is a matter of the feelings, not the nature. This is the reason why Mencius says the nature is good and also says the feelings 'can become good.' This theory originated with Tzu-ssu.''[16]

In my humble opinion, . . . if we thoroughly understand it from this perspective, then it is conclusive that what is called the Seven Feelings does not refer exclusively to material force. Furthermore, Ch'eng I-ch'uan's *Treatise on What Yen Hui Loved to Learn* and Master Chu's treatise on ''Activity and Tranquility in the *Record of Music*'' tally well with the precept of the *Doctrine of the Mean*. Indeed, since Tzu-ssu transmitted and established the discourse to elucidate the proper character of the nature and the feelings, how could it involve any inadequacy? And since the discussion of Masters I-ch'uan, Yen-p'ing, and Hui-an are all like this, then where is the room for later scholars such as us to come up with different ideas?

That being the case, do not the Seven Feelings, combine principle and material force and involve both good and evil? And are not the Four Beginnings those of the Seven Feelings that are in accord with principle and are good? If this is so, then the desire to separate the Four Beginnings and the Seven Feelings as belonging respectively to principle and material force, without any interaction between them, can well be said to be one-sided.

RESPONSE TO SPECIFIC ITEMS

[1] Your argument states: Commiseration, shame and dislike . . . are the nature.

My humble position is: The Four Beginnings certainly issue from the nature comprised of humanity, righteousness, propriety, and wisdom, but the Seven Feelings also issue from the nature comprised of humanity, righteousness, propriety, and wisdom. Otherwise why did Master Chu say that pleasure, anger, sorrow, and joy are feelings and that the state before they are aroused is the nature? Furthermore, why did he say that feelings are the issuance of the nature?

[2] Your argument states: Pleasure, anger, sorrow, and joy . . . emerge occasioned by circumstantial conditions when external things contact one's form and cause an internal movement.

My humble position is: The sentence "External things contact the form and cause an internal movement" comes from the *Treatise on What Yen Hui Loved to Learn*. If we examine the original text, however, it says: "As the form has already been engendered, when external things touch the form, they cause a movement internally. When there is an internal movement, the Seven Feelings emerge."[17] When it says "cause a movement internally," and then says "there is an internal movement," it is referring to the arousing of the mind-and-heart. When the mind-and-heart is aroused, the desires of the nature emerge; these are what we call feelings. This being the case, when feelings appear externally, they may seem to be occasioned by circumstantial conditions, but in fact they issue from within.

[3] Your argument states: As for the issuance of the Four Beginnings . . . it is the commencement of the active manifestation of the nature.

My humble position is: Both the Four Beginnings and the Seven Feelings issue from the mind-and-heart. Since the mind-and-heart is a conjunction of principle and material force, feelings certainly combine both principle and material force. It is not the case that there is a particular distinctive kind of feelings that issue only from principle and not from material force. This point truly calls for one to distinguish the true from the false.

[4] Your argument states: As for the issuance of the Seven Feelings . . . it is the outgrowth of physical form.

My humble position is: *The Record of Music* states: "Humans are born quiet; this is the nature conferred by heaven. When it is stirred by things and moves, these are the desires of the nature." Master Chu says: "The desires of the nature are what we call feelings."[18] This being the case, feelings being stirred by things and moving is a natural principle. For it is due to the fact that there really is a given principle within that there is a match with the stimulus given externally. It is not that there is originally no such principle within, but upon the approach of an external thing, there is a fortuitous match, and the mind-and-heart is aroused and moves.

Since this is so, I am afraid that the sentence, "When external things approach, that which is most susceptible to stimulus and the first to move is our physical form," does not express anything unique to the Seven Feelings. If we are to discuss the matter in terms of being aroused by things and then moving, the Four Beginnings are exactly the same. When the stimulus is a child about to fall into a well, the principle of humanity automatically responds, and the disposition of commiseration is thereby formed. When the stimulus is passing by a shrine or the court, the principle of propriety automatically responds, and a disposition of reverence is thereby formed. In being aroused by things these are no different from the Seven Feelings.

[5] Your argument states: It does not make sense to say that the Seven Feelings are within us . . . the original substance of principle.

My humble position is: When it is within, it is definitely pure heavenly principle. But at the time it can only be called the nature; it cannot be called the feelings. But the moment it is aroused, it becomes feelings, with the differentiation of harmonious and unharmonious. For in the not-yet-aroused state it is exclusively principle, but when it is aroused, it mounts material force to be active. Master Chu's treatise "On Origination, Flourishing, Benefiting, and Firmness" states: "Origination, flourishing, benefiting, and firmness are nature; production, growth, harvest, and storage are the feelings."[19] And again he says: "Humanity, righteousness, propriety, and wisdom are the nature; commiseration, shame and dislike for evil, deference and compliance, and the sense of right and wrong are feelings."[20] Indeed, in his treating production, growth, harvest, and storage as feelings we can see the fact of mounting on material force to be active, and so the Four Beginnings are likewise a matter of material force. It is also stated in Master Chu's answers to his students that commiseration is material force, but that whereby we are capable of commiserating in such a way is principle. This statement is particularly clear, but it refers to the case of the feelings' issuance when material force is compliant; it does not involve the element of error from the turbulence and confusion due to imperfect material force.

In your letter you characterize the Seven Feelings as emerging from circumstantial conditions and being aroused by our physical form. I feel uneasy about these assertions. And I find your reference to the Seven Feelings as being externally stimulated by physical form (and hence not the original substance of principle) particularly unacceptable. In that case the Seven Feelings would be something external to the nature, and Tzu-ssu's reference to them as harmonious would be wrong. But there is something even more out of line. Mencius' feeling of pleasure to the extent that he could not fall asleep was indeed pleasure.[21] Shun's punishment of the four criminals was anger.[22] Confucius' mourning cry was sorrow. When Min-tzu, Tzu-lu, Jan-yu, and Tzu-kung were in attendance upon him and the master was joyous, that was indeed joy.[23] How could these cases not be the original substance of principle? And if one examines the cases of ordinary people, there are also times when heavenly principle is manifest. For instance, when they see their parents and relatives, they spontaneously feel joyful; when they see death, mourning, sickness, and pain, they suddenly feel sad. How can this not be a matter of the original substance of principle? If these cases are all the effects of physical form, then physical form does not have anything to do with the nature or the feelings. Could that be possible?

[6] Your argument states: The Four Beginnings are all good. . . .

My humble opinion is: This is precisely what Master Yen-p'ing referred to when he said the Mencian theory originated from Tzu-ssu.

[7] Your argument states: As for the Seven Feelings, good and evil are not fixed. . . . After they issue and are perfectly measured, they may be called harmonious.

My humble opinion is: Master Ch'eng says, "Before pleasure, anger, sorrow, and joy are aroused, how could they not be good? After they are aroused and have attained perfect measure, in every respect they are nothing but good."[24] Therefore the Four Beginnings are certainly all good, and the Seven Feelings are also all good. Only if they fail to attain due measure after they have been aroused will they lean toward one side and become evil. How could it be said that good and evil are not yet fixed?

Now if you say that "Good and evil are not yet determined," and further say that "When we have them but are not able to exercise proper discernment, then the mind-and-heart will not attain its proper condition, and only after they have issued with proper measure can they be called harmonious," then this makes the Seven Feelings quite superfluous and useless. And what's more, when they have issued but not yet attained perfect measure, what are you going to term them?

And the words "When you have them but are not able to exercise discernment" come from Master Chu's *Commentary on the Great Learning,* chapter 7. Its meaning is that as for the four feelings, anger, fear, pleasure, and worry, they should just arise anew each time; they may not have a prior fixed place in the mind-and-heart. In the *Questions on the Great Learning* it says: "Joy and anger, worry and fear, are responses to stimuli. Beauty or filthiness, bending down or looking up, are based upon things' physical endowments and are functions of the mind. How could there just be some that do not come out correctly? Only in the occurrence of affairs, if there are matters concerning which one does not exercise proper discernment, then it may be impossible to avoid making mistakes in one's response to them or getting swept away by them. Then as for joy and anger, worry and fear, there must first be a movement internally, and then there may be cases in which they do not attain their correct proportions, that is all."[25] This is a matter that pertains to the rectification of the mind-and-heart; quoting it as evidence with regard to the Seven Feelings is a different matter.

Indeed, having repeatedly analyzed the explanations in your letter —not only in respect to precision but also when one checks it against what the sages and worthies meant—if the differences are like this, then as for the statement "Based on its point of origin the referent of each has a particular focus and emphasis," although there seems to be room for doubt, I suspect that it is in fact completely inappropriate.

That being the case, then as for the statements that the Four Beginnings are a matter of principle and the Seven Feelings are a matter of material force, how can we just say that they involve nothing impermissible? What's more, this argument is not just a matter of impermissible terminology. Rather, I suspect that with regard to the real character of the nature and the feelings and the practical application to preserving one's inborn good dispositions and exercising reflection in activity, in all these respects it has impermissible implications. What do you think about it? MK

Yi Hwang's Response: Items of Partial Disagreement
[From *Sa-ch'il i-ki wangbok sŏ* 1:39b–41b]

Your first argument states: The Seven Feelings also issue from humanity, righteousness, propriety, and wisdom.

I would say: This is what I have called approaching what is different and seeing the similarity; in such a case the two can of course be talked about in an undifferentiated manner. But we cannot say that there is only similarity without any difference.

Your third argument states: It is not the case that there is a particular distinctive kind of feelings that only issue from principle and not from material force.

I would say: The issuance of the Four Beginnings is of course not without the involvement of material force. But what Mencius was referring to, in fact, was not the aspect of their issuance by material force. If we say a reference to material force is included, then already it is no longer a description of the Four Beginnings. And furthermore, how could you go on elsewhere in your argument to say that the statement that the Four Beginnings are the issuance of principle should not be changed?

Your fourth argument states: It is not that there is no such principle within, but a fortuitous stimulus from external things arouses the mind-and-heart to activity. And the Four Beginnings are also like the Seven Feelings with respect to how they are aroused.

I would say: This theory is of course correct. But in this paragraph the passages you quote from the *Record of Music* and the sayings of Master Chu are all in what may be described as an undifferentiated manner of discourse. If from this perspective we attack a mode of discourse that makes analytical distinctions, there will be no need to worry about a lack of ammunition! Nevertheless the mode of discourse that makes analytical distinctions is not something I have personally invented out of thin air. The world has had such a principle from the very beginning and the ancients originally had explanations of this sort. Now if we insist upon holding onto one at the expense of the other, would it not be one-sided?

From the perspective of the undifferentiated manner of discourse, the Seven Feelings combine both principle and material force. This is clear enough without wasting too many words. But if we contrast the Seven Feelings with the Four Beginnings and discuss each in terms of its distinctive characteristics, the Seven Feelings are related to material force in the way the Four Beginnings are related to principle. Each of their issuances has its own systematic connections, and each of their names has its particular point of reference. Therefore we can follow their focal points and categorize them separately, that is all. I have never said that the Seven Feelings have nothing to do with principle or that they are aroused according to a fortuitous encounter with external things. And the Four Beginnings are certainly no different from the Seven Feelings with respect to being stimulated by things and then moving. It is only that in the case of the Four Beginnings principle issues them and material force follows it, while in the case of the Seven Feelings material force issues them and principle mounts it.

Your fifth argument states: When it is aroused, it mounts material force to be active. . . . The Four Beginnings are likewise a matter of material force.

I would say: The Four Beginnings are also a matter of material force. You have time and again stressed this point and now you have further cited Master Chu's responses to his students' queries; this matter is abundantly clear. But do you think that the point of Mencius in explaining the Four Beginnings was likewise their issuance by material force? If it is perceived as material force, then in the expressions "the beginning of humanity," "the beginning of righteousness," "the beginning of propriety," and "the beginning of wisdom,"[26] how are we to take the four words, "humanity," "righteousness," "propriety," and "wisdom?" If there is even the slightest admixture of material force, what we have is no longer the original condition of genuine heavenly principle. If they are seen as genuine heavenly principle, then the beginnings that issue from them are definitely not like things compounded of a mixture of water and mud.

In your opinion humanity, righteousness, propriety, and wisdom are terms that apply to the not-yet-aroused condition, and therefore they are genuine principle. The Four Beginnings are terms that apply to the condition after the feelings are aroused; without material force they could not be active, therefore they are also a matter of material force. In my humble opinion, even though we say that the Four Beginnings mount material force, the point Mencius was making was not their mounting material force, but only their issuance by genuine principle. Therefore he spoke of the beginning of humanity and the beginning of righteousness, and later wise men likewise spoke of this as "singling out the good side."

If we insist that the Tao must include material force, the moment we speak of it in that way we are already wading in muddy water and all these passages that have been cited will be irrelevant. The ancients used the analogy of a man going and coming mounted on horseback for the way principle mounts material force in order to be active; this was indeed appropriate. Without the horse, the man cannot go and come; without the man, the horse will miss the way. Man and horse are interdependent and inseparable. People have various perspectives in discussing this situation. Some refer to it in a general way and speak of the traveling; in this case both the man and the horse are implicated. This is like speaking of the Four and the Seven in an undifferentiated manner. Others refer to the man traveling; in this case it is not necessary to refer likewise to the horse, but the horse's traveling is implied. This is like the Four Beginnings. Others might refer to the horse's traveling; in that case it is not necessary to refer likewise to the man, but the man's traveling is implied. This is like the Seven Feelings.

Now, having seen that I talk about the Four and the Seven separately, you time and again attack my position from the perspective of those who talk about them in an undifferentiated manner. This is like hearing someone talking about a man traveling or a horse traveling and emphatically asserting that the man and horse are a unity, so one cannot speak of them separately. When you see me talk about the Seven Feelings from the perspective of the issuance of material force, you emphatically assert that they are also the issuance of principle. This is like hearing someone speak of a horse traveling and insisting he must mention the man traveling. When you see me speak of the Four Beginnings from the perspective of the issuance of principle, then again you emphatically assert their issuance by material force. This is like hearing someone speak of a man traveling and insisting he must mention the horse traveling. This is precisely what Master Chu described as playing a game of hide and seek.

What do you think about this? MK

Yi Hwang's Response: Items of Complete Disagreement
[From *Sa-ch'il i-ki wangbok sŏ* 1:43b–45b]

Your fifth argument states that my letter describing the Seven Feelings as being externally stimulated by physical form (and hence not the original substance of principle) is particularly unacceptable. In that case the Seven Feelings would be something external to the nature. . . . Mencius' feeling of pleasure to the extent that he could not fall asleep . . . was this not the original substance of principle?

I would say: At first I erroneously said, "How could it be that what is externally aroused is physical form but its issuance is the original substance of principle?" What I meant was: How could it be reasonable that when they are aroused, it is a matter of material force, but when it comes to their issuance, it is a matter of principle? But since I felt that the expression was not crystal clear, I have already changed it.

Now in your letter the text of my remarks is changed to state directly: "The Seven Feelings are externally stimulated by physical form (and hence are not the original substance of principle)." That is a far cry from my original intention. And this is followed directly by your indictment: "In that case the Seven Feelings would be something external to the nature." Then do you mean that when Master Chu said, "As for the Seven Feelings, they are the issuance of material force,"[27] he likewise meant the Seven Feelings are something outside the nature? Generally speaking, there are cases where principle issues and material force follows, so these can be spoken of as focusing on principle, that is all; but this does not mean that principle is external to material force. These are the Four Beginnings. There are cases in which material force issues and principle mounts it, so one may speak of them as focusing on material force; but this does not mean that material force is external to principle. These are the Seven Feelings.

The pleasure of Mencius, the anger of Shun, the sorrow and joy of Confucius, these are the issuances of material force in compliance with principle. There is not even an iota of obstruction; therefore the original substance of principle is in a condition of undifferentiated wholeness. The cases of ordinary people being pleased when they see their parents or being sad when they are in mourning is also the issuance of material force in compliance with principle. But because of irregularities in the material force of ordinary people, the original substance of principle cannot be in its genuine and integral condition.

If we discuss the question from this angle, even though we take the Seven Feelings as the issuance of material force, what problem will there be as regards the original substance of principle? Furthermore, how will there be anything to worry about regarding there being no connection between physical form on the one hand and the feelings and nature on the other?

Your fifth argument says: "Your letter states: 'When we have such feelings but are not able to exercise discernment, then the mind-and-heart does not attain its proper condition, and only after it has issued with perfect measure can it be called harmonious,' then this makes the Seven Feelings quite superfluous and useless. And on the contrary they are something that may harm the mind-and-heart."

I would say that in regard to this matter the words and intent of my previous explanation missed the proper context and therefore were problematic. Now I have amended this. I am indebted to you.

But your letter also objects to the "When we have such feelings but are not able to exercise discernment" passage on the grounds that it is a matter pertaining to the rectification of the mind-and-heart, and quoting it as evidence regarding the Seven Feelings is a quite different matter. This seems to be the case, but in fact it is not so. For although this passage belongs to the chapter on the rectification of the mind-and-heart, this one sentence to the effect that joy and anger, worry and fear, may not be permitted a fixed place in the mind-and-heart is an explanation of the problem of the mind-and-heart, that is all. It has not yet addressed the question of rectifying the mind-and-heart.

Indeed, the reason these four easily become harmful to the mind-and-heart is really that the feelings issued by preconditioned material force, although they are originally good, easily slip toward evil, and thus it is so, that is all. As for the Four Beginnings, which are the issuance of principle, how has there ever been this kind of problem?

Moreover, how can you say that the mind-and-heart might have something about which it commiserates, but yet not attain its proper condition, or the mind-and-heart might have something about which it feels shame and dislike, but yet not attain its proper condition? Ch'eng Hao's *Letter on Calming Human Nature* says: "As for that in the human mind-and-heart which is easily aroused but difficult to control, anger is the most extreme. But at a time when one might be angered, one can just forget the anger and reasonably consider the right and wrong of the case; so one can also see that external temptations need not be hated."[28]

Now consider what is referred to as "easily aroused and difficult to control." Would that be principle, or would it be material force? If it were principle, why would it be difficult to control? It is material force; therefore it gallops fast and is difficult to restrain, that is all. Moreover, if anger were the issuance of principle, then how would you have what was said about forgetting anger and considering principle instead? But because it is the issuance of material force he spoke of forgetting anger and considering principle instead. This is what is meant by reining in material force with principle. If this is so, then as for my quoting this passage as evidence that the Seven Feelings belong to the material force category, in which way is it not pertinent?

In the last paragraph of the same section, you discuss the mistake of my theory that, based on their point of origin, the Four Beginnings and the Seven Feelings each have a particular focus or emphasis. And you further say that this argument is not just a matter of impermissible terminology. Rather, you suspect that with respect to the real character of the nature and the feelings and the practical application to preserving one's inborn good dispositions and exercising reflection in activity, in all these respects it has impermissible implications.

I would say: The thesis regarding the point of origin and particular focus can be clarified through the whole context of our debate and needs no further discussion here. As for the questionable points regarding terminology or the real character of the nature and the feelings, where there was the least bit of uneasiness on my part, I have already carefully corrected it due in part to your instruction and in part to my own realization. Seeing that the problematic points have been eliminated, its meaning is luminously transparent and clearly manifest, like open windows in all directions or the ringing of jade. It comes close to avoiding the problem of lumping things together. As for the application to preserving one's inborn good dispositions and exercising reflection in activity, although I cannot venture to be presumptuous about it, I suspect there is nothing that goes so far as to be seriously unacceptable. MK

Ki Taesŭng's Response
[From *Sa-ch'il i-ki wangbok sŏ* 2:9a and 11a]

Comment: Because the expressions in your letter exaggerated certain points, originally I responded superficially in order to clarify that material force is not absent in the Four Beginnings. I did not intend to say that what Mencius was referring to included material force. My explanation definitely did state that at the moment of the nature's issuance as feelings, if material force does not take over, the original goodness of the nature can be directly fulfilled. This truly is what Mencius refers to as the Four Beginnings. For although what are called the Four Beginnings cannot be said to not have material force, at the moment of their manifestation the original substance of heavenly principle genuinely presents and reveals itself without a trace of deficiency; it seems like something devoid of material force. It might be compared with the moon reflected in a pure lake: since the water is especially clear and transparent, the moonlight seems even more brilliant, and the surface and the interior are totally translucent, as if there were no water. Therefore we can say that they are issued forth by principle. We may take a perspective that includes material force, but is that the point Mencius meant to convey?

As for the playing hide and seek that you criticize, although that certainly was not my original intention, my mode of expression does involve this problem. It is something I myself have constantly regretted, but I have not been able to avoid it. I sincerely hope that you, master, will continue to call my attention to it so that I may be warned. . . .

Comment: What I reported as the theory you expressed in your letter was not without inaccuracies. And the statement that there were unacceptable implications regarding the application to preserving the mind's good dispositions and exercising reflection in activity was a casual and reckless expression. I certainly should be concerned about it. But at the time I resorted to such an expression I did have something to call attention to. Now perusing the items of your letter, I see among them that my theses regarding the Seven Feelings' not being exclusively a matter of material force, and regarding good and evil's being not yet determined, have undeservingly met with your approval, and you have also already amended the first letter. Thus my wild and groundless remarks of the previous day have become pointless. There is no need to pursue the matter further. I humbly present this for your lofty scrutiny. MK

Yi I (1536–1584)

Yi I (Yulgok) rivals Yi Hwang for the position of foremost philosopher of the Chosŏn dynasty. He was a great statesman and theorist of government as well as a metaphysical thinker of rare perceptiveness and clarity. In the decade after Yi Hwang's death, Yi I resurrected the position finally abandoned by Ki Taesŭng in the Four-Seven Debate and further developed it in debate with his friend Sŏng Hon (1535–1598).

Yi Hwang and Ki Taesŭng had argued the question in terms of two sets of feelings: the purely good Four Beginnings and the sometimes good and sometimes evil Seven Feelings. In this selection Yi I refers instead to the "Tao Mind" and the "Human Mind," classical terms that likewise referred to normative and good inclinations versus those of a more dubious sort. The basic question—whether this differentiation is founded upon different modal relationships of principle and material force—remains the same, however. Readers may detect a number of further differences not only in the content but also in the character of the intellectuality and concerns of these two great thinkers. MK

Letter to Sŏng Hon
[From *Yulgok chŏnsŏ* 10:11a–18a]

There is a single thread running through both the explanation of principle and material force and the explanation of the Human Mind and the Tao Mind. If one has not comprehended the meaning of the Human Mind and the Tao Mind, it amounts to not comprehending principle and material force. If one has already clearly understood the inseparability of principle and material force, then one can extend that to an understanding of the fact that the Human Mind and Tao Mind do not have a twofold origin. Only if there is something not yet comprehended about the relationship between principle and material force might one perhaps regard them as separate, with each occupying its own distinct place. And thus one might also then question whether in the case of the Human Mind and the Tao Mind there might be two distinct origins. . . .

The treatment of your hesitations in my last letter was so precise in discernment and explication and the analogies so to the point that I would have thought one reading of it could bring agreement. But seeing that even then you still have doubts, it might be best to put the matter aside for a time and read extensively in the writings of the sages and worthies and wait for understanding to come later. I myself got a glimpse of this matter some ten years ago, and from then on, little by little, have thought it out. Every time I read the classics and the commentaries I always read one text in the light of the others. At first there were times when things did not fit together, but afterward they gradually fell into place, until now it had all coalesced and fit together with a decisiveness that is beyond doubt. A hundred thousand most eloquent speakers could not change my understanding. I only regret that my psychological endowment is so coarse that I have not been up to vigorously putting it into practice and making it a reality, for which I continually sigh and reproach myself.

Principle is above forms; material force is on the level of form. The two cannot be separated from each other. If they cannot be separated, then their issuance as function is single and one cannot speak of them as mutually possessing issuing functions. If one says they mutually possess issuing functions, that would mean that when principle issues as function, material force at times might not be right with it, or that when material force issues as function, there might be times when principle is not right with it. In that case the relation of principle and material force would admit of both separation and conjunction and prior and posterior. Activity and tranquility would have a commencement; yin and yang would have a beginning. The error in all this is indeed anything but small!

But principle is nonactive; rather it is material force that has concrete activity. Therefore in the case of feelings that emerge from the original nature and are not disrupted by our physical constitution, they are classed on the side of principle. Those that, although at the beginning emerging from the original nature, are then disrupted by the physical constitution are classed on the side of material force. One cannot get by without such propositions. That which accounts for the original goodness of man's nature is principle; but if it were not for material force, principle, being nonactive, would have no issuance. Then as for the Human Mind and the Tao Mind, are they not indeed both rooted in principle? It is not a matter of the outgrowth of the Human Mind already standing in contrast to principle in the mind-and-heart in the state before it is aroused. The wellspring is single but its outpouring is dual; how could Master Chu not have understood this! It's just that the kinds of expression used to clarify the matter for others all have their own particular focus.

Master Ch'eng said: "It's not correct that good and evil are in the nature as two contrasting items, each with its own emergence."[29] Indeed, good and evil are two distinct things; still there is no rationale whereby they stand in contrast in the mind and each emerge separately. How much more is this so in the case of principle and material force, which are inseparably intermixed. How could there be a rationale whereby they stand in contrast and mutually give issuance! If Master Chu actually thought that principle and material force have as function mutual issuances that could be contrasted with one another and each emerges on its own, then that would mean that Master Chu is also mistaken. But one who could make such an error could not be a Master Chu!

As for developing the terminology of "Human Mind" and "Tao Mind,"[30] how did the sage have any alternative? Principle in its original condition is definitely perfectly good, but it mounts material force to issue as function, and this is where good and evil diverge. If one only sees that it mounts material force and involves both good and evil and does not understand principle in its original condition, then that amounts to not knowing the Great Foundation. If one only sees principle's original condition and does not understand its mounting on material force to issue as function—a condition which may develop into evil—then that is like mistaking the bandit for a son. Therefore the sage was concerned about this matter and categorized the feelings that directly follow from our normative nature in its original conditions as the "Tao Mind" in order to get people to preserve, nurture, and develop it to the fullest extent. The feelings that are disrupted by the effects of our physical constitution and are unable to be the direct consequence of our normative nature in its original condition he categorized as the "Human Mind" in order to get people to examine the excess or deficiency involved in such feelings and moderate them accordingly.

That which moderates them is the Tao Mind. Indeed, concrete form is a part of the nature with which we are endowed by heaven. As for the Human Mind, how is it likewise not good? But its negative connotation is from its involving excess or deficiency and devolving into evil, that is all. If one is able to develop the Tao Mind to its fullest extent and moderate the Human Mind, making the proclivities that attend our physical constitution each follow its proper norm, then whether in activity or tranquility, speech or deeds, there will be nothing that is not of our normative nature in its original condition.

From ancient times this has been the main purport of the sages' and worthies' method of cultivating the mind-and-heart. But how is this in any way related to the theory of the mutual issuance of principle and material force? The problem with Yi Hwang is essentially a matter of just the two words "mutual issuance." How regrettable! Even with all the Old Master's subtlety and precision there was, as it were, a heavy membrane interposed with regard to the Great Foundation. . . .

As for something that cannot be separated from a vessel and has ceaseless activity, water is just the thing. Thus water is just the metaphor for principle. The original clarity of water is like the nature's original goodness. The difference between a clean and dirty vessel is like the differentiation of the physical nature. When the vessel moves, the water moves—which is like material force issuing and principle mounting it. The vessel and the water move together; there is no difference between the vessel moving and the water moving. Nor is there a difference in the issuance of material force and principle, as suggested by the mutual issuance theory. When the vessel moves, the water necessarily moves; the water never moves of itself. Principle is nonactive; it is material force that has activity.

The psychological endowment of a sage is perfectly pure, and his nature is in integral possession of its substance without a single bit of the self-centeredness of selfish human desires. As for the issuance of this nature, therefore, "he can follow his heart's desire without transgressing the norm,"[31] and the Human Mind is likewise the Tao Mind. It's like a perfectly clean vessel filled with water: since there is not a speck of dirt, when it moves and the originally clear water is poured out and flows forth, it remains entirely clear water.

As for the worthy, although his psychophysical endowment is pure, it has not escaped a slight admixture of turbidity. Therefore it must be supplemented by the application of further cultivation before it regains the full perfection of the original nature. As for its issuance, there is that which is the direct consequence of the original nature and is not disrupted by the physical constitution. There is also that which, although it issues from the nature, is also affected by the physical constitution; but although the physical constitution has some effect, the Human Mind submits to what is mandated by the Tao Mind. Therefore the appetites for food and sex also stay on the right track. It is like a vessel filled with water that is basically clean but has not escaped a slight bit of dirt inside: there must be further cleansing before the water regains its original clarity. As for its movement, therefore, sometimes there is clear water that pours out, and the dirt has not yet moved. There are other cases when although clean water comes out, the dirt has already been moved, and so the dirt must be stopped and not allowed to become mixed in, and then the outpouring water can keep its clarity.

One who has no semblance of his original perfection has a psychophysical endowment that has a lot of the turbid and little of the clear in it, much that is impure and little that is pure. The original condition of the nature is overwhelmed, and, moreover, there is no application made to cultivate and perfect it. What issues forth in such a case is for the most part due to the physical constitution; here the Human Mind is in control. Intermittently the Tao Mind emerges mixed in with the Human Mind, but the person does not know how to discern and preserve it, so he consistently gives himself over to the self-centered proclivity of his physical constitution.

When this reaches the point of one's being conquered by the feelings, concupiscence burns hotly, and the Tao Mind is reduced to the Human Mind. It is like an unclean, filthy vessel filled with water: the muddy water has lost its original clarity, and there is moreover no effort to cleanse it. As for its movement, muddy, roiled water comes forth, and one sees no evidence of its having been clean water. There are occasions when the mud has not yet been roiled up and suddenly clear water comes out for a moment, but in the blink of an eye the mud is again roiled up so what was clear again becomes turbid, and what flows forth is all dirty water.

The nature is originally good, but due to influence of the imperfect psychophysical endowment at times it devolves into evil. To regard evil as not the original condition of the nature is permissible; to say that it is not based on the nature is impermissible. The water is originally clear, but due to the roiling up of the mud it ends as a turbid outflow. One may regard the turbidity as not the original condition of water, but one cannot say that the turbid outflow is not that of water.

The middle sort of person's nature falls between that of the worthy and the person who bears no semblance to his original condition. One can understand it by following it out along these lines.

Principle's inseparability from material force is really like the water's being inseparable from the vessel. Now if you would say they mutually have issuances as function, then that would mean that sometimes the vessel would move first and the water would follow and move, sometimes the water would move first and the vessel would follow and move. How in the world could there be a rationale for this!

And if one uses the metaphor of a man mounted on a horse, then the man is the nature and the horse is the psychophysical constitution. The horse's temperament may be docile and good or it may be unruly: this represents the differences of clarity and turbidity, purity and impurity, in the psychophysical endowment. When they go out the gate, sometimes the horse follows the will of the rider and goes out, sometimes the rider leaves it to the horse and goes out. When the horse follows the will of the rider and goes out, it is classed on the side of the man; that is the Tao Mind. When the man leaves it to the horse and goes out, it is classed on the side of the horse; that is the Human Mind. The road in front of the gate is the road of things and affairs as it ought to be traversed. When the rider has mounted the horse but not yet gone out the gate, there is no commencement or sign of either the man leaving it to the horse or the horse following the will of the man: this is the same as there originally being no outgrowths of the Human Mind and the Tao Mind that stand in contrast to one another.

The vital forces of the sage are the same as those of other men: when they are hungry, they desire to eat; when thirsty, they wish to drink; when cold, they want clothing; when they itch, they want to scratch. They likewise are not free from such matters. Therefore the fact that even a sage must have the Human Mind is like the situation of having a horse that has a perfectly docile temperament: Will there not be times when the rider goes forth leaving it to the horse? But the horse is so submissive to the rider's will that it does not wait for the reins to control it but of itself follows the proper road. This is what is meant by the sage's "following the desires of his heart without transgressing the norm,"[32] and the Human Mind being also the Tao Mind.

In the case of ordinary persons, their psychophysical endowment is not perfectly pure, so when the issuance of the Human Mind is not controlled by the Tao Mind it devolves into evil. It is like the rider who goes forth leaving it to the horse and not using the reins for control, so the horse has its way and does not traverse the proper road.

In this line of comparison, there is the case of a horse of the most unruly temperament. Even though the rider tries to control it with the reins, it bucks continually and inevitably runs off into wild groves and thickets of thorns. This is the case of a turbid and impure psychophysical endowment in which the Human Mind is in control and the Tao Mind is covered over and obscured. When the temperament of the horse is so unruly, the horse bucks continually and will not stand quietly for even a moment. This is the condition of the man with a dark and confused mind-and-heart who has never established the Great Foundation.

Even if it is an unruly horse, if by chance it happens to stand still, then, while it is standing still, there is no difference between it and the docile, good horse. This is like the situation of the ordinary man whose mind-and-heart is dark and confused; even though he has not established its substance, there is by chance a period when his mind-and-heart is not yet aroused. At that moment its clear and pure substance is no different from that of a sage.

From this kind of comparison, how can the explanation of the Human Mind and the Tao Mind, and the matter of focusing on principle or focusing on material force, be anything but clear and easy to understand! If one wants to apply it to the mutual issuance thesis, it would be like the man and the horse being in different places when they have not yet gone out the gate and the man mounting the horse after they go out. In some cases the man might go out and the horse follow him; in others the horse might go out and the man follow. The terminology and the rationale both go wrong, and it becomes meaningless. A man and a horse can be separate from one another, however, so the comparison is not quite as close as that of the vessel and water. But water also has concrete form, and in this respect likewise is not comparable to principle which is formless. Similes must be looked at flexibly; one must not get mired down in them.

Concerning the psychophysical nature man receives at birth, there are certainly some cases in which good and evil are already determined. Therefore Confucius said that at birth men's natures are close to being the same, but by the habituation of practice they become far different from one another.[33] And again he said: "The highest kind of wise man and the worst kind of fool do not change."[34] But that is not a matter of the original condition of the fool's nature, but the consequence of his darkness and confusion; hence this cannot be called the equilibrium of the as-yet-unaroused condition of the mind. The not-yet-aroused condition is the nature in its original condition. If there is darkness and confusion, then material force has already disrupted the nature. Therefore one cannot say this is the substance of the nature. . . .

As for your thesis regarding splashing water with the willow switch, it can be said to be seeing concrete things and thinking out the principle, but it seems still incomplete. For water's running downward is a matter of natural principle, but when it splashes it goes up into the hand, and this also is a matter of natural principle. If water only flowed downward and would not go upward even when splashed, that would be contrary to principle. When it splashes upward into the hand, although it is a matter of material force, that whereby it splashes upward into the hand is a matter of principle. Its splashing up into the hand is a matter of principle as mounted on material force. Seeking an original condition other than its mounting on material force is definitely wrong. If one takes cases where it is mounted on material force but the issuance is contrary to the constant nature and calls it the original condition, that too is wrong. But if one sees that which is contrary to the constant nature and straightway takes it as purely the product of material force alone and not something in which principle is present, that too is wrong. As you mentioned, for some evil man to grow old and die peacefully in his room is certainly contrary to what is normal. But when governance is unequal and awards and punishments are not in accord with the proper norm, then there certainly is a rationale whereby evil men get their way and good ones suffer and perish. Mencius said: "When bad government prevails in the kingdom, princes of small power are submissive to those of great, and the weak to the strong. This is the rule of heaven."[35] Indeed not taking into account the greatness or smallness of virtue but only taking small or great in terms of strength and weakness as that which determines victory or defeat, how could that be the original natural condition! It's just that he is speaking in terms of power, that is all. If power works that way, then the principle is also that way, and so he calls it "natural." That being the case, if a certain evil man manages to preserve his life, one may say that such is not the original nature of principle. But if one says it is the sole product of material force and has nothing to do with principle, then it is wrong. Where in the world is there any material force apart from principle?

The wonder that is principle and material force is difficult to understand and also difficult to explain. Principle has only a single wellspring; material force likewise has only a single wellspring. Material force is evolvingly active and becomes diversified and even; principle likewise evolvingly acts and becomes diversified and uneven. Material force does not part from principle; principle does not part from material force. This being the case, principle and material force are a unity. Where can one see any difference? As for what is described as "principle is just principle, material force is just material force," in what can one see that principle is just principle and material force just material force?[36]

I hope you will consider this matter carefully and then compose a response. I would like to find out what you come up with in your understanding of the matter. MK

CHAPTER NINETEEN

Buddhism

O ne of the most important changes from the Koryŏ to the
Chosŏn dynasty was the shift from sponsoring Buddhism
to the Confucianization of the state through the adoption of Neo-
Confucianism, based in particular on the writings of Chu Hsi. Generally, Confucian rulers, except King Sejo (1455–1468) and Queen
Dowager Munjŏng (1501–1565), who acted as a regent to the young
King Myŏngjong from 1545 until her death in 1565, attempted to
suppress all beliefs and practices other than those of Chu Hsi regarding
the nature and patterns of government, society, and people. Thus, as
Confucianism enjoyed unreserved governmental patronage, Buddhism was continuously suppressed and even persecuted. Confucian
scholar-officials during the Chosŏn dynasty wrote treatises to justify
rejecting and persecuting Buddhism, and eminent Buddhist monks
made efforts to defend Buddhism against attacks from the Confucian
view and to find ways to reconcile and integrate their views with
Confucianism. Although the Confucianists's main critical arguments
against Buddhism were based on ethical issues, in fact the government's policy was more concerned with economics.

A notable critic who advocated rejecting Buddhism was Chŏng
Tojŏn (d. 1398), an architect of the Confucian state of Chosŏn. In
1393 King T'aejo confiscated the property of a great many monasteries
and turned the land over to the state. In 1405 King T'aejong abolished
the ecclesiastical posts of *wangsa* (royal preceptor) and *kuksa* (national

preceptor). In 1406 the number of temples was reduced to two hundred and forty-two, and the number of sects was reduced to seven. The number of monks who could live in any given temple was set by the government. Most temples lost their tax-exempt status, and the number of temple attendants was strictly limited. In 1424 King Sejong decreed that the number of temples in the nation be limited to thirty-six and that the seven remaining sects be amalgamated into two authorized schools, the Sŏnjong (Meditation school) and Kyojong (Doctrinal school). In 1492, during the rule of Sŏngjong, the law providing for the ordination of monks was rescinded, and all monks were under pressure to return to lay status. During the reign of Yŏnsangun (1494–1506), many temples and Buddhist images were destroyed, and the protective umbrella of state recognition of Buddhism was withdrawn. The monk examinations and ranks disappeared. Under King Chungjong (1506–1544) the Buddhist department in the state examination system was abolished, and the destruction or appropriation of Buddhist property increased.

In response, some Buddhist thinkers tried to vindicate Buddhism against Confucian criticisms and even attempted to find grounds for reconciliation with Confucianism. The most famous of these thinkers are Kihwa (1376–1433), Pou (1515–1565), and Hyujŏng (1520–1604). It is notable that all three had studied Confucianism before becoming Buddhist monks, which gave them the knowledge and confidence to compare Confucianism with Buddhism. They played a leading role in their times and occupy prominent positions in the history of Chosŏn Buddhism. In general, however, the survival of Buddhism in the Chosŏn dynasty during the period of suppression and persecution should be attributed mostly to the efforts of those monks who devoted themselves to continued study and practice in remote mountain monasteries and to the pious support of lay Buddhists, including both ordinary people and women of the upper class. JW

Kihwa (1376–1433)

Kihwa was one of the eminent Meditation masters who advocated reconciliation among religions in the early Chosŏn dynasty and left behind a number of writings, commenting on Buddhist scriptures and attempting to reconcile Buddhism with Confucianism. The *Hyŏnjŏng non* (Treatise on Manifesting Righteousness), translated here, compares Buddhist principles and their function in the world with Confucianism in order to defend Buddhism against attacks from Confucians and to seek reconciliation. JW

Treatise on Manifesting Righteousness
[From *Hanguk pulgyo chŏnsŏ* 7:217a–225b]

That of which the essence is neither being nor nonbeing, but which pervades both being and nonbeing, and that of which the origin is neither past nor present, but which pervades past and present, is the path.

The causes of being and nonbeing are embedded in one's true nature and emotions. The causes of past and present are embedded in birth and death. One's true nature is originally without emotions, but emotions arise due to true nature becoming deluded. Emotions give rise to the obstruction of wisdom. Thoughts are transformed, and the essence becomes differentiated. Therefore, myriad things are formed, and birth and death begin.

As for emotions, they include defilement and purity, good and evil. Purity and goodness are what give rise to saints; defilement and evil are what produce ordinary people. Therefore, we should know that if emotions do not arise, then neither ordinary people nor saints will be able to flourish.

A bodhisattva is one whose nature may already be enlightened, but whose emotions have not yet completely disappeared. Therefore making the claim that "an enlightened one has emotions" in reference to bodhisattvas—how much more true is this for the two-vehicle adherents of sravakas and pratyekabuddhas! All three-vehicle adherents still have emotions, so how much more do humans, heavenly beings, and various other beings.

The enlightenment of a Buddha is complete, and there is nothing that his wisdom does not include. His purity is consummate, and his emotional troubles have already disappeared. Therefore discussion about emotions cannot be applied to a Buddha. That is why everyone is called a sentient being except a Buddha.

In general, the three or five vehicles are all concerned with controlling the emotions: the vehicles of humans and heavenly beings are concerned with controlling the stain of defilements, whereas the other three vehicles are concerned with controlling the stain of purity. After the stains of defilement and purity are extinguished, one can then approach the realm of great enlightenment by oneself.

By means of maintaining the five abstentions,[1] one is reborn in the realm of humans; by means of maintaining the ten wholesome deeds,[2] one may be reborn in the realm of heavenly beings; by means of the four noble truths[3] and the twelvefold chain of dependent origination,[4] one becomes a member of the two vehicles; by means of the six perfections,[5] one becomes a bodhisattva.

In my view, the ultimate point of the *Tripiṭaka* is only that it causes people to leave emotions and manifest their true nature. Emotions arise in one's true nature like clouds rising in a vast sky. Abandoning emotions and manifesting one's true nature is like clouds opening and manifesting the great blue sky.

Emotions are light and emotions are weighty, just like clouds that are light and clouds that are thick. Clouds differ in lightness and thickness, but they are the same in blocking the light of the sky; emotions can be distinguished as light and weighty, but they are the same in obstructing the light of one's true nature.

When clouds rise, the sun and moon withhold their light, and the world becomes darkened; when clouds open, the light pervades a thousand world-systems and brightens the vast universe. By comparison, Buddhism is like the fresh wind that clears away the floating clouds. Those who want an expansive view but dislike the fresh wind are deluded; those who want pure peace between themselves and others but dislike our path of Buddhism are lost.

If one teaches people to rely on Buddhism and cultivate it, their minds can be accomplished and righteous; their bodies can be accomplished and cultivated; they can manage their homes; they can rectify the nation; and the whole world can be at peace.

A person with sharp capacities can be regarded as a bodhisattva, can be regarded as a sravaka, and can be regarded as a pratyekabuddha; a person with dull capacities can be considered as reborn in heaven and can become a good person. In truth, the world would not be disorderly if Buddhism were practiced like this. Why? Because a Buddhist dislikes the consequences of wrongdoing, all the various evils should be eliminated. Although all evil is not completely eliminated, at least one evil would be abandoned. If one evil is abandoned, then one punishment would disappear. When one punishment disappears at home, then ten thousand punishments vanish in the state.

Delighting in preparing the ground for blessings, one should cultivate various good deeds. Although all the various good deeds are not
completely cultivated, there is the practice of at least one good deed.
To practice one good deed means that one blessing is obtained. When
a blessing flourishes in the home, then ten thousand blessings flourish
in the state.

In general, the five abstentions and the ten wholesome deeds are the
barest minimum in our teaching. Originally these were established for
the people with the lowest capacities. Nevertheless, if anyone practices
these well, then it is not only good for oneself but also beneficial for
others. If there is benefit from these minimal practices, how much
more would arise from the four noble truths and the twelvefold chain
of dependent origination! How much more from the six perfections!

Confucianism regards the five constants[6] as pivotal to the practice
of the Way. The five abstentions that are taught by the Buddha are
identical to the five constants taught by the Confucians: no killing
means humanity; no stealing means righteousness; no sexual misconduct means propriety; no drinking intoxicants means wisdom; no
lying means faith.

But when it comes to the means Confucians use for instructing
people when they do not practice virtue, they govern by means of
punishment. Therefore, it is said: "If the people be led by laws, and
uniformity sought to be given them by punishments, they will try to
avoid the punishment but have no sense of shame. If they be led by
virtue, and uniformity sought to be given them by the rules of propriety, they will have the sense of shame and moreover will become
good."[7] But for persons who are not saintly, it is not possible to "be
led by virtue, and uniformity sought to be given them by the rules of
propriety." Therefore, it is said: "Completing the study of them by
silent meditation, and securing the faith of others without the use of
words, depended on their virtuous conduct."[8] "If the people be led
by laws, and uniformity sought to be given them by punishments,"
one cannot avoid having rewards and punishments. Therefore, it is
said that rewards and punishments are the powerful handle of the
state.

"Completing the study of them by silent meditation, and securing
the faith of others without the use of words" is truly our Buddha's
method of transformation, in addition to displaying cause and effect.
When people are taught by means of rewards and punishment, their
lack of transgression will be on the surface only and that is all. But

when people are taught by means of cause and effect, their minds will become obedient. In today's world, we can see with our own eyes such development taking place. Why? If you motivate people to do good using rewards and prohibit people from evil using punishment, then one who abstains from evil does so out of a feeling of fear and dread, and one who does good does so out of an interest in being rewarded. Therefore, compliance with the teaching is merely superficial and not heartfelt obedience.

If a person wants to know the reason for one's present poverty or wealth, then the seeds planted in the past should be shown; if one wants to know the adversity or blessings of the future, then one should be shown the causes used in the present. Therefore, the wealthy person delights in sowing good seeds in previous lifetimes and works industriously; the poor person repents for not cultivating good in previous lifetimes and exerts himself.

Furthermore, one who seeks happiness in a future life should be untiringly diligent in doing good; one who wants to avoid disaster in a future life must restrain himself from doing evil. It is your choice to disagree. But if you agree, then agree in your mind; never submit merely outwardly. But how can we make everyone submit in their minds? One who cannot submit in his mind should be directed by rewards and punishments at the beginning. This will quickly cause the mind to be happy and to submit sincerely. Therefore, besides the teaching of cause and effect, there is instruction in rewards and punishments. It is said that one who can be accepted should be accepted, and one who must be broken in should be broken in. This is close to Confucianism. Therefore, neither Confucianism nor Buddhism should be abolished.

In fact, when the Buddha was about to die, he used this teaching to instruct both kings and their ministers. In general, he wished them to use his Way to guide everyone in the world and to obtain great assistance from it to govern the world, while also causing them to practice the path of cultivating the truth together. Our Buddha's teachings are only concerned with how to make people follow the function of the Way without distinction between lay people and monks. This means that people do not have to shave their hair or wear different robes to practice the Way. Therefore, it is said, "Freeing people from their bonds through skillful methods is expediently called *samādhi*"; it is also said, "There is no precise dharma named the Supreme Enlightenment."[9] The Buddha's mind is like this. How can his way be considered narrow! If you lack the power of patience, however, it is difficult to live in the mundane world without contamination or to attain the Way while living at home. Therefore the Buddha taught people to leave their homes in order to have them cultivate the practice of radical detachment.

Confucianists say that a man has a home and a woman has a family; inheriting their family estate and not breaking the rites of ancestor worship can be called filial piety. Nowadays Buddhists break from marriage, depart from human duties, go to the mountain forest for a long time, and break the family line forever. How can this be called filial piety? One should look after his parents' well-being day and night and should obediently follow the wishes of the parents at all times. Whenever a person leaves home, he must report to his parents; upon his return, he should present himself to the parents. But, nowadays, Buddhist monks give themselves permission to leave home without even informing their parents; moreover, once they leave, they never return home for the rest of their lives. They do not serve their parents with delicious food while the parents are alive, nor do they plan an elaborate funeral when the parents die. How can this not be unfilial to their parents?

As a test, let us discuss this subject. The unchangeable principle and temporary expedient are the main essentials of the Way. Without the principle there is nothing to maintain constancy; without expedients there is nothing to be used to respond to changing circumstances. Through both, maintaining permanence by the principle and adapting to change by using expedients, eventually the great completion of the Way can be achieved and can manifest itself everywhere. If one does not know how to maintain constancy, one has no way of correcting the human mind. If one does not know how to respond to changing circumstances, one has no way of achieving great works. Now, human beings receive their birth from their parents and owe their survival to the state. Filial piety at home and loyalty to the state are proper duties for a subject and a son. Marriage and memorial services for ancestors are also the great principles of men's cardinal relationships. Without marriage, the principle of reproduction may be annihilated; without memorial services, the tradition of ancestor worship may be extinguished. But to fulfill completely the duties of loyalty and filial piety as a subject and as a son is difficult. To remain married while maintaining righteousness till the end of one's life, to perform ancestor worship with heart and soul, and to abide in perfect purity are also difficult. If one scrupulously keeps his office while at the same time remaining totally dedicated to loyalty and filial piety, and if one continuously upholds righteousness and abides in perfect purity until his death, he will not only not lose his good name while he is alive but will also gain rebirth as a human being after death. This is a result of adhering to the unchangeable way of the principle.

Most people attempt to obtain fame only; very few try to restrain themselves from passion. Most people only want rebirth as a human being and find it difficult to free themselves from endless transmigration. Passion is the root cause of transmigration; lust is the immediate cause of birth. For those people who are no longer in a position to avoid ties to their wives and children, can they possibly cut themselves off from passion? If they cannot remove themselves from passion, can they possibly free themselves from transmigration? If one wants to be free from transmigration, one should first eliminate passion; if one wants to eliminate passion, one should first leave one's wife and children; if one wants to leave one's wife and children, one must abandon the mundane world. If one does not abandon the mundane world, one cannot leave one's wife and children, nor can one eliminate passion and be free from transmigration. Can ordinary people in the secular world achieve these things without the great compassion and expedients of the great saint? Such a person is difficult to find in myriad generations or among millions of people. Now, the condition of passion is similar to the attraction between a magnet and iron. Therefore, if one has no power of fortitude while dwelling in the mundane world, passion is difficult to avoid.

In the case of Śākyamuni, our original master, when he dwelled in the Tuṣita Heaven, he was called Prabhapala, Guardian of Illumination Bodhisattva. When he descended from the Tuṣita Heaven to the palace of the king Suddhodana in ancient India, he was named Siddhartha, Goal Achieved. How can we say that he was a person who had no power of fortitude? We can say that the sun was ashamed and its light was so faint, and the supreme heaven was ashamed and was cleansed through him. Although he had been involved in passion, he had never been contaminated by it. Wishing to be an exemplar for future generations, he, an ideal prince of the great king, acted in an unfilial way and left the palace without informing his parents and entered the Himalayas. There he practiced difficult asceticism without regard for his life. With fortitude he concentrated on meditation without disturbance. Having extinguished completely his emotional ties and attained clearly the true enlightenment, he returned to his native place to greet his father and ascended into heaven to visit his mother in order to preach the dharma and save them both. This is how the sage adapts to circumstances as occasions demand. Although he seemingly acts contrary to the unchangeable principle, he is actually united with the path. Furthermore, the Buddha not only attained all the three knowledges[10] and the six supernatural powers[11] but also completely attained the four wisdoms[12] and the eight liberations.[13] His virtue has spread throughout the world and later generations and has caused the future generations throughout the world to call his parents "the father and mother of the great sage" and to use his family name as their surname. Also those who have entered the homeless life are called offspring of Śākyamuni. How can you not say that this is great filial piety? Didn't Confucius say, "We develop our own personality and practice the Way so as to perpetuate our name for future generations and to give glory to our parents. This is the end of filiality"?[14] The world of later generations since then has been guided by this way, and it has also allowed the world of later generations to be influenced and transformed by it. According to the magnitude of their capacities, people have joined salvation by relying on this dharma. How can this not be called "great compassion"? Didn't Confucius say, "If a man can for one day subdue himself and return to propriety, all under heaven will ascribe perfect virtue to him"?[15]

QUESTION: Every individual who lives in this world should serve his king with complete loyalty and should assist his state with utmost sincerity. But presently the Buddhists do not have an audience with the emperor and do not serve the king and the court. Instead, they dwell in high and remote places, from where they merely sit and watch the success or failure of the state. How could this be called loyalty?

ANSWER: In religion, one who would become a king should first receive the precepts. After purifying his body and mind, he then ascends the throne. Moreover, monks never neglect their prayers for the king and the state at the daily ritual services in the morning and evening. How could this not be called loyalty? Whereas the rulers promote virtue by conferring honors and emoluments and prohibit evil by punishing crimes, we Buddhists instruct people that good deeds bring happiness and evil deeds bring disaster. Therefore those who learn Buddhism will naturally withdraw from evil thoughts and develop good intentions. Although the Buddhists do not confer honors as rewards or awe the people with punishment, our Buddha's teachings cause the people to be transformed. Is this not assisting the king and the state? [217a–219a]. . .

QUESTION: The birth and death of human beings are the beginning and end of human life. Therefore, Confucius only spoke of birth and death of the present life, and never spoke about previous and future lives. Now, the Buddhists talk about the previous life and the next life as well as the period between birth and death; these are called the "three periods of time." In general, the time before birth and after death cannot be seen by the eyes or heard by the ears. Then how can anyone actually see it? Is it not duplicitous to delude the people this way?

ANSWER: The birth and death of human beings may be compared to the transition from day to night. Since there is change, the preceding and the following are naturally completed. For the day, the night that has just passed is the preceding and the night that is coming is the following. For the night, the day that has just passed is the preceding and the day that is coming is the following. As with the transition of day to night, the "three periods of time" (past, present, and future) are naturally accomplished. Since days and nights are like this, the months and years are also similar to this. Since the months and years are like this, birth and death are also similar to this. The reason that the past has no beginning and the future has no end can be understood in this way. The *Book of Changes* says: "It exhibits the past, and teaches us to discriminate the issues of the future."[16] How can the term "past and future" not be the same as "the preceding and the following"? Therefore one who says that the theory of the "three periods of time" is duplicitous has not given sufficient thought to it. [223a–b]. . .

QUESTION: Upon examination of the Buddhist scriptures, one finds that Buddhism emphasizes emptiness and reveres quiescent extinction. Even though the scriptures are twice as meritorious as the *Primary Learning* of Confucianism, they are useless; even though they surpass the *Great Learning,* they are worthless. Therefore, Buddhist scriptures cannot be a prescription of cultivation for oneself nor an aid for government.

ANSWER: Scriptures are implements to carry the Way and prescriptions to transform people. By studying the scriptures, one can discern the path that should be followed or not be followed and one can also learn the propriety that should be practiced or not be practiced. As for the path that should be followed and the propriety that should be practiced, how can we reject them just because they are not our own practices? Have you not heard that there are no two ways in the world and that sages do not have two minds? As for the sages, even when they are separated by thousands of miles and by thousands of generations, their minds do not know the difference. Confucius said, "He had no foregone conclusions, no arbitrary predeterminations, no obstinacy, and no egoism."[17] The *Book of Changes* also says, "When one's resting is like that of the back, and he loses all consciousness of self; when one walks in his courtyard and does not see any person in it."[18] When there is no sense of self and no sense of others, how can there be any defilement? Śākyamuni said: "When there is no sense of self and no sense of others, then by cultivating all good things, enlightenment is immediately attained." This is the reason why the sages' minds are the same even though they live in different generations. As for the words "emptiness" and "annihilation," where are these words cited in the twelvefold divisions of the *Tripiṭaka?* The *Great Precepts* states: "Filial obedience is the law of the supreme way." Filial piety is called the precept; it is also called the restraint. Could this at the same time be called the void? The *Perfect Enlightenment Scripture* says: "The mind flower issues forth brightness and shines upon the world in ten directions."[19] Could this be called annihilation? If one wants to experience what is true and what is false, one must first investigate the scriptures. If one imprudently rejects the scriptures without investigation, he will surely be laughed at by a knowledgeable person. Have you not heard that one who has not studied all the literature of the world cannot correct the ancient and present scriptures? Confucius said: "Filiality is the first principle of heaven, the ultimate standard of earth, the norm of conduct for the people."[20] Is this not what is called the supreme way? This is because, as the *Book of Changes* says, "when acted on, it penetrates forthwith to all phenomena and events under the sky."[21] Is this not what is called the mind shining brightly? What is called illustrious virtue in Confucianism is the same as what is called the wonderful bright mind of Buddhism. What the *Book of Changes* calls "it is still and without movement; but when acted on, it penetrates forthwith to all phenomena and events"[22] is the same as what is called "serene radiance" in Buddhism. What difference is there between the Confucian saying "After cultivating one's own good, one can demand good from others; after eliminating one's own evil, one can correct others' evil" and our

Buddha's teaching "Eliminate evil and cultivate good, and thereby bring benefit to all sentient beings"? Since the principles of what we have discussed in Buddhism and Confucianism are the same, what difference is there in the remainder of these two teachings? To favor self and to slight others, and to be self-righteous and to blame others, are men's common sentiments. A truly learned person will only follow what is righteous. How can the people judge what is right and what is wrong based on their biased view of self and others? Of the three religions (Buddhism, Confucianism, and Taoism), it is Buddhism that is capable of transforming the people without the recourse of conferring honors. This is because of the influence that people feel from the great sageliness and great compassion of the Buddha. The sage ruler Shun "loved to question others, and to study their words, though they might be shallow. He concealed what was bad in them, and displayed what was good."[23] The sage ruler Yü "did homage to the excellent words."[24] If Shun and Yü had encountered the teachings of the Buddha, how could they not have taken refuge in their beauty? Therefore those who think that the Buddha's teachings cannot be the proper means of self-cultivation and of governing the people have not given the matter adequate consideration.

QUESTION: What are the similarities and differences, and the superiority and inferiority, among Taoism, Confucianism, and Buddhism?

ANSWER: The Taoists say, "By taking no action, there is nothing which is not done; be inactive while taking action." The Buddhists say, "Calm but always illuminating; illuminating but always calm." The Confucians say, "According to the *Book of Changes,* with no thought and no action, being calm and unmovable, then one can respond and be in harmony everywhere." One who is calm is never unresponsive; that is to say, he is calm but always illuminating. One who responds harmoniously never experiences absence of calm; that is to say, he is illuminating but always calm. "Taking no action, but there is nothing that is not done" means "being calm and always responsive." "Taking action but there is nothing that is done" means "being responsive but always being calm." Thus, we can say that the teachings of the three religions coincide with each other as if they were spoken from one mouth. But if you want to know the level of their practices, or the similarities and differences of their applications, you should completely purify your mind and cleanse your eye of wisdom. Only then can you comprehend the scriptures of Buddhism, Confucianism, and Taoism and also practice the teachings in daily life.

Confronted with life and death, disaster and blessing, can one reach an understanding by oneself without relying on someone else's explanations? I will not insist upon giving my justification lest one may listen out of fright. [224c–225b] JW/YC

Kim Sisŭp (1435–1493)

Kim Sisŭp is renowned for syncretizing Buddhism and Confucianism. In *Musa* (On No-Thought), Kim, writing under his pen name of Ch'ŏnghanja, comments on Buddhist practices of his time, criticizes those idle Meditation practitioners who were not sincere in their meditation while pretending to be transcendent, and insists on a syncretic approach to Buddhist practices within a secular life of Confucian perspective. JW

On No-Thought
[From *Maewŏltang chip* 16:1a–2b]

Ch'ŏnghanja said: "When ancient men practiced the Way, they devoted every moment of their time as precious and never indulged in idleness. But the people nowadays are indolent and give no thought to it, nor are they anxious about it all day; when can they attain enlightenment?" A guest took issue with this and stated: "The Way is by nature without thought and without anxiety. To think and to be anxious are delusions. Can one think and be anxious while practicing the Way?"

Ch'ŏnghanja said: "That which has no thought or anxiety is the essence of the Way. To be anxious with great care and not be idle are the essentials of its practice. We see all the time in our worldly affairs that neglecting to be anxious leads to the destruction of myriad things. If such is the case, how can one attain the true Way of no delusion through idleness? Therefore, Chi-wen of the state of Lu thought over three times before acting.[25] Confucius set up the 'Nine Items of Thoughtful Consideration.'[26] Tseng Tzu kept a reminder: 'One attains only through anxiety.' Confucius had a precept for profound anxiety. Unless one is an innately intelligent person who does not need to exert himself, how can it be possible for him not to think? The dispositions of men are not the same; some are stupid and ignorant, and some are bright and intelligent. If one is not diligent and steadfast, how can he become equal to superior sages? One must think and be anxious studiously and meticulously, and one must train daily and discipline himself monthly until he attains the realm of enlightenment by himself. Only thereafter can he say that, in the Way, there is no thought and anxiety."

The guest asked: "In the teaching of the world, Confucianism, the ceremonies and customs are clearly arranged in order; and the 'three bonds,'[27] the 'five constants,' the 'eight particulars of the *Great Learning*,'[28] and 'the nine standard rules,'[29] all have a clear logic and order from the beginning to the end. From the bond between father and son to that of ruler and subject, from the investigation of things to the whole kingdom being tranquil and happy, from the honoring of men of virtue and talents to the kindly cherishing of the princes of the states, and from the rulers above to the mass of the people, there is an arranged order to study, by which one learns one thing today and another tomorrow and practices by days and by months until he reaches sagehood. Therefore, the *Book of Changes* praises entering the spiritual realm by fully comprehending the principle, while commentaries on the classics record the importance of careful thinking and clear distinction so that all the affairs in the world are in clear order and not confused. Only then can we dwell in the civilized world and lead a life that is different from that of the birds, the beasts, and the barbarians. Those scholars who are outside of this world, however, have cut their ties with the world and thus lead a life unconcerned with all the anxieties. In such a life, they do not have to bow their heads to their rulers, nor are they obligated to pay respect to their relatives. They enjoy their simple life among birds and beasts free from all worldly desires. Where would they place their mind? What would they think and what would they be anxious about?"

Ch'ŏnghanja answered: "Those who are outside of this world may indeed lead a simple life free from all desires. But until they reach the highest level of cultivation, how can they not think about the direction they should follow? The people in general assume the meaning of Meditation to be dwelling in peaceful leisure; they fail to grasp that the word Meditation also connotes to think and cultivate oneself and to be anxious in calmness. Among all the beings in the world, humans are most spiritual, and their intelligence exceeds that of all other creatures. Although the intellectual capacities of individuals may differ, how can it be possible for a person not to study even for one day and not think even for one day? If one studies and does not think, he will lose what he has studied. If one thinks and does not study, it will be dangerous. When one thinks, he thinks not to have depraved thoughts; he thinks the means by which the Way is attained. When one is anxious, it is not a lunatic anxiety; the anxiety is concerned with the means by which learning is achieved. Even while one hesitates and vacillates, his eyes still can see and his mind still can think to gain gradual self-cultivation. There can never be an end to learning. Therefore, climbing a mountain, one thinks about learning its height; facing water, one thinks about learning its purity; sitting on a rock, one thinks about learning its hardness; looking at a pine tree, one thinks about learning its faithfulness; and viewing the moon, one thinks about learning its brightness. Myriad phenomena appear brightly in the mind and each has certain good points. If we do not study all of them completely and contemplate their mystery so as to reach the realm of spirit, we do not know the ultimate realm of practicing the Way." JW/YC

Pou (1515–1565)

In *Il Chŏng* (Oneness and Correctness), Pou attempts to syncretize all descriptions of worldly views and ways of different lives into what he calls "Oneness and Correctness," overcoming differences among various religious thoughts through his common-sense approach. In this essay, he also tries to harmonize the sectarian views of his social situation with the ultimate principles. JW

On Oneness and Correctness
[From *Hanguk pulgyo chŏnsŏ* 7:581b–c]

Being One is not a simple numeral "one" compared with two or three; it means being genuinely real without falseness. It is the principle of heaven. This principle is void and quiet and has no sign; there are no myriad phenomena in the universe that it does not include. And yet its essence is only one. Things did not begin with two or three. On account of the activities of one energy, the plants grow in spring, days become longer in summer, fruit trees bear fruits in autumn, grains are stored in winter, and it becomes bright in the day and dark at night. From ancient times to the present, there has never been an error in these phenomena even for a moment. Among all the creatures under heaven, all the flying and submerged animals and plants, and the creatures in all colors and shapes, there is none that has not received its life from Oneness, and there has never been a difference even by a hair. This is the reason why the heavenly principle is Oneness at all times, and it is truly real and not false.

Correctness (*chŏng*) is not partial and not depraved; it is pure and unadulterated. It is the mind of men. This mind is quiet and without thinking and is the principle of all the myriad things in the universe. It has nothing that is not proper and its spirit is unambiguous; there is nothing in the myriad things of the universe that is not receptive to it and never has there been a private thought that was partial or depraved. This is why the nature of this Oneness issues forth the feeling of commiseration, the feeling of modesty and complaisance, and the feeling of approving and disapproving. By means of joy, anger, sorrow, and pleasure, myriad things respond accordingly as if reflecting in a mirror, and there has never been even a single mistake. This is why the human mind is by nature correct and pure and is not adulterated.

It is called the principle and it is also called the mind. Although its names may differ, there has never been any difference between the principle of heaven and men and the meaning of Oneness and Correctness. Heaven is man and man is heaven. Likewise, Oneness is Correctness and Correctness is Oneness. Therefore, the essence of man is the essence of heaven, and Oneness is Correctness and Correctness is Oneness. The mind of man is the mind of heaven, and the vital force of man is the vital force of heaven. The auspicious clouds, the bright stars, the light breeze, and the clear moon of heaven and earth have all issued forth from the mind of man and the vital force of man. This is what is meant by saying the myriad things in the universe are originally one with us. Thus, if our mind is correct, the mind of the universe is also correct; if the vital force within us is harmonious, the vital force of the universe is likewise harmonious. How can the meaning of One Correctness be coincidental?

We are only noble men. As we walk, pause, sit, and lie down in day and night, and also as we reflect, call out, think, and give meaning, we must exert ourselves to be in one mind and to be correct at all times. We must not allow the multitude of desires to be mixed and to respond to various things. When emotions emerge from being based on a primordial chaotic nature, then all misfortune will be naturally removed without exorcism, and all good fortune will be completed without prayer. Moreover, our lives can be protected and lengthened, our descendants can be nurtured, and we can eternally enjoy a good position in life during the era of great peace at the time of the heavenly elders and sages. JW/YC

Hyujŏng (1520–1604)

Hyujŏng is generally regarded as the greatest monk of the Chosŏn dynasty. Most of the eminent masters of modern Korean Buddhism trace their dharma lineage back to him. Although he studied the Confucian classics at the National Academy in Seoul, he became a Buddhist monk at the age of nineteen. Having passed the monk examination in 1552, he was appointed director of the Doctrinal school and then director of the Meditation school in 1555. In 1557 he retired to the mountains until 1592 when Japan invaded Korea. Despite his religious beliefs and age—he was then seventy-two—he organized and led a militia largely composed of Buddhist monks to repel the invaders. Because of his successful military exploits, he has become a legendary folk hero even to this day. He is also known as Sŏsan Taesa (Great Master of the Western Mountain).

Surrounded by the hostile environment of the Neo-Confucian orthodoxy of the Chosŏn state, Buddhism was placed in the unenviable position of having to justify its teachings as compatible with the dominant state ideologies. In *Samga kwigam* (Mirror of Three Religions), Hyujŏng attempted to show that the three religions, Confucianism, Taoism, and Buddhism, were ultimately not divergent in transmitting the truth and that the ultimate messages they convey are basically the same. The section on Buddhism in *Samga kwigam,* which is translated here, is often published separately as *Sŏnga kwigam* (Mirror for Meditation Students) and is one of the most widely read Buddhist texts in Korea. Abstracting key passages from various scriptures and adding his own commentaries, Hyujŏng compiled *Sŏnga kwigam* as a guide for the practitioners of meditation. *Sŏn Kyo Kyŏl* (Secrets of Meditation and Doctrine) was compiled also by Hyujŏng on behalf of his disciple Yujŏng (1544–1610). In these two works and many others, Hyujŏng tried to unify the Meditation school and the Doctrinal school in an attempt to revitalize Buddhism in Korea. JW

Mirror for Meditation Students
[From *Hanguk pulgyo chŏnsŏ* 7:619a–625a]

There is one thing here.[30] From the beginning it is clear and divine. It is never born, and it has never disappeared. Neither its name nor its form can be grasped.

The buddhas' and patriarchs' appearance in the world is the same as waves arising where there is no wind.

The dharma has many meanings and people have many different capacities. Therefore, it has been necessary to set forth expedient teachings.

Many different names have been given arbitrarily, such as mind, Buddha, and sentient being. But one must not hold onto names and try to offer explanations. If its essence is right here, that then is correct. If thoughts are stirred up, that is a mistake.

The transmission of mind by the World-Honored One in three places is the purport of meditation. That which he said during his entire life constitutes the way of doctrine. Therefore it is said that meditation is the Buddha's mind and doctrine is his words.

Therefore if one loses it in speech, then "picking up a flower"[31] and "facing a wall"[32] will become merely the traces of doctrine. But if one attains it in his mind, then even the coarse words and petty talk of the world will become the purpose of meditation that has been transmitted separately outside the doctrine. . . . One who seeks Buddha by transcending the mind is off the path. One who is attached to the mind in order to become the Buddha will become a demon. In general, the capacity to forget is the way of the Buddha, while false discrimination belongs to the sphere of demons.[33] Moreover, when discrimination does not arise, then empty luminosity naturally illuminates itself. . . .

The Doctrinal gate only transmits the dharma of the one mind; the Meditation gate only transmits the dharma of seeing one's true nature. The mind is one's true nature, and one's true nature is the mind. (The mind means the original mind of sentient beings and is different from that ignorant mind which is attached to illusory characteristics. One's true nature means the original dharma nature of the one mind—not the nature as contrasted with phenomena.) . . .

Therefore the student should at first clearly discern that the two principles of immutability and adaptability to changing situations, according to the true words of the doctrine, are the intrinsic nature and manifested forms of one's own mind, and that the two paths of sudden enlightenment and gradual cultivation are the beginning and end of one's own practice. Only after this realization should the student lay aside the doctrinal principles and practice the meaning of meditation, carefully holding only to the one thought that appears in his mind. Then he will surely obtain what is there to be attained, and this is what is called the living road to salvation.

In general, students of meditation should practice live words and should not practice dead words. . . .

The Meditation Master Kao-feng [1238–1295] said: "In practicing meditation, one must have three essentials. One is a foundation of great faith. The second is a great firm determination. The third is a great feeling of doubt. If one of these is lacking, then it is like a tripod with a broken leg and becomes useless in the end." . . .

To practice meditation is like the method of tuning a stringed instrument; one must obtain the median between taut and slack. If one makes too much of an effort, then he will be inclined to cling to it too closely; if one forgets about it, he will fall into ignorance. Therefore one should maintain constant alertness. . . .

In general, the practitioners of meditation should remind themselves with the following questions: "Do you recognize the profound generosity of the four blessings of having parents, a ruler, teachers, and benefactors? Do you recognize the ugliness of the human body, made of four elements, that is in steady decline and decay every moment? Do you realize that human life is uncertain from breath to breath? Have you encountered buddhas and patriarchs? Have you felt how rare it is to encounter such a teaching after hearing the Supreme Dharma? . . . Are you determined to carry on the Buddha's wisdom in the present life? Have you resolved to be delivered from birth-and-death through your own dedication? Is your mind unmoved by the eight winds of gain or loss, fame or dispute, joy or sorrow, praise or ridicule? . . . These are the points the practitioners of meditation should check daily."[34] An ancient man said: "If one's present body cannot be saved in his present life, then how can one hope to be saved in the next life?"[35] . . .

The mind is a model for myriad forms. Karma is the reflection of the mind. It is also said that all the myriad things are produced as illusions from the mind. Since the mind originally has no form, how then can things have features? . . .

The scripture says: "To become aware of illusion is to transcend it, and one does not use any expedient means. To transcend illusion is to attain enlightenment, and it has no gradual sequence."

Transcending illusion is like the moon appearing after clouds are cleared. It does not mean that the absence of clouds can be called the moon; instead, where there are no clouds, one can see the moon. It does not mean that nonillusion is the real and unchanging truth; instead, where there is no illusion, one can find the truth.

In general, arising mind and moving thought (speaking falsehood and speaking the truth) are all illusions. . . .

Mind's clean purity is the Buddha. Mind's radiance is the dharma. Mind's nonduality is the saṅgha. Also, the original enlightenment of one's nature is the Buddha. The original nirvana of one's nature is the dharma. The mysterious function of one's nature is the saṅgha. If one suddenly obtains the immediacy of the present moment within oneself, he will at that point realize that originally there are no worldly matters. . . .

An ancient master said: "If one regards the precepts as important as the Buddha, the Buddha will always be present in the world." He also said: "One must regard the precepts as your master (Buddha)."

The scripture says: "If one wishes to escape birth and death, first eliminate greed and all thirst for desire."

The scripture says: "Unhindered, pure wisdom is produced by Meditation concentration." Therefore one should know that transcending the ordinary life into sagehood and passing away in peace while sitting or standing are attained by the power of meditation. So it is said: "If one wishes to seek the sagely path, there is no other way except meditation."

If mind is concentrated, it is able to know everything that comes and goes in the world.

The mind in which thought does not arise is called sitting; the nature that is motionless is called Meditation.

When mind does not rise while seeing phenomena, this is called nonbirth. Nonbirth is called nonthought. Nonthought is called liberation.

When correct mindfulness is not forgotten, no suffering will emerge. It is like saying that if one does not sleep, all dreams will disappear automatically. . . .

When water is pure, a pearl glows; when clouds are cleared, the moon shines brightly. When the three types of karma are purified, all types of merit will converge.

When the poor come and beg, one should give something according to one's situation. The great compassion that treats all others as yourself is the true almsgiving. . . .

If there is no practice of endurance, no accomplishment is possible even with myriad practices.

In general, if you have a humble mind, myriad merits will return to you. . . .

Reciting the Buddha's name by mouth only is mere recitation; only when the Buddha's name is recited with the heart is it true invocation of the Buddha. Therefore, if one merely recites the Buddha's name and fails in the invocation of the Buddha, then it is of no use to the Way. . . .

Listening to the recitation of the scripture is a blessing of joy for all those who read, recite, hear, and uphold the scripture. Our illusory body of flesh is ephemeral, but the practice of reciting scripture is real and will never be in vain.

If one reads the scriptures without reflecting on them within his heart, it will be of no use even though he may read ten thousand scriptures. . . .

The purpose of studying the scriptures is to cultivate one's true nature. Why should one be concerned about his study not being recognized by others? Fundamentally, the Way is to make life wholesome. Why should one be concerned about being utilized by this world? . . .

How could renouncing the world to enter monkhood be a trifling matter? It is not to seek an easy life, nor is it to obtain the necessities of life, nor to seek profit or fame. It is to transcend birth and death, to eliminate sufferings, to perpetuate the life of Buddha's wisdom, to escape from the three realms of existence, and to save sentient beings. . . .

An ancient master said: "Divine light of mind is not obscure but perpetually good and beautiful. All who enter this gate should not retain their knowledge." It is said: "Although a flake of gold is precious, if it falls into an eye, it will obscure the vision." It is also said: "Do not attempt to learn by means of intellect and do not discern by means of discernment."

[Epilogue]

An ancient man said: "Confucianists plant the root, Taoists grow the root, and Buddhists harvest the root." This sequence is shown to you. Now, I have attempted to help beginners to open the three gates of religious tradition so that they can gain access directly. If you can open the eyes of your mind, however, at a later date you will surely laugh loudly and revile this. JWYC

Secrets of Meditation and Doctrine
[From *Hanguk pulgyo chŏnsŏ* 7:657b–658a]

The students of meditation nowadays say: "Meditation is our master's dharma." The students of doctrine say: "Doctrine is our master's dharma." For one dharma, there are two different claims, and so they argue, pointing at a deer and calling it a horse. Alas! Who can solve this problem? Nevertheless, meditation is the mind of the Buddha and doctrine is the words of the Buddha. Doctrine is what reaches wordlessness from words whereas meditation is what reaches wordlessness from wordlessness. What reaches from wordlessness to wordlessness cannot be named, and hence it is arbitrarily called mind. Not knowing its reason, people say that it can be learned by studying and can be obtained by thinking. This is indeed pitiful. People of the Doctrinal tradition say, "In the doctrine, there is also meditation," and quote the phrase: "It emerges not from the sravaka (disciples) vehicle, not from the pratyekabuddha vehicle, not from the bodhi-sattva vehicle, and not from the Buddha vehicle." But this is merely an initiatory phrase for the beginners of meditation, and it is not the real principle of meditation.

The teachings the World-Honored One gave during his life are like casting three types of compassionate nets into the sea of birth-and-death in the triple worlds. By using a small net, shrimps and bivalves are caught (as the Hīnayāna teachings are for human beings and heavenly beings). By using a medium net, breams and trouts are caught (as the teachings of the Middle Vehicle for pratyekabuddhas). By using a big net, whales and sea tortoises are caught (as the complete and sudden teachings are for the Mahāyāna people). It is as if they were being placed altogether on the other shore of nirvana. This is the arranged order of the Doctrinal tradition.

Among those in the sea, there is one extraordinary being whose mane is like red fire, whose claws are like an iron lance, whose eyes shoot sunlight, and whose mouth spits a thunderstorm. When it turns its body over, the sky is filled with white waves, mountains and rivers are shaken, and the sun and the moon are darkened. It transcends the realms of the three kinds of nets, ascends straight up to the blue clouds, and pours out the sweet dew of the compassionate dharma to save all beings (exactly like the capacity of the patriarchs' teaching transmitted outside the doctrine). This is the difference between meditation and the doctrine.

This dharma of meditation was especially transmitted to our Buddha, the World-Honored One, by the patriarch, Chingwi,[36] and is not the stale words of ancient buddhas. Nowadays, among those who erroneously transmit the goal of meditation, some consider the gate of "sudden and gradual" enlightenment the correct lineage; some take the teaching of "complete and sudden" enlightenment to be the essential vehicle; some cite non-Buddhist scriptures to explain the secret meaning of meditation; some frivolously play with karmic consciousness as being the fundamental dimension of meditation; some regard mental light and shadow as the real self, and some even commit unrestrained actions, such as the blind wielding a stick and the deaf shouting without remorse or shame. What is their true mind? How can I dare talk about these transgressions of slander against the dharma?

I say that what is transmitted outside the doctrine cannot be known by studying nor be grasped by thinking. Only after thoroughly devoting one's mind to the extent that its way is totally cut off can it be known. Only after the realization is reached willingly can it be obtained. Have you not heard? When Śākyamuni picked a flower and showed it to the congregation, only Mahākāśyapa smiled. There are these stories told by Meditation masters that have been transmitted to later generations: Bodhidharma said, "it is boundless and not holy"; the Sixth Patriarch said, "to think neither good nor evil"; Huai-jang said, "when a cart is stopped, whip the horse"; Hsing-ssu spoke of "the price of rice in Lu-ling"; Ma-tsu, "drink all the water of the Western River in one gulp"; and Shih-t'ou, "I don't understand Buddha dharma." Moreover, there are Yün-men's sesame bun, Chaochou's drinking tea, T'ou-tzu's selling oil, Hsüan-sha's blank letter, Hsüeh-feng's playing ball, Ho-shan's beating drum, Shen-shan's beating a gong, and Tao-wu's dancing. All these are the same music sung by the ancient buddhas and the patriarchs that have been transmitted especially outside the doctrine. Can it be obtained by thinking? Can it be obtained by deliberation? It is, it can be said, like a mosquito trying to bite the back of an iron ox.

We are now in the last days of the world, and many practitioners are ill equipped for the special transmission outside the doctrine. Therefore, they only value the "complete and sudden approach" to make people see, listen, believe, and understand the use of the Way to produce seeing, hearing, belief, and understanding. They do not value the shortcut approach that has no principles, no meanings, no mind, no words, no taste, and no pattern for searching out a foundation and for breaking the black bucket of ignorance. In this situation, what can we do? Now the masters should face the practitioners of meditation all around the world and use the blade of the wisdom sword to cut through to what is essential. You should not try to bore a hole; instead you should invoke directly the living words of the original shortcut approach to lead them to self-awakening and self-enlightenment. This is the way the religious masters deal with the people. Seeing students who are not making progress, if you immediately try to steer them through preaching, it will cause no small damage to their vision. If a master of meditation violates this dharma in his practice, even though his teaching of dharma may lead to a showering of heavenly flowers, it will be like a lunatic running around at the fringe. If students of meditation believe this dharma of the shortcut approach, then even though they may yet have to achieve enlightenment in this life, they will not be taken to bad places by evil karma upon their death; instead, they will immediately enter the correct path toward enlightenment.

In the past, Ma-tsu's one shout caused the deafness of Po-chang and enabled Huang-po's tongue to spill out. This is the origin of the Lin-chi tradition. You must select the orthodox lineage of meditation. Since your spiritual vision has been clear, I am telling you this in detail. In the future, do not fail to meet the expectations of this elderly monk. If you fail to live up to this elderly monk's expectations, it is a great obligation owed to the buddhas and patriarchs that you fail to meet. Think carefully; think carefully. JW/YC

Notes

1. ORIGINS OF KOREAN CULTURE

1. Diminutive horses that one could ride "without mishap under the lowest branches of a fruit tree." See Edward H. Schafer, *The Golden Peaches of Samarkand* (Berkeley: University of California Press, 1963), p. 68.

2. 59 B.C.

3. Chumong means "able archer."

4. 58 B.C.

5. The eldest of Kŭmwa's seven sons.

6. Chumong becomes Tongmyŏng, "Eastern Light."

7. In an archery contest, Songyang and Tongmyŏng were to shoot a painted deer from a hundred paces.

8. Tongmyŏng did not have musical instruments and had one of his officers steal some from Piryu.

9. Songyang claimed he was the senior ruler because his palace was older; Tongmyŏng confused him by building a palace of decaying wood.

10. Died at the age of forty.

2. THE RISE OF THE THREE KINGDOMS

1. The biography of Wen Yen-po in *Chiu T'ang shu* 61:2360 reads: "Wen Yen-po was transferred to the post of vice-director of the Secretariat (*chung-shu shih-lang*) and enfeoffed as Duke of Hsi-ho Commandery. At that time Ko[gu]ryŏ sent an envoy with tribute of local products. The Eminent Founder (T'ai-tsu) said to his ministers: 'Between name and fact, principle demands that there be perfect correspondence. Ko[gu]ryŏ declared its vassalage

to Sui, but in the end fended off Emperor Yang: what kind of vassal have we here? In our respect for the myriad things we have no desire to be overbearing or lofty; but since we are in possession of the terrestrial vault, it is our task to bring all men together in harmony: why then must we let them declare their vassalage just to exalt and magnify themselves? Let a rescript be drawn up setting forth our concerns in this matter!' Yen-po stepped forward and said, 'The territory east of the Liao was the state of Chi Tzu (Kija) under the Chou, and under the house of Han was Hsüan-t'u Commandery. Thus, prior to Wei and Chin it was nearby and inside the imperial domain: we should not now let it off without a declaration of vassalage. Besides, if we were to contend with Koguryŏ about rites, what would the barbarians of the four quarters have to look up to? Moreover, the Middle Kingdom's attitude toward the barbarians should be like that of the sun toward the planets. In the order of things our downward gaze should favor all the barbarians in equal measure, without any question of demeaning or exalting.' The Eminent Founder thereupon rescinded his order." MR

2. *Tao te ching* 44 (D. C. Lau, trans., *Lao Tzu: Tao Te Ching* [Harmondsworth: Penguin, 1963], p. 105): "Know contentment/And you will suffer no disgrace; Know when to stop/ And you will meet with no danger."

3. Here the names are obliterated.

4. D. C. Lau, p. 68.

5. *Shang shu* (*SPTK*) 3:12a (Legge 3:159).

6. See *Hsin T'ang shu* 220:6202.

3. ANCIENT CUSTOMS AND RELIGION

1. The three treatises are: Nāgārjuna, *Mādhyamika śāstra* (Middle Treatise); *Dvādaśanikāya śāstra* (Twelve Gates Treatise); and Āryadeva, *Śata śāstra* (Hundred Verses Treatise).

2. For the text's authenticity see Jonathan W. Best, "Tales of Three Paekche Monks Who Traveled Afar in Search of the Law," *Harvard Journal of Asiatic Studies* 51 (1991):152–178. *Sanghana and *Vedatta are unidentified reconstructions.

3. One of the sixteen *samādhi* mentioned in the chapter "The Bodhisattva Fine Sound," in the *Scripture of the Lotus Blossom of the Fine Dharma,* trans. Leon Hurvitz (New York: Columbia University Press, 1976), p. 303.

4. *Book of Songs* 196 (Legge 3:334). According to traditional belief, *mingling* caterpillars (the larvae of the moth *Heliothis armigera*) infesting the mulberry are transformed into "sphex" wasps after being carried by the wasps to their nests.

5. Hsi River is another name for the Li River in Hupei.

6. *Chou i* (*SPTK*) 1:3a (Legge, *Yi King,* Sacred Books of the East 16 [Oxford: Clarendon, 1882], p. 411).

7. The date is corrected following *SGYS* 3:125.

8. This took place on 15 September 527 (*SGYS* 3:128).

9. The *Kobon sui chŏn* quoted in *SGYS* gives Sŏl as his surname; Pak is given in *HKSC* 13:523c.

10. *SGYS* 4:181 says "after four years."

11. *SGYS* 4:181 says "two years after the monk built his hermitage."

12. *HKSC* 13:523c says "at the age of twenty-five."

13. *HKSC* also mentions four *Āgamas* and the *Prajñāpāramitā hṛdaya sūtra*.

14. *HKSC* 13:523c gives the year 589.

15. *SGYS* 4:183 says "Sui Yang-ti sent three hundred thousand troops to attack Koguryŏ."

16. Ninth year of Queen Sŏndŏk, rather than the fifty-eighth year of Kŏnbok, which did not exist.

17. *SGYS* 4:183 says, on the authority of the *Kobon sui chŏn,* that he died at the age of eighty-four; *HKSC* 13:524a says "at the age of ninety-nine (630)."

18. *HKSC* 13:524a adds "at Hwangnyong Monastery."

19. In consecration of his future buddhahood.

20. *P'u-sa chieh pen* (*T.* 24, no. 1500):1107a–1110a; (*T.* 24, no. 1501):1110b–1115c.

21. Monks (*bhikṣu*), nuns (*bhikṣuṇī*), laymen (*upāsaka*), and laywomen (*upāsikā*).

22. Monks, nuns, male novices (*śramanera*), female novices (*śramaṇerikā*), and female postulants (*śikṣamānā*).

23. In his *Further Lives of Eminent Monks* (667), Tao-hsüan (596–667) praises Chajang as a "bodhisattva who protects the dharma" (*HKSC* 24:639c22).

24. Four classes of arhats, pratyekabuddhas, and buddhas.

25. Avalokiteśvara is meant.

26. Gods, dragons, yakṣas (supernatural beings), gandharvas (musician demigods), asuras (titans), garuḍas (mythical birds), kinnaras (mythical beings), and mahoragas (great serpents).

27. This is an error. In 562, Sadaham, a *hwarang,* distinguished himself in a war against Great Kaya (*SGYS* 4:39; 44:417–418)

28. The real author is Ku Yin.

4. CONSOLIDATION OF THE STATE

1. An exhortation similar to that in the *Tso Commentary,* Duke Chao 28 (Legge 5:725, 727).

2. When his father killed his elder brother, the duke escaped to the Ti barbarians. After nineteen years he returned to his state of Chin and reigned for nine years; *Shih chi* 39:1656–1659.

3. *Shih chi* 37:1593.

4. *Shang shu* 2:1b (Legge 3:54).

5. *Wei shu* 7A:137; *SGSG* 25:227.

6. This is the title given him by the Liang in 521.

7. Thus his body was placed in a coffin at his death but was not interred

formally for twenty-seven months, the usual period of mourning for a king or queen in Paekche and Koguryŏ (for example, King Kwanggaet'o).

8. *Tso Commentary,* Duke Ch'eng 9 (Legge 4:372).

9. A colonel of carriage and cavalry under Emperor Wen of Han. *Shih chi* 102:2757–2761 (Burton Watson, *Records of Grand Historians of China* 1:539–542).

10. Marquis of P'ing-chin and chancellor under Emperor Ching; *Shih chi* 112:2949–2953 (Watson 2: 219–225).

11. Marquis of P'ing-yang and prime minister under Emperor Hui; *Shih chi* 54:2021–2031 (Watson 1:421–426).

12. *Ch'eng-wu-lang shih yü-shih nei-kung-feng.*

13. *Chu-tao hsing-ying tu-t'ung.*

14. *Sidok.*

15. *KRS* 4:34a.

16. *KRS* 5:1a.

17. *Analects* 9:19 (Arthur Waley, *The Analects of Confucius* [London: Allen & Unwin, 1949], p. 142).

18. *Mencius* 3B:4 (Legge 2:271).

19. An upright official who served both the Northern Chou (557–581) and Sui dynasties (581–618). He died at the age of sixty-eight. His biographies in the *Pei shih* 75 and *Sui shu* 62 do not mention the words to which Ch'oe alludes.

20. Literally, like a duck and a sparrow.

21. *Li chi* 9, "Li yün" (the evolution of *li* on political ideals and ceremonial usages); Legge, *Li Ki,* Sacred Books of the East 27–28 (Oxford: Oxford University Press, 1885), 2:383.

22. Literally "five-bushel rice teaching" from the fixed contribution required from each family.

23. *Han Shu* 71:3039–40. For the translation and commentary on T'ao Ch'ien's poem, "In Praise of the Two Tutors Surnamed Shu," see James R. Hightower, *The Poetry of T'ao Ch'ien* (Oxford: Clarendon Press, 1970), pp. 215–219.

5. THE RISE OF BUDDHISM

1. *HKC* 1:1018a (Peter H. Lee, *Lives of Eminent Korean Monks* [Cambridge: Harvard University Press, 1969], p. 52); *SGYS* 3:122.

2. *HKC* 2:1020c (Lee, p. 76); *SGYS* 4:179–185, 191–194.

3. *SGYS* 3:130–132, 135–136; *Tongguk Yi sangguk chip* 23:7a–12b.

4. *Ta-sheng ch'i-hsin-lun i-chi* (T. 44:1846).

5. In *Wŏnjong mullyu* 22 (*HTC* 103:422a–b) and *SGYS* 4:197–198.

6. *SGSG* 6:61.

7. *SKSC* 5:737a13.

8. Morality, concentration, and wisdom.

9. *Book of Songs* 101 and 158, where the axe stands for a matchmaker.

10. *T.* 10 [279]:68c.

11. See Robert E. Buswell, Jr., *The Formation of Ch'an Ideology in China and Korea: The Vajrasamādhi-Sūtra, a Buddhist Apocryphon* (Princeton: Princeton University Press, 1989), p. 62, n. 50.

12. Preface to *Kŭmgang sammaegyŏng non* (*T.* 34, no. 1730) 1, 34:961a–963a; hereafter cited only by chapter, page, register, and line number where relevant. For a complete study and translation of this scripture (*T.* 9, no. 273, pp. 365c–374b), see Robert E. Buswell, Jr., *The Formation of Ch'an Ideology in China and Korea*.

13. Voidness of characteristics, voidness of voidness, and voidness of both.

14. The pure *dharmadhātu,* which is the manifestation of the ninth immaculate consciousness, and the four wisdoms into which the remaining eight consciousnesses develop.

15. The practice of: (1) the ten faiths; (2) ten abidings; (3) ten practices; (4) ten transferences; (5) ten stages; (6) equal enlightenment.

16. Fixed wisdom (=integrative wisdom), unfixed wisdom (=sublime-observation wisdom), nirvana wisdom (=perfection in action wisdom), ultimate wisdom (=great perfect mirror wisdom).

17. Of buddhahood: the fruition buddha who is endowed with all meritorious qualities (=reward body); the *tathāgatagarbha* buddha (=dharma body); form buddha (=transformation body).

18. The rules of conduct and deportment; the cultivation of all wholesome dharmas; aiding all sentient beings.

19. The path to enlightenment is all-embracing; enlightenment is attained via correct understanding; one enters enlightenment by not differentiating concentration from wisdom.

20. Empty-space liberation; adamantine liberation; *prajñā* liberation.

21. Abiding on the equal-enlightenment state for one hundred, one thousand, or ten thousand aeons.

22. The dharma, reward, and transformation bodies.

23. Existence in the realms of sense desire, subtle form, and formlessness.

24. To avoid unwholesome states that have not yet arisen; to overcome unwholesome states that have already arisen; to develop wholesome states that have not yet arisen; to maintain wholesome states that have already arisen.

25. Concentration of will, mind, effort, and investigation.

26. Wŏnhyo explains that these are four powers inherent in the mind's original enlightenment, which act as the conditions for the observation of the three moral codes given above. The four powers are: (1) the tranquil aspect of original enlightenment, which is distinct from all the defilements and acts as the condition for the perfection of the rules of conduct and deportment; (2) the wholesome aspect of original enlightenment, which conforms with all the wholesome faculties and acts as the condition for the cultivation of all wholesome dharmas; (3) the compassionate aspect of original enlightenment, which

does not abandon any sentient being and acts as the condition that prompts one to help all sentient beings; (4) the wisdom aspect of original enlightenment, which is separate from any mundane characteristic and acts as the condition for freeing the mind from any attachment to the phenomenal characteristics of the three types of moral conduct so that they will conform with thusness. *VS*, p. 370c25–28; *KSGN* 3:991a3–b14.

27. Of cause, effect, path, and extinction.

28. Form, feeling, perception, impulse, consciousness.

29. The fifty evils are another unusual listing found in *VS*. The consciousness aggregate (*vijñānaskandha*) includes eight evils—the eight consciousnesses—as do both the feeling and perception *skandhas*. The impulse *skandha* possesses nine evils: eight associated with mind and one dissociated from it. The form *skandha* possesses seventeen evils: the four primary elements and the thirteen derivative forms. These make a total of fifty evils. *KSGN* 2:981b25–c3.

30. Faith, exertion, mindfulness, concentration, wisdom.

31. The development of the five spiritual faculties into potent forces.

32. Voidness of: the three existences, the six destinies, the characteristics of dharmas, the characteristics of names, and mind and consciousness.

33. Faith, consideration, cultivation, practice, relinquishment.

34. Gods, humans, animals, hungry ghosts, and denizens of hell.

35. Giving, morality, patience, exertion, concentration, and wisdom.

36. Eye, ear, nose, tongue, body, mind.

37. Mindfulness, investigation of dharmas, exertion, joy, serenity, concentration, equanimity.

38. A peculiar classification unique to *VS*. The term appears in *VS* as "great matrix of meaning," which the sutra elucidates as follows: "great" means the four great elements of earth, air, fire, and water; "meaning" refers to such lists as the aggregates, elements, and senses; "matrix" means the original consciousness (*mūlavijñāna*); *VS*, p. 372a21–23. Wŏnhyo interprets these as contemplations on the four gross phenomena (the four great elements), as well as the contemplation of three subtler categories of dharmas (the aggregates, and so forth), making a total of seven meanings. These contemplations lead to the destruction of the beginningless seeds of conceptual proliferation (*prapañca*) within the *mūlavijñāna*; *KSGN* 3:988a4–8, 998c2–11.

39. This sentence is quoted from *VS*, p. 370b23.

40. *VS*, p. 366a28.

41. *VS*, p. 366a29.

42. *Mo-ho po-jo po-lo-mi ching* (*T*. 8, no. 223) 5:251b27–28; quoted in *Ta-chih-tu lun* (*T*. 25, no. 1509) 47:397a13–14. "Shatter" in this quotation should be taken in the sense of "to actualize."

43. *Ta-chih-tu lun* 47:399b2–5.

44. This quotation appears to be a paraphrase of a passage in Ching-ying Hui-yüan's (523–592) *Ta-sheng i chang* (*T*. 44, no. 1851) 13:718a7–8.

45. *Yu-ch'ieh-shih ti lun* (*T.* 30, no. 1579), 11:329b1–2.

46. *VS*, p. 372b21–22.

47. *VS*, p. 373b10–11.

48. *Tao te ching* 1; D. C. Lau, trans., *Lao Tzu: Tao Te Ching* (Harmondsworth: Penguin, 1963), p. 57: "Being the same they are called mysteries/ Mystery upon mystery."

49. The physical eye, the heavenly or divine eye, the wisdom eye, the dharma eye, and the Buddha eye; *Ta-chih-tu lun* 33 (*T.* 25:751b13–20).

50. The unlimited ability to explain each and every dharma; to explain the meaning of each and every dharma; to explain each and every dharma and its meaning via any mode of written expression; and to explain each and every dharma and its meaning via any mode of verbal expression; *Ta-chih-tu lun* 25 (*T.* 25:246a–c).

51. *Wei-mo-chih* in Chih-chien (*T.* 14:519–537) and Kumārajīva (*T.* 14:537–557); *Shuo-wu-kou-ch'eng* in Hsüan-tsang (*T.* 14:557–558). Wŏnhyo calls him "silent bodhisattva" (*T.* 14:551c22). See Robert Thurman, *The Holy Teaching of Vimalakīrti* (University Park: Pennsylvania State University Press, 1976), pp. 77, 131–132, n. 15.

52. When Confucius met Wen-po Hsüeh-tzu, both said nothing to each other. When Confucius was asked the reason by Tzu-lu, the master replied: "With that kind of man, one glance tells you that the Way is there before you. What room does that leave for any possibility of speech?" See Burton Watson, *The Complete Works of Chuang Tzu* (New York: Columbia University Press, 1968), p. 223.

53. The aspect of suchness in one mind and the aspect of arising and ceasing in one mind (*T.* 32:576a5–6).

54. The number 108 is frequently used to indicate abundance.

55. Wŏnhyo stresses the crucial message of the *Śrīmālādevīsiṃhanāda* that essential purity (Buddha nature) is to be seen in phenomenal impurity (people's defilements) based on the tathāgatagarbha theory. See Alex and Hideko Wayman, *The Lion's Roar of Queen Śrīmālā* (New York: Columbia University Press, 1974), pp. 37–55.

56. *Yü-she* is a shortened form of Ayodhya, a palace in ancient India where Queen Śrīmālā lived. Wŏnhyo uses it for the name of the text (*T.* 12:217a11).

57. See his *Yŏlban chongyo* in *T.* 38 (no. 1769):239a–255c.

58. Wŏnhyo wrote four books on Kumārajīva's translation of the *Lotus*, of which the *Pŏphwa chongyo* is the only one extant (*T.* 34 [1725]:870c–875c).

59. *Chin-ku* indicates *chin-kuang-ming* (*T.* 55 [2183]:1153b24).

60. Dharma body, reward (retribution) body, and transformation body.

61. Wŏnhyo wrote four books on the *Avataṃsaka* (*T.* 55:115b–1178c). Only the preface and roll 3 of his *Hwaŏmgyŏng so* have survived (*T.* 85:234c–236a).

62. Two texts bear the same name (*T.* 10 [656]:1–126 and *T.* 24 [1485]:1010b–1023a). Because Wŏnhyo wrote a commentary on *T.* 24, no. 1485, it might be this text.

63. Kumārajīva's translation of *Pañcaviṃśatisāhasrikā prajñāpāramitā sūtra* (*T*. 8, no. 223; see 55, no. 2145, 10). Wŏnhyo's commentary is in *T*. 33, no. 1697:68b–74a.

64. *Mahāvaipulyamahāsaṃnipāta sūtra* (*T*. 8, no. 397:1–407).

65. For a list of the ten monasteries see Ch'oe Ch'iwŏn, *Fa-tsang ho-shang chuan* (*T*. 50, no. 2054):284a–b.

66. For the thirty-two major and eighty minor marks of an enlightened being, see Leon Hurvitz, "Chih-I (538–597): An Introduction to the Life and Ideas of a Chinese Buddhist Monk," *Mélanges chinois et bouddiques* 12 (1962): 353–361.

67. The attendant karmic results are external factors affecting the individual, such as the environment; the primary karmic results are personal factors, such as the body and mind.

68. *Ta-pei chou,* in *Ch'ien-yen ch'ien-pi Kuan-shih-yin p'u-sa t'o-lo-ni shen-chou ching* (*T*. 20, no. 1057):84a–c, 90b–91a; *Ch'ien-shou ch'ien-yen Kuan-shih-yin p'u-sa kuang-ta yüan-man wu-ai ta-pei-hsin t'o-lo-ni ching* (*T*. 20, no. 1060):107b–c.

69. Stanley Weinstein, "A Biographical Study of Tz'u-en," *Monumenta Nipponica* 15 (1959–1960):119–149, especially p. 147.

70. Inaba Shōju, "On Chos-grub's Translation of the *Chieh-shen-mi-ching-shu,*" in *Buddhist Thought and Asian Civilization* (Emeryville, Cal.: Dharma Publishing, 1977), pp. 105–113, especially pp. 110–111.

71. For bibliographical notices see *T*. 55:1139b24 and 1157b11; *SGSG* 8:82.

72. *SKSC* 4:728c7–8.

73. *SGYS* 4:151–152; Cho Myŏnggi, *Silla pulgyo ŭi inyŏm kwa yŏksa* (The Doctrine and History of Silla Buddhism) (Seoul: Sint'aeyang, 1962), pp. 180–196.

74. In his *Yuganon ki* (705), 13 (*T*. 42:1828).

75. *SGYS* 5:220–221; Cho Myŏnggi, pp. 197–220.

76. *SKSC* 4:728a–b.

77. *SKSC* 4:725c17.

78. Read *Chen* for *Cheng.*

79. Leaves of the *pattra* tree (*Laurus cassia*) were used in India as a writing material and refer, by extension, to the Indian Buddhist scriptures.

80. *Wei-mo chieh so-shuo ching* (*T*. 14, no. 475) 2:551c22; *Shuo Wu-kou-ch'eng ching* (*T*. 14, no. 476) 4:578c23.

81. Three natures: imaginariness (*parikalpita*), dependency (*paratantra*), and perfection (*pariniṣpanna*).

82. *Chieh shen-mi ching* (*T*. 16, no. 676) 2:697a23–b8.

83. Listed on pp. 182–183.

84. *Ssu-fen lü* (*T*. 22, no. 1428) 1:569b21–23, c6–9.

85. That is, "explanation of profound mysteries," construed as a genitive *tatpuruṣa*; see the entry in Franklin Edgerton, *Buddhist Hybrid Sanskrit Dictionary* (New Haven: Yale University Press, 1953), p. 558a. The non-Paninean

analysis of six types of Sanskrit compounds can be traced to the *Bṛhad-devata* 2:105, attributed to Śaunaka (c. 400 B.C.), ed. and trans. Arthur A. Mac-Donell, Harvard Oriental Series, 5–6 (Cambridge: Harvard University Press, 1904–1905).

86. Names, sentences, and phonemes are three of the dissociated forces (*cittaviprayuktasaṃskāra*) recognized by the Vaibhāṣika and some subsequent schools. They include several forces that cannot be described as either mental or physical, such as origination and destruction. See Padmanabh S. Jaini, "The Vaibhāṣika Theory of Words and Meanings," *Bulletin of the School of Oriental and African Studies* 22 (1959):95–107; and "The Development of the Theory of the *Viprayukta-saṃskāras*," *BSOAS* 22 (1959):521–447 [sic].

87. *Wei-mo-chieh so-shuo ching* (*T.* 14, no. 475) 1:542b12; compare *Shuo Wu-kuo-ch'eng ching* (*T.* 14, no. 476) 2:564c20–1.

88. *Ch'eng wei-shih lun* (*T.* 31, no. 1585) 1:1a27–b1. Reading *chajǔng* ("self-corroboration") for *chach'e* ("self-essence"), following the Taishō edition. This is the view of Dharmapāla and Sthiramati on the meaning of the transformation of consciousness.

89. Ibid., 2:7b26. The three are the fruition consciousness (the eighth consciousness), the ratiocinative consciousness (the seventh), and the sense consciousnesses (the first through the sixth).

90. Ibid., 1:1b2–3. This is the view of Nanda, Bandhuśri, and others on the meaning of the transformation of consciousness.

91. See *Ch'eng wei-shih lun* 2:6b5.

92. See for instance, *Yu-ch'ieh shih-ti lun* (*T.* 30, no. 1579) 56:607c3–4; 77:725b1–2.

93. *Ta-sheng A-p'i-ta-mo tsa-chi lun* (*T.* 31, no. 1606) 1–5:694a–719a; by Sthiramati (c. A.D. sixth century).

94. See *Ch'eng wei-shih lun* (*T.* 30, no. 1579) 1:3b15.

95. *Tsa A-p'i-t'an hsin lun* (*T.* 28, no. 1552) 10:957b22–23.

96. Ibid., 10:957b24–25.

97. See *A-p'i-ta-mo fa-chih lun* (*T.* 26, no. 1544) 13:981a–b.

98. See *A-p'i-ta-mo chü-she lun* (*T.* 29, no. 1558) 13:981b6–8.

99. *A-p'i-ta-mo shun cheng-li lun* (*T.* 29, no. 1562) 3:346c9–13, by Saṃgha-bhadra (late fourth century).

100. Ibid., 3:346c13–18.

101. *A-p'i-ta-mo-tsang hsien-tsung lun* (*T.* 29, no. 1563) 3:786c6–11, by Saṃghabhadra.

102. See *Ta-T'ang hsi-yü chi* (*T.* 51, no. 2087) 4:891c16–892b3 for the story of the conflict and eventual reconciliation between Saṃghabhadra and Vasubandhu; translated by Samuel Beal, *Buddhist Records of the Western World* (1888; reprint ed., New York: Paragon, 1968), 1:192–196.

103. *Shun cheng-li lun* (*T.* 29, no. 1562) 3:346c17.

104. *A-p'i-ta-mo fa-chih lun* 13:981a27–29.

105. *A-p'i-ta-mo ta-pi-p'o-sha lun* (*T.* 27, no. 1545) 126:659a23–4, 29b1.

106. *Shun cheng-li lun* (*T.* 29, no. 1562) 14:346c17.

107. *She Ta-sheng lun shih* (*T*. 31, no. 1598) 1:380b12–13.

108. *Yu-ch'ieh-shih ti lun* (*T*. 30, no. 1579) 85:772c9–773a1.

109. *Chieh shen-mi ching* 2:697a23–b8.

110. Ibid., 2:697a28–b4.

111. *Miao-fa lien-hua ching* (*T*. 9, no. 262) 2:13c17–18.

112. *Wei-mo-chieh so-shuo ching* (*T*. 14, no. 475) 2:546b; *Shuo Wu-kou-ch'eng ching* (*T*. 14, no. 476) 3:572a–b.

113. *Ta-pan nieh-p'an ching* (*T*. 12, no. 374) 4:385b and passim.

114. *Ta-fang-kuang fo hua-yen ching* (*T*. 9, no. 278) 44–60:676a–788b; compare *Ta-fang-kuang fo hua-yen ching* (*T*. 10, no. 279) 60–80:319a–444c.

115. Robert Buswell would like to thank Professor Alan Sponberg of the University of Montana, a specialist on K'uei-chi and Chinese Fa-hsiang thought, for his detailed suggestions on the translation itself and for information on the central issues. The translation benefited greatly from his valuable advice.

116. Nangnang: the Chinese colony founded during the Han dynasty along the central coast of the Korean peninsula.

117. *Liang* here should read *pi-lang* (*anumāna*), following K'uei-chi's account of Hsüan-tsang's position; see *Yin-ming ju cheng-li lun shu* (*T*. 44, no. 1840) 2:115b25ff.

118. The sixth of the *anaikāntika* types of fallacies of the inferential reason (*hetvābhāsa*) discussed in the *Yin-ming ju cheng-li lun* (*Nyāyapraveśa*). It is normally used to describe that type of fallacy in which two distinct, yet equally valid, reasons lead to contradictory results.

119. The first three elements (*dhātu*) are visual form (*rūpa*), the eye (*cakṣu*), and eye consciousness (*cakṣurvijñāna*).

120. Following K'uei-chi's description of the syllogism in *Yin-ming ju cheng-li lun shu* (*T*. 44, no. 1840) 2:115b26–27. Tsan-ning's versions of the positions of Hsüan-tsang and Sungyŏng garble what is already a complicated issue, and I have found it preferable to render the syllogisms according to K'uei-chi's account.

121. *Yin-ming ju cheng-li lun shu* (*T*. 44, no. 1840) 2:116a6–7.

122. Ibid., 2:116a16–19, with minor variations.

123. *Ta-fang-kuang fo hua-yen ching* (*T*. 9, no. 278) 8:449c14; (*T*. 10, no. 279) 17:89a1–2.

124. "The Interminable," the deepest of the hells.

125. *Ta-sheng chang-chen lun* (*T*. 30, no. 1578) 1:268b21–22.

126. Dharmapāla explains that emptiness is equivalent to the imaginary aspect of dharmas (*parikalpitasvabhāva*), while nonemptiness refers to the perfected and dependent natures of dharmas (*pariniṣpannasvabhāva* and *paratantrasvabhāva*); *Ta-sheng kuang po lun shih-lun* (*T*. 30, no. 1571) 10:248a29–b2. For the relevant passage in the *Sandhinirmocana sūtra*, see *Chieh shen-mi ching* (*T*. 16, no. 676) 1:688c:23–4ff.

127. *P'ien chung-pien lun sung* (*T*. 31, no. 1601) 1:477c8–9, and *P'ien chung-pien lun* (*T*. 31, no. 1600) 1:464a14–15; the translation follows Vasubandhu's exegesis at 464a18–24.

128. *Fo-ti ching lun* (*T.* 26, no. 1530) 4:307a8–9.

129. *Ch'eng wei-shih lun* (*T.* 31, no. 1585) 7:39b1–2.

130. *Ta-sheng chang-chen lun* (*T.* 30, no. 1578) 1:272b2–5.

131. Following K'uei-chi, *Ch'eng wei-shih lun shu-chi* (*T.* 43, no. 1830) 1:234c14.

132. *Ch'eng wei-shih lun* (*T.* 31, no. 1585) 8:46b17–18.

133. *Ta-sheng chang-chen lun* 2:274b9–10.

134. *Ch'eng wei-shih lun* 7:39b17–18.

135. *Ta-sheng chang-chen lun* 2:274a22–24.

136. *Ta-sheng chang-chen lun* 1:270b25–6, c1–4, 11–13; this position was stated earlier at p. 268c19. Several readings have been corrected according to the Taishō edition: Taehyŏn's recension of the text differs markedly here from the Taishō edition.

137. *Ta-sheng kuang po lun shih-lun* (*T.* 30, no. 1571) 4:206c12–13.

138. *Ta-sheng kuang po lun shih-lun* 6:219b27–28.

139. Existence, nonexistence, both, neither; see Bhāvaviveka's Prajñāpradīpa [*Po-jo-teng lun-shih*] (*T.* 30, no. 1566) 15:135a12, commenting on *Mūlamadhyamakakārikā, Chung-lun* (*T.* 30, no. 1565) 2:39a.

140. Perhaps *Chin-kang po-jo lun* (*T.* 25, no. 1510); the passage is untraced.

141. As well as being the ninth of the twelve divisions of the scriptures, *Sūtropadeśas* were also considered treatises so renowned that they were recognized as canonical texts in their own right; see Thomas Watters, *On Yuan Chwang's Travels in India 629–645 A.D.* (London: Royal Asiatic Society, 1904) 1:275.

142. *SGYS* 5:217–219.

143. *SGYS* 4:190–191.

144. *Amitāyurdhyāna* (*Wu-liang-shou ching*), *T.* 12 [365]:341b–346a; Sacred Books of the East 49 (Oxford: Clarendon, 1894), pp. 167–199.

145. *Scripture of the Lotus Blossom of the Fine Dharma,* trans. Leon Hurvitz (New York: Columbia University Press, 1976), pp. 311–319.

146. Or Sunje in *SGYS* 4:202.

147. According to the *SGYS* 4:203, on 25 May 762 both the Guardian of the Earth and Maitreya appeared.

148. For the *Divination Scripture,* see *Li-tai san-pao chi* (*T.* 49, no. 2034) 12:106c, and Whalen Lai, "The *Chan-ch'a ching:* Religion and Magic in Medieval China," in Robert E. Buswell, Jr., ed., *Chinese Buddhist Apocrypha* (Honolulu: University of Hawaii Press, 1990), pp. 175–206, esp. p. 176.

149. To divine the results of the past, present, and future.

6. POETRY AND SONG

1. Also called Sinbang.

7. LOCAL CLANS AND THE RISE OF THE MEDITATION SCHOOL

1. *SKSC* 19:832b–833a gives his dates as 680–756 and says Musang studied under Chih-shen. *Li-tai fa-pao chi* (*T.* 51 [2075]:185a) says his name was given by Hsüan-tsung. Ma-tsu's first teacher was Musang according to the *Yüan-chüeh ching ta-shu ch'ao* (*HTC* 14:279a); see Jan Yün-hua, "Tsung-mi: His Analysis of Ch'an Buddhism," *T'oung Pao* 58 (1972):42–43, and Yamaguchi Zuihō, "Chibetto bukkyō to Shiragi no Kin oshō," in *Shiragi bukkyō kenkyū,* ed. Kin Chiken and Sai Ingan (Tokyo: Sankibo busshorin, 1973), pp. 3–36.

2. *Mahāparinirvāṇa sūtra* (*T.* 12, no. 374) 27:525c25–26.

3. Ibid., 27:525c27–526a1.

4. The *Tsu-t'ang chi* mistakenly reads "eye" (*mok*) for cause.

5. *Chin-kang san-mei ching* (*T.* 9, no. 273):368c19–20.

6. Based on the story of Yajñadatta who thought he had lost his head and searched for it throughout the city before "finding" it; *Shou-leng-yen ching* (*T.* 19, no. 945) 4:121b.

7. *Ta-sheng tsan* (In Praise of Mahāyāna), in *Ching-te ch'uan-teng lu* (*T.* 51, no. 2076) 29:449b. 29.

8. This section appears with some modifications in *Jen-t'ien yen-mu* (The Eyes of Men and Gods) (*T.* 48, no. 2006) 4:322b.

9. *Hsin-hsin ming* (Inscription on Faith in Mind) (*T.* 48, no. 2010) 376b18; a mistaken homophone in the *Tsu-t'ang chi* has been corrected.

10. *Flower Garland Scripture* (*T.* 9, no. 278) 8:449c14; (*T.* 10, no. 279) 17:89a1–2.

11. Following the Flower Garland school's explanation of the *trikāya.* The rest of this paragraph has been moved here from its original location after the second type of attainment of buddhahood.

12. See *Hsin Hua-yen ching lun* (Exposition of the New Translation of the Flower Garland Scripture) (*T.* 36, no. 1739) 3:739a17–18.

13. Ibid., 3:739b26–27.

14. Ibid., 3:739b26.

15. See *Lotus Scripture* (*T.* 9, no. 262) 5:42a–44a passim, especially p. 43b26.

16. A paraphrase of *Lotus Scripture* 5:42b25–26.

17. Sunji places this section in the context of a hypothetical exchange between master and disciple; I summarize only the gist of the discussion.

18. Kangnŭng in Kangwŏn.

19. The word used here, *cho,* ordinarily means "grandfather," but the context seems to support the interpretation "father"; see Kyung-bo Seo (Sŏ Kyŏngbo), *A Study of Korean Zen Buddhism Approached Through the Chodangjip* (Seoul: Poryŏngak, 1973), p. 149.

20. According to the cyclical year, this should be the first year of Ta-chung, as is confirmed by the account in *SGYS.*

21. Actually the first year of Lung-chi.

8. EARLY KORYŎ POLITICAL STRUCTURE

1. Except for the year, all dates in the text are given according to the lunar calendar.

2. Yao and Shun are two mythical Chinese leaders who exemplified the classical ideal of the model ruler.

3. The remainder of this translation is from Hahm Pyong-Choon, *The Korean Political Tradition and Law: Essays in Korean Law and Legal History* (Seoul: Hollym, 1967), pp. 47–51, with minor changes.

4. Title often borne by a village chief of late Silla.

5. Translation, with minor changes, from Michael C. Rogers, "*P'yŏnnyŏn T'ongnok:* The Foundation Legend of the Koryŏ State," *Journal of Korean Studies* 4 (1982–1983):3–72.

6. *Chou i (SPTK)* 4:1a (Legge, *Yi King*, p. 238).

7. Legge 1:295.

8. James Legge, *Li Ki* (Oxford: Oxford University Press, 1885), 1:400.

9. *Yüeh-ling* (monthly ordinances) sets forth month by month the annual events to be conducted by the government in accordance with the seasonal order of the year.

10. The gentleman has four daily routines. In the morning, he attends to government affairs; during the day, he seeks advice; in the evening, he refines government ordinances; and at night he takes care of his health.

11. *Analects* 2:25 (Legge 1:147).

12. Legge 5:218–219.

13. Hou Ching (502–552) was a man of Liang who unsuccessfully tried to establish himself as a Han emperor.

14. Chu I (482–548) was a chief minister of Liang.

15. The highest titular office, often conferred on a high-ranking official in recognition of unusual contributions to the dynasty.

16. Ki Hongsu (1148–1210) and Ch'a Yaksong (d. 1204) were prominent military officials under Ch'oe Ch'unghŏn, whose high-handed military rule saw a serious erosion in the bureaucratic administration of the government dominated by Confucian literati.

17. *Shu* (also read *chu*) was a silver coin used in Liu Sung China (420–479) whose weight equaled one hundred grains of millet.

18. What follows here in the original text is Yi Chibaek's memorial on the same subject, which is found in translation in chapter 12 of this book.

19. *Mencius* 1A:7 (Legge 2:146).

20. Kim Yusin (595–673) was a Silla warrior-aristocrat whose military strategies helped unify the three Korean kingdoms with the aid of T'ang China in the seventh century.

21. Although the text contains only part of the two four-character lines, the complete translation by James Legge is quoted here. See Legge 4:535.

9. KORYŎ SOCIETY

1. The classics are the *Book of Documents, Book of Songs, Book of Changes, Book of Rites*—which includes *Rites of Chou, Ceremonial,* and *Book of Rites*—and *Spring and Autumn Annals.* These five works were later supplemented with four other books: *Analects, Mencius, Great Learning,* and *Doctrine of the Mean.* The three histories are *Historical Records* (*Shih chi*), *History of the Former Han* (*Han shu*), and *History of the Later Han* (*Hou Han shu*).

2. Minister of public works under the first T'ang emperor, Kao-tsu.

3. Rose to be prime minister in the early T'ang dynasty.

4. Li Shen (d. 846) was a poet of T'ang China.

5. One *kŭn* equals six hundred grams.

6. This is obviously an error. The twenty-third year of Munjong was the second year of Hsi-ning.

7. The Three August Sovereigns were Fu-hsi, Shen-nung, and Huang-ti. The mythical five ancient Chinese emperors begin with Huang-ti and end with Yao and Shun.

8. A man of the Later Wei dynasty who was known for his filial piety.

9. Known as one of the twenty-four most filial sons throughout Chinese history.

10. The three texts comprise *Chou li* (Rites of Chou), *I li* (Ceremonial), and *Li chi* (Book of Rites).

11. A candidate (*hyanggong chinsa*) recommended by his district to sit for the examination.

12. Son of Chancellor Kim Injon (d. 1127).

13. *Sanwŏn tongjang,* a position given to a person of provincial origin.

10. MILITARY RULE AND LATE KORYŎ REFORM

1. Yŏn, second son of King Sinjong (1197–1204), did not ascend the throne.

2. Wang U was a great-great-grandson of King Sukchong (1095–1105).

3. One *tu* in modern times equals 316 cubic inches.

4. These are ritual, music, archery, chariot riding, writing, and mathematics.

5. Han Yü and Tu Fu are renowned Chinese literary figures, as are Ch'ü Yüan, Chia I, Li Po, and T'ao Ch'ien, mentioned below.

6. Hsi K'ang and Juan Chi were two of the Seven Sages of the Bamboo Grove in China.

7. One *yang* in modern times equals 1.325 ounces.

8. One *kan* equals 180 centimeters.

9. Hindu's name appears as Hu'tun after 1274. See William Henthorn, *Korea: The Mongol Invasion* (Leiden: Brill, 1963), p. 186, n. 26.

10. Legge 1:411.

11. Ibid.

12. Though phrased in the first person, this quotation is a paraphrase of the original statement found in the *Doctrine of the Mean* (Legge 1:411).

13. These are the main Yüan imperial offices that were used frequently by the Mongols to interfere in Koryŏ affairs.

14. Although Eastern Capital usually refers to Liao-yang, here it means Tung-ning, to which Koryŏ sent an expeditionary force in 1369 to destroy Ch'i-sai-yin Temür and his forces when he rebelled against Koryŏ following the execution of his father, Ki Ch'ŏl.

15. In 1343, Yüan removed and exiled King Ch'unghye (1330–1332 and 1339–1344) because of his licentious and cruel behavior. He died in 1344 while en route to exile.

16. Officials of late Koryŏ.

17. A favored Korean eunuch at the Yüan court who did much harm to Koryŏ. Exiting on horseback was considered outlandish behavior. See *KRS* 122:23a–24b.

18. These granaries were said to have been set up to exploit the peasants through extortion and usury.

19. Probably men like Ko Yongbo, mentioned earlier.

20. The *choŏp* and *kubun* (ancestral occupation and pension) land, though originally granted by the state, became hereditary whereas most other state land grants did not.

21. One *mu* equals approximately 240 square paces in modern times; 6.6 *mu* is about one acre.

22. Bernhard Karlgren, *The Book of Odes* (Stockholm: Museum of Far Eastern Antiquities, 1950), p. 137: "All is well with the rich people, alas for those who are helpless and alone."

23. *Chou i (SPTK)* 4:3b (Legge, *Yi King*, pp. 353–354).

24. One *sŏk* equals 120 catties (160 pounds).

25. *Chou i (SPTK)* 4:4a (Legge, *Yi King*, p. 354).

26. The text mentions six senses but specifies only five.

11. BUDDHISM: THE CH'ŎNT'AE AND CHOGYE SCHOOLS

1. Generality and particularity; identity and difference; integration and distinction.

2. Where the Buddha preached the sixty-chapter version of the *Flower Garland Scripture*.

3. Each resides in all; all reside in one; one resides in all; and all reside in all.

4. Alluding to *Mo-ho chih-kuan* (T. 46, no. 1911) 10a:132a3–4: "Practitioners of Ch'an [Sŏn] only exalt noumenal contemplation; they are attached to the synthesizing quality of the mind, but remain ignorant of names and characteristics and cannot understand even one phrase of the doctrine." My identification of T'ai-ling with Chih-i (538–597) is only tentative; Ŭich'ŏn seems to be referring to someone who practices meditation exclusively and

neglects doctrinal study, in contrast to people like K'uei-chi (Tz'u-en; 632–682), who merely study doctrine and do not meditate.

5. The site where the Buddha preached many of the Mahāyāna scriptures.

6. Ten different aspects of the Flower Garland theory of the unimpeded interpenetration of all phenomena; for the two different lists, see Junjirō Takakusu, *The Essentials of Buddhist Philosophy* (Honolulu: University of Hawaii Press, 1949), pp. 120–121.

7. Fa-tsang's five divisions of the scholastic teachings: Hīnayāna; Mahāyāna inception teachings; Mahāyāna final teachings; sudden teachings; complete teachings.

8. The fundamental meditative subjects in the Flower Garland school: true emptiness; unimpeded interpenetration of principle and phenomena; all-embracing interfusion. See Tu-shun's *Fa-chieh kuan men*, translated in Garma C. C. Chang, *The Buddhist Teaching of Totality: The Philosophy of Hwa Yen Buddhism* (University Park: Pennsylvania State University Press, 1971), pp. 208–223.

9. Chin-shui Ching-yüan (1011–1088). Nineteen works are attributed to Ching-yüan in Ŭich'ŏn's *Sinp'yŏn chejong kyojang ch'ongnok* (*T.* 55, no. 2184, 1166b–1178b passim), but as far as I am aware, none is extant. Two other short texts by Ching-yüan, not listed by Ŭich'ŏn, appear in *T: Fo i-chiao ching lun shu chieh-yao* (*T.* 40, no. 1820), 844c–857b, and *Chin shih-tzu chang yün-chien lei-chieh* (*T.* 45, no. 1880), 663a–667a.

10. Assuming that *pyŏn* (to change), which does not make much sense here, is mistaken for the homophonous *pyŏn* (to distinguish).

11. *Ta-fang-kuang fo hua-yen ching* (*T.* 10, no. 279) 62:333c1–2; P. L. Vaidya, ed., *Gaṇḍavyūha sūtra, Buddhist Sanskrit Texts,* no. 5 (Darbhanga: Mithila Institute, 1960), p. 46.

12. *Ta-fang-kuang fo hua-yen ching* 62:333c14–15; P. L. Vaidya, *Gaṇḍa-vyūha,* ibid.

13. Alluding to *Analects* 17:7 (Legge 1:321).

14. Five pervasive causes and effects: hermeneutical device for explicating the *Flower Garland Scripture*. The eighty rolls of the scripture are divided among these five: (1) producing faith, which prompts people to believe in the fundamental cause of Buddhahood; (2) differentiation, which distinguishes cause from fruition, allowing the student to understand the law of cause and effect; (3) equanimity, in which the student looks equally upon cause and effect; (4) the completion of spiritual practice; (5) access to realization, in which the student has simultaneous insight into both cause and effect.

15. *Lao Tzu* 41; Arthur Waley, *The Way and Its Power: A Study of the Tao Te Ching and Its Place in Chinese Thought* (New York: Grove Press, 1958), p. 193.

16. The *kyŏl* is a unit of land measurement varying according to the quality of the land and equaling from 61 to 138.3 acres. Takeda Yukio, "Shiragi no metsubō to Kōrai-chō no tenkai," *Iwanami kōza: sekai rekishi* (Tokyo: 1970) 9:486.

17. The eighth rank in the nine-rank Buddhist hierarchy. At this rank, a monk can be appointed abbot of a temple.

18. One *pu* equals five feet.

19. The posts are called *changsaeng p'yo,* or "longevity posts." According to Takeda Yukio, these posts had a religious function as shamanistic guardians of the area. They also were boundary markers indicating the distance from various places. Since each post was said to have been maintained by ten households, they may have been part of *changsaeng ko,* the monastery land set aside specifically for loans to the people.

20. Choil is referred to as the *hwahyang cheja* (Incense-lighting Disciple) in the text.

21. Pyŏngong (1178–1234), also known as Hyesim, was Chinul's successor and a major leader of Meditation under the rule of the Ch'oe house.

22. Chingong (d. 1252), also known as Ch'ŏnjin, was the third national preceptor at Songgwang Monastery.

23. The *Platform Scripture* is the collection of sermons delivered by Hui-neng (638–713), the sixth patriarch of the Ch'an school in China. The full title of the book is *The Sermons of the Sixth Patriarch, Great Master Fa-Pao (Liu-tsu ta-shih Fa-Pao t'an-ching),* that is, the scripture of the dharma-jewel platform, an ordination platform. The second work is *The Recorded Sayings of Ta-hui (T.* 47, no 1998), 811b–943a.

24. A minor figure of the Five Dynasties.

25. One *chang* is ten *ch'ŏk* or *cha,* which in modern times is 3.3 meters.

26. Adapted from a verse attributed to the Fourth Ch'an Patriarch Upagupta; *Ching-te ch'uan-teng lu (T.* 51, no. 2076) 1:207b.

27. *Ta-fang-kuang fo hua-yen ching (T.* 10, no. 279) 50:265b10.

28. Four benefactors: those to whom one is beholden for one's spiritual progress. The lists vary: teacher, parent, ruler, supporters; parents, sentient beings, ruler, the three treasures (of the Buddha, his teachings, and his order).

29. The three trainings in moral discipline, mental concentration, and wisdom.

30. *Shou-leng-yen ching (T.* 19, no. 945) 6:131b.

31. Adapted from *Lao Tzu* 48: "Keep on reducing and reducing, until you reach the state of inactivity *(wu-wei)."*

32. Adapted from *Shou-leng-yen ching* 4:121b.

33. A verse by Shih Wu-chu (737–767) in the *Lives of Eminent Monks compiled during the Sung* is identical except for the first line; see *Sung kao-seng chuan (T.* 50, no. 2061) 20:837a17–19.

34. The three disasters of fire, flood, and wind, which strike during the destruction accompanying the end of the age.

35. Past, present, and future.

36. North, south, east, west, northeast, southeast, northwest, southwest, zenith, nadir.

37. This phrase is commonly attributed to Ma-tsu Tao-i (709–788); see *Ching-te ch'uan-teng lu (T.* 51, no. 2076) 6:246b5. For other citations of this

phrase and problems with its traditional attribution, see Robert E. Buswell, Jr., *The Korean Approach to Zen: The Collected Works of Chinul* (Honolulu: University of Hawaii Press, 1983), pp. 234–235, n. 28.

38. *Ta-fang-kuang fo hua-yen ching* (*T.* 10, no. 279) 51:272c23–25; the scripture-volume simile appears at p. 272c7–17.

39. *Hsin Hua-yen ching lun* (*T.* 36, no. 1739) 14:815a3–8.

40. *Hsin Hua-yen ching lun* 15:819a29–b2.

41. *Hsin Hua-yen ching lun* 21:862a7–8.

42. Chinul alludes here to a statement by the fifth patriarch of both the Hua-yen and Ho-tse Ch'an schools, Tsung-mi (780–841): "The scriptures are the Buddha's words. Ch'an is the Buddha's mind." See *Ch'an-yüan chu-ch'üan chi tou-hsü* (*T.* 48, no. 2015) 1:400b10–11.

43. See postface to *Lüeh-shih Hsin Hua-yen ching hsiu-hsing chüeh-i lun* (*T.* 36, no. 1741), 1049c5–13; the previous paragraph appears at p. 1049c4–5.

44. The instruction given by Nan-ch'üan P'u-yüan (748–835) that brought Chao-chou T'ung-shen (778–897) to awakening; see *Ching-te ch'uan-teng lu* (*T.* 51, no. 2976) 10:276c.

45. *Ta-fang-kuang fo hua-yen ching* (*T.* 10, no. 279) 17:89a; see also *Ta-fang-kuang fo hua-yen ching* (*T.* 9, no. 278) 8:449c.

46. Te-shan Hsüan-chien (780–865), a fifth-generation successor in the T'ien-huang branch of the Ch'ing-yüan Hsing-ssu lineage; for his "thirty blows," see *Ching-te ch'uan-teng lu* 15:317c.

47. Lin-chi I-hsüan (d. 866) was the founder of the Lin-chi school of the mature Ch'an tradition; for his four types of Ch'an shout (Kor. *kal*; Ch. *ho*), see *Lin-chi lu* (*T.* 47, no. 1985), 496c.

48. "Groped for our heads": an allusion to the story of Yajñadatta, who one day woke up thinking he had lost his head and went wildly around the city trying to find it. It is used as a simile for the ignorant person who has always had the enlightened nature but assumes in his delusion that he has lost it. See *Shou-leng-yen ching* (*T.* 19, no. 945) 4:121b.

49. *Ta-sheng ch'i-hsin lun* 575b–583b; the text is an original Chinese composition that has nothing to do with the Indian poet and philosopher Aśvaghoṣa (c. A.D. 100).

50. *Liu-tsu t'an-ching* (*T.* 48, no. 2008), 346a–362b; for a synopsis of the problems concerning the Sixth Patriarch Hui-neng (638–713) and his reputed authorship of the text, see Philip B. Yampolsky, *The Platform Sūtra of the Sixth Patriarch* (New York: Columbia University Press, 1967).

51. Huang-mei is the respectful name for the Fifth Patriarch Hung-jen (601–674) after the mountain where he resided.

52. Mount Sumeru, the center of our world system, was considered in traditional Indian cosmology to be surrounded by seven concentric iron mountain ranges. Here Sumeru is contrasted with the lower surrounding ranges to symbolize the distinction in level between principle and phenomenon, absolute and relative truth, and so forth.

53. Long, bushy eyebrows indicated great wisdom; hence monks who use

too many words and end up obfuscating the dharma will lose their eyebrows; see *Pi-yen lu* (*T.* 48, no. 2003) 1:148b2.

54. *Ta-fang-kuang fo hua-yen ching* (*T.* 10, no. 279) 14:72b.

55. Quoted by Tzu-hsüan (d. 1038) in his *Ch'i-hsin lun shu pi hsüeh chi* (*T.* 44, no. 1848) 3:313c27; and see *Aṭṭhasālinī* iii:213, cited in Herbert V. Guenther, *Philosophy and Psychology in the Abhidharma* (Berkeley: Shambhala, 1976), p. 62.

56. Seng-ts'an (d. 606), as attributed in his *Hsin-hsin ming* (*T.* 48, no. 2010), 376b.

57. Pao-chih (418–514), respectfully known as Chih-kung, in his *Shih-erh shih-sung*, in *Ching-te ch'uan-teng lu* 29:450b5.

58. Yung-chia Hsüan-chüeh (665–713), in his *Ch'eng-tao ko* (*T.* 48, no. 2014), 395c.

59. *Ta-sheng ch'i-hsin lun* (*T.* 32, no. 1665), 583a–b.

60. *Chin-kang po-jo p'o-lo-mi ching* (*T.* 8, no. 235), 749b.

61. *Hsin-hsin ming* 376b.

62. Alluding to the Parable of the Burning House from the *Lotus Scripture* (*T.* 9, no. 262) 2:12c–13c; Leon Hurvitz, *Scripture of the Lotus Blossom of the Fine Dharma* (New York: Columbia University Press, 1976), pp. 58–62.

63. By Tan-hsia Tzu-ch'un (1064–1117), from his verse, the *Wan chu-yin*, in *Ching-te ch'uan-teng lu* 30:463b–c.

64. Adapted from Wŏnhyo's *Palsim suhaeng chang:* "The practice of persons who have wisdom is to steam rice grains to prepare rice; the practice of persons without wisdom is to steam sand to prepare rice." *HPC* 1:841b.

65. See *Ta-fang-kuang fo hua-yen ching* (*T.* 10, no. 279) 51:272c.

66. *Ta-fang-kuang Yüan-chüeh hsiu-to-lo liao-i ching* (*T.* 17, no. 842), 914a.

67. Adapted from Ku-ling Shen-tsan, disciple of Po-chang Huai-hai (720–814); in the *Chodang chip*, fasc. 16, in Hyosŏng Cho Myŏnggi Paksa Hwagap Kinyŏm Kanhaeng Wiwŏnhoe, ed., *Pulgyo sahak nonch'ong* (Seoul, 1965), p. 104c25–26.

68. Kāśyapa was the Buddha whose advent immediately preceded that of the Buddha of the present age, Śākyamuni.

69. Verses by later masters in the Meditation school that attempted to point the student to the essential feature in a meditation topic (*kongan*). The commentary to this text explains somewhat cryptically: " 'To finger' (*yŏm*) and shake the web [the general outline of the topic]; to proclaim through verse (*song*) its meaning." See Taedong Pulgyo Yŏnguwŏn, eds., *Yŏmsong sŏrhwa* (Seoul: Poryŏngak, 1970), 1:11. While this commentary is attributed to Koguk Kagun (thirteenth century), it was probably composed by Hyesim himself; see Buswell, *Korean Approach to Zen,* pp. 133–134, n. 66.

70. Ch'oe Hongyun (d. 1229) was a civil official in early thirteenth-century Koryŏ.

71. *Analects* 9:4 (Legge 1:217).

72. The sobriquet of the Sung literatus Chang Shang-ying (1043–1121).

73. The *Ch'i shih-chieh ching* is apparently an alternate title for the *T'ien-ti*

ching (Heaven and Earth Scripture) or the *Tsao-li t'ien-ti ching* (The Creation of Heaven and Earth Scripture). Both are Chinese apocryphal scriptures parallel in content to the *Ching-ching fa-hsing ching,* where the idea of the advent of Mahākāśyapa and others in China is discussed in most detail. See *P'o-hsieh lun* (*T.* 52, no. 2109), 478c8–11; *Pien-cheng lun* (*T.* 52, no. 2110) 1:524b17–19; compare *Kwang Hung-ming chi* (*T.* 52, no. 2103) 8:140a6–8.

74. *Analects* 4:15 (Waley, *The Analects of Confucius,* p. 105).

75. *Analects* 4:8 (Waley, p. 103).

76. *Ching-te ch'uan-teng lu* 6:246b. For other references to this phrase and problems with its traditional attribution to Ma-tsu (Tao-i; 709–788), see Buswell, *Korean Approach to Zen,* pp. 234–235, n. 28.

77. Nieh Tao-chen (fl. 307–312) was the reputed compiler of one of the earliest Buddhist catalogs, the *Chung-ching mu-lu* (Catalog of All the Scriptures), completed about 307–312. Though no longer extant, excerpts are included in *Li-tai san-pao chi* (*T.* 49, no. 2034) 6:66a; see discussion in Hayashiya Tomojirō, *Kyōroku kenkyū* (Tokyo: Iwanami shoten, 1941), pp. 285–304.

78. Tao-an (314–385) compiled the *Tsung-li chung-ching mu-lu,* completed in 374. The catalog is no longer extant, but excerpts appear in *Ch'u san-tsang chi-chi* (*T.* 55, no. 2145), passim; it is treated in Hayashiya, *Kyōroku kenkyū,* pp. 333–451.

79. Ming-ch'üan (fl. 695) was the compiler of the *Ta-Chou kan-ting chung-ching mu-lu* (*T.* 55, no. 2153), 372c–476a.

80. Tao-hsüan (596–667) compiled the *Ta-T'ang nei-tien lu* (*T.* 55, no. 2149), 219a–324a.

81. *Chin-lu,* also known as *Chin shih lu, Chin tsa-lu,* or *Chin shih tsa-lu,* is extant only in citations: see, for example, *Ta-T'ang nei-tien lu* (*T.* 55, no. 2149), 235b, 248c, 254c, 255a, 336c. It was compiled by Shih Tao-liu and completed by his disciple Chu Tao-tsu (346–419); see *Chen-yüan hsin-ting Shih-chiao mu-lu* (*T.* 55, no. 2157) 18:897b.

82. *Wei-lu,* also known as *Wei shih ching lu-mu, Wei shih lu-mu,* or *Wei shih lu,* is also extant only in citations: see, for example, *Ta-T'ang nei-tien lu* 2:248c; 10:336c. Like the *Chin-lu,* it was compiled by Shih Tao-liu and completed by Chu Tao-tsu.

83. (*T.* 55, no. 2154), 477a–723a.

84. Tan (Duke of Chou) and Shih (Duke of Chao) lived at the start of the Chou kingdom in China in 1100 B.C. and helped found that state; Hsiao Ho (d. 193 B.C.) and Ts'ao Ts'an (c. 192–190 B.C.) helped found the Han dynasty (third century B.C.).

85. The service is called Kyŏngch'am meetings.

12. POPULAR BELIEFS AND CONFUCIANISTS

1. These religious festivals date from early in the dynasty. See Wang Kŏn's "Ten Injunctions" in Chapter 8.

2. Min Yŏn eventually rose to be a commissioner of the Security Council and the grand academician of the Chinhyŏn Hall in Koryŏ.

3. Hyŏndo (Hsüan-t'u in Chinese) Commandery, originally established as one of the four Han commanderies, is variously thought to have been located in northern Korea or in Manchuria. Here it may be used to mean Korea in general.

4. Chinhan, an ancient term for the southern region of the Korean peninsula, may here refer to Silla during the Later Three Kingdoms period.

5. Source unidentified.

6. Early T'ang monk, also known as Chang-tsui.

7. A satellite state of Chin situated in the Shantung and Honan area of China.

8. Source unidentified.

9. *Shang Shu* 10:6a and 11:4b (Legge 3:490 and 539).

10. Yao, Shun, and Yü, the legendary founder of the Hsia, were sage rulers. T'ang was the founder of the Shang dynasty (1751–1112 B.C.). Wen, Wu, Ch'eng, and K'ang were the first four kings of the Chou dynasty (c. 1122–256 B.C.) in China.

11. Chieh, Chou, Li (878–842 B.C.), Yu (781–771 B.C.), and the First Emperor of Ch'in (246–210 B.C.) were criticized by historians for their misrule.

12. A Taoist adept of Sung Hui-tsung's reign (1101–1125) in China.

13. One *mal* equals 18 liters.

14. The Two Directorates were the Chancellery (Munha sŏng) and the Security Council (*Milchik* sa). The Milchik sa had earlier been called Chungch'u wŏn.

15. Known in Korean as Yanghyŏn-go, this fund supported students at the National Academy.

16. Legge 3:261.

17. *Mencius* 2A:6 (Legge 2:202).

18. *Analects* 15:8 (Legge 1:297).

19. *Mencius* 2A:2 (Legge 2:189).

20. *Li Chi* (*SPPY*) 7:15a (Legge 2:285).

21. Hu Yüan was a teacher of Ch'eng I (1033–1107), who together with his brother, Hao (1032–1085), laid the metaphysical foundation of Neo-Confucianism in Sung China.

22. Legge 1:416.

23. Tan-fu, Wang-chi, and King Wen were the great-grandfather, grandfather, and father, respectively, of the Duke of Chou.

24. *Mencius* 4B:21 (Legge 2:327).

25. Legge, *Yi King*, p. 374.

26. *Shih chi* 1:3–4.

27. See Bernhard Karlgren, "Legends and Cults in Ancient China," *Bulletin of the Museum of Far Eastern Antiquities* 18 (1946):206–344.

28. *Book of Songs* 303 (Legge 4:636–638).

29. *Book of Songs* 245 (Legge 4:465–472).

30. *Shih chi* 8:341; *Han shu* 1A:1.

31. In 1361, with the collapse of the Yüan dynasty, the Red Turbans swept out of the area north of Korea and briefly occupied Koryŏ's capital.

EARLY CHOSŎN: INTRODUCTION

1. *T'aejong sillok* 14:27a. See also Han Yŏngu, *Chŏng Tojŏn sasang ŭi yŏngu* (A Study of Chŏng Tojŏn's Thought) (Seoul: Seoul taehakkyo, 1973), p. 22.

2. For the view that the commoners were excluded from the civil service examinations, see Yi Sŏngmu, *Chosŏn ch'ogi yangban yŏngu* (A Study of Yangban in Early Chosŏn) (Seoul: Ilchogak, 1980). For the view that commoners were allowed, see Yŏng-ho Ch'oe, *The Civil Examinations and the Social Structure in Early Yi Korea, 1392–1600* (Seoul: Korean Research Center, 1987) and Yu Sŭngwŏn, *Chosŏn ch'ogi sinbunje yŏngu* (A Study of the Social Status System in Early Chosŏn) (Seoul: Ŭryu munhwasa, 1987).

3. See Yi T'aejin, "The Socio-Economic Background of Neo-Confucianism in Korea of the 15th and 16th Centuries," *Seoul Journal of Korean Studies* 2 (December 1989). In this and in other studies, Professor Yi T'aejin of Seoul National University offers interesting arguments to establish his thesis that the rise of Neo-Confucian literati (*sarim*) in Korea was related to the introduction of the Kiangnan methods during the fifteenth and sixteenth centuries; see also his *Hanguk sahoesa yŏngu: nongŏp kisul paltal kwa sahoe pyŏndong* (A Study of Social History in Korea: Agrarian Technology Development and Social Changes) (Seoul: Chisik sanŏpsa, 1987).

4. Ki-baik Lee, *A New History of Korea,* trans. Edward W. Wagner with Edward J. Shultz (Cambridge, Mass.: Harvard University Press, 1984), pp. 217–218.

13. FOUNDING THE CHOSŎN DYNASTY

1. *Shang shu* (*SPTK*) 8:13b (Legge 3:425).

2. *Shang shu* 2:2a (Legge 3:55).

3. *Shang shu* 4:7a (Legge 3:195).

4. *Shang shu* 1;11b Legge 3:49).

5. *Shang shu* 2:8a (Legge 3:72–73).

6. *Mencius* 1B:9 (Legge 2:168).

7. *Shang shu* 6:5a (Legge 3:337).

14. POLITICAL THOUGHT IN EARLY CHOSŎN

1. Legge, *Yi King,* Sacred Books of the East 16 (Oxford: Clarendon, 1882), p. 381. The original text turns the first two sentences around. Instead of "humanity" it reads "men" (*jen*). Chŏng Tojŏn thus emphasizes morality and humanity.

2. *Mencius* 2A:6 (Legge 2:201).

3. Here Chŏng Tojŏn paraphrases the first lines of the chapter on the "great minister" (*ta-tsai*) of the *Rites of Chou*.

4. *Shang shu* (*SPTK*) 8:13b (Legge 3:425).

5. *Han shu* 49:2293–4; the Three Kings are Yü, T'ang, and Wen.

6. *Great Learning* 6 (Legge 1:366).

7. *Sŏnjo sillok* 2:21a.

8. *Shang shu* 2:4a–b (Legge 3:61–62).

9. This is a quotation from Ch'eng I's preface to the *I chuan* (Commentary to the *Book of Changes*). See Wing-tsit Chan, *A Source Book in Chinese Philosophy* (Princeton: Princeton University Press, 1963), p. 570, no. 69.

10. This is a paraphrase of the *Doctrine of the Mean* 23. It emphasizes that only the one who possesses utmost sincerity can develop himself and, by extension, all other living beings in the world, thus assisting the transforming powers of heaven and earth.

11. The meaning of "dark inner room" is not clear. It is an expression from poem 256 in the *Book of Songs* (Legge 4:515).

12. *Chou i* (*SPPY*) 18:3b (Legge, *Yi King*, p. 410).

13. Yi I followed Tung Chung-shu's (c. 179–c. 104 B.C.) theory of historical cycles according to which the founder of a new dynasty had to make certain changes (for example, shifting his residence, assuming a new title, altering the color of the clothing) for marking the new Mandate of Heaven, even though he did not alter the fundamental course of his predecessor. "Simplicity" was correlated with heaven, "refinement" with earth. They were supposed to replace each other periodically in order to correct the abuses that would otherwise develop. See Fung Yu-lan, *A History of Chinese Philosophy* (Princeton: Princeton University Press, 1953) 2:61ff.

14. According to the *Book of Documents*, Chi Tzu refused to acknowledge the sovereignty of King Wu, the founder of Chou (Legge 3:320). Chi Tzu (Kija) thus became the second legendary founder of Korea and made his "Eight Rules" the basis of his rule.

15. *Mencius* 3A:1 (Legge 2:234).

15. CULTURE

1. Son Po-gi, *Hanguk ŭi kohwalcha* (Early Korean Typography) (Seoul: Pojinjae, 1982), chap. 6.

2. They are now known as the *kyemi* (1403) type.

3. Tu Cheng-ts'ang of T'ang.

4. The botanical name of the *hwangyang* tree, also called the *hoeyang* tree, is *Buxus koreana*. Its hard wood is often used for making seals and sculptures.

5. Joseph Needham et al., whose translation is used here, erroneously identified the month as the eighth month. We have deleted brackets in the original.

6. Translation taken from Joseph Needham et al., *The Hall of Heavenly*

Records: Korean Astronomical Instruments and Clocks, 1380–1780 (Cambridge: Cambridge University Press, 1986), pp. 17–18, 23–26.

7. Translation taken from Joseph Needham et al., *The Hall of Heavenly Records*, pp. 18–19.

8. Translation taken from Joseph Needham et al., *The Hall of Heavenly Records*, pp. 19–21.

16. SOCIAL LIFE

1. *Chou i* 9:6a (Legge, *Yi King*, pp.435–436).

2. The "three ways" and "six methods" concern the six realms of hell, hungry spirits, procreation, demons, humans, and heaven.

3. Yü is the state with which Shun was first enfeoffed.

4. The three things are the topknot (*sangt'u*), the headband (*manggŏn*), and the hat (*kat*).

5. This is a paraphrase of *Li chi* (*SPPY*) 25:54b–55a (Legge, *Li Ki*, Sacred Books of the East 27–28 [Oxford: Oxford University Press, 1885] 2:237–238).

6. This is not an exact quotation from the *Ch'un ch'iu*, but a combination of several passages. Its meaning is rather obscure, but both women, Chung Tzu and Ch'eng Feng, were not first wives, and this distinction apparently was expressed by the funeral gifts that were sent for them. See *Spring and Autumn Annals*, Duke Yin 1 (Legge 5:3) and Duke Wen 5 (Legge 5:240).

7. *Book of Songs* 6 (Legge 4:12).

8. See *Reflections on Things at Hand: The Neo-Confucian Anthology Compiled by Chu Hsi and Lü Tsu-ch'ien*, translated, with notes, by Wing-tsit Chan (New York: Columbia University Press, 1967), p. 177.

9. The original Chinese text adds: "Therefore, when the husband dies, she will not marry again." *Li chi* 11:37b (Legge 1:439).

10. "Three obediences" refer to a woman's obedience to her father while a child, to her husband during marriage, and to her son when widowed.

11. In the *Book of Songs* (poems 9 and 10), describing kingly virtue and praiseworthy conduct of young women.

12. The *chao-mu* order was used in ancient China to arrange the spirit tablets in the ancestral hall.

13. *Li chi* 16:57a, translated according to Sŏ Kŏjŏng's paraphrase.

14. Legge 4:431.

17. ECONOMY

1. *Kyŏl* is a unit of land measurement based on acreage as well as soil fertility.

2. See *Sejong sillok* 78:37a–b.

3. Legge 2:227.

4. "Grain in ear" begins about June 7 in the twenty-four fortnightly periods.

5. Kun tried to bring a flood under control, and his son Yü continued the work of dredging and channeling the rivers.

6. *Great Learning* 10:19 (Legge 1:379).

7. About 2 by 40 feet.

8. After a long debate, the king finally agreed to allow trade for fifteen thousand *yang* of Japanese silver at the 1538 price for the sake of maintaining a good relationship with Japan.

18. THOUGHT

1. *Doctrine of the Mean* 22 (Legge 1:415–416).

2. *Doctrine of the Mean* 16:2 (Legge 1:397).

3. *Tao-te ching* 40.

4. Paraphrase of *Huai-nan Tzu* (*SPPY*) 3:1a.

5. *Commentary on Doctrine of the Mean* 1:2.

6. *Doctrine of the Mean* 1:4 (Legge 1:384). Actually it names only four feelings, but they are taken as representative of a conventional list of seven found in the *Book of Rites*.

7. Reference to *Doctrine of the Mean* 1, and *Mencius* 6A:7, respectively.

8. *Mencius* 2A:4 (Legge 2:202).

9. *Mencius* 6A:5 (Legge 2:402).

10. Reference to *Book of Changes* (Legge, *Yi King*, p. 356).

11. Reference to *Analects* 17:2 (Legge 1:318) and *Mencius* 7B:24, respectively.

12. For Tzu-ssu's discussion see *Doctrine of the Mean* 1. English translations of these works may be found in *A Source Book in Chinese Philosophy*, Wing-tsit Chan, trans. (Princeton: Princeton University Press, 1963), pp. 547–550.

13. *Yü-lei* (1473 ed.) 53:17b.

14. *Doctrine of the Mean* 1:4 (Legge 1:384).

15. *Chung-yung huo-wen* (*SPPY*) 14a–b.

16. Source unidentified.

17. *I-ch'uan wen-chi* (*SPPY*) 4:1a.

18. *Li chi* (*SPPY*) 11:8b (Legge, *Li Ki* 2:96) and *Chu Tzu ta-ch'üan* (*SPPY*) 67:8a, respectively.

19. *Chu Tzu ta ch'üan* 67:8a.

20. Ibid.

21. *Mencius* 6B:13 (Legge 2:443).

22. *Shang shu* 1:8a (Legge 3:39).

23. *Analects* 11:10 (Legge 1:240) and 11:13 (Legge 1:241), respectively.

24. *Ts'ui-yen* (*SPPY*) 2:25a.

25. *Ta-hsüeh huo-wen* (Seoul: Kyŏngmunsa, 1977 ed.) 47b.

26. *Mencius* 2A:6 (Legge 2:202–203).

27. *Yü-lei* 53:17b.

28. *Ming-tao wen-chi* (*SPPY*) 3:1b.

29. *I-shu* (*SPPY*) 1:7b.

30. The terms originated in the *Book of Documents* (Legge 3:61), a famous passage that reads: "The human mind is insecure, the mind of the Tao is subtle; be discerning, be undivided. Hold fast to the Mean!"

31. *Analects* 2:4 (Legge 1:147).

32. Ibid.

33. *Analects* 17:3 (Legge 1:318).

34. *Mencius* 4A:7 (Legge 2:296).

35. In *Chu Tzu ta-ch'üan* 46:24b, "Letter to Liu Shu-wen," where Chu Hsi says, "Material force is just material force, the nature is just the nature; they likewise being themselves do not get mixed up together."

19. BUDDHISM

1. No killing, no stealing, no sexual misconduct, no lying, and no drinking intoxicants.

2. The strictures against killing, stealing, sexual incontinence, lying, gossiping, harsh speech, flattery, coveting, hatred, and delusion.

3. All existence is suffering; suffering is caused by selfish craving; the eradication of selfish craving brings about the cessation of suffering and enables one to attain nirvana; and there is a path by which this eradication can be achieved, namely, the discipline of the eightfold path.

4. Ignorance, action, consciousness, name and form, six sense organs, contact, sensation, desire, attachment, existence, birth, and old age and death.

5. Giving, morality, patience, effort, concentration, and wisdom.

6. Humanity, righteousness, propriety, wisdom, and faithfulness.

7. *Analects* 2:3 (Legge 1:146).

8. Legge, *Yi King,* p. 378.

9. *Chin-kang po-jo po-lo-mi ching* (*T.* 8, no. 235) 749b14–15.

10. Knowledge of past lives, the operation of karmic cause and effect, and the extinction of the outflows.

11. Clairvoyance, clairaudience, telepathy, knowledge of all former existences of self and others, the power to be anywhere or do anything at will, and knowledge of extinction of the outflows.

12. "The great perfect mirror wisdom . . . which sees the perfect interfusion of all things; . . . integrative nature wisdom . . . which rises above all distinctions and sees all things impartially without coloring by the ego; . . . wisdom of marvelous observation . . . [and] profound intellectual discrimination; . . . wisdom of the accomplishment of what was to be done." (Robert E. Buswell Jr., *The Korean Approach to Zen: the Collected Works of Chinul* [Honolulu: University of Hawaii Press, 1983], p. 411).

13. Eight forms of salvation as both goal and process of attainment: perception of form while abiding in the fine material sphere; perception of form externally but not internally; confidence through recognition of the beautiful; abiding in the sphere of endless space; abiding in the sphere of unbounded consciousness; abiding in the sphere of nothingness; abiding in the sphere of

neither perception nor nonperception; and abiding in the extinction of perception and feeling.

14. Mary Lelia Makra, trans., *The Hsiao Ching* (New York: St. John's University Press, 1961), p. 2.

15. *Analects* 12:1 (Legge 1:250).

16. Legge, *Yi King,* p. 396.

17. *Analects* 9:4 (Legge 1:217).

18. Legge, *Yi King,* pp. 175–176.

19. *Yüan-chüeh ching* (*T.* 17, no. 842), 920b17–18.

20. Makra, *Hsiao Ching,* p. 14.

21. Legge, *Yi King,* p. 370.

22. Ibid.

23. *Doctrine of the Mean* 6 (Legge 1:388).

24. *Shang shu* 2:6a (Legge 3:66).

25. *Analects* 5:19 (Legge 1:180).

26. *Analects* 16:10 (Legge 1:314).

27. Relations between prince and minister, father and son, and husband and wife.

28. The investigation of things, extension of knowledge, sincerity in thought, rectification of heart, cultivation of person, regulation of family, governance of states, and tranquility and happiness of the state. See *Great Learning* 4–5 (Legge 1:357–359).

29. "The cultivation of their own characters, the honoring of men of virtue and talents, affection toward their relatives, respect toward the great ministers, kind and considerate treatment of the whole body of officers, dealing with the mass of the people as children, encouraging the resort of all classes of artisans, indulgent treatment of men from a distance, and the kindly cherishing of the princes of the States." See *Doctrine of the Mean* 20:11 (Legge 1:408–409).

30. The "One thing" means the absolute and refers to mind in this tradition. In his summation, Hyujŏng said, "The sages of the three religions have all emerged from this phrase." See *Sŏnga kwigam* in *HTC* 112:911a.

31. The phrase "picking up a flower" (K. *yŏmhwa,* Ch. *nien-hua*) and its story have been used in the Meditation tradition to refer to enlightened intuition.

32. "Facing a wall" refers to Sŏn sitting meditation, because of the story that Bodhidharma sat facing a wall in silence at Shao-lin Temple for nine years.

33. See the teaching of Ch'an Master Huang-po in the *Wan-ling lu* (*T.* 48, no. 2012) 387a2.

34. See the writings of Pou in *HPC* 6:676c–677a.

35. *Ta-hui yü-lu* (Recorded Sayings of Ta-hui) (*T.* 47, no. 1998), 942a21–22.

36. Legendary teacher of Śākyamuni.

Glossary

Administrative Codes of Chosŏn. See Chŏng
   Tojŏn.
Ado 阿道. Former Ch'in monk.
Aejang 哀莊王. Silla king, 800–809.
Amitābha 無量光明佛 (Infinite Light);
   or Amitāyus 無量壽佛 (Infinite
   Life).
Amitāyurdhyāna sūtra 觀無量壽經
   (Meditation on the Buddha Amitāyus
   Scripture).
Analects (Lun yü 論語).
Andong 安東 (Koch'ang-gun 古昌郡)
   (North Kyŏngsang).
Andong Kwŏn 安東權. Prominent clan
   from Andong.
Angil 安吉. Silla official.
Anhong 安弘 (Anham 安含). Silla
   monk, d. 640.
An Hyang 安珦. Koryŏ scholar,
   1243–1306.
Anp'yŏng, Prince 安平大君.
   King Sejong's third son and a
   renowned calligrapher,
   1418–1453.
An Sŭng 安勝. Koguryŏ noble, King
   Podŏk 報德王, fl. 670–683.
Anthology of Refined Literature. See Hsiao
   T'ung.
An Yu 安裕. Koryŏ scholar who first

accepted the Neo-Confucianism of
   Chu Hsi, 1243–1306.
Arouse Your Mind and Practice! See
   Wŏnhyo.
Asadal 阿斯達. Tangun's second capital,
   near P'yŏngyang or in Hwanghae.
Asaṅga 無着. Elder brother of
   Vasubandhu, fourth century.
   Mahāyānasaṃgraha 攝大乘論. A
   systematic exposition of the
   Consciousness-Only system attributed
   to him.
Assembly of the Eight Prohibitions. See
   P'algwanhoe.
Assembly of One Hundred Seats
   (Paekkojwa hoe 百高座會).
automatic striking clepsydra. See
   chagyŏngnu.
Avalokiteśvara 觀音. Bodhisattva Who
   Observes the Sounds of the World,
   Sound Observer.
Awakening of Faith. See Wŏnhyo.

Bhāvaiveka 清辨. Indian opponent of
   Paramārtha's Yogācāra philosophy, c.
   500–570.
Bodhisattvabhūmi 菩薩地持經 (Stages of
   Bodhisattva Practice).

Bodhiruci 菩提流支. Indian translator of Buddhist texts into Chinese, sixth century.

Bone rank system 骨品制.

Book of Changes (*I ching* 易經; *Chou i* 周易).

Book of Documents (*Shu ching* 書經, *Shang shu* 尚書).

Book of Filial Piety (*Hsiao ching* 孝經).

Book of Rites (*Li chi* 禮記).

Book of Songs (*Shih ching* 詩經).

Buddhist schools:

Ch'ŏnt'ae (T'ien-t'ai 天台).
Consciousness-Only 唯識.
Disciplinary (Vinaya 律).
Divine Seal 神印.
Flower Garland 華嚴.
Meditation 禪.
Pŏpsang (Fa-hsiang 法相).
Pure Land 淨土.
Three Treatise 三論.
Yogācāra 瑜伽.

ch'ach'aung 次次雄 (*chach'ung* 慈忠). "High chief".

Chach'o 自超. Muhak, royal preceptor, 1327–1405.

Ch'adŭk, Lord 車得公. Silla minister, fl. 661–680.

chagyŏngnu 自擊漏. Automatic striking clepsydra.

Chajang 慈藏. Silla monk, c. 636–645.

Ch'am 參. Ts'an, minister of Wiman Chosŏn.

Chan-ch'a shan-o yeh-pao ching 占察善惡業報經 (Scripture That Divines the Requital of Wholesome and Unwholesome Actions).

chang 丈. 3.3 meters, ten *ch'ŏk*.

Ch'ang 昌 (Sin Ch'ang 辛昌). Thirty-third ruler of Koryŏ; legitimacy denied by Chosŏn, 1388–1389.

Ch'angbok Monastery 昌福寺 (Kyŏnggi).

Ch'ang Chori 倉助利. Koguryŏ minister, late third century.

Changdanggyŏng 藏唐京. Place associated with Tangun.

Chang[gang] 長降. Ugo's son, assistant king of Old Chosŏn.

Changhwa, Queen 莊和王后. Wife of Wang Kŏn.

changmun 場門. Market.

Chang Nan-hsien 張南軒 (Chang Shih 張栻). Sung scholar, 1133–1180.

Ch'angnyŏng 昌寧 (South Kyŏngsang).

Chang Pogo 張保皐. Silla thalassocrat, d. 846.

Chang Tsai 張載. Sung philosopher, 1020–1077.

changwŏn 壯元. Top honor in the examinations.

Chang Yŏngsil 蔣英實. Chosŏn inventor, d. 1455.

Chao-chou 趙州. T'ang meditation master, 778–897.

Chao Ts'o 鼂錯. Han official, d. 154. B.C.

Chech'ŏn 提川. (North Ch'ungch'ŏng).

Cheju 濟州. On Cheju Island, the largest island in southern Korea.

Ch'eng Hao 程顥. Sung philosopher, 1032–1085.

Ch'eng I 程頤. Sung philosopher, 1033–1107.

Ch'eng-kuan 澄觀. T'ang great master, 738–739.

Chen-p'an 眞番. Chinbŏn, Han commandery.

Chen Te-hsiu 眞德秀. Sung philosopher, 1178–1235.

Chewang ungi 帝王韻記. *See* Yi Sŭnghyu

Chia I 賈誼. Han poet and statesman, 201–169 B.C.

Chieh 桀. Bad last ruler of Hsia.

Chih-i 智顗. T'ien-t'ai master, 538–597.

Chih-shan village 赤山村 (Wen-teng hsien 文登縣).

Chih-tsang 智藏. T'ang San-lun master, 549–623.

Chihye 智惠. Silla nun.

Chih-yen 智儼. T'ang Hua-yen master, 602–668.

Chimyŏng 智明. Silla monk.

Chindŏk 眞德女王. Silla queen, 647–654.

Chingong 眞公. Ch'ŏnjin, Koryŏ monk, d. 1252.

Chingwi 眞歸. Legendary teacher of Śākyamuni.

Ch'ing-yüan Hsing-ssu 青原行思. T'ang Ch'an master, d. 740.

Chinhan 辰韓. One of the Three Han, annexed by Silla.

Chinhŭng 眞興王. Silla king, 540–567.

Chinja 眞慈. Silla monk.

Chinp'yo 眞表. Silla monk.

Chinp'yŏng 眞平王. Silla king, 579–631.

chinsa 進士. Licentiate in literature.

Chinul 知訥. National Preceptor Pojo 普照國師, eminent Koryŏ monk, 1158–1210.

ch'inyŏng 親迎. Welcome the bride into house.

Chiphyŏnjŏn 集賢殿. Hall of Worthies, a royal research institute under King Sejong.

chipsabu 執事部. "State secretariat," Silla.

Chiri, Mount 智異山. Mountain in southwestern Korea.

Ch'isu 緇秀. Koryŏ monk, late eleventh century.

Chi-tsang 智藏. Sui/T'ang monk of the Three Treatise school, 549–623.

Chit'am-ni 支塔里 (Hwanghae).

Chi Tzu 箕子 (Kija).

Chiwŏn 智遠. Silla chief of clerics.

ch'ŏch'ŏp 妻妾. Main wife and concubine.

Cho Chun 趙浚. Chosŏn official who helped found the Chosŏn dynasty, 1346–1405.

> *Kyŏngje yukchŏn* 經濟六典 (Six Codes of Governance).

Cho Ch'ung 趙冲. Koryŏ official, 1171–1220.

Ch'oe 最. Tsui, Old Chosŏn prince, d. 106.

Ch'oe Cha 崔滋. Koryŏ scholar, 1188–1260.

> *Pohan chip* 補閑集 (Supplementary Jottings in Idleness, 1254).

Ch'oe Ch'iwŏn 崔致遠. Silla writer, b. 857.

> *Kyewŏn (p'ilgyŏng) chip* 桂苑筆耕集 (Plowing the Cassia Grove with a Writing Brush).

Ch'oe Ch'ung 崔冲. Koryŏ scholar, 984–1068.

Ch'oe Ch'unghŏn 崔忠獻. Koryŏ general, d. 1219.

Ch'oe Ch'ungsu 崔忠粹. Brother of Ch'oe Ch'unghŏn, d. 1197.

Ch'oe Haenggwi 崔行歸. Koryŏ writer, fl. 967.

Ch'oe Hang 崔沆. Koryŏ military leader, d. 1257.

Ch'oe Hang 崔恒. Chosŏn official, 1409–1474.

Ch'oe Hongyun 崔洪胤. Koryŏ official, d. 1229.

Ch'oe Malli 崔萬理. Chosŏn official who opposed the use of *hangŭl*, fl. 1419–1444.

Ch'oe Nubaek 崔婁伯. Koryŏ official, twelfth century.

Ch'oe Ŏnwi 崔彥撝. Silla/Koryŏ official, 868–944.

Ch'oe Sŭngno 崔承老. Koryŏ official, 927–989.

Ch'oe Sŭngu 崔承祐. Silla scholar, fl. 890–918.

Ch'oe U 崔瑀 (I 怡). Koryŏ military leader, d. 1249.

Ch'oe Ŭi 崔竩. Koryŏ military leader, d. 1258.

Ch'oe Ŭng 崔凝. Koryŏ official, 898–932.

Ch'oe Yŏng 崔瑩. Koryŏ loyalist general, 1316–1388.

Ch'oe Yuch'ŏng 崔惟清. Koryŏ writer, 1095–1174.

> 白鷄山玉龍寺贈諡先覺國師碑銘 (Stele Inscription Conferring the Posthumous Title Precognizant National Preceptor).

Cho Hanbo 曹漢輔 (Manggidang 忘機堂). Chosŏn scholar, fl. 1473–1533.

ch'ŏk 尺. About one foot, 28 centimeters.

Cho Kwangjo 趙光祖. Chosŏn official and leader of the 1519 Recommendation Examination, 1482–1519.

chokpo 族譜. Genealogy.

chŏksŏ 嫡庶. Primary and secondary sons.

Chŏksŏng 赤城. (North Ch'ungch'ŏng).

Cholbon 卒本. Cholbon Puyŏ, Koguryŏ.

Chŏlla 全羅. Province in southwestern Korea.

Chŏllo 絕奴部. Koguryŏ clan.

ch'on 寸. One-tenth of one *ch'ŏk*, one inch.

Ch'ŏnch'aek 天頤. National Preceptor Chinjŏng 眞靜國師, early fourteenth century.

Sŏnmun pojang nok 禪門寶藏錄.

chŏng 正. Correctness.

Chŏngbang 政房. Personnel Authority.

Chŏngbang 正方. Koguryŏ monk.

Chŏng Chisang 鄭知常. Koryŏ official, d. 1135.

Chŏng Chungbu 鄭仲夫. Koryŏ general, d. 1178.

Chŏngdong haengsŏng 征東行省. Eastern Expedition Field Headquarters.

Ch'ŏnghae 清海. Military base on Wan Island 莞島.

chŏnghak 正學. Right learning.

Chŏng Ch'angson 鄭昌孫. Chosŏn official, 1402–1487.

Chŏng Ch'o 鄭招. Chosŏn official, d. 1434.

Ch'ŏngho-ri 清湖里. (Northeast of P'yŏngyang).

Chŏng Inji 鄭麟趾. Chosŏn official, 1396–1478.

ch'ongjae 冢宰. Prime minister.

Chŏngjong 定宗. Koryŏ king, 945–949.

Chŏng Kasin 鄭可臣. Koryŏ official, d. 1298.

Chŏng Mongju 鄭夢周. Koryŏ loyalist, 1337–1392.

ch'ŏngŏ 薦擧. Recommendation appointment.

Chŏngok 全谷 (Kyŏnggi).

chongpŏp 宗法. Clan laws.

Chŏngsaam 政事嚴. Administration Rock, Paekche council.

Ch'ŏngsong, Mount 青松山. Sacred place in Silla.

Chŏng T'ak 鄭擢. Koryŏ official, 1363–1423.

Chŏng T'ak 鄭琢. Chosŏn official, 1526–1605.

Chŏng Tojŏn 鄭道傳. Chosŏn official who assisted Yi Sŏnggye in founding the new dynasty, d. 1398.

Chosŏn kyŏngguk chŏn 朝鮮經國典 (Administrative Codes of Chosŏn).

Pulssi chappyŏn 佛氏雜弁 (Discourse on Buddha).

Simgi ip'yŏn 心氣理篇 (Mind, Material Force, and Principle).

chŏngŭm 正音. "Correct Sounds"; See also *hangŭl*.

Chŏng Yŏn 鄭淵. Chosŏn official, fl. 1420.

chŏnsikwa 田柴科. "Stipend land law".

Chosŏn 朝鮮. Dynasty that ruled Korea from 1392 to 1910.

Chosŏn t'ongbo 朝鮮通寶. Currency of Korea.

Chou 紂. Bad last ruler of Shang.

Chou, Duke of 周公. Regent to King Ch'eng of Chou, d. 1094 B.C.

Chou Tun-i 周敦頤. Sung philosopher, 1017–1073.

Ch'ŏyong 處容. Son of the dragon king.

Chuang Tzu 莊子. c. 399–295 B.C.

Ch'uhang 箒項. Silla general.

Chu Hsi 朱熹. Sung philosopher, 1130–1200.

ch'ŭgugi 測雨器. Rain gauge.

chujaso 鑄字所. Type foundry.

Chukchi 竹旨. Silla *hwarang*, fl. 649–670.

Chumong 朱蒙. King Tongmyŏng of Koguryŏ, 37–19 B.C.

Chun 準. Old Chosŏn king, d. 194 B.C.

Chu Sebung 周世鵬. Chosŏn organizer of the first private academy, 1495–1554.

Chun, Duke of Yŏngnyŏng 永寧公綧. Koryŏ royalty, 1223–1283.

Ch'ungch'ŏng 忠淸道. Province in south central Korea.

Chungjong 中宗. Chosŏn king, 1506–1544.

Ch'ungnyŏl 忠烈王. Koryŏ king, 1274–1308.

Ch'ungsŏn 忠宣王. Koryŏ king, 1308–1313.

Ch'ungsuk 忠肅王. Koryŏ king, 1313–1330; 1332–1339.

Chunjŏng 俊貞 (Kyojŏng 姣貞). Silla *wŏnhwa*, d. 576.

Chu Tzu chia-li 朱子家禮. Family Rites of Chu Hsi.

Chu Tzu yü-lei 朱子語類. Classified Conversations of Chu Hsi.

Classified Collection of Medical Prescriptions. See *Ŭibang yuch'wi*.

Commentary on the *Treatise on the Awakening of Faith.* See *Wŏnhyo*.

Compendium of Mahāyāna. See Asaṅga.

Compilation of Native Korean Prescriptions. See *Hyangyak chipsŏng pang*.

Comprehensive Mirror of the Eastern
Kingdom. See Sǒ Kǒjǒng.
Confucius 孔子. 551–479 B.C.
Crow Taboo Day 烏忌日 (*taldo* 怛忉).
Silla annual function.

Daruhaci 達魯花赤. Military governor.
Daśabhūmika sūtra 十地經 (Scripture
Concerning the Ten Stages).
"Dedication" 獻花歌 (by an old man).
Dharmapāla 護法. Indian commentator
of *Vijñaptimātratasiddhi śāstra* c.
530–561.
*Diagram of the Dharmadhātu According to
the One Vehicle.* See Ūisang.
*Diagrammatic Treatises for the
Commencement of Learning.* See Kwǒn
Kŭn.
Diamond Scripture 金剛般若波羅蜜經
(Diamond Cutter, *Vajracchedikā
prajñāpāramitā sūtra*).
Director of Treasury. See *P'an samsa sa.*
Directorate General of Policy Formation.
See *Kyojǒng togam.*
Doctrine of the Mean (Chung yung 中庸).

Eastern Okchǒ 東沃沮.
"Eleven Poems on the Ten Vows of the
University Worthy Bodhisattva." See
Kyunyǒ.
Ennin 圓仁. Japanese Tendai monk,
794–864.
Erh ya 爾雅. Lexical work.
Exemplar of Korean Medicine. See Hǒ
Chun.
Explanation of Profound Mysteries Scripture.
See Sandhinirmocana *sūtra.*
Explanations of Vimalakīrti Scripture. See
Vimalakīrtinirdeśa *sūtra.*
*Exposition of the Adamantine Absorption
Scripture.* See Wǒnhyo.

Fa-lang 法郎. San-lun master, 507–581.
Fa-shang 法上. Northern Ch'i monk.
Fa-tsang 法藏. T'ang Hua-yen master,
643–712.
Fairy Peach Mount 仙桃山. Mount
Sǒndo, West Mountain.
Five Classics 五經. *Book of Changes, Book
of Documents, Book of Songs, Book
of Rites,* and *Spring and Autumn
Annals.*

"Five Commandments for Laymen"
世俗五戒 (by Wǒngwang).
Flower Garland Scripture 華嚴經
(*Avataṃsaka sūtra*).
Four Books 四書. *Analects, Great
Learning, Doctrine of the Mean,* and
Mencius.
Four-Seven Debate. See Sǒng Hon and
Yi Hwang.
Fu Yüeh 傅說. Wise minister of Yin.

Gangō-ji 元興寺 (formerly Hōkō-ji,
Nara).
Golden Glow Scripture. See
Suvarṇaprabhāsottama *sūtra.*
Great Learning (Ta hsüeh 大學).
Guardian of the Earth Scripture
地藏菩薩經.
Gyōnen 凝然. Japanese Kegon monk,
1240–1321.

Haeburu 解夫婁. King of North Puyǒ.
Haedong ch'iltae rok 海東七代錄. Record
of Seven Generations in Korea.
Haein Monastery 海印寺 (South
Kyǒngsang).
Haemosu 解慕漱. Father of Chumong.
Haga Mountain 下柯山 (North
Kyǒngsang).
Hall of Illustrating the Cardinal Principles
(Myǒngnyundang 明倫堂).
hallim 翰林. Court diarist.
Hallimwǒn 翰林院. Royal Academy of
Letters.
Hamgyǒng 咸鏡道. Province in
northeastern Korea.
Han Anin 韓安仁. Koryǒ scholar, d.
1122.
hangŭl 한글. "Great Letters," Korean
alphabet.
Han Ǒnguk 韓彦國. Koryǒ scholar.
Han Ŭm 韓陰. Han Yin, Old Chosǒn
minister.
Hanyang 漢陽. Seoul.
Ha Yun 河崙. Chosǒn official,
1347–1416.
head ranks (*tup'um* 頭品).
Historical Record of the Three Kingdoms.
See Kim Pusik.
History of Koryǒ. See Koryǒ sa.
Hǒ Cho 許稠. Chosǒn official,
1369–1439.

Hŏ Chun 許浚. Chosŏn physician, d. 1615.

Tongŭi pogam 東醫寶鑑 (Exemplars of Korean Medicine, 1610).

Hōkō-ji 法興寺. Built by Soga no Umako with Paekche help, 596.

Hong Hon 洪渾. Chosŏn official, 1517–1580.

Hongmungwan 弘文館. Office of Special Advisers.

hop 合. One-tenth of a pint.

Ho-shan 禾山. T'ang Ch'an master.

Hŏ Yŏp 許曄. Chosŏn official, 1517–1580.

Hsiao Sun-ning 蕭遜寧. Khitan commander.

Hsiao T'ung 蕭統. Crown prince of Liang, 501–531.

Wen hsüan 文選 (Anthology of Refined Literature).

Hsien-pi 鮮卑. Proto-Mongolian people.

Hsi K'ang 嵇康. One of Seven Worthies of the Bamboo Grove, 223–262.

Hsiung-nu 匈奴. Turkish-speaking nomads.

Hsüan-sha Shih-pei 玄沙師備. T'ang Ch'an master, 835–908.

Hsüan-tsang 玄奘. T'ang translator of Vijñānavāda, 596–664.

Hsüan-tsung 玄宗. T'ang emperor, 712–756.

Hsüan-t'u 玄菟. Hyŏndo, Han commandery.

Hsü Ching 徐兢. Sung official, 1091–1153.

Kao-li t'u-ching 高麗図經 (Illustrated Account of Koryŏ, 1123).

Hsüeh-feng I-ts'un 雪峯義存. T'ang Ch'an master, 822–908.

Huang-po 黃蘗. T'ang Ch'an master, d. 890.

Hui-neng 慧能. Sixth patriarch of Chinese Ch'an, 638–713.

Hui-ssu 慧思. Founder of the T'ien-t'ai school, 515–577.

Hŭijong 熙宗. Koryŏ king, 1204–1211.

Hui-tsung 徽宗. Sung emperor, 1100–1125.

Hŭkhoja 黑胡子. "Dark Serimdian," Koguryŏ monk.

Hŭngdŏk 興德王. Silla king, 826–836.

Hŭngguk Monastery 興國寺 (Yangju, Kyŏnggi).

Hŭngnyun Monastery 興輪寺 (built 544).

hungu 勳舊. Meritorious elites in early Chosŏn.

Hunmin chŏngŭm 訓民正音. Correct Sounds to Instruct the People, by King Sejong.

hwabaek 和白. "Council of nobles," Silla.

Hwangch'o Pass 黃草嶺 (South Hamgyŏng).

Hwanghae 黃海道. Province northwest of Seoul.

Hwangnyong Monastery 皇(黃)龍寺 (built 553–645).

Hwanin 桓因. Heavenly god, father of Hwanung.

Hwanung 桓雄. Father of Tangun.

hwarang 花郎 (*kuksŏn* 國仙).

Hwarang segi. *See* Kim Taemun.

Hwarindang 活人堂. Hall of Helping People.

hyangga 鄉歌. Silla songs.

hyanggyo 鄉校. County school.

hyangni 鄉吏. Local clerks.

hyangsi 鄉試. Village market.

Hyangyak chesaeng chipsŏng pang 鄉藥濟生集成方 (Collection of Native Prescriptions to Save Life).

Hyangyak chipsŏng pang 鄉藥集成方 (Compilation of Native Korean Prescriptions, 1433).

Hyangyak kani pang 鄉藥簡易方. (Simple Prescriptions for Folk Medicine, by Kwŏn Chunghwa).

Hyech'ŏl 惠哲. Silla meditation master.

Hyech'ong 惠聰. Esō, Paekche monk, fl. 595–615.

Hyegong 惠空. Silla monk, fl. 579–647.

Hyegwan 慧灌. Ekan, Koguryŏ monk, fl. 625–672.

Hyehyŏn 慧顯. Paekche monk, 570–627.

Hyein 惠仁. Paekche Vinaya master.

Hyeja 慧慈. Eji, Koguryŏ monk, d. 622.

Hyejong 惠宗. Koryŏ king, 943–945.

Hyeryang 惠亮. Koguryŏ monk, d. 623.

Hyesim 慧諶. Koryŏ meditation monk, 1178–1234.

Sŏnmun yŏmsong chip 禪門拈頌集 (Collection of the Meditation School's Explanatory Verses).

Hyesuk 惠宿. Silla *hwarang*/monk, fl. 600.

hyŏn 縣. County.

Hyŏngwang 玄光. Paekche monk, fl. 539–575.

Hyŏnjong 顯宗. Koryŏ king, 1009–1031.

Hyujŏng 休靜 (Great Master Sŏsan 西山大師). Eminent Chosŏn monk, 1520–1604.

   Sŏnga kwigam 禪家龜鑑 (Mirror for Meditation Students).

   Samga kwigam 三家龜鑑 (Mirror of the Three Religions).

   Sŏn kyo kyŏl 禪教訣 (Secrets of Meditation and Doctrine).

i 理 (*li*). Principle.

Ich'adon 異次頓 (Pak Yŏmch'ok 朴厭髑 or Kŏch'adon 居次頓). Silla minister/martyr, 506–527.

idu 吏讀. Ancient Korean transcription system.

Igŭm 伊金. Buddhist monk, late fourteenth century.

I-hsing 一行. T'ang monk-mathematician, 682–727.

i-ki (*i-ki ron* 理氣論). Debate.

Illustrated Conduct of the Three Bonds. See Samgang haengsil to.

Im Ch'un 林椿. Koryŏ scholar, late twelfth century.

Im Kyŏngch'ŏng 林景清. Koryŏ scholar.

Im Kyŏngsuk 任景肅. Koryŏ scholar.

Im Kyŏnmi 林堅味. Koryŏ general eliminated by Yi Sŏnggye in 1388.

Im Wan 林完. Koryŏ official.

Im Wŏnhu 任元厚. Koryŏ official, 1089–1156.

Im Wŏnjun 任元濬. Chosŏn official, 1423–1500.

Im Yu 任濡. Koryŏ scholar, 1150–1213.

Injo 仁祖. Chosŏn king at the time of Manchu invasion, 1623–1649.

Injong 仁宗. Koryŏ king, 1122–1146.

Inscription on the Image of the Thus Come One of Infinite Life 阿彌陀如來造像記 (Kamsan Monastery 甘山寺).

Iŏm 利嚴. Silla meditation master, 866–932.

Iphak tosŏl. See Kwŏn Kŭn.

Irŏm 日嚴. Koryŏ monk, late twelfth century.

Iryŏn 一然. Koryŏ meditation master, 1206–1289.

   Samguk yusa 三國遺事 (Memorabilia of the Three Kingdoms).

isagŭm 尼師今. "King," Silla.

Japan (Wa, Wae 倭).

Jōtō 常騰. Japanese Kegon monk, 740–815.

Juan Chi 阮籍. One of Seven Worthics of the Bamboo Grove, 210–263.

Kaero 蓋鹵王. Paekche king, 455–475.

Kaesŏng 開城. Kaegyŏng or Songak, Koryŏ capital.

kahun 家訓. House Rules.

Kakhun 覺訓. Koryŏ monk, early thirteenth century.

   Haedong kosŭng chŏn 海東高僧傳 (Lives of Eminent Korean Monks, 1215).

Kamsan Monastery 甘山寺 (built in 719 in Kyŏngju; not extant).

kan 間. 180 centimeters.

Kangch'ung 康忠. Wang Kŏn's ancestor.

Kang Hŭian 姜希顏. Chosŏn official and accomplished poet, calligrapher, and painter, 1417–1464.

Kanghwa Island 江華島 (Kyŏnggi).

Kang Kamch'an 姜邯贊. Koryŏ general, 948–1031.

Kang-mu 綱目. Abridged Essentials, abbreviated title of *Tzu-chih t'ung-chien kang-mu.*

Kangsu 強首. Silla writer, d. 692.

Kao-tsu 高祖. T'ang emperor, 618–626.

Karak 駕洛 (Kaya 伽倻). Federation, 42–562.

kawi 嘉俳. Silla festival.

ke-yi 格義. "Matching the meaning."

ki 氣 (*ch'i*). Material force.

Khitan 契丹.

Ki Ch'ŏl 奇轍. Koryŏ official, d. 1356.

Kihwa 己和. Chosŏn monk, 1376–1433.

   Hyŏnjŏng non 顯正論 (Treatise on Manifesting Righteousness).

kiin 其人. Koryŏ hostage system.

Kim Alchi 金閼智. Progenitor of royal Kim clan in Silla.

Kim Chigyŏng 金之慶. Chosŏn official, 1419–1485.

Kim Chisŏng 金志誠 (Kim Chijŏn 金志全). Silla minister, d. c. 720.

Kim Ch'o 金貂. Koryŏ official.

Kim Ch'unch'u 金春秋. King T'aejong Muyŏl, 654–661.

Kim Ch'wiryŏ 金就礪. Koryŏ military official, d. 1234.

Kim Hujik 金后稷. Silla minister, fl. 579–631.

Kim Hŭmun 金歆運. Silla *hwarang*, d. 655.

Kim Hŭn 金昕. Silla scholar, 803–849.

Kim Injun 金仁俊. Koryŏ slave ruler, d. 1268.

Kim Inmun 金仁問. Silla diplomat and general, 629–694.

Kim Kagi 金可紀. Silla scholar, d. 859.

Kim Panggyŏng 金方慶 Koryŏ official, 1212–1300.

Kim Pin 金鑌. Chosŏn scientist, d. 1455.

Kim Puch'ŏl 金富轍 (Puŭi 富儀). Koryŏ scholar, d. 1136.

Kim Pusik 金富軾. Koryŏ historian, 1075–1151.

Samguk sagi 三國史記 (Historical Record of the Three Kingdoms, 1146).

Kim Sisŭp 金時習. Chosŏn scholar and versatile writer, 1435–1493.

Musa 無思 (On No-Thought).

Kim Taemun 金大問. Silla scholar, early eighth century.

Hwarang segi 花郎世記 (Annals of the Hwarang).

Kim Taesŏng 金大成. Silla minister, d. 774.

Kim Ton 金墩. Chosŏn official, 1385–1440.

Kim T'ongjŏng 金通精. Koryŏ official, d. 1170.

Kim Ungyŏng 金雲卿. Silla official, fl. 821–841.

Kim Yakchin 金躍進. Koryŏ military official.

Kim Yangdo 金良図. Silla general, d. 670.

Kim Yŏngyu 金永濡. Chosŏn official, 1418–1494.

Kim Yusin 金庾信. Silla general, 595–673.

Ki Taesŭng 奇大升 (Kobong 高峰). Chosŏn scholar, initiated the Four-Seven debate with Yi Hwang, 1527–1572.

Kŏch'ilbu 居柒夫. Silla minister, fl. 545–576.

Kogi 古記. Old Record.

Kogukch'ŏn 故國川王. Koguryŏ king, 179–196.

Koguryŏ 高句麗. 37 B.C.–668.

Kohŭng 高興. Paekche scholar, fl. 375.

Kojong 高宗. Koryŏ king, 1213–1259.

kongjŏn 公田. "Public land."

Kongmin 恭愍王. Koryŏ king, 1351–1374.

Kongyang 恭讓王 The last Koryŏ king, 1389–1392.

Koryŏ 高麗. 918–1392.

Koryŏ sa 高麗史. History of Koryŏ, 1451.

kŏsŏgan 居西干 (*kŏsŭrhan* 居瑟邯). "Founder/king."

Ko Yakhae 高若海. Chosŏn official, 1377–1443.

Kṣitigarbha 地藏. "Guardian of the earth."

K'uei-chi 窺基. T'ang Fa-hsiang master, 632–682.

Kukchagam 國子監. National University, Koryŏ.

kuksa 國師. National preceptor.

kuksŏn 國仙. National practitioner of native traditions.

kukt'ong 國統. National overseer.

Kulp'ori 屈浦里. (North Hamgyŏng).

Kumārajīva 鳩摩羅什. Most eminent translator of Buddhist texts into Chinese, 344–413.

Kŭmgang, Mount 金剛山. Sacred place in Silla.

Kŭmwa 金蛙. King Haeburu's son.

Kun 郡. County.

kŭn 斤. Six hundred grams in Chosŏn.

Kungye 弓裔 (Kim Kungye 金弓裔). Rebel leader, d. 918.

kunjŏn 軍田. Military land.

kwajŏn 科田. "Rank land."

Kwak Chonjung 郭存中. Chosŏn official.

Kwallŭk 觀勒 (Kanroku). Paekche monk, fl. 602–624.

Kwanch'ang 官昌 (Kwanjang 官狀). Silla *hwarang*, 645–660.

Kwangdŏk 廣德. Silla monk, fl. 661–681.

Kwanggaet'o 廣開土王. Koguryŏ king, 391–413.

Kwanghak 廣學. Koryŏ monk.

Kwangjong 光宗. Koryŏ king, 949–975.

Kwanna, Lady 貫那夫人. Jealous wife in Koguryŏ.

Kwanno 灌奴部. Koguryŏ clan.

Kwisan 貴山. Silla general, d. 602.

Kwŏn Ch'ae 權採. Chosŏn official, 1399–1438.

Kwŏn Che 權踶. Chosŏn official, 1387–1445.

Kwŏn Chunghwa 權仲和. Koryŏ-Chosŏn official, 1322–1408.

Kwŏn Kŭn 權近. Chosŏn official and Neo-Confucian scholar, 1352–1409.

Iphak tosŏl 入學図說 (Diagrammatic Treatises for the Commencement of Learning).

Kwŏn Nam 權擥. Chosŏn official, 1416–1465.

Ŭngjesi chu 應制詩註 (Commentary on Poems Written at Royal Command).

Kwŏn Pu 權溥. Koryŏ official, 1262–1346.

Kyebaek 階伯. Paekche general, d. 660.

Kyerim 鷄林. Forest of the Cock, old name of Kyŏngju, Silla.

Kyeru 桂婁部. Koguryŏ clan.

Kyeryong, Mount 鷄龍山 (central Korea, near Taejŏn).

Kyesu 罽須. Kogukch'ŏn's son.

Kyojŏng togam 教正都監. Directorate General of Policy Formation.

kyŏl 結. Land measurement based on acreage and soil fertility, about two and a quarter acres of top grade field.

Kyŏmik 謙益. Paekche Vinaya master, fl. 526.

kyŏngdang 扃堂. Koguryŏ private school.

Kyŏngdŏk 景德王. Silla king, 742–765.

Kyŏngguk taejŏn 經國大典. National Code.

Kyŏnghŭng 憬興. Silla monk, fl. 681–692.

Kyŏngje yukchŏn. See Cho Chun.

Kyŏngjong 景宗. Koryŏ king, 975–981.

Kyŏngju 慶州. Silla capital; Eastern Capital 東都 in Koryŏ.

Kyŏngsang 慶尙道. Province in southeast Korea.

Kyŏngsun 敬順王. Last Silla king, 927–935.

Kyŏng Taesŭng 慶大升. Koryŏ general, 1154–1183.

Kyŏngwŏn 慶源. Former name of Inch'ŏn, Kyŏnggi.

kyŏngyŏn 經筵. Royal lecture.

Kyŏnhwŏn 甄萱. Ruler of Later Paekche, d. 936.

kyorin 交隣. Neighborly relations with Japan.

Kyosŏgwan 校書館. Office of Editorial Review.

Kyunyŏ 均如. Koryŏ great master and poet, 923–973.

普賢十種願王歌十一章 (Eleven Poems on the Ten Vows of the Universally Worthy Bodhisattva).

Lao Tzu 老子. Ancient Chinese philosopher of Taoism, third century B.C.

Lao Tzu (Tao Te Ching 道德經 The Way and Its Power).

Larger Sukhāvatīvyūha 無量壽經.

Liao-tung 遼東.

Ling-hu Ch'eng 令狐澄, *Hsin-lo kuo-chi* 新羅國記 (Record of Silla).

Lion's Roar of Queen Śrīmālā Scripture, The 勝鬘獅子吼一乘大方便廣經 (*Śrīmālādevīsiṃhanāda sūtra*).

Li T'ung 李侗 (Yen-p'ing 延平). Sung scholar, 1088–1158.

Li T'ung-hsüan 李通玄. T'ang Buddhist scholar, 635–730.

Liu Hsiang 劉向. Han scholar, 77–6 B.C.

Lives of Eminent Korean Monks. See Kakhun.

Lives of Eminent Monks Compiled During the Sung. See Tsan-ning.

Lo Cheng-an 羅整菴 (Ch'in-shun 欽順). Ming scholar, 1465–1547.

Lo-lang 樂浪 (Nangnang). Han commandery.

Lotus Scripture 妙法蓮華經 (Scripture of the Lotus Blossom of the Fine Dharma, *Saddharmapundarika sūtra*).

Luxuriant Dike 菁堤. (Ch'ŏngje in Yŏngch'ŏn North Kyŏngsang).

Mahan 馬韓. One of the Three Han, destroyed by Paekche.

Maitreya 彌勒. Future Buddha who resides in Tuṣita Heaven.

mal 말. 18 liters.

Mangi 亡伊. Koryŏ peasant rebel in 1176–1177.

mangjong 芒種. "Grain in ear."

mangniji 莫離支. "High minister," Koguryŏ.

Manjŏk 萬積. Koryŏ slave rebel, d. 1198.

Mañjuśrī 文殊. Bodhisattva of wisdom.

Manŏn pongsa 萬言封事. *See* Yi I.

maripkan 麻立干. "Great chief," Silla.

Maun Pass 磨雲嶺 (South Hamgyŏng).

Ma-tsu 馬祖. Musang's disciple, 709–788.

"Meeting with Bandits" 遇賊歌 (by Yŏngjae 永才, fl. 785–798).

Memorabilia of the Three Kingdoms. See Iryŏn.

middle people 中人 (*chungin*).

Mich'uhol 彌鄒忽 (Inch'ŏn).

Milbon 密本. Silla monk.

minjŏn 民田. People's land.

Min Kimun 閔起文. Chosŏn official, 1511–1574.

Min Yŏn 閔頔. Koryŏ official, 1269–1335.

Mirim-ri 美林里 (Northeast of P'yŏngyang).

Mirror for Meditation Students. See Hyujŏng.

Moho 靺鞨. Malgal, Tungusic people in Manchuria, later founded Parhae and Chin; also Suksin, Ŭmnu, Mulgil.

Mokchong 穆宗. Koryŏ king, 997–1009.

Mu 武王. Paekche king, 600–641.

mu 畝. About 240 square paces; 6.6 *mu* is one acre.

Muak, Mount 毋岳. Musan; in Seoul.

Muan 務安. County in Chŏlla.

much'ŏn 舞天. "Dancing to heaven," Ye festival.

Muhak 無學 (Chach'o 自超). 1327–1405.

Mujin yukcho so. See Yi Hwang.

Munjong 文宗. Koryŏ king, 1046–1083.

Munjong 文宗. Chosŏn king and the eldest son of King Sejong, 1450–1452.

Munjŏng 文定王后. Queen dowager and promotor of Buddhism, 1501–1565.

munkwa 文科. Higher civil examination.

Munmu 文武王. Silla king, 661–681.

munmyŏng 問名. Asking name of bride's mother.

Muryŏng 武寧王. King Sama 斯麻王, Paekche king, 501–523.

Musang 無相. Silla meditation master, 680–762.

Muyŏl 武烈王. T'aejong Muyŏl, Silla king, 654–661.

Muyŏm 無染. Silla meditation master, 800–888.

Musŏlt'o ron 無舌士論 (Treatise on the Tongueless Realm).

Myoch'ŏng 妙清. Koryŏ monk, d. 1135.

Myohyang Mountains 妙香山 (northwestern Korea).

Myŏngjong 明宗. Chosŏn king, 1545–1567.

Myŏngnang 明郎. Silla monk, fl. 632–668.

naejangjŏn 內庄田. "Royal estate land."

Nāgārjuna 龍樹. Founder of the Middle Way school, c. 150–250.

Naju 羅州. South Chŏlla.

Nak, Mount 洛山. Silla's Potalaka, home of Sound Observer.

Naktong River 洛東江. One of five great rivers in Korea.

Namgyŏng 南京. Southern Capital, Seoul.

Namhae 南解王. Silla king, 4–24.

Nam Kon 南袞. Chosŏn official, 1471–1527.

Nam Kŭp 南汲. Chosŏn official, fl. 1421.

Nammo 南毛. Silla *wŏnhwa*.

nangjung 郎中. Official of the fifth rank.

Nan-yang Hui-chung 南陽慧忠. Heir of the Sixth Patriarch, d. 776.

napch'ae 納采. Rite of betrothal.

napkil 結吉. Divining the bride's qualities.

napp'ye 納幣. Sending wedding gifts.

National Academy (*kukhak* 國學 in Silla and Koryŏ, *Taehakkam* 大學監 in

Silla, *Sŏnggyungwan* 成均館 in Chosŏn).

National Code. See Kyŏngguk taejŏn.

New Catalog of the Teachings of All the Schools. See Ŭich'ŏn.

New Vinaya 毗曇新律. Translated by Kyŏmik.

Nihon shoki 日本書紀 (Chronicle of Japan, 720).

Nirvāṇa Scripture 大般涅槃經.

No Chungnye 盧仲禮. Chosŏn physician, fl. 1423.

nogŭp 祿邑. "Stipend village."

Noin 老人 (Lu-jen). Old Chosŏn minister.

Nokchin 祿眞. Silla minister, early ninth century.

nongjang 農莊. "Agriculture estate."

No Sŏksung 盧碩崇. (Koryŏ general, twelfth century).

Nulchi 訥祇王. Silla king, 417–458.

Odae, Mount 五臺山 (Kangwŏn).

"Ode to Knight Kip'a" 讚耆婆郎歌 (by Ch'ungdam).

Office of Editorial Review (*Kyosŏgwan* 校書館).

Office of the Censor-General (*Saganwŏn* 司諫院).

Office of the Inspector-General (*Sahŏnbu* 司憲府).

Office of Special Advisers (*Hongmungwan* 弘文館).

Oji Mount 亏知山. Sacred place in Silla.

Okchŏ 沃沮. Ancient Korean tribe in northeastern Korea.

Old Chosŏn 古朝鮮.

Ŏmjang 嚴莊. Silla monk, seventh century.

Ondal 溫達. Koguryŏ general, d. 590.

Onjo 溫祚. Tongmyŏng's third son, founder of Paekche, 18 B.C.–A.D. 28.

O Sejae 吳世才. Koryŏ scholar, late twelfth century.

Ŏ Sukkwŏn 魚叔權. Chosŏn writer and interpreter of Chinese, fl. 1525–1554.

P'aegwan chapki 稗官雜記 (Storyteller's Miscellany).

O Sukpi 吳淑庇. Koryŏ rebel, d. 1197.

osŭngp'o 五升布. Five-ply cloth used as a medium of exchange.

O Yŏnch'ong 吳延寵. Koryŏ official, 1055–1116.

Pae Chungson 裵仲孫. Koryŏ general, d. 1273.

Paegak, Mount 白岳山 (Kunghol 弓忽, Kŭmmidal 今彌達).

Paegundong sŏwŏn 白雲洞書院. White Cloud Grotto Academy, the first private academy in Chosŏn; later Sosu sŏwŏn 紹修書院.

Paekche 百濟. 18B.C.–660.

Paek Munbo 白文寶. Koryŏ official, d. 1374.

Paek Suhan 白壽翰. Koryŏ official, d. 1135.

Pai-chang Huai-hai 百丈懷海. T'ang Ch'an master, 720–814.

Pak Chinjae 朴晋材. Koryŏ general, d. 1207.

Pak Ch'o 朴礎. Koryŏ-Chosŏn scholar.

Pak Ch'ungwŏn 朴忠元. Chosŏn official, 1507–1581.

Pak Hyŏkkŏse 朴赫居世. Founder of Silla, 57 B.C.–A.D. 4.

Pak Illyang 朴寅亮. Koryŏ writer, 1047–1096.

Sui chŏn 殊異傳 (Tales of the Extraordinary).

Pak Inbŏm 朴仁範. Silla writer, late ninth century.

Pak Ko 朴翔. Chosŏn official, fl. 1401.

Pak P'aengnyŏn 朴彭年. Chosŏn official, 1417–1456.

Pak Sŏ 朴犀. Koryŏ military officer, thirteenth century.

Pak Sŏngmyŏng 朴錫命. Chosŏn official, 1370–1406.

Pak Sumun 朴守紋. Chosŏn official.

Palgi 發岐. King Kogukch'ŏn's brother, d. 198.

P'algwanhoe 八關會. Assembly of the Eight Prohibitions, popular Buddhist ritual mixed with indigenous beliefs.

Pan Ku 班固 Han historian, 32–92.

Han shu 漢書 (History of the Former Han).

P'an samsa sa 判三事司. Director of Treasury.

Paramārtha 眞諦. Translator of Buddhist texts into Chinese, 499–569.

Parhae 渤海. Multiethnic kingdom in Manchuria, 698–926.

P'ayak 波若. Koguryŏ monk, 562–613.

Peach Blossom Girl 桃花女. Silla beauty, fl. late sixth century.

Perfection of Wisdom Scriptures. See *Prajñāpāramitā sūtras.*

Personnel Authority. See *Chŏngbang.*

Personal Security Force (*tobang* 都房).

P'ijŏn 皮田. Sacred place in Silla.

p'il 匹. Cloth measurement unit, about 2 by 40 feet, "bolt."

Piryu 沸流. Tongmyŏng's second son.

po 洑. River embankment irrigation method.

Podŏk 普德. Koguryŏ monk, fl. 642–668.

Poje Monastery 普濟寺 (Kaesŏng, Kyŏnggi).

Pŏmil 梵日. Great Master T'onghyo 通曉大師, d. 889.

Pomungak 寶文閣. Pomun Hall.

pongwan 本貫. Place of clan origin.

Pongsang 烽上王. Koguryŏ king, 292–300.

Pŏphŭng 法興王. Wŏnjong 原宗, Silla king, 514–540.

Pŏpkong 法空. King Pophŭng's Buddhist name.

Pou 普雨. Chosŏn monk, 1515–1565.

Il chŏng 一正 (Oneness and Correctness).

Prajñāpāramitā sūtras 般若波羅蜜經.

protection appointment (*ŭm* 蔭).

Pulguk Monastery 佛國寺 (built 751).

pun 分. One-tenth of an inch.

Punhwang Monastery 芬皇寺 (completed 634).

Pusan 釜山. Port in Kyŏngsang.

Pusŏk Monastery 浮石寺. Built in 676 by Ŭisang in Yŏngju, North Kyŏngsang.

Puyŏ 夫餘. Ancient kingdom of the Tungusic people in Manchuria considered proto-Korean.

P'yŏngan 平安道. Province in northwestern Korea.

Pyŏngong. See Hyesim.

P'yŏngwŏn 平原王. Koguryŏ king, 559–590.

P'yŏngyang 平壤. Western Capital.

Pyŏnhan 弁韓. Pyŏnjin 弁辰, one of the Three Han, annexed by Silla.

Pyŏn Hyomun 卞孝文. Chosŏn official, b. 1396.

Pyŏn Kyeryang 卞季良. Chosŏn official, 1369–1431.

"Questions and Answers with Chief of Clerics Chiwŏn." See Tŏŭi.

recommendation appointment (*ch'ŏngŏ* 薦舉).

Record of the Dharma Jewel in Successive Generations (*Li-tai fa-pao chi* 歷代法寶記, compiled during the T'ang).

Record of the Mañjuśrī Stūpa 妙吉祥塔記 (Haein Monastery).

Record of an Oath Made in the Year Imsin 壬申誓記石.

"Requiem" 祭亡妹歌 (by Wŏlmyŏng 月明).

Revised and Augmented Gazeteer of Korea (*Sinjŭng Tongguk yŏnji sŭngnam* 新增東國輿地勝覽).

royal lectures (*kyŏngyŏn* 經筵).

Sabi 泗沘. Paekche capital, Puyŏ 扶餘 in South Ch'ungch'ŏng.

Sabul Mountain 四佛山 (North Kyŏngsang).

Sach'ŏnwang Monastery 四天王寺 (completed 679).

sadae 事大. Respect for the senior state, referring to Korea's relationship to China.

Sadaham 斯多含. *Hwarang*, fl. 562.

sadang 祠堂. Domestic shrine.

sado 司徒. Grand instructor.

saengwŏn 生員. Licentiate in classics.

Saganwŏn 司諫院. Office of the Censor-General.

sahwa 士禍. Literati purges.

sajŏn 私田. "Private land."

Sal River 薩水 (Ch'ŏngch'ŏn 清川江).

Samantabhadra 普賢. Bodhisattva Universally Worthy.

Samga kwigam. See Hyujŏng.

samgang 三綱. Three bonds.

Samgang haengsil to 三綱行實図 (Illustrated Conduct of the Three Bonds).

samjong 三從. "Three obediences" for a
woman.

Sam pyŏlch'o 三別抄. Special Patrol
Troops.

Sandhinirmocana sūtra 解深密經.
Explanation of Profound Mysteries
Scripture.

Sang Chin 尙震. Chosŏn official,
1493–1564.

sangdaedŭng 上大等. Chief minister, Silla.

sangjwap'yŏng 上佐平. Prime minister,
Paekche.

Sangwŏn 祥原 (South P'yŏngan).

San-kuo chih 三國志 (by Ch'en Shou,
233–297).

Sansang 山上王. Koguryŏ king,
196–227.

sarim 士林. Neo-Confucian literati in
early Chosŏn.

Sartaq 撒禮塔. Mongol general, d. 1232.

sarye 四禮. Four rites.

Sasŏmsŏ 司贍署. Office of Currency
Management.

Sat'aek Chijŏk 沙宅智積. Paekche
noble.

*Scripture on Benevolent Kings (Jen-wang
ching* 仁王經).

*Scripture of the Buddha's Recompense of
Kindness* 佛報恩經.

*Secrets of Meditation and Doctrine. See
Hyujŏng.*

sega 世家. Ruling family.

Sejo 世祖. Chosŏn king who usurped
the throne from his nephew, 1455–
1468.

Sejong 世宗. Great king of Chosŏn,
1418–1450.

Seng-chüan 僧詮. Sŭngnang's disciple, c.
512.

Shen-shan Seng-mi 神山僧密. T'ang
Ch'an master, c. ninth century.

Shih chi 史記 (Records of the Historian
by Ssu-ma Ch'ien).

Shih-t'ou Hsi-ch'ien 石頭希遷.
Important early Ch'an master,
700–790.

Shih-tsu 世祖. Kublai Khan, 1260–1294.

Shoku Nihongi 續日本紀 (Further
Chronicles of Japan by Sugano
Mamichi et al., completed 797).

Shōtoku 聖德太子. Japanese prince,
574–622.

Shun 舜. Legendary ruler of China, third
millennium B.C.

sigŭp 食邑. Estate.

sijang 市場. Market.

Siksānanda 實义難陀. Khotanese
translator of Buddhist texts into
Chinese, 652–710.

Silla 新羅. 57 B.C.–935.

*Simple Prescription for Folk Medicine. See
Hyangyak kani pang.*

Sim Yŏnwŏn 沈連源. Chosŏn official,
1491–1558.

Sin Ch'ojung 申處中. Chosŏn licentiate.

Sin Chŏm 申點. Chosŏn official, fl.
1572.

Sinhaeng 神行. Silla monk, d. 799.

Sinmu 神武王. Silla king, 839.

Sinmun 神文王. Silla king, 681–692.

Sin Sukchu 申叔舟. Chosŏn official,
1417–1475.

Sin Ton 辛旽 (P'yŏnjo 遍照). Koryŏ
monk, d. 1371.

Six Codes of Governance. See Cho Chun.

sodo 蘇塗 (sottae). Sacred area.

Soga no Umako 蘇我馬子. Chief
minister under Suiko, d. 626.

Sogyŏk chŏn 昭格殿. Office of Taoist
Rites.

Sŏ Hŭi 徐熙. Koryŏ official, 940–998.

sŏk 石. Grain unit, about 5.12 U.S.
bushels; ten *mal* makes one *sŏk* or *sŏm,*
160 pounds; "picul."

Sŏkchang-ni 石壯里 (South Ch'ungch'ŏng).

Sŏ Ko 徐固. Chosŏn official.

Sŏ Kŏjŏng 徐居正. Chosŏn official and
writer, 1420–1488.

Sŏ Kyŏngdŏk 徐敬德. Chosŏn
philosopher, 1489–1546.

Sŏl Ch'ong 薛聰. Silla systematizer of *idu*
writing, c. 660–730.

Sŏl Kyedu 薛罽頭. Silla official, fl. 621.

Sŏl Sun 偰循. Chosŏn official, d. 1435.

Sŏndŏk 善德女王. Silla queen, 632–646.

Sŏng 聖王. Paekche king, 523–554.

Songdo 松都 (Kaesŏng, Kaegyŏng
開京). Koryŏ capital.

Sŏnggyungwan 成均館. National
Academy.

sŏnghak 聖學. Sage learning.

Song Hon 成渾 (Ugye). Chosŏn scholar,
1535–1598.

Sŏng Hyŏn 成俔. Chosŏn official,
1439–1504.

Sŏngjong 成宗. Koryŏ king, 981–997.

Sŏngjong 成宗. Chosŏn king,
1469–1494.

Sŏng Kan 成侃. Chosŏn official,
1427–1456.

"Song of Ch'ŏyong" 處容歌 (by
Ch'ŏyong).

"Song of the Comet" 彗星歌 (by
Yungch'ŏn).

"Song of Tuṣita Heaven" 兜率歌 (by
Wŏlmyŏng).

"Song of Yangsan" 陽山歌 (anonymous).

*Songs of Flying Dragons. See Yongbi ŏch'ŏn
ka.*

Songyang 松讓王. King of Piryu.

Sŏnjo 宣祖. Chosŏn king at the time of
Japanese invasion, 1567–1608.

Sŏn kyo kyŏl 禪教訣. *See* Hyujŏng.

Sŏngi 成己 (Ch'eng I). Old Chosŏn
minister.

Sŏnmun pojang nok. See Ch'ŏnch'aek.

Sŏnmun yŏmsong chip. See Hyesim.

Sŏrabŏl 徐羅伐 (Sŏbol 徐伐; Sara 斯羅;
Saro 斯盧).

Sound Observer. *See* Avalokiteśvara.

Sorim Monastery 小林寺 (North
Kyŏngsang).

Sŏrwŏn 薛原 (*hwarang*).

Sŏ Sŏn 徐選 (Chosŏn official,
1367–1433).

Sosurim 小獸林王. Koguryŏ king,
371–384.

Sosu sŏwŏn 紹修書院. First private
academy in Korea, originally
Paegundong sŏwŏn.

Southern Capital 南京. Seoul.

South Hall Council 南堂 (*namdang*). Silla
council.

Sosŏng 昭聖王. Silla king, 799–800.

sŏwŏn 書院. Private academy.

Spring and Autumn Annals (ch'un ch'iu
春秋).

Ssangsŏng 雙城. Mongol commandery,
Hamgyŏng.

Ssu-ma Ch'ien 司馬遷. Compiler of *Shih
chi*, c. 145–90 B.C.

Stages of Yoga Practice. See Yogācārabhūmi.

state councillors 宰樞 (*chaech'u*).

"Statesmanship" 安民歌 (by
Ch'ungdam).

Straight Talk on Farming (Nongsa chiksŏl
農事直說, ordered by Sejong).

Sukchong 肅宗. Koryŏ king, 1095–1105.

Suksin 肅慎 (Su-shen). Ancestors of the
Jürchen and Moho.

Sundo 順道. Former Ch'in monk.

sŭng 升. Grain volume unit, one-tenth of
a *tu.*

Sŭngjang 勝莊 Sheng-chuang, fl.
703–713.

Sŭngjŏn 勝詮. Silla monk, fl. 701.

Sŭngnang 僧郎. Koguryŏ monk, early
fifth or early sixth century.

Sungyŏng 順璟. Silla monk, fl. 666–667.

Sung Fu 宋復. "Memorial Inscription to
Wŏnch'ŭk" 大周西明寺故大德
圓測法師佛舍利塔并序.

Sunji 順之. Silla meditation master, c.
859.

Sunno 順奴部. Koguryŏ clan.

Suro 首露王. Karak/Pon Kaya king,
42–199.

Suro, Lady 水路夫人. Wife of Lord
Sunjŏng 純貞公.

Suvarṇaprabhāsottama sūtra
金光明最勝王經 (Golden Glow
Scripture).

Ta-chih-tu lun 大智度論 (Great
Perfection of Wisdom Treatise).

Taean 大安. Silla monk, late seventh
century.

T'aebaek Mountain 太白山.

T'aebong 泰封. One of the Later Three
Kingdoms.

taedaero 大對盧. "Chief minister,"
Koguryŏ.

Taedong River 大同江. Present name of
P'ae River.

Taegu 大矩. Silla monk and compiler.

taegukt'ong 大國統. Great national
overseer.

T'aehyŏn 太賢. Taehyŏn, fl. 753–774.

Sŏng yusingnon hakki 成唯識論學記
(Study Notes to the *Treatise on the
Completion of Consciousness Only*).

T'aejo 太祖. Founder of Koryŏ dynasty,
918–943.

T'aejo 太祖. Founder of Chosŏn dynasty,
1392–1398.

T'aejong 太宗. Chosŏn king, 1400–1418.

Tai-fang 帶方. (Taebang). Han commandery.

T'ai-tsung 太宗. T'ang emperor, 626–649.

Tamuk 曇旭. Paekche Vinaya master.

Tanch'ŏn 端川. Site of silver mine.

T'ang 湯. Virtuous founder of Shang.

Tangun 檀君 (Tangun Wanggŏm 王儉). Legendary founder of Korea.

Tangun kogi 檀君古記 (Old Record of Tangun).

Tanjong 端宗. Chosŏn king who was deposed by Sejo, 1452–1455.

tano 端午. Fifth day of the fifth month festival.

Tao-hsüan 道宣. T'ang monk, 596–667.

Hsü kao-seng chuan 續高僧傳 (Further Lives of Eminent Monks).

Tao-wu Yüan-chih 道吾圓智. T'ang Ch'an master, 769–835.

T'arhae 脫解王. Silla king, 57–80.

Tattvasiddhi 成實論 (Treatise on the Completion of Truth).

tax villages or fief (*sigŭp* 食邑).

"Ten Injunctions" 十訓要.

Three Kings 三后/王. King Yü of Hsia, King T'ang of Shang, and King Wen of Chou.

tobang 都房. Personal Security Force.

Todŭng 道登. Koguryŏ monk, fl. 628–646.

Tojang 道藏. Paekche monk, fl. 675–730.

tohak 道學. Learning of the Way.

Tŏkch'ŏn 德川 (North P'yŏngan).

T'ongdo Monastery 通度寺. Built in 646, North Kyongsang.

Tongdo sŏngnip ki 東都成立記 (Record of the Establishment of the Eastern Capital, by An Hong 安弘).

Tongguk Yi sangguk chip. See Yi Kyubo.

tongmaeng 東盟. Koguryŏ national assembly.

Tongsamdong 東三洞 (near Pusan).

Top'yŏngŭisasa 都評議司事. Privy Council.

Tosŏn 道詵. National Preceptor Sŏngak 先覺國師, 827–898.

Toŭi 道義. Wŏnjŏk 元寂, d. 825.

"Questions and Answers with Chief of Clerics Chiwŏn."

T'ou-tzu Ta-tung 投子大同. T'ang Ch'an master, 819–914.

Treatise on Manifesting Righteousness. See Kihwa.

Treatise on the Completion of Consciousness-Only. See Hsüan-tsang.

Ts'an-ning 贊寧. Monk from Northern Sung, 919–1002.

Sung kao-seng chuan 宋高僧傳 (Lives of Eminent Monks Compiled During the Sung, 988).

Tso Commentary 左傳.

Tsongkhapa 宗喀巴. Tibetan monk-scholar, 1357–1419.

Tsushima 對馬. Japanese islands whose inhabitants traded at Korean ports.

Tsu-t'ang chi 祖堂集 (Collection from the Hall of Patriarchs).

tu 斗. One-fifteenth of a small or one-twentieth of a large *sŏk*, "peck."

T'u-chüeh 突厥. Turks.

Tung Chung-shu 董仲舒. Han philosopher, 179–104? B.C.

Tung-i 東夷. Eastern Barbarians.

Tung-shan Liang-chieh 洞山良价. T'ang Ch'an master, 807–869.

Tunryun 遁倫 (Toryun 道倫). Disciple of T'aehyŏn.

Tzu-chih t'ung-chien 資治通鑑 (Comprehensive Mirror for Aid in Government, by Ssu-ma Kuang, pub. 1086).

Tzu-ssu 子思. Confucius's grandson, 491–432 B.C.

U 禑 (Sin U 辛禑). Thirty-second ruler of Koryŏ, legitimacy denied by Chosŏn. 1374–1388.

Ugŏ 右渠 (Yu-ch'ü). Old Chosŏn king, d. 108 B.C.

Ŭibang yuch'wi 醫方類聚 (Classified Collection of Medical Prescriptions, by Kim Yemong et al).

Ŭich'ŏn 義天. National Preceptor Taegak 大覺國師, 1055–1101.

Sinp'yŏn chejong kyojang ch'ongnok 新編諸宗教藏總錄 (New Catalog of the Teachings of All the Schools).

Ŭijong 毅宗. Koryŏ king, 1146–1170.

Ŭijŏngbu 議政府. State Council.

Ŭisang 義湘. Eminent Silla monk, 625–702.

Ilsŭng pŏpkye to 一乘法界図 (Diagram of the Dharmadhātu According to the One Vehicle); also *Pŏpkye tosŏ in* 法界図書印.

Paekhwa toryang parwŏn mun 白花道場発願文 (Vow Made at the White Lotus Enlightenment Site).

Ŭiyŏn 義淵. Koguryŏ monk, fl. 576.

Ŭlchi Mundŏk 乙支文德. Koguryŏ general, fl. 612.

Ŭl P'aso 乙巴素. Koguryŏ minister, d. 203.

Unggi 雄基 (North Hamgyŏng).

Ungmyŏn 郁面. Devout slave girl.

U T'ak 禹倬. Koryŏ exeget of Ch'eng-Chu school, 1262–1342.

Various Rites (Chü li 曲禮).

Vasubandhu 世親. Expounder of Yogācāra school, c. 400–480.

Vimalakīrti nirdeśa sūtra 維摩詰所説經 (Explanations of Vimalakīrti Scripture).

Wang Kŏn 王建. Founder of Koryŏ, 918–943.

Wang Kyŏp 王峽. Old Chosŏn general.

Wang Yang-ming 王陽明. Ming philosopher, 1472–1529.

Wan Island 莞島 (off South Chŏlla).

Wansan 完山 (Chŏnju, North Chŏlla).

Wei lüeh 魏略 (A Brief Account of Wei, by Yü Huan 魚豢).

Wen-ti 文帝. Han emperor, 180–157 B.C.

Wen, King 文王. Founder of Chou, 1171–1122 B.C.

Wen Yen-po 溫彦博. T'ang official, fl. 626–649.

Western Capital 西京 (P'yŏngyang).

wi 衞. Military division.

Wiman 衞滿. King of Wiman Chosŏn, 194 B.C.–?

Wŏnch'ŭk 圓測. Eminent Silla monk, 542–640.

Commentary on the *Explanation of Profound Mysteries Scripture* 解深密經疏.

Wŏngwang 圓光. Eminent Silla monk, 542–640.

Wŏnhyo 元曉. Most celebrated Silla monk, 617–686.

Palsim suhaeng chang 発心修行章 (Arouse Your Mind and Practice!).

Taesŭng kisillon so 大乘起信論疏 (Commentary on the *Treatise on the Awakening of Faith*).

Kŭmgang sammaegyŏng non 金剛三昧經論 (Exposition of the Adamantine Absorption Scripture).

Ijangŭi 二障義 (Meaning of Two Obstructions).

Simmun hwajaeng non 十門和諍論 (Treatise on Ten Approaches to the Reconciliation of Doctrinal Controversy).

Wŏnjong 元宗. Koryŏ king, 1259–1274.

Wŏnsŏng 元聖王. Silla king, 785–798.

Wu, King 武王. Founder of Chou, 1121–1116 B.C.

Wu-chu 無住. Musang's disciple, 714–774.

Wu family shrine 武氏祠堂 (Chia-hsiang hsien 嘉祥縣).

Yalu River 鴨綠江.

yang 兩 (tael).

yangban 兩班 Literati class.

yangbu 兩部. Chancellery and Security Council.

yangin 良人. Commoner.

Yang-shan Hui-chih 仰山慧寂. T'ang Ch'an master, 803–887.

Yang Sŏngji 梁誠之. Chosŏn official, 1415–1482.

Yang-ti 煬帝. Sui emperor, 604–617.

Yao 堯. Legendary ruler of China, third millennium B.C.

Ya pyŏlch'o 夜別抄. Special Night Patrol Troops.

Yejong 睿宗. Koryŏ king, 1105–1122.

Yemaek 濊貊 (Ye 濊). Designates proto-Korean people, known as Eastern Ye during the Late Han.

Yemungwan 藝文館. Office of Royal Decrees.

Yen 燕 Chinese state bordering Korea, destroyed 222 B.C. by Ch'in.

Yen-kuan Ch'i-an 塩官齊安. T'ang Ch'an master, 750–842.

Yesan-jin 禮仙鎮 (South Ch'ungch'ŏng).

Yesŏng River 禮成江. (Kyŏnggi).

Yi Chadŏk 李資德. Koryŏ official.

Yi Chagyŏm 李資謙. Koryŏ official, d. 1126.

Yi Chahyŏn 李資玄. Koryŏ official, 1061–1125.

Yi Changyong 李藏用. Koryŏ minister, 1201–1272.

Yi Chayŏn 李子淵. Koryŏ scholar, d. 1086.

Yi Chehyŏn 李齊賢. Koryŏ official and scholar, 1287–1367.

Hyohaeng nok 孝行錄 (Record of Filial Behavior).

Yi Chi 李至. Chosŏn official, d. 1414.

Yi Chibaek 李知白. Koryŏ official.

Yi Chik 李稷. Chosŏn official, 1362–1431.

Yi Ch'ŏn 李蕆. Chosŏn official, 1376–1451.

Yi Chungwi 李仲位. Chosŏn official.

Yi Hwang 李滉 (T'oegye 退溪). Chosŏn Neo-Confucian philosopher, 1501–1570.

Mujin yukcho so 戊辰六條疏 (Memorial on Six Points Presented in 1568).

Yi I 李珥 (Yulgok 栗谷). Chosŏn Neo-Confucian philosopher, 1536–1584.

Manŏn pongsa 萬言封事 (Memorial in Ten Thousand Words).

Yi Illo 李仁老. Koryŏ poet, 1152–1220.

P'ahan chip 破閑集 (Jottings to Break Up Idleness, 1254).

Yi Kae 李塏. Chosŏn official, 1417–1456.

Yi Ki 李芑. Chosŏn official.

Yi Ko 李顗. Koryŏ military officer, d. 1171.

Yi Kŏ 李蘧. Chosŏn official.

Yi Kongno 李公老. Koryŏ official, d. 1224.

Yi Kŭkton 李克墩. Chosŏn official, 1435–1503.

Yi Kyubo 李奎報. Koryŏ writer, 1168–1241.

Tongguk Yi sangguk chip 東國李相國集 (Collected Works of Minister Yi of Korea, 1241–1251).

Yi Munjin 李文眞. Koguryŏ scholar, fl. 600.

ying 楹. Pillar.

Yi Ŏnjŏk 李彥迪. Chosŏn scholar and Neo-Confucianist, 1491–1553.

Yi Saek 李穡. Koryŏ scholar, 1328–1396.

Yi Sajŭng 李思曾. Chosŏn official, fl. 1560.

Yi Sŏllo 李善老. Chosŏn official, early fifteenth century.

Yi Sŏnggye 李成桂. Founder of Chosŏn, 1335–1408; ruled 1392–1398.

Yi Sunsin 李舜臣. Chosŏn admiral, 1545–1598.

Yi Sŭnghye 李承休. Koryŏ writer, 1224–1300.

Chewang ungi 帝王韻記 (Rhymed Record of Emperors and Kings).

Yi Tamji 李湛之. Koryŏ scholar, late twelfth century.

Yi Ŭibang 李義方. Koryŏ rebel, d. 1174.

Yi Ŭimin 李義旼. Koryŏ rebel, d. 1196.

Yi Yŏnggyŏn 李永肩. Naju magistrate, fl. 1470.

Yogācārabhūmi 瑜伽師地論 (Stages of Yoga Practice).

Yŏm Hŭngbang 廉興邦. Koryŏ official eliminated by Yi Sŏnggye, d. 1388.

Yŏm Kyŏngae 廉瓊愛. Wife of Ch'oe Nubaek, d. 1146.

Yŏndŭnghoe 燃燈會. Lantern Festival.

Yŏngan 永安. Old name for Hamgyŏng.

Yongbi ŏch'ŏn ka 龍飛御天歌 (Songs of Flying Dragons, 1445–1447).

Yŏngch'ŏn 永川 (North Kyŏngsang).

yŏnggo 迎鼓. Puyŏ festival.

Yŏnggwan 靈觀. Chosŏn monk, 1485–1571.

Yŏngju 英州 (North Hamgyŏng).

Yŏngmyo Monastery 靈廟寺 (completed 635).

Yŏn (Ch'ŏn) Kaesomun 淵(泉)蓋蘇文. Koguryŏ general, d. 665.

Yŏnno 涓奴部. Koguryŏ clan.

Yŏnsangun 燕山君. Tyrannical ruler of Chosŏn deposed by a coup, 1494–1506.

Yü 禹. Virtuous founder of Hsia.

Yüan-chüeh ching 圓覺經 (Perfect Enlightenment Scripture).

Yü Chung-wen 于仲文. Sui general.

Yüeh-shan Wei-yen 藥山惟儼. Main disciple of Shih-t'ou, 745–828.

Yu Hŭich'un 柳希春. Chosŏn official, 1513–1577.

Yu Hyot'ong 俞孝通. Chosŏn official, fl. 1408–1431.

Yu Kwan 柳觀. Chosŏn official, 1346–1433.

Yu Kyŏng 柳璥. Koryŏ scholar, 1211–1289.

Yun Hoe 尹淮. Chosŏn official, 1380–1436.

Yun Kae 尹漑. Chosŏn official, 1494–1566.

Yun Kwan 尹灌. Koryŏ leader, d. 1111.

Yün-men Wen-yen 雲門文偃. T'ang Ch'an master, d. 949.

Yun Ŏni 尹彦頤. Koryŏ official, 1090–1149.

Yun Sindal 尹莘達. Chosŏn official.

Yun Ŭnbo 尹殷輔. Chosŏn official, 1468–1544.

Yu Paeksun 柳伯淳. Chosŏn official, fl. 1410.

Yuri 儒理王. Silla king, 24–57.

Yuryu 儒留. Chumong's eldest son, King Yuri 琉璃王, 19 B.C.–A.D. 18.

Yu Sŏk 廋晢. Koryŏ official, c. 1086–1100.

Yu Taesu 俞大修. Chosŏn official, 1546–1586.

Yü-wen Shu 于文述. Sui general.

Zenshu 善珠. Japanese monk, 723–797.

Bibliography

THREE KINGDOMS AND UNIFIED SILLA

BUDDIST AND EAST ASIAN SOURCES

Works in Buddhist canonical collections are listed by titles; other East Asian sources are alphabetized by author.

A-p'i-ta-mo chü-she lun 阿毘達磨俱世論. *T.* 29, no. 1558: 1a–159b.

A-p'i-ta-mo fa-chih lun 阿毘達磨發智論. *T.* 26, no. 1554: 918b–1031c.

A-p'i-ta-mo shun cheng-li lun 阿毘達磨順正理論. *T.* 29, no. 1562: 329a–775c.

A-p'i-ta-mo-tsang hsien-tsung lun 阿毘達磨藏顯宗論. *T.* 29, no. 1563: 777a–977c.

A-p'i-ta-mo ta-pi-p'o-sha lun 阿毘達磨大毘婆沙論. *T.* 27, no. 1545: 1a–1004a.

Ch'en Shou. *San-kuo-chih.* 三國志. 4 vols. Peking: Chung-hua shu-chü, 1959.

Ch'eng wei-shih lun 成唯識論. *T.* 31, no. 1585: 1a–60a.

Ch'eng wei-shih lun shu-chi 成唯識論述記. *T.* 43, no. 1830: 229a–606c.

Chieh shen-mi ching 解深密經. *T.* 16, no. 676: 688b–711b.

Chin-kang san-mei ching 金剛三昧經. *T.* 9, no. 273: 365c–374b.

Ching-te ch'uan-teng lu 景德傳燈錄. *T.* 51, no. 2076: 196b–467a.

Cho Myŏnggi. *Silla pulgyo ŭi inyŏm kwa yŏksa* 新羅佛教의 理念과 歷史. Seoul: Sint'aeyangsa, 1962.

Ch'oe Ch'iwŏn. *Kyewŏn p'ilgyŏng chip* 桂苑筆耕集 (*SPTK*).

Chung lun 中論. *T.* 30, no. 1564: 1a–39c.

Fa-tsang ho-shang chuan 法藏和尚傳 (Ch'oe Ch'iwŏn). *T.* 50, no. 2054: 280c–286c.

Fan Yeh et al. *Hou Han shu* 後漢書. 12 vols. Peking: Chung-hua shu-chü, 1963.

Fo-ti ching lun 佛地經論. *T.* 26, no. 1530: 291b–328c.

Hae simmilgyŏng so 解深密經疏 (Wŏnch'ŭk). *HTC* 34: 291a–476a.

Hsin-hsin ming 信心銘. *T.* 48, no. 2010: 376b–377a.

Hsin Hua-yen ching lun 新華嚴經論 (Li T'ung-hsüan). *T.* 36, no. 1739: 721a–1008b.

Huš kao-seng chuan 續高僧傳 (Tao-hsüan). *T.* 50, no. 2060: 425a–707a.

Haedong kosŭng chŏn 海東高僧傳 (Kakhun). *T.* 50, no. 2065: 1015a–1023a.

Hwang Suyŏng, ed. *Chŭngbo Hanguk kŭmsŏk yumun* 增補韓國金石遺文. Seoul: Ilchisa, 1978.

Hwaŏm ilsŭng pŏpkye to 華嚴一乘法界図 (Ŭisang). *T.* 45, no. 1887A: 711a–716a.

Iryŏn. *Samguk yusa* 三國遺事 (Ch'oe Namsŏm ed.). Seoul: Minjung sŏgwan, 1954.

Kim Pusik. *Samguk sagi* 三國史記 (Yi Pyŏngdo ed.). 2 vols. Seoul: Ŭryu munhwasa, 1977.

Kŭmgang sammaegyŏng non 金剛三昧經論 (Wŏnhyo). *T.* 34, no. 1730: 961a–1008a.

Kyunyŏ chŏn 均如傳 (Hyŏngnyŏn chŏng). *KT* 47: 259c–262c.

Li-tai san-pao chi 歷代三寶記 (Fei Ch'ang-fang). *T.* 49, no. 2034: 22c–127c.

Liu Hsü et al. *Chiu T'ang shu* 舊唐書. 16 vols. Peking: Chung-hua shu-chü, 1975.

Miao-fa lien-hua ching 妙法蓮華經. *T.* 9, no. 262: 1a–62b.

Mun Myŏngdae. "Silla Hwaŏmgyŏng sagyŏng kwa kŭ pyŏnsangdo ŭi yŏngu, 1." 新羅華嚴經寫經과그變相図의研究. *Hanguk hakpo* 14 (1979): 27–64.

Ou-yang Hsiu et al. *Hsin T'ang shu* 新唐書. 20 vols. Peking: Chung-hua shu-chü, 1975.

"Paekhwa toryang parwŏn mun" 白花道場發願文 (Ŭisang). *HPC* 2: 9a.

"Paekkyesan Ongnyongsa chŭngsi sŏngak kuksa pimyŏng" 白鷄山玉龍寺贈諡先覺國師碑銘 (Ch'oe Yuch'ŏng). *Tong munsŏn* 117: 18b–22b.

Palsim suhaeng chang 發心修行章 (Wŏnhyo). *HPC* 1: 841a–c.

Pan Ku. *Han shu* 漢書. 20 vols. Peking: Chung-hua shu-chü, 1962.

Pien chung-pien lun 辯中邊論. *T.* 31, no. 1600: 464b–477b.

Pien chung-pien lun sung 辯中邊論頌. *T.* 31, no. 1601: 477c–480b.

Po-jo-teng lun shih 般若燈論釋. *T.* 30, no. 1566: 50c–136a.

She Ta-sheng lun shih 攝大乘論釋. *T.* 31, no. 1598: 380a–499b.

Shou-leng-yen ching 首楞嚴經. *T.* 19, no. 945: 105b–155b.

Shun chung lun 順中論. *T.* 30, no. 1565: 39c–50b.

Shuo Wu-kou-ch'eng ching 說無垢稱經. *T.* 14, no. 476: 557c–588a.

Sŏ Kŏjŏng et al. *Tong munsŏn* 東文選. 3 vols. Seoul: Kyŏnghŭi ch'ulp'ansa, 1966–1967.

Sŏnmun pojang nok 禪門寶藏錄 (Ch'ŏnch'aek). *HTC* 113: 492b–502b.

Sŏng yusingnon hakki 成唯識論學記 (T'aehyŏn). *HTC* 80: 1a–3a.

Ssu-ma Ch'ien. *Shih chi* 史記. 10 vols. Peking: Chung-hua shu-chü, 1974.

Sung kao-seng chuan 宋高僧傳 (Tsan-ning). *T.* 50, no. 2061: 710b–900a.

Ta-chih-tu lun 大智度論. *T.* 25, no. 1509: 59a–496a.

Ta-Chou Hsi-ming ssu ku ta-te Yüan-ts'e (Wŏnch'ŭk) fa-shih fo she-li t'a-ming ping-hsü 大周西明寺故大德圓測法師佛舍利塔銘并序 (Sung Fu), in *Chin-shi ts'ui-pien* 金石萃編 (1805 ed.). 146: 34b–37a.

Taesŭng kisillon sogi hoebon 大乘起信論疏記回本. *HTC* 71: 310b–351a.

Ta-fang-kuang fo hua-yen ching 大方廣佛華嚴經 (Buddhabhadra). *T.* 9, no. 278: 395a–788b.

Ta-fang-kuang fo hua-yen ching. (Sikṣānanda). *T.* 10, no. 279: 1a–444c.

Ta-pan nieh-p'an ching 大般涅槃經. *T.* 12, no. 374: 365a–852b.

Ta-sheng chang-chen lun 大乘掌珍論. *T.* 30, no. 1578: 268a–278b.

Ta-sheng ch'i-hsin-lun i-chi 大乘起信論義記 (Fa-tsang). *T.* 44, no. 1846: 240c–287b.

Ta-sheng kuang po lun shih-lun 大乘廣百論釋論. *T.* 30, no. 1571: 187a–250b.

Ta-sheng A-p'i-ta-mo tsa-chi lun 大乘阿毘達磨雜集論. *T.* 31, no. 1606: 663a–774a.

Ta-T'ang hsi-yü chi 大唐西域記. *T.* 51, no. 2087: 867b–947c.

Tsa A-p'i-t'an hsin lun 雜阿毘曇心論. *T.* 28, no. 1552: 869c–965c.

Tsu-t'ang chi (Chodang chip) 祖堂集. *Hyosŏng Cho Myŏnggi paksa hwagap kinyŏm pulgyo sahak nonch'ong.* Seoul: Tongguk University Press, 1965. Appendix, pp. 1a–129a.

Wei-mo-chieh so-shuo ching 維摩詰所說經. *T.* 14, no. 475: 537a–557b.

Wu-liang-shou ching 無量壽經. *T.* 12, no. 365: 340b–346b.

Wŏnjong mullyu 圓宗文類 (Ŭich'ŏn). *HTC* 103: 393a–431a.

Yamaguchi, Zuihō. "Chibetto Bukkyō to Shiragi no Kin oshō." In *Shiragi bukkyō kenkyū* 新羅佛教研究, ed. Kin Chiken and Sai Ingan. Tokyo: Sankibō busshorin, 1973, pp. 3–36.

Yi Kyubo. *Tongguk Yisangguk chip* 東國李相國集. Seoul: Tongguk munhwasa, 1958.

Yi Nŭnghwa. *Chosŏn pulgyo t'ongsa* 朝鮮佛教通史. 2 vols. Seoul: Sinmungwan, 1918.

Yin-ming ju cheng-li lun shu 因明入正理論疏. *T.* 44, no. 1840: 91b–143a.

Yŏlban chongyo 涅槃宗要 (Wŏnhyo). *T.* 38, no. 1769: 239a–255c.

Yu-ch'ieh-shih ti lun 瑜伽師地論. *T.* 30, no. 1579: 279a–882a.

WESTERN LANGUAGE SOURCES

Beal, Samuel. *Buddhist Records of the Western World.* London: Truebner, 1884. Reprint. New York: Paragon, 1968.

Best, Jonathan W. "Tales of Three Paekche Monks Who Traveled Afar in Search of the Law." *Harvard Journal of Asiatic Studies* 51, no. 1 (1991): 139–197.

Buswell, Robert E., Jr. *The Formation of Ch'an Ideology in China and Korea: The Vajrasamādhi-Sūtra—A Buddhist Apocryphon.* Princeton: Princeton University Press, 1989.

Edgerton, Franklin. *Buddhist Hybrid Sanskrit Dictionary*. New Haven: Yale University Press, 1953.

Hurvitz, Leon. "Chih-i (538–597): An Introduction to the Life and Ideas of a Chinese Buddhist Monk." *Mélanges chinois et bouddiques* 12 (1962).

——. *Scripture of the Lotus Blossom of the Fine Dharma*. New York: Columbia University Press, 1976.

Inaba, Shōju. "On Chos-grub's Translation of the *Chieh-shen-mi-ching-shu*." In Leslie S. Kawamura and Keith Scott, eds., *Buddhist Thought and Asian Civilization: Essays in Honor of Herbert V. Guenther on His Sixtieth Birthday*, 105–113. Emeryville, Calif.: Dharma Publishing, 1977.

Jaini, Padmanabh S. "The Vaibhāṣika Theory of Words and Meanings." *Bulletin of the School of Oriental and African Studies* 22 (1959): 95–107.

——. "The Development of the Theory of the *Viprayukta-saṃskāras*." *Bulletin of the School of Oriental and African Studies* 22 (1955): 521–447.

Jan, Yüan-hua. "Tsung-mi: His Analysis of Ch'an Buddhism." *T'oung Pao* 58 (1972): 1–50.

Lai, Whalen. "The *Chan-Ch'a ching*: Religion and Magic in Medieval China." In Robert E. Buswell, Jr., ed., *Chinese Buddhist Apocrypha*, 175–206. Honolulu: University of Hawaii Press, 1990.

Lau, D. C. *Lao Tzu: Tao Te Ching*. Harmondsworth: Penguin, 1963.

Legge, James. *The Chinese Classics*. 5 vols. Hong Kong: Hong Kong University Press, 1960.

——. *Li Ki*. 2 vols. Sacred Books of the East 27–28. Oxford: Oxford University Press, 1885.

MacDonell, Arthur A. *Bṛhad-devata*. Harvard Oriental Series 5–6. Cambridge: Harvard University Press, 1904–5.

Schafer, Edward H. *The Golden Peaches of Samarkand: A Study of T'ang Exotics*. Berkeley: University of California Press, 1963.

Seo, Kyung-bo. *A Study of Korean Zen Buddhism Approached Through the Chodangjip*. Seoul: Poryŏngak, 1973.

Takakusu, Junjirō. *Amitāyurdhyāna sūtra*. Sacred Books of the East 49. Oxford: Clarendon, 1894.

Thurman, Robert. *The Holy Teaching of Vimalakīrti*. University Park: University of Maryland Press, 1976.

Waley, Arthur. *The Analects of Confucius*. London: Allen & Unwin, 1949.

——. *The Book of Songs*. London: Allen & Unwin, 1954.

Watson, Burton. *The Complete Works of Chuang Tzu*. New York: Columbia University Press, 1968.

——. *Records of the Grand Historian of China*. 2 vols. New York: Columbia University Press, 1961.

Watters, Thomas. *On Yuan Chwang's Travels in India (629–645 A.D.)*. 2 vols. London: Royal Asiatic Society, 1904.

Wayman, Alex and Hideko. *The Lion's Roar of Queen Śrīmālā*. New York: Columbia University Press, 1974.

Weinstein, Stanley. "A Biographical Study of Tz'u-en." *Monumenta Nipponica* 15 (1959–60): 119–149.

Koryŏ

BUDDHIST AND EAST ASIAN SOURCES

Ch'an-yüan chu-ch'üan chi tou-hsü 禪源諸詮集都序 (Tsung-mi). *T.* 48, no. 2015: 399a–413c.

Ch'eng-tao ko 證道歌 (Yung-chia Hsüan-chüeh). *T.* 48, no. 2014: 395c–396c.

Chen-yüan hsin-ting shih-chiao mu-lu 貞元新定釋教目錄. *T.* 55, no. 2157: 771a–1048a.

Ch'i-hsin lun shu pi-hsüeh-chi 起信論疏筆削記 (Tzu-hsüan). *T.* 44, no. 1848: 297a–409b.

Chingak kuksa ŏrok 眞覺國師語錄. P'ŏngch'ang, Kangwŏn: Pojesa, 1940.

Ching-te ch'uan-teng lu 景德傳燈錄. *T.* 51, no. 2076: 196b–467a.

Chin-kang po-jo p'o-lo-mi ching 金剛般若波羅蜜經. *T.* 8, no. 235: 748c–766c.

Chin shih-tzu chang yun-chien lei-chieh 金師子章雲間類解 (Ching-yuan). *T.* 45, no. 1880: 663a–667a.

Ch'oe Cha. *Pohan chip* 補閑集. In *Koryŏ myŏnghyŏn chip*. Seoul: Kyŏngin munhwasa, 1972.

Chŏng Inji et al. *Koryŏ sa* 高麗史. 3 vols. Seoul: Yŏnse taehakkyo Tongbanghak yŏnguso, 1955–1961.

Chŏng Tojŏn. *Sambong chip* 三峯集. 2 vols. Seoul: Kyŏngin munhwasa, 1987.

Chōsen Sōtokufu. *Chōsen kinseki sōran* 朝鮮金石總覽. 2 vols. Keijō: Chōsen sōtokufu, 1919.

Chou i 周易 (*SPTK*).

Ch'u san-tsang chi-chi 出三藏記集. *T.* 55, no. 2145: 1a–114a.

Fo i-chiao ching-lun-shu chieh-yao 佛遺教經論疏節要 (Ching-yuan). *T.* 40, no. 1820: 844c–857b.

Hanguk pulgyo chŏnsŏ. Seoul: Poryŏngak, 1972.

Hayashiya Tomojirō. *Kyōroku kenkyū* 經錄研究. Tokyo: Iwanami shoten, 1941.

Hsin-hsin ming 信心銘 (Seng-ts'an). *T.* 48, no. 2010: 376b–377a.

Hsin Hua-yen ching lun 新華嚴經論 (Li T'ung-hsüan). *T.* 36, no. 1739: 721a–1008b.

Hsü Ching. *Hsüan-ho feng-shih Kao-li t'u-ching* 宣和奉使高麗図經. Seoul: Asea munhwasa, 1972.

Im Ch'un. *Sŏha chip* 西河集. In *Koryŏ myŏnghyŏn chip*. Seoul: Kyŏngin munhwasa, 1972.

Iryŏn. *Samguk yusa* 三國遺事 (Ch'oe Namsŏn ed.). Seoul: Minjung sŏgwan, 1954.

Kim Chongsŏ et al. *Koryŏsa chŏryo* 高麗史節要. Hōsa bunko ed. Tokyo: Gakushūin, 1960.

Kim Pusik. *Samguk sagi* 三國史記 (Yi Pyŏngdo ed.). 2 vols. Seoul: Ŭryu munhwasa, 1977.

Kuang hung-ming chi 廣弘明集. *T.* 52, no. 2103: 97a–361a.

Kwŏn Kŭn. *Iphak tosŏl* 入學図說. Tr. Kwŏn Tŏkchu. Seoul: Ŭryu munhwasa, 1974.

Lin-chi lu 臨濟錄. *T.* 47, no. 1985: 495c–506c.

Li-tai san-pao chi 歷代三寶記. *T.* 49, no. 2034: 22c–127c.

Liu-tsu t'an-ching 六祖壇經. *T.* 48, no. 2008: 347c–365a.

Lüeh-shih Hsin Hua-yen ching hsiu-hsing tz'u-ti chüeh-i lun 略釋新華嚴經修行次第決疑論. *T.* 36, no. 1741: 1012a–1048c.

Mo-ho chih-kuan 摩訶止觀. *T.* 46, no. 1911: 1a–140c.

No Sasin et al. *Sinjŭng Tongguk yŏji sŭngnam* 新增東國輿地勝覽. Seoul: Tongguk munhwasa, 1964.

Palsim suhaeng chang 發心修行章 (Wŏnhyo). *HPC,* 1: 841a–c.

Pien-cheng lun 辯正論. *T.* 52, no. 2110: 490b–550c.

Pi-yen lu 碧巖錄. *T.* 48. no. 2003: 140a–225c.

P'o-hsieh lun 破邪論. *T.* 52, no. 2109: 474c–489c.

Shou-leng-yen ching 首楞嚴經. *T.* 19, no. 945: 106b–155b.

Sinp'yŏn chejong kyojang ch'ongnok 新編諸宗教藏總錄 (Ŭich'ŏn). *T.* 55, no. 2184: 1166a–1178c.

Sŏ Kŏjŏng et al. *Tong munsŏn* 東文選. 3 vols. Seoul: Kyŏnghŭi ch'ulp'ansa, 1966–1967.

Sung kao-seng chuan 宋高僧傳. *T.* 50, no. 2061: 710b–900a.

Ta-sheng ch'i-hsin lun 大乘起信論. *T.* 32, no. 1666: 575b–591c.

Ta-Chou kan-ting chung-ching mu-lu 大周刊定衆經目錄 (Ming-ch'uan). *T.* 55, no. 2153: 372c–476a.

Taedong pulgyo yŏnguwŏn, ed. *Yŏmsong sŏrhwa* 拈頌說話. Seoul: Poryŏngak, 1970.

Taegak kuksa munjip 大覺國師文集. Photolithographic reprint of 1939 Haeinsa woodblock. Seoul, 1974.

Ta-fang-kuang fo hua-yen-ching 大方廣佛華嚴經 (Buddhabhadra). *T.* 9, no. 278: 395a–788b.

Ta-fang-kuang fo hua-yen-ching (Sikṣānanda). *T.* 10, no. 279: 1a–444c.

Ta-fang-kuang Yüan-chüeh hsiu-to-lo liao-i ching 大方廣圓覺修多羅了義經. *T.* 17, no. 842:

Takeda Yukio. "Shiragi no metsubō to Kōrai-chō no tenkai" 新羅の滅亡と高麗朝の展開. *Iwanami kōza: sekai rekishi* 岩波講座：世界歷史. Tokyo: 1970, 9: 486.

Ta-T'ang nei-tien lu 大唐內典錄 (Tao-hsüan). *T.* 55, no. 2149: 219b–342a.

T'ongdosa chi 通度寺誌. Seoul: Asea munhwasa, 1979.

Tsu-t'ang chi 祖堂集. *Hyosŏng Cho Myŏnggi paksa hwagap kinyŏm pulgyo sahak nonch'ong.* Seoul: Tongguk University Press, 1965. Appendix, pp. 1a–129a.

Yi Chehyŏn. *Yŏgong p'aesŏl* 櫟翁稗說. In *Koryŏ myŏnghyŏn chip.* Seoul: Kyŏngin munhwasa, 1972.

Yi Hongjik. *Kuksa taesajŏn* 國史大事典. Seoul: Paengmansa, 1972.

Yi Illo. *P'ahan chip* 破閑集. In *Koryŏ myŏnghyŏn chip.* Seoul: Kyŏngin munhwasa, 1972.

Yi Kyubo. *Tongguk Yi sangguk chip* 東國李相國集. Seoul: Tongguk munhwasa, 1958.

WESTERN LANGUAGE SOURCES

Buswell, Robert E., Jr. *The Korean Approach to Zen: The Collected Works of Chinul.* Honolulu: University of Hawaii Press, 1983.

Chang, Garma C. C. *The Buddhist Teaching of Totality: The Philosophy of Hwa Yen Buddhism.* University Park: Pennsylvania State University Press, 1971.

Guenther, Herbert V. *Philosophy and Psychology in the Abhidharma.* Berkeley, Ca.: Shambhala, 1976.

Hahm Pyong-Choon. *The Korean Political Tradition and Law.* Seoul: Hollym, 1967.

Henthorn, William. *Korea: The Mongol Invasions.* Leiden: Brill, 1963.

Hurvitz, Leon. *Scripture of the Lotus Blossom of the Fine Dharma.* New York: Columbia University Press, 1976.

Karlgren, Bernhard. "Legends and Cults in Ancient China." *Bulletin of the Museum of Far Eastern Antiquities* 18 (1046): 206–344.

———. *The Book of Odes.* Stockholm: Museum of Far Eastern Antiquities, 1950.

Lee, Ki-baek. *A New History of Korea.* Translated by Edward W. Wagner with Edward J. Shultz. Cambridge: Harvard University Press, 1984.

Legge, James. *The Chinese Classics.* 5 vols. Hong Kong: Hong Kong University Press, 1970.

———. *Li Ki.* 2 vols. Sacred Books of the East 27–28. Oxford: Oxford University Press, 1885.

———. *Yi King.* Sacred Books of the East 16. Oxford: Clarendon Press, 1882.

Liao, W. K., trans. *Complete Works of Han Fei Tzu.* London: Probsthain, 1959.

Rogers, Michael C. "*P'yŏnnyŏn T'ongnok*: The Foundation Legend of the Koryŏ State." *Journal of Korean Studies* 4 (1982–83): 3–72.

Takakusu, Junjirō. *The Essentials of Buddhist Philosophy.* Honolulu: University of Hawaii Press, 1949.

Vaidya, P. L., ed. *Gandavyūha sūtra, Buddhist Sanskrit Texts.* No. 5. Darbhanga: Mithila Institute, 1960.

Waley, Arthur. *The Way and Its Power: A Study of the Tao Te Ching and Its Place in Chinese Thought.* New York: Grove Press, 1958.

Yampolsky, Philip B. *The Platform Sūtra of the Sixth Patriarch.* New York: Columbia University Press, 1967.

Early Chosŏn

BUDDHIST AND EAST ASIAN SOURCES

Andong Kwŏnssi sebo. 安東權氏世譜. 3 vols. Andong: Sŏnghwabo chungganso, 1928.

Ch'eng Hao. *Ming-tao wen-chi* 明道文集. In *Erh Ch'eng ch'üan-shu* (*SPPY*).

Ch'eng Hao and Ch'eng I. *Erh Ch'eng ch'üan-shu* 二程全書 (*SPPY*).

Ch'eng I. *I-ch'uan wen-chi* 伊川文集. In *Erh Ch'eng Ch'üan-shu.*

Ch'oe Hang. *T'aehŏjŏng munjip* 太虛亭文集. 1625 ed. Kyujanggak collection.

Cho Kwangjo. *Chŏngam chip* 靜庵集. In *Yijo ch'oyŏp myŏnghyŏn chip sŏn,* pp. 1–181.

Chŏng Inji et al. *Koryŏ sa* 高麗史. 3 vols. Seoul: Yŏnse taehakkyo, Togbanghak yŏnguso, 1955.

Chŏng Tojŏn. *Sambong chip* 三峯集. 2 vols. Seoul: Kyŏngin munhwasa, 1987.

Chosŏn wangjo sillok 朝鮮王朝實錄. 48 vols. Seoul: Kuksa p'yŏnch'an wiwŏnhoe, 1970.

Chungjong sillok 中宗實錄. In *Chosŏn wangjo sillok,* vols. 14–19.

Chu Hsi. *Chung-yang huo-wen* 中庸或問. Reprint of *SPPY*. Seoul: Kyŏngmunsa, 1977.

——. *Chu Tzu ta-ch'üan* 朱子大全. Reprint of *SPPY*. Taipei: Cheng-chung shu-chü, 1970.

——. *Chu Tzu yü-lei* 朱子語類. Reprint of 1473 ed. Taipei: Cheng-chung shu-chü, 1962.

——. *Ta-hsüeh huo-wen* 大學或問. Reprint. Seoul: Kyŏngmunsa, 1977.

Han Yŏngu. *Chŏng Tojŏn sasang ŭi yŏngu* 鄭道傳思想의研究. Seoul: Seoul taehakkyo, 1973.

Hanguk yuhak charyo chipsŏng 韓國儒學資料集成 Pae Chongho, ed. 3 vols. Seoul: Yŏnse taehakkyo, 1980.

Hŏ Chun. *Tongŭi pogam* 東醫寶鑑. Reprint. Seoul: Namsadang, 1976.

Huai-nan Tzu 淮南子 (*SPPY*).

Hunmin chŏngŭm 訓民正音. Pak Chongguk, ed. Reprint. Seoul: Chŏngŭmsa, 1982.

Hyujŏng. *Sŏn kyo kyŏl* 禪教歌. HPC 7: 657b–658b.

——. *Samga kwigam* 三家龜鑑. HPC 7: 616a–625a.

——. *Sŏnga kwigam* 禪家龜鑑. HPC 7: 625b–631c.

Ki Taesŭng. *Kobong chip* 高峯集. In *Hanguk yuhak charyo chipsŏng,* 1: 229–266.

Kihwa. *Hyŏnjŏng non* 顯正論. HPC 7: 217a–225c.

Kim Sisŭp. *Maewŏltang chip* 梅月堂集. Seoul: Sejong taewang kinyŏm saŏphoe, 1978.

Kwŏn Kŭn. *Iphak tosŏl* 入學図說. Tr. Kwŏn Tŏkchu. Seoul: Ŭryu munhwasa, 1974.

Kyŏngguk taejŏn 經國大典. Seoul: Chūsūin, 1934.

Munjong sillok 文宗實錄. In *Chosŏn wangjo sillok,* vol. 6.

Myŏngjong sillok 明宗實錄. In *Chosŏn wangjo sillok*, vols. 19–21.

No Sasin et al. *Sinjŭng Tongguk yŏji sŭngnam* 新增東國輿地勝覽. Seoul: Tongguk munhwasa, 1957.

Ŏ Sukkwŏn. *P'aegwan chapki* 稗官雜記. Seoul: Chōsen kosho kankōkai, 1909.

Pan Ku. *Han shu* 漢書. 20 vols. Peking: Chung-hua shu-chü, 1962.

Pou. *Il chŏng* 一正. *HPC* 7: 581b–c.

Sa-ch'il i-ki wangbok sŏ 四·七理氣往復書. In *Hanguk yuhak charyo chipsŏng*, 1: 233–260.

Sejo sillok 世祖實錄. In *Chosŏn wangjo sillok*, vols. 7–8.

Sejong sillok 世宗實錄. In *Chosŏn wangjo sillok*, vols. 2–6.

Sin Sukchu. *Pohanjae chip* 保閑齋集. Seoul: Chōsenshi henshūkai, 1937.

Sŏ Kŏjŏng et al. *Tongguk t'onggam* 東國通鑑. Seoul: Chosŏn kwangmunhoe, 1911.

———. *Tong munsŏn* 東文選. 3 vols. Seoul: Kyŏnghŭi ch'ulp'ansa, 1966–1967.

Sŏ Kyŏngdŏk. *Hwadam chip* 花潭集. In *Yijo ch'oyŏp myŏnghyŏn chip sŏn*, pp. 183–243.

Sŏng Hyŏn. *Hŏbaektang chip* 虛白堂集. n.d.

———. *Yongjae ch'onghwa* 慵齋叢話. Seoul: Koryŏ taehakkyo, 1963.

Sŏngjong sillok 成宗實錄. In *Chosŏn wangjo sillok*, vols. 8–12.

Sŏnjo sillok 宣祖實錄. In *Chosŏn wangjo sillok*, vols. 21–25.

T'aejo sillok 太宗實錄. In *Chosŏn wangjo sillok*, vol. 1.

T'aejong sillok 太祖實錄. In *Chosŏn wangjo sillok*, vols. 1–2.

Yang Sŏngji. *Nulchae chip* 訥齋集. Reprint Seoul: Asea munhwa yŏnguso, 1973.

Yi Hwang. *T'oegye chŏnsŏ* 退溪全書. Seoul: Sŏnggyungwan taehakkyo, Taedong munhwa yŏnguwŏn, 1958.

Yi I, *Yulgok chŏnsŏ* 栗谷全書. Seoul: Sŏnggyungwan taehakkyo, Taedong munhwa yŏnguwŏn, 1958.

Yi Ŏnjŏk. *Hoejae chip* 晦齋集. In *Hanguk yuhak charyo chipsŏng*, 1: 63–73.

Yi Sŏngmu. *Chosŏn ch'ogi yangban yŏngu* 朝鮮初期兩班研究. Seoul: Ilchogak, 1980.

Yi T'aejin. *Hanguk sahoesa yŏngu: nongŏp kisul paltal kwa sahoe pyŏndong* 韓國社會史研究農業技術發達과社會變動. Seoul: Chisik sanŏpsa, 1987.

Yijo ch'oyŏp myŏnghyŏn chip sŏn 李朝初葉名賢集選. Seoul: Sŏnggyungwan taehakkyo, Taedong munhwa yŏnguwŏn, 1959.

Yu Hŭich'un. *Miam ilgi ch'o* 眉巖日記抄. Vol. 3. Seoul: Chōsenshi henshūkai, 1938.

Yu Sŭngwŏn. *Chosŏn ch'ogi sinbunje yŏngu* 朝鮮初期身分制研究. Seoul: Ŭryu munhwasa, 1987.

WESTERN LANGUAGE SOURCES

Chan, Wing-tsit, trans. *Reflections on Things at Hand: The Neo-Confucian Anthology Compiled by Chu Hsi and Lü Tsu-ch'ien*. New York: Columbia University Press, 1967.

Fung, Yu-lan. *A History of Chinese Philosophy.* Derk Bodde, trans. Princeton: Princeton University Press, 1953.

Lee, Ki-baek. *A New History of Korea.* Translated by Edward W. Wagner with Edward J. Shultz. Cambridge: Harvard University Press, 1984.

Legge, James. *The Chinese Classics.* 5 vols. Hong Kong: Hong Kong University Press, 1960.

———. *Li Ki.* 2 vols. Sacred Books of the East, 27–28. Oxford: Oxford University Press, 1885.

———. *Yi King.* Sacred Books of the East, 16. Oxford: Clarendon, 1899.

Makra, Mary Lelia, trans. *The Hsiao Ching.* New York: St. John's University Press, 1961.

Needham, Joseph, et al. *The Hall of Heavenly Records: Korean Astronomical Instruments and Clocks, 1380–1780.* Cambridge: Cambridge University Press, 1986.

Yi, T'aejin. "The Socio-Economic Background of Neo-Confucianism in Korea of the 15th and 16th Centuries." *Seoul Journal of Korean Studies* 2 (1989): 39–63.

Index